Walter Bagehot (1826–1877), banker, economist, political thinker and commentator, critic and man of letters, was Victorian England's most versatile genius. Bagehot, writes Sir William Haley in his introduction to the literary essays, is a writer "that no generation has yet been able to ignore", and in the past decade interest in his thought has greatly increased. The publication of The Collected Works of Walter Bagehot, edited by Mr. St. John-Stevas, a leading authority on Bagehot's life and thought, is therefore timely, and the publication of the first two volumes in 1966 was hailed as a major literary event.

The present volumes, containing Bagehot's historical essays, constitute a further important instalment of the nine volume edition. They will be followed by two volumes covering his political writings, two more on his economic thought, and a final volume which will include his letters and miscellaneous publications. Much new material has been included in the present edition which will enable the contemporary reader to assess Bagehot at his true worth for the first time.

In the historical volumes, the reader will find a brilliant and vividly etched series of portraits of eighteenth and nineteenth century statesmen from Bolingbroke to Disraeli. Unlike many of his contemporaries, Bagehot viewed the eighteenth century with sympathetic interest and his assessments are thus free of the prejudices which marred their writing. The nineteenth century portraits are even more fascinating since they give a contemporary assessment of the virtues and defects of their subjects, many of whom were known to Bagehot personally. Bagehot was not a trained historian and was primarily interested in the characters of those he wrote about, which in part explains why these essays still retain their freshness and interest.

Included in these volumes are many essays which have for the first time been attributed to Bagehot. Nearly forty articles on the American Civil War and another twenty on Napoleon III have been rescued from the oblivion of old issues of *The Economist* and placed in circulation once again. They will be of interest both to the historian and the general reader.

This edition of Bagehot sets out to include everything he wrote which is of lasting value and interest. The aim has been to give the essays in their original form or in the form last revised by Bagehot. No effort has been spared to establish definitive and authoritative texts. The edition will make the complete Bagehot available for the first time. Its thoroughness and meticulous scholarship make it a major contribution to nineteenth century studies.

Mr. Norman St. John-Stevas, author of "Walter Bagehot: a study of his life and thought" is a graduate of Oxford and Cambridge and a former fellow of the Yale Law School. Mr. St. John-Stevas was for five years political correspondent of *The Economist* and has been Conservative Member of Parliament for Chelmsford since 1964.

THE COLLECTED WORKS OF
WALTER BAGEHOT

VOLUME THREE

THE COLLECTED WORKS OF
WALTER BAGEHOT

EDITED BY

Norman St John-Stevas

The Historical Essays
(in two volumes) with an introduction by
Jacques Barzun

VOLUME THREE

THE ECONOMIST LONDON

The Collected Works of Walter Bagehot
This volume first published 1968
This edition © The Economist 1968

PRINTED AND BOUND IN ENGLAND BY
HAZELL WATSON AND VINEY LTD
AYLESBURY, BUCKS
set in Monotype Fournier 11/12 point

THE COLLECTED WORKS OF
WALTER BAGEHOT

VOLUMES I & II · LITERARY ESSAYS
VOLUMES III & IV · HISTORICAL
VOLUMES V & VI · POLITICAL
VOLUMES VII & VIII · ECONOMIC
VOLUME IX · LETTERS & MISCELLANY

CONTENTS

Volume Three

15

EDITOR'S PREFACE

My first duty is to express my appreciation and gratitude to Professor Jacques Barzun, the Provost of Columbia University, New York, for his kindness in having written the introduction to this volume. I am also grateful to Mr. Michael Churchman (who is married to a relative of Walter Bagehot) for contributing his perceptive article on Bagehot's attitude to the American Civil War. I would also like to thank Mr. Donald Tyerman of *The Economist* and Miss Mary Sullivan for their invaluable help in reading proofs.

The principles on which the editing of these volumes are being carried out have been set out by me in Volume I and I will not repeat them here, save to say that no effort has been spared to establish as accurate and complete a text as possible. This volume contains Bagehot's 'historical' essays. This was not, of course, his classification, and there is inevitably some overlap between these and his 'political' writings, but it is I think an improvement on the previous division between 'literary' and 'biographical' writings which has been in use. I have divided the essays into sections and within each section have arranged them in a chronological order according to their subject matter rather than the date on which they were written. Thus the first section, which is made up of Bagehot's writings on British statesmen and others, starts with his essay on Bolingbroke and ends with an article on Robert Lowe. This section includes a number of essays which have never before been attributed to Bagehot including studies of Bright, Gladstone and Disraeli. These and other newly attributed essays in this volume have all been selected by me from *The Economist* and attributed to Bagehot on internal evidence. I have unfortunately not been able to check them against *The Economist* contributors' books since these were destroyed on May 11 1941 when the newspaper's premises were burnt down after an air raid. Fortunately Bagehot's style is so distinctive that this has not been too difficult a task and in cases of doubt I have not included the articles.

The second section is made up of Bagehot's writings on Napoleon III from the *Letters on the Coup D'État* written in 1851 down to his final reflections on the Empire in 1874. Apart from the *Letters* themselves and two other articles these articles have never before been included in a Bagehot edition. In an introductory note to this section I describe Bagehot's connection with Napoleon III and analyse the development of his thought on the Second Empire.

The third section deals with the American Civil War on which Bagehot wrote extensively. His sister-in-law, Mrs. Russell Barrington, records in her biography that in 1861 alone, Bagehot wrote thirty-one articles on the Civil War.[1] I have identified all these and the other Civil War articles which Bagehot wrote, many of them of only ephemeral interest. Others are of considerable importance for the light they throw on contemporary English attitudes to the Civil War and for Bagehot's general reflections on American politics. I have accordingly included thirty-seven articles covering the whole course of the Civil War. They should be of value to historians and others interested in the period.

The fourth section is made up of Bagehot's essays on foreign statesmen. There are of necessity fewer of these since *The Economist* had special contributors such as Nassau Senior who dealt with foreign affairs. Finally I have included the essay on the eccentric Henry Crabb Robinson which is quite unclassifiable and therefore has a section on its own, which would have caused wry amusement both to its subject and its author.

Originally I had intended to include all the historical essays in one volume, but my researches uncovered so many articles worth preserving that it has been necessary to add an additional volume. The plan is now more symmetrical with two volumes each being devoted to the literary, historical, political and economic essays and a final single volume to letters and miscellany.

In presenting these essays I have tried to keep as near as possible to their original form of publication. I have therefore kept footnotes to the minimum and added them only where explanation is essential. For the same reason I have not referenced or corrected Bagehot's quotations, and they appear as he wrote them. They were not intended as 'academic' references but were the products of a well

---

[1] See 'The Life of Walter Bagehot' (London, 1918), p. 351.

stocked mind, recalling past reading. Bagehot's essays were not academic exercises but the products of a journalist of genius engaged in the affairs of his time. In editing his collected works I have had this constantly in mind.

1 Hampstead Square   NORMAN ST JOHN-STEVAS

December 1967

NOTE ON THE TEXT

THE basic text followed for those essays which were not reproduced in *Estimates of Some Englishmen and Scotchmen** has been the text in the original journal of publication, the *National, Fortnightly, Inquirer, The Economist,* or whatever it happened to be. The original articles have been photostated in each case. They have then, when appropriate, been compared with the text used by Forrest Morgan in his *The Works of Walter Bagehot* published by the Travelers Insurance Company of Hartford Connecticut in 1891,** and also with R. H. Hutton's 'Biographical Studies' first published in 1881. Sometimes a Morgan or Hutton rendering has been preferred but if so this is always indicated in the text. Any major points of difference between the different texts have been noted in footnotes. The punctuation has in a number of instances been corrected and modernised. Introductory notes have been included as an aid to the general reader. The use of capitals has been kept to a minimum and Bagehot's use of capitals which was highly erratic has not in general been followed. They are used for proper names and where the text appears to require them.

When the essays had been reprinted in *Estimates of Some Englishmen and Scotchmen,* the *Estimates* text has been used as the basic text as this was the text finally revised by Bagehot. This text has been compared with the original and any differences noted in footnotes. Comparison has been carried out with the Hutton and Morgan texts. Bagehot's footnotes are indicated by an asterisk, editor's footnotes are numbered. In most cases it is obvious from the text that the numbered footnotes are the editor's but where there is an ambiguity 'Ed' has been added. The first footnotes in the longer essays is usually a joint Bagehot and editor footnote. The aim in presenting the text has been to give the essays in their original form or in the form as last revised by Bagehot.

The essays have been identified by external evidence save for the

* 'Estimates of Some Englishmen and Scotchmen' was a collection of essays published by Bagehot in 1858.
** Two impressions appear to have been published, the first in 1889.

following which have been attributed by me to Bagehot on internal indications: 'Lord Palmerston at Bradford' (1864), the first essay on Richard Cobden (1863), 'Mr. Bright at Manchester' (1866), 'Mr. Bright's Return to Parliament' (1871), 'Mr. Gladstone's Resolutions' (1868), 'Mr. Gladstone's Chapter of Autobiography' (1868), 'Mr. Gladstone's Ministry' (1874), 'Mr. Disraeli's Administration' (1868), the articles on the fourteenth and fifteenth Earls of Derby (1869 and 1872), 'Mr. Mill's Address to the Electors of Westminster' (1865), 'Mr. Mill on Ireland' (1868), 'Mr. Goschen's Acceptance of Office' (1865). Of the essays on Napoleon III all save the 'Letters on the French Coup D'Ètat', 'Caesareanism as it now exists' (1865), and 'The Emperor Napoleon' (1873), have been attributed on internal evidence. The same is true of the articles on the American Civil War with the exception of 'The American Constitution at the Present Crisis' (1861). In the section on foreign statesmen the articles on Thiers (1872) and King Leopold I of the Belgians (1865) have been attributed on internal evidence.

BAGEHOT AS HISTORIAN

by Jacques Barzun

'ADAM SMITH as a Person'; 'Why Mr. Disraeli Has Succeeded'—only a genius would propose to himself such enigmas and attempt to resolve them for the public. Bagehot, the proposer of these and other riddles of modern history, has been conceded genius often and willingly enough, yet he remains a shadowy figure in that part of the public mind where reputations are considered settled. The difficulty about Bagehot seems to be not his merits but his role. What is he? 'Polymath' is not an acceptable answer; rather, it prolongs the doubt: Economist? Journalist? Political Scientist? Historian? Metaphysician? Liberal? Conservative? Which or how many of these must we apply to Bagehot to 'place' him? Nor is this all: if a man has been dead nearly a hundred years and is 'well-known' without being known well, a certain impatience arises at the mere mention of his name. It would be better for him to exchange his ambiguous position for one of complete obscurity. It is easier to pull Kierkegaard out of nowhere and establish his complex presence than to revise our judgments of those who have only half entered the Pantheon, whose nose and cheekbone only are showing, like Shakespeare's in Ingres's painting of the Apotheosis of Homer.

Bagehot is of course in part responsible for the uncertainty of his posthumous fame. He made two capital mistakes—one, the mistake of bearing a name puzzling to pronounce; the other, the mistake of dying at 51, before the variety and superiority of his mind could force themselves on public opinion by the necessary repetition of tenets and attitudes. A strong but simple mind can make its mark in twenty years; a subtle and humorous mind, endowed always with binocular vision, needs a much longer span as well as a series of emphatic interpreters. Double views are not quickly popular; they were not at all so in Bagehot's time, an age which was trying hard to be single-minded, and which accordingly preferred sermons and prophecies to the historian's temper in essay form. The historical temper moreover tends to choose subjects, past or present, that seem to the amateur of belles-lettres ephemeral or best left to experts: Bagehot is credited with a masterpiece called *The English Constitution*, but who wants to read about that?

The subjects treated in this volume will readily call forth the same disdainful fears of the literary mind. At first sight what we have here is the work of a political historian—more especially a parliamentary historian—whose 'period' goes from the age of Queen Anne to that of Gladstone, Bismarck, Lincoln, and Napoleon III. It seems as if only a specialist of the same species could feel a natural urge to read such histories, no matter how rapid the narrative and accessible the prose. And even a specialist might shy off, on the ground that later research and more modern views leave Bagehot's writings only an antiquarian interest. All this would be true if Bagehot's subject at any time were solely what the title of the particular work declares—the English Constitution, Bolingbroke as a Statesman, or Caesareanism as it now Exists. But to a candid reader the most casual dip into Bagehot's pages reveals something quite different. Bagehot is indeed a political historian whose subject is Gladstone or the Reform Act of 1832, but his subject is also, and always, political man. Or to put the same fact in other words, what interests Bagehot is the mainspring of political action, the elusive principles of man's behaviour in the social state. As a twentieth-century student of Bagehot has remarked, one willingly turns over the dusty files of *The Economist* for Bagehot's 'special gifts of generalisation. One never loses touch with the institutions Bagehot is describing nor the people who infuse them.' For example: 'Few latter-day [business]-cycle theorists, even those who have explicitly dealt with the so-called "psychological factors", have permitted themselves such a bland and relevant observation as: "All people are most credulous when they are most happy." The easy interplay of persons, institutions, and theory in Bagehot's exposition makes the abstraction from it of a formal structure difficult, as well as something of a violation.'[1] In short, he who will listen to Bagehot's tales of half-forgotten events will receive, besides the knowledge of those events and their participants, a new wisdom and a unique pleasure.

[1] Walt W. Rostow, 'Bagehot and the Trade Cycle,' in *The Economist, 1843–1943*, London, 1943, 157–8.

II

To define his scope rather than his philosophy I have called Bagehot a parliamentary historian. The term is convenient but perhaps unduly limiting: Bagehot's concern was with the fate of free political institutions. The bent of his mind and the span of his life conspired to supply his subject matter and its perplexing questions. He had vividly before him, actually or through memoirs of the recent past, the procession of England's great ministers since Bolingbroke. His recital of their merits, their characters, and their vicissitudes puts together a story of the most stable and yet most flexible government of the great age which comes to a close with Bagehot's own career. Toward the end of that period, and coinciding with his mature years, Bagehot had as contrast the spectacle of two other governments, equally rational but not so stable: the Caesarian democracy of Napoleon III, which foundered in 1870, and the American federal republic, which was rent by civil war and had not been reconstructed when Bagehot died in 1877.

Bagehot was thus the witness and the judge of the first attempts to reconcile liberty and stability, self-government by the mass of industrialised mankind and the pursuit of increasingly complex policies. These difficulties, not to say contradictions, are still with us. They exercised Bagehot's imagination, because like a dramatist he felt within himself that the opposing ideals, parties, and human impulses were equally right. And this explains his singular character, which some have mistaken for that of the cynic. Born with the gifts and moods of an *esprit d'élite*, he championed the virtue of stupidity and defended 'the right to be a Philistine'. Conversely, when the Philistine mind sinks into its congenial litter of facts and figures (which Bagehot is well able to handle), Bagehot rouses that mind by a call for principle and theory: 'as the argument is often more difficult than the illustration, it is apt not to be used; and political economy is in danger of dissolving into statistics, which is much as if anecdotes of animals were substituted for the science of biology.'[2]

In a word, Bagehot is the Socratic ironist in politics; though as we shall see, he is not a mere critic of others' conceptions but develops one of his own. Like his peers—Carlyle, Mill, Arnold, and Ruskin—Bagehot knew that the task of his age was at once to embody and to prevent revolution; that is, to promote yet restrain change, so as to

[2] 'Professor Cairnes' (1875).

direct it. The stolid, cautious, unimaginative members of society will huddle together and do what they can to prevent revolution by merely sitting still; the restless spirits, lit by generous hope or merely fanatical from rancour, will not wait for inching reforms but will want to establish the perfect state by an overnight coup. Neither party, neither temperament, will ever have the genius to act at any time in deliberate opposition to its own habit. The only hope lies in the politics of equilibrium, the art by which one or more leading men can move the poised mass a little way toward goals that they dimly see.

Hence Bagehot's writing about statesmen and politicians: their importance is calculable; their circumstances instructive. The theorist, knowing that the idea of perpetual revolution is fundamental to modern societies, uses contemporary examples to illuminate past conflicts and vice versa. When, for instance, Bagehot wants to draw the character of Harley while telling the life of Bolingbroke, the historian puts the appropriate modern words in Harley's mouth: '"I do not wish in this House," he would say in our age, "to be a party to any extreme course. Mr. Gladstone brings forward a great many things which I cannot understand; I assure you he does. There is more in that bill about tobacco than he thinks; I am confident there is. Money is a serious thing, a *very* serious thing. And I am sorry to say Mr. Disraeli commits the party very much; he avows sentiments which are injudicious; I cannot go along with him. . . . Great orators are very well; but as I said, how is the revenue?"' [3]

This perennial cowardice of conservatism was magnified by the great fear that followed the French Revolution of 1789 and the wars of Napoleon; this fear became the major premise, as it were, of the nineteenth century: 'A whole generation in England, and indeed in Europe, was so frightened by the Reign of Terror that they thought it could only be prevented by another Reign of Terror. . . . In England we had a state of opinion which did the work of one without one; nine-tenths of the English people were above all things determined to put down "French principles"; and unhappily "French principles" included what we should now consider obvious improvements and rational reforms. They would not allow the most cruel penal code which any nation ever had to be mitigated—they did not wish justice to be questioned; they would not let the mass of the people be educated, or at least only so that it came to nothing; they would not alter

---

[3] 'Bolingbroke as a Statesman' (1863).

anything which came down from their ancestors, for in their terror they did not know but there might be some charmed value even in the most insignificant thing: and after what they had seen happen in France, they feared that if they changed a single iota all else would collapse.'[4]

This description prepares us to understand the first reform of Parliament in 1832. But we are wrong if we expect that Bagehot will then produce the liberal historian's familiar effect of Light After Darkness. On the contrary, he is a severe critic of 1832 and of Lord Althorp, the mere politician who against his will saw the Act through: 'He was a man so picturesquely out of place in a great scene that if a great describer gets hold of him he may be long remembered.'[5] The grave defect of 1832 for Bagehot is that in making reforms it began the destruction of political diversity and put in its place the principle that the change most to be desired is an increase in the power of numbers. Here the same analyst who has shown us the virtue of a Harley in adhering to common sense against the visions of 'brilliant and vehement men' demonstrates the limitations of common sense when men such as Althorp 'guide legislative changes in complex institutions. Being without culture, they do not know how these institutions grew; being without insight, they only see one half of their effect; being without foresight, they do not know what will happen if they are enlarged; being without originality, they cannot devise anything new to supply if necessary the place of what is old. . . . Such men are admirably suited to early and simple times.—English history is full of them, and England has been made mainly by them; but they fail in later times, when the work of the past is accumulated, and no question is any longer simple.'[6]

Knowing history to be irreversible, Bagehot is worried—as we are —by the conditions that first produce the mass man, then give him power, and finally face him with complex predicaments. Bagehot knows as well as we do that 'the greater power of the working-classes' made for less cruelty and blindness in government, for the diffusion of 'a sweeter and better spirit throughout society'. But the price seems to him high when he foresees that before long there will be 'only one sort of vote and only one size of constituency . . . then the reign of monotony will be complete'.[7] The prediction had certainly come true

[4] 'Lord Althorp and the Reform Act of 1832' (1876).
[5] *Ibid.*   [6] *Ibid.*   [7] *Ibid.*

seventy years later, when the representation of the Universities was abolished, when the Liberal party was but a remnant between two political groups competing less for the nation's support than for the possession of the same welfare programme, and when the voters hardly cared which they chose. A. P. Herbert, reviewing his career as a University member had by then confirmed Bagehot's judgment and shown in repeated instances of inaction and injustice the practical effects of this loss of variety.[8]

By his assorted examples from English history, Bagehot illustrates what we now all perceive about modern life: it sows uniformity and reaps monotony. He may therefore be of greater use to us when in the other half of his doctrine he reminds us that 'the common mass of plain sense is the great administrative agency of the world';[9] that 'the constitutional statesman' is not a man of original ideas but 'a man of common opinions and uncommon abilities'.[10] Bagehot is so sure of the importance of this truth that he repeats it in varied forms—'the powers of a first-rate man and the creed of a second-rate man.'[11] And again: 'So long as constitutional statesmanship consists in recording the views of a confused nation, so long as success in it is confined to minds plastic, changeful, administrative, we must hope for no better man.'[12]

This is a hard lesson for the finer spirits of our century, who were reared upon the belief in theory as the hope of the world, who studied Marx and now wish for 'a philosophy of democracy', or who toil at a statistical science of man. It should seem as if our advanced times and those intricate problems facing complex institutions ought to be dealt with by intellect linked with expertise. Yet it is not so. To begin with, the people do not want it so. They rarely choose or do not long support the men of intellect. They prefer an inarticulate general to an elegant and witty phrase-maker; they respond to the hard, plain, fighting words of a President to whom abstraction is almost unknown, but who nonetheless led a nation briskly through dangerous times; they worship an organiser of resistance and victory whose politics in peacetime were always dubious; they love youth, vigour, and idealism, but cannot sustain that love so well as they relish the comfort of being administered by common sense and political know-how.

[8] A. P. Herbert, *Independent Member*, London, 1950.
[9] 'Lord Palmerston' (1865).   [10] 'The Character of Sir Robert Peel' (1856).
[11] *Ibid.*   [12] *Ibid.*

And even apart from the people, in whom ultimate power is vested, the leaders of society, men of influence and wealth and education do not want intellect and theory to lead them. They trust and prefer the 'common opinions allied to uncommon abilities'. Dash and brilliance tire them out in the end or make them suspicious from the start. Bagehot (in one of his brilliant defences of dullness), gives us the explanation when he criticises Robert Lowe: 'The faculty of disheartening adversaries by diffusing on occasion an oppressive atmosphere of business-like dullness is invaluable to a parliamentary statesman. But these arts Mr. Lowe does not possess. He cannot help being brilliant; the quality of his mind is to put everything in the most lively, most exciting, and most startling form. He cannot talk that monotonous humdrum which men scarcely listen to, which lulls them to sleep, but which seems to them "the sort of thing you would expect", which they suppose is "all right." And Mr. Lowe's mode of using general principles not only is not that which a parliamentary tactician would recommend, but is the very reverse of what he would advise: Mr. Lowe always ascends to the widest generalities . . . ; the middle principles, in which most minds feel most reality and on which they find it most easy to rest, have no charms for him; he likes to go back to the bone, to the abstract, to the attenuated. And if he left these remote principles in their remote unintelligibility, he would not suffer so much: but he makes the dry bones live; he wraps them in illustrations which Macaulay might envy. And he is all the more effective because he uses our vernacular tongue. [His] phrases . . . will be long remembered and will longer impair his influence with grave, quiet, and influential persons. Mr. Lowe startles those who do not like to be startled, and does not compose those who wish to be composed. . . .'[13]

There are exceptions to the generality implied by this description, and Bagehot is quick to note them. They belong to the class he calls 'dictators', as distinguished from 'administrators'. Dictators, as he uses the term, legitimately occur in representative government: they are needed in moments of crisis, usually in times of war. William Pitt was such a dictator, and unlike the administrator of ordinary times was a man of ideas—'a fresh stock of youthful thought such as no similar statesman has ever possessed . . .' But it was not the possession of ideas or the coloring they imparted to his proposals that made

[13] 'Mr. Lowe as Chancellor of the Exchequer' (1871).

Pitt the great man he was in Bagehot's eyes. No: 'The characteristic merit of Pitt is that in the midst of obvious cares, in the face of most keen, most able, and most stimulated opposition, he applied his whole power to the accomplishment of great but practicable schemes.'[14]

That such men as Pitt emerge and succeed—men of ideas and abilities both—naturally leads the political thinker to ask himself why dictators should not be the regular thing. To help him examine the question Bagehot had, as I have said, the example of Napoleon's nephew over the Channel, an example that Europe was to repeat, with variations, a good many times in our century. Bagehot dealt with Louis-Napoleon's Caesarism in a dozen or more essays, and from the early days of both their careers. Young Bagehot, aged 26, was in Paris in 1852 when the Paris republicans were trying to oppose the coup d'état. As correspondent for a liberal newspaper, and himself of liberal convictions, one might have supposed that his articles would attack the usurper and express the familiar liberal indignation. Not so Bagehot. He wrote home an account of events and causes showing that a dictatorship was at once inevitable and useful. But he also helped the republicans build their barricades. In a word, apart from all reasoned preferences, law and the orderly conduct of business must come first, by force if all other appeals fail.

In after days, without changing beliefs, Bagehot was unsparing in his criticism of the emperor. He could see that Napoleon III led not only France but a party spread throughout all nations; the new 'intelligent despotism' was creating a genre, and the Emperor was 'the crowned democrat of Europe'. Yet Bagehot was convinced that such a government could serve only 'crude and immediate' purposes. It could not endure, and Bagehot predicted its fall a full year before the war that led to the humiliation of Sedan.[15]

It was the democratic, or rather the populist, strength of the new despotism that Bagehot apprehended. Apropos of Napoleon III's last plebiscite Bagehot gives a definition to bear in mind when we read him on this topic of the new political force: 'Democracy seems to us to consist as often as not in the free use of the people's name *against* the vast majority of the people.'[16] He has no love for what he calls

---

[14] 'William Pitt' (1861).
[15] *The Economist*, August 22, November 28, December 5 1863; August 7 1869.
[16] *Ibid.*, May 14 1870.

'democratic autocracies', by which he means one-party systems based on periodic voting suitably rigged. A free government, for Bagehot, 'lives by discussion, a free press has its life in argument and dissertation'. Any other rule 'is sure to be an *uneasy* government. It prohibits daily and efficient discussion, and the instructed classes, who love discussion, who delight in argument, who love the noble play of mind upon mind, become its irreconcilable enemies.' The conclusion is that 'free government involves privilege, because it requires that more power should be given to the instructed than to the uninstructed'.[17]

Bagehot wrote these words before free public education had been legislated—let alone taken effect upon the industrial masses; and he naturally shared the disquiet of his most thoughtful and liberal contemporaries, from Tocqueville to Matthew Arnold, at the prospect of political power passing wholly into the hands of the illiterate multitude. Before 1885 no example of successful rule by the many existed, unless it was the unedifying one of the Roman plebs. All agreed that government by consent was desirable and that consent implied the participation of all, as voters and potential legislators. But what would the practising of that theory bring about when the uninstructed masses were suddenly loosed? This question, like the others that Bagehot met with clarity and concreteness, confronts us still in the new nations of the post-war world. Moral and material civilization are not always in parallel, and even moderately free institutions require the moral more than the material. Bagehot was certain that the English polity in the nineteenth century was based, not upon the aristocracy of birth, but 'on property and, through property, upon education and intelligence'.[18] Well, education and property have since his day tamed the monster of 'democracy' as the word was then used. The industrial masses have not turned into a Roman plebs in those countries where a parliamentary tradition existed or was begun. And despite all that can be said against their choice of leaders when judged by Plato's standard of philosopher kings, the nations of the Western world have been 'deferential' in Bagehot's sense: the people have deferred to education and ability and have shown a remarkable detective instinct for integrity or the lack of it. Thus under all the changes of a hundred years our political history is continuous with that which Bagehot studied and from which he extracted so many profound lessons.

[17] *The Economist*, September 5 1863.   [18] *Ibid.*

III

If Bagehot were only political and enamoured of England alone, he should still command our attention. But he is much more. He is, throughout his political narratives, a cultural historian as well, a psychologist, a literary artist, and—ahead of his time—a philosopher of the pragmatic or existential school. He always sees man as a whole and as part of another whole that we call society, culture, 'the times'. This is doubtless why Bagehot deprecated systems, in the writing of history as in the conduct of politics. The logic of words, the results of analysis, the predictions of experience, are continually being falsified by new fact. 'So complex is life,' he writes apropos of Adam Smith, 'that this Scotch professorship [of Moral Philosophy], though in a superficial view wasteful, . . . was nevertheless on the whole exceedingly useful. It not only induced him to study as a part of his vast scheme the particular phenomena of wealth, but it gave him an excellent opportunity of seeing those phenomena and of learning how to explain them.'[19] Bagehot then limns in a characteristic page the advantages that Glasgow offered for Smith's purpose in the second half of the eighteenth century.

One could give innumerable other examples of Bagehot's power to condense in a few lines a state of affairs, cultural, psychological, or other. One thinks of the portrait of Lord Althorp as a representative Englishman; the summary of the merits of Scottish education; the definitions of the orator and the agitator in the sketch of Cobden and of the scientist in the 'Macaulay'; and the wonderful sequence of pictures in the tremendous retrospect on Brougham. The variety and momentum are those of history itself—or such is the truthful illusion. But there is also coherence in these portraits of persons and places, because they proceed from a central and, as one may surmise, instantaneous vision of the subject: it has the unity of an organic birth; a kernel idea lives in each essay or part of an essay that makes its germinative force felt throughout, sometimes by repetition. Thus Brougham has a demonic eye; Bolingbroke is an Alcibiades; Gladstone is a didactic and dogged Christian. Of his own father-in-law Bagehot wrote with affection and admiration yet with a cool judgment that supplies another informing idea: 'Through life it was one of his re-

[19] 'Adam Smith as a Person' (1876).

markable peculiarities to be a *very animated* man, talking by preference and by habit on *inanimate* subjects.'[20]

Bagehot himself could perhaps be described as having performed miracles to animate the inert matters of trade and finance. But what differentiates him from a lively economist is this being possessed of, and by, the historical sense. He is always 'applying the historical method' (which includes the biographical), as he tells us casually in opening his discussion of *The Wealth of Nations*. He believes that understanding depends on knowing the history of things and he assumes that the pastness of the past is an ordinary perception. Yet how few people reading Robert Peel's *Memoirs* on their appearance would think first as Bagehot does: 'Most people have looked over old letters; they have been struck with the change of life, with the doubt on things now certain, the belief in things now incredible, the oblivion of what now seems most important, the strained attention to departed detail, which characterize the mouldering leaves.'[21] Most people do not muse in any such way. They merely think 'how strange, how quaint, how funny!' They notice a gap in their comprehension but they do not sort out its causes nor bridge it with imaginative links. For the intellectual knowledge that something is old is not the same as the bodily sense of the passage of time. That sense Bagehot had to an almost morbid degree. It is a kind of philosophical anguish that pierces through his masculine prose: 'Our grandfathers and their fathers quarrelled for two generations as to the Peace of Utrecht; but only an odd person here and there could now give an account of its provisions. The most cultivated lady would not mind asking, 'the peace of Utrecht! yes—what was that?' ... Even now, the dust of forgetfulness is falling over the Congress of Vienna and the peace of Paris; we are forgetting the last great pacification as we have wholly forgotten the pacification before that: in another fifty years 'Vienna' will be as 'Utrecht', and Wellington be no more than Marlborough.'[22]

The true historian, clearly, is he who, at once studious and sensitive, is not content with satisfying his intellectual curiosity about the gap he feels between Now and Then, but who like an actor adapts his feelings to the lines of each situation until he can reproduce and make others understand it. We have just seen Bagehot helping his reader

[20] 'Memoir of the Right Hon. James Wilson' (1860).
[21] 'The Character of Sir Robert Peel' (1856).
[22] 'Bolingbroke as a Statesman' (1863).

measure the remoteness of Bolingbroke by mentioning the Congress of Vienna, only half a century in the past. When he comes to deal with that past he finds the extraordinary words to evoke it: 'The years immediately succeeding the great peace were years of sullenness and difficulty. The idea of the war had passed away; the thrill and excitement of the great struggle were no longer felt. . . . Altogether, we had vanquished Napoleon, but we had no pleasure in what came after him.'[23]

This capacity for re-creating the feel at the same time as the fact is not learned from seminars and manuals. It is a gift, the gift of the associative imagination. Who but Bagehot would have thought of digressing superbly for a whole page about Byron in order to make plain the figure of Sir Robert Peel? Bagehot also has the gift of framing successive images in such short compass that some of them may escape the mind that too eagerly follows the plot. Thus a summing up of the industrial revolution and the rise of a new bourgeoisie is given us in ten lines: 'Sir Robert's father and grandfather were two of the men who created Lancashire. No sooner did the requisite machinery issue from the brain of the inventor than its capabilities were seized on by strong, ready, bold men of business, who erected it, used it, devised a factory system, combined a factory population—created, in a word, that black industrial region of whose augmenting wealth and horrid labour tales are daily borne to the genial and lazy south. Of course it cannot be said that mill-makers invented the middle classes. . . .'[24]

The historical temper liberates the possessor from provincialism in the same way that the actor's temperament liberates from a straitlaced morality, by a multiplication of imaginary sympathies. Bagehot is occasionally unjust to the French and the North Americans, on political grounds, but he is not a Victorian moralist or spiritual Little Englander. In the last century, only his fellow historians Macaulay and Froude would have felt the same freedom to write: 'We see in Bolingbroke's case that a life of brilliant licence is compatible with a life of brilliant statesmanship; that licence itself may even be thought to quicken the imagination for oratorical efforts; that an intellect similarly aroused may, at exciting conjunctures, perceive possibilities which are hidden from duller men; that the favourite of society will be able to use his companionship with men and his power over women so as much to aid his strokes of policy. . . .'[25]

[23] 'Lord Brougham' (1857).   [24] 'The Character of Sir Robert Peel' (1856).
[25] 'Bolingbroke as a Statesman' (1863).

Bagehot's awareness that human life is social life, his zest for its minute accidents and intimate vagaries, is what makes him quote his subjects so frequently, use anecdotes about them, invent conversations, and dramatise their ideas. One often suspects that the introductory words 'someone once said' or 'it is told of —' are only cloaks for Bagehot's modesty when he has found the transfixing phrase. His genuine quotations, be it said in passing, are generally inexact—as in Montaigne, Hazlitt, and other men of wide reading and strong imagination, whose knowledge is not copied from the source and pasted together but has grown into their memory. In the process the words of another are unconsciously refitted to the new use, and in Bagehot seldom objectionably; for as he said of Lord Lyndhurst, 'there was no laxity in his intellect; everything there was braced and knit'.[26]

In no one more than in an historical essayist is this natural cohesion of ideas necessary. History is multifarious, occasions to digress and explain beckon on every side, disputed points engage the polemical instincts. But the essay affords no room to sort out and indulge these temptations as the writer of a book can do, with his procession of chapters, footnotes, and appendices. It is therefore not by chance that of the three historians I have named as equals, Bagehot is the great abridger. Macaulay stretched to the limit the very long essay which is almost a monograph; Froude shines more in his books than in his 'Short Studies', which are uneven. But leaving the greatness of Froude to the care of his masterly biographer,[27] I believe the contrast between Bagehot and Macaulay instructive about both. In his essay of 1856 on Macaulay, Bagehot comes as near to being unjust as his generous nature will permit. Out of emulation verging on rivalry, he finds Macaulay an unsatisfactory historian, a 'pictorial' narrator and no more. Macaulay, in effect, is denied imagination and understanding, which is as much as to say that he is no historian, only a chronicler. This is absurd; and in remarks scattered through the later essays Bagehot fortunately revises his first harsh judgment. Indeed, he defends Macaulay from accusations very like his own, and twenty years after the original critique, he is able to define Macaulay's greatness and chief defect. In naming that defect, Bagehot (though he did not set out to do so) indicates his own special merit: '... there is this fundamental likeness between Macaulay and Adam Smith: that they can both

[26] 'What Lord Lyndhurst Really Was' (1863).
[27] *James Anthony Froude*, by Waldo Hilary Dunn, Oxford, 1961–63, 2 vols.

describe practical matters in such a way as to fasten them on the imagination, and not only get what they say read, but get it remembered and make it part of the substance of the reader's mind ever afterwards. ... What Macaulay does for us in history—at least what he does best— [is to] engrave indelibly the main outlines and the rough common-sense of the matter. ...' So much for Macaulay's strength; now for his defect as Bagehot sees it: 'the osteology' of the subject is not enough; so the critic hopes that '. . . other more refining and perhaps in some respects more delicate minds may add the nicer details, and explain those wavering, flickering, inconstant facts of human nature which are either above common-sense or below it.'[28]

When one considers that if a written history is to impress its form and meaning upon the mind it must eliminate much that is flickering and inconstant in events and in men—that is, must reduce the chaos to an intelligible pattern—one concludes that Bagehot's ideal poses a literary difficulty, a problem of style. Only in that sense is the 'more refining, more delicate' mind required, and it is not because Macaulay was less perceptive or because Bagehot had less common sense that their historical writings differ. Rather, it is that in Bagehot—and thanks to Macaulay's earlier effort at liberation—historical prose has taken a further step away from neo-classic form, and while retaining a certain oratorical strength has come nearer the fluency of colloquial speech. This quality, which we now praise above all others, is what led a contemporary reviewer of Bagehot's earliest Essays to call him 'childish and indescribably trivial'.

IV

To be sure, one could argue that Hazlitt had liberated—had 'finalised'—English prose to the fullest extent one could wish, and before Macaulay. Bagehot himself must have been acknowledging Hazlitt's influence on his own style when he maintained against contemporary opinion that 'Hazlitt was a much greater writer than Charles Lamb.'[29] But Hazlitt's prose is best suited to the essay of opinion, the discontinuous musings and assertions of the strong mind which has long since tasted its observations and now imparts them. Narration is another task, for which continuity, close-knit summaries, and change of pace without loss of momentum are indispensable. What Bagehot

[28] 'Adam Smith as a Person' (1876).   [29] 'Henry Crabb Robinson' (1869).

learned from Hazlitt is freedom and naturalness in phrase-making. Bagehot sometimes errs on the side of pedagogic repetition, but he is also one of the great English epigrammatists; his wit and his aphorisms are not sought; they spring from his sustained attention to the matter in hand, his turning over and over the object which his common sense readily classifies, but in which the refining eye discovers new lights that call forth the flashing words. This being so, to quote the maxim apart from the details it illuminates is to change its tone and weaken its force. Yet the temptation to collect maxims is great:

'You cannot calm the passions of men by defining their words.'

'Nothing is so cruel as fear.'

'The great obstacle to originality is the English nation.'

'Politicians . . . may appeal to posterity; but of what use is posterity? Years before that tribunal comes into life, your life will be extinct; it is like a moth going into Chancery.'

The same pleasure arises from the short phrases that cap a just analysis: 'a certain dexterous insincerity'; 'a taint of subtlety'; 'a mind to receive the daily deposits of insensibly changing opinion'; 'the sure sagacity of his masculine mind'; 'incessant men'. And often, in a less emphatic voice, the wit shades into humour, as when after reporting a peasant's encomium on Lord Althorp's knowledge of sheep, Bagehot adds: 'he delighted to watch a whole flock pass, and seemed to know them as if he had lived with them'. And again, out of introspective wisdom: 'Before the fear of ridicule and the touch of reality, the illusions of youth pass away, and with them goes all intellectual courage. We have no longer the hardihood, we have scarcely the wish, to form our own creed, to think our own thoughts, to act upon our own belief: we try to be sensible, and we end in being ordinary.'[30]

This note of melancholy in Bagehot does but translate into feeling the sensation of the passage of time. The historian is, next to the religious, the closest observer of mortality, and when he is not of a grim or ascetic cast of mind, he is most likely to be passionately humorous, full of a sad gaiety. He is the double man who, because he also understands workaday business and mankind's sound reasons for short views and self-interest, appears simultaneously as mystic and cynic. Being once alone at breakfast with a small boy who hesitated to break an egg with his spoon, Bagehot encouraged him: 'Hit it hard

[30] 'William Pitt' (1861).

on the head. It has no friends.'[31] To know Bagehot is to catch the mingled laughter and despair in that remark. The words define the essence of politics under any government: whoever does not gather his friends around him and make their voices heard will suffer like the egg; but the chief pleasure in life is to perceive this among other fated conditions and give them shape in philosophic words.

Such was the impulse that moved Bagehot not only to write but to correct history. It is the moralist's task to say: 'Look! it is not as you thought,' and this without a set notion that things are better or worse than the legend or the convention affirms. Pitt was better than his fame, and so was Bolingbroke; Lyndhurst and Althorp were worse. Gladstone's character was different from what it appeared, Disraeli's achievement more limited. And while showing that crystallised reputations needed reshaping, Bagehot found innumerable commonplaces to destroy and to replace with truer generalities. Matthew Arnold was among the earliest to praise in Bagehot this 'concern for the simple truth', the truth which is always so hard to extract from confusion and sophistication and to fortify against their tide-like return.

Bagehot had that ambition: to influence a change of thought, to exert power over the minds of men as Adam Smith and—less happily, in Bagehot's view—Burke had done. But he knew how chancy such an endeavour was: 'I am afraid I am callous, possibly proud, and do not care for mere general reputation. . . . First-rate fame, the fame of great productive artists is a matter of ultimate certainty, but no other fame is. Posterity cannot take up little people, there are so many of them. Reputation must be acquired at the moment, and the circumstances of the moment are matters of accident.'[32]

Besides, the metaphysical and passionate strain in him conspired with his love of nonsense and of conversation to make impossible the pose or mask by which an ambitious character captures the public attention. Had Bagehot not been tied to the heavy duties of a banker and financial analyst, had he written historical essays and literary criticism *ex cathedra*, he might soon have formed a following. But he might also have acquired the rigidity that spoils much Victorian work. What is invaluable now is what his own time took for waywardness, though it was to him 'the noble play of mind': 'I get tired of either

---

[31] Quoted in Norman St John-Stevas, *Walter Bagehot*, Eyre & Spottiswoode, London, 1959, p. 1.
[32] Letter to Eliza Wilson, January 4 1858.

sense or nonsense if I am kept very continuously to either, and like my mind to undulate between the two as it likes best.'[33]

Beneath this indulgence there was in Bagehot a very accurate idea of the forces at work within the human mind and of the worth of each; he says of Byron: 'There is a kind of eruption of ideas from a subterconscious world; the whole mental action is volcanic.'[34] And for himself he declares: 'The deepest part of the soul after a little revolts at anything merely intellectual. Such things seem trivial and unworthy when forced on us as substitutes for what is deeper.'[35]

V

Looking over the entire body of Bagehot's work, one is entitled to ask: 'What sort of historical writings are these? Are they good history; and if so, for what purposes and occasions?' If historiography consists only in specialised, professional work, that is, in the laying out of complete, up-to-date, verified information, then clearly the essays in this volume are not history, not scholarship. They never pretended to be, though offered as true and in fact full of truths. Whoever wants the complete parliamentary history of England, done according to the latest canons and convictions, had better begin with J. H. Plumb's volumes on Walpole and continue with the many works of his many colleagues in chronological sequence, down to the latest lives of Curzon, Baldwin, Asquith, Sir Charles Dilke, and the rest. By doing that instead of reading Bagehot one will learn much more—and much less. For when one goes to the classic writers of history one looks for something else than tested information. It is there, solid in part, needing amendment in other parts; but what one really seeks is a unique sense of life suffusing an ordered presentation of past times and men. The point of view may no longer be accepted, it may never have been commonly held—no matter: such writings are in fact the only ones that overcome error and fashion and can still tell us something about ourselves. They possess what Niebuhr, the historian of Rome, called 'that immediate expression of reality which emanates from life'— and which rarely emanates from anything else.

Bagehot, it is clear, is not a classic historian in the same sense as Gibbon, Macaulay, Carlyle, or Michelet: essays are not volumes. But

[33] *Ibid.*, February 1 1858.   [34] 'The Character of Sir Robert Peel' (1856).
[35] Letter to Eliza Wilson, February 14 1858.

his work is not the less historical for his being among the great *users* of history—the moralists such as Plutarch and Montaigne, the political theorists such as Montesquieu and Burke—all of whom are concerned with the truth about man, and all of whom thereby answer the sceptic's question 'Why study the past?' Nowadays the answer needs steady repeating, for the sceptic's mood prevails, being very much that of the scientist—only the present is real, only the future matters. History is irregular and uncertain: what can it teach us? Surely 'the truth about man' lies in experimental (or at least statistical) studies.

The sufficient answer is that it lies also—and mainly—in the recital of how men have behaved in circumstances which the student of history, the *politique et moraliste* in the manner of Bagehot, makes us understand. The simple spectacle of character in motion toward purpose, quite apart from parallels and preachments, is a force that acts on the beholder and—like art—leaves him a changed man. Whether changed for the better or not is his affair. That he will be less gay or more serene, harder of heart or wiser, depends on his temperament. What is sure is that if he pursues the reading of history in the masters he will find himself addicted to a pleasure he cannot give up.

Henry St John, Viscount Bolingbroke
Introductory note

Henry St John, first Viscount Bolingbroke (1678–1751) was born at Battersea, the only son of Sir Henry St John and Lady Mary Rich. The elder St John held the manors of Battersea and Wandsworth. The son was educated at Eton and, it is said, at Christ Church, Oxford, but there is no record of this. In 1701 he became M.P. for the borough of Wootton-Bassett, supporting Harley and the Tory party. He was appointed to prepare and bring in a bill for the security of Protestant succession to the throne. From 1704–8 he was Secretary-at-War; in 1710 he became Secretary of State, and in 1710 was M.P. for Berkshire. He was created Viscount Bolingbroke in 1712. Bolingbroke went to France in 1712 to make the final arrangements for peace after the French war, and again he took charge of peace negotiations in 1713 when the Treaty of Utrecht was signed. On the accession of George I, Bolingbroke was dismissed from office. In 1714 a motion for his impeachment was carried, a bill of attainder passed, and his name erased from the role of peers. He fled to France and became Secretary of State to James the Pretender. He left the Pretender's service in 1716 and for a while lived in France until in 1723 he was pardoned and returned to England. He joined Walpole's party but became estranged from him because Walpole opposed an act permitting Bolingbroke to inherit and acquire real estate. Bolingbroke retired to France where he wrote essays upon history in the form of letters to friends, and upon political subjects. Bolingbroke died at Battersea in 1751.

Bolingbroke as a Statesman[1]

W H O now reads Bolingbroke? was asked sixty years ago. Who knows any thing about him? we may ask now. Professed students of our history or of our literature may have special knowledge; but out of the general mass of educated men, how many could give an intelligible account of his career? How many could describe even vaguely his character as a statesman? Our grandfathers and their fathers quarrelled for two generations as to the peace of Utrecht; but only an odd person here and there could now give an account of its provisions. The most cultivated lady would not mind asking, 'The peace of Utrecht! yes,— what was that?' Whether Mr. St. John was right to make that peace; whether Queen Anne was right to create him a peer for making it; whether the Whigs were right in impeaching him for making it,— the mass of men have forgotten. So is history *un*made. Even now the dust of forgetfulness is falling over the Congress of Vienna and the peace of Paris; we are forgetting the last great pacification as we have wholly forgotten the pacification before that; in another fifty years 'Vienna' will be as 'Utrecht,' and Wellington be no more than Marlborough.

In the mean time, however, Mr. Macknight has done well to collect for those who wish to know the principal events of Bolingbroke's career. There was no tolerable outline of them before; and in some respects this is a good one. Mr. Macknight's style is clear, though often ponderous; his remarks are sensible, and he has the great merit of not being imposed on by great names and traditional reputations. The defect of the book is, that he takes too literary a view of politics and politicians; that he has not looked closely and for himself at real political life; that he therefore misses the guiding traits which show what in Queen Anne's time was so like our present politics, and what so wholly unlike. We shall venture in the course of this article to

[1] *The Life of Henry St John Viscount Bolingbroke, Secretary of State in the reign of Queen Anne.* By Thomas Macknight, author of the 'History of the Life and Times of Edmund Burke.' This essay was first published in the *National Review* for April 1863, Volume XVI, pp. 389–426.

supply some general outline of the controversies that were to be then decided, and of the political forces which decided them; for unless these are distinctly imagined, a reader of the present day cannot comprehend why such a man as Bolingbroke was at one moment the most conspicuous and influential of English statesmen, and then for years an exile and a wanderer.

We must own, however, that it is not the intrinsic interest even of events once so very important as the war of the Grand Alliance and the peace of Utrecht which tempts us to write this article. It is the interest of Bolingbroke's own character. He tried a great experiment. There lurks about the fancies of many men and women an imaginary conception of an ideal statesman, resembling the character of which Alcibiades has been the recognised type for centuries. There is a sort of intellectual luxury in the idea which fascinates the human mind. We like to fancy a young man in the first vigour of body and in the first vigour of mind, who is full of bounding enjoyment, who is fond of irregular luxury, who is the favourite of society, who excels all rivals at masculine feasts, who gains the love of women by a magic attraction, but who is also a powerful statesman, who regulates great events, who settles great measures, who guides a great nation. We seem to outstep the *mœnia mundi*, the recognised limits of human nature, when we conceive a man in the pride of youth to have dominion of the pursuits of age, to rule both the light things of women and the grave things of men. Human imagination so much loves to surpass human power, that we shall never be able to extirpate the conception. But we may examine the approximations to it in life. We see in Bolingbroke's case that a life of brilliant licence is really compatible with a life of brilliant statesmanship; that licence itself may even be thought to quicken the imagination for oratorical efforts; that an intellect similarly aroused may, at exciting conjunctures, perceive possibilities which are hidden from duller men; that the favourite of society will be able to use his companionship with men and his power over women so as much to aid his strokes of policy, but, on the other hand, that these secondary aids and occasional advantages are purchased by the total sacrifice of a primary necessity; that a life of great excitement is incompatible with the calm circumspection and sound estimate of probability essential to great affairs; that though the excited hero may perceive distant things which others overlook, he will overlook near things that others see; that though he may be stimulated to great speeches which others could not make, he will also be irritated to petty speeches which others would not; that he will attract enmities, but not confidence; that he will not observe how few and plain are the alternatives of common business, and how little even genius can enlarge them; that his prosperity will be a wild dream of unattainable possibilities, and his adversity a long regret that those possibilities are departed. At any rate, such was Bolingbroke's career. We have better evidence about him than about any similar statesman, for the events in which he was concerned were large, and he has given us a narrative of them from his own hand; and a summary retrospect of his career will not be worthless, if it show what sudden brilliancy and what incurable ruin such a life as his, with such a genius as his, was calculated to ensure.

Bolingbroke's father was a type of his generation. He was a rake of the Restoration. Charles the Second is the only king of England who has had both the social qualities which fitted him to be the head of society, and the immoral qualities which fitted him to corrupt society. His easy talk, his good anecdotes, his happy manners, his conversancy with various life, made Whitehall the 'best club' of that time. What sort of life he encouraged men to lead there we all know. Bolingbroke's father learned of him all the evil which he could learn. It was not singular that he committed excesses of dissipation; but it was rather singular that he committed what was thought to be murder. He stabbed a man in a drunken broil, and if Burnet can be trusted, only escaped from the gallows by a great bribe. He dawdled on at the coffee-houses far into Queen Anne's time, a memorial of extinct profligacy, and a spectacle and a wonder to a graver generation.

Bolingbroke's mother was a daughter of the Earl of Warwick; but she died early, and his father married again, so that we hear very little about her. If the silence of his biographers may be trusted as evidence, she exercised but little influence upon his infancy or upon his life.

The most influential preceptors of Bolingbroke's boyhood were his grandmother and grandfather, who also were not unusual characters in their generation. The former was a serious and moderate royalist, the latter was a serious but moderate Puritan. Bolingbroke's father apparently did not much like keeping house: it must have interfered with his pleasures, and marred the life of coffee-houses. The whole direction of Bolingbroke s mind was given to his grave grandfather and grandmother. In after-times, when he was a prominent Tory and professed high-churchman, satirists used to say that he was brought up among 'Dissenters.' And it is probable that his grandmother, who was the daughter of the celebrated Oliver St. John, the great parliamentary lawyer and chief-justice, was far from being in opinion what a high Anglican divine would term a 'church-woman.' Bolingbroke himself used to relate terrible stories of having been compelled to read the sermons of Puritan divines. But, as far as our slight information goes, he did not suffer more than in any moderately 'serious' family of our own time. All serious families were then thought to have a little taint of Dissent; and Bolingbroke was probably very sensitive to the partial dullness of a semi-puritanical religion.

At any rate, we have no doubt it was said (and his elder relatives much grieved at it) that 'the boy was gone wrong, like his father.' When he came out into the world, he astonished his associates by his license. He had been at Eton and Oxford, but he had not learnt, what is often learned there, a decorum in profligacy. To what precise enormities his license extended is immaterial, and cannot now be known. Goldsmith had talked to an old gentleman who related that Bolingbroke and his companions, in a drunken frolic, ran 'naked through the Park.' But this is hardly credible; and probably Goldsmith's informant was one of the many old people who believe, that the more wonderful the stories they tell, the more wonderful they themselves become. But at any rate his outrages attracted censure. He did not, like his father, belong to his generation. The age of King William tolerated much that we tolerate no longer; but it was not like the first years of Charles the Second. There was no longer a headlong recoil from Puritan strictness, and the Crown was on the side at least of apparent morality; as is usual in England, grave decorum and obvious morals had a substantial influence, and against these Bolingbroke offended.

He wrote poetry too, and the sort of poetry can only be appreciated by reading Locke's celebrated warning against that art, and the connexions which it occasions. Bolingbroke's verses are addressed to a Clara A—, an orange-girl, who pretended to sell that fruit near the Court of Requests, but who really had other objects. She was a lady of what may be called mutable connexions; and the object of Bolingbroke's verses is to induce her to give them up and adhere to him only. He says:

> No, Clara, no; that person and that mind
> Were formed by Nature, and by Heaven designed

For nobler ends: to these return, though late;
Return to these, and so avert thy fate.
Think, Clara, think; nor will that thought be vain;
Thy slave, thy Harry, doom'd to drag his chain
Of love ill-treated and abused, that he
From more inglorious chains might rescue thee:
Thy drooping health restored by his fond care,
Once more thy beauty its full lustre wear;
Moved by his love, by his example taught,
Soon shall thy soul, once more with virtue fraught,
With kind and generous truth thy bosom warm,
And thy fair mind, like thy fair person, charm.
To virtue thus and to thyself restored,
By all admired, by one alone adored,
Be to thy Harry ever kind and true,
And live for him who more than dies for you.

One would like to know what the orange-girl thought of all this; but it would seem he was lavish of money as well as of verses.

At twenty-two he married. We do not know much about his money-matters; and, as his father and grandfather were both alive, his means could not have been at all large, especially as his expenses had been great. But his wife had certainly a considerable fortune. She was descended from a clothier called Jack of Newbury, who had made a fortune several generations before, and was one of the coheiresses of Sir Henry Winchescomb, who had large property. What sort of person she was does not very clearly appear. But it does appear that the match was an unhappy one. He said she had a bad temper, with what truth we cannot ascertain now; and she said he was a bad husband, which was unquestionably true. He had been a rake before marriage, and did not cease afterwards. He could drink more wine than any one in London, and continued that too. A kind of connexion was kept up between them for many years, but it was a dubious and unhappy connexion. We may suppose, however, that when he was a great statesman she derived some glory, if little happiness, from him; and he certainly received a large income from her property during very many years.

At the age of twenty-eight Bolingbroke entered the House of Commons. Before that time he had done nothing to prove himself a man of great ability. At school and college he had done well, and had laid up perhaps a greater store of classical knowledge than those around him knew of. When abroad for a year or so, he had learned to speak French unusually well and unusually easily. But since he had been of age and in the world, his vices had been great, and he had not done much to compensate for them. Probably his boon companions considered him very clever; but then sober men rated very low the judgment of those companions. His skill in writing poetry had not been greater than most people's, and his choice of subjects had been worse. Until now he had had no opportunity of showing great talents, and much opportunity of showing considerable vices.

In the House of Commons it was otherwise. His handsome person, long descent, and aristocratic mien set off a very remarkable eloquence, which seems to have been very ready even at the first. Years afterwards he was the model to whom Lord Chesterfield pointed in all the arts of manner and expression. 'Lord Bolingbroke,' he tells us, 'without the least trouble, talked all day long full as elegantly as he wrote;' 'he adorned whatever subject he either spoke or wrote upon by the most splendid eloquence; not a studied and laboured eleoquence, but by such a flowing happiness of diction which (from care perhaps at first) was become so habitual to him, that even his most familiar conversations, if taken down in writing, would have borne the press without the least correction either as to method or style.' 'He had the most elegant politeness and good-breeding which ever any courtier or man of the world was blessed with.'

Nor did he neglect matter in the pursuit of manner. In later life he wrote some characters of the two great orators of antiquity which showed how acutely he had studied them. He turned aside from the commonplace topics, from their language and their manner, to comment on their acquaintance with all the topics of their time, and on the practical style in which they discuss practical questions. No one can read those delineations without perceiving that the writer is speaking of an art which he has himself practised. Those who knew how little studious Bolingbroke's habits were, appear to have been surprised at the information he displayed. But his excitable life rather promoted than forbad brief crises of keen study; his parts were quick, his language vague, though imposing, and he could always talk very happily on subjects of which he only knew a very little.

The time was favourable to a great orator. The Tory party was exactly in the state in which it has been in our own time. It had many votes and no tongue. Our county system tends to prevent our county magnates from ruling England. Stringent limitations are laid down which narrow the electoral choice, and tend to exclude available talent. It is wise and natural that the landed interest should choose to be represented by landed gentlemen; a community of nature between representatives is desirable and inevitable. But our counties are more exacting than this: each county requires that the member shall have land within the county, and as in each the number of candidates thus limited is but small, unsuitable ones must be chosen. We have left off expecting eloquence from a county member. Grave files of speechless men have always represented the land of England. In Queen Anne's time too, as in our own time, a lingering prejudice haunted rural minds, and inclined them to prefer stupid magnates that shared it to clever ones who were emancipated from it. Bolingbroke, like Mr. Disraeli, found the Tory party in a state of dumb power; like him, too, he became its spokesman and obtained its power.

Bolingbroke came into parliament just at the end of King William's reign, and was at once forced into contact with the two subjects which were to occupy almost exclusively his active life. The reign of King William, which was about to end, and that of Queen Anne, which was just about to begin, were filled by two of the greatest topics which can occupy a period. The first of these was a question of dynasty. Our revolution has been called the 'minimum of a revolution;' and in the eyes of a political philosopher so it is. It altered but little in the substance of our institutions and in our positive law. But to common people, when it happened, the change was great. Even now the detail of our parliamentary system is not much understood by the poorer part of the public, and they care for it but little; the Queen and her family, and the Prince of Wales and the Princess Alexandra, mainly interest them. The person of the sovereign embodies to them constitution, law, power. But our revolution changed the sovereign. The only political name and idea known to rural hamlets were taken away, and another name and idea were substituted in its stead. Jacobites went about saying that there was one king whom God had made, and another king whom Parliament had made. At this moment, though the dogma of hereditary right has been confuted for ages, though it has been laughed at for ages, though parliaments have prohibited it, though divines have been impeached for preaching it, though it is a misdemeanour to maintain it, the tenet still lives in ordinary minds. In Somersetshire and half the quiet counties the inhabitants would say that Queen Victoria ruled by the right of birth and the grace of God, and not by virtue of an Act of Parliament. They still think that she has a divine right to the crown, and not a right by statute only. If the old creed of the Jacobites is still so powerful, what must have been its force in Queen Anne's time? That generation has seen the change from 'God's king' to 'man's king,' and very many of them did not like it. Shrewd men said that England was prosperous under the revolutionary government; common sense said that an ill-born king who governed well was better than a well-born king who governed ill; Whigs said that England was free after the revolution, and would have been enslaved but for the revolution; yet on the simple superstition of many natural minds the force of these arguments was lost. They admitted the advantage of liberty and of prosperity, but they would not renounce 'the Lord's anointed for a mess of pottage.'— Happily this political feeling was counteracted by a religious feeling. The hatred to popery supported the successful and rebellious king, who was a Protestant, against the unsuccessful and legitimate king, who was a papist. But the strength so obtained was precarious; it might cease at any time. The 'Pretender' might change his religion, and reports were continually circulated that he had done so, or was to do so. The existing dynasty could not be strong while its best support in the most natural minds was the continued profession of one religion by a person who had very strong motives to profess another.

The question of dynasty was the prominent question in Bolingbroke's age; such a question must always be the first where it exists. The question, who shall be king, can never be secondary. But it had a formidable rival. All through King William's and all through Queen Anne's time, the English mind was occupied with almost the only question which could compete with the question, who should be king of England—the question, whether there ought or ought not to be war with France. Frequent battles, daily hopes of battles, daily arguments whether there should be battles or not, kept even the greatest domestic question out of our thoughts.

On both these subjects Bolingbroke was compelled to critical action in his first parliament. The question of dynasty was in a very odd and very English complexity. It might have been thought to be a question of bare alternatives, and to have been susceptible of no compromise. *Either* Parliament had no power to choose a sovereign upon grounds of expediency, *or* it might choose any sovereign who was expedient.

If King James might be expelled at all, it could only be because he was a bad king, and in order to put in a better king. On principle, Parliament was either powerless or omnipotent. But this clear decisive logic has never suited Englishmen. As for King William, indeed, no one could say he was any sort of king except a parliamentary king; but his heir was the Princess Anne. 'Surely, it was thought, she and her children had *some* divine right—a little, if not much? She had no right by birth certainly, for her father and her brother came before her; she was not the nearest heir, but she was the nearest Protestant heir; she was not the eldest son of the last king, but she was his eldest daughter that was living.' These facts do not seem to be very material to us now, but at the time they were critically material. Half the population probably believed that it would be right,—not merely expedient, but right in some high mystic sense,—to obey Anne and her children. They were not only ready, but were anxious, to take her for the root of a new dynasty. But the Fates seemed capriciously determined to defeat their wishes. Anne had thirteen children, and all the thirteen died. At the death of the Duke of Gloucester, who was the last of them, some further settlement was necessary, and what it should be was decided in Bolingbroke's first parliament.

On this subject he ought to have been a Whig of the Whigs. His books are full of such expressions as the 'chimera of prerogative;' 'the slavish principles of passive obedience and non-resistance which had skulked' in old books till the reign of James I. And he has stated the Whig conception of the revolution as well as any one, if not better. 'If,' he says, 'a divine, indefeasable, hereditary right to govern a community be once acknowledged; a right independent of the community, and which vests in every successive prince immediately on the death of his predecessor, and previously to any engagement taken on his part towards the people; if the people once acknowledge themselves bound to such princes by the ties of passive obedience and non-resistance, by an allegiance unconditional, and not reciprocal to protection; if a kind of oral law, or mysterious cabbala, which pharisees of the black gown and the long robe are always at hand to report and interpret as a prince desires, be once added, like a supplemental code, to the known laws of the land: then, I say, such princes have the power, if not the right, given them of commencing tyrants; and princes who have the power, are prone to think that they have the right. Such was the state of king and people before the revolution.' He could have no horror of popery, for he regarded all the historical forms of Christianity with an impartial scepticism; he probably thought it more gentlemanly than Presbyterianism, and not more absurd than Anglicanism. He ought to have been ready to obey whatever king was most eligible upon grounds of rational expediency.

The proposal of the Whigs, too, was as moderate as it was possible for it to be. As public opinion required, they selected the next Protestant heir. They passed over all the children of James II, who were Catholics, the descendants of Henrietta, daughter of Charles I, who were Catholics, the elder descendants of Elizabeth, the daughter of James I, who were Catholics, and found the Princess Sophia, a younger daughter of Elizabeth, who was a very clever and accomplished lady, and who, if she had any religion, was a Protestant. All the reasonable and prudent part of the nation were in favour of this scheme. The Whigs were of course in favour of it, for it was their scheme. Harley, at the head of the moderate Tories, strenuously supported it. But it was not popular with the unthinking masses, and perhaps could not be. Half or more than half the believers in divine right were ready, as we have explained, to pay obedience to Queen Anne as a sort of consecrated queen; she was at any rate a princess born of a real king and queen in real England; we had always been used to her. But a search in Germany for the sort of Protestants we were likely to find there was not pleasant to the mass of Englishmen; and of the strong-minded old lady that had been discovered nothing whatever was commonly known. After all, too, there was no certainty that in future we should be obeying the nearest Protestant heir. We were passing over several Catholic families; and if hereafter any one of them were to become a Protestant—according to *principle*, or what was called such, we must obey him as our king.

Though the choice of the Hanoverian family as heirs to the Crown was prudent, wise, and statesmanlike, there was no strong popular sentiment by which it was firmly based, and no neat popular phrase by which it could in argument be precisely supported. In a word, unthinking people of the common sort did not much like the House of Hanover, and a mass of ill-defined prejudice accumulated against it. Of this prejudice Bolingbroke made himself the organ. He did not share it, or try to share it. But, finding a large and speechless party, he thought he could become at once politically important by saying for them that which they could not say for themselves. The scheme was successful. He became at once important in Parliament, because he was the eloquent spokesman of many inaudible persons.

In foreign policy, Bolingbroke's tactics were the same. The aggression of France was the natural terror of lovers of liberty at that time. Louis XIV was as ready to use his power without scruple against free nations as Napoleon; and his power, though not equal to that of Napoleon at his zenith, was greater than that of Napoleon at most times, and than that of any other French sovereign at any time. The King of Spain, too, was about to die; it was to be feared that he would name as his heir Philip, the grandson of Louis, and few doubted but that Louis, notwithstanding an express renunciation of all such claims by treaty, would permit his grandson to accept the throne.[2] Nor was the Spain of 1700 merely the Spain of our time. She was much more powerful. She possessed the 'California' of that age, a vast empire in South America, producing gold and silver, which were then thought to be magically potent substances, for the whole civilised world. She possessed, too, Sicily, and Naples, and Milan, and Belgium; and popular imagination, which ever clings to decaying grandeur, still believed that Spain itself was a nation of great power—was still able, as in former generations, to obtain ascendency in Europe. The *terror*, for such it was, of liberal politicians then was, that this vast inheritance would practically fall into the dominion of Louis XIV.—that it would belong to a Bourbon prince brought up under his eye, and slavishly in subjection to him. The Whigs contended that this calamity should be prevented, if possible, by an amicable partition of Spain, by giving France as little as possible, and that little in places as little important as possible. If no such amicable arrangement were possible, they said, it must be prevented by a war. The Tories did not like war; did not like partition treaties. They did not love France, but they were not anxious to oppose France. In that age we were uneducated in foreign policy; the mass of men had no distinct conception of Continental transactions, nor was reason reinforced very distinctly by antipathy. We hated France, it is true, but we hated Holland also; she was our rival in commerce, and our enemy—sometimes our successful enemy—in naval warfare; and to vanquish the French by the aid of the Dutch did not gratify an unmixed animosity.[3] The anti-revolutionary part of the nation did not care for liberty, for that was the code of the Whigs

---

[2] The *National Review* has 'of it' for 'the throne'—p. 399.
[3] Both Morgan and Hutton have 'did not greatly gratify our animosity'.

and the basis of the revolution. In a word, though there was little distinct or rational opinion opposed to a war with France, there was much indistinct and crude prejudice. Of this too Bolingbroke became the organ.

In the later part of his life he did not attempt to defend his first notion of foreign policy. He says: 'I have sometimes considered, in reflecting on these passages, what I should have done, if I had sat in parliament at that time; and have been forced to own myself, that I should have voted for disbanding the army then; as I voted in the following parliament for censuring the partition treaties. I am forced to own this, because I remember how imperfect my notions were of the situation of Europe in that extraordinary crisis, and how much I saw the true interest of my own country in a half light. But, my lord, I own it with some shame; because in truth nothing could be more absurd than the conduct we held. What! because we had not reduced the power of France by the war, nor excluded the house of Bourbon from the Spanish succession, nor compounded with her upon it by the peace; and because the house of Austria had not helped herself, nor put it into our power to help her with more advantage and better prospect of success—were we to leave that whole succession open to the invasions of France, and to suffer even the contingency to subsist of seeing those monarchies united? What! because it was become extravagant, after the trials so lately made, to think ourselves any longer engaged by treaty, or obliged by good policy, to put the house of Austria in possession of the whole Spanish monarchy, and to defend her in this possession by force of arms, were we to leave the whole at the mercy of France? If we were not to do so, if we were not to do one of the three things that I said above remained to be done, and if the Emperor put it out of our power to do another of them with advantage; were we to put it still more out of our power, and to wait unarmed for the death of the king of Spain? In fine, if we had not the prospect of disputing with France, so successfully as we might have had it, the Spanish succession, whenever it should be open; were we not only to show by disarming, that we would not dispute it at all, but to censure likewise the second of the three things mentioned above, and which King William put in practice, the compounding with France, to prevent if possible a war, in which we were averse to engage?' The truth doubtless is, that Bolingbroke never believed, or much believed, these absurdities. As he was the spokesman of the

Tories, he advocated, and was compelled to advocate, the vague notions which they not unnaturally held, and these were prejudices imbibed by habit, not opinions elaborated by effort. That his mode of advocacy was very skilful, we may easily believe. His speeches have perished; but their merit may be conjectured. He is in his writings a great master of *specious* statement. Accessory arguments and subordinate facts seem of themselves to fall precisely where they should fall. He has the knack of never *making* a case; the case always seems made for him; he seems to be giving it its most suitable expression, but to be doing no more. In the greater part of his writings which were written late in life, except when he defends the peace of Utrecht, he had no tenet to defend in which he took a keen interest. He had not the habits suitable to abstract thought, or the genius for it. He is apt, therefore, to embody meagre thoughts in excellent words; to develop long arguments from sparse facts. He had a pleasure in writing, and he had little to say. But when his passions were eager, when his interest was vivid, when the very dissipation of his life quickened his excitability, when the topic of discussion was critically important to himself,—we may well believe his advocacy to have been effective. He could ever say what he pleased, and in early life he had much to say which he well knew and for which he much cared.

A blunder of Louis' for several years simplified English politics. At the death of James the Second, he acknowledged his son, the 'Pretender,' as king of England; and he could have done him no greater harm. The English people were not very sure of abstract rights, but they were very sure of practical applications. Whether they had a right to choose a king for themselves might be doubtful, but it was clear that the king of France had no such right. Whoever might be our king, it certainly should not be his *protégé*. War with France became popular. The King of Spain was dead; as was feared, he had left the vast inheritance of Spain to Louis' grandson; and war with France became expedient. It was declared accordingly.

The death of William simplified politics still further. Bolingbroke himself may explain this. 'The alliances,' he tells us, 'were concluded, the quotas were settled, and the season for taking the field approached, when King William died. The event could not fail to occasion some consternation on one side, and to give some hopes on the other; for, notwithstanding the ill success with which he made war generally, he was looked upon as the sole centre of union that could keep together the great confederacy then forming; and how much the French feared from his life had appeared a few years before, in the extravagant and indecent joy they expressed on a false report of his death. A short time showed how vain the fears of some, and the hopes of others, were. By his death, the Duke of Marlborough was raised to the head of the army, and indeed of the confederacy; where he, a new, a private man, a subject, acquired by merit and by management a more deciding influence than high birth, confirmed authority, and even the crown of Great Britain, had given to King William. Not only all the parts of that vast machine, the grand alliance, were kept more compact and entire, but a more rapid and vigorous motion was given to the whole; and, instead of languishing or disastrous campaigns, we saw every scene of the war full of action. All those wherein he appeared, and many of those wherein he was not then an actor—but abettor, however, of their action—were crowned with the most triumphant success. I take with pleasure this opportunity of doing justice to that great man, whose faults I knew, whose virtues I admired; and whose memory, as the greatest general and as the greatest minister that our country or perhaps any other has produced, I honour.' The war absorbed England for several years. For the first time in our history, we were the centre of a great confederacy, and our general was the victorious leader, in great battles, of miscellaneous armies. It was then that we first acquired that great name as a military people, which, notwithstanding our small numbers and small armies, we have since supported, and that a great foresight, a minute diligence, and a splendid courage in modern war, were first combined in an Englishman. Marlborough was in one respect more fortunate than Wellington. Napoleon must always be the first military figure of his generation, but throughout the last century the whole Continent talked of the wars of Marlborough; for he was the most fascinating as well as the most successful general in them.

During the first eight years of Marlborough's wars, the English nation was nearly united. A war always unites a people: the objector to it becomes a kind of traitor to his country; he seems to be a favourer of the enemy, even though he is not. Not only Harley, a moderate Tory, but Bolingbroke, an extreme Tory, took office in the war-ministry. It is true there was no dereliction of party principle in their doing so, either as such principle was then understood, or as it is understood now. Marlborough himself had never been a Whig; and

Godolphin, the head of the treasury and first minister for the home administration, had ever been a Tory. But though plain party-ties might not be violated by a Tory support of Marlborough's wars, a sort of sentiment was violated. The war was a Whig war, and could only be carried on by Whig support. Ere long Godolphin and Marlborough were compelled to give the Whigs a large share in the actual administration. The ministry became a composite one. Though many Tories remained in it, yet its essence and its spirit were Whig. It was carrying on the sort of war which one party in the state had extolled for years, and which the antagonist party had deprecated for years. It has been called after its cause. It has been called the Whig ministry of Godolphin and Marlborough, the two leading Tories of the age.

The place which Bolingbroke accepted was that of Secretary at War, which brought him into contact with the best business of the time, with that sort of business upon which most depended. As far as appears, he did it well, and the official experience he then acquired must have been inestimable to him afterwards. There is much which no statesman can in truth know, and much more which he will not be thought to know, unless he has gone through a certain necessary official education, and learned to use certain conventional official expressions; this sort of knowledge Bolingbroke now acquired. But it was not by success or failure in office desk-work that the movements of his life were to be regulated.

The Whigs naturally did not quite like the subordinate position which they occupied in a ministry which was carrying out a Whig policy. They thought it hard that Tories should be paid for Whig measures; that the glory of delivering Europe should be given, not to Whigs, who had striven to deliver it, but to Tories, who would have liked not to deliver it. Their support was necessary to Godolphin and to Marlborough, and they gradually raised the price of that support. Early in 1708, most of the remaining Tories were turned out, and Bolingbroke among them. Except the two chiefs, Godolphin and Marlborough, the ministry became a Whig ministry almost exclusively.

That Bolingbroke did not like to be turned out is probable, but he professed to like it. He sought refuge in retirement; he professed to study philosophy, and passed much of his time in the country, and in reading; such professions from a man of great ambition and lax life were ridiculed. A friend suggested that he should write this motto over his favourite rural retreat:

From business and the noisy world retired,
Nor vexed by love, nor by ambition fired,
Gently I wait the call of Charon's boat,
Still drinking like a fish, and amorous like a goat.

And Swift says he could hardly bear the jest, for he was a man rather
sensitive to ridicule. And though satirists might laugh at his medita-
tions and his studies, and though he permitted them to derange very
little his pleasure or his vices, there is no doubt but that they were
real, and that they were valuable. Doubtless, too, though he was only
twenty-eight, he was a little tired of subordinate office. His disposition
was very impatient, and his sense of personal dignity very considerable.
Even so patient a pattern of routine diligence as Sir Robert Peel
rejoiced as a young man to be for a year or so out of office. His mind,
he acknowledged, widened, and his capacity to think for himself
improved. If Peel, who was made to toil in the furrow, felt this,
Bolingbroke, who was made to exult in the desert, might well feel it.
During three years he really read much and thought much.

But a great change was at hand. The war with France was still
successful and still popular, but it might be doubted if it was still
necessary. We had weakened France so much, that it might be
questionable if she wanted weakening more. Our victories had destroyed her prestige; and the results of these victories had weakened
her vigour. Sensible men began to inquire what was to be the time,
what the occasion, and what the terms of peace.

The ministry, indeed, appeared to be firm, but it was firm in appearance only. The conditions of ministerial continuance differed in that
age in a most material respect from the present conditions. Now the
House of Commons, in almost all cases, prescribes imperatively not
only what measures shall be taken, but what men shall take them; it
chooses both policy and ministers. In Queen Anne's time Parliament
had acquired an almost complete ascendancy in policy; it could fix
precisely whether there should be war or no war, peace or no peace; it
had acquired a perfect control upon legislation, and a nearly perfect
control upon internal administration. But it had no choice, or but little,
in the selection of persons. *What* was to be done Parliament settled,
but *who* was to do it the Queen settled.

Queen Anne had done so at her accession. Though she was engaged
in a Whig war, she removed the Whig ministers whom she found in
office. She appointed as supreme generalissimo over the war abroad,

and real prime minister over matters of state at home, the Duke of Marlborough, not because of his discretion or his acquaintance with business, or his military genius, but because his wife was her early friend and her special favourite. As the Duke of Wellington justly observed, the Duke of Marlborough *was* the English government; he was not liable to be thwarted, or misconstrued, or neglected; his operations in Flanders were never cramped by the home-government, as the operations of the Duke of Wellington in Spain were cramped. He appointed the Lord High Treasurer Godolphin; he placed the treasury, then even more than now the supreme internal office, in Godolphin's hands, because he was connected with him by domestic ties, because they had long acted together, because he had great confidence in his financial ability. The Duke of Marlborough was not only great because of his wife, but absolute because of his wife.

By a kind of compensation the source of his power was the cause also of his downfall. The Queen and the Duchess quarrelled, as was natural. The Duchess was virulent and obtrusive, and the Queen was sensitive and sullen. The Queen had a strong sense of personal dignity, which the Duchess used to outrage. The Duchess, who was clever, thought the Queen a fool, and scarcely forebore to look and say so. From early habit the friendship lasted much longer than could have been thought likely, but it could not last for ever. As it was breaking up, a small force produced a large effect. The Queen, Swift says, had not a 'stock of amity' for more than one person at a time:[4] she commonly cared but little for every body save one; but she required one. The Duchess had placed at court a poor relative of her own, a Miss Hill, whom both she and the Queen regarded as a petty dependent, a *real* maid, who would be useful and lie on the floor when peeresses and young ladies of quality were useless and went to bed. As she was humble and artful, she acquired influence: she was never in the way and never out of the way. She was always pleasant to the Queen, and the Duchess was commonly unpleasant. The consequence was certain. The abject new favourite soon supplanted the querulous old favourite.

A very curious man took advantage of this. Wits and satirists have been fond of describing Robert Harley; but perhaps they have not described him very well. They have made a heap of incongruities of him. They have told us that, being bred a Puritan, and retaining

4 Hutton has 'a stock of amity to serve above one object at a time'.

59

till his death much of the Puritan phraseology, he yet became the favourite leader of high churchmen and Tories; that being a muddle-headed dawdle, he gained a great reputation for the transaction of business; that having an incapacity for intelligible speech, he became an influential orator in parliament; that being a puzzle-headed man, of less than average ability, and less than average activity, he long ruled a great party, for years ruled the court, and was at last Prime Minister of England.

It is very natural that brilliant and vehement men should depreciate Harley, for he had nothing which they possess, but had every thing which they commonly do not possess. He was by nature a moderate man. In that age they called such a man a trimmer, but they called him ill. Such a man does not consciously shift or purposely trim his course. He firmly believes that he is substantially consistent. 'I do not wish in this house,' he would say in our age, 'to be a party to any extreme course. Mr. Gladstone brings forward a great many things which I cannot understand; I assure you he does. There is more in that bill of his about tobacco than he thinks; I am confident there is. Money is a serious thing, a *very* serious thing. And I am sorry to say Mr. Disraeli commits the party very much. He avows sentiments which are injudicious. I cannot go along with him, nor can Sir John. He was not taught the Catechism; I know he was not. There is a want of sound and sober religion,—and Sir John agrees with me,—which would keep from distressing the clergy, who are very important. Great orators are very well; but, as I said, how is the revenue? And the point is, not to be led away and to be moderate, and not to go to an extreme. As soon as it seems *very* clear, then I doubt. I have been many years in parliament, and *that* is my experience.' We may laugh at such speeches, but there have been plenty of them in every English parliament. A great English divine has been described as always leaving out the principle upon which his arguments rested; even if it was stated to him, he regarded it as far-fetched and extravagant. Any politician who has this temper of mind will always have many followers; and he may be nearly sure that all great measures will be passed more nearly as he wishes them to be than as great orators wish. Harley had this temper, and he enjoyed its results. He always had a certain influence over moderate Whigs when he was a Tory, and over moderate Tories when he was a Whig. Nine-tenths of men are more afraid of violence than of any thing else; and inconsistent moderation is always popular, because of all qualities it is most opposite to violence,—most likely to preserve the present safe existence.

Harley's moderation, which was influential because it was un-affected, was assisted by two powers which brilliant people despise, because in general they do not share them. Harley excelled in the forms of business. There is distinct evidence that official persons preferred his management of the treasury to that of Lord Godolphin, who preceded him, or Sir Robert Walpole, who succeeded him. In real judgment and substantial knowledge of affairs, there was doubtless no comparison; Godolphin was the best financier of his generation, and Walpole was the best not only of his own but of many which came after him. But the ultimate issue of business is not the part of it which most impresses the officials of a department. They understand how business is conducted better than what comes of it. The states-man who gives them no trouble,—who coincides with that which they recommend,—who thinks of the things which they think of, is more satisfactory to his mere subordinates than a real ruler, who has plans which others do not share, and whose mind is occupied by large considerations, which only a few can appreciate, and only experience can test. In his own time, both with the Tory party, and with moderate Whigs, Harley's reputation as a man of business was a means of influence which, on the same scene and in our own day, could hardly be surpassed.

But it was surpassed in his own day. In personal questions, as we have explained, the Parliament in Queen Anne's time was only a subordinate power; the court was the principal and the determining power. Now the faculty of business is but secondary in all courts; the faculty of intrigue is the main source of real influence. To be able to manage men, to know with whom to be silent, to know with whom to say how much, to be able to drop casual observations, to have a sense of that which others mean, though they do not say,—to be aware what Lady A. is in secret planning, though she says the very opposite, —to know that Lord B. has no influence, though he seems most potent,—to know that little C. is a wire-puller, and can get you any thing, though he looks mean and though no one knows;—in a word, to understand, to feel, to be unable to help feeling, the *by-play* of life, is the principal necessity for a success in courts. It is the instinct of management which is not to be shown even in conversation, far less in writing or speculation, but yet which rules all small societies.

Harley possessed it, and the obscure but potent talents of business also; and we need seek no farther explanation why he was one of the most successful men in his own time.

Harley was some sort of relative to Miss Hill (or Mrs. Masham, for she married), the rising favourite of Queen Anne's time. He was the favourite leader of all moderate Tories; and, on the whole, though not without grumblings from extreme men, the most important leader of the Tory party. He had been turned out when Bolingbroke was turned out, and he wished to return. The fly was brought to the spider. Mrs. Masham, the new favourite, asked Harley what counsel she should give the Queen. He said, Turn out the Whigs; and meant, Bring *me* in.

The Queen was inert, for that was her nature; and the evident popularity and the glorious success of the Whig war naturally staggered her. But the Whigs made an error. The high-church and semi-high-church party had enormous power in the nation; they had always advocated non-resistance before the revolution, and though they had taken the oaths to King William's government, they did not like to think that they were supporting a government which was conspicuously rebellious, which began in resistance to legitimate authority. Of course the fact was so. King William invaded England with Dutch troops, and was joined by English rebels; but the divine right of princes, and the duty of unconditional obedience, retained much influence over most of the clergy and over many of the laity. If the Whigs had been wise, they would have offended this powerful sentiment as little as possible. High churchmen were certainly powerful, but were necessarily inert; they had no distinct course to recommend; they *would* have done much, but they *could* do nothing. They had assented to the existing government, and though their assent might be unwilling and ungracious, the existing government should have let them alone. The Whigs adopted the reverse course. A foolish parson expressed with unusual folly the sentiments of the great majority of his order. The Commons, at the instigation of the Whigs, actually impeached him at the bar of the Lords. In their folly they used against a pious and innocuous fool the extreme remedy which the Constitution provides for the final punishment of impious and dangerous traitors. The country was in a ferment; the Tory party were active; the moderate classes were alarmed; the clergy were incensed; the Whigs became unpopular.

62

Harley seized the opportunity. He persuaded Mrs. Masham to persuade the Queen that now was the moment to gratify her new antipathy to her old favourite; that now she should punish the Duchess of Marlborough; that now she should dismiss the Whig ministry. She did so. He came in himself, and made Bolingbroke a secretary of state, and the first member in the House of Commons.

It has been said, and is very likely, that Harley would have preferred to retain in office the quiet and moderate Whigs, and not to bring in Bolingbroke, an extreme and unquiet Tory. The Whig party, however, was compact, and held together; it must be expelled as a whole, or retained as a whole. If it had been wholly retained, Harley could not have come in; and he was therefore obliged to ally himself with the aggravated Tories, and with Bolingbroke, who had made himself their mouthpiece. It only completes the mingled character of Bolingbroke to repeat the legend of the time, that his acceptance of office was heard with gladness, not only in grave manor-houses, and by severe high churchmen, but in more unmentionable places and by more questionable persons. Some ladies of much beauty and little virtue, so runs the legend, were heard to say, 'Bolingbroke is minister. He has six thousand guineas a year. Six thousand guineas, and all for us.' The auspices of such a ministry were not good.

The public aspect of affairs was, however, in the most critical particular very favourable. While the French war lasted, indeed, the new ministry must be perplexed. They must either retain the Duke of Marlborough as general-in-chief, which was not pleasant, as he was the chief of the party opposed to them, and since probably Mrs. Masham did not wish it; or they must dismiss the Duke in the midst of victory, and find a new general, who might be defeated. But this painful alternative was temporary only. The English nation had been sated with sieges and victories, and more than sated with taxes and with debt; it was disposed to peace. The new ministry came therefore into the enjoyment of a great inheritance, the greatest that has ever fallen to a new ministry. France had been so reduced by Marlborough's victories that she was ready to consent to a peace which a few years before she would have thought most shameful, which a few years before we should have thought most honourable. The new ministry were to make that peace.

The preliminary difficulty soon assumed its worst shape. It became necessary to dismiss the Duke of Marlborough; and, as might be expected, the Duke of Ormond, who succeeded him, was much less successful. There was happily no great defeat, but there were minor disasters, which were magnified by the contrast with past glories. We had been used to a great exploit every year, and we were now asked to be thankful at not being defeated very much. The contrast was painful, and the necessity of making peace became greater than ever.

Up to this time Bolingbroke had been the most successful politician of his age, and almost of any age, in England. He had, it is true, no influence at court. Queen Anne distrusted him; she liked decorous men of regulated life. But, though little over thirty, he was the leader of the House of Commons; the first orator there; the second minister in the cabinet; the favourite minister of the most ardent section of his party,—a section just strengthened by an election. The fame of his oratory filled London; and the fame of his genius filled the country. Mr. Pitt excepted, no Englishman has risen so high and so rapidly under our parliamentary system. It was at this crisis that his eager nature and his life of excitement began to prepare his downfall, as they had prepared his rise.

The official management of the foreign negotiations was in the hands of Bolingbroke. Lord Dartmouth, the other secretary of state, could speak no French, and Harley, the prime minister, could speak but little; but Bolingbroke spoke it well. Harley, too, had no directing ability. He had the defects of Lord Aberdeen: he was moderate and useful and judicious. But he could not upon the spur of the moment strike out a distinct policy. Other statesmen must create before he can decide on their creations. Bolingbroke was to devise how a peace should be made.

A plain and strongheaded statesman—such a statesman as Walpole or as Palmerston—would have had little difficulty. France was most anxious to make peace; and it mattered but little for England or for Europe what were the precise conditions of it. There are occasions when a war itself does its own work, and does it better than any pacification. The Crimean war was an instance of this. That war thoroughly destroyed the prestige of Russia, and the pernicious pre-dominance of Russia. At the end of it, what were to be the conditions of peace was almost immaterial. The wars of Marlborough had done their work also. We had gone to war to prevent the acquisition of overbearing power by Louis XIV; if a grandson who was devoted to him had succeeded to Spain and the Spanish empire while France was unexhausted, he would have been a despot in Europe; he would have been terrible to us as Napoleon was terrible. But nine years of continuous defeat had exhausted France, and Louis XIV was now a vanquished and decayed old man. At his death the crown of France would pass to Louis XV, who was an infant; it was not much to be feared that the policy of France and the policy of Spain would be dangerously connected because their kings were second cousins. Possibly, indeed, Louis XV might die, and the King of Spain might come to the throne of France. But this was a remote and contingent danger; it would have been unwise in our ancestors to lavish blood and spend treasure because a prince might die young who really lived to be extremely old. The true object of the war had been accomplished by the war itself, and the substantial task of making a peace was therefore very easy.

The accessories of the task, too, it would seem, were easy also. As we had been victorious in a first-rate war, it was right that we should be dignified in the final pacification. It was right that we should be ready, that we should even be anxious, to make peace; but, at any rate, France, who was vanquished, ought to seem equally anxious. Since, in part, the war was a war to reduce her influence over the European imagination, the manner of making peace was at least as material as the terms of it. We were principal members of a great league, and we had stirred up a part of Spain to resist the French King of Spain. We were bound to keep clear faith with our allies, and bound not to desert brave provinces who had relied principally on our protection.

Bolingbroke was too eager to perceive these plain considerations. He sent a man to Paris to ask for peace; and the French minister was so astounded that he would hardly believe the man. He owned afterwards that, when he was asked the preliminary question, 'Do you want a peace?' it seemed to him like asking a lingering invalid whether he wanted to recover. He could hardly bring himself to believe that Bolingbroke's messenger was duly authorised.

The previous life of that messenger certainly was not such as to gain him credit. He was a French abbé named Gaultier, who had been a French spy, and perhaps still was so, in England. He was an acute plausible person, very fat, and not very respectable, and altogether as unlikely a person to be sent from a victorious nation to a defeated nation as could be imagined.

Nevertheless the Abbé Gaultier was so sent. He said to Torcy, the

French minister, 'Do you want a peace? I bring you the means of treating independently of the Dutch, who are unworthy of His Majesty's kindness and the honour he has done them in addressing himself to them so many times to restore peace to Europe.' In an ordinary alliance, such a clandestine reconciliation with the enemy, and such a secret desertion of allies, would have been plainly dishonest. There would have been little to say for it, and very few would have been willing to say that little. But the Grand Alliance was not an ordinary one. Its acute framers had perceived the difficulty of their task. They had foreseen the difficulty of retaining in firm cohesion a miscellaneous league of scattered states. They had adopted the best expedient at their disposal: they had prohibited the very commencement of exclusive negotiation by individual states. Their words are as clear as words can be. They are these: 'Neutri partium fas sit, Bello semel suscepto, de Pace sum Hoste tractare nisi conjunctim et communicatis conciliis cum altera Parte.' These words expressly forbid such secret missions as those of Gaultier, and were inserted expressly to forbid them.

The separate treaty with Holland was even more express: it said that 'no negotiation shall be set on foot by one of the allies without the concurrence of the other; and that each ally shall continually, and from time to time, impart to the other every thing which passes in the said negotiation.' And yet it was especially from Holland that Bolingbroke was anxious, by every secret disguise, and every diplomatic artifice, to conceal his negotiation. He hoped, by a separate and secret peace, to obtain commercial advantages for the English, in which the Dutch should have no share.

Even after the first mission of Gaultier had terminated, there was an intricate series of secret negotiations, in which he and Prior were employed for us, and Mesnager for the French. Prior expressly required on our behalf 'that the secret should be inviolably kept till allowed by both parties to be divulged;' and the French minister wrote to Bolingbroke: 'It wholly depends upon the secrecy and good use you will make of the entire confidence he testifies to the Queen of Great Britain; and the King of France extols the firmness of the Queen, and sees with great pleasure the new marks of resolution she shows.' It was impossible to desert our allies more absolutely or more dishonourably. It was impossible to violate an express treaty more audaciously or more corruptly.

Nor was the secret negotiation a mere crime; it was also a miserable blunder. Diplomacy could hardly commit a greater. There was a splendid, a nearly unexampled power of compelling France to make a good peace. There was a great coalition against her, which had always been victorious under Eugene and Marlborough; which had obtained such successes as no Englishman had imagined; which had reduced France to a pitch of shame, degradation, and weakness, that surprised her most sanguine enemies, and depressed her most sanguine friends. So long as the coalition was compact, the coalition was all-powerful. But by the mere act of commencing a separate negotiation, Bolingbroke dissolved the coalition. There could be no mutual trust after that. The principal member of the league deserted the league, and its bond was immediately disunited. We all know what would have been the consequences if England had acted thus in the last war. Suppose Lords Grey and Grenville had come in before the campaign of 1814; suppose that they had sent a secret emissary to Napoleon; suppose that they had offered a separate peace without Spain, or Austria, or Russia. We know that Napoleon would again have been a principal potentate in Europe, for the coalition which alone could extirpate him would have been dissolved.

The truth of these remarks is written on the very face of the treaty of Utrecht, and is obvious in every part of the negotiation of it. A few months before Louis had been willing to abandon Spain and to abandon his grandson. He had said, 'If you can take Spain from him, take it; I will not help him.' But the allies were not content. They required that Louis should compel his grandson to resign; and this he considered dishonourable. But at Utrecht it was not even proposed that Philip should abandon Spain; that the House of Bourbon should possess Spain, was a conceded and admitted principle. We had dissolved the European confederacy, and we could not hope to attain its objects.

Nor was the desertion of the other powers combined with us in the Grand Alliance our only desertion, or our worst. All these powers were states of some magnitude, and some were states of great magnitude; they would be able to go on as they had always gone on,—to shift for themselves, as they had always shifted. But we also deserted others who were not so independent. We had incited the Catalans in the north-east of Spain to resist the French King of Spain; we had promised them in express terms our support and aid; for a long time we had given them that aid. But at the peace of Utrecht we deserted them. The Catalans made a brave resistance; but a small province could do nothing against a great nation. The Catalans were soon overcome, and deprived of all their liberties. Throughout Europe, and doubtless throughout England also, there were many murmurs against our policy. We had encouraged a brave people to rebel; we had even threatened if they did not rebel; and when they did rebel, we deserted them. If, at present, France and England were to incite the Poles to rebel against Russia, they hardly *could* desert them: the public opinion of the world is now so powerful; in Queen Anne's time public opinion could only murmur, but it did murmur. The peace of Utrecht, men said, was a base crime as well as a gross blunder.

But why, it will be asked, did Bolingbroke commit so gross a blunder? What reasons could have rendered it plausible to him. The principal answer is the principal key to his character. With many splendid gifts, he was exceedingly defective in cool and plain judgment. He failed where in all ages such men as Alcibiades have failed. Whether by nature he was much gifted with judgment, we cannot tell; the probability is that he was about as well gifted as other men. But his life was such as to render a cool judgment impossible. 'His fine imagination,' says Lord Chesterfield, 'was often heated and exhausted with his body in celebrating and almost deifying the prostitute of the night; and his convivial joys were pushed to all the extravagancy of frantic bacchanals.' Swift tells graphic stories of his drinking till his associates could drink no longer, and his being left at three in the morning calling for 't'other flask.' Many men may lead gross lives and keep cool heads, but such are not men of Bolingbroke's temperament. A man like Walpole, or a man like Louis Napoleon, is protected by an unsensitive nature from intellectual destruction. But such a man as Bolingbroke, whose nature is warm and whose imagination is excitable, imbibes the eager poison into the very heart of his mind. Such is our protection against the possibilities of an Alcibiades. No one who has not a vivid imagination can succeed in such a career; and any man of vivid imagination that career would burn away and destroy. Cold men may be wild in life and not wild in mind. But warm and eager men, fit to be the favourites of society, and fit to be great orators, will be erratic not only in conduct but in judgment. They will see men 'like trees walking.'

Bolingbroke's excitement did not prevent his working. He laboured many hours and wrote many letters. He often complains of the number of hours he has been at his desk, and of the labours which were thrown upon him. But his work probably only excited him the more; for a time *vires acquirit eundo* is the law of such wild strength. In the course of the negotiations he went to Paris, became the idol of society there, and used his social advantages efficiently for political purposes. To dazzle people more, he learned, or pretended to learn, the Spanish language, to read such diplomatic documents as were written in it. But such minor excellencies could not mend the incurable badness of a peace commenced by a surrender of the best we had to surrender, by a dissolution of our alliance. A plain strong-headed man would have left alone the accessory advantages, and succeeded in the main point. Without Spanish and without French Walpole would have made a good peace; Bolingbroke could not do so with both.

Bolingbroke, too, had a scheme, as imaginative and excited men will have. He knew that in relinquishing Spain to the House of Bourbon, he was giving the opponents of peace a great argumentative advantage. The mass of mankind, who judge by visible symbols, considered that a peace by which the King whom we had opposed should reign in Spain, and by which the King whom we had proposed did not reign there, as a gross failure. In sound argument, it was probably right for us to concede. As we have explained, the war had accomplished its own work; France was excessively weakened, and there was little fear of present danger from her. If by a possible death the crown of France should fall to the King of Spain, it would be time enough then to prevent the same person from reigning in the two kingdoms. The treaty of Utrecht provides that the same prince shall not reign in both; and, if necessary, we could go to war to enforce the treaty. The Bourbon King was popular in Spain, and was preferred by the Spaniards to any one else. It would have been hard to dislodge him. But Bolingbroke did not like to rely on these plain arguments. He hoped to make the peace popular by an appeal to our commercial jealousy, by gaining mercantile advantages for ourselves which our rivals the Dutch did not share. He obtained for us the celebrated Assiento contract, giving us the right of carrying Negro slaves to the West Indies, and also certain privileges which would have given our manufacturers great advantage in the French markets. He hoped this commercial bribe would silence the national conscience; that it would induce us to forget our treachery to our allies, our desertion of the

Catalans, and the establishment of the House of Bourbon in Spain; he hoped it would make the peace popular.

He was disappointed. The reception of that peace by the nation, and especially by the Tory party, was very like the reception of Mr. Disraeli's great budget.[5] A great secret had been long paraded of something which was to please every body; it was divulged, and it pleased nobody. Bolingbroke may himself describe the effect that his work produced on the more moderate portion of his party:

'The whimsical or the Hanover Tories continued zealous in appearance with us till the peace was signed. I saw no people so eager for the conclusion of it. Some of them were in such haste, that they thought any peace preferable to the least delay, and omitted no instances to quicken their friends who were actors in it. As soon as the treaties were perfected and laid before the Parliament, the scheme of these gentlemen began to disclose itself entirely. Their love of the peace, like other passions, cooled by enjoyment. They grew nice about the construction of the articles, could come up to no direct approbation, and, being let into the secret of what was to happen, would not preclude themselves from the glorious advantage of rising on the ruins of their friends and of their party.'

Nothing could be more natural than their conduct. The moderate Tory party, and most sensible men, wished for a satisfactory peace made in a satisfactory manner; they wished for dignity in diplomacy, and desirable results. They were disappointed. After a war which every one was proud of, we concluded a peace which no one was proud of, in a manner that every one was ashamed of.

The commercial treaties on which Bolingbroke relied, so far from helping him, were a hindrance to him. The right of taking slaves to the West Indies was indeed popular: the day for anti-slavery scruples had not commenced. But, in return for the privileges which the French gave to our manufacturers, we had given many privileges to them. We had established an approximation to free-trade, and every one was aghast. The English producer clamoured for protection, and he has seldom clamoured in vain. The commercial treaties required the consent of Parliament, and were rejected. If Bolingbroke had been a free-trader upon principle, his convictions might have consoled him. But he professed to know nothing of commerce, and did know nothing. His books are full of nonsense on such topics: he hated the City

[5] Morgan and Hutton have the additional words 'of 1852'.

because they were Whigs, and he hated the Dutch because he had deserted them; and these were his cardinal sentiments on mercantile affairs. He speaks of 'matters, such as that of commerce, which the negotiators of the peace of Utrecht could not be supposed to understand.' Certainly he did not understand them. He only directed his subordinates to get out of the French as much for ourselves, and as little for the Dutch as possible.

'Instead of gathering strength,' says Bolingbroke, 'either as a ministry or as a party, we grew weaker every day. The peace had been judged with reason to be the only solid foundation whereupon we could erect a Tory system; and yet when it was made, we found ourselves at a full stand. Nay the very work, which ought to have been the basis of our strength, was in part demolished before our eyes, and we were stoned with the ruins of it.'

In our time he would have been really stoned. The fierce warlike disposition of the English people would not have endured such dishonour. We may doubt if it would have endured any peace. It certainly would not have endured the best peace, unless it were made with dignity and with honesty. We should have been wildly elated by Marlborough's victories, and little in a mood to bear shame and to be guilty of desertion. The English people has been much the same for centuries. In country manor-houses, where a son had been killed for the cause which was sacrificed—in alehouses, where men were used to hear of glorious victories—in large towns, where the wrongs of injured races like the Catalans were understood—through a whole nation, which has ever been proud, brave, and honourable, a mean peace, effected by desertion, must have been abhorred. It was merely endured because it was made, and because in those days, when communication was slow, public opinion, as in America now, did not distinctly form itself till the crisis for action was over. But though for the moment endured, it was long abhorred. For very many years half our political talk was coloured by it. It was to the Tories what the coalition between Lord North and Fox was to the Whigs,—a principal operating cause in excluding them from office during fifty years.

And, what for the time was worse, the Tory ministry of the moment was disunited. 'Whilst this was doing,' says Bolingbroke, 'Harley looked on, as if he had not been a party to all which had passed; broke now and then a jest, which savoured of the inns of court, and the bad company in which he had been bred; and on those occasions where his station obliged him to speak of business, was absolutely unintelligible.' In reality Harley disliked his position. He had always been a moderate man, respected by moderate men; he had the reputation of a man of care and judgment, and he had thriven by that reputation. On a sudden he became a party to a disreputable peace, at which even moderate Whigs were frantic, for which even moderate Tories could not vote. That the negotiations had commenced by artifice and deceit did not horrify him much, for he was a man much given to stratagem. But he knew also that the negotiation had ended in conspicuous meanness and unpopular concessions; he felt that his reputation for judgment was weakened. All shrewd observers knew that there would soon be disunion between Harley, the old head of the moderate Tories, and Bolingbroke, the present head of the extreme Tories. Swift, who was a very shrewd observer, and who was close at hand, knew that there was already disunion.

Before the treaties had been discussed by, and the commercial part of them rejected in, the House of Commons, Bolingbroke made another error. He left the House of Commons. Harley had been created Earl of Oxford, and he could not endure to be inferior to him. There was much delay in conferring the peerage, and he was very angry at it. He was, Oxford says, 'in the utmost rage against the Treasurer, Lady Masham, and without sparing the greatest,' and made 'outrageous speeches.' A wise friend would have observed to him that no greater kindness could have been done him than to refuse him a peerage altogether. The great but gradual revolution which was consummated in the time of Walpole was then beginning to be apparent. Before Queen Anne's time our most conspicuous statesmen had been, during the most important part of their lives, members of the House of Lords; since Queen Anne's time they have at similar periods been usually members of the House of Commons. There are several causes for this, but the principal is one on which Bolingbroke has often commented. From time immemorial the Commons have been the guardians of the public purse; and whenever the public purse was to be touched, they have always been the first body in the state. But before the revolution they were seldom wanted. They granted the King, at the commencement of his reign, an estimated revenue, which was supposed to be adequate to the estimated expenditure in time of peace. As our wealth was rapidly increasing, it was often more than sufficient. In time of war the House of Commons must be applied to; new money was needful for new expenses; but the ordinary expenditure went on every year without their being consulted or required. The expense of William's wars and Queen Anne's wars made a great change: taxation became larger than it had ever been, though very small as it seems to us now. Since that time the estimated revenue which the crown yearly enjoyed, without additional parliamentary aid, has scarcely ever been adequate to the estimated expenditure. There has yearly been a budget, and yearly a recourse to the House of Commons. The position of a minister in the House of Commons has therefore greatly risen. Nine years out of ten the nation could at present dispense with a House of Lords—though a useful it is an auxiliary power; but every year we want a House of Commons, for it has to grant funds of primary necessity. The minister who can manage the Commons, and extract from them the necessary moneys, has, then, become our most necessary minister.

The change was just beginning; for Walpole, Bolingbroke's schoolfellow and parliamentary rival, ruled their generation by his parliamentary and financial abilities. But Bolingbroke was too eager and impetuous to foresee the action of this powerful but obscure cause. The tradition had been, that the Peers were superior to the Commons, and he adhered to this tradition. He was angry till he obtained his peerage.

Nor was he satisfied when he did obtain it. He was made a Viscount only, and Harley had been made an Earl. He could not bear to be inferior to him in any thing, especially as there was an extinct earldom in his own family. He was vexed, angry, and dissatisfied. Once he went out of town, and would attend to no business for days. He was angry too with the press. The peace of Utrecht was attacked and assailed, and it was his peace. It is true that Bolingbroke should have been able to bear literary comments, even when rather bitter. He was himself through life an unscrupulous writer, using the press without reluctance and without cessation. He was then employing Swift, the most bitter writer of libels, both political and personal, that can be conceived. He lived with Swift in intimacy, and printed his libels.[6] He gave him political information and ideas, and praised him when he used them so as most to hurt his adversaries. He ought to have been able to bear any thing, yet he could bear nothing. He prosecuted many more persons than it was usual to prosecute then, and far more than

---

[6] The *National Review* has 'pointed' instead of 'printed'.

any who have been prosecuted since. He thought, with a continental wit, that 'a press is free when government newspapers are licentious.' He thought that every thing should be said for him, and that nothing should be said against him. The copyists of Alcibiades are commonly irritable, for neither their nature nor their habits teach them forbearance.

But neither Bolingbroke's disunion with his principal colleague nor the attacks of the press were his greatest danger. He was in the worst political position which can be imagined. As we have explained, the principal question of the age was a question of dynasty: after the peace with France it was the sole great question; it is in the nature of a topic so absorbing to swallow up every subject of minor interest. There were only two solutions of the problem possible. The law prescribed one, and a sort of superstition prescribed another. The Act of Settlement said that the House of Hanover was to succeed Queen Anne; the doctrine of non-resistance said that the Pretender was to succeed her. The Jacobites adhered to the doctrine of non-resistance. The Whigs adhered to the Act of Parliament. Both these parties had a definite solution of the principal topic of the hour. But between these fluctuated the great mass of the Tory party, who did not like the House of Hanover because it had no hereditary right, who did not like the Pretender because he was a Roman Catholic. This party objected to both possible solutions: they lived in the vague hope that the Pretender might turn Protestant—that some unforeseen circumstance would intervene—that Queen Anne would last their time. For persons in a private station such a state of mind was very possible and very natural. But it was of this very party that Bolingbroke was the spokesman and the leader, and he was a minister. He could not well remain without a distinct policy. Queen Anne, though not old, was often ill. She was suspected to be, and we now know she was, very near her death. He must make a choice.

Yet which king was Bolingbroke to choose? If he chose the House of Hanover, he himself ought not to be minister. This was the Whig candidate; this was the candidate whom his party disliked—at whom they murmured—whom they declined to support. A Tory ministry which should bring in the House of Hanover was like a Derbyite ministry that should propose free-trade or reform of Parliament. It was a ministry which tried to maintain its existence by denying its party tenets. Probably in those times a Tory ministry could not have

74

done what we have seen them do in our own time. Party spirit ran much stronger in Queen Anne's time than in ours. The political contentions of London were like the contests at a borough election now. At three o'clock on the polling day it is very difficult to change your politics and keep your character. So it was in London then. A fierce strife raged. Whig society and Tory society were separated like two hostile camps, and a deserter from one to the other was sure of contemptuous hatred from those he left, and a contemptuous patronage from those to whom he came. Bolingbroke could not do even once that which Mr. Disraeli has done twice.

Bolingbroke's enemies have been very anxious to fix on him a formed design to bring in the Pretender. He would doubtless have been very glad to do so, if he could have formed a coherent scheme. But he could not. Oxford was far too moderate and timid a man to break the law, or to plan to break it. He had himself supported the Act of Settlement. He knew that the Hanoverian succession, though not popular to the imagination of any class, was acceptable to the reason of the most thinking class. He knew that the aristocracy, the large towns, and all the cultivated part of the community, were in favour of it. He knew that, as the aristocratic classes had the command of the House of Lords, of the small boroughs, and of very many counties, as the great towns were of themselves favourable, the House of Hanover was sure of a majority in Parliament. He knew that the general vulgar, and especially the rural vulgar, who were favourable to the House of Stuart, though numerically strong, were but weak in parliamentary representation. He was probably a party to some covert intrigues, for intrigue was intrinsically agreeable to him; but in reality he was too timid to abandon the plain and legal course for a tortuous and illegal one. Bolingbroke had, on the other hand, a constitutional predilection for violent courses, and no particular objection to an illegal course. If he could have turned out Oxford,—if he could have carried his party with him, he would certainly have contrived some scheme for proclaiming the Pretender at Queen Anne's death. But even he was not mad enough to commit himself to a definite plan before he knew that he should have the power to execute it. In the meantime 'Tom Harley,' the Prime Minister's brother, exactly expressed the position of the ministry. 'We ought,' he said, 'to be better or worse with Hanover than we are.' The case, as men saw it then, was simple. The Queen was approaching daily to the grave. The ministry in power were uncertain what to do in the event of her death. They had 'no settled intention' of breaking the law, Bolingbroke tells us; but he does not venture to contend that they had a settled intention of obeying it. They were drifting to a crisis without a plan.

Nor was Bolingbroke comfortable while the Queen lived. She herself did not like him. A smaller person has never been placed by the caprice of fate amid great affairs than the 'good Queen Anne.' She had not, Swift says, 'a sufficient stock of amity' for more than one person at a time; she was always choosing a favourite upon whom to concentrate her affections exclusively. Her comprehension was as limited as her affections. She seriously objected, it is said, to one minister for appearing before her in a tie-wig instead of a full-bottom; and even if this anecdote has been exaggerated by continual narration, it expresses the sort of objections which ruled her mind and determined her conduct. She had a strong objection to all license; decorum was a sort of morality to her, as to most great ladies; she would have been much puzzled to fix where manners ended and where morals began. Bolingbroke was license personified; and therefore she distrusted and disliked him. She did not altogether approve, either, of the peace of Utrecht. She probably did not understand the details, but she evidently understood that it was a 'perplexing matter,' and 'not the sort of thing to which she had been accustomed under Lord Marlborough.' The original strength of the Tory ministry had been in the Queen's predilection for Miss Hill, afterwards Lady Masham; Harley ruled Miss Hill, and Miss Hill ruled the Queen. But the Queen was not quite sure about Miss Hill. One of her tastes was a taste for aristocracy; and she was half ashamed of having taken a great liking to a waiting-maid who had been placed about her. She had an old predilection also for the Duchess of Somerset, by birth the last of the Percys, whose husband was a Whig. Swift was never easy as to the effect of this friendship. He said, the 'Duchess of Somerset is a proud woman, but I will pull her down;' so he libelled her, which did not make her more propitious to him or his masters. There was always a danger that the ex-waiting-maid, on whom all depended, should be discarded, as the Duchess of Marlborough had been discarded; that the Duchess of Somerset might become prime favourite in her stead; that the policy of the government, and all the persons of our rulers, should be again changed by the inexplicable caprice of a quiet old lady.

And Bolingbroke had another difficulty. The distrust of him was not confined to Queen Anne. It extended through his party, and was an inevitable result of his peculiar position. He was an eloquent man without prejudices, speaking the prejudices of men who could not speak. But the speechless client and the eloquent advocate differ in nature so much that they can never much like or well understand the other. The Tory party knew that when Bolingbroke expressed their favourable conviction, he did not himself believe a word of what he was saying. And they could not tell what he did believe. And being for the most part regular men of middle life from the agricultural counties, they did not much like to trust as their leader a young man of loose life about town. After the peace of Utrecht, especially, he could not tell what they would think, and they could not tell what he would do. They could never have anticipated his doing any thing so mean as that, and he could never understand what disgrace there was in so obvious a diplomatic stratagem as breach of faith. In our own time, it is easy to vex Tories. You have only to ask, 'What is Dizzy's next move?' Such short words would not have suited our formal ancestors. But many a courteous Whig, doubtless, asked many a Tory, 'What is to be my Lord Bolingbroke's next fine stroke of policy?' and the Tory could not have known what to say. So long as Oxford was at the head of affairs, common men felt that there was still something ordinary about the government. But if Bolingbroke were to become sole minister, or chief minister, we should be subjected to the bold schemes of undiluted genius.

In this difficult position Bolingbroke showed great ability. He could not, indeed, remove its irremovable defects. He could not declare for the House of Hanover; and he could not declare for the House of Stuart. He could not remove the dislike which a dull queen, and a dull party, felt for a brilliant man. But what could be done he did. He showed great parliamentary ability, and was ever ready with wonderful eloquence. He pleased his party by a schism bill, agreeable to High Churchmen, and disagreeable to Dissenters. He obtained the favour of the waiting-maid, if he could not obtain that of the Queen, her mistress. Miss Hill (or Lady Masham, as she now was) was a sort of relation of Oxford's; and this had first brought them together. For a long time the union was firm; he gave her much counsel and some money, and she gave him much power. But Oxford had a conscience, or vestiges of a conscience, in the use of public money. He was not ready to give Miss Hill, or Miss Hill's brother, all that they wanted.

Swift puts it that he was too careful of the public interest for the corruption of the time; as we should put it, he would not bribe without limit against the public interest out of the public treasury. But Bolingbroke had no scruples: he bid higher; he gave Miss Hill and 'Jack Hill' all he could, and promised that they should have more if they would make him first minister and maintain him as such. He himself may tell the result: 'The Earl of Oxford was removed on Tuesday; the Queen died on Sunday. What a world is this, and how our fortune banters us!' Such was the close of three years of intrigue. He had bribed the waiting-maid just when the mistress was no more.

Nor at the moment was this the worst. The Queen's distrust of Bolingbroke had lasted till her death. The white staff—the 'magic wand,' as Bolingbroke calls it, long disused in English politics, but then the symbol of the Lord High Treasurer and of the Prime Minister— had been taken from Oxford, but it had not been given to any one. Bolingbroke could not gain it for himself. It was arranged that the treasury should be put into commission, as it had been in King William's time, and as it always now is. Bolingbroke was to continue secretary of state, and be in fact principal minister; yet he was not to have the indefinite power of the Lord-Treasurer,—the mystic power of the white staff. But on her death-bed Queen Anne felt that Bolingbroke could not be trusted even so far. She was dying, and knew that she was dying. She doubtless felt it was her duty to place the administration in the hands of some one who would obey the law on her death. She did not like the family of Hanover; she had the most keen repugnance to the presence of any of them in England during her life. She could not endure to see her successor close at hand, and it probably never struck her as a matter of duty to save the country from a possible convulsion of civil war. She was a very little-minded woman, but at the same time she was a decorous woman, and a well-meaning woman. She would not have planned or dared or wished to break the law which she had passed. As death was coming upon her, she knew that the practical premiership of Bolingbroke would endanger the security of the Act of Settlement. Of all statesmen he was least likely to obey it, and therefore most unfit to be Prime Minister when it was of critical importance to obey it. Obscurely, perhaps, but effectually, Queen Anne felt this. She gave the white staff to Shrewsbury, and Bolingbroke's three days of premiership were at an end.

Probably Bolingbroke felt the disaster the more that he was obliged to seem to assent to it. Shrewsbury had been acting as confidential adviser to the Queen for some time, to Bolingbroke's dismay. He knew, he said, how he stood with Oxford—that was open war; but how he stood with Shrewsbury he did not know. As soon as the Queen was despaired of, the Privy Council was summoned, and by ordinary rule only those summoned should attend; a ministry thus secures a Privy Council of chosen friends. But at this meeting two Whig dukes, the Duke of Somerset and the Duke of Argyll, attended, though not summoned, and by their influence the Council was induced to ask the Queen to make Shrewsbury High Treasurer; and Bolingbroke was obliged to assent. Neither in the nation nor at the court had he substantial influence or effectual power.

He had in truth no alternative. A frantic bishop, Atterbury, bishop of Rochester, wanted him to proclaim the Pretender. But Boling-broke, though a hot-headed statesman, had a notion of law and a perception of obvious consequences. He was not a hot-headed divine: he knew that by law George I must be proclaimed at once; he knew that Shrewsbury, who wielded the white staff, which every one would obey, would at once proclaim George I. He knew that he could not himself command the obedience of a watchman. All the force of government had at once passed from him, and he acquiesced in the new order of things. He assisted at the proclamation of George I.

The law had indicated the steps which should be taken in case of the Queen's death, and before her successor could be brought over from Germany. A document was produced by the Hanoverian minister, naming Lords Justices, who were to administer the government until the arrival of George I. Of these Lords Justices, Bolingbroke, of course, was not one. They were all sound Whigs, and steady friends to the House of Hanover. As Bolingbroke had for four years been wielding the force of government so as to give pain to them, they immediately began to exercise it so as to give pain to him. They appointed Addison as their secretary; desired all documents to be addressed to him; and, though Bolingbroke was still in high office, and had at the last moment been real Prime Minister, they kept him waiting at their door with studied circumstances of indignity, which were much remarked on then, and which much tried his philosophy.

It would, however, have been well for Bolingbroke if mere in-dignities like these had been all which was in store for him, or all which he deserved. When Parliament met, zealous Whigs naturally began to murmur a good deal as to the past. Bolingbroke had ruled them hardly during his reign. His ministry had removed Marlborough from his appointments; his ministry had expelled Walpole from the House of Commons. Walpole would most likely have said that the Whig 'innings' had arrived, and that the actions of their predecessors must be scrutinised. Bolingbroke for a time affected to fear nothing. Oxford went to and fro in London, and Bolingbroke followed his example. All at once he changed his policy. He appeared at the theatre in state, and took pains while there to attract attention; went home, changed his dress, and fled to France.

In truth, he was thoroughly frightened. He declared that 'his blood was,' he understood, 'to have been the cement of a new alliance' between the moderate Tories and the Whigs. Some have traced this notion to the hints of Marlborough, but it was most likely due as much to Bolingbroke's own conscience. He knew well that the secret negotiations prior to the peace of Utrecht would not bear even fair scrutiny. He knew that they were now to be subjected to hostile scrutiny. Even from impartial judges he could only expect condemnation, and his case would now be tried by his enemies. His life, indeed, was in no danger. Neither the nation nor the party opposed to him were inclined to bloodshed; but he felt he was in danger of something. His guilty conscience magnified the possibilities of punishment; to escape them, he did exactly what was worst for his reputation; though it was as much as pleading guilty, he fled.

He was attainted as a traitor in his absence, and there may be legal doubt as to whether the attainder was deserved. That a minister who advises his sovereign to violate a treaty, and who violates it accordingly, is worthy of severe punishment, will be admitted by every one; and that Bolingbroke had done this is beyond question or dispute. But this offence does not amount to high treason, and the details of an incidental transaction as to the town of Tournay had to be pressed into the service; and it required much stretching to make these amount even to a constructive treason. But whatever might be the legal correctness or the incorrectness of the precise punishment inflicted on Bolingbroke is scarcely material now. He well deserved a bill of 'Pains and Penalties;' and whether he was or was not visited with the very penalty that was most suitable, does not matter much.

On Bolingbroke's arrival in France, he looked about him for awhile. He was at once solicited by the emissaries of the Pretender, but he deliberated for some time, and it would have been wiser for him to have deliberated longer. He well knew that though there was much latent Jacobite sentiment in England, there was no good material for a Jacobite rebellion. Many squires and rectors and peasants would have been glad to see the legitimate king restored; but their zeal was not very active; it belonged to the region of traditional sentiment and vague prejudice rather than to that of practical and vigorous life. The House of Hanover had the force of government and the *sense* of the country in its favour. It was in possession, and Bolingbroke was aware that the Jacobites, without trusted leaders, without organisation or arms, could not expel it from possession. He knew all this well, but his passions were too strong for his judgment; from excitability, restlessness, and rage, he joined the Pretender. He must be busy, and hoped, or half-hoped to be revenged on his enemies.

He could not, however, long agree with his new associates. The descent from actual office to imaginary office was too sudden; to many men it was pleasing to be secretary of state to a mock king, but it was very painful to one who had just been secretary to a real queen. His contempt, too, for the Irish associates of the Pretender was unbounded. He saw that they were hot-headed and ignorant men,—who knew nothing of the country which they hoped to rule,—whom that country would not endure for a day. He knew that the Roman Catholics in England were a small and unpopular body, and their aid more dangerous than their enmity. The genuine Jacobites distrusted him also. He said that they were untrustworthy because they were fools, and they said that he was untrustworthy because he was a traitor. This could not last; after a brief interval, he left the Pretender and his court: they began to slander him, and he began to speak much evil of them.

With his secession from the Jacobites Bolingbroke's active career ends. He was afterwards only an aspirant for a career. He was, after several years, permitted to return to England, and to enjoy his estate though he was an attainted traitor; but the attainder was not reversed, and while it was in force he could not take his seat in the House of Lords, or hold any office whatever. He wrote much against Walpole, but he did not turn out Walpole. On one occasion he was much mortified because Pulteney and the practical opponents of Walpole said that the support of his name rather weakened than strengthened them. He gave in a long memorial of suggestions to George I; but the King said they were 'bagatelles.' He then fancied that he should become minister because of the support of Lady Suffolk, George II's mistress; but Lady Suffolk had no influence, and Queen Caroline, who had predominant influence, supported Walpole. He then hoped to be minister under the Prince of Wales, George II's son, and wrote a treatise on a 'Patriot King' for that prince's use. But George II outlived his son; and he was saved the mortification of seeing how little that small prince would have carried out his great ideas. Though he survived Queen Anne more than thirty years, he never after her death attained in England to a day's power. Three years of eager unwise power, and thirty-five of sickly longing and impotent regret,—such, or something like it, will ever be in this cold modern world the fate of an Alcibiades.

Adam Smith

Introductory note

Adam Smith (1723–1790) was born at Kirkcaldy, Scotland, the only child of Adam Smith, writer to the signet (the Scots equivalent of a barrister), and Margaret Douglas. He was educated at the burgh school in Kirkcaldy, at Glasgow University, and at Balliol College, Oxford. In 1751 he was elected to the chair of logic at Glasgow, and in 1752 transferred to the chair of moral philosophy, lecturing on theology, ethics, jurisprudence, and political institutions. The fame of his lectures brought him a tutorship to the Duke of Buccleuch, and during his travels with the Duke he met Hume, Turgot, and others in Paris, and Voltaire at Geneva. In 1767 he settled in Kirkcaldy on a pension from the Duke of Buccleuch. Smith's great work *The Wealth of Nations*, which initiated the study of political economy as a separate science, was published in 1776. He died in Edinburgh in 1790.

Adam Smith as a Person[1]

Of Adam Smith's Political Economy almost an infinite quantity has been said; but very little has been said as to Adam Smith himself. And yet not only was he one of the most curious of human beings, but his books can hardly be understood without having some notion what manner of man he was. There certainly are economical treatises that go straight on, and that might have been written by a calculating machine. But *The Wealth of Nations* is not one of these. Any one 'who would explain what is in it, and what is not in it, must apply the historical method,' and state what was the experience of its author and how he worked up that experience. Perhaps, therefore, now that there is a sort of centenary of Adam Smith, it may not be quite amiss to give a slight sketch of him and of his life, and especially of the peculiar points in them that led him to write the book which still in its effects, even more than in its theory, occupies mankind.

The Founder of the science of business was one of the most un-businesslike of mankind. He was an awkward Scotch professor, apparently choked with books and absorbed in abstractions. He was never engaged in any sort of trade, and would probably never have made sixpence by any if he had been. His absence of mind was amazing. On one occasion, having to sign his name to an official document, he produced not his own signature, but an elaborate imitation of the signature of the person who signed before him; on another, a sentinel on duty having saluted him in military fashion, he astounded and offended the man by acknowledging it with a copy—a very clumsy copy no doubt—of the same gestures. And Lord Brougham preserves other similar traditions. 'It is related,' he says, 'by old people in Edinburgh that while he moved through the Fishmarket in his accustomed attitude—that is with his hands behind his back, and his head in the air—a female of the trade exclaimed, taking him for an idiot broken loose, 'Hech sirs, to see the like o' him to be aboot. And yet he is well eneugh put on' (dressed). It was often so too in society. Once,

[1] This essay was first published in the *Fortnightly Review* for July 1 1876, Volume XX [N.S.], pp. 18–42.

during a dinner at Dalkeith, he broke out in a long lecture on some political matters of the day, and was bestowing a variety of severe epithets on a statesman, when he suddenly perceived his[2] nearest relative sitting opposite, and stopt; but he was heard to go on muttering 'Deil care, Deil care, it's all true." ' And these are only specimens of a crowd of anecdotes.

The wonder that such a man should have composed *The Wealth of Nations*, which shows so profound a knowledge of the real occupations of mankind, is enhanced by the mode in which it was written. It was not the exclusive product of a lifelong study, such as an absent man might, while in seeming abstraction, be really making of the affairs of the world. On the contrary, it was in the mind of its author only one of many books, or rather a single part of a great book, which he intended to write. A vast scheme floated before him much like the dream of the late Mr. Buckle as to a *History of Civilisation*, and he spent his life accordingly, in studying the origin and progress of the sciences, the laws, the politics, and all the other aids and forces which have raised man from the savage to the civilised state. The plan of Adam Smith was indeed more comprehensive even than this. He wanted to trace not only the progress of the race, but also of the individual; he wanted to show how each man being born (as he thought) with few faculties, came to attain to many and great faculties. He wanted to answer the question, how did man—race or individual—come to be what he is? These immense dreams are among the commonest phenomena of literary history; and as a rule, the vaster the intention the less the result. The musings of the author are too miscellaneous, his studies too scattered, his attempts too incoherent, for him to think out anything valuable, or to produce anything connected. But in Adam Smith's case the very contrary is true; he produced an enduring particular result in consequence of a comprehensive and diffused ambition. He discovered the laws of wealth in looking for 'the natural progress of opulence' and he investigated the progress of opulence as part of the growth and progress of all things.

The best way to get a distinct notion of Adam Smith's scheme is to look at the other works which he published besides *The Wealth of Nations*. The greatest, and the one which made his original reputation, was *The Theory of Moral Sentiments*, in which he builds up the whole moral nature of man out of a single primitive emotion-sympathy, and

[2] i.e. the statesman's—Ed.

in which he gives a history of ethical philosophy besides. With this are commonly bound up *Some Considerations concerning the first Formation of Languages*, which discuss how 'two savages who had never been taught to speak, but had been bred up remote from the society of man, would naturally begin their converse.' Then there is a very curious *History of Astronomy*, left imperfect; and another fragment on the *History of Ancient Physics*, which is a kind of sequel to that part of the *History of Astronomy* which relates to the ancient astronomy; then a similar essay on *Ancient Logic and Metaphysics*; then another on the nature and development of the fine, or, as he calls them, *The Imitative Arts*, *Painting*, *Poetry*, *and Music*, in which was meant to have been included a history of the theatre—all forming part, his executors tell us, 'of a plan he had once formed for giving a connected history of the liberal and elegant arts.' And he destroyed before his death the remains of the book, *Lectures on Justice*, 'in which,' we are told by a student who heard them, 'he followed Montesquieu in endeavouring to trace the gradual progress of jurisprudence, both public and private, from the rudest to the most refined ages, and to point out the effects of those arts which contribute to subsistence and to the accumulation of property in producing correspondent alterations in law and government;' or, as he himself announces it at the conclusion of *The Moral Sentiments* 'another discourse' in which he designs 'to endeavour to give an account of the general principles of law and government, and of the different revolutions they have undergone in the different ages and periods of society, not only in what concerns justice, but in what concerns police, revenue, and arms, and whatever else is the subject of law.' Scarcely any philosopher has imagined a vaster dream.

Undoubtedly it is a great literary marvel that so huge a scheme, on so many abstract subjects, should have produced anything valuable, still more that it should have produced what has been for a whole century a fundamental book on trade and money—at first sight, the least fit for a secluded man to treat at all, and which, if he did treat of them, would seem more than any other to require from him an absorbed and exclusive attention. A little study of the life of Adam Smith, however, in some degree lessens the wonder; because it shows how in the course of his universal studies he came to meet with this particular train of thought, and how he came to be able to pursue it effectually.

Adam Smith was born early in the first half of the eighteenth century, at Kirkcaldy in Scotland, on the 5th June, 1723. His father died before he was born; but his mother, who is said to have been a woman of unusual energy and ability, lived to be very old, and to see her son at the height of his reputation as a philosopher. He was educated at school in the usual Scotch way, and at the University of Glasgow; and at both he is said, doubtless truly, to have shown an unusual facility of acquisition, and an unusual interest in books and study. As we should also expect, a very strong memory, which he retained till the last, showed itself very early. Nothing, however, is known with precision as to the amount of knowledge he acquired in Scotland, or as to his place among his contemporaries. The examination system, which nowadays in England discriminates both so accurately, has in Scotland never been equally developed, and in Adam Smith's time had never been heard of there at all.

His exceptional training begins at the next stage. There is at the University of Glasgow a certain endowment called the Snell exhibition, after the name of its founder, which enables the students selected for it to study for some years at the University of Oxford. Of these exhibitioners Adam Smith became one, and as such studied at Oxford for as many as seven years. As might be expected, he gives the worst account of the state of the university at that time. In the sketch of the history of education which forms so odd an episode in *The Wealth of Nations*, he shows perpetually that he thought the system which he had seen at Oxford exceedingly bad, and its government excessively corrupt. 'If,' he says, 'the authority to which a teacher is subject resides in the body corporate of the college or university of which he is himself a member, and in which the greater part of the other members are, like himself, persons who either are or ought to be teachers, they are likely to make a common cause, to be all very indulgent to one another, and every man to consent that his neighbour may neglect his duty, provided he is himself allowed to neglect his own.' 'In the University of Oxford the greater part of the public professors have for these many years given up altogether even the pretence of teaching.' And he adds, 'In England, the public schools are much less corrupted than the universities. In the schools, the youth are taught, or at least may be taught, Greek and Latin. That is everything which the masters pretend to teach, or which it is expected they should teach. In the universities, the youth neither are taught, nor can always find the means of being taught, the sciences which it is the business of these incorporated bodies to teach.' And he retained through life a fixed belief that endowments for education tended only to the 'ease' of the teacher, and not to the advantage of the learner. But though he says he had the means of learning little at Oxford, he certainly, in fact, learnt much. 'Greek,' as Sydney Smith says, 'never crossed the Tweed in any force;' but Adam Smith incessantly shows a real familiarity with Greek books and a sound accumulation of Greek learning. Very likely his erudition would not bear much comparison with what is now carried away from Balliol. If we compare him with a more recent Snell exhibitioner, Sir William Hamilton, we shall see that Greek teaching has enormously advanced in the time between them; but, on the other hand, if we compare Adam Smith with Scotch philosophers, of purely Scotch education, say with Reid or Hume, we cannot help seeing that his acquaintance with Greek things belongs, both in quantity and in quality, to an order altogether superior to theirs.

For the vast works which Adam Smith contemplated, a sound knowledge of Greek was, as he must have felt, far more necessary than any other kind of knowledge. The beginnings of nine-tenths of all philosophy are to be found there, and the rudiments of many other things. But for the purpose of the great task which he actually performed, Adam Smith learned at Oxford something much more valuable than Greek. He acquired there a kind of knowledge and sympathy with England, in which the other eminent Scotchmen—especially literary Scotchmen—of his time were often very deficient. At that time the recollection of the old rivalry between the two countries had by no means died away; there was still a separate Scotch philosophy and a separate literature; and when it happened, as it perpetually did, that Scotch writers were not thought so much of in England as they thought they ought to be, they were apt to impute their discredit to English prejudice, and to appeal to France and Paris to correct the error. Half Hume's mind, or more than half, was distorted by his hatred of England, and his love of France. He often could not speak of English things with tolerable temper, and he always viewed French ones with extravagant admiration. Whether Adam Smith altogether liked this country may perhaps be doubted—Englishmen then hated Scotchmen so much—but he had no kind of antagonism to her, and quite understood that in most economical respects she was then exceedingly superior to France. And this exceptional sympathy and knowledge we may fairly ascribe to a long and pleasant residence in England. For his great work no qualification was more necessary; *The Wealth of Nations* would have been utterly spoiled if he had tried (as Hume incessantly would have tried) to show that, in industrial respects, England might not be better than France, or at any rate was not so very much better.

The Snell foundation at Oxford has often been an avenue to the English Church, and it seems to have been intended that Adam Smith should use it as such. The only anecdote which remains of his college life may be a clue to his reasons for not doing so. He is said to have been found by his tutor in the act of reading Hume's *Philosophical Essays*, then lately published, and to have been reproved for it. And it is certain that any one who at all sympathised with Hume's teaching in that book would have felt exceedingly little sympathy with the formularies of the Church of England, even as they were understood in the very Broad Church of that age. At any rate, for some reason or other, Adam Smith disappointed the wishes of his friends, gave up all idea of entering the Church of England, and returned to Scotland without fixed outlook or employment. He resided, we are told, two years with his mother, studying no doubt, but earning nothing, and visibly employed in nothing. In England such a career would probably have ended in his 'writing for the booksellers,' a fate of which he speaks in *The Wealth of Nations* with contempt. But in Scotland there was a much better opening for philosophers. The Scotch universities had then, as now, several professorships very fairly paid, and very fairly distributed. The educated world in Scotland was probably stronger a century ago than it ever was before or since. The Union with England had removed the aristocracy of birth which over-shadowed it before, and commerce had not yet created the aristocracy of wealth which overshadows it now. Philosophical merit had there-fore then in Scotland an excellent chance of being far better rewarded than it usually is in the world. There were educated people who cared for philosophy, and these people had prizes to give away. One of those prizes Adam Smith soon obtained. He read lectures, we are told, under the patronage of Lord Kames, an eminent lawyer who wrote books on philosophy, that are still quoted, and who was no doubt deeply inter-ested in Adam Smith's plans of books on the origin and growth of all arts and sciences, as these were the topics which he himself studied and handled. Contrary to what might have been expected, these lectures were very successful. Though silent and awkward in social life, Adam Smith possessed in considerable perfection the peculiarly Scotch gift of abstract oratory. Even in common conversation, when once moved, he expounded his favourite ideas very admirably. As a teacher in public he did even better; he wrote almost nothing, and though at the beginning of a lecture he often hesitated, we are told, and seemed 'not to be sufficiently possessed of the subject,' yet in a minute or two he became fluent, and poured out an interesting series of animated arguments. Commonly, indeed, the silent man, whose brain is loaded with unexpressed ideas, is more likely to be a successful public speaker than the brilliant talker who daily exhausts himself in sharp sayings. Adam Smith acquired great reputation as a lecturer, and in consequence obtained two of the best prizes then given to philosophers in Scotland —first the professorship of logic, and then that of moral philosophy, in the University of Glasgow.

The rules, or at any rate the practice, of the Scotch universities, seem at that time to have allowed a professor in either of these chairs, great latitude in the choice of his subject. Adam Smith during his first year lectured on rhetoric and *belles lettres* 'instead of on logic,' and in the chair of moral philosophy he expounded, besides the theory of duty, a great scheme of social evolution. The beginnings of *The Wealth of Nations* made part of the course, but only as a fragment of the immense design of showing the origin and development of cultivation and law; or, as we may perhaps put it, not inappropriately, of saying how, from being a savage, man rose to be a Scotchman. This course of lectures seems to have been especially successful. So high, we are told, was his reputation as a professor, 'that a multitude of students from a great distance resorted to the university merely upon his account. Those branches of science which he taught became fashionable' in the city, 'and his opinions were the chief topics of discussion in clubs and literary societies. Even the small peculiarities of his pronunciation and manner of speaking became frequently the objects of imitation.' This is the partial recollection of an attached pupil in distant years;—it may be over-coloured a little—but even after a fair abatement it is certainly the record of a great temporary triumph and local success.

That the greater part of the lectures can have been of much intrinsic merit it is not easy now to believe. An historical account 'of the general principles of law and government, and of the different revolutions which they have undergone in the different ages and periods of society,' would be too great a task for a great scholar of the ripest years and with all the accumulated materials of the present time, and it was altogether beyond the strength of a young man a century ago;—not to say that he combined it with an account of the origin of the moral faculties, a theory of *belles lettres*, and other matters. The delivery of that part of the course which was concerned with wealth and revenue may have been useful to him, because it compelled him to bring his ideas on those subjects into a distinct form. Otherwise, being a bookish man, he might have been too absorbed in bookish matters, and neglected what can only be taught by life for that which is already to be learned from literature. But at the time this was only a minor merit;—the main design of the lectures was only an impossible aim at an unbounded task.

So complex, however, is life, that this Scotch professorship, though in a superficial view wasteful, and likely to exhaust and hurt his mind by demanding[3] the constant efflux of inferior matter, was, nevertheless, on the whole exceedingly useful. It not only induced him to study as a part of his vast scheme the particular phenomena of wealth, but it gave him an excellent opportunity of seeing those phenomena and of learning how to explain them. It was situated at Glasgow, and Glasgow, though a petty place in comparison with its present magnitude, was nevertheless a considerable mercantile place according to the notions of those times. The Union with England had opened to it the trade with our West Indian colonies, as well as with the rest of the English empire, and it had in consequence grown rapidly and made large profits. That its size was small, as we should think now, was to a learner rather an aid than a disadvantage. A small commerce is more easily seen than an immense one; that of Liverpool or London now is so vast that it terrifies more than excites the imagination. And a small commerce, if varied, has almost as much to teach as a large one; the elements are the same though the figures are smaller, and the less the figures the easier are they to combine. An inspection of Liverpool now would not teach much more than an inspection of Glasgow a hundred years ago, and the lessons of modern Liverpool would be much more difficult to learn. But the mere sight of the phenomena of the Glasgow[4] commerce was but a small part of the advantage to Adam Smith of a residence at Glasgow. The most characteristic and most valuable tenets of Adam Smith are, when examined, by no means of a very abstract and recondite sort. We are, indeed, in this generation not fully able to

---

³ I have inserted 'demanding'—Ed. ⁴ I have inserted 'Glasgow'—Ed.

appreciate the difficulty of arriving at them. We have been bred up upon them; our disposition is more to wonder how any one could help seeing them, than to appreciate the effort of discovering them. Experience shows that many of them—the doctrine of free trade for example—are very uncongenial to the untaught human mind. On political economy the English-speaking race is undoubtedly the best instructed part of mankind; and, nevertheless, in the United States and in every English-speaking colony, protection is the firm creed of the ruling classes, and free trade is but a heresy. We must not fancy that any of the main doctrines of Adam Smith were very easily arrived at by him because they seem very obvious to us. But, on the other hand, although such doctrines as his are too opposed to many interests and to many first impressions to establish themselves easily as a dominant creed, they are quite within the reach and quite congenial to the taste of an intelligent dissenting minority. There was a whole race of mercantile freetraders long before Adam Smith was born; in his time the doctrine was in the air; it was not accepted or established;—on the contrary, it was a tenet against which a respectable parent would probably caution his son;—still it was known as a tempting heresy and one against which a warning was needed. In Glasgow there were, doubtless many heretics. Probably in consequence of the firm belief in a rigid theology, and of the incessant discussion of its technical tenets, there has long been, and there is still, in the south of Scotland, a strong tendency to abstraction and argument[5] quite unknown in England. Englishmen have been sometimes laughing at it, and sometimes gravely criticising it for several generations: Mr. Buckle wrote half a volume on it: Sydney Smith alleged that he heard a Scotch girl answer in a quadrille, 'But, my lord, as to what ye were saying as to love in the *aib*stract,' and so on. Yet, in spite both of ridicule and argument, the passion for doctrine is still strong in southern Scotland, and it will take many years more to root it out. At Glasgow in Adam Smith's time it had no doubt very great influence; a certain number of hard-headed merchants were believers in free trade and kindred tenets. One of these is still by chance known to us. Dr. Carlyle, whom Mr. Gladstone not unhappily described as a 'gentleman clergyman' of the Church of Scotland, tells us of a certain Provost Cochrane, to whom Adam Smith always acknowledged his obligations, and who was the founder and leading member of a club 'in which the express design was

[5] This should perhaps be 'abstract argument' rather than 'abstraction and argument.'

to inquire into the nature and principles of trade in all its branches, and to communicate their knowledge on that subject to each other.' From this club Adam Smith not only learned much which he would never have found in any book, but also in part perhaps acquired the influential and so to say practical way of explaining things which so much distinguishes *The Wealth of Nations.* Mr. Mill says he learned from his intercourse with East India directors the habit of looking for, and the art of discovering, 'the mode of putting a thought which gives it easiest admittance into minds not prepared for it by habit;' and Adam Smith probably gained something of this sort by living with the Glasgow merchants, for no other book written by a learned professor shows anything like the same power of expressing and illustrating arguments in a way likely to influence minds like theirs. And it is mainly by his systematic cultivation of this borderland between theory and practice that Adam Smith attained his pre-eminent place and influence.

But this usefulness of his Scotch professorship was only in the distant future. It was something for posterity to detect, but it could not have been known at the time. The only pages of his professional work which Adam Smith then gave to the public were his lectures on moral philosophy, in what an Englishman would consider its more legitimate sense. These formed the once celebrated *Theory of Moral Sentiments,* which, though we should now think them rather pompous, were then much praised and much read. For a great part, indeed, of Adam Smith's life they constituted his main title to reputation. *The Wealth of Nations* was not published till seventeen years later; he wrote nothing else of any importance in the interval; and it is now curious to find that when *The Wealth of Nations* was published, many good judges thought it not so good as *The Theory of Moral Sentiments,* and that the author himself was by no means certain that they were not right.

The Theory of Moral Sentiments was, indeed, for many years, exceedingly praised. One sect of philosophers praised it, as it seems to me, because they were glad of a celebrated ally, and another because they were glad of a celebrated opponent: the first said, 'see that so great an authority as Adam Smith concurs with us;' and the second replied, 'but see how very weak his arguments are; if so able an arguer as Adam Smith can say so little for your doctrines, how destitute of argumentative grounds those doctrines must be.' Several works in the history of philosophy have had a similar fate. But a mere student of philosophy who cares for no sect, and wants only to know the truth, will nowadays, I think, find little to interest him in this celebrated book. In Adam Smith's mind, as I have said before, it was part of a whole; he wanted to begin with the origin of the faculties of each man, and then build up that man—just as he wished to arrive at the origin of human society, and then build up society. His *Theory of Moral Sentiments* builds them all out of one source, sympathy, and in this way he has obtained praise from friends and enemies. His friends are the school of 'moral sense' thinkers, because he is on their side, and believes in a special moral faculty, which he laboriously constructs from sympathy; his enemies are the Utilitarian school, who believe in no such special faculty, and who set themselves to show that his labour has been in vain, and that no such faculty has been so built up. One party says the book is good to gain authority for the conclusion, and the other that you may gain credit[6] by refuting its arguments. For unquestionably its arguments *are* very weak, and attractive to refutation. If the intuitive school had had no better grounds than these, the Utilitarians would have vanquished them ages since. There is a fundamental difficulty in founding morals on sympathy; an obvious confusion of two familiar sentiments. We often sympathise where we cannot approve, and approve where we cannot sympathise. The special vice of party spirit is that it effaces the distinction between the two; we sympathise with our party, till we approve its actions. There is a story of a Radical wit in the last century who was standing for Parliament, and his opponent, of course a Tory, objected that he was always *against* the king whether right or wrong, upon which the wit retorted that on his own showing the Tory was exposed to equal objection since he was always *for* the king whether right or wrong. And so it will always be. Even the wisest party men more or less sympathise with the errors of their own side; they would be powerless if they did not so; they would gain no influence if they were not of like passions with those near them. Adam Smith could not help being aware of this obvious objection; he was far too able a reasoner to elaborate a theory without foreseeing what would be said against it. But the way in which he tries to meet the objection only shows that the objection is invincible. He sets up a supplementary theory—a little epicycle—that the sympathy which is to test good morals must be the sympathy of an 'im-

---

[6] The *Fortnightly* has 'to gain credit' for 'that you may gain credit'—p. 27.

partial spectator.' But, then, who is to watch the watchman? Who is to say when the spectator is impartial, and when he is not? If he sympathises with one side, the other will always say that he is partial. As a moralist, the supposed spectator must warmly approve good actions, and warmly disapprove bad actions; as an impartial person he must never do either the one or the other. He is a fiction of inconsistent halves; if he sympathizes he is not impartial, and if he is impartial he does not sympathize. The radical vice of the theory is shown by its requiring this accessory invention of a being both hot and cold, because the essence of the theory is to identify the passion which loves with the sentiment which approves.

But although we may now believe *The Theory of Moral Sentiments* to be of inconsiderable philosophical value, and though it would at first sight seem very little likely to contribute to the production of *The Wealth of Nations*, yet it was, in fact, in a curious way most useful to it. The education of young noblemen has always been a difficulty in the world, and many schemes have been invented to meet it. In Scotland, a hundred years ago, the most fashionable way was to send them to travel in Europe, and to send with them some scholar of repute to look after their morals and to superintend their general education. The guardians of the great border nobleman, the Duke of Buccleugh, were in want of such a tutor to take him such a tour, and it seems to have struck them that Adam Smith was the very person adapted for the purpose. To all appearance an odder selection could hardly have been made. Adam Smith was, as we have seen, the most absent of men, and an awkward Scotch professor, and he was utterly unacquainted with the continent. He had never crossed the English Channel in his life, and if he had been left to himself would probably never have done so. But one of the guardians was Charles Townshend, who had married the young Duke's mother. He was not much unlike Mr. Disraeli in character, and had great influence at that time. He read *The Theory of Moral Sentiments*, and Hume writes to Adam Smith: 'Charles Townshend, who passes for the cleverest fellow in England, is so taken with the performance that he said to Oswald he would put the Duke under the author's care, and would make it worth his while to accept of that charge. As soon as I heard this I called on him twice with a view of talking with him about the matter, and of convincing him of the propriety of sending that young nobleman to Glasgow; for I could not hope that he could offer you any terms which would tempt you to renounce your professorship. But I missed him. Mr. Townshend passes for being a little uncertain in his resolutions, so perhaps you need not build much on this sally.' Mr. Townshend was, however, this time in earnest, and the offer was made to Adam Smith. In our time there would have been an insuperable difficulty. He was a professor of great repute, they were asking him to give up a life-professorship that yielded a considerable income, and they would have hardly been able to offer him anything equally permanent. But in the eighteenth century there was a way of facilitating such arrangements that we do not now possess. The family of Buccleugh had great political influence, and Charles Townshend, the Duke's father-in-law, at times possessed more; and accordingly the guardians of the young duke therefore agreed that they should pay Adam Smith £200 a year till they should get him an equal office of profit under the Crown;—a person apparently more unfit for the public service could not easily have been found; but in that age of sinecures and pensions it was probably never expected that he should perform any service;—an arrangement more characteristic of the old world, and more unlike our present world, could hardly have been made. The friends of the young Duke might, not unnaturally, have had some fears about it; but, in fact, for his interests it turned out very well. Long afterwards, when Adam Smith was dead, he wrote:—'In October, 1766, we returned to London, after having spent near three years together without the slightest disagreement or coolness; on my part with every advantage that could be expected from the society of such a man. We continued to live in friendship till the hour of his death; and I shall always remain with the impression of having lost a friend whom I loved and respected, not only for his great talents, but for every private virtue.' Very few of Charles Townshend's caprices were as successful. Through life there was about Adam Smith a sort of lumbering *bonhomie* which amused and endeared him to those around him.

To Adam Smith the result was even better. If it had not been for this odd consequence of *The Theory of Moral Sentiments*, he might have passed all his life in Scotland, delivering similar lectures and clothing very questionable theories in rather pompous words. He said in after life that there was no better way of compelling a man to master a science than by setting him to teach it. And this may be true of the definite sciences. But nothing can be conceived worse for a man of inventive originality than to set him to roam over huge subjects like law, morals, politics, and civilisation, particularly at a time when few good data for sound theories on such subjects are at hand for him to use. In such a position the cleverer the man, the worse are likely to be the consequences: the wider his curiosity and the more fertile his mind, the surer he is to pour out a series of gigantic conjectures of little use to himself or to any one. A one-eyed man with a taste for one subject, even at this disadvantage, may produce something good. The limitation of his mind may save him from being destroyed by his position; but a man of large interests will fail utterly. As Adam Smith had peculiarly wide interests, and as he was the very reverse of a one-eyed man, he was in special danger; and the mere removal from his professorship was to him a gain of the first magnitude. It was of cardinal importance to him to be delivered from the production of incessant words and to be brought into contact with facts and the world. And as it turned out, the caprice of Charles Townshend had a singular further felicity. It not only brought him into contact with facts and the world; but with the most suitable sort of facts, and for his purpose the best part of the world.

The greater part of his three years abroad were naturally spent in France. France was then by far the greatest country on the continent. Germany was divided and had not yet risen; Spain had fallen; Italy was of little account. In one respect, indeed, France was relatively greater than even at the time of her greatest elevation, the time of the first Napoleon. The political power of the first empire was almost unbounded, but it had no intellectual power; under it Paris had ceased to be an important focus of thought and literature. The vehement rule which created the soldiers also stamped out the ideas. But under the mild government of the old *régime*, Paris was the principal centre of European authorship. The deficiency of the old *régime* in eminent soldiers and statesmen only added to the eminence of its literary men. Paris was then queen of two worlds, in that of politics by a tradition from the past, and in literature by a force and life vigorously evidenced in the present. France therefore thus attracted the main attention of all travellers who cared for the existing life of the time; Adam Smith and his pupil spent the greater part of their stay abroad there. And as a preparation for writing *The Wealth of Nations* he could nowhere else have been placed so well. Macaulay says that 'ancient abuses and new theories' flourished together in France just before the meeting of the States-General in greater vigour than they had been seen combined before or since. And the description is quite as true economically as politically; on all economical matters the France of that time was a sort of museum stocked with the most important errors.

By nature then, as now, France was fitted to be a great agricultural country, a great producer and exporter of corn and wine; but her legislators for several generations had endeavoured to counteract the aim of nature, and had tried to make her a manufacturing and an exporting country. Like most persons in those times, they had been prodigiously impressed by the high position which the maritime powers, as they were then called (the comparatively little powers of England and Holland), were able to take in the politics of Europe. They saw that this influence came from wealth, that this wealth was made in trade and manufacture, and therefore they determined that France should not be behindhand, but should have as much trade and manufacture as possible. Accordingly they imposed prohibitive or deterring duties on the importation of foreign manufactures; they gave bounties to the corresponding home manufactures. They tried, in opposition to the home-keeping bent of the French character, to found colonies abroad. These colonies were, according to the maxim then everywhere received, to be markets for the trade and nurseries for the commerce of the mother country;—they were mostly forbidden to manufacture for themselves, and were compelled to import all the manufactures and luxuries they required from Europe exclusively in French ships. Meanwhile, at home, agriculture was neglected. There was not even a free passage for goods from one part of the country to another. As Adam Smith himself describes it—

'In France, the different revenue laws which take place in the different provinces, require a multitude of revenue-officers to surround, not only the frontiers of the kingdom, but those of almost each particular province, in order either to prevent the importation of certain goods, or to subject it to the payment of certain duties, to the no small interruption of the interior commerce of the country. Some provinces are allowed to compound for the gabelle or salt-tax. Others are exempted from it altogether. Some provinces are exempted from the exclusive sale of tobacco, which the farmers-general enjoy through the greater part of the kingdom. The *Aides*, which correspond to the excise in England, are very different in different provinces. Some provinces are exempted from them, and pay a composition or equivalent. In those in which they take place and are in farm, there are many local duties which do not extend beyond a particular town or district. The *Traites*, which correspond to our customs, divide the kingdom into three great parts; first, the provinces subject to the tarif of 1664, which are called the provinces of the five great farms, and under which are comprehended Picardy, Normandy, and the greater part of the interior provinces of the kingdom; secondly, the provinces subject to the tarif of 1667, which are called the provinces reckoned foreign, and under which are comprehended the greater part of the frontier provinces; and, thirdly, those provinces which are said to be treated as foreign, or which, because they are allowed a free commerce with foreign countries, are in their commerce with the other provinces of France subjected to the same duties as other foreign countries. These are Alsace, the three bishopricks of Metz, Toul, and Verdun, and the three cities of Dunkirk, Bayonne, and Marseilles. Both in the provinces of the five great farms (called so on account of an antient division of the duties of customs into five great branches, each of which was originally the subject of a particular farm, though they are now all united into one), and in those which are said to be reckoned foreign, there are many local duties which do not extend beyond a particular town or district. There are some such even in the provinces which are said to be treated as foreign, particularly in the city of Marseilles. It is unnecessary to observe how much, both the restraints upon the interior commerce of the country, and the number of the revenue officers must be multiplied, in order to guard the frontiers of those different provinces and districts, which are subject to such different systems of taxation.'

And there were numerous attendant errors, such as generally accompany a great protective legislation, but which need not be specified in detail.

In consequence, the people were exceedingly miserable. The system of taxation was often enough by itself to cause great misery. 'In the provinces,' says Adam Smith, 'where the personal *taille* on the farmer is imposed, the farmer is afraid to have a good team of horses or oxen, but endeavours to cultivate with the meanest and most wretched instruments of husbandry that he can.' The numerous imposts on the land due from the peasantry to the nobles had the same effect even then—most of the country was practically held in a kind of double ownership; the peasant cultivator had usually, by habit if not by law, a fixed hold upon the soil, but he was subject in the cultivation of it to innumerable exactions of varying kinds, which the lord could change pretty much as he chose. 'In France,' continues Adam Smith, so oddly contrary to everything which we should say now, 'the inferior ranks of the people must suffer patiently the usage which their superiors choose to inflict on them.' The country in Europe where there is now, perhaps, the most of social equality was then the one in which there was, perhaps, the least.

And side by side with this museum of economical errors there was a most vigorous political economy which exposed them. The doctrines of Free Trade had been before several times suggested by isolated thinkers, but by far the most powerful combined school of philosophers who incessantly inculcated them were the French *Économistes*. They delighted in proving that the whole structure of the French laws upon industry was utterly wrong; that prohibitions ought not to be imposed on the import of foreign manufactures; that bounties ought not to be given to native ones; that the exportation of corn ought to be free; that the whole country ought to be a fiscal unit; that there should be no duty between any province; and so on in other cases. No one could state the abstract doctrines on which they rested everything more clearly. 'Acheter, c'est vendre,' said Quesnay, the founder of the school, 'vendre, c'est acheter.' You cannot better express the doctrine of modern political economy that 'trade is barter.' 'Do not attempt,' Quesnay continues 'to fix the price of your products, goods, or services; they will escape your rules. Competition alone can regulate prices with equity; it alone restricts them to a moderation which varies little; it alone attracts with certainty provisions where they are wanted or labour where it is required.' 'That which we call dearness is the only remedy of dearness: dearness causes plenty.' Any quantity of sensible remarks to this effect might be disinterred from these writers. They were not always equally wise.

As the prime maxim of the ruling policy was to encourage commerce and neglect agriculture, this sect set up a doctrine that agriculture was the only source of wealth, and that trade and commerce contributed nothing to it. The labour of artificers and merchants was sterile; that of agriculturists was alone truly productive. The way in which they arrived at this strange idea was, if I understand it, something like this: they took the whole agricultural produce of a country, worth say £5,000,000 as it stood in the hands of the farmer, and applied it thus:—

First, as we should say, in repayment of capital spent in wages, &c.	£3,000,000
Secondly, in payment of profit by way of hire of capital say, or as subsistence to himself	500,000
Total outlay . . .	£3,500,000

But that outlay of £3,500,000 has produced a value of £5,000,000; there is therefore an overplus over and above the outlay of £1,500,000; and this overplus, or *produit net* as the *Économistes* call it, goes to the landlord for rent, as we should call it. But no other employment yields any similar *produit net*. A cotton spinner only replaces his own capital, and obtains his profit on it; like the farmer (as they said), he pays the outlay, and he gains a profit or subsistence for himself. But he does no more. There is no extra overplus as in farming; no balance, after paying wages and hiring capital; nothing to go to any landlord. In the same way commerce is, according to this system, transfer only—the expense of distribution is paid; the necessary number of capitalists and of labourers are maintained, but that is all; there is nothing beyond the wages, and beyond the profit. In agriculture only is there a third element —a *produit net*.

From this doctrine the *Économistes* drew two inferences, one very agreeable to agriculturists, the other very disagreeable; but both exactly opposite to the practice of their government. *First*, they said, as agriculture was the exclusive source of all wealth, it was absurd to depress it or neglect it, or to encourage commerce and manufacture in place of it. They had no toleration for the system of finance and commercial legislation which they saw around them, of which the one object was to make France a trading and manufacturing country, when nature meant it to be an agricultural one. *Secondly*, they inferred that most, if not all, the existing taxes in France were wrong in principle. 'If,' they argued, 'agriculture is the only source of wealth, and if, as we know, wealth only can pay taxes, then all taxes should be imposed on agriculture.' They reasoned: 'In manufactures there is only a necessary hire of labour, and a similar hire of capital, at a cost which cannot be diminished; there is in them no available surplus for taxation. If you attempt to impose taxes on them, and if in name you make them pay such taxes, they will charge higher for their necessary work. They will in a roundabout way throw the burden of those taxes on agriculture. The *produit net* of the latter is the one real purse of the state;

no other pursuit can truly pay anything, for it has no purse. And therefore,' they summed up, 'all taxes, save a single one on the *produit net*, were absurd. They only attempted to make those pay who could not pay; to extract money from fancied funds, in which there was no money.' All the then existing taxes in France, therefore, they proposed to abolish, and to replace them by a single tax on agriculture only.

As this system was so opposed to the practice of the Government, one would have expected that it should have been discountenanced, if not persecuted, by the Government. But, in fact, it was rather favoured by it. Quesnay, the founder of the system, had a place at court, and was under the special protection of the King's mistress, who was then the King's government. M. de Lavergne has quoted a graphic description of him. 'Quesnay,' writes Marmontel, 'well lodged in a small *appartement* in the *entresol* of Madame de Pompadour, only occupied himself from morning till night with political and agricultural economy. He believed that he had reduced the system to calculation, and to axioms of irresistible evidence; and as he was collecting a school, he gave himself the trouble to explain to me his new doctrine, in order to make me one of his proselytes. I applied all my force of comprehension to understand those truths which he told me were self evident; but I found in them only vagueness and obscurity. To make him believe that I understood that which I really did not understand, was beyond my power; but I listened with patient docility, and left him the hope that in the end he would enlighten me, and make me believe his doctrine. I did more; I applauded his work, which I really thought very useful, for he tried to recommend agriculture in a country where it was too much disdained, and to turn many excellent understandings towards the study of it. While political storms were forming and dissolving above the *entresol* of Quesnay, he perfected his calculations and his axioms of rural economy, as tranquil and as indifferent to the movements of the Court, as if he had been a hundred leagues off. Below, in the *salon* of Madame de Pompadour, they deliberated on peace or war—on the choice of generals—on the recall of ministers; while we in the *entresol* were reasoning on agriculture, calculating the *produit net*, or sometimes were dining gaily with Diderot, D'Alembert, Duclos, Helvetius, Turgot, Buffon; and Madame de Pompadour, not being able to induce this troup of philosophers to come down to her *salon*, came herself to see them at table, and to chat

ADAM SMITH AS A PERSON

with them.' An opposition philosophy has rarely been so petted and well treated. Much as the reign of Louis XVI differed in most respects from that of Louis XV, it was like it in this patronage of the *Économistes*. Turgot was made Minister of Finance, to reform France by applying their doctrines.

The reason of this favour to the *Économistes* from the Government was, that on the question in which the government took far the most interest the *Économistes* were on its side. The daily want of the French government was more power; though nominally a despotism, it was feeble in reality. But the *Économistes* were above all things anxious for a very strong government; they held to the maxim, everything *for* the people—nothing *by* them; they had a horror of checks and counter-poises and resistances; they wished to do everything by the *fiat* of the sovereign. They had, in fact, the natural wish of eager speculators, to have an irresistible despotism behind them, and supporting them; and with the simplicity which marks so much of the political specula-tions of the eighteenth century, but which now seems so childlike, they never seemed to think how they were to get their despot, or how they were to ensure that he should be on their side. The painful experience of a hundred years has taught us that influential despotisms are not easy to make, and that good ones are still less so. But in their own time nothing could be more advantageous to the *Économistes* than to have an eager zeal for a perfect despotism; in consequence they were patronised by the greatest existing authority, instead of being discountenanced by it.

This account of the *Économistes* may seem to a reader who looks at Adam Smith exclusively by the light of modern political economy to be too long for their relation to him. But he would not have thought so himself. He so well knew how much his mind had been affected by them and by their teaching, that he at one time thought of dedicating *The Wealth of Nations* to Quesnay, their founder; and though he relinquished that intention, he always speaks of him with the greatest respect. If, indeed, we consider what Glasgow is now, still more what it must have been a hundred years ago, we shall comprehend the degree to which this French experience—this sight of a country so managed, and with such a political economy—must have excited the mind of Adam Smith. It was the passage from a world where there was no *spectacle* to one in which there was the best which the world has ever seen, and simultaneously the passage from the most Scotch of ideas to others the most un-Scotch. A feeble head would have been upset in the transit, but Adam Smith kept his.

From France he went home to Scotland, and stayed quietly with his mother at his native town of Kirkcaldy for a whole ten years. He lived on the annuity from the Duke of Buccleugh, and occupied himself in study only. What he was studying, if we considered *The Wealth of Nations* as a book of political economy only, we might be somewhat puzzled to say. But the contents of that book are, as has been said, most miscellaneous, and in its author's mind it was but a fragment of an immensely larger whole. Much more than ten years' study would have been necessary for the entire book which he contemplated.

At last, in 1776, *The Wealth of Nations* was published, and was, on the whole, well received. Dr. Carlyle, indeed, preserves an impression that, in point of style, it was inferior to *The Theory of Moral Sentiments*. But all competent readers were agreed as to the great value of the substance. And almost everybody will probably now think, in spite of Dr. Carlyle, that the style is very much better than that of *The Moral Sentiments*. There is about the latter a certain showiness and an 'air of the professor trying to be fascinating,' which are not very agreeable; and, after all, there is a ponderous weight in the words which seems to bear down the rather flimsy matter. But the style of *The Wealth of Nations* is entirely plain and manly. The author had, in the interval, seen at least a little of the living world and of society, and had learnt that the greatest mistake is the trying to be more agreeable than you can be, and that the surest way to spoil an important book is to try to attract the attention of, to 'write down' to, a class of readers too low to take a serious interest in the subject. A really great style, indeed, Adam Smith's certainly is not. Lord Mansfield is said to have told Boswell that he did not feel, in reading either Hume or Adam Smith, that he was reading English at all; and it was very natural that it should be so. English was not the mother tongue of either. Adam Smith had, no doubt, spoken somewhat broad Scotch for the first fourteen or fifteen years of his life; probably he never spoke anything that could quite be called English till he went to Oxford. And nothing so much hampers the free use of the pen in any language as the incessant remembrance of a kindred but different one; you are never sure the idioms nature prompts are those of the tongue you would speak, or of the tongue you would reject. Hume and Adam Smith exemplify the difficulty in opposite ways. Hume is always idiomatic, but his idioms are constantly wrong; many of his best passages are, on that account, curiously grating and puzzling; you feel that they are very like what an Englishman would say, but yet that, after all, somehow or other, they are what he never would say;—there is a minute seasoning of imperceptible difference which distracts your attention, and which you are for ever stopping to analyse. Adam Smith's habit was very different. His style is not colloquial in the least. He adheres to the heavy 'book' English which he had found in the works of others, and was sure that he could repeat in his own. And in that sort of style he has eminent merit. No one ever has to read him twice to gather his meaning;[7] no one can bring much valid objection to his way of expressing that meaning; there is even a sort of appropriateness, though often a clumsy sort, in his way of saying it. But the style has no intrinsic happiness; no one would read it for its own sake; the words do not cleave to the meaning, so that you cannot think of them without it, or it without them. This is only given to those who write in the speech of their childhood, and only to the very few of those—the five or six in every generation who have from nature the best grace, who think by inborn feeling in words at once charming and accurate.

Of *The Wealth of Nations* as an economical treatise, I have nothing to say now; but it is not useless to say that it is a very amusing book about old times. As it is dropping out of immediate use from change of times, it is well to observe that this very change brings it a new sort of interest of its own. There are few books in which there may be gathered more curious particulars of the old world. I cull at random almost that 'a broad wheel waggon, attended by two men, and drawn by eight horses,' then 'in about six weeks time carried and brought trade between London and Edinburgh;'—that in Adam Smith's opinion, if there were such an effectual demand for grain as would require a million tons of shipping to import it, the 'navy of England,' the mercantile navy of course, would not be sufficient for it;—that 'Holland was the great emporium of European goods;' that she was, in proportion to the land and the number of inhabitants, by far the richest country in Europe; that she had the greatest share of the ocean-carrying trade; that her citizens possessed £40,000,000 in the French and English funds;—that in Sheffield no master cutler can have more than one apprentice, by a bye-law of the corporation, and in Norfolk and Norwich no weaver more than two;—that if Adam Smith's eyes

---

[7] The *Fortnightly* has 'No one even has to read twice in him to gather meaning.'—p. 36.

served him right, 'the common people in Scotland, who are fed with oatmeal, are in general neither so strong nor so handsome as the same class of people in England, who are fed with wheaten bread, and that they do not look or work as well;' that, which is odder still, the porters and coalheavers in London, and those unfortunate women who live by prostitution—the strongest men and the most beautiful women, perhaps, in the British dominions—are from the lowest rank of people in Ireland, and fed with the potato; and that £1,000 share in India stock 'gave a share not in the plunder, but in the appointment of the plunderers of India;'—that 'the expense of the establishment of Massachussetts Bay, before the commencement of the late disturbances,' that is, the American war, 'used to be about £18,000 a year, and that of New York, £4,500;' that all the civil establishments in America did not at the same date cost £67,000 a year;—that 'in consequence of the monopoly of the American colonial market,' the commerce of England, 'instead of running in a great number of small channels, has been taught to run principally in one great channel;'—that 'the territorial acquisitions of the East India Company, the undoubted right of the Crown,' 'might be rendered another source of revenue more abundant, perhaps, than all' others from which much addition could be expected;—that Great Britain is, perhaps, since 'the world began, the only state which has extended its empire' 'without augmenting the area of its resources;'—that, and this is the final sentence of the book, 'If any of the provinces of the British empire cannot be made to contribute towards the support of the whole empire, it is surely time that Great Britain should free herself from the expense of defending those provinces in time of war, and of supporting any part of their civil or military establishments in time of peace, and endeavour to accommodate her future views and designs to the real mediocrity of her circumstances.' A strange passage, considering all that has happened since, and all the provinces which we have since taken. No one can justly estimate *The Wealth of Nations* who thinks of it as a book of mere political economy, such as Quesnay had then written, or as Ricardo afterwards wrote; it is really both full of the most various kinds of facts and of thoughts often as curious on the most various kinds of subjects.

The effect of the publication of *The Wealth of Nations* on the fortunes of its author was very remarkable. It gave the Duke of Buccleugh the power of relieving himself of his annuity, by performing the equivalent clause in the bargain; he obtained for Adam Smith a commissionership of customs for Scotland—an appointment of which we do not know the precise income, but which was clearly, according to the notions of those times, a very good one indeed. A person less fitted to fill it could not indeed easily have been found. Adam Smith had, as we have seen, never been used to pecuniary business of any kind; he had never even taken part in any sort of action out of such business; he was an absent and meditative student. It was indeed during his tenure of this office that, as I have said, he startled a subordinate who asked for his signature, by imitating the signature of the last commissioner, instead of giving his own—of course in pure absence of mind. He was no doubt better acquainted with the theory of taxation than any other man of his time; he could have given a minister in the capital better advice than any one else as to what taxes he should or should not impose. But a commissioner of customs, in a provincial city, has nothing to do with the imposition of taxes, or with giving advice about them. His business simply is to see that those which already exist are regularly collected and methodically transmitted, which involves an infinity of transactions requiring a trained man of detail. But a man of detail Adam Smith certainly was not— at least of detail in business. Nature had probably not well fitted him for it, and his mode of life had completed the result, and utterly unfitted him. The appointment that was given him was one in which the great abilities which he possessed were useless, and in which much smaller ones, which he had not, would have been of extreme value.

But in another respect this appointment has been more blamed than I think is just. However small may be the value of Adam Smith's work at the Custom House, the effect of performing it and the time which it occupied prevented him from writing anything more. And it has been thought that posterity has in consequence suffered much. But I own that I doubt this exceedingly. Adam Smith had no doubt made a vast accumulation of miscellaneous materials for his great design. But these materials were probably of very second-rate value. Neither for the history of law, nor of science, nor art, had the preliminary work been finished, which is necessary before such a mind as Adam Smith's can usefully be applied to them. Before the theorising philosopher must come the accurate historian. To write the history either of law or science or art is enough for the life of any single man: neither have as yet been written with the least approach to completeness. The best of the fragments on these subjects, which we now have, did not exist in Adam Smith's time. There was, therefore, but little use in his thinking or writing at large about them. If he had set down for us some account of his residence in France, and the society which he saw there, posterity would have been most grateful to him. But this he had no idea of doing; and nobody would now much care for a series of elaborate theories, founded upon facts insufficiently collected.

Adam Smith lived for fourteen years after the publication of *The Wealth of Nations*, but he wrote nothing, and scarcely studied anything. The duties of his office, though of an easy and routine character, which would probably have enabled a man bred to business to spend much of his time and almost all his mind on other things, were, we are told, enough 'to waste his spirits and dissipate his attention.' And not unnaturally, for those who have ever been used to give all their days to literary work rarely seem able to do that work when they are even in a slight degree struck and knocked against the world; only those who have scarcely ever known what it is to have unbroken calm are able to accomplish much without that calm. During these years Adam Smith's life passed easily and pleasantly in the Edinburgh society of that time—a very suitable one, for it was one to which professors and lawyers gave the tone, and of which intellectual exertion was the life and being. Adam Smith was it is true no easy talker—was full neither of ready replies nor of prepared replies. He rather liked to listen, but if he talked—and traps it is said were laid to make him do so—he could expound admirably on the subjects which he knew, and also (which is quite as characteristic of the man as we see him in his works), could run up rapid theories on such data as occurred to him, when, as Dugald Stewart tells us in his dignified dialect, 'he gave a loose to his genius upon the very few branches of knowledge of which he only possessed the outlines.'

He died calmly and quietly, leaving directions about his manuscripts and such other literary things, and saying, in a melancholy way, 'I meant to have done more.' The sort of fame which *The Wealth of Nations* has obtained, and its special influence, did not begin in his lifetime, and he had no notion of it. Nor would he perhaps have quite appreciated it if he had. His mind was full of his great scheme of the origin and history of all cultivation; as happens to so many men, though scarcely ever on so great a scale, aiming at one sort of reputation, he attained another. To use Lord Bacon's perpetual illustration, like

Saul, he 'went in search of his father's asses, and he found a kingdom.'

Adam Smith has been said to belong to the Macaulay type of Scotchmen, and the saying has been thought a paradox, particularly by those who, having misread Macaulay, think him a showy rhetorician, and not having at all read Adam Smith, think of him as a dry and dull political economist. But the saying is true, nevertheless. Macaulay is anything but a mere rhetorical writer—there is a very hard kernel of business in him; and Adam Smith is not dry at all—the objection to him is that he is not enough so, and that the real truth in several parts of his subject cannot be made so interesting as his mode of treatment implies. And there is this fundamental likeness between Macaulay and Adam Smith, that they can both describe practical matters in such a way as to fasten them on the imagination, and not only get what they say read, but get it remembered and make it part of the substance of the reader's mind ever afterwards. Abstract theorists may say that such a style as that of Adam Smith is not suitable to an abstract science; but then Adam Smith has carried political economy far beyond the bounds of those who care for abstract science or who understand exactly what it means. He has popularised it in the only sense in which it can be popularised without being spoiled; that is, he has put certain broad conclusions into the minds of hard-headed men, which are all which they need know, and all which they for the most part will ever care for, and he has put those conclusions there ineradicably. This, too, is what Macaulay does for us in history, at least what he does best; he engraves indelibly the main outlines and the rough common sense of the matter. Other more refining and perhaps in some respects more delicate minds, may add the nicer details and explain those wavering, flickering, inconstant facts of human nature which are either above common sense or below it. Both these great Scotchmen excelled in the 'osteology of their subject,' a term invented by Dr. Chalmers, a third great Scotchman who excelled in it himself; perhaps, indeed, it is a idiosyncrasy of their race.

Like many other great Scotchmen—Macaulay is one of them—Adam Smith was so much repelled by the dominant Calvinism in which he was born that he never voluntarily wrote of religious subjects, or, as far as we know, spoke of them. Nothing, indeed, can repel a man more from such things than what Macaulay called the 'bray of Exeter Hall.' What can be worse for people than to hear in their youth arguments, alike clamorous and endless, founded on ignorant interpretations of inconclusive words? As soon as they come to years of discretion all instructed persons cease to take part in such discussions, and often say nothing at all on the great problems of human life and destiny. Sometimes the effect goes farther; those subjected to this training become not only silent but careless. There is nothing like Calvinism for generating indifference. The saying goes that Scotchmen are those who believe most or least; and it is most natural that it should be so, for they have been so hurt and pestered with religious stimulants, that it is natural they should find total abstinence from them both pleasant and healthy. How far this indifference went in Adam Smith's case we do not exactly know, but there is no reason to think it extended to all religion; on the contrary, there are many traces of the complacent optimism of the eighteenth century—a doctrine the more agreeable to him because, perhaps, it is the exact opposite of Calvinism —and which was very popular in an easy-going age, though the storms and calamities of a later time dispelled it, and have made it seem to us thin and unreal. The only time when Adam Smith ever came near to theological discussion was by a letter on Hume's death, in which he said that Hume, one of his oldest friends, was the best man he had ever known—perhaps praise which was scarcely meant to be taken too literally, but which naturally caused a great storm. The obvious thing to say about it is that it does not indicate any very lofty moral standard, for there certainly was no sublime excellence in Hume, who as Carlyle long ago said, 'all his life through did not so much morally live as critically investigate.' But though the bigots of his time misunderstood him, Adam Smith did not by so saying mean to identify himself with irreligion or even with scepticism.

Adam Smith's life, however, was not like Macaulay's—'a life without a lady.' There are vestiges of an early love affair, though but vague ones. Dugald Stewart, an estimable man in his way, but one of the most detestable of biographers, for he seems always thinking much more of his own words than of the facts he has to relate, says: 'In the early part of Mr. Smith's life, it is well known to his friends that he was for several years attached to a young lady of great beauty and accomplishment.' But he does not tell us who she was, and 'has not been able to learn' 'how far his addresses were favourably received,' or, in fact, anything about the matter. It seems, however, that the lady died unmarried, and in that case the unsentimental French novelists say that the gentleman is not often continuously in earnest, for that 'a lady cannot be *always* saying No!' But whether such was the case with Adam Smith or not we cannot tell. He was a lonely, bookish man, but that may tell both ways. The books may be opposed to the lady, but the solitude will preserve her remembrance.

If Adam Smith did abandon sentiment and devote himself to study, he has at least the excuse of having succeeded. Scarcely any writer's work has had so much visible fruit. He has, at least, annexed his name to a great practical movement which is still in progress through the world. Free Trade has become in the popular mind almost as much his subject as the war of Troy was Homer's; only curious inquirers think of teachers before the one any more than of poets before the other. If all the speeches made at our Anti-Corn Law League were examined, I doubt if any reference could be found to any preceding writer, though the name of Adam Smith was always on men's lips. And in other countries it is the same. Smith-ism is a name of reproach with all who do not hold such doctrines, and of respect with those who believe them; no other name is used equally or comparably by either. So long as the doctrines of protection exist—and they seem likely to do so, as human interests are what they are and human nature is what it is— Adam Smith will always be quoted as the great authority of Anti-Protectionism—as the man who first told the world the truth so that the world could learn and believe it.

And besides this great practical movement Adam Smith started a great theoretical one also. On one side his teaching created Mr. Cobden and Mr. Bright, on another it rendered possible Ricardo and Mr. Mill. He is the founder of that analysis of the 'great commerce' which in England we now call political economy, and which, dry, imperfect, and unfinished as it is, will be thought by posterity one of the most valuable and peculiar creations of English thought. As far as accuracy goes Ricardo no doubt began this science, but his whole train of thought was suggested by Adam Smith, and he could not have written without him. So much theory and so much practice have rarely, perhaps never, sprung from a single mind.

Fortunate in many things, Adam Smith was above all things fortunate in his age. Commerce had become far larger, far more striking, far more world-wide than it ever was before, and it needed an effectual explainer. A vigorous Scotchman with the hard-headedness and the abstractions of his country, trained in England and familiar with France, was the species of man best fitted to explain it, and such a man was Adam Smith.

The Centenary of
'The Wealth of Nations'[1]

'THE WEALTH OF NATIONS,' which was published in 1776, is this
year just a hundred years old, and the English Political Economy Club
gave on Wednesday a dinner in celebration of the fact, at which they
had the remarkable honour of entertaining the French Minister of
Finance, who came from Paris for the purpose, and who made on the
occasion a most admirable and suitable speech. No compliment could
have been more suitable for a dinner in celebration of the beginning
of the most effectual of political philosophies, and the one which has
by far the most affected the intercourse of nations.

Nothing beforehand,—nothing if we look at the matter with the
eyes, say, of the year 1770, could have seemed more unlikely than that
Adam Smith should have succeeded in such an achievement. Political
economy is, above all things, the theory of business, and if ever there
was an eminent man who pre-eminently was not a man of business it
was Adam Smith. He was a bookish student who never made a sixpence, who was unfit for all sorts of affairs, and whose absence of mind
is hardly credible. He once astonished a sentinel who did him some
kind of military salute by drawing himself up and giving with perfect
gravity a fac-simile salute in return. On another occasion, when he
had to put his signature to an official document, instead of doing so
he copied with slow and elaborate care the name of the person who
had signed before him. And these acts are but specimens of his life.
If the townsmen of Kirkcaldy—the little place where *The Wealth of
Nations* was written—had been told to select the townsman who was
most unlikely, as far as externals went, to tell this world how to make
money, most likely they would have selected Adam Smith, whose
writings have, in fact, caused more money to be made and prevented
more money from being wasted, than those of any other author.

[1] This article was first published in *The Economist* for June 3 1876, Volume XXXIV
pp. 649–51.

That there had been various preceding political economies, more than the common world much remembers, rather enhances the wonder. Unquestionably, many hardheaded men, and some sects of writers, can be mentioned who approached more or less nearly to the general doctrines now accepted as the true theory of commerce. What sort of 'natural selection,' then, made Adam Smith's political economy so much more successful than that of all others? Why was this most unlikely-looking Scotch student the 'favoured' philosopher whose name was to be annexed for all time to the true theory of trade?

One great piece of good fortune to Adam Smith was his time. Historians of science remark that most great discoveries are based on large collections of new facts. And this was the case with trade in the eighteenth century. There was then a much vaster, a much wider, and much more varied commerce than the world had ever seen in any preceding time. And its contents were catalogued and were commented upon in a quantity and with an accuracy which there had been nothing like before. 'Political Arithmetic,' as statistics were then called, was no doubt then very small in comparison with the mass of figures to which it has grown now; but still it existed, and existed for the first time—at least, in any connected bulk—and that existence was a sign of the recent extension of commerce and of the changed place it began to take in men's minds. Adam Smith was singularly fortunate among philosophers, for he had a new world to explain and new data for explaining it.

And he had also a world to conquer. The new commerce which had grown up had done so in spite of any law which could be framed to prevent it—not that such had been in the least the intention of legislators. On the contrary, they were most anxious to develop trade, and to make the nations rich which were subject to them; but they had pursued a wrong, though very natural, method. Seemingly, the most obvious person to consult on matters of trade, is the trader; the person who, at first sight, seems likely to know most about a thing, is the person who makes it; and, accordingly, the European governments had taken counsel with the producer. But, unhappily, the producer was just the wrong person to consult. What he wanted was a high price for his article, and a monopoly of the market in which to sell it; and the laws he recommended were inevitably framed, more or less, to obtain his wishes; whereas, the interest of the nations which the governments were trustees for, and which they were sincerely desirous to serve, was a 'low price,' unrestricted competition from abroad, and a freedom for every one to buy or sell everything at home. The legislative success of Adam Smith's philosophy has transcended that of all other philosophers very much from this. He found a world in which the interests of the buyer were supposed to be secured by laws, framed at the suggestion of the seller, and he was able to show, not by mere elaborate argument—though he gave that too—but also by an unsurpassed store of living illustrations, that these laws worked ill, and were sure to do so, because they were framed in the wrong person's interest. To use a homely illustration, Adam Smith was so fortunate as to find a world in 'which the cat had the custody of the cream,' and to have had unprecedented facilities for showing the absurdity of the arrangement.

And when we look more closely at the matter, we find notwithstanding the outside impression, that he was a person singularly fitted to do this. He belonged to what—calling the group from the representative most familiar to us—we may call 'the Macaulay type of Scotchmen.' He possessed in combination,—exactly that power of lucid exposition, that eager interest in his subject, that immense power of illustrating it from all quarters, and that hard kind of predominant— we might almost say—intolerant common sense, of which every reader of Mr. Trevelyan's excellent biography will just now have in his mind an almost perfect specimen. Many persons are now deterred from reading *The Wealth of Nations* by the dullness of modern books of political economy, but most of it really consists of some of the most striking and graphic writing in the language. And its defect, like that of several other great works of the eighteenth century, is rather that it tries to make its subject more interesting than it ought to be, and not to dwell on the dull standpoints of the truth, though these are often the most important parts of all. But perhaps for its peculiar time and purpose this defect was almost a merit. It gained a hearing from the mass of mankind, who always think they ought to be able to understand even the most complex subjects with little effort, and so brought home approximate truth to those most concerned in its application. A student familiar with abstractions may prefer teaching like Ricardo's, which begins in dry principles, and which goes with unabbreviated reasoning to conclusions that are as dry. But such students are very rare. Teaching like Adam Smith's, imperfect and external as from its method it is, vitally changes the minds and maxims of thousands to whom an abstract treatise is intolerable.

Three other circumstances, too, helped Adam Smith. First—He was educated in England—educated, we mean, as a young man; and though Oxford may have taught him little of book learning in comparison with what she ought, as he always said she did, she gave him—for he lived there several years—a sort of familiarity with English things, and of sympathy with English life, which the Scotchmen of that day often wanted. Anyone who will compare Hume's way of treating an English subject with Adam Smith's, will at once feel the contrast. Hume without disguise hates the whole thing; Adam Smith—though, no doubt, even in him there are unextinguished vestiges of the old feud between the countries—abounds in kindly understanding, and seems always to remember that he spent a happy youth in England, though possibly not one of the elaborate book-training which he coveted.

Secondly—Adam Smith lived for years in Glasgow, then even a commercial city of intelligence, and was a member of a club of merchants, 'in which the express design was to inquire into the nature and principles of trade in all its branches, and to communicate their knowledge on that subject to each other.' A set of strongheaded merchants, trained as the Scotchmen have ever since the Reformation been, in abstract reasoning, would be sure to argue out something near to Free-trade—and tradition preserves the name of a certain 'Provost Cochrane,' to whom Adam Smith always said he was under great obligations. This club and the atmosphere of Glasgow life, probably taught him more than he was aware of, not so much in the way of definite ideas and conclusions, as in the way of 'putting business things,' so that men of business can understand them—an art which a man cannot learn in his study, for books will never teach it, but which Adam Smith pre-eminently possessed, and which is an essential pre-requisite to his characteristic work. Lastly—Adam Smith resided in France a considerable time in middle life, which not only brought him into contact with the French *Economistes*, who had like him, a Free-trade doctrine, and traces of whose influence curiously leavening the original Scotch substance of the thought, are everywhere to be found in *The Wealth of Nations*, but also generally widened his culture, excited his mind, and in those days of the old *régime*, introduced him to an almost complete specimen of commercial morbid anatomy on the greatest scale, showing how a treasury which ought to be full might be made empty, and how a nation which ought to have been rich and happy might be made and kept poor and miserable.

As far as England is concerned, most of the legislative effects of the work of Adam Smith are complete. He thought the adoption of a Free-trade legislation as unlikely as the creation of a 'Utopia,' but yet it has been established. The fetters in which pre-existing laws bound our commerce, have been removed, and the result is that we possess the greatest, the most stable, and the most lucrative commerce which the world has ever seen. Deep as was Adam Smith's conviction of the truth of his principles, the history of England for the last thirty years would have been almost inconceivable to him. Thirty years ago Carlyle and Arnold had nearly convinced the world of the irrecoverable poverty of our lower classes. The 'condition of England question,' as they termed it, was bringing us fast to ruin. But, in fact, we were on the eve of the greatest prosperity which we have ever seen, or perhaps any other nation. And it was to the repeal of the Corn Laws in 1846, and to the series of changes of which this was the type, and the most important, that we owe this wonderful contrast. The nature and the direction of the result Adam Smith would have unquestionably accepted; but the magnitude and the rapidity—the 'figures and the pace'—would have been far beyond his imagination. Even to us, with the aid of our modern experience of large transactions, they are amazing, and no mind trained in the comparatively slow and and small school of the eighteenth century, would, a hundred years since, have been able to think them possible.

In almost all other countries much remains to be done in the alteration of the laws in the way that Adam Smith would have suggested. The English race have gone into many countries, and have there done many wonderful things, but they have not been able to take their Free-trade principles with them. Everywhere 'Protection' rises like a weed from the soil; the wish to consult, and the habit of being guided by the producer, are as strong in the United States in 1876 as ever they were in England in 1776; and almost all our colonies partake the same spirit. Probably no one can over-estimate the loss of wealth and the diminution of happiness which this unhappy ignorance causes. A rational tariff in America would have done more indirectly to make American industry stable and prosperous, and directly to advance the growth of wealth and industry, than anything else which could be named. And yet an irrational and pernicious tariff seems fixed upon the United States for many years.

In Europe there has not been for many years any symptom of commercial progress so good as the presence of M. Léon Say—the French Finance Minister—at Adam Smith's festival. The circumstances of France are for the moment very difficult; a very large revenue must be raised, and in this case, as in all similar ones, much of it will have to be raised not in the best way. But it is much that the guidance of such immense affairs should be in the hands of one who is thoroughly imbued with wise opinions, and much that they should no longer be at the mercy of M. Thiers, the last statesman in Europe, perhaps, who avers that he is 'a Protectionist on principle,' and who only wishes that the 'tall chimnies' of some favoured producer should smoke and thrive, no matter at what cost to the consumer, or at what ruin to other industries.

And though in England the legislative work of Adam Smith has nearly come to an end, there is much else which we have yet to learn from him,—at any rate, from the spirit of his teacher, if not from its letter. Though a political economist, he was not a mere economist—or, rather, he was the antithesis of one as we now think of him. Great as his work has been, he said, with much melancholy, not long before his death, 'I meant to have done more.' *The Wealth of Nations* was but a part of a much larger work in which he meant to treat something like what we should now call the 'evolution' of human society and of human improvement. He discovered, as it has been put, 'the natural progress of opulence while looking for the natural progress of all things.' And he was disappointed to think that he finished so little of so great a scheme. In this critics, instructed by longer experience, will not agree with him. These great plans are the bane of philosophy; 'the master mind,' as has been profoundly said, 'shows itself in limitation,' and, fortunate as Adam Smith was in many ways, it is his greatest good fortune that fate constrained and compelled him to it. But, nevertheless, this wider design in which *The Wealth of Nations* began, is one of its peculiar features and one which we now-a-days much want Adam Smith to complete. The world is too much divided between economists, who think only of 'wealth,' and of sentimentalists, who are never so sure they are right as when they differ from what political economy teaches. Now of course it is true that there are some things, though not many things, more important than money, and a nation may well be called on to abandon the maxims which would produce the most money, for others which would promote some of these better ends. The case is much like that of health in the body. There are unquestionable circumstances in which a man may be called on to endanger and to sacrifice his health at some call of duty. But for all that bodily health is a most valuable thing, and the advice of the physician as to the best way of keeping it is very much to be heeded, and in the same way, though the wealth is occasionally to be foregone, and the ordinary rules of industry abandoned, yet still national wealth is in itself and in its connections a great end, and economists who teach us how to arrive at it are most useful. Nor were they ever so useful as now, when there is a tendency to magnify the occasional exceptions to their doctrines into the rule. Their teaching, being based on hard fact, is often most painful to human nature, and accordingly in every age a whole race of socialists will gainsay and oppose it. They are like pleasant doctors who teach people to eat and drink too much, only they have higher pretensions, and say you must not think of health only; there are things which are higher than health, and so they appeal at once to the higher aspirations of humanity and to its lower weaknesses. We must not be deluded into thinking that the characteristic work of Adam Smith is over because the laws of which he disapproved are repealed. Perhaps there never was a time in which we more needed to combine a stern and homely sagacity resembling his, with the far-reaching aims and ample knowledge for which he was so remarkable.

William Pitt

Introductory note

William Pitt (1759–1806) was born at Hayes, Kent, the second son of William Pitt, first earl of Chatham, and of Hester Grenville. He was educated at Pembroke College, Cambridge, and was called to the Bar at Lincoln's Inn in 1780. He became M.P. for Appleby in 1781. He became Chancellor of the Exchequer under Shelburne upon Rocking-ham's death in 1782, and when Shelburne was overthrown by the coalition of North and Fox and the ministry dismissed in 1783, Pitt was made Prime Minister in December of that year, at the age of twenty-five. He had great difficulty in forming a ministry, and was then often defeated in Parliament, but he refused to dissolve Parliament until he was sure that public feeling was on his side. He won an overwhelming majority at the general election of 1784. He now took measures to reduce the national debt and made great reductions in customs duties. Pitt was disturbed by the spread of republican ideas in England following the outbreak of the French Revolution, and this coloured his attitude to the French demand for the opening of the Scheldt, which led to war with France in 1793. Pitt sought to oppose France by a series of European coalitions which were not successful and which imposed a heavy burden of taxation on the country. How-ever, after the end of the war on the Continent in 1797, a second series of alliances drove the French back to the Rhine.

At the outbreak of the Irish rebellion of 1798, Pitt renewed the suspension of the Habeas Corpus Act and passed other coercive measures. The Irish Parliament was united to that of Great Britain in 1800. Pitt sought to complete his Irish policy by introducing a measure of Catholic emancipation, but found George III so obdurate in oppos-ing him that he resigned in 1801. He agreed to support Addington's administration but gradually came into opposition to it and re-entered office in 1804 on Addington's resignation, though without the support of most of his former allies among the Whigs. He formed a third coalition with Russia, Austria, and Sweden, which brought about a war with Spain. The battle of Austerlitz sundered the coalition he built up, and the news of it contributed to his death. Pitt died at Putney in 1806.

William Pitt[1]

Lord Stanhope's *Life of Mr. Pitt* has both the excellencies and the defects which we should expect from him, and neither of them are what we expect in a great historical writer of the present age. Even simple readers are becoming aware that historical investigation, which used to be a sombre and respectable calling, is now an audacious pursuit. Paradoxes are very bold and very numerous. Many of the recognised 'good people' in history have become bad, and all the very bad people have become rather good. We have palliations of Tiberius, eulogies on Henry VIII, devotional exercises to Cromwell, and fulsome adulation of Julius Cæsar and of the first Napoleon. The philosophy of history is more alarming still. One school sees in it but a gradual development of atheistic belief, another threatens to resolve it all into 'the three simple agencies, starch, fibrin, and albumen.' But in these exploits of audacious ingenuity and specious learning Lord Stanhope has taken no part. He is not anxious to be original. He travels, if possible, in the worn track of previous historians; he tells a plain tale in an easy plain way; he shrinks from wonderful novelties; with the cautious scepticism of true common sense; he is always glad to find that the conclusions at which he arrives coincide with those of former inquirers. His style is characteristic of his matter. He narrates with a gentle sense and languid accuracy, very different from the stimulating rhetoric and exciting brilliancy of his more renowned contemporaries.

In the present case Lord Stanhope has been very fortunate both in his subject and in his materials. Mr. Pitt has never had even a decent biographer, though the peculiarities of his career are singularly inviting to literary ambition. His life had much of the solid usefulness of modern times, and not a little also of the romance of old times. He was skilled in economical reform, but retained some of the majesty of old-world eloquence. He was as keen in small figures as a rising politician

[1] *Life of the Right Honourable William Pitt,* By Earl Stanhope, Author of the 'History of England from the Peace of Utrecht.' This essay was first published in the *National Review* for July 1861, Volume XIII, pp. 179–228.

now, yet he was a despotic premier at an age when, in these times, a politician could barely aspire to be an under-secretary. It is not wonderful that Lord Stanhope should have been attracted to a subject which is so interesting in itself, and which lies so precisely in the direction of his previous studies. From his high standing and his personal connections, he has been able to add much to our minuter knowledge. He has obtained from various quarters many valuable letters which have not been published before. There is a whole series from George III to Mr. Pitt, and a scarcely less curious series from Mr. Pitt to his mother. We need not add that Lord Stanhope has digested his important materials with great care; that he has made of them almost as much as could be made; that he has a warm admiration and a delicate respect for the great statesman of whom he is writing. His nearest approach to an ungentle feeling is a quiet dislike to the great Whig families.

Mr. Pitt is an example of one of the modes in which the popular imagination is, even in historical times, frequently and easily misled. Mankind judge of a great statesman principally by the most marked and memorable passage in his career. By chance we lately had the honour to travel with a gentleman who said that Sir Robert Peel was the 'leader of the Whigs;' and though historical evidence will always prevent common opinion from becoming so absurd as this, it is undeniable that, in the popular fancy of younger men, Sir Robert Peel is the Liberal minister who repealed the corn-laws, and carried Catholic Emancipation. The world is forgetting that he was once the favourite leader of the old Tory party—the steady opponent of Mr. Canning, and the steady adherent of Lord Sidmouth and Lord Eldon. We remember his great reforms, of which we daily feel the benefit; we forget that, during a complete political generation, he was the most plausible supporter of ancient prejudices, and the most decent advocate of inveterate abuses. Mr. Pitt's fate has been very similar, but far less fortunate. The event in his life most deeply implanted in the popular memory is his resistance to the French Revolution; it is this which has made him the object of affection to extreme Tories, and of suspicion and distrust to reasonable Liberals. Yet no rash inference was ever more unfounded and more false. It can be proved that in all the other part of Mr. Pitt's life the natural tendency of his favourite plan was uniformly Liberal; that at the time of the French Revolution itself, he only did what the immense majority of the

English people, even of the cultivated English people, deliberately desired; that he did it anxiously, with many misgivings, and in opposition to his natural inclinations; that it is very dubious whether, in the temper of the French nation and the temper of the English nation, a war between them could by possibility have been avoided at that juncture; that in his administration and under his auspices the spirit of legislative improvement which characterises modern times may almost be said to begin; that he was the first English minister who discussed political questions with the cultivated thoughtfulness and considerate discretion which seem to characterise us now; that in political instruction he was immeasurably superior to Fox, and that, in the practical application of just principles to ordinary events, he was equally superior to Burke.

There are two kinds of statesmen to whom, at different times, representative government gives an opportunity and a career—dictators and administrators. There are certain men who are called in conjunctures of great danger to save the state. When national peril is imminent, all nations have felt that it was needful to select the best man who could be found—for better, for worse; to put unlimited trust in him; to allow him to do whatever he wished, and to leave undone whatever he did not approve of. The qualities which are necessary for a dictator are two,—a commanding character and an original intellect. All other qualities are secondary. Regular industry, a conciliatory disposition, a power of logical exposition and argumentative discussion, which are necessary to a parliamentary statesman in ordinary times, are not essential to the selected dictator of a particular juncture. If he have force of character to overawe men into trusting him, and originality of intellect sufficient to enable him to cope with the pressing, terrible, and critical events with which he is selected to cope, it is enough. Every subordinate shortcoming, every incidental defect, will be pardoned. 'Save us!' is the cry of the moment, and, in the confident hope of safety, any deficiency will be overlooked, and any frailty pardoned.

The genius requisite for a great administrator is not so imposing, but it is, perhaps, equally rare, and needs a more peculiar combination of qualities. Ordinary administrators are very common: every-day life requires and produces every-day persons. But a really great administrator thinks not only of the day but of the morrow; does not only what he must but what he wants; is eager to extirpate every abuse, and on the watch for every improvement; is on a level with the highest political thought of his time, and persuades his age to be ruled according to it—to permit him to embody it in policy and in laws. Administration in this large sense includes legislation, for it is concerned with the far-seeing regulation of future conduct, as well as with the limited management of the present. Great dictators are doubtless rare in political history; but they are not more so than great administrators, such as we have just defined them. It is not easy to manage any age; it is not easy to be on a level with the highest thought of any age; but to manage that age according to that highest thought is among the most insuperable and arduous difficulties of the world. The intellectual character of a dictator is noble but simple; that of a great administrator and legislator is complex also.

The exact description of Mr. Pitt is, that he had in the most complete perfection the faculties of a great administrator, and that he added to it the commanding temperament, though not the creative intellect, of a great dictator. He was tried by long and prosperous years, which exercised to the utmost his peculiar faculties, which enabled him to effect brilliant triumphs of policy and of legislation: he was tried likewise by a terrible crisis, with which he had not the originality entirely to cope, which he did not understand as we understand it now, but in which he showed a hardihood of resolution and a consistency of action which captivated the English people, and which impressed the whole world.

A very slight survey of Mr. Pitt's career is all we have room for here; indeed, it is not easy within the compass of an article to make any survey, however slight; but we hope at least to show that peculiar training, peculiar opportunity, and peculiar ability, combined to make him what he was.

It may seem silly to observe that Mr. Pitt was the son of his father, and yet there is no doubt that it was a critical circumstance in the formation of his character. When he was born, as Lord Macaulay has described, his father's name was the most celebrated in the whole civilised world; every post brought the news of some victory or some great stroke of policy, and his imagination dwelt upon the realities before him. 'I am glad I am not the eldest son,' he said, 'I should like to speak in the House of Commons, like papa.' And there are other sayings indicating an early ambition and an early consciousness of power. There is nothing extraordinary in this. Most boys are conceited; most boys have a wonderful belief in their own power. 'At sixteen,' says Mr. Disraeli, 'every one believes he is the most peculiar man who ever lived.' And there is certainly no difficulty in imagining Mr. Disraeli thinking so. The difficulty is not to entertain this proud belief, but to keep it; not to have these lofty visions, but to hold them. Manhood comes, and with it come the plain facts of the world. There is no illusion in them; they have a distinct teaching: 'The world,' they say definitely, 'does not believe in you. You fancy you have a call to a great career, but no one else even imagines that you fancy it. You do not dare to say it out loud.' Before the fear of ridicule and the touch of reality the illusions of youth pass away, and with them goes all intellectual courage. We have no longer the hardihood; we have scarcely the wish to form our own creed, to think our own thought, to act upon our own belief; we try to be sensible, and we end in being ordinary; we fear to be eccentric, and we end in being commonplace. It is from this fate that the son of a commanding prime minister is at any rate preserved; the world thinks about him; the world alludes to him. He can speak 'in the grand style,' and he will not be laughed at, or not much. When we wonder at the indomitable resolution and the inflexible self-reliance which Mr. Pitt through life displayed, we may lessen our wonder by remembering that he never endured the bitter ignominy of youth; that his self-confidence was never disheartening by being 'an unknown man;' that he early received from fortune the inestimable permission *to be himself.*

The education of Mr. Pitt was as favourable to the development of his peculiar powers as his position. The public education of England has very great merits, and is well fitted for the cultivation of the average Englishman; but one at least of the qualities which fit it for training ordinary men unfit it for training an extraordinary man. Its greatest value to the mass of those who are brought up in it is the diminution of their self-confidence. They are early brought into a little but rough world, which effects on a small scale what the real world will afterwards effect still more thoroughly on a large one. It teaches boys who are no better than other boys that they are no better than other boys; that the advantages of one are compensated by the advantages of others; that the world is a miscellaneous and motley medley, in which it is not easy to conquer, and over which it is impossible to rule. But it is not desirable that a young man in Pitt's position should learn this lesson. If you are to train a man to be Prime Minister at five-and-twenty, you must not dishearten his self-confidence, though it be over-weening; you must not tame his energy, though it seem presumptuous. Ordinary men should and must be taught to fear the face of the world; they are to be guided by its laws and regulated by its manners; the one exceptional man, who is in his first youth to rule the world, must be trained not to fear it, but to despise it.

The legitimate food of a self-relying nature is early solitude, and the most stimulating solitude is solitude in the midst of society. Mr. Pitt's education was of this kind entirely. He was educated at home during his whole boyhood. He was sent to Cambridge at a most unusually early age. He lived there almost wholly with Mr. Pretyman, his tutor. 'While Mr. Pitt was undergraduate,' writes that gentleman, 'he never omitted attending chapel morning and evening in the public hall, except when prevented by indisposition. Nor did he pass a single evening out of the college-walls; indeed, most of his time was spent with me.' During his whole residence at the University, Mr. Pretyman continues, 'I never knew him spend an idle day, nor did he ever fail to attend me at the appointed hour.' He did not make any friends, scarcely any social acquaintances, till he had taken his degree. He passed very much of his time, his tutor tells us, in very severe study, and very much of it, as we may easily believe, in the most absorbing of early pleasures—the monotonous excitement of ambitious anticipation. On an inferior man this sort of youth could have had but one effect—it must have made him a prig. But it had not that effect on Pitt. It contributed to make him a shy, haughty, and inaccessible man. Such he emerged from Cambridge, and such he continued through life to be; but he was preserved from the characteristic degradation of well-intentioned and erudite youth by two great counteracting influences,—a strong sense of humour and a genuine interest in great subjects. His sense of fun was, indeed, disguised from the vulgar by a rigid mask of grave dignity; but in private it was his strongest characteristic. 'Don't tell me,' he is said to have said, 'of a man's being able to talk sense; every one can talk sense: can he talk nonsense?' And Mr. Wilberforce, the most cheerful of human beings, who had seen the most amusing society of his generation, always declared that Pitt's wit was the best which he had ever known. And it was likely to be; humour gains much by constant suppression, and at no time of life was Pitt ever wanting in dexterous words. No man who really cares for great things, and who sees the laughable side of little things, ever becomes a 'prig.'

While at Cambridge likewise Pitt paid, as his tutor tells us, great attention to what are now, in popular estimation, the characteristic studies of the place. His attainments in mathematics were probably not much like the elaborate and exact knowledge which the higher wranglers now yearly carry away from the University, but they were considerable for his time, and they comprehended the most instructive part of the subject, the first principles; a vague hope, too, is expressed that he may read Newton's *Principia* 'after some summer circuit,' which, as we may easily suppose, was not realised.

Though the tutor's information is not very exact, we may accept his general testimony that Pitt was a good mathematician, according to the academic standing of that day. There is, indeed, strong corroborative evidence of the fact in Mr. Pitt's financial speeches. It is not easy to draw out the evidence in writing, and it would be very tiresome to read the evidence if it were drawn out; but a skilful observer of the contrast between educated and uneducated language will find in Pitt many traces of mathematical studies. Raw argument and common-sense correctness come by nature, but only a preliminary education can give the final edge to accuracy in statement, and the last nicety to polished and penetrating discussion. In later life the facile use of financial rhetoric was as familiar to Mr. Pitt as to Mr. Gladstone.

His classical studies were pursued upon a plan suggested by his father, which was certainly well adapted for the particular case, though it would not be good for mankind in general. A sufficient experience proves that no one can be taught any language thoroughly and accurately except by composition in it; and Mr. Pitt had apparently never practised any sort of composition in Greek or Latin, whether verse or prose. But for the purpose of disciplining a student in *his own* language, the reverse practice of translating from the classical languages is the best single expedient which has ever been made use of. And to this Mr. Pitt was trained by his father from early boyhood. He was taught to read off the classics into the best English he could find, never inserting a word with which he was not satisfied, but waiting till he found one with which he *was* satisfied. By constant practice he became so ready that he never stopped at all; the right word always presented itself immediately. When he was asked in later life how he had acquired the mellifluous abundance of appropriate language with which he amazed and charmed the House of Commons, it was to this suggestion of his father that he at once imputed it.

To the probably unconscious influence of the same instructor we may ascribe his early interest in parliamentary conflict. We have before quoted the naïve expression of his boyish desire to be in the House of Commons. There is a still more curious story of him in very early youth. It is said, 'He was introduced, on the steps of the throne in the House of Lords, to Mr. Fox, who was his senior by ten years, and already in the fulness of his fame. Fox used afterwards to relate that, as the discussion proceeded, Pitt repeatedly turned to him and said, "But surely, Mr. Fox, that might be met thus:" or, "Yes, but he lays himself open to retort." What the particular criticisms were Fox had forgotten; but he said that he was much struck at the time by precocity of a lad who through the whole sitting was thinking only how all the speeches on both sides could be answered.'

Nor were his political studies confined to the studious cultivation of oratorical language, or to a thorough acquisition of the art of argumentative fence; he attended also to the *substance* of political science. He was the first great English statesman who read, understood, and valued *The Wealth of Nations*. Fox had 'no great opinion of *those* reasonings;' and the doctrines of Free Trade, though present, like all great political ideas, to the overflowing mind of Burke, were, like all his ideas, at the daily mercy of his eager passions, and his intense and vivid imagination. Mr. Pitt, as it would seem, while still at college, acquired and arranged them with the collected consistency which was the characteristic of his mind. So thorough a training, in the superficial accomplishments, the peculiar associations, and the abstract studies of political life, has not perhaps fallen to the lot of any other English statesman.

Nor was the political opportunity of Mr. Pitt at all inferior to his political training. The history of the first twenty years of the reign of George III is a history of his struggles with the aristocratic proprietors of parliamentary boroughs. Neither the extension of the power of the Crown, nor the maintenance of the political ascendency of the Whig families, was very popular with the nation at large; the popular element in the constitution was for the most part neutral in the conflict; it reserved the greater part of its influence for objects more interesting to itself; but between the two parties, between the Crown and the great borough proprietors, the strife was eager, intense, and unremitting.

As we some time since had occasion to explain at length,[2] the situa-

[2] Morgan and Hutton have 'As the present writer has elsewhere explained.'

tion in which a constitutional king was placed under the old system of an unreformed Parliament was more than an energetic man could endure. According to the theory of that government, the patronage of the Crown was to be used to purchase votes in Parliament, and to maintain a parliamentary majority by constant bargains with borough proprietors. But *who* is to use the patronage? The theory assumes that it is to be used by the minister of the day. According to it, the head of the party which is predominant in Parliament is to employ the patronage of the Crown for the purpose of confirming that predominance. But suppose that the Crown chooses to object to this; suppose that the King for the time being should say, 'This patronage is mine; the places in question are places in my service; the pensions in question are pensions from me: I will myself have at least some share in the influence that is acquired by the conferring of those pensions, and the distribution of those places." George III actually did say this. He was a king in one respect among a thousand; he was willing to do the work of a Secretary of the Treasury; his letters for very many years are filled with the petty details of patronage; he directed who should have what, and stipulated who should not have any thing. This interference of the King must evidently in theory, and did certainly in fact, destroy the efficiency of the alleged expedient. Very much of the patronage of the Crown went, not to the adherents of the Prime Minister, because they were his adherents, but to the King's friends, because they were his friends. Many writers have been very severe on George III. for taking the course which he did take, and have frequently repeated the well-known maxims, which show that what he did was a deviation from the constitution. Very likely it was; but what is the use of a constitution which takes no account of the ordinary motives of human nature? It was inevitable that an ambitious king, who had industry enough to act as he did, would so act. Let us consider his position. He was invested with authority which was apparently great. He was surrounded by noblemen and gentlemen who passed their life in paying him homage, and in professing perhaps excessive doctrines of loyal obedience to him. When the Duke of Devonshire, or the Duke of Bedford, or the Duke of Newcastle, approached the royal closet, they implied by words and manner that he had immeasurably more power than they had. In fact, it was expected that he should have immeasurably less. It was expected that, though these noblemen daily acknowledged that he was their superior, he should constantly act as if he were their inferior. The Prime Minister was in reality appointed by them, and it was expected that the King should do what the Prime Minister told him; that he should assent to measures on which he was not consulted; that he should make peace when Mr. Grenville said peace was right; that he should make war whenever Mr. Grenville said war was right; that he should allow the offices of his household and the dignities of his court to be used as a means for the support of cabinets whose members he disliked, and whose policy he disapproved of. It is evident that no man who was not imbecile would be content with such a position. It is not difficult to bear to be without power, it is not very difficult to bear to have only the mockery of power; but it is unbearable to have real power, and to be told that you must content yourself with the mockery of it; it is unendurable to have in your hands an effectual instrument of substantial influence, and also to act day by day as a pageant, without any influence whatever. Human nature has never endured this, and we may be quite sure that it never will endure it. It is a fundamental error in the "esoteric theory" of the Tory party, that it assumed the King and the Prime Minister to be always of the same mind, while they often were of different minds.'

By a series of stratagems George III. at last obtained, in the person of Lord North, a minister who combined a sufficient amount of parliamentary support with an unlimited devotion to the royal pleasure. He was a minister of great ability, great parliamentary tact, unbounded good humour, and *no* firmness. He yielded every thing to the intense, eager, petty incisiveness of his sovereign. The King was the true minister for all purposes of policy and business. Lord North was only the talking minister of the present French Assemblies, who is bound to explain and to defend measures which he did not suggest, and about which he was not consulted.

It is difficult to say how long Lord North's government might not have continued, if it had not been for the military calamities of the American War. That war had been very popular at its commencement, and continued popular as long as it was likely to be successful; it became unpopular as soon as it was likely to fail. The merchants began to murmur at the stoppage of trade. The country gentlemen began to murmur at the oppressive burden of war-taxes. The nation began to reconsider its opinion as to the justice of the quarrel, as soon as it appeared that our military efforts would probably be disastrous. Lord

North shared in these feelings; he did not believe the war would succeed; no longer hoped it would succeed; no longer thought that there was any motive for continuing to carry it on, but for several years he did continue to carry it on. The will of George III was a very efficient force on every one just about him, and the personal ascendency over many men intellectually far his superiors is a curious example of the immense influence of a distinct judgment and inflexible decision, with fair abilities and indefatigable industry, and placed in close contact with great men and great affairs.

At length, in March 1782, the calamitous issue of the American War became too evident, and Lord North resigned. Lord Holland gives us a curious history of the mode in which he announced to the House that he was no longer Prime Minister: 'I have heard my uncle Fitzpatrick give a very diverting account of the scene that passed in the House of Commons on the day of Lord North's resignation, which happened to be a remarkably cold day, with a fall of snow. A motion of Lord Surrey's, for the dismissal of Ministers, stood for that day, and the Whigs were anxious that it should come on before the resignation of Lord North was officially announced, that his removal from office might be more manifestly and formally the act of the House of Commons. He and Lord Surrey rose at the same instant; after much clamour, disorder, and some insignificant speeches on order, Mr. Fox, with great quickness and address moved, as the most regular method of extricating the House from its embarrassment, 'That Lord Surrey be now heard." But Lord North, with yet more admirable presence of mind, mixed with pleasantry, rose immediately and said, "I rise to speak to that motion;" and, as his reason for opposing it, stated his resignation and the dissolution of the Ministry. The House, satisfied, became impatient, and after some ineffectual efforts of speakers on both sides to procure a hearing, an adjournment took place. Snow was falling, and the night tremendous. All the members' carriages were dismissed, and Mrs. Bennet's room at the door was crowded. But Lord North's carriage was waiting. He put into it one or two of his friends, whom he had invited to go home with him, and turning to the crowd, chiefly composed of his bitter enemies, in the midst of their triumph, exclaimed, in this hour of defeat and supposed mortification, with admirable good-humour and pleasantry, "I have my carriage. You see, gentlemen, the advantage of being in the secret. Good night." '

Such acquiescent *bonhomie* is admirable, no doubt; but easy good-nature is no virtue for a man of action, least of all for a practical politician in critical times. It was Lord North's 'happy temper' which first made him the mean slave of George III, which afterwards induced him to ally himself with the most virulent assailants of that monarch and, at a preceding period, of himself.

When Lord North resigned, it was natural that the leaders of the Opposition should come at once into predominant power; but a ministerial crisis in the early part of George III's reign was never permitted to proceed in what is now fixed as the constitutional etiquette. The King always interfered with it. On this occasion the only political party who could take office was that which, under the judicious guidance of Lord Rockingham, and supported by the unequalled oratory of Fox and Burke, had consistently opposed the American War. But the leaders of this party were personally disliked by George III. Lord Rockingham he had once before called 'one of the most insignificant noblemen in my service.' Mr. Fox, from a curious combination of causes, he hated. Accordingly, though it was necessary for him to treat with Lord Rockingham and his friends, he did not treat with them directly. He employed as an intermediate agent Lord Shelburne, the father of the present Marquis of Lansdowne, a politician whom it is not difficult to describe, but whom it is difficult really to understand. Policemen tell us that there is such a character as a 'reputed thief,' who has never been convicted of any particular act of thievery. Lord Shelburne was precisely that character in political life; every one always said he was dishonest, but no particular act of dishonesty has ever been brought home to him. It is not for us now to discuss the dubious peculiarities of so singular a character. But it will be admitted that it was a most unfortunate one for conducting the delicate personal negotiations inevitable on the formation of a cabinet, and that it specially unfitted the person believed to possess it to be a good go-between between a king who hated an Opposition and an Opposition who distrusted the King. The inevitable result followed: every member of the incoming party was displeased with the King; every one disbelieved the assertions of Lord Shelburne; every one distrusted the solidity of a ministry constructed in a manner so anomalous. A ministry, however, was constructed, of which Lord Shelburne and Lord Rockingham were both members; and both, Mr. Fox said, intended to be Prime Ministers.

Lord Rockingham must evidently have been a man of very fine and delicate judgment. He could not speak in the House of Lords, and his letters are rather awkwardly expressed; but those who compare the history of the Whig party for some years before his death with the history of that party for some years after it, and those who compare the career of Burke for the same two periods, will perceive that both over the turbulence of the great party and the turbulence of the great orator the same almost invisible discretion exercised a guiding and restraining control. After Lord Rockingham's death, both the Whig party and Mr. Burke committed great errors and fell into lamentable excesses, which were entirely unlike any thing which happened while he was yet alive. If he had been permitted to exercise a composing influence, it is possible that the Ministry we have described might have lasted; but, unfortunately, within three months after its formation he fell ill and died. Mr. Fox, who had just been quarrelling with Lord Shelburne, refused to serve under him and sent in his resignation; and his example was followed by Burke, and by most of the followers of Lord Rockingham.

Lord Shelburne, however, still intended to be Prime Minister. The King was in his favour. The Whigs had no great aristocratic leader. The Duke of Portland, who was put forward as such, had no powers of speech and but feeble powers of thought. There was no difference of political opinion which need have separated any Whig from Shelburne. He was therefore justified in hoping that if he persevered, he might rally round him in no long time the greater part of the Whig party, notwithstanding the secession of its present leaders. He doubtless hoped also, by taking advantage of the various influences of the Crown, to attach to himself very many of the followers of Lord North, who were the old adherents of the Crown. But these were anticipations only. For the moment he was more completely separated from the parliamentary ability of his age than any minister has since been. He came into office in opposition to Lord North and one great party; he remained in office in opposition to Fox and Burke, the leaders of the other great party. The trained leaders of the old Ministry and the trained leaders of the old Opposition were both opposed to him. If he decided to remain Prime Minister, it was necessary for him to take some bold step. He did so. He made Mr. Pitt Chancellor of the Exchequer and the Leader of the House of Commons, though he was but twenty-three.

Such a singular good fortune has never happened to any English statesman since parliamentary government in this country has been consolidated into its present form, and it is very unlikely that any thing like it can ever happen again. Perhaps no man of twenty-three could get through the quantity of work that is now required to fill the two offices of Finance Minister and Leader of the House of Commons. In Pitt's time the Chancellor of the Exchequer (he himself tells us) needed no private secretary; he had no business requiring any. The Leader of the House of Commons did not even require one-tenth part of the ready available miscellaneous information which he must now have at his command, and most of which cannot be learned from any books. To fill the offices which Mr. Pitt filled at twenty-three, it would in this age be necessary that a man should have a trained faculty of transacting business rapidly, which no man of twenty-three can have; and that he should have also a varied knowledge of half a hundred subjects, which no college can teach, and which no book of reference will ever contain. Mr. Pitt, however, met with no difficulty. Though the finances of the country had been disordered by the American War, and though the Ministry was daily assailed by the dexterous good-humour of Lord North, and the vehement invectives of Fox and Burke, 'the boy,' as they called him, was successful in his budget, and successful in his management of the House of Commons. It soon, however, became evident that Lord Shelburne's Ministry could not stand long. There were three parties in the House, and a coalition of any two was sufficient to outnumber any one. According to a calculation preserved in a letter from Gibbon, every thing depended on the decision of Mr. Fox. If he returned to the Government, it would be strong; if he allied himself with Lord North, it must fail. He did ally himself with Lord North, and Lord Shelburne resigned.

The coalition between Fox and Lord North is not defended even by Lord John Russell, who defends almost every act in the political life of his great hero. Indeed, it was not likely that he would defend it; for to it we owe the almost unbroken subjection of the Whigs, and the almost unbroken reign of the Tories, for five-and-twenty years.

No political alliance in English history has been more unpopular than this coalition. For once the King and the people were on the same side, and that side the right side. During by far the greater part of his reign the wishes of George III were either opposed to the wishes of his people, or the wishes of the two, though identical, were pernicious. During the first part of his reign his attempts to increase the royal influence were generally unpopular; during the latter part, he and his people were both favourable to the American War and to the French War, with what result history shows. But at the period of which we are speaking both the prominent prejudices of the King and the deepest feelings of the people were offended by the same event. The Coalition deeply annoyed the King. It was hateful to him that his favourite, Lord North, who had been his confidential minister for years, who was enriched with the marks of his bounty and good-will, who was the leader of many politicians, always biased in favour of the Crown, and always anxious to support its influence, if they could,—should after all ally himself with Mr. Fox, who had opposed the Crown for years; who had called its latent influence 'an infernal spirit;' who was the leader of the party opposed to the American War, and therefore, in the King's view, of the party which had advocated treason and abetted the disruption of the empire; who, worse than all, was the companion and encourager of the Prince of Wales in every species of dissipation; who introduced him to haunts and countenanced him in habits which made the very heart of an economical and decorous monarch horrified and angry; who at that very moment was endeavouring to make 'capital,' as we should now say, out of the political prospects and present influence of his profligate associate. George III used to call the 'coalition ministry' his 'son's ministry;' and he could not embody his detestation of it in terms more expressive, to those who knew their meaning. On the other hand, the people were not unnaturally offended also. The Coalition brought into very clear prominence the most characteristic weakness of our unreformed constitution. Though it professed to be, and really was, a popular constitution, the people could not be induced to believe that they had much concern in it. The members chosen by popular election were a minority; those nominated by aristocratic and indirect influence were a majority. Accordingly most men believed, or were prone to believe, that the struggles in Parliament were faction-fights for place and power; that the interest of the nation had little to do with them, or nothing; that they were contests for political power, and for the rich pecuniary rewards which influential office then conferred. The Coalition seemed to prove that this was so even to demonstration. If there ever had been a *bonâ fide*, and not a simulated, struggle in Parliament, it was the struggle between Fox and Lord North. They had opposed one another for years; Fox had heaped on Lord North every term of invective, opprobrium, and contempt; Lord North had said every thing which a good-natured and passive man *could* say in reply. They had taken different sides both on the obvious question which had been the dividing and critical one of the last few years, and on the latent question which was the real one underlying the greater part of the controversies of the age and giving to them most of their importance. Lord North was the great parliamentary advocate of the American War; Fox was its most celebrated and effective opponent. Lord North was the most decent agent, and the most successful coöperator, whom George III had yet found in his incessant policy of maintaining and augmenting the power of the Crown. Fox was known to be opposed to that policy with all his mind, soul, and strength; he was known to be have heaped upon that policy every bitter term of contempt, opprobrium, and execration which the English language contains; he was known to have incurred the bitter hatred of George III by so doing. With these facts before them, what could the nation infer when they saw these two statesmen combine for the evident purpose of obtaining immediate office? They could only say what they did. They said at once that the coalition must be dishonest if the previous opposition had been real, and that the coalescing statesmen were utterly untrustworthy if that opposition had been simulated.

The government of the Coalition was not, however, destined to be durable. George III was a dangerous man to drive to extremity; though without great creative ability, he had dexterous powers of political management, cultivated by long habit and experience; he had an eager obstinacy allied to the obstinacy of insanity; it was not safe to try him too far. The Coalition Government, however, tried him as far as it was possible. They framed an India Bill giving the patronage of India to commissioners, to be from time to time nominated by Parliament, to be irremovable by the Crown, the first of whom were to be nominated by themselves. The King was enraged at a scheme so injurious to his secret influence. He considered that it was a scheme for enabling Mr. Fox to buy votes in Parliament. Lord Fitzwilliam, his intimate political friend, was to be at the head of the new Board; and it was expected, perhaps intended, that the Board should be an independent instrument of parliamentary power at the service of the aristocratic Whigs, and in daily opposition to the influence of the Crown,—to that personal influence which George III had all his life been hoarding and acquiring. The people were almost as much enraged at the scheme as the King himself. They thought that the politicians who had just formed a corrupt coalition to obtain office were now providing a corrupt expedient for retaining that office: 'Being dishonest themselves,' it was said, 'they are providing themselves with the means of purchasing the votes of others who are dishonest likewise.' The exact value of these accusations we have not space to estimate now; something might certainly be said in extenuation of them, if it were needful; but at the time the popular feeling was powerfully excited by them; they were expressed by Pitt with marvellous force and marvellous variety, and reëchoed through the nation.

The parliamentary influence of the Coalition Government, which was supported by the greater part of the borough proprietors, both Whig and Tory, was, however, sufficient to carry their India Bill through the House of Commons by majorities which would now be considered very large. It reached the House of Lords; and would have passed that House too, if George III had not taken one of the most curious steps in our constitutional history. He wrote on a card: 'His Majesty allowed Earl Temple to say that whoever voted for the India Bill was not only not his friend, but would be considered by him as an enemy; and if these words were not strong enough, Earl Temple might use whatever words he might deem stronger and more to the purpose.'

Such was the influence of the Crown; such was especially the personal influence which George III had acquired by steady industry and incessant attention to the personalities of politics, that the fate of the India Bill in the Lords very soon became dubious; 'the bishops wavered;' the stanchest followers of Lord North especially, being high Tories, became uncertain; and in the end the bill was rejected by a majority of ninety-five over seventy-six.

Nor did the King's active influence stop here. The Coalition Ministry did not resign; although their principal measure had been rejected in the Lords, they kept their places; they induced the House of Commons to resolve that it was a breach of the privilege of Parliament to attempt to influence votes in either House by announcing 'any opinion or pretended opinion of his Majesty.' The Ministry was passive in its place; but George III was never deterred by minor difficulties. He sent his commands at midnight to Mr. Fox and Lord North to deliver up the seals of office, and to send them by their under-secretaries, as he must decline to see them in person. By this parliamentary *coup d'état* he broke up an administration which, though unpopular in the country, was supported by the 'great owners' of parliamentary influence and an overwhelming majority in the House of Commons.

But who was to come in? That the King could turn out the old Ministry was very clear, for he had done so; but that he could form a ministry that could last in such circumstances seemed unlikely; that he could form any ministry at all was not evident. Political expectation was very eager. As soon as the House met on the day after midnight dismissal, a new writ was moved for the borough of Appleby, 'in the room of the Right Honourable William Pitt, who, since his election has accepted the office of First Lord of the Treasury and Chancellor, of the Exchequer.' The announcement was received with laughter, for it seemed unlikely that an ambitious boy (such was the speech of the time) should be able to carry on the government, and to lead the House of Commons in the face of an adverse majority, in direct opposition to the most experienced statesmen, the most practised debaters, and the most skilful manœuverers of his age.

Mr. Pitt was only twenty-five, and he had no one to rely on. Mr. Dundas was a useful subordinate and an efficient man of business; but he was not a great statesman or a great orator, and he *was* a Scotch adventurer. In the Lords, Mr. Pitt was confident of the support of Lord Temple, who had effected the defeat of the India Bill by the use of the King's name; but Lord Temple wanted to be paid. He had great borough connections, which gave him permanent claims on every government; he had just turned out the old Government, which gave him a peculiar claim upon the favour of the new. He asked for a dukedom, and was refused. The King thought he had asked too much, and perhaps believed that it would be most dangerous at that critical moment to give the highest of honorary rewards to the principal agent in an alarming act of royal influence. At any rate, the application was declined, and Lord Temple resigned. Mr. Pitt was thus left almost alone. His cabinet consisted but of seven persons, and he himself was the only member of the House of Commons among those seven.

Everybody expected that Parliament would be immediately dissolved. As Mr. Pitt was evidently in a minority in the House of Commons which then existed, it was confidently believed that he would at once see whether he would not have a majority in a new House of Commons. He was too wary, however, to do so. In that age public opinion formed itself slowly and declared itself slowly. The nation, as far as it had an opinion, was in favour of the new administration; but in many parts of the country there was no opinion. Delay was in favour of the side which had the advantage in telling argument; and so strong were the objections of reasonable and moderate men to the coalition between Fox and Lord North,—so entirely was their India Bill interpreted by the help of that connection, and regarded in its relation to it,—that every day's discussion made converts. The members for close boroughs, and for counties in which individual interest predominated, were, it is true, a majority in the House of Commons, and they adhered for the most part to the Coalition. But the strength so obtained was always weak at a trying crisis. The same influences acted on the borough proprietors which acted upon others, and they never liked to be opposed to the national will when it was distinctly declared. Nor had the extreme partisans of either party ever liked the coalition of the two parties. The warmest Whigs were alienated from Fox, and the strongest Tories were alienated from Lord North. The majority of Fox began to waver, and the minority of Pitt began to augment. Every division showed a tendency in the same direction. Pitt maintained the struggle with dauntless courage, and unbounded dialectical dexterity, against all the orators in the House of Commons. The event began to be doubtful. In the unreformed Parliament no more was necessary. A large section of every party was attached to it by the hope of patronage; it had been bought by pro- mises of that patronage. As we formerly explained,[3] the strength so obtained was unstable. 'It especially failed at the moment at which it was especially wanted. A majority in Parliament which is united by a sincere opinion, and is combined to carry out that opinion, is in some sense secure. As long as that opinion is unchanged, it will remain; it can only be destroyed by weakening the conviction which binds it together. A majority which is obtained by the employment of patron- age is very different; it is combined mainly by *an expectation*. Sir Robert Walpole, the great master in the art of dispensing patronage, defined gratitude as an anticipation of future favours; he meant that the majority which maintained his administration was collected, not by recollection, but by hope: they thought not so much of favours which were past as of favours which were to come. At a critical moment this

---

[3] Morgan and Hutton have 'As the present writer has elsewhere explained.' The *National Review* has 'As we formerly explained.'—p 214.

bond of union was ordinarily weak.' As soon as it seemed likely that Mr. Pitt would be victorious, the selfish part of the followers of the Coalition,—a very large part,—began to go over to Mr. Pitt. The last motion of Mr. Fox was carried by a majority of *one*.

Mr. Pitt then saw that his time was come; he dissolved Parliament, and his triumph was complete. The popular feeling was overwhelming. It prevailed even in the strongholds of the Whig aristocracy. 'Thus in Norfolk,' says Lord Stanhope, 'the late member had been Mr. Coke, lord of the vast domains of Holkham, a gentleman who, according to his own opinion, as stated in his address to the county, had played "a distinguished part" in opposing the American War. But notwithstanding his alleged claims of distinction, and his much more certain claims of property, Mr. Coke found it necessary to decline the contest.' But of all the contests of this period, the most important in that point of view was for the county of York. That great county, not yet at election times severed into Ridings, had been under the sway of the Whig houses. Bolton Abbey, Castle Howard, and Wentworth Park had claimed the right to dictate at the hustings. It was not till 1780 that the spirit of the county rose. 'Hitherto,'—so in that year spoke Sir George Savile,—'I have been elected in Lord Rockingham's dining-room. Now I am returned by my constituents.' And in 1784 the spirit of the county rose higher still. In 1784 the independent freeholders of Yorkshire boldly confronted the great houses, and insisted on returning, in conjunction with the heir of Duncombe Park, a banker's son, of few years and of scarcely tried abilities, though destined to a high place in his country's annals—Mr. Wilberforce. With the help of the country-gentlemen, they raised the vast sum of £18,662 for the expense of the election; and so great was their show of numbers and of resolution, that the candidates upon the other side did not venture to stand a contest. Wilberforce was also returned at the head of the poll by his former constituents at Hull. 'I can never congratulate you enough on such glorious success,' wrote the Prime Minister to his young friend. One hundred and sixty followers of Mr. Fox lost their seats, and were called 'Fox's martyrs.' The majority for Pitt in the new Parliament was complete, overwhelming, and enthusiastic.

The constitutional aspects of the events of 1784 has been much discussed, and well merits discussion. It is certain that George III did much which was, according to the good notions now fixedly established, thoroughly unconstitutional: it is certain that scarcely any one will, upon any constitutional doctrines, new or old, defend the 'card' displayed by Lord Temple. But, if we had room to argue the subject, we think it might be shown that it would have been inexpedient to apply, in the year 1784, the strict constitutional maxims on which we should act in the year 1861; that the beneficial relations, and that the inevitable relations of the Parliament and the Crown were different then from that which they are now; that under such an aristocratic legislature as the unreformed Parliament principally was, it was needful that the Crown should sometimes intervene, when the opinion of Parliament was opposed to the opinion of the people; that in times when public opinion was formed but slowly, it was advisable that the Crown should do so, not by an instant dissolution of the House of Commons, as we should now exact, but by a deferred dissolution, which would enable the thinking part of the community to reflect, and give the whole country, far and near, time to form a real judgment.

But at present we have to deal with the events of 1784, not in their relation to the constitution of England, but in their relation to the life of Mr. Pitt. They were the completion of his opportunity. But a short time previously the political isolation of Lord Shelburne had made him Chancellor of the Exchequer at a boyish age; the isolation of George III now made him Prime Minister while still very young. The first good fortune would have been a marvel in the life of any other man, but was nothing to the marvel of the second. By a strange course of great incidents, he was in the most commanding position which an English subject has ever occupied since parliamentary government was thoroughly established in the country. The victory was so complete that the mercenaries of the enemy had deserted to his standard. The Crown was necessarily on his side, for he alone stood between George III and the hated Coalition, which he had discarded and insulted; the people were on his side, from a hatred of the official corruption of which they considered his opponents to be the representatives and the embodiments, from a firm belief in his true integrity, from a proud admiration of his single-handed courage and audacious self-reliance. He had the power to do what he would.

Nor was this all. The opportunity was not only a great opportunity, but was an opportunity in the hands of *a young man*. Half of our greatest statesmen would have been wholly unprepared for it. When Lord Palmerston was in office in the spring of 1857 with a large majority, a shrewd observer, now no longer among us, said, 'Well, it is a large majority; but what is he to do with it?' He did not know himself; by paltry errors and frivolous haughtiness he frittered it away immediately. An old man of the world has no great objects, no telling enthusiasm, no large proposals, no noble reforms; his advice is that of the old banker, 'Live, sir, from day to day, and don't trouble yourself!' Years of acquiescing in proposals as to which he has not been consulted, of voting for measures which he did not frame, and in the wisdom of which he often did not believe, of arguing for proposals from half of which he dissents,—usually de-intellectualise a parliamentary statesman before he comes to half his power. From all this Pitt was exempt. He came to great power with a fresh mind. And not only so. He came into power with the cultivated thought of a new generation. Too many of us scarcely remember how young a man he was. He was born in 1759, and might have well been in the vigour of life in 1830. Lord Sidmouth, his contemporary, did not die till after 1840; he was younger than his cousin, Mr. Thomas Grenville, who long represented in London society the traditions of the past, and who died in 1846. He governed men of the generation before him. Alone among English statesmen, while yet a youth he was governing middle-aged men. He had the power of applying the eager thought of five-and-twenty, of making it rule over the petty knowledge and trained acquiescence of five-and-fifty. Alone as yet, and alone perhaps for ever in our parliamentary history, while his own mind was still original, while his own spirit was still unbroken, he was able to impose an absolute yoke on acquiescent spirits whom the world had broken for him.

We have expended so much space on a delineation of the peculiar opportunities which Mr. Pitt enjoyed, that we must be very concise in showing how he used them. Three subjects then needed the attention of a great statesman, though none of them were so pressing as to force themselves on the attention of a little statesman. These were, our economical and financial legislation; the imperfection of our parliamentary representation; and the unhappy condition of Ireland. Pitt dealt with all three.

Our economical legislation was partly in an uncared-for state, and partly in an ill-cared-for state. Our customs-laws were a chaos of confusion. Innumerable Acts of Parliament had been passed on temporary occasions and for temporary purposes; blunders had been discovered in them; other Acts were passed to amend those blunders; those other Acts contained other blunders; new corrective legislation was required, and here too there were errors, omissions, and imperfections. And in so far as our economical legislation was based upon a theory, that theory was a very mistaken one; it was the theory of Protection. The first duty of the English legislature, it was believed, was to develop English industry, and to injure foreign industry. Our manufactures, it was thought, could be made better by Acts of Parliament; the manufactures of our rivals it was believed could be made worse. The industry of the nation worked in a complicated network of fetters and bonds.

Mr. Pitt applied himself vigorously to this chaos. He brought in a series of resolutions consolidating our customs-laws, of which the inevitable complexity may be estimated by their number. They amounted to 133, and the number of Acts of Parliament which they restrained or completed was much greater. He attempted, and successfully, to apply the principles of Free Trade, the principles which he was the first of English statesmen to learn from Adam Smith, to the actual commerce of the country, and to the part of our commerce which afforded the greatest temptations to a philosophic statesman, and presented the greatest accumulation of irritable and stupid prejudice. France and England were near one another, but had no trade with one another; no such trade at least as two countries so different in soil, in climate, and in natural aptitude, ought to have. So far from either nation much wishing to trade with the other, neither wished to depend on the other for any thing. The national dignity was supposed to be compromised by buying from an ancient rival. Mr. Pitt, however, framed a treaty which, if its consequences had not been swept away with so much else, both good and evil, in the European storm of the French Revolution, would have been quoted as the true commencement of free-trade legislation; would have been referred to as we now refer to the tentative reforms of Huskisson, and to the earlier budgets of Sir Robert Peel. So little was the subject then understood, even by those most likely to understand it, that both Fox and Burke opposed the treaty with virulence and vehemence; declaring that France was our natural enemy, and that it was unworthy of any one who pretended to be a statesman to create a 'peddling traffic,' and maintain 'huckstering' relations with her.

The financial reputation of Pitt has greatly suffered from the absurd praise which was once lavished on the worst part of it. The dread of national ruin from the augmentation of the national debt was a sort of nightmare in that age; the evil was apparent, and the counteracting force was not seen. No one perceived that English industry was yearly growing with an accelerating rapidity; no one foresaw that in a few years it would be aided by a hundred wonderful inventions—by the innumerable results of applied science; no one comprehended that the national estate was augmenting far faster than the national mortgage.[4] The popular mind was apprehensive, and wished to see some remedy applied to what seemed to be an evident and dangerous evil. Mr. Pitt sympathised with the general apprehension, and created the well-known 'Sinking Fund.' He proposed to apply annually a certain fixed sum to the payment of the debt, which was in itself excellent, but he omitted to provide real money to be so paid. The only source out of which debt can be defrayed, as every one now understands, is a surplus revenue; out of an empty exchequer no claims can ever be liquidated by possibility: an excess of income over outlay is a prerequisite of a true repayment. Mr. Pitt, however, not only did not see this, but persuaded a whole generation that it was not so. He proposed to borrow the money to pay off the debt, and fancied that he thus diminished it. He had framed a puzzle in compound interest, which deceived himself, and every one who was intrusted with the national finances, for very many years.

The exposure of this financial juggle, for though not intended to be so, such in fact it was, has reacted very unfavourable upon Mr. Pitt's deserved fame. It was so long said 'that he was a great financier *because* he invented the Sinking Fund,' that it came at last to be believed that he could not be a great financier inasmuch as he had invented it. So much merit had been claimed for something bad, that no search was made for any thing good. But an accurate study of these times will prove that Pitt was really one of the greatest financiers in our history, that he repaired the great disorders of the American War, that he restored a surplus revenue, that he understood the true principles of taxation, that he even knew that the best way to increase a revenue from the consumption of the masses is to lower the rate of duty and develop their consuming power.

The subject of parliamentary reform is the one with which, in Mr. Pitt's early days, the public most connected his name, and is also that

[4] Morgan and Hutton have 'burden' for 'mortgage'.

with which we are now least apt to connect it. We have so long and so often heard him treated as the great Conservative minister, that we can hardly realise to ourselves that he was an unsparing and ardent reformer. Yet such is the indisputable fact. He proposed the abolition of the worst of the rotten boroughs fifty years before Lord Grey accomplished it. The period was a favourable one for reform. The failure of the American War had left behind it a bitter irritation and an anxious self-reproach. Why had we, with our great wealth, our great valour, our long experience, failed in what seemed a trivial enterprise? Why had we been put to shame in the face of Europe? Why had we been forced to humble ourselves in the face of Europe? Why had we been compelled to make an ignominious peace? Why had we, as one of the greatest of civilised states, failed to conquer a raw and unknown colony? The popular answer was, that our arms had been unsuccessful because our government was corrupt. The practical working of our unreformed Constitution has been tersely described as the barter of patronage for power; the parliamentary majorities of that age were kept by an incessant commerce between the proprietors of seats who sold and the Secretary of the Treasury who bought. In the present day refined arguments are often brought forward to justify or to palliate the system of government. But whatever may be the abstract worth of those arguments, their practical worth is not great. They will never convince the mass of men; they will never satisfy the unsophisticated instinct of ordinary men; they will not remove their natural distrust of what they believe to be unpatriotic selfishness; they will not lessen their conscientious repugnance to that which they call corruption. After the disasters of the American War this feeling was very strong and very diffused. An unpopular tree was judged of by unpopular fruits; our calamities were evident, and our corruption was conspicuous. A most distinct association of the two was formed in the popular mind. Of this Mr. Pitt took advantage. If the strong counteracting influence of the French Revolution had not changed the national opinion, he would unquestionably have amended our parliamentary representation. Even after the French Revolution he never changed his own opinion; he considered that the time was not favourable for what we now call organic changes; and he judged wisely, for the mass of the nation was wildly and frantically Conservative; but he did not abandon his early principles: he never became a 'Pittite.'

The state of Ireland was a more pressing difficulty than our financial confusion, our economical errors, or our parliamentary corruption. It had an independent legislature, which might at any time take a dangerously different view of national interests, of the expediency of a peace, or the expediency of a war, from the English Parliament. That legislature was a Protestant legislature in the midst of a Catholic people; it was the legislature of a small and hated minority in the midst of an excitable, tumultuous oppressed people. The mass of the Irish Catholics believed that the mass of the property, which belonged in fact to the Protestants, was in strict right theirs; they believed that they were the true owners of the soil, and that the Protestants were intruders; they believed that they had a right to govern the country, and that the Protestants were usurpers; they believed that the Church which the State supported was a heretic Church; that the Church which the State did not support was the true Church—the only true Church in Christendom. In every parish the distinction between Protestant and Catholic was periodically ruled by the most critical of tests—the pecuniary test. The collection of the tithe in detail over the country from the Catholic population for the Protestant Church was the source of chronic confusion and incessant bloodshed. Mr. Pitt proposed to remedy all these evils in turn, and effectually. He proposed to remedy the most immediate and pressing cause of trouble throughout the country by changing—as has since been done—the periodical extortion of the Irish tithe from the hostile farmer into an equivalent payment by a rent-charge, which could be easily collected, and could give rise to no disgraceful scenes. He proposed to put the Catholic majority and the Protestant minority upon a perfect equality so far as civil rights were concerned. He was desirous that Catholics should be eligible to all offices, and be electors for all offices. He was ready likewise to destroy the prevalent religious agitation at its very root, by paying the ministers of the church of the poor as well as the ministers of the church of the rich. He proposed at once to remedy the national danger of having two Parliaments, and to remove the incredible corruption of the old Irish Parliament, by uniting the three kingdoms in a single representative system, of which the Parliament should sit in England. He framed, in a word, a scheme which would have cured the internal divisions of Ireland, which would have united her effectually to the empire without impairing her real liberty.

Of these great reforms he was only permitted to carry a few into execution. His power, as we have described it, was great when his reign commenced, and very great it continued to be for very many years; but the time became unfavourable for all forward-looking statesmanship,—for every thing which could be called innovation. The French Revolution and the French War destroyed for many years our national taste for political improvement. But notwithstanding these calamities, Pitt achieved some part of all his cherished schemes save one. No opportunity would have enabled Pitt to effect, no particular situation[5] would have suggested these great reforms to Pitt, if he had not had certain more than ordinary tendencies and abilities—the tendencies and abilities of a great administrator. Contrary to what might at first sight be supposed, using the word "administrator" in its most enlarged sense,—in the sense in which we used it at the commencement of this article,—the *first* qualification of the highest administrator is, that he should think of something which he need not think of,—of something which is not the pressing difficulty of the hour. For inferior men no rule could be so dangerous. Ambitious mediocrity is dangerous mediocrity: ordinary men find what they must do amply enough for them to do; the exacting difficulty of the hour, which will not be stayed, which must be met, absorbs their whole time and all their energies. But the ideal administrator has time, has *mind*—for that is the difficulty—for something more; he can do what he must, and he *will* do what he wishes. This is Mr. Pitt's peculiarity among the great English statesmen of the eighteenth century. As a rule, the spirit of Sir Robert Walpole ruled over all these statesmen. They respected his favourite maxim, *quieta non movere;* to deal shrewdly and adroitly with what must be dealt with; to leave alone whatever might be left alone; to accumulate every possible resource against the inevitable difficulties of the present moment, and never to think or dream or treat of what was not inevitable;—these were then, as always, the justifiable aims of commonplace men. They did *their* possible; they did all that they could with their strength and their faculties in their day and generation. The philosophy of the time, with its definite problems and its unaspiring tendencies, encouraged them; it made them unalive to the higher possibilities they were forgetting, to the higher duties they were half-consciously half-unconsciously passing over. It was with reference to this oblivious neglect of the future, this short-sighted absorption in the present, that Dr. Arnold

[5] The *National Review* has 'peculiar situation'—p. 222, but 'particular situation' seems preferable.

called this century the 'misused trial-time of modern Europe.' It is the distinctive characteristic of Pitt, that, having a great opportunity, having power such as no parliamentary statesman has ever had, having in his mind a fresh collection of youthful thought such as no similar statesman has ever possessed,—he applied *that* power steadily and perseveringly to embody that thought. To persons who think but slightly this may seem only a very slight merit. The first remark of many a commonplace man would be, 'If I had great power, I would carry out my own ideas.' A modern Socrates, if there were such a person, would answer: 'But, my good friend, what are your ideas?' When explained to an exact and scrutinising questioner, still more when confronted with the awful facts—the inevitable necessities of the real world,—these 'ideas' would melt away; after a little while the commonplace person, who was at first so proud of them, would cease to believe that he ever entertained them; he would say, 'Men of *business* do not indulge in those speculations.' The characteristic merit of Pitt is, that in the midst of harassing details, in the midst of obvious cares, in the face of most keen, most able, and most stimulated opposition, he applied his whole power to the accomplishment of great but practicable schemes.

The marvel, or at any rate the merit, is greater. Pitt was by no means an excited visionary. He had by no means one of those minds upon which great ideas fasten as a fanaticism. There was among his contemporaries a great man, who was in the highest gifts of abstract genius, in the best acquisitions of political culture, far superior to him. But in the mind of Burke great ideas were a supernatural burden, a superincumbent inspiration. He saw a great truth, and he saw nothing else. At all times, with the intense irritability of genius, in later years with the extreme one-sidedness of insanity, he was content, in season and out of season, with the great visions which had been revealed to him, with the great lessons which he had to teach, and which he could but very rarely induce any one to hear. But Pitt's mind was the extreme contrast to this. He had an extreme discretion, tested at the most trying conjectures. In 1784, when he had no power, when there was a hostile majority in the House of Commons, when he had no sure majority in the House of Lords, when the support of the King, which he undeniably had, was an undeniable difficulty;—for he did not intend to be a second Lord North; he did not intend to be a servitor of the Palace; he would not have stooped to carry out measures which he disapproved of; he would not have been willing to enunciate measures as to which he had not been consulted;—at this very moment with most of the constitutional powers against him, with the very greatest greatly against him, with no useful part of it truly for him,—he never made a false step; he guided the most feeble administration of modern times so ably and so dexterously that in a few months it became the strongest. A mind with so delicate a tact as this is entitled to some merit for adhering to distant principles. It is those who understand the present that feel the temptation of the present; it is those who comprehend the hour that feel the truly arduous, though upon paper it may seem the petty, difficulty of thinking beyond the hour. It is no merit in those who cannot have the present to attempt to act for posterity. There is nothing else left to them; they have no other occupation open to them. But it is a great merit in those who can have what is plain, apparent, and immediate, to think of the unseen, unasking, impalpable future.

It is this singular discretion which is Mr. Pitt's peculiar merit, because he belongs to the class of statesmen who are most apt to be defective in that discretion. He was an oratorical statesman; and an oratorical statesman means, *ex vi termini*, an excitable statesman. His art consists in the successful power to give in a more than ordinary manner the true feelings and sentiments of ordinary men; not their superficial notions, nor their coarser sentiments, for with these any inferior man may deal, but their most intimate nature, that which in their highest moments is most truly themselves. How is the exercise of this art to be reconciled with terrestrial discretion? Is the preacher to come down from his pedestal? is he who can deal worthily with great thoughts to be asked also to deal fittingly with small details? is it possible that the same mind which can touch the hearts of all men can also be alive to the petty interests of itself? is the microscopic power to be added to the telescopic power? is the capacity for careful management to be added to the power of creating unbounded enthusiasm? Yet this is the perpetual difficulty of parliamentary statesmen. A dry man can do the necessary business; an excitable man can give to the popular House of Parliament the necessary excitement. Mr. Pitt was able, with surpassing ability and surpassing ease, to do both; scarcely any one else has been so.

This great parliamentary position he owed to a combination of parliamentary abilities, of which only one or two can be, within our necessary limits, distinctly specified, but one or two of which are very prominent.

First, his singular oratorical power. He was, Lord Macaulay tells us, 'at once the one man who could explain a budget without notes, and who could speak that most unmeaningly evasive of human compositions, a Queen's speech, offhand.' He had the eloquence of business both in its expressive and its inexpressive forms; and he had likewise the eloquence of character; that is, he had the singular power, which not half a dozen men in a generation possess, of imparting to a large audience the exact copy of the feelings, the exact impress of the determination, with which they are themselves possessed. On a matter of figures, 'Pitt said so,' was enough; on a question of legislative improvement, an apathetic Parliament caught some interest from his example; in the deepest moments of national despair, an anxious nation could show some remains of their characteristic courage, from his bold audacity, and unwearied, inflexible, and augmenting determination.

No man could have achieved this without a sanguine temperament, and accordingly good observers pronounced Mr. Pitt the most sanguine man they had ever known. In no stage of national despondency, in no epoch of national despair, was his capacity of hope, one of the important capacities for great men in anxious affairs, ever shaken. At the crisis of his early life, Lord Temple's resignation, which seemed the last possible addition to the coalition of difficulties under which he was labouring, is said to have deprived him of sleep; but nothing else ever did so after his power attained its maturity, and while his body retained its strength.

Over the House of Commons, too, his anxious love of detail had an influence which will not surprise those who know how sensitive that critical assembly is to every sort of genuineness, and how keenly watchful it is for every kind of falsity. The labour bestowed on his reform of the Customs Acts, on his Indian measures, on his financial proposals from year to year, is matter of history; no one can look with an instructed eye at these measures without instantly being conscious of it. In addition to his other great powers, Mr. Pitt added the rare one of an intense power of work, in an age when that power was rarer than it is now, and in a Parliament where the element of dandies and idlers was far more dominant than it has since become.

Nor would this enumeration of Pitt's great parliamentary qualities be complete; it would want, perhaps, the most striking and obvious characteristic if we omitted to mention Pitt's well-managed shyness and his surpassing pride.

In all descriptions of Pitt's appearance in the House of Commons, a certain aloofness fills an odd space. He is a 'thing apart,' different somehow from other members. Fox was the exact opposite. He was a good fellow; he rolled into the House fat, good-humoured, and popular. Pitt was spare, dignified, and reserved. When he entered the House, he walked to the place of the Premier, without looking to the right or to the left, and he sat at the same place. He was ready to discuss important business with all proper persons, upon all necessary occasions; but he was not ready to discuss business unnecessarily with any one, nor did he discuss any thing but business with any, save a very few intimate friends, with whom his reserve at once vanished, and his wit and humour at once expanded, and his genuine interest in all really great subjects was at once displayed. In a popular assembly this sort of reserve rightly manipulated is a power. It is analogous to the manner which the accomplished author of *Eöthen* recommends in dealing with Orientals: 'it excites terror and inspires respect.' A recent book of memoirs illustrates it. During Addington's administration, a certain rather obscure 'Mr. G.' was made a privy-councillor, and the question was raised in Pitt's presence as to the mode in which he could have obtained that honour. Some one said, 'I suppose he was always talking to the Premier, and bothering him.' Mr. Pitt quietly observed, 'In *my* time I would much rather have made him a privy-councillor *than have spoken to him.*' It is easy to conceive the mental exhaustion which this well-managed reserve spared him, the number of trivial conversations which it economised, the number of imperfect ambitions which it quelled before they were uttered. An ordinary man could not of course make use of it. But Pitt at the earliest period imparted to the House of Commons the two most important convictions for a member in his position: he convinced them that he would not be the King's creature, and that he desired no pecuniary profit for himself. As he despised royal favour and despised real money, the House of Commons thought he might well despise them.

We have left ourselves no room to speak of Mr. Pitt's policy at the time of the French Revolution. It would require an essay of considerable length to do it substantial justice; and when Lord Stanhope has completed these volumes, we hope to have a more fitting opportunity. But we may observe that the crisis which that revolution presented to an English statesman was one rather for a great dictator than for a great administrator. The English people were at first in general pleased with the commencement of the French Revolution. 'Anglo-manie,' it seemed, had been prevalent on the Continent; the English Constitution it was hoped would be transplanted; the fundamental principles of the English Revolution it was, at any rate, hoped would be imitated. The essay of Burke by its arguments, the progress of events by an evident experience, proved that such would not be the history. What was to come was uncertain. There was no precedent on the English file; the English people did not know what they ought to think; they were ready to submit to any one who would think for them. The only point upon which their opinion was decided was, that the French Revolution was very dangerous; that it had produced awful results in France; that it was no model for imitation for sober men in a sober country. They were ready to concede any thing to a statesman who allowed this, who acted on this, who embodied this in appropriate action.

Mr. Pitt saw little further than the rest of the nation; what the French Revolution was he did not understand; what forces it would develop he did not foresee; what sort of opposition it would require he did not apprehend. He was, indeed, on one point much in advance of his contemporaries. The instinct of uncultivated persons is always towards an intemperate interference with any thing of which they do not approve. A most worthy police-magistrate in our own time said that 'he intended to put down *suicide*.' The English people, in the very same spirit of uncultured benevolence, wished to 'put down the French Revolution.' They were irritated at its excesses; they were alarmed at its example; they conceived that such impiety should be punished for the past and prohibited for the future. Mr. Pitt's natural instinct, however, was certainly in an entirely opposite direction. He was by inclination and by temperament opposed to all war; he was very humane, and all war is inhuman; he was a great financier, and all war is opposed to well-regulated finance. He postponed a French war as long as he could; he consented to it with reluctance, and continued it from necessity.

Of the great powers which the sudden excitement of democratic revolutions would stimulate in a nation which seemed exhausted, Mr. Pitt knew no more than those who were around him. Burke said that, as a military power, France was 'blotted from the map of Europe;' and though Pitt, with characteristic discretion, did not advance any sentiment which would be so extreme, or any phrase which would adhere so fixedly to every one's memory, it is undeniable that he did not anticipate the martial power which the new France, as by magic, displayed; that he fancied she would be an effete country; that he fancied he was making war with certain scanty vestiges of the *ancien régime*, instead of contending against the renewed, excited, and intensified energies of a united people. He did not know that, for temporary purposes, a revolutionary government was the most powerful of all governments; for it does not care for the future, and has the entire legacy of the past. He forgot that it was possible, that from a brief period of tumultuous disorder, there might issue a military despotism more compact, more disciplined, and more overpowering than any which had preceded it or any which has followed it.

But, as we have said, the conclusion of a prolonged article is no place for discussing the precise nature of Mr. Pitt's anti-revolutionary policy. As has been observed, he did not comprehend the Revolution in France; as Lord Macaulay has explained, with his habitual power, he over-rated the danger of a revolution in this country; he entirely over-estimated the power of the democratic assailants, and he entirely under-estimated the force of the conservative, maintaining, restraining, and, if need were, reactionary, influence. He saw his enemy, but he did not see his allies. But it is not given to many men to conquer such difficulties; it is not given to the greatest of administrators to apprehend entirely new phenomena. A highly imaginative statesman, a man of great moments and great visions, a greater Lord Chatham, might have done so, but the educated sense and equable dexterity of Mr. Pitt failed. All which he could do he did. He burnt the memory of his own name into the continental mind. After sixty years, the French people still half believe that it was the gold of Pitt which caused half their misfortunes; after half a century it is still certain that it was Pitt's indomitable spirit and Pitt's hopeful temper which was the soul of every continental coalition, and the animating life of every anti-revolutionary movement. He showed most distinctly how potent is the influence of a commanding character just when he most exhibited the characteristic contraction of even the best administrative intellect.

Lord Brougham

Introductory note

Henry Peter Brougham, Baron Brougham and Vaux (1778–1868), was born in Edinburgh, the eldest son of Henry Brougham and Eleanor Syme. He was educated at Edinburgh High School and at Edinburgh University. Brougham passed advocate in 1800, and went on the southern circuit. In 1802 Brougham, Jeffrey and Sydney Smith founded the *Edinburgh Review*, to the first issue of which Brougham contributed three articles. He became a member of Lincoln's Inn in 1803 and supported himself largely by writing for the *Edinburgh Review*. His earlier articles had been scientific; he now wrote on political and economic subjects with the intention of adopting a political career. He was called to the Bar in 1808 and went on the northern circuit, but he had small success in the courts until he had made his mark in politics. In 1810 he became M.P. for Camelford, and for Winchelsea in 1815. Brougham had already won Wilberforce's good opinion by his sympathy with the anti-slavery movement; only a few months after he had entered Parliament Brougham moved an address to the Crown on slavery. He drew attention in Parliament to the need for retrenchment and a sound commercial policy, and to the importance of popular education. When she became Queen, the Princess of Wales, who constantly consulted Brougham, appointed him her attorney-general, and he defended her during her trial in 1820. Brougham urged the government to resist the dictation of the Holy Alliance in Europe in 1824, pointing out the iniquity of the French invasion of Spain and the tyranny of the Austrians in Italy. In the same year Brougham proposed the vote of censure on the government of Demerara, which was a milestone in the history of abolition.

When Canning succeeded Lord Liverpool in 1827, Brougham left the opposition benches and joined the ministerial side. In 1828 Brougham brought in a scheme of reform which enormously improved the system of common-law procedure. Upon Wellington's accession in 1828, Brougham returned to the opposition, though he vigorously upheld Wellington and Peel in their efforts to secure Catholic emancipation. Brougham became M.P. for Knaresborough and for Yorkshire in 1830, and in the same year he was elevated to the peerage and became Lord Chancellor. He effected great legal reforms, especially in the court of chancery; he substituted the judicial committee of the privy council for the court of delegates, and he instituted the central criminal court. Brougham lost office at the dismissal of Melbourne's government in 1834; after the re-establishment of Melbourne's ministry in 1835 Brougham virtually led the opposition in the House of Lords until he gradually withdrew from politics altogether.

Brougham's interest in popular education was very practical. He published in 1825 *Observations on the Education of the People*, a plan for the publication of cheap and useful works, which was carried out by the Society for the Diffusion of Useful Knowledge. Brougham also helped to found London University in 1828. He took a leading part in education debates in the Commons and brought forward several bills for developing the educational system.

Brougham died at Cannes in 1868.

Lord Brougham[1]

It was a bold, perhaps a rash idea, to collect the writings of Henry Brougham. They were written at such distant dates; their subjects are so various; they are often so wedged into the circumstances of an age, —that they scarcely look natural in a series of volumes. Some men, doubtless, by a strong grasp of intellect, have compacted together subjects as various; the fingermarks of a few are on all human knowledge; others, by a rare illuminative power, have lit up as many with a light that seems peculiar to themselves: *Franciscus Baconus sic cogitavit* may well illustrate an *opera omnia*. But Lord Brougham has neither power; his restless genius has no claim to the still illuminating imagination; his many-handed, apprehensive intelligence is scarcely able to fuse and concentrate. Variety is his taste, and versatility his power. His career has not been quiet. For many years rushing among the details of an age, he has written as he ran. There are not many undertakings bolder than to collect the works of such a life and such a man.

The edition itself seems a good one. The volumes are convenient in size, well printed, and fairly arranged. The various writings it contains have been revised, but not over-revised, by their author. It is not, however, of the collection that we wish to speak. We would endeavour, so far as a few hasty pages may serve, to delineate the career and character of the writer. The attempt is among the most difficult. He is still among us; we have not the materials, possibly not the impartiality, of posterity. Nor have we the familiar knowledge of contemporaries; the time when Lord Brougham exerted his greatest faculties is beyond the political memory of younger men. There are no sufficient books on the events of a quarter of a century ago, we have only traditions; and this must be our excuse if we fall, or may seem to fall, into error and confusion.

The years immediately succeeding the great peace were years of sullenness and difficulty. The idea of the war had passed away; the

[1] *Works of Henry Lord Brougham, F.R.S., Member of the National Institute of France and the Royal Academy of Naples,* London and Glasgow: Griffin and Co. This essay was first published in the *National Review* for July 1857, Volume V, pp. 164–96.

thrill and excitement of the great struggle were no longer felt. We had maintained, with the greatest potentate of modern times, a successful contest for existence; we had our existence, but we had no more; our victory had been great, but it had no fruits. By the aid of pertinacity and capital, we had vanquished genius and valour; but no visible increase of European influence followed. Napoleon said, that Wellington had made peace as if he had been defeated. We had delivered the Continent; such was our natural idea: but the Continent went its own way. There was nothing in its state to please the everyday Englishman. There were kings and emperors; 'which was very well for foreigners, they had always been like that; but it was not many kings could pay ten per cent income-tax.' Absolutism, as such, cannot be popular in a free country. The Holy Alliance, which made a religion of despotism, was scarcely to be reconciled with the British constitution. Altogether we had vanquished Napoleon, but we had no pleasure in what came after him. The cause which agitated our hearts was gone; there was no longer a noise of victories in the air; continental affairs were dead, despotic, dull; we scarcely liked to think that we had made them so; with weary dissatisfaction we turned to our own condition.

This was profoundly unsatisfactory. Trade was depressed; agriculture ruinous; the working classes disaffected. During the war, our manufacturing industry had grown most rapidly; there was a not unnatural expectation that, after a general peace, the rate of increase would be accelerated. The whole Continent, it was considered, would be opened to us; Milan and Berlin decrees no longer excluded us; Napoleon did not now interpose between 'the nation of shopkeepers' and its customers; now he was at St. Helena, surely those customers would buy? It was half-forgotten that they could not. The drain of capital for the war had been, at times, heavily felt in England; there had been years of poverty and discredit; still our industry had gone on, our workshops had not stopped. We had never known what it was to be the seat of war, as well as a power at war. We had never known our burdens enormously increased, just when our industry was utterly stopped; disarranged as trading credit sometimes was, it had not been destroyed. No conscription had drained us of our most efficient consumers. The Continent, south and north, had, though not every where alike, suffered all these evils; its population were poor, harassed, depressed. They could not buy our manufactures, for they had no money. The large preparations for a continental export lay on hand;

our traders were angry and displeased. Nor was content to be found in the agricultural districts. During the war, the British farmer had inevitably a monopoly of this market; at the approach of peace, his natural antipathy to foreign corn influenced the legislature. The Home Secretary of the time had taken into consideration, whether 76s. or 80s. was such a remunerating price as the agriculturist should obtain, and a corn-law had passed accordingly. But no law could give the farmer famine-prices, when there was scarcity here and plenty abroad. There were riots at the passing of the 'Bread-tax,' as it was; in 1813, the price of corn was 120s.; the rural mind was sullen in 1816, when it sunk to 57s. The protection given, though unpopular with the poor, did not satisfy the farmer.

The lower orders in the manufacturing districts were, of necessity, in great distress. The depression of trade produced its inevitable results of closed mills and scanty employment. Wages, when they could be obtained, were very low. The artisan population was then new to the vicissitudes of industry: how far they are, even now, instructed in the laws of trade, recent prosperity will hardly let us judge; but, at that time, they had no doubt that it was the fault of the State, and if not of particular statesmen, then of the essential institutions, that they were in want. They believed the Government ought to regulate their remuneration, and make it sufficient. During some straitened years of the war, the name of 'Luddites' became known. They had principally shown their discontent by breaking certain machines, which they fancied deprived them of work. After the peace, the records of the time are full of 'Spencean Philanthropists,' 'Hampden Clubs,' and similar associations, all desiring a great reform—some of mere politics, others of the law of property and all social economy. Large meetings were every where held, something like those of the year 1839: a general insurrection, doubtless a wild dream of a few hot-brained dreamers, was fancied to have been really planned. The name 'Radical' came to be associated with this discontent. The spirit which, in after-years, clamoured distinctly for the five points of the Charter, made itself heard in mutterings and threatenings.

Nor were the capitalists, who had created the new wealth, socially more at ease. Many of them, as large employers of labour, had a taste for Toryism; the rule of the people to them meant the rule of their work-people. Some of the wealthiest and most skilful became associated with the aristocracy; but it was in vain with the majority to attempt it. Between them and the possessors of hereditary wealth, there was fixed a great gulf; the contrast of habits, speech, manners, was too wide. The two might coincide in particular opinions; they might agree to support the same institutions; they might set forth, in a Conservative creed, the same form of sound words: but, though the abstract conclusions were identical, the mode of holding them—to borrow a subtlety of Father Newman's—was exceedingly different. The refined, discriminating, timorous immobility of the aristocracy was distinct from the coarse, dogmatic, keep-downishness of the manufacturer. Yet more marked was the contrast, when the opposite tendencies of temperament had produced, as they soon could not but do, a diversity of opinion. The case was not quite new in England. Mr. Burke spoke of the tendency of the first East Indians to Jacobinism. They could not, he said, bear that their present importance should have no proportion to their recently-acquired riches. No extravagant fortunes have, in this century, been made by Englishmen in India; but Lancashire has been a California. Families have been created there, whose names we all know, which we think of when we mention wealth; some of which are now, by lapse of time, passing into the hereditary caste of recognised opulence. This, however, has been a work of time; and, before it occurred, there was no such intermediate class between the new wealth and the old. 'It takes,' it is said that Sir Robert Peel observed, 'three generations to make a gentleman.' In the mean time, there was an inevitable misunderstanding; the new cloth was too coarse for the old. Besides this, many actual institutions offended the eyes of the middle class. The state of the law was opposed both to their prejudices and interests: that you could only recover your debts by spending more than the debt, was hard; and the injury was aggravated, the money was spent in 'special pleading' —'in putting a plain thing so as to perplex and mislead a plain man.' 'Lord Eldon and the Court of Chancery,' as Sydney Smith expressed it, 'sat heavy on mankind.' The existence of slavery in our colonies, strongly supported by a strong aristocratic and parliamentary influence, offended the principles of middle-class Christianity, and the natural sentiments of simple men. The cruelty of the penal law—the punishing with death sheep-stealing and shop-lifting—jarred the humanity of that second order of English society, which, from their habits of reading and non-reading, may be called, *par excellence*, the scriptural classes. The routine harshness of a not very wise executive did not mitigate the feeling. The *modus operandi* of government appeared coarse and oppressive.

We seemed to pay, too, a good deal for what we did not like. At the close of the war, the ten per cent income-tax was of course heavily oppressive. The public expenditure was beyond argument lavish; and it was spent in pensions, sinecures ('them idlers' in the speech of Lancashire), and a mass of sundries, that an economical man of business will scarcely admit to be necessary, and that even now, after countless prunings, produce periodically 'financial reform associations,' 'administrative leagues,' and other combinations which amply testify the enmity of thrifty efficiency to large figures and muddling management. There had remained from the eighteenth century a tradition of corruption, an impression that direct pecuniary malversation pervaded the public offices; an idea true in the days of Rigby or Bubb Dodington, but which, like many other impressions, continued to exist many years after the facts in which it originated had passed away. Government, in the hands of such a man as Lord Liverpool, was very different from Government in the hands of Sir Robert Walpole: respectability was exacted: of actual money-taking there was hardly any. Still, especially among inferior officials, there was something to shock modern purity. The size of jobs was large: if the Treasury of that time could be revived, it would be depressed at the littleness of whatever is perpetrated in modern administration. There were petty abuses too in the country—in municipalities—in charitable trusts—in all outlying public moneys, which seemed to the offended man of business, who saw them with his own eyes, evident instances confirming his notion of the malpractices of Downing Street. 'There are only five little boys in the school of Richester; they may cost £200, and the income is £2,000, and the trustees don't account for the balance; which is the way things are done in England: we keeps an aristocracy,' &c. The whole of this feeling concentrated into a detestation of rotten boroughs. The very name was enough: that Lord Dover, with two patent sinecures in the Exchequer and a good total for assisting in nothing at the Audit Office, should return two members for one House, while Birmingham, where they made buttons,—'as good buttons as there are in the world, Sir,'—returned no members at all, was an evident indication that Reform was necessary. Mr. Canning was an eloquent man; but 'even *he* could not say that a decaying stump was the *people*.' Gatton and Old Sarum became unpopular.

The source of power seemed absurd, and the use of power was tainted. Side by side with the incipient Chartism of the Northern operative, there was growing daily more distinct and clear the Manchester philosophy, which has since expressed itself in the Anti-Corn-Law League, and which, for good and evil, is now an element so potent in our national life. Both creeds were forms of discontent. And the counterpoise was wanting. The English Constitution has provided that there shall always be one estate raised above the storms of passion and controversy, which all parties may respect and honour. The King is to be loved. But this theory requires, for a real efficiency, that the throne be filled by such a person as can be loved. In those times it was otherwise. The nominal possessor of the crown was a very old man, whom an incurable malady had long sequestered from earthly things. The actual possessor of the royal authority was a voluptuary of over-grown person, now too old for healthy pleasure, and half-sickened himself at the corrupt pursuits in which, nevertheless, he indulged perpetually. His domestic vices had become disgracefully public. Whatever might be the truth about Queen Caroline, no one could say she had been well treated. There was no loyalty on which suffering workers, or an angry middle class, could repose: all through the realm there was a miscellaneous agitation, a vague and wandering discontent.

The official mind of the time was troubled. We have a record of its speculations in the life of Lord Sidmouth, who more than any one perhaps embodied it. He had been Speaker, and was much inclined to remedy the discontent of the middle classes by 'naming them to the House.' A more conscientious man perhaps has never filled a public position. If the forms of the House of Commons had been intuitively binding, no one could have obeyed them better: the 'mace' was a 'counsel of perfection' to him; all disorder hateful. In the Home Office it was the same. The Luddites were people who would not obey the Speaker. Constituted authority must be enforced. The claims of a suffering multitude were not so much neglected as unappreciated. A certain illiberality, as we should now speak, pervades the whole kind of thought. The most striking feature is an indisposition, which by long indulgence has become an inability, to comprehend another person's view, to put oneself in another's mental place, to think what he thinks, to conceive what he inevitably is. Lord Sidmouth referred to the file. He found that Mr. Pitt had put down disaffection by severe measures. Accordingly, he suspended the Habeas-Corpus Act, passed six Acts, commended a Peterloo massacre, not with conscious unfeelingness, but from an absorbed officiality, from a knowledge that this was what 'the department' had done before, and an inference that this must be done again. As for the reforming ideas of the middle classes, red tape had never tied up such notions: perhaps it was the French Revolution over again: you could not tolerate *them*.

Between such a dominant mind as this, and such a subject mind as has been described, there was a daily friction. The situation afforded obvious advantages to enterprising men. Its peculiarity did not escape the shrewd eyes of John Lord Eldon. 'If,' said the Conservative Chancellor, 'I were to begin life again, d——n my eyes, but I would begin as an agitator.' Henry Brougham did so begin. During the war he had distinguished himself in the exposition of the grievances of the trading interest. Our Government had chosen a mode of carrying it on specially fitted to injure our commerce. 'Napoleon had said, that no vessel should touch a British port, and then enter a French one, or one under French control. The Orders in Council said, that no vessel whatever should enter any such port without having first touched at some port of Great Britain.' The natural results were the annihilation of our trade with the Continent, and a quarrel with the United States. The merchants of the country were alarmed at both consequences. Perhaps until then men hardly knew how powerful our trading classes had become. Meetings were held in populous places; petitions in great numbers—an impressive and important thing in those times—were presented. Wherever foreign commerce existed, the discontent expressed itself in murmurs. The forms of the House of Commons were far more favourable than they now are to an action from without; and this is not unnatural, since there had been as yet but few actions from without, and it has not been necessary to have a guard against them. The petitions, as has been said, were numerous; and on the presentation of each there was a speech from the member presenting it, trying to bring on a debate, and suggesting topics which might irritate the ministry and convince the country. Mr. Brougham was always in his place.* 'Hardly an hour passed without detecting some false statement or illogical argument; hardly a night passed without gaining some convert to the cause of truth.' The result was decisive. 'Although opposed by the whole weight of the Government both in

---

* This and the following quotations are from the Speeches of Lord Brougham and the Introduction to them, published in 1838; the latter were written by himself.

public and out of doors; although at first vigorously resisted by the energy, the acuteness, the activity, and the expertness, which made Mr. Perceval one of the first debaters of his day; although, after his death, the struggle was maintained by the father of the system, with all his fire and with his full knowledge of the subject,—nay, although the Ministry risked their existence on the question, the victory remained with the petitioners.[2] The Orders in Council were abolished, and the efficacy of agitation proved. 'The session of 1816 offered an example yet more remarkable of the same tactics being attended with signal success. On the termination of the war, the Government were determined, instead of repealing the whole income-tax, which the law declared to be 'for and during the continuance of the war, and no longer,' to 'retain one-half of it.' 'As soon as this intention was announced, several meetings were held.' Some petitions were presented. Mr. Brougham declared that, if the motion 'were pressed on Thursday, he should avail himself of the forms of the House.' Of course the unpopularity of paying money was decisive: the income-tax fell. The same faculty of aggression, which had been so successful in these instances, was immediately so applied as to give voice to the sullenness of the country; to express forms of discontent as real, though not with an object as determinate. Mr. Brougham did not understate his case: 'There is one branch of the subject which I shall pass over altogether,—I mean the *amount* of the distresses which are now universally admitted to prevail over almost every part of the empire. Upon this topic all men are agreed; the statements connected with it are as unquestionable as they are afflicting.' Nor did he shrink from detail. 'I shall suppose,' he observed to the House, 'a farm of 400 acres of fair good land, yielding a rent of from £500 to £600 a-year.' 'It will require a four years' course,—200 acres being in corn, 100 in fallow, and 100 in hay and grass;' and he seems to prove that at least it *ought* not to answer, 'independently of the great rise in lime and all sorts of manure.' The commercial mania of the time takes its turn in the description. 'After the cramped state in which the enemy's measures and our own retaliation (as we termed it) had kept our trade for some years, when the events of spring 1814 suddenly opened the Continent, a rage for exporting goods of every kind burst forth, only

---

[2] I have inserted the words 'the struggle was maintained by' which do not appear in the *National Review*. The 'father of the system' is a reference to Mr. James Stephen, grandfather of Sir James Fitzjames Stephen.—Ed.

to be explained by reflecting on the previous restrictions we had been labouring under, and only to be equalled (though not in extent) by some of the mercantile delusions connected with South American speculations. Every thing that could be shipped was sent off; all the capital that could be laid hold of was embarked. The frenzy, I can call it nothing less, after the experience of 1806 and 1810, descended to persons in the humblest circumstances, and the farthest removed, by their pursuits, from commercial cares. It may give the committee some idea of this disease, if I state what I know to have happened in one or two places. Not only clerks and labourers, but menial servants, engaged the little sums which they had been laying up for a provision against old age and sickness; persons went round tempting them to adventure in the trade to Holland, and Germany, and the Baltic; they risked their mite in the hopes of boundless profits; it went with the millions of the more regular traders: the bubble soon burst, like its predecessors of the South Sea, the Mississippi, and Buenos Ayres; English goods were selling for much less in Holland and the north of Europe, than in London and Manchester; in most places they were lying a dead weight without any sale at all; and either no returns whatever were received, or pounds came back for thousands that had gone forth. The great speculators broke; the middling ones lingered out a precarious existence, deprived of all means of continuing their dealings either at home or abroad; the poorer dupes of the delusion had lost their little hoards, and went upon the parish the next mishap that befel them; but the result of the whole has been much commercial distress— a caution now absolutely necessary in trying new adventures—a prodigious diminution in the demand for manufactures, and indirectly a serious defalcation in the effectual demand for the produce of land.' Next year he described as the worst season ever known. The year 1812, a year before esteemed one of much suffering, rose in comparison to one of actual prosperity. He began with the 'clothing, a branch of trade which, from accidental circumstances, is not as depressed as our other great staples;' he passed to the iron trade, &c. &c. He dilated on the distress, the discontent, and suffering of the people. Of course the Government were to blame. He moved that the 'unexampled' difficulties of trade and manufactures were 'materially increased by the policy pursued with respect to our foreign commerce,—that the continuance of these difficulties is in a great degree owing to the severe pressure of taxation under which the country labours, and which ought by every practicable means to be lightened,—that the system of foreign policy pursued by his Majesty's ministers has not been such as to obtain for the people of this country those commercial advantages which the influence of Great Britain in foreign countries fairly entitled them to expect.' As became a pupil of the Edinburgh University, Mr. Brougham was not averse to political economy. He was ready to discuss the theory of rent or the corn-laws. He made a speech, which he relates as having had a greater success than any other which he made in Parliament, in support of Mr. Calcraft's amendment, to 'substitute £192,638. 4s. 9d. for £385,276. 9s. 6d., the estimate for the household troops.' Foreign policy was a favourite topic. Almost unsupported, as he said some years after, he attacked the Holy Alliance. Looking back through the softening atmosphere of reminiscence, he almost seems to have a kindness for Lord Castlereagh. He remembers with pleasure the utter 'courage with which he exposed himself unabashed to the most critical audience in the world, while incapable of uttering any thing but the meanest matter, expressed in the most wretched language;' nor has he 'forgotten the kind of pride that mantled on the fronts of the Tory phalanx, when, after being overwhelmed with the fire of the Whig Opposition, or galled by the fierce denunciations of the Mountain, or harassed by the splendid displays of Mr. Canning, their chosen leader stood forth, and presenting the graces of his eminently patrician figure, flung open his coat, displayed an azure ribbon traversing a snow-white chest, and declared 'his high satisfaction that he could now meet the charges against him face to face, and repel with indignation all that his adversaries had been bold and rash enough to advance.' But the 'Mr. Brougham' of that time showed no admiration; no denunciations were stronger than his; no sarcasm impinged more deeply; if the 'noble lord in the blue ribbon' wished any one out of the House, the 'man from the Northern Circuit' was probably that one. Kings and emperors met with little mercy: and later years have shown how little was merited by the petty absolutism and unthinking narrowness of that time. That Mr. Brougham indissolubly connected the education movement with his name every body knows; but scarcely any one remembers how unpopular that movement was. Mr. Windham had said, some years before, 'That the diffusion of knowledge was proper might be supported by many good arguments; but he confessed he was a sceptic on that point. It was said, Look at the state of the savages as compared with ours. A savage among savages was *very well*, and the difference was only perceived when he came to be introduced into civilised society.' 'His friend, Dr. Johnson, was of opinion, that it was not right to teach reading beyond a certain extent in society.' The same feeling continued. Mr. Peel, in his blandest tones, attacked the education committee. Lord Stowell, not without sagacity, observed, 'If you provide a larger amount of high-cultivated talent than there is a demand for, the surplus is very likely to turn sour.' Such were the sentiments of some of the best scholars of that era; and so went all orthodox sentiment. That education was the same as republicanism, and republicanism as infidelity, half the curates believed. But in spite of all this opposition, perhaps with more relish on account of it, Mr. Brougham was ever ready. He was a kind of prophet of knowledge. His voice was heard in the streets. He preached the gospel of the alphabet; he sang the praises of the primer all the day long. 'Practical observations,' 'discourses,' 'speeches,' exist, terrible to all men now. To the kind of education then advocated there may be objections. We may object to the kind of 'knowledge' then most sought after; but there can be no doubt that those who then laboured in its behalf must be praised for having inculcated, in the horrid heat of the day, as a boring paradox what is now a boring commonplace. Our space would fail us if we were to attempt to recount his labours on the slavery question, on George IV and Queen Caroline, or his hundred encounters with the routine statesmen. The series commenced at the peace; but it continued for many years. Is not its history written in the chronicles of Parliament? You must turn the leaves—no unpleasant reading—of those old debates, and observe how often Mr. Brougham's name occurs, and on what cumbrous subjects, before you can estimate the frequency of his attacks and the harassing harshness of his labour. One especial subject was his more than any other man's—law reform. He had Romilly and Mackintosh as fellow-labourers in the amelioration of the penal code; he had their support, and that of some others, in his incessant narrations of the grievances of individuals, and denunciations of the unfeeling unthinkingness of our home administration; but no man grappled so boldly—we had almost said so coarsely—with the crude complexities of our civil jurisprudence: a rougher nature, a more varied knowledge of action than we must expect of philanthropists were needed for that task. The subject was most difficult to deal with. The English commerce and civilisation had grown up in the meshes of a half-feudal code, further complicated with the curious narrowness and spirit of chicane which haunt every where the law-courts of early times. The technicality which produced the evil made the remedy more difficult. There was no general public opinion on the manner of reform; the public felt the evil, but no one could judge of the efficacy of a remedy, save persons studious in complicated learning, who would hardly be expected to show how that learning could be rendered useless,—hardly, indeed, to imagine a world in which it did not exist. The old creed, that these ingenious abuses were the last 'perfection of reason,' still lingered. It must give Lord Brougham some pride to reflect how many of the improvements which he was the first to popularise, if not to suggest, have been adopted,—how many old abuses of detail, which he first indicated to Parliament, exist no longer,— how many more are now admitted by every body to be abuses, though the mode of abolition is contested. The speech on law reform, which he published in the collected edition of his speeches, is nearly a summary of all that has been done or suggested in common or civil law reform for the last thirty years. The effect which so bold an attack on so many things by a single person produced in that conservative time was prodigious. 'There never was such a nuisance as the man is,' said an old lawyer whom we knew; and he expressed the feeling of his profession. If we add, that beside all these minor reforms and secondary agitations, Mr. Brougham was a bold advocate of Catholic emancipation and parliamentary reform—the largest heresies of that epoch—we may begin to understand the sarcasm of Mr. Canning: 'The honourable and learned gentleman having, in the course of his parliamentary life, supported or proposed *almost every species of innovation* which could be practised on the constitution, it was not very easy for ministers to do any thing without seeming to borrow from him. Break away in what direction they would, whether to the right or to the left, it was all alike. "Oh," said the honourable gentleman, "I was there before you; you would not have thought of that if I had not given you a hint." In the reign of Queen Anne, there was a sage and grave critic of the name of Dennis, who in his old age got it into his head that he had written all the good plays which were acted at that time. At last a tragedy came forth with a most imposing display of hail and thunder. At the first peal, Dennis exclaimed: "That is my thunder!" So with the honourable and learned gentleman; there was no noise astir for the good of mankind in any part of the world, but he instantly claimed it for his thunder.' We may have wearied our readers with these long references to old conflicts, but it was necessary. We are familiar with the aberrations of the ex-Chancellor; we forget how bold, how efficacious, how varied was the activity of Henry Brougham.

There are several qualities in his genius which make such a life peculiarly suited to him. The first of these is an aggressive impulsive disposition. Most people may admit that the world goes ill; old abuses seem to exist, questionable details to abound. Hardly any one thinks that any thing may not be made better. But how to improve the world, to repair the defects, is a difficulty. Immobility is a part of man. A sluggish conservatism is the basis of our English nature. '*Learn*, my son,' said the satirist, 'to bear tranquilly the calamities of others.' We easily learn it. Most men have a line of life, and it imposes certain duties which they fulfil; but they cannot be induced to start out of that line. We dwell in 'a firm basis of content.' 'Let the mad world go its own way, for it will go its own way.' There is no doctrine of the English Church more agreeable to our instinctive taste than that which forbids all works of supererogation. 'You did a thing without being obliged,' said an eminent statesman; 'then that must be wrong.' We travel in the track. Lord Brougham is the opposite of this. It is not difficult to him to attack abuses. The more difficult thing for him would be to live in a world without abuses. An intense excitability is in his nature. He must 'go off.' He is eager to reform corruption, and rushes out to refute error. A tolerant placidity is altogether denied to him.

And not only is this excitability eager, it is many-sided. The men who have in general exerted themselves in labours for others, have generally been rather of a brooding nature; certain ideas, views, and feelings have impressed themselves on them in solitude; they come forth with them among the crowd: but they have no part in its diversified life. They are almost irritated by it. They have no conception except of their cause; they are abstracted in one thought, pained with the dizziness of a heated idea. There is nothing of this in Brougham. He is excited by what he sees. The stimulus is from without. He saw the technicalities of the law-courts; observed a charitable trustee misusing the charity moneys; perceived that George IV oppressed Queen Caroline; went to Old Sarum. He is not absorbed in a creed: he is pricked by facts. Accordingly his activity is miscellaneous. The votary of a doctrine is concentrated, for the logical consequences of a doctrine are limited. But an open-minded man, who is aroused by what he sees, quick at discerning abuses, ready to reform any thing which he thinks goes wrong,—will never have done acting. The details of life are endless, and each of them may go wrong in a hundred ways.

Another faculty of Brougham (in metaphysics it is perhaps but a phase of the same) is the faculty of easy anger. The supine placidity of civilisation is not favourable to animosity. A placid Conservative is perhaps a little pleased that the world is going a *little* ill. Lord Brougham does not feel this. Like an Englishman on the Continent, he is ready to blow up any one. He is a Jonah of detail; he is angry at the dust of life, and wroth with the misfeasances of *employés*. The most reverberating of bastinadoes is the official mind basted by Brougham. You did *this* wrong; why did you omit *that?* document C ought to be on the third file; paper D is wrongly docketed in the ninth file. Red tape will scarcely succeed when it is questioned; you should take it as Don Quixote did his helmet, without examination, for a most excellent helmet. A vehement industrious man proposing to untie papers and not proposing to spare errors is the terror of a respectable administrator. 'Such an unpracticable man, Sir, interfering with the *office*, attacking private character, messing in what cannot concern him.' These are the jibes which attend an irritable anxiety for the good of others. They have attended Lord Brougham through life. He has enough of misanthropy to be a philanthropist.

How much of this is temper, and how much public spirit, it is not for any one to attempt to say. That a natural pleasure in wrath is part of his character, no one who has studied the career of Brougham can doubt. But no fair person can doubt either that he has shown on many great occasions—and, what is more, on many petty occasions—a rare zeal for the public welfare. He may not be capable of the settled calm by which the world is best administered. There is a want of consistency in his goodness, of concentration in his action. The gusts of passion pass over him, and he is gone for a time you can scarcely say where. But though he is the creature of impulse, his impulses are often generous and noble ones. No one would do what he has done, no one could have the intense motive power to do what he has done, without a large share of diffused unselfishness. The irritation of the most acute excitability would not suffice. It is almost an axiom in estimates of human nature, that in its larger operations all that nature must concur. Doubtless there is a thread of calculation in the midst of his impulses; no man rises to be Lord-Chancellor without, at least in lulls and intervals of impulse, a most discriminating and careful judgment of men and things and chances. But after every set-off and abatement, and without any softening of unamiable indications, there will yet remain—and a long series of years will continue to admire it—an eager principle of disinterested action.

Lord Brougham's intellectual powers were as fitted for the functions of a miscellaneous agitator as his moral character. The first of these, perhaps, is a singular faculty of conspicuous labour. In general, the work of agitation proceeds in this way: a conspicuous, fascinating popular orator is ever on the surface, ever ready with appropriate argument, making motions, attracting public attention; beneath and out of sight are innumerable workers and students, unfit for the public eye, getting up the facts, elaborating conclusions, supplying the conspicuous orator with the *data* on which he lives. There is a perpetual controversy, when the narrative of the agitation comes to be written, whether the merit of what is achieved belongs to the skilful advocate who makes a subtle use of what is provided for him, or the laborious inferiors and juniors who compose the brief and set in order the evidence. For all that comes before the public, Lord Brougham has a wonderful power; he can make motions, addresses, orations, when you wish and on what you wish. He is like a machine for moving amendments. He can keep at work any number of persons under him. Every agitation has a tendency to have an office; some league, some society, some body of labourers must work regularly at its details. Mr. Brougham was able to rush hither and thither through a hundred such kinds of men, and gather up the whole stock of the most recent information, the extreme decimals of the statistics, and diffuse them immediately with eager comment to a listening world. This may not be, indeed is not, the strictest and most straining kind of labour; the anxious, wearing, verifying, self-imposed scrutiny of scattered and complicated details is a far more exhausting task; it is this which makes the eye dim and the face pale and the mind heavy. The excitement of a multifarious agitation will carry the energies through much; the last touches, and it is these which exhaust, need not be put on any one subject. Yet, after all deductions, such a career requires a quantity far surpassing all that most men have of life and *verve* and mind.

Another advantage of Lord Brougham, is his extreme readiness;

what he can do, he can do at a moment's notice. He has always had this power. Lord Holland, in his memoirs referring to transactions which took place many years ago, gives an illustration of it. 'The management of our press,' he is speaking of the question of the general election of 1807, 'fell into the hands of Mr. Brougham. With that active and able individual I had become acquainted through Mr. Allen in 1805. At the formation of Lord Grenville's ministry, he had written, at my suggestion, a pamphlet called the *State of the Nation*. He subsequently accompanied Lord Rosslyn to Lisbon. His early connection with the Abolitionists had familiarised him with the means of circulating political papers, and given him some weight with those best qualified to co-operate in such an undertaking. His extensive knowledge, his extraordinary readiness, his assiduity and habits of composition, enabled him to correct some articles, and to furnish a prodigious number himself. With partial and scanty assistance from Mr. Allen, myself, and one or two more, he in the course of a few days filled every bookseller's shop with pamphlets,—most London newspapers, and all country ones without exception, with paragraphs,—and supplied a large portion of the boroughs throughout the kingdom with handbills adapted to the local interests of the candidates, and all tending to enforce the conduct, elucidate the measures, or expose the adversaries of the Whigs.'

Another power which was early remarked of Brougham, and which is as necessary as any to an important leader in great movements, is a skilful manipulation of men. Sir James Mackintosh noted in his Journal on the 30th of January 1818: 'The address and insinuation of Brougham are so great, that nothing but the bad temper which he cannot always hide could hinder him from mastering every body as he does Romilly. He *leads* others to his opinion; he generally appears at first to concur with theirs, and never more than half opposes it at once. This management is helped by an air of easy frankness that would lay suspicion itself asleep. He will place himself at the head of an opposition among whom he is unpopular; he will conquer the House of Commons, who hate, but now begin to fear him.' An observer of faces would fancy he noted in Lord Brougham this pliant astuteness marred by ill-temper. It has marked his career.

Another essential quality in multifarious agitation is an extreme versatility. No one can deny Lord Brougham this. An apparently close observer has described him: 'Take the routine of a day, for instance.

In his early life he has been known to attend, in his place in court, on circuit, at an early hour in the morning. After having successfully pleaded the cause of his client, he drives off to the hustings, and delivers, at different places, eloquent and spirited speeches to the electors. He then sits down in the retirement of his closet to pen an address to the Glasgow students, perhaps, or an elaborate article in the *Edinburgh Review*. The active labours of the day are closed with preparation for the court business of the following morning; and then, in place of retiring to rest, as ordinary men would after such exertions, he spends the night in abstruse study, or in social intercourse with some friend from whom he has been long separated. Yet he would be seen, as early as eight on the following morning, actively engaged in the court, in defence of some unfortunate object of government persecution; astonishing the auditory, and his fellow-lawyers no less, with the freshness and power of his eloquence. A fair contrast with this history of a day, in early life, would be that of one at a more advanced period; say, in the year 1832. A watchful observer might see the new Lord Chancellor seated in the court over which he presided, from an early hour in the morning until the afternoon, listening to the arguments of counsel, and mastering the points of cases with a grasp of mind that enabled him to give those speedy and unembarrassed judgments that have so injured him with the profession. If he followed his course, he would see him, soon after the opening of the House of Lords, addressing their lordships on some intricate question of law, with an acuteness that drew down approbation even from his opponents; or, on some all-engrossing political topic, casting firebrands into the camp of the enemy, and awakening them from the complacent repose of conviction to the hot contests with more active and inquiring intellects. Then, in an hour or so, he might follow him to the Mechanics' Institution, and hear an able and stimulating discourse on education, admirably adapted to the peculiar capacity of his auditors; and towards ten, perhaps, at a Literary and Scientific Institution in Marylebone, the same Proteus-like intellect might be found expounding the intricacies of physical science with a never-tiring and elastic power. Yet, during all those multitudinous exertions, time would be found for the composition of a discourse on natural theology, that bears no marks of haste or excitement of mind, but presents as calm a face as though it had been the laborious production of a contemplative philosopher.' We may differ in our estimate of the *quality* of these various efforts; but no one can deny to him who was capable of them a great share in what Adam Smith mentioned as one of the most important facilities to the intellectual labourer,—a quickness in 'changing his hand.'

Nor would any of these powers be sufficient, without that which is, in some sense, the principle of them all—an enterprising intellect. In the present day this is among the rarest gifts. The speciality of pursuits is attended with a timidity of mind. Each subject is given up to men who cultivate it, and it only; who are familiar with its niceties, and absorbed in its details. There is no one who dares to look at the whole. 'I have taken *all* knowledge to be my province,' said Lord Bacon. The notion, and still more the expression, of it seems ridiculous now. The survey of each plot in the world of knowledge is becoming more complete. We shall have a plan of each soon, on a seven-inch scale; but we are losing the picturesque pictures of the outside and surface of knowledge in the survey of its whole. We have the petty survey, as we say, but no chart, no globe of the entire world; no bold sketch of its obvious phenomena, as they strike the wayfarer and impress themselves on the imagination. The man of the speciality cannot describe the large outlines; he is too close upon the minutiæ; he does not know the relations of other knowledge, and no one else dares to infringe on his province—on the 'study of his life'—for fear of committing errors in detail which he alone knows, and which he may expose. Lord Brougham has nothing of this cowardice. He is ready to give, in their boldest and most general form, the rough outlines of knowledge as they strike the man of the world, occupied in its affairs and familiar with its wishes. He is not cooped up in a single topic, and he has no dread of those who are. He may fall into error, but he exhibits a subject as it is seen by those who know other subjects, by a man who knows the world; he at least attempts an embracing conception of his topic, he makes you feel its connection with reality and affairs. He has exhibited this virtue at all stages of his career, but it was most valuable in his earlier time. There is no requisite so important as intellectual courage in one who seeks to improve all things in all ways.

His oratory also suits the character of the hundred-subject agitator well. It is rough-and-ready. It abounds in sarcasm, in vituperation, in aggression. It does not shrink from detail. It would batter any thing at any moment. We may think as we will on its merits as a work of art, but no one can deny its exact adaptation to a versatile and rushing agitator—to a tribune of detail.

The deficiencies of Brougham's character—in some cases they seem but the unfavourable aspect of its excellencies—were also fitted for his first career. The first of these, to say it in a sentence, is the want of a thinking intellect. A miscellaneous agitator must be ready to catch at any thing, to attack every thing, to blame any one. This is not the life for a mind of anxious deliberation. The patient philsopher, who is cautious in his positions, dubious of his data, slow in his conclusions, must fail at once. He would be investigating while he should attack, inquiring while he should speak. He could not act[3] upon a chance; the moment of action would be gone. A sanguine and speedy intellect, ready to acquire by its very idea, all but excludes the examining, scrupulous, hesitating intellect which reflects.

Nor would a man of very sensitive judgment endure such a career. An agitator must err by excess; a delicate nature errs by defects. There is a certain coarseness in the abusive breed. A Cleon should not feel failure. No man has ever praised very highly Lord Brougham's judgment; but to have exceedingly improved it would perhaps have impaired his earlier utility. You might as fitly employ some delicate lady as a rough-rider, as a man of a poising refining judgment in the task of a grievance-stater.

Harsh nerves, too, are no disadvantage. Perhaps they are essential. Very nice nerves would shrink from a scattered and jangled life. Three days out of six the sensitive frame would be jarred, the agitator would be useless. It is possible, indeed, to imagine that in a single noble cause something that would light up the imagination, that would move the inner soul, a temperament the most delicate, a frame that is most poetic, might well be interested absorbingly. A little of such qualities may be essential. The apostle of a creed must have the nature to comprehend that creed; his fancy must take it in, his feelings realise it, his nature absorb it. To move the finer nature, you need the deeper nature. Perhaps even in a meaner cause, in something which should take a hold on the moving mob, sway the masses, rule the popular fancy, rough as the task of the mob-orator is, you require the delicate imagination. One finds some trace of it—still more of what is its natural accompaniment, a sweet nature—buried in the huge frame and coarse exterior of O'Connell. No unpoetic heart could touch the Irish people. Lord Brougham is prose itself. He was described many years ago, as excelling all men in a knowledge of the course of exchange.

[3] The *National Review* has 'state' instead of 'act'.—p. 181.

'He is,' continued the satirist, 'apprised of the exact state of our exports and imports, and scarce a ship clears out its cargo at Liverpool or Hull but he has the notice of the bill of lading.' To explain the grievances of men of business needs no poetic nature. It scarcely needs the highest powers of invective. There is something nearly ridiculous in being the 'Mirabeau of sums.'

There is a last quality, which is difficult to describe in the language of books, but which Lord Brougham excels in, and which has perhaps been of more value to him than all his other qualities put together. In the speech of ordinary men it is called 'devil;' persons instructed in the German language call it 'the dæmonic element.' What it is one can hardly express in a single sentence. It is most easily explained by physiognomy. There is a glare in some men's eyes which seems to say, 'Beware, I am dangerous; *noli me tangere.*' Lord Brougham's face has this. A mischievous excitability is the most obvious expression of it. If he were a horse, nobody would buy him; with that eye, no one could answer for his temper. Such men are often not really resolute, but they are not pleasant to be near in a difficulty. They have an aggressive eagerness which is formidable. They would kick against the pricks sooner than not kick at all. A little of the demon is excellent for an agitator.

His peculiar adaptation to his peculiar career raised Mr. Brougham, in a few years, to a position such as few men have ever obtained in England—such as no other man perhaps has attained by popular agitation. When he became member for Yorkshire, in 1830, he was a power in the country. The cause which he was advocating had grown of itself. The power of the middle classes, especially of the commercial classes, had increased. Lord Eldon was retiring. Lord Sidmouth had retired. What we now call liberality was coming into fashion. Men no longer regarded the half-feudal constitution as a 'form of thought.' Argument was at least thought fair. And this seems likely and natural. No one can wonder that the influence of men of business grew with the development of business, and that they adopted the plain, straightforward, cautious creed, which we now know to be congenial to them. It is much more difficult to explain how reform became a passion. The state of the public mind during the crisis of the Reform Bill is one which those who cannot remember it cannot understand. The popular enthusiasm, the intense excitement, the rush of converts, the union of rectors and squires with those against whom they had respectively so long preached and sworn, the acclamation for the 'whole bill and nothing but the bill,' are become utterly strange. As the first French Assembly in a single night abolished with public outcry the essential abuses of the old *régime*, so our fathers at once, and with enthusiasm, abolished the close boroughs and the old representation, the lingering abuses of half-feudal England. The present Frenchmen are said not to comprehend the 4th of August: we can hardly understand the year '32. An apathy has fallen upon us. But we can nevertheless, and without theorising, comprehend what an advantage such an enthusiasm was to the Liberals of that time. Most Whig ministries have been like low-church bishops. There is a feeling that the advocates of liberty ought scarcely to coerce; they have ruled, but they seem to deny the succession by which they ruled; they have been distrusted by a vague and half-conservative sentiment. In the tumult of 1832 all such feelings were carried away. Toryism was abolished with delight.

Mr. Brougham was among the first to share the advantage. There is a legend, that in the first Whig ministry Lord Brougham was offered the post of Attorney-General, and that he only replied by disdainfully tearing up the letter containing the offer. Whether the anecdote be literally true or not, we cannot say. The first of the modern Whig ministries is in the post-historical period. We have not yet enough of contemporary evidence to be sure of its details: years must pass before the memoir-writers can accumulate. But in spirit the tale is doubtless accurate. Lord Grey did not wish to make Mr. Brougham Lord-Chancellor, and Mr. Brougham refused any inferior place as beneath his merits and his influence. The first Whig ministry were, indeed, in a position of some difficulty. The notion that a successful opposition, as such, should take the reins of administration, has been much derided: 'Sir,' said a sceptic on this part of constitutional government, 'I would as soon choose for a new coachman the man who shied stones best at my old one!' And, without going the length of such critics, it must be allowed that the theory may produce odd results, when the persons summoned by their victory to assume office have been for many years in opposition. The party cannot have acquired official habits; the traditions of business cannot be known to them; their long course of opposition will have forced into leadership men hardly fitted for placid government. There is said to have been much of this feeling when Lord Grey's ministry were installed; it seemed as if that 'old favourite of the public,' Mr. Buckstone, were called to license plays.

Grave Englishmen doubted the gravity of the administration. To make Lord Brougham Chancellor was, therefore, particularly inconvenient. He was too mobile: you could not fancy him droning. He had attacked Lord Eldon during many years, of course; but did he know law? He was a most active person; but would he sit *still* upon the woolsack? Of his inattention to his profession men circulated idle tales. 'Pity he hadn't known a little law, and then he would have known a little of every thing,' was the remark of one who certainly only knows one thing. A more circumstantial person recounted that, when Brougham had been a pupil of Sir Nicholas Tindal, in the Temple, an uncle of his, having high hopes of his ability, asked the latter: 'I hope my nephew is giving himself up, soul and body, to his profession?' 'I do not know any thing,' replied the distinct special-pleader, 'as to his *soul*, but his body is very seldom in my chambers.' Putting aside with contempt this surface of tales, it could not be denied that Mr. Brougham's practice at the bar,—large and lucrative as it was—immense as was the energy required to maintain it at the same time with his other labours,—had yet not shown him to possess the finest discretion, the most delicate tact of the advocate. Mr. Scarlett stole verdicts away from him. 'He strikes hard, Sir,' said an attorney; 'but he strikes wrong.' The appointment scarcely strengthened the ministry of the time. Mr. Brougham was a hero; Lord Brougham was 'a necessity.' It was like Mr. Disraeli being Chancellor of the Exchequer.

After the lapse of years, and with the actual facts before us, it is not difficult to see how far these anticipations have been falsified, and how far they have been justified by the result. All the notions as to Lord Brougham's ignorance of law may at once be discarded. A man of his general culture and vigorous faculties, with a great memory and much experience in forensic business, is no more likely to be ignorant of the essential bookwork of law than a tailor to be ignorant of scissors and seams. A man in business must be brought in contact with it; a man of mind cannot help grasping it. No one now questions that Lord Brougham was and is a lawyer of adequate attainments. But, at the same time, the judgments which supply the conclusive proof of this—the complete refutation of earlier cavillers—also would lead us to deny him the praise of an absolutely judicial intellect. Great judges may be divided into two classes,—judges for the parties, and judges for the lawyers. The first class of these are men who always decide the particular case before them rightly; who have a nice insight into all that concerns it, are acute discerners of fact, accurate weighers of testimony, just discriminators of argument. Lord Lyndhurst is perhaps as great a judge in this kind as it is easy to fancy. If a wise man had a good cause, he would prefer its being tried before Lyndhurst to its being tried before any one else. For the 'parties,' if they were to be considered in litigation, no more would be needed. By law-students, however, and for the profession, something more is desired. They like to find, in a judicial decision, not only a correct adjustment of the particular dispute in court, but also an ample exposition of principles applicable to other disputes. The judge who is peculiarly exact in detecting the precise peculiarities of the case before him, will be very apt to decide only what is essential to, absolutely needed by, that case. His delicate discrimination will see that nothing else is necessary; he will not bestow conclusions on after-generations; he will let posterity decide its own controversies. A judge of different kind has a professional interest in what comes before him: it is in his eyes not a pitiful dispute whether A or B is entitled to a miserable field, but a glorious opportunity of deciding some legal controversy on which he has brooded for years, and on which he has a ready-made conclusion. Accordingly, his judgments are in the nature of essays. They are, in one sense, applicable to the matter in hand—they decide it correctly; but they go so much into the antecedents of the controversy—give so much of principle—that the particular facts seem a little lost: the general doctrine fills the attention. No one can read a judgment of the late Lord Cottenham without feeling that it fixed the law on the matter in hand upon a defined basis for future years; very likely he finds an authority for the case which has occurred in his practice: he does not stay to inquire whether the litigants appreciated the learning; perhaps they did not—possibly they would have preferred that a more exclusive prominence should be given to themselves. Now Lord Brougham has neither of these qualities; his intellect wants the piercing precision which distinguishes the judge—the unerring judge—of the case then present; and, though competently learned, he has never been absorbed in his profession as a judge of 'principle' almost always must be. A man cannot provide a dogma suiting all the cases of the past, and deciding all the cases for the future, without years of patient reflection. His mind must be stored with doctrines. No one can fancy this of Lord Brougham. He is not to be thought of as giving still attention to technical tenets, years of brooding consideration to an abstract jurisprudence. Accordingly, though an adequate, and, in his time—for his speed cleared off arrears—a most useful judge, he cannot be said to attain the first rank in the judicial scale; and such we believe is the estimation of the world.

Of the political duties of the Chancellor, and Lord Brougham's performance of them, it is not easy to speak. Many of them are necessarily secret; and the history of those times cannot yet be written. That he showed wonderful energy, zeal, and power, no one can doubt; nor that the essential defects of his character soon showed him but little qualified for an administrator. In the year 1802, Francis Horner anticipated, that if 'an active career were opened to Brougham, he would show a want of prudence and moderation;' and it is curious to read, as a commentary on it, what the Duke of Wellington wrote to Sir Robert Peel, on the 15th November 1835: 'His Majesty mentioned that Lord Brougham* had threatened he would not put the great seal to a Commission to prorogue the Parliament;' and afterwards correcting himself: 'It appears that Lord Brougham did not make the threat that he would not prorogue the Parliament, but that Lord Melbourne said he was in such a state of excitement that he might take that course.' We must wait for Lord Brougham's memoirs before we know the exact history of that time; but all the glimpses we get of it show the same picture of wildness and eccentricity.

The times—the most nearly revolutionary times which England has long seen—were indeed likely to try an excitable temperament to the utmost; but at the same time they afforded scope to a brilliant manager of men, which only such critical momentary conjunctions can do. Mr. Roebuck gives a curious instance of this:

The necessity of a dissolution had long been foreseen, and decided on by the ministers; but the King had not yet been persuaded to consent to so bold a measure; and now the two chiefs of the administration were about to intrude themselves into the royal closet, not only to advise and ask for a dissolution, but to request the King on the sudden—on this very day, and within a few hours—to go down and put an end to his parliament in the midst of the session, and with all the ordinary business of the session yet unfinished. The bolder mind of the Chancellor took the lead, and Lord Grey anxiously solicited him to *manage* the King on the occasion. So soon as they were admitted, the Chancellor, with some care and circumlocution, pro-

* The editors of Sir Robert Peel's Memoirs have left this name in blank; but if they had wished it not to be known, they should have suppressed the passage. Everybody knows who held the great seal at that time.

pounded to the King the object of the interview they had sought. The startled monarch no sooner understood the drift of the Chancellor's somewhat periphrastic statement, than he exclaimed in wonder and amazement against the very idea of such a proceeding. 'How is it possible, my lords, that I can after this fashion repay the kindness of parliament to the Queen and myself? They have just granted me a most liberal civil-list, and to the Queen a splendid annuity in case she survives me.' The Chancellor confessed that they had, as regarded his Majesty, been a liberal and wise parliament, but said that nevertheless their further existence was incompatible with the peace and safety of the kingdom. Both he and Lord Grey then strenuously insisted upon the absolute necessity of their request, and gave his Majesty to understand, that this advice was by his ministers unanimously resolved on; and that they felt themselves unable to conduct the affairs of the country in the present condition of the parliament. This last statement made the King feel that a general resignation would be the consequence of a further refusal; of this, in spite of his secret wishes, he was at the moment really afraid, and therefore he, by employing petty excuses, and suggesting small and temporary difficulties, soon began to show that he was about to yield. 'But, my lords, nothing is prepared; the great officers of state are not summoned.' 'Pardon me, sir,' said the Chancellor, bowing with profound apparent humility, 'we have taken the great liberty of giving them to understand that your Majesty commanded their attendance at the proper hour.' 'But, my lords, the crown, and the robes, and other things needed, are not prepared.' 'Again I most humbly entreat your majesty's pardon for my boldness,' said the Chancellor; 'they are all prepared and ready,—the proper officers being desired to attend in proper form and time.' 'But, my lords,' said the King, reiterating the form in which he put his objection, 'you know the thing is wholly impossible; the guards, the troops, have had no orders, and cannot be ready in time.' This objection was in reality the most formidable one. The orders to the troops on such occasions emanate always directly from the King, and no person but the King can in truth command them for such service; and as the Prime Minister and daring Chancellor well knew the nature of royal susceptibility on such matters, they were in no slight degree doubtful and anxious as to the result. The Chancellor therefore, with some real hesitation, began again as before, 'Pardon me, sir, we know how bold the step is that, presuming on your great goodness, and your anxious desire for the safety of your kingdom, and happiness of your people, we have presumed to take. I have given orders, and the troops are ready.' The King started in serious anger, flamed red in the face, and burst forth with, 'What, my lords, have you dared to act thus? Such a thing was never heard of. You, my Lord Chancellor, ought to know that such an act is treason, high treason, my lord.' 'Yes, sir,' said the Chancellor, 'I do know it; and nothing but my thorough knowledge of your Majesty's goodness, of your paternal anxiety for the good of your people, and my own solemn belief that the safety of the state depends upon this day's proceedings, could have emboldened me to the performance of so unusual, and, in ordinary circumstances, so improper a proceeding. In all humility, I submit myself to your Majesty, and am ready in my own person to bear all the blame, and receive all the punishment which your Majesty may deem needful; but I again entreat your Majesty to listen to us and to follow our counsel, and as you value the security of your crown and the peace of your realms, to yield to our most earnest solicitations.' After some further expostulations by both his ministers, the King cooled down and consented. Having consented, he became anxious that every thing should be done in the proper manner, and gave minute directions respecting the ceremonial. The speech to be spoken by him at the prorogation was ready prepared and in the Chancellor's pocket. To this he agreed, desired that every body might punctually attend, and dismissed his ministers for the moment with something between a menace and a joke upon the audacity of their proceeding.

With the fall of Lord Melbourne's first administration terminated Lord Brougham's administrative career. As every one knows, on the defeat of Sir Robert Peel and the subsequent return of the Whigs to power, he was not invited to resume office. Since that time,—for now more than twenty years,—he has had to lead the life, in general the most trying to political reputation, perhaps to real character and more than any other alien to the character of his mind and the tendencies of his nature. We have had many recent instances how difficult it is to give what is variously termed an 'independent support,' and a 'friendly opposition,' to a government of which you approve the general tendencies, but are inclined to criticise the particular measures. The Peelites and Lord John Russell have for several years been in general in this position, and generally with a want of popular sympathy. As they agree with the Government in principle, they cannot take, by way of objection, what the country considers broad points; their suggestions of detail seem petty and trivial to others,—the public hardly think of such things; but men who have long considered a subject, who have definite ideas and organised plans, can scarcely help feeling an eager interest in the smallest minutiæ of the mode of dealing with it: sometimes they discern a real importance undiscerned by those less attentive; more commonly, perhaps, they fancy there is something peculiarly felicitous in contrivances settled by themselves and congenial to their habits or their notions. Lord Brougham was in a position to feel this peculiarly. The various ideas which he had struggled for in earlier life were successful one by one; the hundred reforms he suggested were carried; the hundred abuses he had denounced were abolished. The world which *was*, was changed to the world which *is*; but it was not changed by him. That he should have been favourably disposed to the existing liberal administrations was not likely; the separation was too recent, perhaps too abrupt. An eager and excitable disposition is little likely to excel in the measured sentences, the chosen moments, the polished calm of the *frondeur*. Accordingly, the life of Brougham for many years has not been favourable to his fame. On particular occasions, as on the abolition of Negro apprenticeship, he might attain something of his former power. But, in general, his position has been that of the agitator whose measure is being substantially carried, yet with differences of detail aggravating to his temper and annoying to his imagination. Mr. Cobden described Sir Robert Peel's mode of repealing the corn-laws with the microscopic sliding-scale for three years, as seventeen-and-sixpence on the demand of the Anti-Corn-Law League, and good security for the other half-crown. Yet excitable men at that very moment clamoured for the last half-crown; they could not bear the modification, the minute difference from that on which they had set their hearts. We must remember this in relation to what is now most familiar to us in the life of Lord Brougham. To a man so active, to be out of action is a pain which few can appreciate; that other men should enter into your labours is not pleasant; that they should be Canningites does not make it any better. We have witnessed many escapades of Lord Brougham; we perhaps hardly know his temptations and his vexations.

Such is the bare outline of the career of Lord Brougham. A life of early, broken, various agitation; a short interval of ordinary administration,—occurring, however, at a time singularly extraordinary; a long old age secluded from the actual conduct of affairs, and driven to distinguish itself by miscellaneous objection and diversified sarcasm. Singular stories of eccentricity and excitement, even of something more than either of these, darken these latter years. On these we must not dwell. There are many aspects of his varied character, a few of which we should notice by themselves.

The most connected with his political life is his career as a law reformer. We have spoken of his early labours on this subject; we have said, that few men who have devoted themselves to nothing else have exposed so many abuses, propounded so many remedies; that one of his early notions is a schedule of half, and much more than half, that has been, or will be, done upon a large portion of the subject. But here praise must end. The completed, elaborated reforms by which Lord Brougham will be known to posterity are few, are nothing in comparison with his power, his industry, and his opportunities. There is nothing, perhaps, for which he is so ill qualified. The bold vehement man who exposes an abuse has rarely the skilful, painful, dissecting power which expunges it. Lord Brougham once made a speech on conveyancing. 'I should not,' said, on the next day, an eminent professor of that art, 'like him to draw a deed relating to my property.' A law reformer, in order that his work may be perfect, requires the conveyancing abilities. He must be able to bear in mind the whole topic,—draw out what is necessary of it on paper,—to see what is necessary,—to discriminate the rights of individuals,—to distinguish, with even metaphysical nicety, the advantage he would keep from the abuse he would destroy. He must elaborate enacting clauses which will work in the complicated future, repealing clauses which will not interfere with the complicated machinery of the past. His mind must be the mind of a codifier. A rushing man, like Lord Brougham, must not hope to have this. A still and patient man, in quiet chambers, apt in niceties, anxious by temperament, precise in habit, putting the last extreme of perfection on whatever he may attempt, is the man for the employment. You must not expect this quiet precision from an agitator. There is the same difference as that between the striking pugilist[4] and the delicate amputating operator.

The same want of repose has impaired his excellence in a pursuit to which, at first sight, it seems much less needful—the art of oratory. We are apt to forget that oratory is an imaginative art. From our habits of business, the name of rhetoric has fallen into disrepute: our greatest artists strive anxiously to conceal their perfection in it; they wish their address in statement to be such that the effect seems to be produced by that which is stated, and not by the manner in which it is stated. But not the less on that account is there a real exercise of the imagination in conceiving of the events of a long history, in putting them forward in skilful narration, each fact seeming by nature to fall into its place, all the details appearing exactly where they should,— a group, to borrow a metaphor from another art, collecting itself from

4 Morgan and Hutton have 'hand-striking' pugilist.

straggling and desultory materials. Still more evidently is the imagination requisite in expressing deep emotions, even common emotions,
or in describing noble objects. Now, it seems to be a law of the imagination that it only works in a mind of stillness. The noise and crush of
life jar it. 'No man,' it has been said, 'can say, I *will* compose poetry;'
he must wait until—from a brooding, half-desultory inaction—poetry
may arise, like a gentle mist, delicately and of itself.

> I waited for the train at Coventry;
> I hung with grooms and porters on the bridge
> To watch the three tall spires; and there I shaped
> The city's legend into this.[5]

Lord Brougham would not have waited so. He would have rushed up
into the town; he would have suggested an improvement, talked the
science of the bridge, explained its history to the natives. The quiet
race would think twenty people had been there. And of course, in
some ways this is admirable; such life and force are rare; even the
'grooms and porters' would not be insensible to such an aggressive
intelligence,—so much knocking mind. But in the mean time no lightly-
touched picture of old story would have arisen on his imagination. The
city's legend would have been thrust out: the 'fairy frostwork' of the
fancy would have been struck away: there would be talk on the school-
ing of the porter's eldest boy. The rarity of great political oratory
arises in a great measure from this circumstance. Only those engaged
in the jar of life have the material for it; only those withdrawn into a
brooding imagination have the faculty for it. M. Lamartine has drawn
a striking picture of one who had the opportunity of action and the
dangerous faculty of leisure: 'Vergniaud s'envirait dans cette vie
d'artiste, de musique, de déclamation et de plaisirs; il se pressait de
jouir de sa jeunesse, comme s'il eût le pressentiment qu'elle serait
sitôt cueillie. Ses habitudes étaient méditatives et paresseuses. Il se
levait au milieu du jour; il écrivait peu et sur des feuilles éparses; il
appuyait le papier sur ses genoux comme un homme pressé qui se
dispute le temps; il composait ses discours lentement dans ses rêveries
et les retenait à l'aide de notes dans sa mémoire; il polissait son
éloquence à loisir, comme le soldat polit son arme au repos.' This is
not the picture of one who is to attain eminence in stirring and com-

[5] Tennyson, *Godiva*—Ed.

bative times: harsher men prevailed; a mournful fate swallowed up his delicate fancies. He died, because he was idle; but he was great, because he was idle. Idleness with such minds is only the name for the passive enjoyment of a just-moving imagination.[6]

We should only weary our readers with a repetition of what has been said a hundred times already, if we tried to explain that Lord Brougham has nothing of this. His merit is, that he was never idle in his life. He must not complain if he has the disadvantage of it also. That he was a most effective speaker in his great time, is of course undoubted. His power of sarcasm, his amazing readiness, his energetic vigour of language, made him, if not a very persuasive, at least a most formidable orator. His endless animation must tell even to excess upon his audience. But he has not acted wisely for his fame in publishing his speeches. They have the most unpardonable of all faults,—the fault of dullness. It is scarcely possible to read them. Doubtless, at the time their influence was considerable; they may even have been pleasant, as you like to watch the play of a vicious horse; but now, removed from the hearing of the speaker's voice,—out of the way of the motions of his face and the glare of his eye,—even their evil-speaking loses its attractiveness. The sarcasm seems blunt,—the denunciation heavy. They are crowded with a detail which may have been, though acute observers say it was not, attractive at the time, but which no one can endure now. Not only do you feel that you are bored, but you are not sure that you are instructed. An agitator's detail is scarcely to be trusted. His facts may be right, but you must turn historian in order to test them; you must lead a life of state-papers and old letters to know if they are true. It is perhaps possible for the imagination of man to give an interest to any considerable action of human life. A firmly-drawing hand may conduct us through the narration,—an enhancing touch enliven the details; but to achieve this with contested facts in a combative life is among the rarest operations of a rare power. The imagination has few tasks so difficult. To Lord Brougham, least of all, has it been possible to attract men by the business detail and cumbrous aggressions of the last age. His tone is too harsh. He has shattered his contemporaries, but he will not charm posterity.

Lord Brougham has wished to be known not only as an orator but as a writer on oratory. He has written a 'Discourse' on ancient oratory, recommending, and very deservedly, its study to those who

---

[6] Morgan and Hutton have 'justly moving imagination'.

would now excel in the art; and there is no denying that he has rivalled the great Greek orator; at least in one of his characteristic excellencies. There is no more manly book in the world than Brougham's Speeches; he always 'calls a spade a spade,' the rough energy strikes; we have none of the tawdry metaphor, or half-real finery of the inferior orators, there is not a simile which a man of sense should not own. Nevertheless, we are inclined to question whether his studies on the ancient oratory, especially on the great public oration of Demosthenes, have been entirely beneficial to him. These masterly productions were, as every one knows, the eager expression of an intense mind on questions of the very best interest; they have accordingly the character of vehemence. Speaking on subjects which he thought involved the very existence of his country, he could not be expected to speak very temperately; he did not, and could not admit, that there was fair ground for difference of opinion; that an equally patriotic person, after proper consideration, could by possibility arrive at an opposite conclusion. The circumstances of the parliamentary orator in this country are quite different; a man cannot discuss the dowry of the princess royal, the conditions of the Bank charter, as if they were questions of existence—all questions arising now present masses of fact, antecedents in blue-books, tabulated statistics, on which it is impossible that there should not be a necessity for an elaborate inquiry—that there should not be discrepancy of judgment after that inquiry. The Demosthenic vehemence is out of place. The calm didactic exposition, almost approaching to that of the lecturer, is more efficacious than the intense appeal of an eager orator. That 'Counsellor Broom was all in a fume,' is a line in one of the best ludicrous poems of a time rather fertile in such things; on points of detail it is ridiculous to be in a passion; on matters of business it is unpersuasive to be enthusiastic; even on topics less technical, the Greek oratory is scarcely a model to be imitated precisely. A certain nonchalant ease pervades our modern world—we affect an indifference we scarcely feel; our talk is light, almost to affectation; our best writing is the same; we suggest rather than elaborate, hint rather than declaim. The spirit of the ancient world was very different —the tendency of its conversation probably was, to a rhetorical formality, an haranguing energy; certainly it is the tendency of its written style. 'With every allowance,' says Colonel Mure, 'for the peculiar genius of the age in which the masterpieces of Attic prose were produced,—a consideration which must always have a certain weight in literary judgments,—still, the impartial modern critic cannot but discern in this pervading rhetorical tone a defect, perhaps the only serious defect, in the classical Greek style. . . . It certainly is not natural for the historian or the popular essayist to address his readers in the same tone in which the defender of a client, or the denouncer of a political opponent, addresses a public assembly.' So great a change in the general world, in the audience to be spoken to, requires a change in the speaker. The light touch of Lord Palmerston is more effective than the most elaborated sentences of a formal rhetorician. Of old, when conversation and writing were half oratorical, oratory might be very oratorical; now that conversation is very conversational, oratory must be a little conversational. In real life, Lord Brougham has too much of the orator's tact not to be half aware of this; but his teaching forgets it.

That Lord Brougham should have adopted a theory enjoining vehemence in oratory, is an instance to be cited by those who hold that a man's creed is a justification for his inclinations. He is by nature over-vehement, and what is worse, it is not vehemence of the best kind; there is something of a scream about it. People rather laughed at his kneeling to beseech the peers. No one quite feels there is real feeling in what he reads and hears, it seems like a machine going. Lord Cockburn has an odd anecdote. An old judge, who loved dawdling, disliked the 'discomposing qualities' of Brougham. His revenge consisted in sneering at Brougham's eloquence, by calling it or him *the Harangue*. 'Well, gentlemen, what did *the Harangue* say next? Why it said this (misstating it); but here, gentlemen, *the Harangue* was wrong and not intelligible.' We have some feeling for the old judge. If you take a speech of Brougham, and read it apart from his voice, you have half a notion that it is a gong going, eloquence by machinery, an incessant talking *thing*.

It is needless to point out how completely an excitable ungenial nature, such as we have so much spoken of, incapacitates Lord Brougham for abstract philosophy. His works on that subject are sufficiently numerous, but we are not aware that even his most ardent admirers have considered them as works of really the first class; it would not be difficult to extract from the *Political Philosophy*, which is probably the best of them, singular instances of inconsistency and of confusion. The error was in his writing them: he who runs may *read*, but it does not seem likely he will think. The brooding disposition, and the still investigating intellect, are necessary for consecutive reasonings on delicate philosophy.

The same qualities, however, fit a man for the acquisition of general information. A man who is always rushing into the street will become familiar with the street. One who is for ever changing from subject to subject will not become painfully acquainted with any one, but he will know the outsides of them all, and the road from each to the other. Accordingly, all the descriptions of Lord Brougham, even in his earliest career, speak of his immense information. Mr. Wilberforce, in perhaps the earliest printed notice of him, recommended Mr. Pitt to employ him in a diplomatic capacity, on account of his familiarity with languages, and the other kinds of necessary knowledge. He began by writing on porisms;[7] only the other day he read a paper on some absurdities imputed to the integral calculus, in French, at Paris. It would be in the highest degree tedious to enumerate all the subjects he knows something of. Of course, an extreme correctness cannot be expected. 'The most *mis*informed man in Europe,' is a phrase of satire; yet, even in its satire, it conveys a compliment to his information.

An especial interest in physical science may be remarked in Brougham, as in most men of impressible minds in his generation. He came into life when the great discoveries in our knowledge of the material world were either just made, or on the eve of being made. These enormous advances, which have been actually made in material civilisation, were half anticipated. There was a vague hope in science. The boundaries of the universe, it was hoped, would move. Active, ardent minds were drawn with extreme action[8] to the study of new moving power; a smattering of science was immeasurably less common then than now, but it exercised a stronger dominion, and influenced a higher class of genius. It was new, and men were sanguine. In the present day, younger men are perhaps repelled into the opposite extreme. We live among the marvels of science, but we know how little they change us. The essentials of life are what they were. We go by the train, but we are not improved at our journey's end. We have railways, and canals, and manufactures,—excellent things, no doubt, but they do not touch the soul. Somehow, they seem to make life more superficial. With a half-wayward dislike, some in the present generation

---

[7] Mathematical propositions concerned with the conditions that will render a given problem capable of innumerable solutions.—Ed.
[8] Morgan and Hutton have 'extreme hope' for 'extreme action'.

have turned from physical science and material things. 'We have tried these, and they fail,' is the feeling. 'What is the heart of man the better for galvanic engines and hydraulic presses? Leave us to the old poetry and the old philosophy; there is at least a life and a mind.' It is the day after the feast. We do not care for its delicacies; we are rather angry at its profusion: we are cross to hear it praised. Men who came into active life half a century ago were the guests invited to the banquet; they did not know what was coming, but they heard it was something gorgeous and great; they expected it with hope and longing. The influence of this feeling was curiously seen in the Useful Knowledge Society, the first great product of the educational movement in which Lord Brougham was the most ardent leader. No one can deny that their labours were important, their intentions excellent, the collision of mind which they created most beneficial. Still, looking to their well-known publications, beyond question the knowledge they particularly wished to diffuse is, according to the German phrase, 'factish.' Hazlitt said, 'they confounded a knowledge of useful things with useful knowledge.' An idea, half unconscious, pervades them, that a knowledge of the detail of material knowledge, even too of the dates and shell of outside history, are extremely important to the mass of men; that all will be well when we have a cosmical ploughboy, and a mob that knows hydrostatics. We shall never have it; but even if we could, we should not be much the better. The heart and passions of men are moved by things more within their attainment; the essential nature is stirred by the essential life; by the real actual existence of love, and hope, and character, and by the real literature which takes in its spirit, and which is in some sort its undefecated essence. Thirty years ago the preachers of this now familiar doctrine were unknown; nor was their gospel for a moment the one perhaps most in season. It was good that there should be a more diffused knowledge of the material world; and it was good, therefore, that there should be partisans of matter, believers in particles, zealots for tissue, who were ready to incur any odium and any labour that a few more men might learn a few more things. How a man of incessant activity should pass easily to such a creed is evident. He would see the obvious ignorance. The less obvious argument, which shows that this ignorance, in great measure inevitable, was of far less importance than would be thought at first sight, would never be found by one who moved so rapidly.

We have gone through now, in some hasty way, most of the lights in which Lord Brougham has been regarded by his contemporaries. There is still another character in which posterity will especially think him. He is a great memoirist. His *Statesmen of George III* contains the best sketches of the political men of his generation, one with another, which the world has, or is likely to have. He is a fine painter of the exterior of human nature. Some portion of its essence requires a deeper character; another portion, more delicate sensations; but of the rough appearance of men as they struck him in the law-court and in parliament,—of the great debater struggling with his words,—the stealthy advocate gliding into the confidence of the audience,—the great judge unravelling all controversies, and deciding by a well-weighed word all complicated doubts,—of such men as these, and of men engaged in such tasks as these, there is no greater painter perhaps than Brougham. His eager aggressive disposition brought him into collision with conspicuous men; his skill in the obvious parts of human nature has made him understand them. A man who has knocked his head against a wall,—if such an illustration is to be hazarded,—will learn the nature of the wall. Those who have passed fifty years in managing men of the world, will know their external nature, and, if they have literary power enough, will describe it. In general, Lord Brougham's excellence as a describer of character is confined to men whom he had thus personally and keenly encountered. The sketches of the philosophers of the eighteenth century, of French statesmen, are poor and meagre. He requires evidently the rough necessities of action to make him observe. There is, however, a remarkable exception. He preserves a singularly vivid recollection of the instructors of his youth; he nowhere appears so amiable as in describing them. He is over-partial, no doubt; but an old man may be permitted to reverence, if he can reverence, his schoolmaster.

This is all that our limits will permit us to say of Lord Brougham: on so varied a life, at least on a life with such varied pursuits, one might write to any extent. The regular biographer will come in after years. It is enough for a mere essayist to sketch, or strive to sketch, in some rude outline, the nature of the man.

The Death of Lord Brougham[1]

S OME one said of the quiet old age of Wilkes that he was a 'Volcano burnt out,' and much the same is true of Brougham. Of so little importance was his death, and so natural was it that a man of nearly ninety should die, that the event was not even telegraphed to England from the South of France where it happened. Perhaps, if years ago, in the eager vigour of his genius, he had been told that such would be the end, it would have been one of the keenest pains he ever could have felt. His love of fame, as his friends would call it; his vanity, as his enemies would say (if, indeed, his real enemies have not now all died out),—would have felt more than most things the fact of quiet and silent extinction.

No one, however, who knows, whether by memory or by study, the recent political history of England, can hear with indifference that 'Henry Brougham,' as men used to call him, is no more. His name carries us back to a period which seems far longer ago than in years it is, to the time before the Reform Bill of 1832. It was in the reign of Toryism, after the peace, that Lord Brougham gained his renown, and those are the years of his life that will live in history. What the Toryism of that time was—how short-sighted and how ignorant—is almost forgotten. Dr. Arnold used to call the eighteenth century the 'misused trial time of modern Europe;' it would be much truer to call the years from 1815 to 1832 the misused trial time of the Tory party in England. They had a remarkable advantage; the French war had ended in a splendid victory; and the ministry who had managed the war naturally gained the credit. Their rule was popular in the country. If they had governed with intelligence and moderation—if they had governed as Mr. Pitt governed before, and Mr. Canning tried to govern afterwards —subsequent history might have been much changed. But they governed in the spirit of Lord Eldon and Lord Sidmouth; they made no concessions; they tried to keep *everything* as it was; they made the

---

[1] This article was first published in *The Economist* for May 16 1868, Volume XXVI, pp. 555—6.

existing Government responsible for every kind of abuse; they not only upheld the prerogative of the Crown and the power of the House of Lords, but cheating in charities and death for petty larceny. We wish the Marquis of Salisbury would leave the Great Eastern Railway to other hands, and write the history of the Tories after the peace. We should then know—not from a Liberal who must be prejudiced, but from a Tory attached to real Toryism—how narrow were the opinions, and how pernicious was the conduct, of those who ruled when Toryism was predominant. They would amend no grievance, because it might impair the English Constitution, and so they made themselves and the Constitution responsible for all grievances.

This was just the opportunity for a great agitator, and Lord Brougham had the gifts of a great agitator. If you take up the volumes of the old debates in Parliament, you will not turn many pages without finding Mr. Brougham calling attention to some grievance, and proposing some reform. Slavery, the state of the representation, the cruelty of the criminal law, the cost of the civil law, the harsh acts of an unsympathising administration—all these, and a hundred similar subjects, were for ever on his lips. A wonderful versatility and vast physical power were at his command, and he used them in the cause of the people. There was nothing democratic in his principles; on the contrary, like most of the original Edinburgh reviewers, he held some opinions which would now be thought much too inclined to aristocracy. But he had a strong sense of justice, an intense dislike of human misery, an overpowering impulse to expose fraud, an utter contempt for stupid administration; and these were the qualities then wanting. A Liberal politician is said to have observed in Lord Palmerston's time, when some one regretted the decline of energy in the Liberal party—'Ah! we could be as great men as our fathers if we had but their grievances;' and in this respect Lord Brougham was very happy, for he lived in the age of grievances, and had every faculty fitted to expose them.

Lord Brougham had the first great essential of an agitator—the faculty of easy anger. He was sure that he did well to be angry on a hundred occasions. To the end of his life—in the peaceful repose of a long old age—he kept this faculty. There was a vicious look about him always; 'if he was a horse, no one would buy him with that eye,' some one is reported to have said; and many persons who joined with him in benevolent undertakings were unpleasantly reminded by sudden outbreaks that philanthropy and conciliation are by no means always united. To the last, a sudden eruption was apt to terrify his quiet co-operators. But in his zenith, a bad temper was of singular use. He could, without any notice, state a grievance with appropriate indignation; most men require an interval to prepare their wrath, but Lord Brougham's was always boiling and only needed a vent. If others could find the occasion of complaint he could always add the vehemence.

In later life, his natural gifts were not so suited to his circumstances. There was something unfitting—so it was thought and so perhaps it was—in making a great agitator Lord Chancellor; it seemed like making a field preacher Archbishop of Canterbury. No doubt Lord Brougham was a very fair judge, and the stories which were once circulated as to his incompetence have long ceased to be believed. But, at the same time, he was not a great judge. No one will ever refer to his judgments as materials for future decisions; they contain long and rolling sentences, but they are defective in compact principle. It requires the meditation of a life to be a master of legal principle, and Lord Brougham never meditated, least of all upon law. Nor had he the fine tact for truth, in fact, which has distinguished some judges. At the bar he never was a good 'verdict getter,' as the phrase is; he never had the precise instinct of the very words in which to present to a jury the particular case, which some men, otherwise greatly his inferiors, largely possessed. He talked about and about the point, but he did not delicately hit it without apparent effort, and as if by accident. The same want of intuitive perception followed him to the bench; he was inferior to Lyndhurst as a judge, just as he was inferior to Scarlett as an advocate.

In Brougham's case, as in so many, his defects were the exaggerations of his merits. Versatility was his great power, and he was always trying to do everything and to do everything at once. When he was Chancellor he wrote a treatise on hydrostatics, which had to be much altered, if not rewritten, before it could see the light; and the records of the time are full of anecdotes, in part exaggerated but in substance true, of the universality of his efforts and the eccentricity of his transitions. Why precisely he had to leave political life has never been stated on authority; but it was, doubtless, connected with the feverishness of his energy, and the incalculability of his actions.

A still more evil genius induced him to attempt 'political philosophy.' A poorer book or a worse was never written by a man of great abilities and great political experience than his elaborate treatise on that subject. The Tory lawyers used to say of him—'He means to decide well; he tries to think, but he can't.' And his political philosophy proves that upon remote, abstract subjects he really could not think. He was not quiet enough, and could not keep still. His philosophical reflections are always pompous, and when new mostly nugatory. By a happy thought, however, he has attained a literary fame likely to last. He roughly sketched for the 'Edinburgh Review' some outlines of men whom he had known. This was some thirty years ago; but even then he was an old statesman dwelling on the past, and losing his hold upon the present. These sketches have been expanded and republished, and are as pleasant reading as any one is likely to find. He had, so to say, knocked against every considerable man of his time, and his retentive memory preserved an accurate note of the collision. Upon history these 'sketches' will probably have a decisive effect, for the agreeable books are those which historians read most thoroughly, and which fasten most upon their minds. Probably Lord Brougham little thought that it was by these hasty sketches—the casual task of some waste hour—that he would gain his most lasting influence, yet even now they are the only writings of his which are read; his treatises and speeches no one touches.

In quality Lord Brougham's life may be easily rivalled, but not in quantity. No one is likely to press so much life into the same time as he did into his first fifty years. There was in him, and in some of his contemporaries too, a certain titanic energy, an unresting, superfluous, nervous power, which the present generation do not possess, and which some of them envy. The race seems to have grown smaller and weaker if finer, like the second race of Greek deities as compared with the first. There are many men who can do better things than Lord Brougham, but no living Englishman is probably his equal in incessant vigour, vehement passion, and many-handed energy.

Lord Althorp
Introductory note

John Charles Spencer, Viscount Althorp and Earl Spencer (1782–1845), the eldest son of George John, second Earl Spencer, and of Lavinia Bingham, was born at Spencer House, St. James, London. In childhood he was left to the care of servants; in 1790 he went to Harrow, and from 1800–2 was at Trinity College, Cambridge. He had by this time acquired the passionate enthusiasm for field sports which he retained all his life. He became M.P. for Okehampton in 1804; M.P. for St. Albans in 1806, and was M.P. for Northamptonshire 1806–34. For many years he seldom spoke in Parliament or interested himself in politics at all, devoting himself to the Pytchley hunt, racing, and prize fights, but his admiration for Fox eventually drew him into active politics. He began to study economic history and working-class grievances, supporting Huskisson and Joseph Hume, and in 1830 became leader of the Whig opposition in the Commons. In December of that year he became Chancellor of the Exchequer and leader of the lower House under Earl Grey, after Wellington's resignation. He returned to office with an increased Whig majority in 1831, and when the Lords rejected the Reform Bill in October, he showed his zeal for the Bill by the energy with which he rallied his followers. He saw the Bill pass the Lords in June, 1832. At the rise of Peel, Spencer began to lose influence and retained office only very reluctantly until he succeeded to the Earldom in 1834. He then withdrew from politics to his country pursuits, reappearing only in 1841 to speak in favour of the repeal of the Corn Laws. Lord Althorp died at Wiseton Hall, Northamptonshire, in 1845.

Lord Althorp and the Reform Act of 1832[1]

'ALTHORP carried the Bill,' such is the tradition of our fathers, 'the Bill,' of course, being *the* Bill to them—the great Reform Act of 1832, which was like a little revolution in that generation,—which really changed so much, and which seemed to change so much more. To have been mainly concerned in passing so great a measure seems to many of the survivors of that generation, who remember the struggles of their youth and recall the enthusiasm of that time, almost the *acme* of fame. And in sober history such men will always be respectfully and gravely mentioned, but all romance has died away. *The* Bill is to us hardly more than other bills; it is one of a great many Acts of Parliament which in this day, partly for good and partly for evil, have altered the ever-varying constitution of England. The special charm, the charm which to the last you may see that Macaulay always felt about it, is all gone. The very history of it is forgotten. Which of the younger generation can say what was General Gascoigne's amendment, or who were the 'waverers,' or even how many Reform 'Bills' in those years there were? The events for which one generation cares most are often those of which the next knows least. They are too old to be matters of personal recollection, and they are too new to be subjects of study: they have passed out of memory, and they have not got into the books. Of the well-informed young people about us, there are very many who scarcely know who Lord Althorp was.

And in another respect this biography has been unfortunate. It has been kept too long. The Reform Act of 1867 has shed a painful light on the Reform Act of 1832, and has exhibited in real life what philosophers said were its characteristic defects. While these lingered in the books they were matters of dull teaching, and no one cared for them; but now Mr. Disraeli has embodied them, and they are living

---

[1] This essay was first published in the *Fortnightly Review* for November 1876, Volume XX [N.S.], pp. 574–600. In form it was a review of 'Memoir of John Charles, Viscount Althorp, third Earl Spencer. By the late Sir Denis Le Marchant, Bart. London: Richard Bentley and Son, 1876.' Oddly enough there is no mention of this in the heading of the original *Fortnightly* article.

among us. The traditional sing-song of mere eulogy is broken by a sharp question. Those who study that time say, 'Althorp, you tell us, passed the Bill. It was his frankness and his high character and the rest of his great qualities which did it. But was it good that he should have passed it? Would it not have been better if he had not possessed those fine qualities? Was not some higher solution possible? Knowing this Bill by its fruits, largely good, but also largely evil, might we not have had a better Bill? At any rate, if it could not be so, show *why* it could not be so. Prove that the grave defects in the Act of 1832 were necessary defects. Explain how it was that Althorp had no choice, and then we will admire him as you wish us.' But to this biographer—a man of that time, then in the House of Commons on the Whig side, and almost, as it were, on the skirts of the Bill—such questions would have seemed impossible. To him, the Act of 1832 is still wonderful and perfect—the great measure which *we* carried in *my* youth; and as for explaining defects in it, he would have as soon thought of explaining defects in a revelation.

But if ever Lord Althorp's life is well written, it will, I think, go far to explain not only why the Reform Bill was carried, but why that Bill is what it was. He embodies all the characteristic virtues which enable Englishmen to effect well and easily great changes in politics: their essential fairness, their 'large roundabout common sense,' their courage, and their disposition rather to give up something than to take the uttermost farthing. But on the other hand also he has all the characteristic English defects: their want of intellectual and guiding principle, their even completer want of the culture which would give that principle, their absorption in the present difficulty, and their hand-to-mouth readiness to take what solves it without thinking of other consequences. And I am afraid the moral of those times is that these English qualities as a whole—merits and defects together—are better suited to an early age of politics than to a later. As long as materials are deficient, these qualities are most successful in hitting off simple expedients, in adapting old things to new uses, and in extending ancient customs; they are fit for instantaneous little creations, and admirable at bit-by-bit growth. But when, by the incessant application of centuries, these qualities have created an accumulated mass of complex institutions, they are apt to fail, unless aided by others very different. The instantaneous origination of obvious expedients is of no use when the field is already covered with the heterogeneous growth of complex past expedients; bit-by-bit development is out of place unless you are sure which bit should and which bit should not be developed; the extension of customs may easily mislead when there are so many customs; no immense and involved subject can be set right except by faculties which can grasp what is immense and scrutinise what is involved. But mere common sense is here matched with more than it can comprehend, like a schoolboy in the differential calculus;—and absorption in the present difficulty is an evil, not a good, for what is wanted is that you should be able to see many things at once, and take in their bearings, not fasten yourself on one thing. The characteristic danger of great nations, like the Romans or the English, which have a long history of continuous creation, is that they may at last fail from not comprehending the great institutions which they have created.

No doubt it would be a great exaggeration to say that this calamity happened in its fulness in the year 1832, and it would be most unfair to Lord Althorp to cite him as a complete example of the characteristics which may cause it; but there was something in him of those qualities, and some trace in 1832 of that calamity—enough in both cases to be a warning. Only a complete history of the time can prove this; but perhaps in a few pages I may a little explain and illustrate it.

Let us first get, both as more instructive and as less tedious than analysis, a picture of the man as he stood in the principal event of his life. A good drawer has thus painted him. Lord Jeffrey, the great Edinburgh reviewer, who was an able lawyer and practical man of business in his day, though his criticism on poetry[2] has not stood the test of time, was Lord Advocate in the Reform Ministry of 1830, and he is never tired of describing Lord Althorp:—'There is something,' he writes, 'to me quite delightful in his calm, clumsy, courageous, immutable probity, and it seems to have a charm for everybody.' 'I went to Althorp,' he writes, 'again, and had a characteristic scene with that most honest, frank, true, and stout-hearted of God's creatures. He had not come down-stairs, and I was led up to his dressing-room, with his arms (very rough and hairy) bare above the elbows, and his beard half-shaved and half staring through the lather, with a desperate razor in one hand, and a great soap-brush in the other. He gave me the loose finger of his brush hand, and with the usual twinkle of his bright eye and radiant smile, he said,"You need not be anxious about your Scotch bills to-night, for we are no longer his Majesty's minis-

[2] I have substituted 'poetry' for 'party'.—Ed.

ters." And soon after he writes again, at an after stage of the ministerial crisis, 'When they came to summon Lord Althorp to a council on the Duke's giving in, he was found in a shed with a groom busy oiling the locks of his fowling-pieces, and lamenting the decay into which they had fallen during his ministry.' And on another occasion he adds what may serve as an intellectual accompaniment to these descriptions, 'Althorp, with his usual frankness, gave us a pretended confession of his political faith, and a sort of creed of his political morality, and showed that though it was a very shocking doctrine to promulgate, he must say that he had never sacrificed his own inclinations to a sense of duty without repenting it, and always found himself more substantially unhappy for having employed himself for the public good.' And some one else at the time said, 'The Government cannot be going out, for Althorp looks so very dismal.' He was made (as we learn from this volume) a principal minister, contrary to his expectation and in opposition to his wish. He was always wanting to resign; he was always uncomfortable, if not wretched, and the instant he could he abandoned politics, and would never touch them again, though he lived for many years. And this, though in appearance he was most successful, and was almost idolised by his followers and friends.

At first this seems an exception to one of nature's most usual rules. Almost always, if she gives a great faculty she gives also an enjoyment in the use of it. But here nature had given a remarkable power of ruling and influencing men—one of the most remarkable (good observers seem to say) given to any Englishman of that generation; and yet the possessor did not like, but on the contrary, much disliked to use it. The explanation, however, is, that not only had nature bestowed on Lord Althorp this happy and great gift of directing and guiding men, but, as if by some subtle compensation, had added what was, under the circumstances, a great pain to it. She had given him a most sluggish intellect—only moving with effort, and almost suffering, —generally moving clumsily, and usually following, not suggesting. If you put a man with a mind like this—especially a sensitive, conscientious man such as Lord Althorp was—to guide men quickly through complex problems of legislation and involved matters of science, no wonder that he will be restive and wish to give up. No doubt the multitude wish to follow him; but where is he to tell the multitude to go? His mind suggests nothing, and there is a pain and puzzle in his brain.

Fortune and education had combined in Lord Althorp's case to develop his defects. His father and mother were both persons of great cultivation, but they were also busy people of the world, and so they left their son to pick up his education as he could. A Swiss footman, who did not know English very well, taught him to read, and 'was his sole instructor and most intimate associate till he went to Harrow.' His father, too, being a great fox-hunter, he clearly cared more, and was more occupied with hounds and animals, as a young boy, than with anything else; and he lived mainly with servants and people also so occupied, from which, as might be expected, he contracted a shyness and awkwardness which stayed with him through life. When he went to Harrow the previous deficiencies of his education were, of course, against him, and he seems to have shown no particular disposition to repair them. As far as can now be learnt he was an ordinary strong-headed and strong-willed English boy, equal to necessary lessons, but not caring for them, and only distinguished from the rest by a certain suppressed sensibility and tenderness, which he also retained in after years, and which softened a manliness that would otherwise have been rugged, and which saved him from being unrefined.

At Cambridge his mother, as it appears, suddenly, and for the first time, took an interest in his studies, and told him she should expect him to be high at his first college examination. And this seems to have awakened him to industry. The examination was on mathematics, which suited him much better than the Harrow classics, and he really came out high in it. The second year it was the same, though he had good competitors. But there his studies ended. His being a nobleman at that time excluded him from the university examinations, and he was far too apathetic to work at mathematics, except for something of the sort, and his tutor seems to have discouraged his doing so. Then, as since, the bane of Cambridge has been a certain incomplete and rather mean way of treating great studies, which teaches implicitly, if not plainly, that it was as absurd to learn the differential calculus in and for itself as it would be to keep a ledger for its own sake. On such a mind as Lord Althorp's, which required as much as possible to be awakened and kept awake to the interest of high studies, no external surroundings could have been more fatal. He threw up his reading and took to hounds, betting, and Newmarket, and to all which was then, even if not since, thought to be most natural, if not most proper, in a young nobleman.

As far as classical studies are concerned he probably lost nothing. He was through life very opaque to literary interests, and in his letters and speeches always used language in the clumsiest way. But he had—perhaps from his childish field-sports—a keen taste for animals and natural history, which nowadays would have been developed into a serious pursuit. And as it was he had an odd craving for figures, which might have been made something of in mathematics. 'He kept,' we are told, 'an account of every shot he fired in the course of a year, whether he missed or killed, and made up the book periodically.' He would not pass the accounts of the Agricultural Society without hunting for a missing threepence; and when Chancellor of the Exchequer he used, it is said, 'to do all his calculations, however complicated, alone in his closet,' which his biographer thinks very admirable, and contrasts with the habit of Mr. Pitt, 'who used to take a Treasury clerk into his confidence,' but which was really very absurd. It is not by such mechanical work that great budgets are framed, and a great minister ought to know what *not* to do himself, and how to use, for everything possible, the minds of others. Still there is much straightforward strength in this, if also some comic dulness.

If Lord Althorp's relatives did not give him a very good education, they did not make up for it by teaching him light accomplishments. They sent him the 'grand tour,' as it was then called; but he was shy and awkward, seems to have had no previous preparation for foreign society, would not go into it, and returned boasting that he could not speak French. His mother—a woman of great fashion and high culture —must have sighed very much over so uncourtly and so 'English' an eldest son.

Then, in the easy way of those times—it was in 1804—he was brought into Parliament for Okehampton, a nomination borough, some 'Mr. Strange,' a barrister, retiring in his favour, and his interest being strong, he was made a lord of the Treasury. But the same apathy to intellectual interests which showed itself at college clung to him here also. He showed energy, but it was not the energy of a man of business. He passed, we are told, 'the greatest part of his time in the country, and when he attended at the Treasury, which was very rarely, and only on particular occasions to make up a Board, he returned home immediately afterwards. Indeed, he used to have horses posted on the road from London to Althorp, and often rode down at night, as soon as the House had risen, in order that he might hunt with

the Pytchley the next morning.' 'On these occasions,' says another
account, 'he had no sleep, and often the hacks which he rode would
fall down on the road.' And years afterwards the old clerks of the
office used to tell of the rarity and brevity of his visits to the department, and of the difficulty of getting him to stay;—all which shows
force and character, but still not the sort of character which would fit
a man to be Chancellor of the Exchequer. But though he had much of
the want of culture, Lord Althorp had none of the unfeelingness which
also the modern world is getting somehow to attach to the character
of the systematic sportsman. On the contrary, he was one of the many
instances which prove that this character may be combined with an
extreme sensibility to the sufferings of animals and man. He belonged
to the class of men in whom such feelings are far keener than usual,
and his inner character approached to the 'Arnold type,' 'for to hear
of cruelty or injustice pained him' almost 'like a blow.'

He, it seems, kept a hunting journal, which tells how his hounds
found a fox at Parson's Hill, and 'ran over old Naseby field to Althorp
in fifty minutes, and then, after a slight check, over the finest part of
Leicestershire;' and all that sort of thing. But probably it does not
tell one very natural consequence which happened to him from such a
life. Being a somewhat uncouth person, addicted to dogs and horses—
a 'man's man,' as Thackeray used to call it—he did not probably go
much into ladies' society, and was not very aggressive when he was
there. But men who do not make advances to women are apt to become victims to women who make advances to them, and so it was
with Lord Althorp. He married a Miss Acklom, a 'Diana Vernon' sort
of person, 'rather stout, and without pretension to regular beauty;'
but nevertheless, it is said, 'with something prepossessing about her—
clever, well read, with a quick insight into the character of others,
and with much self-dependence.' And this self-dependence and thought
she showed to her great advantage in the principal affair of her life.
Lord Althorp's biographer is sure, but does not say how, that the first
declaration of love was made by the lady; he was, it seems, too shy
to think of such a thing. As a rule, marriages in which a young nobleman is actively captured by an aggressive lady are not domestically
happy, though they may be socially useful, but in this case the happiness seems to have been exceptionally great; and when she died, after
a few years, he suffered a very unusual grief. 'He went,' we are told, 'at
once to Winton, the place where he had lived with her, and passed

several months in complete retirement, finding his chief occupation in reading the Bible,' in which he found, at first, many grave difficulties, such as the mention of the constellation 'Orion' by the prophet Amos, and the high place (an equality with Job and David) given by Ezekiel to the prophet Daniel when still a young man, 'and before he had proved himself to be a man of so great a calibre as he certainly did afterwards.' On these questions, he adds, 'I have consulted a Mr. Shepherd, the clergyman here, but his answers are not satisfactory.' Happily, however, such a man is not at the mercy of clergymen's answers, nor dependent[3] upon petty details of ancient prophets. The same sensibility which made him keenly alive to justice and injustice in things of this world, went further, and told him of a moral government in things not of this world. No man of or near the Arnold species was ever a sceptic as to, far less an unbeliever in, ultimate religion. New philosophies are not wanted or appreciated by such men, nor are book arguments of any real use, though these men often plod over them as if they were; for in truth an inner teaching supersedes everything, and for good or evil closes the controversy; no discussion is of any effect or force; the court of appeal, fixed by nature in such minds, is peremptory in belief, and will not hear of any doubt. And so it was in this case. Through life Lord Althorp continued to be a man strong, though perhaps a little crude, in religious belief; and thus gained at the back of his mind a solid seriousness which went well with all the rest of it. And his grief for his wife was almost equally durable. He gave up not only society, which perhaps was no great trial, but also hunting—not because he believed it to be wrong, but because he did not think it seemly or suitable that a man after such a loss should be so very happy as he knew that hunting would make him.

Soon after his marriage he had begun to take an interest in politics, especially on their moral side, and of course the increased seriousness of his character greatly augmented it. Without this change, though he might have thought he might have been occasionally useful in outlying political questions, probably he would have had no grave political career, and his life never would have been written. But the sort of interest which he took in politics requires some explanation, for though his time is not very long ago, the change of feeling since then is vast.

'If any person,' said Sir Samuel Romilly, the best of judges, for he

3 I have inserted 'dependent'.—Ed.

lived through the times and was mixed up, heart and soul, in the matters he speaks of, 'if any person be desirous of having an adequate idea of the mischievous effects which have been produced in this country by the French Revolution and all its attendant horrors, he should attempt some reforms on humane and liberal principles. He will then find not only what a stupid dread of innovation, but what a savage spirit, it has infused into the minds of his countrymen.' And very naturally, for nothing is so cruel as fear. A whole generation in England, and indeed in Europe, was so frightened by the Reign of Terror that they thought it could only be prevented by another Reign of Terror. The Holy Alliances, as they were then called, meant this and worked for this. Though we had not in name such an alliance in England, we had a state of opinion which did the work of one without one. Nine-tenths of the English people were above all things determined to put down 'French principles,' and unhappily 'French principles' included what we should all now consider obvious improvements and rational reforms. They would not allow the most cruel penal code which any nation ever had to be mitigated; they did not wish justice to be questioned; they would not let the mass of the people be educated, or at least only so that it came to nothing; they would not alter anything which came down from their ancestors, for in their terror they did not know but there might be some charmed value even in the most insignificant thing; and after what they had seen happen in France, they feared that if they changed a single iota all else would collapse.

Upon this generation, too, came the war passion. They waged, and in the main—though with many errors—waged with power and spirit, the war with Napoleon; and they connected this with their horror of liberal principles in a way which is now very strange to us, but which was very powerful then. We know now that Napoleon was the head of a conservative reaction, a bitter and unfeeling reaction, just like that of the contemporary English; but the contemporary English did not know this. To the masses of them he was *Robespierre à cheval*, as some one called him—a sort of Jacobin waging war, in some occult way, for liberty and revolution, though he called himself Emperor. Of course the educated few gradually got more or less to know that Napoleon hated Jacobins and revolution, and liberty too, as much as it is possible to hate them; but the ordinary multitude, up to the end of the struggle, never dreamed of it. Thus in an odd way the war passion of the time strengthened its conservative feeling; and in a much more usual way it did so too, for it absorbed men's minds in the story of battles and the glory of victories, and left no unoccupied thought for gradual improvement and dull reform at home. A war time, also, is naturally a harsh time; for the tale of conflicts which sometimes raises men above pain, also tends to make men indifferent to it; the familiarity of the idea ennobles but also hardens.

This savageness of spirit was the more important because, from deep and powerful economical agencies, there was an incessant distress running through society, sometimes less and sometimes more, but always, as we should now reckon, very great. The greatest cause of this was that we were carrying on, or trying to carry on, a system of Free Trade under a restrictive tariff: we would not take foreign products, and yet we wished to sell foreigners ours. And our home market was incessantly disordered. First the war and then the Corn-Laws confined us chiefly to our own soil for our food, but that soil was of course liable to fail in particular years, and then the price of food rose rapidly, which threw all other markets into confusion—for people must live first, and can only spend the surplus, after paying the cost of living, upon everything else. The fluctuations in the demand for our manufactures at home were ruinously great, though we were doing all we could to keep them out of foreign markets, and the combined effect was terrible. And the next great cause was that we were daily extending an unprecedented system of credit without providing a basis for it, and without knowing how to manage it. There was no clear notion that credit, being a promise to pay cash, must be supported by proportionate reserves of cash held in store; and that as bullion is the international cash, all international credit must be sustained by a store of bullion. In consequence all changes for the worse in trade, whether brought on by law or nature, caused a destruction of confidence, and diffused an uneasy moral feeling which made them far worse than they would have been otherwise. The immense fluctuations in our commerce, caused by protection, were aggravated by immense fluctuations in our credit, and the combined result was unspeakably disastrous.

During the French war these causes were not so much felt. Trade was better, because we were creating a foreign market for ourselves. Just as lately, by lending to a miscellaneous mass of foreign countries, we enabled those countries to buy of us, so in the great war, by large subsidies and huge foreign expenditure, we created a 'purchasing power' which was ultimately settled by our manufactures. We had nothing else to settle it with; if we did not send them direct, we must use them to buy the bullion, or whatever else it might be which we did send directly. This 'war demand,' of which so much is said in the economical literature of those years, of course ceased at the peace; and as we declined to take foreign products in exchange for ours, no substitute for it could be found, and trade languished in consequence. Agriculture, too, was worse after the peace, for the natural protection given by the war was far more effective than the artificial protection given by the Corn-Laws. The war kept out corn almost equally whatever was the price, but the Corn-Laws were based on the 'sliding scale,' which let in the corn when it became dear. Our farmers, therefore, were encouraged to grow more corn than was enough for the country in good years, which they could not sell; and they did not get a full price in bad years, for the foreign corn came in more and more as the price rose and rose. Though the protection availed to hurt the manufacturer, it was not effectual in helping the farmer. And the constant adversity of other interests, by a reflex action, also hurt him. Committees on agricultural distress, and motions as to the relief of trading distress, alternate in the parliamentary debates of those years. Our credit system, too, was in greater momentary danger after the peace than before; for during the war it was aided by a currency of inconvertible paper, which absolved us from the necessity of paying our promises in solid cash, though at very heavy cost in other ways, both at the instant and afterwards.

These fluctuations in trade and agriculture of course told on the condition of the working classes. They were constantly suffering, and then the 'savage spirit' of which Sir Samuel [Romilly] has spoken showed itself at its worst. Suffering, as usual, caused complaint, and this complaint was called sedition. The *Habeas Corpus* Act was suspended, harsh laws were passed, and a harsher administration incited to put it down. It could not be put down. It incessantly smouldered and incessantly broke out, and for years England was filled with the fear of violence, first by the breakers of the law and then by the enforcers of it.

Resistance to such a policy as this was most congenial to a nature half unhinged by misfortune, and always in itself most sensitive and opposed to injustice. Even before his wife's death, Lord Althorp had begun to exert himself against it; and afterwards he threw the whole vigour not only of his mind but of his body into it. So far from running away perpetually to hunt as in old times, he was so constant in his attendance in Parliament that tradition says hardly any one, except the clerks at the table, was more constantly to be seen there. He opposed all the Acts by which the Tory Government of the day tried to put down disaffection instead of curing it, and his manly energy soon made him a sort of power in Parliament. He was always there, always saying what was clear, strong, and manly; and therefore the loosely-knit opposition of that day was often guided by him; and the ministers though strong in numerical majority, feared him, for he said things that the best of that majority understood in a rugged English way, which changed feelings, even if it did not alter votes. He was a man whom every one in the House respected, and who therefore spoke to prepossessed hearers. No doubt, too, the peculiar tinge which grief had given to his character added to his influence. He took no share in the pleasures of other men. Though a nobleman of the highest place, still young, as we should now reckon (he was only thirty-six when Lady Althorp died), he stood aloof from society which courted him, and lived for public business only; and therefore he had great weight in it, for the English very much value obviously conscientious service, and the sobered foxhunter was a somewhat interesting character.

He had not indeed any clear ideas of the cause of the difficulties of the time, or of the remedies for them. He did no doubt attend much to economical questions; and his taste for figures, shown before in calculating the ratio of his good shots to his bad, made statistical tables even pleasing to him. His strong sense, though without culture and without originality, struggled dimly and sluggishly with the necessary problems. But considering that he lived in the days of Huskisson and Ricardo, his commercial ideas are crude and heavy. He got as far as the notion that the substitution of direct taxes for the bad tariff of those days would be 'a good measure,' but when he came to apply the principle he failed from inability to work it out. Nor did years of discussion effectually teach him. In his great budget of 1832—the first which the Whigs had made for many years, and at which therefore every one looked with unusual expectation—he proposed to take off a duty on tobacco, and to replace it by a tax on the transfer of real and funded property, together with a tax on the import of raw cotton; and it was the necessity of having to withdraw the largest part of this plan, that more than anything else first gave the Whigs that character for financial incapacity which clung to them so long. A crude good sense

goes no way in such problems, and it is useless to apply it to them. The other economical problem of the time, how to lay a satisfactory basis for our credit, Lord Althorp was still less able to solve, and excusably so; for the experience which has since taught us so much did not exist, and the best theories then known were very imperfect. The whole subject was then encumbered with what was called the 'currency question,' and on this Lord Althorp's views were fairly sensible, but no more.

I have said what may seem too much of the distresses of the country fifty or sixty years ago, not only because the mode in which he dealt with them is the best possible illustration of Lord Althorp's character, but also because some knowledge of them is necessary to an understanding of 'parliamentary reform,' as it was in his time, on account, of which alone any one now cares for him. The 'bill,' if I may say so, for these miseries of the country was sent in to the old system of parliamentary representation; and very naturally. The defenders of that system of necessity conceded that it was anomalous, complex, and such as it would have been impossible to set up *de novo*. But they argued that it was practically successful, worked well, and promoted the happiness of the people better than any other probably would. And to this the inevitable rejoinder at the time was: 'The system does not work well; the country is not happy; if your system is as you say to be judged by its fruits, that system is a bad system, for its fruits are bad, and the consequences everywhere to be seen in the misery around us.' Upon many English minds which would have cared nothing for an apparent work of theoretical completeness, this 'practical' way of arguing, as it was called, pressed with irresistible strength.

The unpopularity was greater because a new generation was growing up with 'other thoughts' and 'other minds' than that which had preceded it. Between 1828 and 1830, a new race came to influence public affairs, who did not remember the horrors of the French Revolution, and who had been teased to death by hearing their parents talk about them. The harsh and cruel spirit which those horrors had awakened in their contemporaries became itself by the natural law of reaction an object of disgust and almost of horror to the next generation. When it was said that the old structure of Parliament worked well, this new race looked not only at the evident evils amid which they lived, but at the oppressive laws and administration by which their fathers had tried to cure those evils; and they 'debited' both to the account of the old Parliament. It was made responsible for the mistaken treatment as well as for the deep-rooted disease, and so the gravest clouds hung over it.

The Duke of Wellington too (the most unsuccessful of Premiers as well as the most successful of generals), broke the Tory party —the natural party to support this system—into fragments. With a wise renunciation both of his old principles and of his fixed prejudices he had granted 'Catholic emancipation,' and so offended the older and stricter part of his followers. They accused him of treachery, and hated him with a hatred of which in this quiet age, when political passion is feeble, we can hardly form an idea. And he then quarrelled, also, with the best of the moderate right—Mr. Huskisson and the Canningites. He had disliked Mr. Canning personally when alive, he hated still more the liberal principles which he had begun to introduce into our foreign policy, and he was an eager, despotic man who disliked difference of opinion; so just when he had broken with the most irrational section of his party, he broke with its most rational members too and left himself very weak. No one so much, though without meaning it, aided the cause of parliamentary change, for he divided and enfeebled the supporters of the old system; he took away the question of Catholic Emancipation which before filled the public mind; and he intensified the unpopularity of all he touched by the idea of a 'Military Premier,' for which we should not care now, but which was odious and terrible then when men still feared oppression from the Government.

Upon minds thus predisposed the French Revolution of 1830 broke with magical power. To the young generation it seemed like the fulfilment of their dreams.

> The meagre, stale, forbidding ways
> Of custom, law, and statute took at once
> The attraction of a country in romance,

And lively natures thought that they might be

> Called upon to exercise their skill,
> Not in Utopia, subterranean fields,
> Or some secluded island, heaven knows where,
> But in the very world, which is the world
> Of all of us.[4]

[4] Wordsworth 'Prelude'.—Ed.

And even to soberer persons this new revolution seemed to prove that change, even great change, was not so mischievous as had been said—that the good of 1789 might be gained without the evil, and that it was absurd not to try reform when the unreformed world contained so much which was miserable and so much which was difficult to bear. Even a strong Tory ministry might have been overthrown, so great was the force of this sudden sentiment; the feeble ministry of the Duke of Wellington fell at once before it; and the Whigs were called to power.

Their first act was to frame a plan of parliamentary reform, and that which they constructed was many times larger than anything which any one expected from them. All those who remember those times say that when they heard what was proposed they could hardly believe their ears. And when it was explained to the House of Commons, the confusion, the perplexity, and the consternation were very great. Reform naturally was much less popular in the assembly to be reformed than it was elsewhere. The general opinion was that if Sir Robert Peel had risen at once and denounced the bill as destructive and revolutionary he might have prevented its being brought in. Another common opinion in the House was that the 'Whigs would go out next morning.' But the bill had been framed by one who, with whatever other shortcomings and defects, has ever had a shrewd eye for the probable course of public opinion. 'I told Lord Grey,' says Lord Russell, 'that none but a large measure would be a safe measure.' And accordingly, as soon as its provisions came to be comprehended by the country, there was perhaps the greatest burst of enthusiasm which England has ever seen (certainly the greatest enthusiasm for a law, though that for a favourite person may sometimes have risen as high or higher). A later satirist has spoken of it as the 'Great bill for giving everybody everything,' and everybody almost seems to have been as much in favour of it as if they were to gain everything by it. Agricultural counties were as eager as manufacturing towns; men who had always been Tories before were as warm as Liberals. The country would have 'the bill, the whole bill, and nothing but the bill.'

But this enthusiasm did not of itself secure the passing of the bill; there were many obstacles in the way, which it took months to overcome, and which often made many despair. First the bill was not one of which the political world itself strongly approved; on the contrary, if left to itself, that world would probably have altogether rejected it.

It was imposed by the uninitiated on the initiated, by the many on the few; and inevitably those who were compelled to take it did not like it. Then the vast proposals of the ministry deeply affected many private interests. In 1858 I heard an able politician say, 'The best way for a Government to turn itself out is to bring in a Reform bill; the number of persons whom every such bill must offend is very great, and they are sure to combine together, not on Reform, but on something else, and so turn out the Government.' And if there was serious danger to a ministry which ventured to propose such petty reforms as were thought of in 1858, we can imagine the magnitude of the danger which the ministry of 1832 incurred from the great measure they then brought in. One member, indeed, rose and said, 'I am the proprietor of Ludgershall, I am the member for Ludgershall, I am the constituency of Ludgershall, and in all three capacities I assent to the disfranchisement of Ludgershall.' But the number of persons who were so disinterested was small.[5] The Bill of 1832 affected the franchise of every constituency, and, therefore, the seat of every member; it abolished the seats of many, and destroyed the right of nomination to seats also possessed by many; and nothing could be more repugnant to the inclinations of most. A House of Commons with such a bill before it was inevitably captious, unruly, and difficult to guide. And even if there had been or could have been a House of Commons which at heart liked the bill, there would still have been the difficulty, that many other people then most influential did not much like it. A great many members of the Cabinet which proposed it, though they believed it to be necessary, did not think it to be desirable. The country would have some such measure, and therefore they proposed this. 'Lord Palmerston and Mr. Grant,' says Lord Russell, 'had followed Mr. Canning in his opposition to Parliamentary Reform. Lord Lansdowne and Lord Holland had never been very eager on the subject.' Lord Brougham did not approve of the disfranchisement of nearly so many boroughs, and others of the Cabinet were much of the same mind. Their opinion was always dubious, their action often reluctant, and, according to Mr. Greville, some of the most influential of them being very sensitive to the public opinion of select political society were soon 'heartily ashamed of the whole thing.'

The House of Lords, too, was adverse, not only as an assembly of men mostly rich and past middle age is ever adverse to great political

[5] The *Fortnightly Review* has 'rare' for 'small'.—p. 586.

change, or as a privileged assembly is always hostile to any movement which may destroy it, but for a reason peculiar to itself. The English House of Lords, as we all know, is not a rigid body of fixed number like the upper chambers of book constitutions, but an elastic body of unfixed number. The Crown can add to its members when it pleases and as it pleases. And in various ways which I need not enumerate now, this elasticity of structure has been of much use, but in one way it does much harm. The Crown for this purpose means the ministry; the ministry is appointed by a party, and is the agent of that party, and therefore it makes peers from its own friends all but exclusively. Under a Tory government more than nine-tenths of the new peers will be Tory; under a Whig government more than nine-tenths will be Whig; and if for a long course of years either party has been continuously, or nearly so, in power, the House of Lords will be filled with new members belonging to it. And this is a serious inconvenience, because the longer any party has been thus in power, the more likely it is to have to go out and lose power, and the new ministry which comes in, and the new mode of thought which that ministry embodies, finds itself face to face with a House of Peers embodying an antagonist mode of thought, and formed by its enemies. In 1831 this was so, for the Tories had been in office almost without a break since 1784, had created peers profusely, who were all Tories, and added the Irish elective peers who, from the mode of election, were all Tories too. In consequence the Reform movement of 1831 and 1832 found itself obstinately opposed to a hostile House of Lords, whose antagonism aided the reluctance diffused through the House of Commons, and fostered the faint-heartedness common in the Cabinet. The King, too, who had begun by being much in favour of reform, gradually grew frightened. His correspondence with Lord Grey gives a vivid picture of a well-meaning, but irresolute man, who is much in the power of the last speaker, who at last can be securely relied on by no one, and who gives incessant (and as it seems unnecessary) trouble to those about him. The rising republicanism of the day will find in these letters much to serve it; for however convinced one may be, on general grounds, that English royalty was necessary to English freedom at that time, it is impossible not to be impatient at seeing how, month after month in a great crisis, when there was so much else to cause anxiety and create confusion, one stupid old man should have been able to add so much to both.

And all through the struggle the two effects of the new French Revolution were contending with one another. Just as it aroused in young and sanguine minds (and the majority of the country was just then disposed to be sanguine) the warmest hopes, in minds oppositely predisposed it aroused every kind of fear. Old and timid people thought we should soon have in England 'Robespierre and the guillotine.' Indeed, in a way that it is rather amusing now to consider, the French horrors of 1793 are turned into a kind of intellectual shuttlecock by two disputants. One says, 'See what comes of making rash changes, how many crimes they engender, and how many lives they lose!' 'No' replies the other, 'see what comes of not making changes till too late, for it was delay of change, and resistance to change, which caused those crimes and horrors.' Nor were these unreal words of mere rhetoric. They told much on many minds, for what France had done and would do then naturally filled an immense space in men's attention, as for so many years not long since Europe has been divided into France and anti-France.

With all these obstacles in its way the ministry of 1831 had the greatest difficulty in carrying the Reform Bill. I have not space to narrate, even in the briefest way, the troubled history of their doing so. Parliamentary debates are generally dull in the narration, but so great was the excitement, and so many were the relieving circumstances, that an accomplished historian will be able to make posterity take some sort of exceptional interest in these. The credit of the victory, such as it is, must be divided between many persons; Lord Grey managed the King, and stood first in the eye of the country; Lord Russell contributed the first sketch of the bill, containing all its essential features, both good and bad, and he introduced the first bill into the House of Commons; the late Lord Derby then first showed his powers as a great debater. But the best observers say that Lord Althorp carried the Bill: he was Leader of the House at the time, and the main strain of ruling one of the most troubled of Parliaments was on him. His biographer, Sir James le Marchant, who was present at the debates, says:—

Lord Althorp's capacity as a leader had been severely tested throughout this tremendous struggle, and it extorted the praise even of his political opponents. I recollect Sir Henry Hardinge saying, 'It was Althorp carried the bill. His fine temper did it. And in answer to a most able and argumentative speech of Crocker, he rose and merely said, "that he had made some calculations which he considered as entirely conclusive in refutation of the right honourable gentleman's arguments which he had mislaid, but if the House would be guided by his advice they would reject the amendment"—which they accordingly did. There is no standing against such influence as this. The Whigs ascribed Lord Althorp's influence not to his temper alone, but to the confidence felt by the House in his integrity and sound judgment, an opinion so universal that Lord Grey was induced by it to press upon him a peerage that he might take charge of the bill in the committee of the Lords; and the design was abandoned not from any hesitation or unwillingness on the part of Lord Althorp, but from the difficulty of finding a successor to him in the Commons.'

So bad a speaker, with so slow a mind, has never received so great a compliment in a scene where quickness and oratory seem at first sight to be the most abolutely requisite of qualities.[6] But it is no doubt a great mistake to imagine that these qualities are the true essentials to success of this kind. A very shrewd living judge says, after careful reflection, that they are even hurtful. 'A man,' says Mr. Massey in his history, 'who speaks seldom, and who speaks ill, is the best leader of the House of Commons.' And no doubt the slow-speeched English gentlemen rather sympathize with slow speech in others. Besides, a quick and brilliant leader is apt to be always speaking, whereas a leader should interfere only when necessary, and be therefore felt as a higher force when he does so. His mind ought to be like a reserve fund; not invested in showy securities, but sure to be come at when wanted, and always of stable value. And this Lord Althorp's mind was; there was not an epigram in the whole of it; everything was solid and ordinary. Men seem to have trusted him much as they trust a faithful animal, entirely believing that he would not deceive if he could, and that he could not if he would.

And what, then, was this great 'Bill'—which it was so great an achievement to pass? Unfortunately this is not an easy question to answer shortly. The 'Bill' destroyed many old things and altered many old things, and we cannot understand its effects except in so far as we know what these old things were.

'A variety of rights of suffrage,' said Sir James Mackintosh, 'is the principle of the English representation.' How that variety began is not at all to the present purpose; it grew as all English things grow—

[6] In the *Fortnightly Review* this sentence was mistakenly printed as part of the quotation from Sir James le Marchant.—p. 589.

by day-to-day alterations from small beginnings; and the final product was very different from the first beginning, as well as from any design which ever at any one time entered any one's mind. There always was a great contrast between the mode of representation in boroughs and in counties, because there was a great contrast in social structure between them. The 'knight of the shire' was differently chosen from the 'burgess of the town,' because the 'shire' was a different sort of place from the town, and the same people could not have chosen for the two—the same people not existing in the two. The borough representations of England, too, 'struggled up'—there is hardly any other word to describe it—in a most irregular manner. The number of towns which sent representatives is scarcely ever the same in any two of our oldest Parliaments. The sheriff had a certain discretion, for the writ only told him to convene 'de quolibet burgo duos burgenses,' and did not name any towns in particular. Most towns then disliked the duty and evaded it if possible, which seems to have augmented the sheriff's power, for he could permit or prevent the evasion as much as he chose. And at a very early period great differences grew up between the ways of election in the towns which were always represented. There seems to have been a kind of 'natural selection;' the most powerful class in each borough chose if it could at each election, and if any class long continued the most powerful, it then acquired customary rights of election which came to be unalterable. Nor was there any good deciding authority to regulate this confusion. The judge of elections was the 'House of Commons' itself, and it often decided not according to law or evidence, but as political or personal influence dictated. And rights of election thus capriciously recognised became binding on the borough for ever. As might be expected the total result was excessively miscellaneous. The following are the franchises of the boroughs in two counties as legislators of 1832 found them:—

SOMERSETSHIRE.

BRISTOL .	.	Freeholders of 40s., and free burgesses.
BATH	.	Mayor, aldermen, and common councilmen only.
WELLS .	.	Mayor, masters, burgesses, and freemen of the seven trading companies of the said city.
TAUNTON .	.	Potwallers, not receiving alms or charity.
BRIDGEWATER .	.	Mayor, aldermen, and twenty-four capital burgesses of the borough paying scot and lot.

ILCHESTER	. .	Alleged to be the inhabitants of the said town paying scot and lot which the town called potwallers.
MINEHEAD	. .	The parishioners of Dunster and Minehead, being housekeepers in the borough of Minehead, and not receiving alms.
MILBORN PORT.	.	The capital bailiffs and their deputies, the number of bailiffs being nine, and their deputies being two; in the commonalty, stewards, their number being two; and the inhabitants thereof paying scot and lot.

LANCASHIRE.

LANCASTER	. .	Freemen only.
WIGAN .	. .	Free burgesses.
CLITHEROE	. .	Freeholders, resident and non-resident.
LIVERPOOL	. .	Mayor, bailiffs, and freemen not receiving alms.
PRESTON .	. .	All the inhabitants.

Nothing could be more certain than that a system which was constructed in this manner must sooner or later need great alteration. Institutions which have grown from the beginning by adaptation may last as long as any if they continue to possess the power of adaptation. The force which created them still exists to preserve them. But in this case the power of adaptation was gone. A system of representation made without design was fixed as eternal upon a changing nation; and somehow or other it was sure to become unsuitable. Nothing could be more false in essence than the old anti-reform arguments as far as they affected the 'wisdom of our ancestors;' for the characteristic method of our ancestors had been departed from. Our ancestors changed what they wanted bit by bit, just when and just as they wanted. But their descendants were forbidden to do so; they were asked to be content not only with old clothes but with much patched old clothes, which they were denied the power to patch again. And this sooner or later they were sure to refuse.

In 1832 a grave necessity existed for changing it. The rude principle of natural selection by which it had been made, insured that at least approximately the classes most influential in the nation would have a proportionate power in the legislature[7]; no great class was likely to be denied anything approaching to its just weight. But now that a system framed in one age was to be made to continue unchanged

[7] The *Fortnightly Review* has 'legislation' instead of 'legislature'.—p. 591.

through after ages there was no such security. On the contrary, the longer the system went on without change the more sure it was to need change. Some new class was sure in course of time to grow up for which the fixed system provided no adequate representatives; and the longer that system continued fixed, the surer was this to happen, and the stronger was it likely that this class would be. In 1832, such a class had arisen of the first magnitude. The trading wealth of the country had created a new world which had no voice in Parliament comparable to that which it had in the country. Not only were some of the greatest towns, like Birmingham and Manchester, left without any members at all, but in most other towns the best of the middle class felt that they had no adequate power; they were either extinguished by a franchise too exclusive, or swamped by one too diffused; either way, they were powerless.

There was equal reason to believe that by the same inevitable course of events some class would come to have more power in Parliament than it should. The influence which gave the various classes their authority at the time in which the machinery of our representation was framed, would be sure in time to ebb away, wholly or in part, from some of them. And in matter of fact they did so. The richer nobility and the richer commoners had come to have much more power than they ought. The process of letting the most influential people in a borough choose its members, amounted in time to letting the great nobleman or great commoner to whom the property of the town belonged, choose them. And many counties had fallen into the direction of the same hands also, so that it was calculated, if not with truth, at any rate with an approach to it, that one hundred and seventy-seven lords and gentlemen chose as many as three hundred and fifty-five English members of Parliament. The parliamentary power of these few rich peers and squires was much too great when compared with their share in the life of the nation, just as that of the trading class was too weak; the excess of the one made the deficiency of the other additionally difficult to bear; and the contrast was more than ever galling in the years from 1830 to 1832, because just then the new French Revolution had revived the feud between the privileged classes and the non-privileged. The excessive parliamentary power of these few persons had before been a yoke daily becoming heavier and heavier, and now it could be endured no longer.

The reform 'Bill' amended all this. It abolished a multitude of nomination boroughs, gave members to large towns and cities, and changed the franchise, so that in all boroughs at any rate, the middle classes obtained predominant power. And no one can deny that the good so done was immense; indeed, no one does now deny it, for the generation of Tories that did so has passed away. No doubt the Reform Act did not produce of itself at once the new heaven and new earth which its more ardent supporters expected of it. It did nothing to remove the worst evils from which the country suffered, for those evils were not political but economical; and the classes whom it enfranchised were not more economically instructed than those whom they superseded. The doctrine of protection then reigned all through the nation, and while it did so no real cure for those evils was possible. But this Act, coming as it did when a new political generation was prepared to make use of it, got rid entirely of the 'cruel spirit' by which our distresses had been repressed before, and which was as great an evil as those distresses themselves, introduced many improvements, municipal reform, tithe reform, and such like, in which the business-like habit of mind due to the greater power of the working classes, mainly helped and diffused a sweeter and better spirit through society.

But these benefits were purchased at a price of the first magnitude, though, from the nature of it, its payment was long deferred. The reformers of 1832 dealt with the evils of their time, as they would have said, in an English way, and without much thinking of anything else. And exactly in that English way, as they had under their hands a most curious political machine which had grown without design, and which produced many very valuable, though not very visible effects, they, without thought, injured and destroyed some of the best of it.

First, the old system of representation, as we have seen, was based on a variety of franchises. But, in order to augment the influence of the middle class, the reformers of 1832 destroyed that variety; they introduced into every borough the £10 household franchise, and with a slight exception which we need not take account of, made that franchise the only one in all boroughs. They raised the standard in the boroughs in which it was lower than £10, and lowered it in those where it was higher; and in this way they changed the cardinal principle of the system which they found established, substituting uniformity as the rule instead of variety.[8]

[8] The *Fortnightly Review* has 'which they found for the established uniformity as a rule instead of variety'—p. 593, but since this does not make sense it has been altered.

And this worked well enough at first, for there was not for some years after 1832 much wish for any more change in our constituencies. But in our own time we have seen the harm of it. If you establish any uniform franchise in a country, then it at once becomes a question, What sort of franchise is it to be? Those under it will say that they are most unjustly excluded; they will deny that there is any real difference between themselves and those above; they will show without difficulty that some whom the chosen line leaves out are even better than those which it takes in. And they will raise the cry so familiar in our ears—the cry of class legislation. They will say, Who are these ten-pound householders, these arbitrarily chosen middle class men, that they should be sole electors? Why should they be alone enfranchised and all others practically disfranchised, either by being swamped by their more numerous votes or by not having votes at all? The case is the stronger because one of the most ancient functions of Parliament, and especially the Commons House of Parliament, is the reformation of grievances. This suited very well with the old system of variety; in that miscellaneous collection of constituencies every class was sure to have some members who represented it. There were then working-class constituencies sending members to speak for them,—'men,' says Mackintosh, 'of popular talents, principles, and feelings; quick in suspecting oppression, bold in resisting it, not thinking favourably of the powerful; listening almost with credulity to the complaints of the humble and the feeble, and impelled by ambition when they are not prompted by generosity to be defenders of the defenceless.' And in cases of popular excitement, especially of erroneous excitement, this plan insured that it should have adequate expression, and so soon made it calm. But the legislation of 1832 destroyed these working-men's constituencies; 'they put the country,' as it was said afterwards, 'under ten-pounders only.' And in consequence there are in our boroughs now nothing but working-class constituencies; there are no longer any ten-pound householders at all. There is throughout our boroughs a uniform sort of franchise, and that the worst sort—a franchise which gives the predominance to the most ignorant and the least competent, if they choose to use it. The middle classes have as little power as they had before 1832, and the only difference is, that before 1832 they were ruled by those richer than themselves, and now they are ruled by those poorer.

No doubt there is still an inequality in the franchise between counties and boroughs—the sole remnant of the variety of our ancient system. But that inequality is much more difficult to defend now when it stands alone, than it was in old times when it was one of many. And the 'ugly rush' of the lower orders which has effaced the 'hard and fast' line established in 1832 threatens to destroy this remnant of variety. In a few years probably there will be but one sort of franchise throughout all England, and the characteristic work of 1832 will be completely undone; the middle classes, whose intelligence Macaulay praised, and to whom he helped to give so much power, will have had all that power taken away from them.

No doubt, too, there is still a real inequality of influence, though there is a legal equality of franchise. The difference of size of boroughs gives more power to those in the small boroughs than to those in the large. And this is very valuable, for elections for large boroughs are costly, and entail much labour that is most disagreeable. But here, again, the vicious precedent of establishing uniformity set in 1832 is becoming excessively dangerous. Being so much used to it people expect to see it everywhere. There is much risk that before long there may be only one sort of vote and only one size of constituency all over England, and then the reign of monotony will be complete.

And, secondly, the reformers of 1832 committed an almost worse error in destroying one kind of select constituency without creating an intellectual equivalent. We are not used nowadays to think of nomination boroughs as select constituencies, but such, in truth, they were, and such they proved themselves to be at, perhaps, the most critical period of English history. Lord Russell, no favourable judge, tells us 'that it enabled Sir Robert Walpole to consolidate the throne of the House of Hanover amid external and internal dangers.' No democratic suffrage would then have been relied on for that purpose, for the mass of Englishmen were then more or less attached to their hereditary king, and they might easily have been induced to restore him. They had not, indeed, a fanatical passion of loyalty towards him, nor any sentiment which would make them brave many dangers on his behalf; but there was much sluggish and sullen prejudice which might have been easily aroused to see that he had his rights, and there were many relics of ancient loyal zeal which might have combined with that prejudice and ennobled it. Nor did the people of that day much care for what we should now call parliamentary government. The educated opinion of that day was strongly in favour of the House of

Hanover; but the numerical majority of the nation was not equally so; perhaps it would have preferred the House of Stuart. But the higher nobility and the richer gentry possessed a great power over the opinions of Parliament because many boroughs were subject to their control, and by exerting that power they, in conjunction with the trading classes, who were then much too weak to have moved by themselves, fixed the House of Hanover on the throne, and so settled the freedom of England. These boroughs at that time, for this purpose as select constituencies, were of inestimable value, because they enabled the most competent opinion in England to rule without dispute, when, under any system of diffused suffrage, that opinion would either have been out-voted or almost so.

And to the last these boroughs retained much of this peculiar merit. They were an organ for what may be called specialized political thought, for trained intelligence busy with public affairs. Not only did they bring into Parliament men of genius and ability, but they kept together a higher political world capable of appreciating that genius and ability when young, and of learning from it when old. The Whig party, such as it was in those days especially, rested on this parliamentary power. In them was a combination of more or less intelligent noblemen of liberal ideas and aims, who chose such men as Burke, and Brougham, and Hume,[9] and at last Macaulay, to develop those ideas and to help to attain those aims. If they had not possessed this peculiar power, they would have had no such intellectual influence; they would have simply been gentlemen of what we now think good ideas, with no special means of advancing them. And they would not have been so closely combined together as they were; they would have been scattered persons of political intelligence. But having this power they combined together, lived together, thought together, and the society thus formed was enriched and educated by the men of genius whom it selected as instruments, and in whom in fact it found teachers. And there was something like it on the government side, though the long possession of power, and perhaps the nature of Toryism, somewhat modified its characteristics.

The effect is to be read in the parliamentary debates of those times. Probably they are absolutely better than our own. They are intrinsically a better discussion of the subjects of their day than ours are of our subjects. But however this may be, they are beyond a question rela-

[9] Morgan has 'Horner' for 'Hume'.—Ed.

tively better. General knowledge of politics has greatly improved in the last fifty years, and the best political thought of the present day is much superior to any which there was then. So that, even if our present parliamentary debates retained the level of their former excellence, they would still not bear the same relation to the best thought of the present that the old ones bear to the best thought of the past. And if the debates have really fallen off much (as I am sure they have), this conclusion will be stronger and more certain.

Nor is this to be wondered at. If you lessen the cause you will lessen the effect too. Not only are not the men whom these select constituencies brought into Parliament now to be found there, but the society which formed those constituencies, and which chose those men, no longer exists. The old parties were combinations partly aristocratic, partly intellectual, cemented by the common possession and the common use of political power. But now that the power is gone the combinations are dissolved. The place which once knew them knows them no more. Any one who looks for them in our present London and our present politics will scarcely find much that is like them.

This society sought for those whom it thought would be useful to it in all quarters. There was a regular connection between the 'Unions,' —the great debating societies of Oxford and Cambridge—and Parliament. Young men who seemed promising had even a chance of being competed for by both parties. We all know the line which the wit of Brooks's made upon Mr. Canning—

> The turning of coats so common is grown,
> That no one would think to attack it;
> But no case until now was so flagrantly known
> Of a schoolboy's turning his jacket.

This meant that it having been said and believed that Mr. Canning, who had just left Oxford, was to be brought into Parliament by the Whig opposition, he went over to Mr. Pitt, and was brought in by the Tory ministry. The Oxford Liberals of our generation are quite exempt from similar temptations. So far from their support in Parliament being craved by both sides, they cannot enter Parliament at all. When many of these tried to do so in the autumn of 1867, their egregious failure was one of the most striking events of that remarkable time.

There was a connection too then between the two parts of the public service now most completely divided—the permanent and the parliamentary civil services. Now, as we all know, the chief clerks in the Treasury and permanent heads of departments never think of going into Parliament; they regard the parliamentary statesmen who are set to rule over them much as the Bengalees regard the English—as persons who are less intelligent and less instructed than themselves, but who nevertheless are to be obeyed. They never think of changing places any more than a Hindoo thinks of becoming an Englishman. But in old times, men like Lord Liverpool, Sir George Rose, and Mr. Huskisson were found eminent in the public offices, and in consequence of that eminence were brought into Parliament. The party in office were then, as now, anxious to obtain competent help in passing measures of finance and detail, and they then obtained it thus, whereas now their successors do not obtain it at all.

There was then, too, a sort of romantic element in the lives of clever young men which is wholly wanting now. Some one said that Macaulay's was like a life in a fairy tale—he opens a letter which looks like any other letter, and finds that it contains a seat in Parliament. Gibbon says that just as he was destroying an army of barbarians, Sir Gilbert Elliot called and offered him a seat for Liskeard. Great historians will never probably again be similarly interrupted. The effect of all this was to raise the intellectual tone of Parliament. At present the political conversation of members of Parliament—a few of the greatest excepted—is less able and less striking than that of other persons of fair capacity. There is a certain kind of ideas which you hardly ever hear from any other educated person, but which they have to talk to their constituents, and which, if you will let them, they will talk to you too. Some of the middle-aged men of business, the 'soap-boilers,' as the London world disrespectfully calls them, whom local influence raises to Parliament, really do not seem to know any better; they repeat the words of the hustings as if they were parts of their creed. And as for the more intellectual members who know better, no one of good manners likes to press them too closely in argument on politics any more than he likes to press a clergyman too strictly on religion. In both cases the *status* in the world depends on the belief in certain opinions, and therefore it is thought rather ill-bred, except for some great reason, to try to injure that belief. Intellectual deference used to be paid to members of Parliament, but now, at least in London, where the species is known, the remains of that deference are rare.

The other side of the same phenomenon is the increased power of the provinces, and especially of the constituencies. Any gust of popular excitement runs through them instantly, grows greater and greater as it goes, till it gains such huge influence that for a moment the central educated world is powerless. No doubt, if only time can be gained, the excitement passes away; something new succeeds, and the ordinary authority of trained and practised intelligence revives. But if an election were now to happen at an instant of popular fury, that fury would have little or nothing to withstand it. And, even in ordinary times, the power of the constituencies is too great. They are fast reducing the members, especially the weaker sort of them, to delegates. There is already, in many places, a committee which often telegraphs to London hoping that their member will vote this way or that, and the member is unwilling not to do so, because at the next election, if offended, the committee may, perchance, turn the scale against him. And this dependence weakens the intellectual influence of Parliament, and of that higher kind of mind of which Parliament ought to be the organ.

We must remember that if now we feel these evils we must expect ere long to feel them much more. The Reform Act of 1867 followed in the main the precedent of 1832; and year by year we shall feel its consequences more and more. The two precedents which have been set will of necessity, in the English world, which is so much guided by precedent, determine the character of future Reform Acts. And if they do the supremacy of the central group of trained and educated men which our old system of parliamentary choice created, will be completely destroyed, for it is already half gone.

I know it is thought that we can revive this intellectual influence. Many thoughtful reformers believe that by means of Mr. Hare's system of voting, by the cumulative suffrage, the limited suffrage, or by some others like them, we may be able to replace that which the legislation of 1832 began to destroy, and that which those who follow them are destroying. And I do not wish to say a word against this hope. On the contrary, I think that it is one of the most important duties of English politicians to frame these plans into the best form of which they are capable, and to try to obtain the assent of the country to them. But the difficulty is immense. The reformers of 1832 destroyed intellectual constituencies in great numbers without creating any new ones, and without saying, indeed without thinking, that it was desirable to create any. They thus by conspicuous action, which is the most influential of political instruction, taught mankind that an increase in the power of numbers was the change most to be desired in England. And of course the mass of mankind are only too ready to think so. They are always prone to believe their own knowledge to be 'for all practical purposes' sufficient, and to wish to be emancipated from the authority of the higher culture. What we have now to do, therefore, is to induce this self-satisfied, stupid, inert mass of men to admit its own insufficiency, which is very hard; to understand fine schemes for supplying that insufficiency, which is harder; and to exert itself to get those ideas adopted, which is hardest of all. Such is the duty which the reformers of 1832 have cast upon us.

And this is what of necessity must happen if you set men like Lord Althorp to guide legislative changes in complex institutions. Being without culture, they do not know how these institutions grew; being without insight, they only see one half their effect; being without foresight, they do not know what will happen if they are enlarged; being without originality, they cannot devise anything new to supply if necessary the place of what is old. Common sense no doubt they have, but common sense without instruction can no more wisely revise old institutions than it can write the Nautical Almanac. Probably they will do some present palpable good, but they will do so at a heavy cost; years after they have passed away, the bad effects of that which they did, and of the precedents which they set, will be hard to bear and difficult to change. Such men are admirably suited to early and simple times. English history is full of them, and England has been made mainly by them, but they fail in later times when the work of the past is accumulated, and no question is any longer simple. The simplicity of their one-idea'd minds, which is suited to the common arithmetic and vulgar fractions of early societies, is not suited, indeed rather unfits them for the involved analysis and complex 'problem-papers' of later ages.

There is little that in a sketch like this need be said of Lord Althorp's life after the passing of the Reform Act. The other acts of Lord Grey's ministry have nothing so memorable or so characteristic of Lord Althorp that anything need be said about them. Nor does any one in the least care now as to the once celebrated mistake of Mr. Littleton in dealing with O'Connell, or Lord Althorp's connection with it. Parliamentary history is only interesting when it is important constitutional history, or when it illustrates something in the character of some interesting man. But the end of Lord Althorp's public life was very curious. In the November of 1834 his brother, Lord Spencer, died, and as he was then leader of the House of Commons a successor for him had to be found. But William IV, whose liberal partialities had long since died away, began by objecting to every one proposed, and ended by turning out the Ministry—another event in his reign which our coming republicans will no doubt make the most of. But I have nothing to do with the King and the constitutional question now. My business is with Lord Althorp. He acted very characteristically,—he said that a retirement from office was to him the 'cessation of acute pain,' and never afterwards would touch it again, though he lived for many years. Nor was this an idle affectation, far less indolence. 'You must be aware,' he said once before, in a letter to Lord Brougham, 'that my being in office is nothing less than a source of misery to me. I am perfectly certain that no man ever disliked it to such a degree as I do; and, indeed, the first thing that usually comes into my head when I wake is how to get rid of it.' He retired into the country and occupied himself with the rural pursuits which he loved best, attended at quarter sessions, and was active as a farmer. 'Few persons,' said an old shepherd, 'could compete with my lord in a knowledge of sheep.' He delighted to watch a whole flock pass, and seemed to know them as if he had lived with them. 'Of all my former pursuits,' he wrote, just after Lady Althorp's death, and in the midst of his grief, 'the only one in which I now take any interest is breeding stock; it is the only one in which I can build castles in the air.' And as soon as he could, among such castles in the air he lived and died. No doubt, too, much better for himself than many of his friends, who long wanted to lure him back to politics. He was wise with the solid wisdom of agricultural England; popular and useful; sagacious in usual things; a model in common duties; well able to advise men in the daily difficulties which are the staple of human life. But beyond this he could not go. Having no call to decide on more intellectual questions, he was distressed and pained when he had to do so. He was a man so picturesquely out of place in a great scene that if a great describer gets hold of him he may be long remembered; and it was the misfortune of his life that the simplicity of his purposes and the reliability of his character raised him at a great conjuncture to a high place for which nature had not meant him, and for which he felt that she had not.

Lord Lyndhurst

Introductory note

John Singleton Copley, Baron Lyndhurst (1772–1863) was born in Boston, Massachusetts. He was the son of John Singleton Copley, the portrait-painter, and of Susannah Farnum Clarke. Copley the younger was brought to England in 1775, and in 1790 entered Trinity College, Cambridge. He was called to the bar in 1804 and joined the midland circuit. He became a serjeant-at-law in 1813, and in 1817 was engaged by the Crown as prosecuting counsel. From 1818–26 he was a Tory M.P. In 1819 he became Solicitor-General, and in 1820 conducted the trial of Arthur Thistlewood for treason, and that of Queen Caroline before the Lords. He was knighted, and from 1824–6 was Attorney-General, and in 1826 became Master of the Rolls. In 1827 he was created Baron Lyndhurst, and from 1827–30 was Lord Chancellor. From 1831–4 he was Chief Baron of the Exchequer, and was Lord Chancellor for a third time in 1834–5. He took a leading part in the debates in the Lords between 1835–41. From 1841–6 he was again Lord Chancellor. Lord Lyndhurst died at Turville in 1863.

What Lord Lyndhurst really was[1]

A GREAT *phenomenon* has passed away from English public life. Not long since Lord Lyndhurst observed—'My Lords, I well remember the breaking out of the French Revolution in 1789, the death of Louis the Sixteenth, and the course of the consequent events.' There is not, perhaps, a conspicuous public man now in Europe who could say this; certainly there is none in England. The picturesque features of Lord Lyndhurst's mind and character made the phenomenon still more striking. The characteristic of his intellect was the combination of great force and great lucidity. Every sentence from him was full of light and energy. His face and brow were, perhaps, unrivalled in our time for the expression of the pure intellect, and he preserved the physical aptitude for public oratory to an old age when most men are scarcely fit for mere conversation. To the very extremity of a protracted life, what is very rare, he both looked and was a great man. The intellect was undimmed, and the power of expression hardly abated. There is no such man left.

It is very natural that such a man should have lived till his career should be half a myth or a legend. Few indeed of those who during the last few years gazed on that remarkable face, had any distinct conception of the life which had been led by the person they saw. The singular vigour of his conversation charmed those who resorted to him, and they were led to believe a man who talked so very well, could hardly have acted very ill. The lives which have been put forth in the newspapers, carefully prepared, like those of most old men, are merely panegyrics. For once the physical vigour of a long old age has redeemed in public estimation the errors and vices of a long life. But it is not so that history should be written; it is in no strain of panegyric that an impartial observer can review the career of Lord Lyndhurst.

The beginning of the public life of Lord Lyndhurst was towards

[1] This article was first published in *The Economist* for October 17 1863, Volume XXI, pp. 1150–1.

the end of the long reign of the Tory party. Sir George Lewis justly observed 'that the Tories in 1815 had an immense balance of popularity, arising from the successful issue of the great war, and that they managed to spend it most completely before 1830.' They governed, as all Conservatives even would now admit, in precisely the wrong spirit. They governed, not in the spirit of Mr. Pitt, but in the spirit of Lord Eldon. They maintained not only the main institutions of the country which were acceptable and popular, but also the minutest abuses which in the course of years had clung to those institutions. They connected the name of the Tory party with every petty abuse and misdemeanour throughout the country. They would alter nothing, and they would let nothing be altered. When public meetings were convened to express public opinion, the organs of the government cried out sedition, and talked as if a 'French Revolution' were going to break out here. By this stupid (there is no milder epithet that is fitting) and narrow-minded policy, the Tories caused the outburst of public opinion, which carried the Reform Bill. Their best organs have admitted as much of late years. 'A few more drops,' said the 'Quarterly Review,' not long since, 'of Eldoninine,' 'and we should have had the People's Charter.' The Tory party kept the nation in such tight and painful fetters, that it was driven wild, and rose and broke them. If the Tories will permit *no* improvement, so went the national idea, we must have an end of Toryism.

All this was excusable and natural in men like Lord Eldon. He had been a Tory from his youth, and he had been confirmed in Toryism by the events of the French Revolution. When the peace came, and a new generation sprung up, he was too old to change his creed. He honestly believed that it was necessary to resist every innovation, no matter of what sort, and to maintain everything, no matter of what kind. In Lord Eldon such conduct was natural and excusable. But it was not natural in a young man of great intelligence in the next generation. Able young men well knew that this illiberal Toryism was out of place, and an anachronism. It was in 1818, when the effects of this system were beginning to be plainly visible, that Lord Lyndhurst chose to connect himself with it.

He did so under circumstances of great suspicion. He had held—loosely, we apprehend—some sort of ultra-Liberal opinions. He had been, at any rate, in the habit of talking in that style at young men's parties and the circuit mess. He was a Liberal if he was anything;

and charges continued to be made against him for many years of having deserted his principles. It is, indeed, utterly inconceivable that Lord Lyndhurst should have believed Toryism such as Toryism was in 1818. He would have no title to fame if he had believed it. His claim is an intellectual claim. He is said, and justly said, to have had, when he chose to exert it, an intellect of the highest cultivation, more fitted than almost any other in his time for the perception of the truth,—a first-rate judicial mind, with culture and experience far transcending the ordinary judicial range. It is inconsistent with this claim that he should really have been on the wrong side in all the important questions of his time. It is absurd to say that the greatest political intellect of his time— and some such claim as this might be justly made for Lord Lyndhurst —really believed that the Catholics should not be emancipated; that the Corn Laws should be maintained; that there should be no reform in Parliament; that the narrow system of 1818 was a perfect or even an endurable system. We do not mean to charge him with acting contrary to his principles: that charge was made years ago, but was the exaggerated charge of political opponents, who saw that there was something to blame, but in their eagerness and haste overdid their accusation. The true charge is that he had no principles, that he did not care to have opinions. If he had applied his splendid judicial faculties to the arguments for Free Trade or for Catholic emancipation, he would soon enough have discovered the truth. But he never did apply them. There is a story of a clever young official 'who said it was *inconvenient* to have opinions.' And this exactly expresses Lord Lyndhurst's life and sentiments. They tell a story which may be true or false, but is certainly characteristic, of what he said as to the Act which bears his name, forbidding a man to marry a deceased wife's sister. The real object of that Act was to please certain particular people who had married their sisters-in-law, and, as it stands to this day, it legalises all antecedent marriages. As it was originally brought in, it legalised subsequent marriages also. Persons conversant with the clergy and strict people represented to Lord Lyndhurst that there would be an outcry against this. He replied: 'Put it the other way, then forbid the future marriages; I am sure I do not care which way it is.' He wanted to serve a temporary purpose, and he did so always. He regarded politics as a game, to be played first for himself, and then for his party. He did not act contrary to his opinion, but he did not care to form a true opinion.

This was the explanation of his joining the Tories. *Not* to join them was poverty then; to join them was wealth. They were firmly fixed in office. As the satirist then sang—

> Nought's constant in the human race,
> Except the Whigs *not* getting into place.

As was the pleasant habit of that time, the Government picked out Mr. Copley, a clever young lawyer, and gave him a seat in Parliament. He accepted it, though he had no more formed opinion that Toryism was true than he had that Mahometanism was true. He took up the opinions of the existing Government and advocated them, and to the end of his life would have thought it 'nonsense and rubbish' to act otherwise.

Probably, however, he would have acted more profitably if he had acted more conscientiously. It really was a case when honesty was the best policy. If he had paid a fair attention to the subjects of his time, he would have been on what all parties now admit to be the right side. If he had a sincere wish to improve and benefit mankind, he would have been forward in the ranks of the Liberal party who were then employed in doing so. The chances of life are various, but most likely he would have had his reward. The Whigs wanted a first-rate judge, who was also a first-rate politician. During their long period of power they have never possessed one. The Whigs have been in power, roughly speaking, five-and-twenty years out of the last thirty. If Lord Lyndhurst had been their leader instead of the Tory leader, he would have had far more of what he valued, more power and influence, more wealth, and greater station. He would have been among the foremost of the winners instead of being among the foremost of the losers. There was nothing which he would have liked so much. There was nothing which he appreciated so much as success in the game of political life,—nothing that he despised and detested like want of success.

It is pleasant to turn to a more favourable topic. Many duties Lord Lyndhurst may have neglected, or despised, or disowned; but one duty, and a neglected one, he performed better, perhaps, on the whole, than any man in his generation. He had the most *disciplined* intellect of his time. There is in every one of his productions evidence not only of natural sinewy strength, but of careful culture and intellectual gymnastic. Lord Brougham tells a story of finding him occupied over the integral calculus for amusement's sake years ago. Every line of his speeches tells how well he understood, and how well he acted on the manly principles of Greek oratory. Few men led a laxer life; few men to the very end of their life were looser in their conversation; but there was no laxity in his intellect. Everything there was braced and knit. Great oratory is but a transitory art; few turn even to the best speeches of the past and even the best of them are so clogged with the detail of the time, that they are dull and wearisome to a hasty posterity. Few will recur to Lyndhurst's speeches, but those who do so will find some of the best, if not the very best specimens, in English, of the best manner in which a man of great intellect can address and influence the intellects of others. Their art, we might almost say their merit, is of the highest kind, *for* it is concealed. The words seem the simplest, clearest, and most natural that a man could use. It is only the instructed man who knows that he could not himself have used them, and that few men could.

Such was the great man whom we have just buried; great in power, but not great in the use of power; a politician, not a statesman; a man of small principle and few scruples. Of him far more truly than of Burke it may be said that 'to party he gave up what was meant for mankind.' He played the game of life for low and selfish objects, and yet, by the intellectual power with which he played, he redeemed that game from its intrinsic degradation.

237

Sir Robert Peel

Introductory note

Robert Peel (1788–1850) was born at Chamber Hall, Lancashire, the eldest son of Robert (afterwards Sir Robert) Peel, politician, and of Ellen Yates. He was educated at Harrow and Christ Church, Oxford. In 1809 his father bought a Tory seat in Parliament for him at Cashel. He was Under-Secretary for War and the Colonies from 1810–12, and then Chief Secretary for Ireland until 1818. In 1815 he had successfully opposed Catholic emancipation and had established a constabulary for preservation of the peace. In 1817 he became M.P. for Oxford University. He rejoined Lord Liverpool's ministry as Home Secretary in 1822; about this time he had begun to mistrust rigid Toryism as a political creed. After bringing about important reforms in criminal law, he resigned over Catholic emancipation, but upon Canning's death in 1827 he laboured to reunite the Tory party. He joined Wellington's ministry as Home Secretary and Leader of the House of Commons in 1828, and seeing that the country was determined on Catholic emancipation, he introduced a bill in 1829 granting the measure. In 1829 he was M.P. for Westbury, and in 1830 and 1833 for Tamworth. In 1830 he resigned office on the defeat of Wellington's government. He became Premier in 1834, holding the offices of First Lord of the Treasury and Chancellor of the Exchequer, but confronted in the Commons by a hostile majority, he resigned office in 1835. He retired to opposition and gradually built up the party which was to become the Conservative party, its policy being to maintain intact the constitution of the Church and State. Peel formed a ministry in 1841, and in 1842 introduced his first budget, which was designed to reduce indirect taxation and make good the temporary deficiency by imposing an income tax. By 1846 he had repealed or reduced more than a thousand duties, and by this lightening of imposts on trade had ensured a leading position in the world for English trade. Until 1845 Peel had steadily opposed Corn Law repeal, but when the harvest failed and famine threatened, he introduced a measure for the ultimate repeal of the Corn Laws. He failed to carry his Cabinet with him and resigned in December, but the same month resumed office and in January 1846 introduced his bill for the repeal of the Corn Laws. It was passed the following June, but Peel was now defeated over his Irish bill. He resigned office, and after a few years in opposition, during which he considered himself the guardian of Free Trade, he died in London in 1850.

The Character of Sir Robert Peel[1]

MOST people have looked over old letters. They have been struck with the change of life, with the doubt on things now certain, the belief in things now incredible, the oblivion of what now seems most important, the strained attention to departed detail, which characterise the mouldering leaves. Something like this is the feeling with which we read Sir Robert Peel's memoirs. Who now doubts on the Catholic question? It is no longer a 'question.' A young generation has come into vigorous, perhaps into insolent life, who regard the doubts that were formerly entertained as absurd, pernicious, delusive. To revive the controversy was an error. The accusations which are brought against a public man in his own age are rarely those echoed in after times. Posterity sees less or sees more. A few points stand out in distinct rigidity; there is no idea of the countless accumulation, the collision of action, the web of human feeling, with which, in the day of their life, they were encompassed. Time changes much. The points of controversy seem clear; the assumed premises uncertain. The difficulty is to comprehend 'the difficulty.' Sir Robert Peel will have to answer to posterity, not for having passed Catholic emancipation when he did, but for having opposed it before; not for having been precipitate, but for having been slow; not for having taken 'insufficient securities' for the Irish Protestant Church, but for having endeavoured to take security for an institution too unjust to be secured by laws or lawgivers.

This memoir has, however, a deeper aim. Its end is rather personal than national. It is designed to show, not that Sir Robert did what was externally expedient—this was probably too plain—but that he himself really believed what he did to be right. The scene is laid, not in Ireland, not in the county of Clare, not amid the gross triumphs[2] of

---

[1] *Memoirs*, by the Right Hon. Sir Robert Peel, Bart., M.P., &c. Published by the Trustees of his Papers, Lord Mahon (now Lord Stanhope) and the Right Hon. Edward Cardwell, M.P. Part I. *The Roman Catholic Question*, 1828–9. This essay was first published in the *National Review* for July 1856, Volume III, pp. 146–74. It was later included in *Estimates of Some Englishmen and Scotchmen.*
[2] The *Estimates* text has 'triumph'.

O'Connell, or the outrageous bogs of Tipperary, but in the Home
Office, among files and papers, among the most correctly-docketed
memoranda, beside the minute which shows that justice A should be
dismissed, that malefactor O ought not to be reprieved. It is labelled
'My Conscience,' and is designed to show that 'my conscience'[3] was
sincere.

Seriously, and apart from jesting, this is no light matter. Not only
does the great space which Sir Robert Peel occupied during many
years in the history of the country entitle his character to the anxious
attention of historical critics, but the very nature of that character itself,
its traits, its deficiencies, its merits, are so congenial to the tendencies
of our time and government, that to be unjust to him is to be unjust
to all probable statesmen. We design to show concisely how this is.

A constitutional statesman is in general a man of common opinions
and uncommon abilities. The reason is obvious. When we speak of a
free government, we mean a government in which the sovereign
power is divided, in which a single decision is not absolute, where
argument has an office. The essence of the 'gouvernement des avocats,'
as the Emperor Nicholas called it, is that you must persuade so many
persons. The appeal is not to the solitary decision of a single statesman;
not to Richelieu or Nesselrode alone in his closet; but to the jangled
mass of men, with a thousand pursuits, a thousand interests, a thousand
various habits. Public opinion, as it is said, rules; and public opinion
is the opinion of the average man. Fox used to say of Burke: 'Burke is a
wise man; but he is wise too soon.' The average man will not bear this.
He is a cool, common person, with a considerate air, with figures in
his mind, with his own business to attend to, with a set of ordinary
opinions arising from and suited to ordinary life. He can't bear novelty
or originalities. He says: 'Sir, I never heard such a thing *before* in my
life;' and he thinks this a *reductio ad absurdum.* You may see his taste
by the reading of which he approves. Is there a more splendid monu-
ment of talent and industry than *The Times?* No wonder that the average man—that any one—believes in it. As Carlyle observes: 'Let the
highest intellect able to write epics try to write such a leader for the
morning newspapers, it cannot do it; the highest intellect will fail.'
But did you ever see any thing there you had never seen before? Out
of the million articles that everybody has read, can any one person

---

[3] The *Estimates* text has 'conduct' instead of the second 'conscience' which has been
substituted.

trace a single marked idea to a single article? Where are the deep theories, and the wise axioms, and the everlasting sentiments which the writers of the most influential publication in the world have been the first to communicate to an ignorant species? Such writers are far too shrewd. The two million, or whatever number of copies it may be, they publish, are not purchased because the buyers wish to know new truth. The purchaser desires an article which he can appreciate at sight; which he can lay down and say: 'An excellent article, very excellent; exactly *my own* sentiments.' Original theories give trouble; besides, a grave man on the Coal Exchange does not desire to be an apostle of novelties among the contemporaneous dealers in fuel;— he wants to be provided with remarks he can make on the topics of the day which will not be known *not* to be his; that are not too profound; which he can fancy the paper only reminded him of. And just in the same way, precisely as the most popular political paper is not that which is abstractedly the best or most instructive, but that which most exactly takes up the minds of men where it finds them, catches the floating sentiment of society, puts it in such a form as society can fancy would convince another society which did not believe,—so the most influential of constitutional statesmen is the one who most felicitously expresses the creed of the moment, who administers it, who embodies it in laws and institutions, who gives it the highest life it is capable of, who induces the average man to think: 'I could not have done it any better, if I had had time myself.'

It might be said that this is only one of the results of that tyranny of commonplace which seems to accompany civilisation. You may talk of the tyranny of Nero and Tiberius; but the real tyranny is the tyranny of your next-door neighbour. What law is so cruel as the law of doing what he does? What yoke is so galling as the necessity of being like him? What *espionage* of despotism comes to your door so effectually as the eye of the man who lives at your door? Public opinion is a permeating influence, and it exacts obedience to itself; it requires us to think other men's thoughts, to speak other men's words, to follow other men's habits. Of course, if we do not, no formal ban issues, no corporeal pain, the coarse penalty of a barbarous society, is inflicted on the offender; but we are called 'eccentric;' there is a gentle murmur of 'most unfortunate ideas,' 'singular young man,' 'well-intentioned, I dare say; but unsafe, sir, quite unsafe.' The prudent, of course, conform. The place of nearly every body depends on the opinion of every one else. There is nothing like Swift's precept to attain the repute of a sensible man: 'Be of the opinion of the person with whom at the time you are conversing.' This world is given to those whom this world can trust. Our very conversation is infected. Where is now the bold humour, the explicit statement, the grasping dogmatism of former days? They have departed; and you read in the orthodox works dreary regrets that the *art* of conversation has passed away. It would be as reasonable to expect the art of walking to pass away. People talk well enough when they know to whom they are speaking. We might even say, that the art of conversation was improved by an application to new circumstances. 'Secrete your intellect, use common words, say what you are expected to say,' and you shall be at peace. The secret of prosperity in common life is to be commonplace on principle.

Whatever truth there may be in these splenetic observations, might be expected to show itself more particularly in the world of politics. People dread to be thought unsafe in proportion as they get their living by being thought to be safe. 'Literary men,' it has been said, 'are outcasts;' and they are eminent in a certain way notwithstanding. 'They can say strong things of their age; for no one expects they will go out and act on them.' They are a kind of ticket-of-leave lunatics, from whom no harm is for the moment expected; who seem quiet, but on whose vagaries a practical public must have its eye. For statesmen it is different—they must be thought men of judgment. The most morbidly agricultural counties were aggrieved when Mr. Disraeli was made Chancellor of the Exchequer. They could not believe he was a man of solidity; and they could not comprehend taxes by the author of *Coningsby*, or sums by an adherent of the Caucasus. 'There is,' said Sir Walter Scott, a 'certain hypocrisy of action, which, however it is despised by persons intrinsically excellent, will nevertheless be cultivated by those who desire the good repute of men.' Politicians, as has been said, live in the repute of the commonalty. They may appeal to posterity; but of what use is posterity? Years before that tribunal comes into life your life will be extinct. It is like a moth going into Chancery. Those who desire a public career, must look to the views of the living public; an immediate exterior influence is essential to the exertion of their faculties. The confidence of others is your *fulcrum*. You cannot, many people wish you could, go into Parliament to represent yourself. You must conform to the opinions of the electors; and they, depend on it, will not be original. In a word, as has been most wisely observed, 'under free institutions it is necessary occasionally to defer to the opinions of other people; and as other people are obviously in the wrong, this is a great hindrance to the improvement of our political system, and the progress of our species.'

Seriously, it is a calamity that this is so. Occasions arise in which a different sort of statesman is required. A year or two ago we had one of these. If any politician had come forward in this country, on the topic of the war with prepared intelligence, distinct views, strong will, commanding mastery, it would have brought support to anxious intellects, and comfort to a thousand homes. None such came. Our people would have statesmen who thought as they thought, believed as they believed, acted as they would have acted. They had desired to see their own will executed. There came a time when they had no clear will, no definite opinion. They reaped as they had sown. As they had selected an administrative tool, of course it did not turn out an heroic leader.

If we wanted to choose an illustration of these remarks out of all the world, it would be Sir Robert Peel. No man has come so near our definition of a constitutional statesman,—the powers of a first-rate man and the creed of a second-rate man. From a certain peculiarity of intellect and fortune, he was never in advance of his time. Of almost all the great measures with which his name is associated, he attained great eminence as an opponent before he attained even greater eminence as their advocate. On the Corn-Laws, on the currency, on the amelioration of the criminal code, on Catholic emancipation,—the subject of the memoir before us,—he was not one of the earliest labourers, or quickest converts. He did not bear the burden and heat of the day; other men laboured, and he entered into their labours. As long as these questions remained the property of first-class intellects, as long as they were confined to philanthropists or speculators, as long as they were only advocated by austere intangible Whigs, Sir Robert Peel was against them. So soon as these same measures, by the progress of time, the striving of understanding, the conversion of receptive minds, became the property of second-class intellects, Sir Robert Peel became possessed of them also. He was converted at the conversion of the average man. His creed was, as it had ever been, ordinary; but his extraordinary abilities never showed themselves so much. He forthwith wrote his name on each of those questions; so that it will be remembered as long as they are remembered.

Nor is it merely on these few measures that Sir Robert Peel's mind must undoubtedly have undergone a change. The lifetime of few Englishmen has been more exactly commensurate with a change of public opinion—a total revolution of political thought. Hardly any fact in history is so incredible as that forty and a few years ago England was ruled by Mr. Perceval. It seems almost the same as being ruled by the *Record* newspaper. He had the same poorness of thought, the same petty Conservatism, the same dark and narrow superstition. His quibbling mode of oratory seems to have been scarcely agreeable to his friends; his impotence in political speculation moves the wrath— destroys the patience of the quietest reader now. Other ministers have had great connections, or great estates, to compensate for the con- tractedness of their minds. Mr. Perceval was only a poorish *nisi prius* lawyer, and there is no kind of human being so disagreeable, so teasing, to the gross Tory nature. He is not entitled to any glory for our war- like successes: on the contrary, he did his best to obtain failure by starving the Duke of Wellington, and plaguing him with petty vexa- tions. His views in religion inclined to that Sabbatarian superstition which is of all creeds the most alien to the firm and genial English nature. The mere fact of such a premier being endured shows how deeply the whole national spirit and interest was absorbed in the contest with Napoleon, how little we understood the sort of man who should regulate its conduct—'in the crisis of Europe,' as Sidney Smith said, 'he safely brought the Curates' Salaries Improvement Bill to a hearing'—and it still more shows the horror of all innovation which the recent events of French history had impressed on our wealthy and comfortable classes. They were afraid of catching revolution, as old women of catching cold. Sir Archibald Alison to this day holds that revolution is an infectious disease, beginning no one knows how, and going no one knows where. There is but one rule of escape, explains the great historian, 'Stay still, don't move; do what you have been accustomed to do, and consult your grandmother on every thing.' In 1812 the English people were all persuaded of this theory. Mr. Perceval was the most narrow-minded and unaltering man they could find: he therefore represented their spirit, and they put him at the head of the state.

Such was the state of political questions. How little of real thoughtfulness was then applied to what we now call social questions cannot be better illustrated than by the proceedings on the occasion of Mr. Perceval's death. Bellingham, who killed him, was, whether punishable or not, as clearly insane as a lunatic can be who offends against the laws of his country. He had no idea of killing Mr. Perceval particularly. His only idea was, that he had lost some property in Russia; that the English government would never repay him his loss in Russia; and he endeavoured to find some cabinet minister to shoot as a compensation. Lord Eldon lived under the belief that he had nearly been the victim himself, and told some story of a borrowed hat and an assistant's great coat to which he ascribed his preservation. The whole affair was a monomaniac delusion. Bellingham had no ground for expecting any repayment. There was no reason for ascribing his pecuniary ruin to the government of that day any more than to the government of this day. Indeed, if he had been alive now, it would have been agreed that he was a particularly estimable man. Medical gentlemen would have been examined for days on the doctrine of 'irresistible impulse,' 'moral insanity,' 'instinctive pistol-discharges,' and every respectful sympathy would have been shown to so curious an offender. Whether he was punishable or not may be a question; but all will now agree that it was not a case for the punishment of death. In that day there was no more doubt that he ought to be hung than there would now be that he ought on no account to be hung. The serious reasons, of which the scientific theories above alluded to are but the exaggerated resemblance, which indicate the horrible cruelty of inflicting on those who do not know what they do the extreme penalty of suffering meant for those who perpetrate the worst they can conceive, are in these years so familiar that we can hardly conceive their being unknown. Yet the Tory historian[4] has to regret that the motion, so earnestly insisted on by his counsel, to have the trial postponed for some days, to obtain evidence to establish his insanity, was not acceded to; that a judicial proceeding, requiring beyond all others the most calm and deliberate consideration, should have been hurried over with a precipitation which, if not illegal, was at least unusual; and a noble lord 'improved' the moment of the assassination by exclaiming to the peers in opposition, 'You see, my lords, the consequence of your agitating the question of *Catholic emancipation.*' To those who now know England, it seems scarcely possible this could have occurred here only forty-four years since. It

[4] Alison.—Ed.

was in such a world that Sir Robert Peel commenced his career. He was under-secretary of state for the colonies at the time of Mr. Perceval's assassination.

We cannot, however, believe that, even if Mr. Perceval had lived, his power would have very long endured. It passed to milder and quieter men. It passed to such men as Lord Liverpool and Mr. Peel. The ruling power at that time in England, as for many years before, as even in some measure, though far less, now, was the class of aristocratic gentry; by which we do not mean to denote the House of Lords exclusively, but to indicate the great class of hereditary landed proprietors, who are in sympathy with the upper House on cardinal points, yet breathe a somewhat freer air, are more readily acted on by the opinion of the community, more contradictable by the lower herd, less removed from its prejudices by a refined and regulated education. From the time of the revolution, more or less, this has been the ruling class in the community; the close-borough system and the county system giving them mainly the control of the House of Commons, and their feelings being in general, as it were, a mean term between those of the higher nobility and the trading public of what were then the few large towns. The rule of the House of Lords was rather mediate than direct. By the various means of influence and social patronage and oppression familiar to a wealthy and high-bred aristocracy, the highest members of it, of course, exercised over all below them a sure and continual influence: it worked silently and commonly on ordinary questions and in quiet times; yet it was liable to be overborne by a harsher and ruder power when stormy passions arose, in the days of wars and tumults. The largest amount of administrative power has indeed been rarely in the hands of the highest aristocracy, and in a great measure for a peculiar reason: that aristocracy will rarely do the work, and can rarely do the work.[5] The enormous pressure of daily-growing business which besets the governors of a busy and complicated community is too much for the refined habits, delicate discrimination, anxious judgment, which the course of their life developes in the highest classes, and with which it nourishes the indolence natural to those who have this world to enjoy. The real strain of the necessary labour has generally been borne by men of a somewhat lower grade, trained by an early ambition, a native aptitude, a hardy competition,

[5] Both Morgan and Hutton start this sentence off 'So far as the actual selection of visible rulers go'.

to perform its copious tasks. Such men are partakers of two benefits. They are rough and ready enough to accomplish the coarse enormous daily work: they have lived with higher gentlemen enough to know and feel what such persons think and want. Sir Robert Walpole is the type of this class. He was a Norfolk squire, and not a nobleman; he was bred a gentleman, and yet was quite coarse enough for any business. His career was what you would expect. For very many years he administered the government much as the aristocracy wished and desired. *They* were, so to speak, the directors of the company which is called the English nation; they met a little and talked a little: but Sir Robert was the manager, who knew all the facts, came every day, saw everybody, and was every thing.

Passing over the time of Lord Liverpool, of whom this is not now the place to speak, some such destiny as this would in his first political life have appeared likely to be that of Sir Robert Peel. If an acute master of the betting art had been asked the 'favourite' statesman who was likely to rule in that generation, he would undoubtedly have selected Sir Robert. He was rich, decorous, laborious, and had devoted himself regularly to the task. There was no other such man. It was likely, at least to superficial observers, that his name would descend to posterity as the 'Sir Robert' of a new time;—a time changed, indeed, from that of Walpole, but resembling it in its desire to be ruled by a great administrator, skilful in all kinds of business and transactions, yet associated with the aristocracy; by one unremarkable in his opinions, but remarkable in his powers. The fates, however, designed Peel for very different destiny; and to a really close observer there were signs in his horoscope which should have clearly revealed it. Sir Robert's father and grandfather were two of the men who created Lancashire. No sooner did the requisite machinery issue from the brain of the inventor than its capabilities were seized on by strong, ready, bold men of business, who erected it, used it, devised a factory system, combined a factory population—created, in a word, that black industrial region, of whose augmenting wealth and horrid labour tales are daily borne to the genial and lazy south. Of course it cannot be said that mill-makers invented the middle classes. The history of England perhaps shows that it has not for centuries been without an unusual number of persons with comfortable and moderate means. But though this class has ever been found among us, and has ever been more active than in any other similar country, yet to a great extent it was scattered, headless, motionless. Small rural out-of-the-way towns, country factories few and far between, concealed and divided this great and mixed mass of petty means and steady intelligence. The huge heaps of manufacturing wealth were not to be concealed. They at once placed on a level with the highest in the land—in matters of expenditure, and in those countless social relations which depend upon expenditure—men sprung from the body of the people, unmistakeably speaking its language, inevitably thinking its thoughts. It is true that the first manufacturers were not democratic. Sir Robert Peel, the statesman's father—a type of the class—was a firm, honest, domineering Conservative; but, however on such topics they may so think, however on other topics they may try to catch the language of the class to which they rise, the grain of the middle class will surely show itself in those who have risen from the middle class. If Mr. Cobden were to go over to the enemy, if he were to offer to serve Lord Derby *vice* Disraeli disconcerted, it would not be possible for him to speak as the hereditary landowner speaks. It is not that the hereditary landowner knows more;—indeed, either in book-learning or in matters of observation, in acquaintance with what has been, or is going to be, or what now is, the owners of rent are not superior to the receivers of profits; yet their dialect is different—the one speaks the language of years of toil, and the other of years of indolence. A harsh laboriousness characterises the one, a pleasant geniality the other. The habit of industry is ingrained in those who have risen by it; it modifies every word and qualifies every notion. They are the βάναυσοι[6] of work. Vainly, therefore, did the first manufacturers struggle to be Conservatives, to be baronets, to be peers. The titles they might obtain, their outward existence they might change, themselves in a manner they might alter; but a surer force was dragging them and those who resembled them into another region, filling them with other thoughts, making them express what people of the middle classes had always obscurely felt, pushing forward this new industrial order by the side, or even in front of the old aristocratic order. The new class has not, indeed, shown itself republican. They have not especially cared to influence the machinery of government. Their peculiarity has been, that they wished to see the government administered according to the notions familiar to them in their business life. They have no belief in mystery or magic; probably they have never appreciated the political influence

6 'Mechanics'.—Ed.

of the imagination; they wish to see plain sense applied to the most prominent part of practical life. In his later career, the second Sir Robert Peel was the statesman who most completely and thoroughly expressed the sentiments of this new dynasty;—instead of being the nominee of a nobility, he became the representative of a transacting and trading multitude.

Both of these two classes were, however, equally possessed by the vice or tendency we commented on at the outset. They each of them desired to see the government carried on exactly according to their own views. The idea on which seems to rest our only chance of again seeing great statesmen, of placing deep deferential trust in those who have given real proofs of comprehensive sagacity, had scarcely dawned on either. The average man had, so to say, varied; he was no longer of the one order, but of an inferior; but he was not at all less exacting or tyrannical. Perhaps he was even more so; for the indolent gentleman is less absolute and domineering than the active man of business. However that may be, it was the fate of Sir Robert Peel, in the two phases of his career, to take a leading share in carrying out the views, in administering the creed, first of one and then of the other.

Perhaps in our habitual estimate of Peel we hardly enough bear this in mind. We remember him as the guiding chief of the most intelligent Conservative government that this country has ever seen. We remember the great legislative acts which we owe to his trained capacity, every detail of which bears the impress of his practised hand; we know that his name is pronounced with applause in the great marts of trade and seats of industry; that even yet it is muttered with reproach in the obscure abodes of squires and rectors. We forget that his name was once the power of the Protestant interest, the shibboleth by which squires and rectors distinguished those whom they loved from those whom they hated; we forget that he defended the Manchester Massacre, the Six Acts, the Imposition of Tests, the rule of Orangemen. We remember Peel as the proper head of a moderate, intelligent, half-commercial community; we forget that he once was the chosen representative of a gentry untrained to great affairs, absorbed in a great war, only just recovering from the horror of a great revolution.

In truth, the character of Sir Robert Peel happily fitted him both to be the chosen head of a popular community, imperiously bent on its own ideas, and to be the head of that community in shifting and changing times. Sir Robert was at Harrow with Lord Byron, who has left the characteristic reminiscence: 'I was always in scrapes, Peel never.' And opposed as they were in their fortunes as boys and men, they were at least equally contrasted in the habit and kind of action of their minds. Lord Byron's mind gained every thing it was to gain by one intense, striking effort. By a blow of the imagination he elicited a single bright spark of light on every subject, and that was all. And this he never lost. The intensity of the thinking action seemed to burn it on the memory, there to remain alone. But he made no second effort; he gained no more. He always avowed his incapability of continuous application: he could not, he said, learn the grammar of any language. In later life he showed considerable talents for action; but those who had to act with him observed that, versatile as were his talents, and mutable as his convictions had always seemed to be, in reality he was the most stubborn of men. He heard what you had to say, assented to all you had to say; and the next morning returned to his original opinion. No amount of ordinary argumentative resistance was so hopeless as that facile acquiescence and instantaneous recurrence. The truth was, that he was,—and some others are similarly constituted,— unable to retain anything which he did not at any rate *seem* to gain by the unaided single rush of his own mind. The ideas of such minds are often not new, very often they are hardly in the strictest sense original; they really were very much suggested from without, and preserved in some obscure corner of memory, out of the way and unknown; but it remains their characteristic that they seem to the mind of the thinker to be born from its own depths, to be the product of its latent forces. There is a kind of eruption of ideas from a subterconscious world. The whole mental action is volcanic; the lava flood glows in *Childe Harold;* all the thoughts are intense, flung forth, vivid. The day after the eruption the mind is calm; it seems as if it could not again do the like; the product only remains, distinct, peculiar, indestructible. The mind of Peel was the exact opposite of this. His opinions far more resembled the daily accumulating insensible deposits of a rich alluvial soil. The great stream of time flows on with all things on its surface; and slowly, grain by grain, a mould of wise experience is unconsciously left on the still, extended intellect. You scarcely think of such a mind as acting; it seems always acted upon. There is no trace of gushing, overpowering, spontaneous impulse; everything seems acquired. The thoughts are calm. In Lord Byron, the very style—dashing, free, incisive—shows the bold impulse from which it came. The stealthy accumulating words of Peel seem like the quiet leavings of an outward tendency, which brought these, but might as well have brought others. There is no peculiar stamp either, in the ideas. They might have been any one's ideas. They belong to the general diffused stock of observations which are to be found in the civilised world. They are not native to the particular mind, nor 'to the manner born.' Like a science, they are credible or incredible by all men equally. This *secondary* character, as we may call it, of intellect, is evidently most useful to a statesman of the constitutional class, such as we have described him. He insensibly and inevitably takes in and imbibes, by means of it, the ideas of those around him. If he was left in a vacuum, he would have no ideas. The primary class of mind that strikes out its own belief would here be utterly at fault. It would want something which other men had; it would discover something which other men would not understand. Sir Robert Peel was a statesman for forty years; under our constitution, Lord Byron, eminent as was his insight into men, and remarkable as was his power, at least for short periods, of dealing with them, would not have been a statesman for forty days.

It is very likely that many people may not think Sir Robert Peel's mind so interesting as Lord Byron's. They may prefer the self-originating intellect which invents and retains its own ideas, to the calm receptive intellect which acquires its belief from without. The answer lies in what has been said—a constitutional statesman must sympathise in the ideas of the many. As the many change, it will be his good fortune if he can contrive to change with them. Statesmen may not live under hermetical seals. Like other men, they must be influenced by the opinions of other men. How potent is this influence, those best know who have tried to hold ideas different from the ideas of those around.

In another point of view also Sir Robert Peel's character was exactly fitted to the position we have delineated. He was a great administrator. Civilisation requires this. In a simple age work may be difficult, but it is scarce. There are fewer people, and everybody wants fewer things. The mere tools of civilisation seem in some sort to augment work. In early times, when a despot wishes to govern a distant province, he sends down a satrap on a grand horse, with other people on little horses; and very little is heard of the satrap again unless he send back some of the little people to tell what he has been doing. No great labour of superintendence is possible. Common rumour and casual complaints are the sources of intelligence. If it seem certain that the province is in a bad state, satrap No. 1 is recalled, and satrap No. 2 sent out in his stead. In civilised countries the process is different. You erect a *bureau* in the province you want to govern; you make it write letters and copy letters; it sends home eight reports per diem to the head *bureau* in St. Petersburg. Nobody does a sum in the province without somebody doing the same sum in the capital, to 'check him,' and see that he does it correctly. The consequence of this is, to throw on the heads of departments an amount of reading and labour which can only be accomplished by the greatest natural aptitude, the most efficient training, the most firm and regular industry. Under a free government it is by no means better, perhaps in some respects it is worse. It is true that many questions which, under the French despotism, are referred to Paris, are settled in England on the very spot where they are to be done, without reference to London at all. But as a set-off, a constitutional administrator has to be always consulting others, finding out what this man or that man chooses to think; learning which form of error is believed by Lord B., which by Lord C.; adding up the errors of the alphabet, and seeing what portion of what he thinks he ought to do, they will all of them together allow him to do. Likewise, though the personal freedom and the individual discretion which free governments allow to their subjects seem at first likely to diminish the work which those governments have to do, it may be doubted whether it does so really and in the end. Individual discretion strikes out so many more pursuits, and some supervision must be maintained over each of those pursuits. No despotic government would consider the police force of London enough to keep down, watch, and superintend such a population; but then no despotic government would have such a city as London to keep down. The freedom of growth allows the possibility of growth; and though liberal governments take so much less in proportion upon them, yet the scale of operations is so much enlarged by the continual exercise of civil liberty, that the real work is ultimately perhaps as immense. While a despotic government is regulating ten per cent. of ten men's actions, a free government has to regulate one per cent. of a hundred men's actions. The difficulty, too, increases. Any body can understand a rough despotic community;—a small buying class of nobles, a small selling class of traders, a large producing class of serfs, are much the same in all quarters of the globe; but a free intellectual community is a complicated network of ramified relations, interlacing and passing hither and thither, old and new,—some of fine city weaving, others of gross agricultural construction. You are never sure what effect any force or any change may produce on a frame-work so exquisite and so involved. Govern as you may, it will be a work of great difficulty, labour, and responsibility; and no man who is thus occupied ought ever to go to bed without reflecting, that from the difficulty of his employment he may, probably enough, have that day done more evil than good. What view Sir Robert Peel took of these duties, he has himself informed us.

'Take the case of the Prime Minister. You must presume that he reads every important despatch from every foreign court. He cannot consult with the Secretary of State for Foreign Affairs, and exercise the influence which he ought to have with respect to the conduct of foreign affairs, unless he be master of everything of real importance passing in that department. It is the same with respect to other departments; India, for instance; how can the Prime Minister be able to judge of the course of policy with regard to India, unless he be cognisant of all the current important correspondence? In the case of Ireland and the Home Department it is the same. Then the Prime Minister has the patronage of the Crown to exercise, which you say, and justly say, is of so much importance and of so much value; he has to make inquiries into the qualifications of the persons who are candidates; he has to conduct the whole of the communications with the Sovereign; he has to write, probably with his own hand, the letters in reply to all persons of station who address themselves to him; he has to receive deputations on public business; during the sitting of Parliament he is expected to attend six or seven hours a day, while Parliament is sitting, for four or five days in the week; at least he is blamed if he is absent.'

The necessary effect of all this labour is, that those subject to it have no opinions. It requires a great deal of time to have opinions. Belief is a slow process. That leisure which the poets say is necessary to be good, or to be wise, is needful for the humbler task of allowing respectable maxims to take root respectably. The 'wise passiveness' of Mr. Wordsworth is necessary in very ordinary matters. If you chain a man's head to a ledger, and keep him constantly adding up, and take a pound off his salary whenever he stops, you can't expect him to have a sound conviction on Catholic emancipation, tithes, and original ideas on the Transcaucasian provinces. Our system, indeed, seems expressly provided to make it unlikely. The most benumbing thing to the intellect is routine; the most bewildering is distraction: our system is a distracting routine. You see this in the description just given, which is not exhaustive. Sir Robert Peel once asked to have a number of questions carefully written down which they asked him one day in succession in the House of Commons. They seemed a list of every thing that could occur in the British empire, or to the brain of a member of Parliament. A premier's whole life is a series of such transitions. It is rather wonderful that our public men have any minds left, than that a certain unfixity of opinion seems growing upon them.

We may go further on this subject. A great administrator is not a man likely to desire to have fixed opinions. His natural bent and tendency is to immediate action. The existing pressing circumstances of the case fill up his mind. The letters to be answered, the documents to be filed, the memoranda to be made, engross his attention. He is angry if you distract him. A bold person who suggests a matter of principle, or a difficulty of thought, or an abstract result that seems improbable in the case 'before the board,' will be set down as a speculator, a theorist, a troubler of practical life. To expect to hear from such men profound views of future policy, digested plans of distant action, is to mistake their genius entirely. It is like asking the broker of the Stock Exchange what will be the price of the funds this day six months? His whole soul is absorbed in thinking what that price will be in ten minutes. A momentary change of an eighth is more important to him than a distant change of a hundred eighths. So the brain of a great administrator is naturally occupied with the details of the day, the passing dust, the granules of that day's life; and his unforeseeing temperament turns away uninterested from reaching speculations, from vague thought, and from extensive and far-off plans. Of course, it is not meant that a great administrator has absolutely no general views; some indeed he must have. A man cannot conduct the detail of affairs without having some plan which regulates that detail. He cannot help having some idea, vague or accurate, indistinct or distinct, of the direction in which he is going, and the purpose for which he is travelling. But the difference is, that this plan is seldom his own, the offspring of his own brain, the result of his own mental contention; it is the plan of some one else. Providence generally bestows on the working adaptive man a quiet adoptive nature. He receives insensibly the suggestions of others; he hears them with willing ears; he accepts them with placid belief. An acquiescent credulity is inherent in such men; they cannot help being sure that what every one says must be true; the *vox populi* is a part of their natural religion. It has been made a matter of wonder that Peel should have belonged to the creed of Mr. Perceval and Lord Sidmouth. Perhaps, indeed, our existing psychology will hardly explain the process by which a decorous young man acquires the creed of his era. He assumes its belief as he assumes his costume. He imitates the respectable classes. He avoids an original opinion, like an *outré* coat; a new idea, like an unknown tie. Especially he does so on matters of real concern to him, on those on which he knows he must act. He acquiesces in the creed of the orthodox agents. He scarcely considers for himself; he acknowledges the apparent authority of dignified experience. He is, he remembers, but the junior partner in the firm; it does not occur to him to doubt that those were right who were occupied in its management years before him. In this way he acquires an experience which more independent and original minds are apt to want. There was a great cry when the Whigs came into office, at the time of the Reform Bill, that they were not men of business. Of course, after a very long absence from office, they could not possess a technical acquaintance with official forms, a trained facility in official action. This Sir Robert Peel acquired from his apprenticeship to Mr. Perceval. His early connection with the narrow Conservative party has been considered a disadvantage to him; but it may well be doubted whether his peculiar mind was not more improved by the administrative training than impaired by the contact with prejudiced thoughts. He never could have been a great thinker; he became what nature designed, a great agent.

In a third respect also Sir Robert Peel conformed to the type of a constitutional statesman; and that third respect also seems naturally to lead to a want of defined principle, and to apparent fluctuation of opinion. He was a great debater; and of all pursuits ever invented by man for separating the faculty of argument from the capacity of belief, the art of debating is probably the most effectual. Mr. Macaulay tells us that, in his opinion, this is 'the most serious of the evils which are to be set off against the many blessings of popular government. The keenest and most vigorous minds of every generation, minds often admirably fitted for the investigation of truth, are habitually employed in producing arguments such as no man of sense would ever put into a treatise intended for publication,—arguments which are just good enough to be used once, when aided by fluent delivery and pointed language. The habit of discussing questions in this way necessarily reacts on the intellects of our ablest men, particularly of those who are introduced into Parliament at a very early age, before their minds have expanded to full maturity. The talent for debate is developed in such men to a degree which, to the multitude, seems as marvellous as the performances of an Italian *improvvisatore*. But they are fortunate indeed if they retain unimpaired the faculties which are required for close reasoning, or for enlarged speculation. Indeed, we should sooner expect a great original work on political science,—such a work, for example, as *The Wealth of Nations*,—from an apothecary in a country town, or from a minister in the Hebrides, than from a statesman, who, ever since he was one-and-twenty, had been a distinguished debater in the House of Commons.' But it may well be doubted whether there is not in the same pursuit a deeper evil, hard to eradicate, and tending to corrupt and destroy the minds of those who are beneath its influence. Constitutional statesmen are obliged not only to employ arguments which they do not think conclusive, but likewise to defend opinions which they do not believe to be true. Whether we approve it or lament it, there is no question that our existing political life is deeply marked by the habit of advocacy. Perhaps fifteen measures may annually, on an average, be brought in by a cabinet government of fifteen persons. It is impossible to believe that all members of that cabinet agree in all those measures. No two people agree in fifteen things; fifteen clever men never yet agreed in any thing; yet they all defend them, argue for them, are responsible for them. It is always quite possible that the minister who is strenuously defending a bill in the House of Commons may have used in the Cabinet the very arguments which the Opposition are using in the House; he may have been overruled without being convinced; he may still think the conclusions he opposes better than those which he inculcates. It is idle to say that he ought to go out; at least it amounts to saying that government by means of a cabinet is impossible. The object of a committee of that kind is to agree on certain conclusions; if every member after the meeting were to start off according to the individual bent and bias of his mind, according to his own individual discretion or indiscretion, the previous concurrence would have become childish. Of course, the actual measure proposed by the collective voice of several persons is very different from what any one of these persons would of himself wish; it is the result of a compromise between them. Each, perhaps, has obtained some concession; each has given up something. Every one sees in the actual proposal something of which he strongly disapproves; every one regrets the absence of something which he much desires. Yet on the whole, perhaps, he thinks the measure better than no measure; or at least he thinks that if he went out, it would break up the government; and imagines it to be of more consequence that the government should be maintained than that the particular measure should be rejected. He concedes his individual judgment. No one has laid this down with more distinctness than Sir Robert Peel;—'Supposing a person at a dinner-table to express his private opinion of a measure originating with a party with whom he is united in public life, is he, in the event of giving up that private opinion out of deference to his party, to be exposed to a charge almost amounting to dishonesty? The idea is absurd.—What is the every-day conduct of government itself? Is there any one in this House so ignorant as to suppose that on all questions cabinet ministers, who yield to the decision of their colleagues, speak and act in Parliament in strict conformity with the opinions they have expressed in the Cabinet? If ministers are to be taunted on every occasion that they hold opinions in the Cabinet different from what they do in this House, and if Parliament is to be made the scene of these taunts, I believe I should not be going too far in saying, the House would have time for little else. It is the uniform practice with all governments, and I should be sorry to think the practice carries any stain with it, for a member of the administration who chances to entertain opinions differing from those of the majority of his colleagues, rather than separate himself from them, to submit to be overruled, and even though he do not fully concur in their policy, to give his support to the measures which, as an administration, they promulgate. I will give the House an instance of this fact. It was very generally reported on a late occasion, that upon the question of sending troops to Portugal a strong difference of opinion took place in the Cabinet. Now would it, I ask, be either just or fair to call on those who, in the discussion of the Cabinet, had spoken in favour of sending out troops to aid the cause of Donna Maria, to come down, and in Parliament advocate that measure in opposition to the decision of their colleagues? No one would think of doing so.' It may not carry a stain; but it is a painful idea.

It is evident, too, that this necessarily leads to great apparent changes of opinion—to the professed belief of a statesman at one moment being utterly different from what it seems to be at another moment. When a government is founded, questions A, B, C, D, are the great questions of the day,—the matters which are obvious, pressing,—which the public mind comprehends. X, Y, Z, are in the background, little thought of, obscure. According to the received morality, no statesman would hesitate to sacrifice the last to the first. He might have a very strong personal opinion on X, but he would surrender it to a colleague as the price of his co-operation on A or B. A few years afterwards times change. Question A is carried, B settles itself, C is forgotten, X becomes the most important topic of the day. The statesman who conceded X before, now feels that he no longer can concede it; there is no equivalent. He has never in reality changed his opinion, yet he has to argue in favour of the very measures which he endeavoured before to argue against. Everybody imagines he has changed, and without going into details, the secrecy of which is esteemed essential to confidential co-operation, it is impossible that he can evince his consistency. No one can doubt that this is a very serious evil, and it is plainly one consequent on or much exaggerated by a popular and argumentative government. It is very possible for a conscientious man, under a bureaucratic government, to co-operate with the rest of a council in the elaboration and execution of measures many of which he thinks inexpedient. Nobody asks him his opinion; he has not to argue, or defend, or persuade. But a free government boasts that it is carried on in the face of day. Its principle is discussion; its habit is debate. The consequence is, that those who conduct it have to defend measures they disapprove, to object to measures they approve, to appear to have an accurate opinion on points on which they really have no opinion. The calling of a constitutional statesman is very much that of a political advocate; he receives a new brief with the changing circumstances of each successive day. It is easy to conceive a cold sardonic intellect, moved with contempt at such a life, casting aside the half-and-half pretences with which others partly deceive themselves, stating any thing, preserving an intellectual preference for truth, but regarding any effort at its special advocacy as the weak aim of foolish men, striving for what they cannot attain. Lord Lyndhurst has shown us that it is possible to lead the life of Lord Lyndhurst. One can conceive, too, a cold and somewhat narrow intellect, capable of forming, in any untroubled scene, an accurate plain conviction, but without much power of entering into the varying views of others; little skilled in diversified argument; understanding its own opinion, and not understanding the opinions of others;—one can imagine such a mind pained, and cracked, and shattered, by endeavouring to lead a life of ostentatious argument in favour of others' opinions, of half-concealment of its chill unaltering essence. It will be for posterity to make due allowance for the variance between the character and the position of Lord John Russell.

Sir Robert Peel was exactly fit for this life. The word which exactly fits his oratory is—specious. He hardly ever said any thing which struck you in a moment to be true; he never uttered a sentence which for a moment any body could deny to be plausible. Once, when they were opposed on a railway-bill, the keen irascibility of Lord Derby stimulated him to observe, 'that *no one* knew like the right honourable baronet how to *dress up* a case for that House.' The art of statement, the power of detail, the watching for the weak points of an opponent, an average style adapting itself equally to what the speaker believed and what he disbelieved, a business air, a didactic precision for what it was convenient to make clear, an unctuous disguise of flowing periods, and 'a deep sense of responsibility' for what it was convenient to conceal—an enormous facility,—made Sir Robert Peel a nearly unequalled master of the art of political advocacy. For his times he was perhaps quite unequalled. He might have failed in times of deep outpouring patriotic excitement; he had not nature enough to express it. He might have failed in an age when there was nothing to do, and when elegant personality and the *finesse* of artistic expression were of all things most required. But for an age of important business, when there were an unusual number of great topics to be discussed, but none great enough to hurry men away from their business habits, or awaken the most ardent passion or the highest imagination, there is nothing like the oratory of Peel,—able but not aspiring, firm but not exalted, never great but ever adequate to great affairs. It is curious to know that he was trained to the trade.

'Soon after Peel was born, his father, the first baronet, finding himself rising daily in wealth and consequence, and believing that money in those peculiar days could always command a seat in Parliament, determined to bring up his son expressly for the House of Commons. When that son was quite a child, Sir Robert would frequently set him on the table, and say, "Now, Robin, make a speech, and I will give you this cherry." What few words the little fellow produced were applauded; and applause stimulating exertion, produced such effects that, before Robin was ten years old, he could really address the company with some degree of eloquence. As he grew up, his father constantly took him every Sunday into his private room, and made him repeat, as well as he could, the sermon which had been preached. Little progress in effecting this was made, and little was expected *at first;* but by steady perseverance the habit of attention grew powerful, and the sermon was repeated almost *verbatim.* When at a very distant day the senator, remembering accurately the speech of an opponent, answered his arguments in correct succession, it was little known that the power of so doing was originally acquired in Drayton church.'

A mischievous observer might say that something else had remained to Sir Robert Peel from these sermons. His tone is a trifle sermonic. He failed where perhaps alone Lord John Russell has succeeded—in the oratory of conviction.

If we bear in mind the whole of these circumstances; if we picture in our minds a nature at once active and facile, easily acquiring its opinions from without, not easily devising them from within, a large placid adaptive intellect, devoid of irritable intense originality, prone to forget the ideas of yesterday, inclined to accept the ideas of to-day,— if we imagine a man so formed cast early into absorbing exhausting industry of detail, with work enough to fill up a life, with action of itself enough to render speculation almost impossible,—placed too in a position unsuited to abstract thought, of which the conventions and rules require that a man should feign other men's thoughts, should impugn his own opinions,—we shall begin to imagine a conscientious man destitute of convictions on the occupations of his life—to comprehend the character of Sir Robert Peel.

That Sir Robert was a very conscientious man is quite certain. It is even probable that he had a morbid sense of administrative responsibility. We do not say that he was so weighed down as Lord Liverpool, who is alleged never to have opened his letters without a pang of foreboding that something had miscarried somewhere; but every testimony agrees that Sir Robert had an anxious sense of duty in detail. Lord Wellesley, in the memoir before us, on an occasion when it would have been at least equally natural to speak of administrative capacity and efficient co-operation, mentions only 'the real impressions which your kindness and high character have fixed in my mind.' The circumstances of his end naturally produced a crowd of tributes to his memory, and hardly any of them omit his deep sense of the obligations of action. The characteristic too is written conspicuously on every line of these memoirs. Disappointing and external as in some respects they seem, they all the more evidently bear witness to this trait. They read like the conscientious letters of an ordinary practical man; the great statesman has little other notion than that it is his duty to transact his business well. As a conspicuous merit, the Duke of Wellington, oddly enough according to some people's notions at the time, selected Peel's veracity: 'In the whole course of my communication with him I have never known an instance in which he did not show the strictest preference for truth. I never had, in the whole course of my life, the slightest reason for suspecting that he stated any thing which he did not firmly believe to be the fact. I could not sit down without stating what I believe, after a long acquaintance, to have been his most striking characteristic.' Simple people in the country were a little astonished to hear so strong a eulogy on a man for not telling lies. They were under the impression that people in general did not. But those who have considered the tempting nature of a statesman's pursuits, the secrets of office, the inevitable complication of his personal relations, will not be surprised that many statesmen should be without veracity, or that one should be eulogised for possessing it. It is to be remarked, however, in mitigation of so awful an excellence, that Sir Robert was seldom 'in scrapes,' and that it is on those occasions that the virtue of veracity is apt to be most severely tested. The same remark too is applicable to the well-praised truthfulness of the Duke himself.

In conjunction with the great soldier, Sir Robert Peel is entitled to the fame of a great act of administrative conscience. He purified the Tory party. No one disputes that, during the long and secure reign which the Tories enjoyed about the beginning of the century, there was much of the corruption naturally incident to a strong party with many adherents to provide for, uncontrolled by an effectual Opposition, unwatched by a great nation. Of course, too, any government commencing in the last century would inevitably have adhering to it various *remanet* corruptions of that curious epoch. Then flourished those mighty sinecures and reversions, a few of which still remain to be the wonder and envy of an unenjoying generation. The House of

Commons was not difficult then to manage. There is a legend that a distinguished Treasury official of the last century, a very capable man, used to say of any case which was hopelessly and inevitably bad: 'Ah, we must apply our majority to this question;' and no argument is so effectual as the mechanical, calculable suffrage of a strong unreasoning party. There were doubtless many excellent men in the Tory party, even in its least excellent days; but the two men, to whom the party, as such, owes most of purification were the Duke of Wellington and Sir Robert Peel. From the time when they became responsible for the management of a Conservative government, there was no doubt, in office or in the nation, that the public money and patronage were administered by men whom no consideration would induce to use either for their personal benefit; and who would, as far as their whole power lay, discourage and prevent the corrupt use of either by others. The process by which they succeeded in conveying this impression is illustrated by a chapter in the Dean of York's[7] *Memoir of Peel*, in which that well-known dignitary recounts the temptations which he applied to the political purity of his relative:

While Peel was secretary for Ireland, I asked him to give a very trifling situation, nominally in his gift, to a worthy person for whom I felt an interest. He wrote me word that he was really anxious to oblige me in this matter, but that a nobleman of much parliamentary interest, who supported the government, insisted upon his right to dispose of all patronage in his own neighbourhood. So anxious was Peel to show his good will towards me, that he prevailed upon the Lord-Lieutenant to ask as a favour from the aforesaid nobleman that the situation might be given to my nominee; but the marquis replied, that the situation was of no value, yet, to prevent a dangerous precedent, he must refuse the application.

In times long after, when Sir Robert Peel became Prime Minister, I asked him often in the course of many years for situations for my sons, which situations were vacant and in his immediate gift. I subjoin three letters which I received from him on these subjects; they were written after long intervals and at different periods, but they all speak the same language:

'Whitehall, December 20 (no date of year).

My dear Dean of York,—I thank you for your consideration of what you deem the unrequited sacrifice which I make in the public service. But I beg to say, that my chief consolation and reward is the *consciousness* that my exertions are disinterested—that I have considered official patronage as a

---

[7] William Cockburn, Peel's brother-in-law.—Ed.

public trust, to be applied to the reward and encouragement of public service, or to the less praiseworthy, but still necessary, purpose of promoting the general interests of the government. That patronage is so wholly inadequate to meet the fair claims of a public nature that are daily presented for my consideration, and that constitute the chief torment of office, that I can only overcome the difficulties connected with the distribution by the utmost forbearance as to deriving any personal advantage from it. If I had absolute control over the appointment to which you refer, I should apply it to the satisfaction of one or other of the engagements into which I entered when I formed the government, and which (from the absolute want of means) remain unfulfilled. But I have informed the numerous parties who have applied to me on the subject of that appointment, that I felt it to be my duty, on account of the present condition of the board and the functions they have to perform, to select for it some experienced man of business connected with the naval profession, or some man distinguished in that profession.

Believe me, my dear Dean, affectionately yours,

ROBERT PEEL.'

I applied again for another place of less importance; the answer was much as before.

'Whitehall, April 5, 1843.

MY DEAR DEAN OF YORK,—I must dispose of the appointment to which you refer upon the same principle on which I have uniformly disposed of every appointment of a similar nature.

I do not consider patronage of this kind (and, indeed, I may truly say it of all patronage) as the means of gratifying private wishes of any one. Those who have made locally great sacrifices and great exertions for the maintenance of the political cause which they espouse, have always been considered fairly entitled to be consulted in respect to the disposal of local patronage, and would justly complain if, in order to promote the interests of a relative of my own, I were to disregard their recommendations. It would subject me to great personal embarrassment, and be a complete departure from the rule to which I have always adhered.

All patronage of all descriptions, so far from being of the least advantage personally to a minister, involves him in nothing but embarrassment.

Ever affectionately yours,

ROBERT PEEL.'

I publish one more letter of the same kind, because all these letters exhibit the character of the writer, and contain matters of some public interest. The distributor of stamps died in the very place where my son was resident, and where he and I had exerted considerable interest in assisting the government members. I thought that now, perhaps, an exception might be made to the

general rule, and I confidently recommended my eldest son for the vacancy.
The following was the answer:

'Whitehall, May 1.

My dear Dean,—Whatever arrangements may be made with respect to
the office of distributor of stamps, lately held by Mr. ——, I do not feel
myself justified in appropriating to myself any share of the local patronage
of a county with which I have not the remotest connection by property, or
any other local tie.

There are three members for the county of —— who support the government; and, in addition to the applications which I shall no doubt have from
them, I have already received recommendations from the Duke of —— and
Earl ——, each having certainly better claims than I have personally for
local appointments in the county of ——.

I feel it quite impossible to make so complete a departure from the
principles on which I have invariably acted, and which I feel to be nothing
more than consistent with common justice, as to take ——shire offices for
my own private purposes.

Very faithfully yours,
Robert Peel.'

These letters show the noble principle on which Sir Robert's public life
was founded. I am quite sure that he had a great regard for my sons. He
invited them to his shooting-quarters, was pleased to find them amusement,
and made them many handsome presents; but he steadily refused to enrich
them out of the public purse merely because they were his nephews. Many
Prime Ministers have not been so scrupulous.

And clearly *one* divine wishes Sir Robert Peel had not been so.

The changes of opinion which Sir Robert Peel underwent are often
cited as indications of a want of conscientiousness. They really are,
subject, of course, to the preceding remarks, proofs of his conscientiousness. We do not mean in the obvious sense of their being opposed
to his visible interest, and having on two great occasions destroyed
the most serviceable party organisation ever ruled by a statesman in a
political age; but in a more refined sense, the timeliness of his transitions may, without overstraining, be thought a mark of their *bona
fides*. He could not have changed with such felicitous exactness if he
had been guided by selfish calculation. The problems were too great
and too wide. There have, of course, been a few men,—Talleyrand or
Theramenes are instances,—who have seemed to hit, as if by a political
sense, the fitting moment to leave the side which was about to fall,
and to join the side which was about to rise. But these will commonly

be found to be men of a very different character from that of Peel. Minds are divided into open and close. Some men are so sensitive to extrinsic impressions, pass so easily from one man to another, catch so well the tone of each man's thought, use so well the opportunities of society for the purposes of affairs, that they are, as it were, by habit and practice, metrical instruments of public opinion. Sir Robert was by character, both natural and acquired, the very reverse. He was a reserved, occupied man of business. In the arts of society, in the easy transition from person to person, from tone to tone, he was but little skilled. If he had been left to pick up his rules of conduct by mere social perception and observation, his life would have been a life of miscalculations; instead of admiring the timeliness of his conversions, we should wonder at the perversity of his transitions. The case is not new. In ancient times, at a remarkable moment, in the persons of two selfish men of genius, the open mind was contrasted with the close. By a marvellous combination of successive manœuvres, Julius Cæsar rose from ruin to empire; the spoiled child of society—sensitive to each breath of opinion—ever living among, at least, the externals of enjoyment—always retaining, by a genial kindliness of manner, friends from each of the classes which he variously used. By what the vulgar might be pardoned for thinking a divine infatuation, Pompeius lost the best of political positions, threw away every recurring chance, and died a wandering exile. As a reserved ungenial man, he never was able to estimate the feeling of the time. 'I have only to stamp with my foot when the occasion requires, to raise legions from the soil of Italy!' were the words of one who could not, in his utmost need, raise a force to strike one blow for Italy itself. The fate of Pompeius would have been that of Peel, if he too had played the game of selfish calculation. His changes, as it has been explained, are to be otherwise accounted for. He was always anxious to do right. An occupied man of business, he was converted when other men of business in the nation were converted.

It is not, however, to be denied, that a calm and bland nature like that of Peel is peculiarly prone to self-illusion. Many fancy that it is passionate imaginative men who most deceive themselves; and of course they are more tempted,—a more vivid fancy and a more powerful impulse hurry them away. But they know their own weakness. 'Do you believe in ghosts, Mr. Coleridge?' asked some lady. 'No, ma'am, I have seen too many,' was the answer. A quiet calm nature, when it is tempted by its own wishes, is hardly conscious that it is tempted. These wishes are so gentle, quiet, as it would say, so 'reasonable,' that it does not conceive it possible to be hurried away into error by them. Nor *is* there any hurry. They operate quietly, gently, and constantly. Such a man will very much believe what he wishes. Many an imaginative outcast, whom no man would trust with sixpence, really forms his opinions on points which interest him by a much more intellectual process—at least has more purely intellectual opinions beaten and tortured into him—than the eminent and respected man of business, in whom every one confides, who is considered a model of dry judgment, of clear and passionless equanimity. Doubtless Sir Robert Peel continued to believe that the Corn-Laws were beneficial when no one in the distrusted classes even fancied that they were so.

It has been bitterly observed of Sir Robert Peel, that he was 'a Radical at heart;' and, perhaps with a similar thought in his mind, Mr. Cobden said once, at a League meeting, 'I do not altogether like to give up Peel. You see he is a Lancashire man.' And it cannot be questioned that, strongly opposed as Sir Robert Peel was to the Reform Bill, he was really much more suited to the reformed than to the unreformed House of Commons. The style of debating in the latter was described by one who had much opportunity for observation, Sir James Mackintosh, as 'continuous animated after-dinner discussion.' The House was composed mainly of men trained in two great schools, on a peculiar mode of education, with no great real knowledge of the classics, but with many lines of Virgil and Horace lingering in fading memories, contrasting oddly with the sums and business with which they were necessarily brought side by side. These gentlemen wanted not to be instructed, but to be amused; and hence arose what, from the circumstance of their calling, may be called the class of conversationalist statesmen. Mr. Canning was the type of these. He was a man of elegant gifts, of easy fluency, capable of embellishing any thing, with a nice wit, gliding swiftly over the most delicate topics; passing from topic to topic like the *raconteur* of the dinner-table, touching easily on them all, letting them all go as easily; confusing you as to whether he knows nothing, or knows everything. The peculiar irritation which Mr. Canning excited through life was at least in part owing to the natural wrath with which you hear the changing talk of the practised talker running away about all the universe; never saying any thing which indicates real knowledge, never saying any thing which at the very moment can be shown to be a blunder; ever on the surface, and ever ingratiating itself with the superficial. When Mr. Canning was alive, sound men of all political persuasions—the Duke of Wellington, Lord Grey—ever disliked him. You may hear old Liberals to this day declaring he was the greatest charlatan who ever lived, angry to imagine that his very ghost exists; and when you read his speeches yourself, you are at once conscious of a certain dexterous insincerity which seems to lurk in the very felicities of expression, and to be made finer with the very refinements of the phraseology. Like the professional converser, he seems so apt at the *finesse* of expression, so prone to modulate his words, that you cannot imagine him putting his fine mind to tough thinking, really working, actually grappling with the rough substance of a great subject. Of course, if this were the place for an estimate of Mr. Canning, there would be some limitation, and much excuse to be offered for all this. He was early thrown into what we may call an aristocratic debating society, accustomed to be charmed, delighting in classic gladiatorship. To expect a great speculator, or a principled statesman, from such a position, would be expecting German from a Parisian, or plainness from a diplomatist. He grew on the soil on which he had been cast; and it is hard, perhaps impossible, to separate the faults which are due to it and to him. He and it have both passed away. The old delicate Parliament is gone, and the gladiatorship which it loved. The progress of things, and the Reform Bill which was the result of that progress, have taken, and are taking, the national representation away from the university classes, and conferring it on the practical classes. Exposition, arithmetic, detail, reforms,—these are the staple of our modern eloquence. The old boroughs which introduced the young scholars are passed away; and even if the young scholars were in parliament, the subjects do not need the classic tact of expression. Very plain speaking suits the 'passing tolls,' 'registration of joint-stock companies,' finance, the post-office. The petty regulation of the details of civilisation, which happily is the daily task of our government, does not need, does not suit, a *recherché* taste or an ornate eloquence. As is the speech, so are the men. Sir Robert Peel was inferior to Canning in the old parliament; he would have been infinitely superior to him in the new. The aristocratic refinement, the nice embellishment, of the old time were as alien to him as the detail and dryness of the new era were suitable. He was admirably fitted to be where the Reform Bill placed him. He was fitted to work and explain; he was not able to charm or to amuse.

In its exact form this kind of eloquence and statesmanship is peculiar to modern times, and even to this age. In ancient times the existence of slavery forbade the existence of a middle-class eloquence. The Cleon who possessed the tone and the confidence of the tradesmen was a man vulgar, coarse, speaking the sentiments of a class whose views were narrow and whose words were mean. So many occupations were confined to slaves, that there was scarcely an opening for the sensible, moderate, rational body whom we now see. It was, of course, always possible to express the sentiments and prejudices of persons in trade. It is new to this era, it seems created for Sir Robert Peel to express those sentiments, in a style refined, but not too refined; which will not jar people of high cultivation, which will seem suitable to men of common cares and important transactions.

In another respect Sir Robert was a fortunate man. The principal measures required in his age were 'repeals.' From changing circumstances, the old legislation would no longer suit a changed community; and there was a clamour first for the repeal of one important act, and then of another. This was suitable to the genius of Peel. He could hardly have created any thing. His intellect, admirable in administrative routine, endlessly fertile in suggestions of detail, was not of the class which creates, or which readily even believes an absolutely new idea. As has been so often said, he typified the practical intelligence of his time. He was prone, as has been explained, to receive the daily deposits of insensibly-changing opinion; but he could bear nothing startling; nothing bold, original, single, is to be found in his acts or his words. No result could be so appropriate to such a mind as a conviction that an existing law was wrong. The successive gradations of opinion pointed to a clear and absolute result. When it was a question, as in the case of the Reform Bill, not of simple abolition, but of extensive and difficult reconstruction, he 'could not see his way.' He could be convinced that the anti-Catholic laws were wrong, that the currency laws were wrong; that the commercial laws were wrong; especially he could be convinced that the *laissez-faire* system was right, and the real thing was to do nothing; but he was incapable of the larger and higher political construction. A more imaginative genius is necessary to deal with the consequences of new creations, and the structure of an unseen future.

This remark requires one limitation. A great deal of what is called legislation is really administrative regulation. It does not settle what is to be done, but *how* it is to be done; it does not prescribe what our institutions shall be, but directs in what manner existing institutions shall work and operate. Of this portion of legislation Sir Robert Peel was an admirable master. Few men have fitted administrative regulations with so nice an adjustment to a prescribed end. The Currency Act of 1844 was an instance of this. If you consult the speeches by which that bill was introduced and explained to Parliament, you certainly will not find any very rigid demonstrations of political economy, or dry compactness of abstract principle. Whether the abstract theory of the supporters of that act be sound or unsound, no exposition of it ever came from the lips of Peel. He assumed the results of that theory; but no man saw more quickly the nature of the administrative machinery which was required. The separation of the departments of the Bank of England, the limitation of the country issues, though neither of them original ideas of Sir Robert's own mind, yet were not, like most of his other important political acts, forced on him from without. There was a general agreement among the received authorities in favour of a certain currency theory; the administrative statesman saw much before most men what was the most judicious and effectual way of setting it at work and regulating its action.

We have only spoken of Sir Robert Peel as a public man; and if you wish to write what is characteristic about him, that is the way to do so. He was a man whom it requires an effort to think of, as engaged in any thing but political business. Disraeli tells us that some one said that Peel was never happy except in the House of Commons, or while doing something which had some relation to something to be done there. In common life we continually see some men as it were scarcely separable from their pursuits: they are as good as others, but their visible nature seems almost all absorbed in a certain visible calling. When we speak of them we are led to speak of it, when we would speak of it we are led insensibly to speak of them. It is so with Sir Robert Peel. So long as constitutional statesmanship is what it is now, so long as its function is the recording the views of a confused nation, so long as success in it is confined to minds plastic, changeful, administrative,—we must hope for no better man. You have excluded the profound thinker; you must be content with what you can obtain— the business-gentleman.

Lord Palmerston

Introductory note

Henry John Temple, third Viscount Palmerston (1784–1865), was born at Broadlands, Hampshire. He was the elder son of Henry Temple, second Viscount Palmerston, M.P., by his second wife, Mary Mee. The third viscount succeeded to the peerage in 1802. He was educated at Harrow; in Edinburgh, where he was sent to board with Dugald Stewart and attend his lectures; and at St. John's College, Cambridge, where he went in 1803. In 1807 he became Tory M.P. for Newport, Isle of Wight. He was Lord of the Admiralty in the Portland administration. In 1809 he accepted the Secretaryship for War from Perceval, which he retained throughout successive administrations until 1828. He was elected M.P. for Cambridge University in 1811 and held the seat until 1831, when he was rejected owing to his support of parliamentary reform. After occupying two other seats, he became M.P. for Tiverton in 1835, which seat he retained until his death. In 1829 he made his first great speech on foreign affairs, attacking the government's policy on Portugal and Greece. He supported Catholic emancipation. In 1830 he became Foreign Secretary in Lord Grey's administration, and retained this office for eleven years with only a short break during Peel's administration. In 1830–31 he effected the independence of Belgium, and in the next decade supported Spain and Portugal against pretenders to those realms; supported Turkey against the encroachments of Russia; and made a treaty with Russia, Austria, and Prussia to defend Turkish territory against the Egyptians. In 1840–41 he declared war against China and annexed Hong Kong. In 1841 he effected the slave-trade convention. In 1846, after five years in opposition, Palmerston again became Foreign Secretary in Lord John Russell's administration. In that year he preserved Swiss independence from Austrian and French interference. In 1849 he supported Turkey, at the risk of war, in her refusal to give up to Russia and Austria certain refugees. In 1850 he compelled Greece to accept his terms in the Pacifico affair, and blockaded the Piraeus, on which occasion he made one of his most famous speeches and defeated both English and foreign attempts to overthrow him. He had already earned Queen Victoria's disapproval by his independent action, and when he expressed his approval of Napoleon's *coup d'état* in 1851, he was dismissed by Lord John Russell. In 1852 he became Home Secretary in Lord Aberdeen's ministry. On the outbreak of the Crimean War he proposed a campaign, but the conduct of the war was refused him by Aberdeen, at which Russell resigned, and the ministry fell in 1855. Palmerston now became Prime Minister at a time of great difficulty and danger. He agreed to the Treaty of Paris in 1856 under pressure from France and Austria. He was defeated on the Chinese war question, but at the general election of 1857 was returned to power with an increased majority. He was defeated in 1858 over the Conspiracy to Murder Bill, but returned as Prime Minister in 1859. He supported Italy's advance towards independence, and strengthened the national defences. Palmerston maintained English neutrality during the American Civil War. He died at Brocket Hall, Hertfordshire in 1865.

Lord Palmerston[1]

LORD PALMERSTON only died on Wednesday, and already the world is full of sketches and biographies of him. It is very natural that it should be so, for he counted for much in English politics: his personality was a power, and it is natural that every one should at his death seek to analyse what we used to have, and what we have now lost. We will do so, but remembering how often the tale has been told, we will be as brief as possible.

Lord Derby happily said that *he* was born in the 'pre-scientific' period, and Lord Palmerston was so even more. He was, it is true, a boarder at Dugald Stewart's, and we believe transcribed at least a part of the lectures on political economy of that philosopher, lately published. But the combined influence of interior nature and the surrounding situation was too strong. His real culture was that of living languages and the actual world. He was the best French scholar among his contemporaries,—so much so that when he went to Paris in 1859, the whole society which fancied he was an imperious and ignorant Englishman, was charmed by the grace of his expression. His English in all his speeches was sound and pure, and in his greater efforts almost fastidiously correct. The *feeling* for language, which is one characteristic of a great man of the world, was very nice in Lord Palmerston and very characteristic.

It was from the actual knowledge of men—from close specific contact—that Lord Palmerston derived his data. We have heard grave men say with surprise, 'He always has an anecdote to cap his argument.' He begins, 'I knew a man once,' and the anecdotes had no trace of the garrulity of age: they were real illustrations of the matter in hand. They were the chosen instances of a man who thought in instances. Some men think, as the philosophers say, by 'definition'; others by 'type'; Lord Palmerston, like an animated man, used to the animated world, thought in examples, and hardly realised abstract words.

[1] This article was first published in *The Economist* for October 21 1865, Volume XXIII, pp. 1265–6.

It was because of this that in international matters—the only ones for which in youth he cared—he was a great practical lawyer. He knew, what hardly any one knows, the subject-matter. He knew the *cases* with which during a long life he had to deal. To most men international law is a matter of precedent and words; to him it was a matter of personal adventure and reality. Some people, not unqualified to judge, have said that his opinion on such matters was as good as any law officer's. He might not have studied Vattel or Wheaton so closely as some; but he had, which is far better, followed with a keen interest the actual and necessary practice of present nations.

It was this sort of worldly sympathy and worldly education which gave Lord Palmerston his intelligibility. He was not a common man, but a common man might have been cut out of him. He had in him all that a common man has and something more. And he did not at all despise, as some philosophers teach people to do, the common part of his mind. He was profoundly aware that the common mass of plain sense is the great administrative agency of the world, and that if you keep yourself in sympathy with this you win, and if not you fail. Sir George Lewis used to say that just as Demosthenes declared action to be the first, second, and third thing in a statesman, so intelligibility is the first, second, and third thing in a constitutional statesman. It is to us certainly the first, second, and third thing in Lord Palmerston. This is not absolutely eulogistic. No one resembled less than Lord Palmerston the fancied portrait of an ideal statesman laying down in his closet plans to be worked out twenty years hence, and to be appreciated twenty years hence. He was a statesman for the moment. Whatever was not wanted now, whatever was not practicable now, whatever would not *take* now, he drove quite out of his mind. The prerequisites of a constitutional statesman have been defined as the 'powers of a first-rate man, and the creed of a second-rate man.' The saying is harsh, but it is expressive. Lord Palmerston's creed was never the creed of the far-seeing philosopher; it was the creed of a sensible and sagacious, but still common-place man. His objects were common objects: what was uncommon was the will with which he pursued them.

No man was better in action, but no man was more free from the pedantry of business. People, he has been heard to say, have different minds. 'When I was a young man, the Duke of Wellington made an appointment with me at half-past seven in the morning, and some one asked me, "Why, Palmerston, how will you keep that engagement?" "Oh," I said, "of course, the easiest thing in the world. I shall keep it the last thing before I go to bed." ' He knew that the real essence of work is concentrated energy and that people who really have that in a superior degree by nature, are independent of the forms and habits and artifices by which less able and active people are kept up to their labour.

Lord Palmerston prided himself on his foreign policy, on which we cannot now pronounce a judgment. But it is not upon this that his fame will rest. He had a great difficulty as a foreign minister. He had no real conception of any mode of life except that with which he was familiar. His idea, his fixed idea, was that the Turks were a highly-improving and civilised race, and it was impossible to beat into him their essentially barbaric and unindustrial character. He would hear anything patiently, but no corresponding ideas were raised in his mind. A man of the world is not an imaginative animal, and Lord Palmerston was by incurable nature a man of the world. Keenly detective in what he could realise by experience—utterly blind, dark, and impervious to what he could not so realise. Even the best part of his foreign policy was alloyed with this defect. The mantle of Canning had descended on him, and the creed and interests of Canning. He was most eager to use the strong influence of England to support free institutions—to aid 'the Liberal party' was the phrase in those days—everywhere on the Continent. And no aim could be juster and better; it was the best way in which English strength could be used. But he failed in the instructed imagination and delicate perception necessary to its best attainment. He supported the Liberal party when it was bad and the country unfit for it, as much as when it was good and the nation eager for it. He did not define the degree of his sympathy, or apportion its amount to the comparative merits of the different claims made on it. According to the notions of the present age, too, foreign policy should be regulated by abstract, or at least comprehensive principles, but Lord Palmerston had no such principles. He prided himself on his exploits in Europe, but it is by his instincts in England that he will be remembered.

It was made a matter of wonder that Lord Palmerston should begin to rule the House of Commons at seventy, and there is no doubt he was very awkward at first in so ruling it. Sir James Graham, and other judges of business management, predicted that 'the thing would fail,' and that a new government would have to be formed. But the truth is, that though he had been fifty years in the House of Commons, Lord Palmerston had never regularly attended it, and even still less attended *to* it. His person had not been there very much, and his mind had been there very little. He answered a question on his own policy, or made a speech, and then went away. Debate was not to him, as to Mr. Pitt, or Mr. Gladstone, a matter of life and pleasure. Mr. Canning used to complain, 'I can't get that three-decker Palmerston to bear down.' And when he was made Leader of the House, it came out that he hardly knew, if he did know, the forms of the House. But it was a defect of past interest, not a defect of present capacity. He soon mastered the necessary knowledge, and as soon as he had done so, the sure sagacity of his masculine instincts secured him an unconquerable strength.

Something we wished to say more on these great gifts, and something, too, might be said as to the defects by which they were alloyed. But it is needless. Brevity is as necessary in a memorial article as in an epitaph. So much is certain:—We shall never look upon his like again. We may look on others of newer race, but his race is departed. The merits of the new race were not his merits; their defects are not his. England will never want statesmen, but she will never see in our time *such* a statesman as Viscount Palmerston.

Lord Palmerston at Bradford[1]

LORD PALMERSTON encountered at Bradford a slight but unmistakeable indication that his popularity is not universal. A certain number of
working men agreed to receive him in solemn silence, and to abstain
from every sort of cheering and congratulation. Sir F. Crossley, the
chairman of the reception dinner, rather defended the working men
for so doing. In the hands of a less consummate man of the world these
elements of dissatisfaction might easily have exploded into something
unpleasant. Lord Palmerston let them alone, said not a word of Reform
or any other topic of possible difference, and made himself as agreeable
as he could. The last is no difficulty to him. He gave pleasure at Bradford, for he gives pleasure wherever he goes. His admirable manner,
his long experience of the world, his wealth of social anecdote, though
great helps, are not the main secret of his unfailing social success. The
principal cause is the nature of man. He is liked because he is *likeable*.
By a native gift, some men please other men, just as other men dis-
please them. 'Good fellows' are born, not made: Lord Palmerston
was so born. Wherever he goes he carries with him a happy attraction,
which makes his friends more friendly, and prevents most opponents
from displaying their hostility. By a skilful use of these natural
advantages, he evaded the difficulty at Bradford so completely that
distant and superficial observers have scarcely discovered it; but the
difficulty was not the less real, and it is instructive to examine the
causes of it.

First. It is inevitable that a Prime Minister such as Lord Palmerston
should not be popular with persons or constituencies of *any* extreme
opinion. He is the favourite Premier of moderate and commonplace
men, and exactly on that account those who hold bold and unusual
opinions do not like him. He represents, not the characteristic and
typical element of either party, but the neutral, the common, the pervading elements which are diffused through the moderate men of all

[1] This article was first published in *The Economist* for August 13 1864, Volume XXII,
p. 1018.

parties. Three-fourths of both parties, perhaps, prefer him as Prime
Minister to any other man, but on both sides of the House there is a
section which, for that very reason, dislikes him. Those who think
most people all wrong, cannot like a statesman whom most men think
quite right. The few zealots of extreme Toryism and extreme Liberalism combine to hate a Premier whom the mixed many, that are
destitute of extreme zeal, much admire, because they imagine that, in
this respect at least, he is akin to themselves.

But besides this inevitable quality of his peculiar position, Lord
Palmerston has other peculiarities which make him disagreeable to
many members of his own party. What Mr. Cobden and Mr. Bright
think of him, we know; and the same feeling, though not to the same
extent, undeniably influences many others. Lord Palmerston represents, above all things, *London*,—that easy worldly Belgravian crowd,
which we can none of us describe or define, but which we all know so
well. Now, that semi-aristocratic and half-frivolous world is not
popular with men of business. Grave men who have made much
money do not like to be thought inferior to light men who have made
no money, who have inherited but little, and who only know how to
spend that which they have. Lord Palmerston, we once heard a good
observer say, 'believes in hunting and shooting,' and naturally he is
not agreeable to those who were not bred to the life which those
amusements typify. His mode of illustrating the advantage of railways
expresses the man precisely. He does not accumulate rural statistics;
he makes up a story of the London world. 'Formerly,' he says, 'when a
gentleman asked a friend in London to come down to him in the
country, the friend came with things to last him for a fortnight or three
weeks, and took perhaps a week on the journey. Now, if one gentleman meets another, say in St. James's street, he says, "I shall have some
good shooting next week. Will you come down to me and spend a few
days?" His friend replies, "Oh by all means. I shall be charmed. What
is the station nearest your house?" The first speaker rejoins, "Why,
I am not very well off at present in regard to railway communication—
the nearest station is 16 miles from my house. But it is a good road.
You will get a nice fly, and you can come very well." Upon this the
invited guest says, "Did you say it was Tuesday you asked me for?"
"Yes," says the country gentleman, "I think you told me you were
free." "The fact is," answers the friend, "I have a very bad memory,
and now I think of it I am very sorry, but I have a particular engage-

ment for that day,—some other time I shall be happy to go to you."
And so away he goes, and offers himself as a visitor to some other
friend, who has got a station within one or two miles of his house.'
Lord Palmerston knows St. James's street better than any one else,
but an energetic manufacturer who hates St. James's street, who hates
the clubs and 'all that life,' does not like him the better, but the worse,
on that account. Deep under the superficial controversies of English
society, there is a struggle between what we may call the Northern and
business element of English society, and the Southern and aristocratic
element. Lord Palmerston is at heart and to the core a *Southerner*, and,
therefore, the zealots of the opposite party never like, even if they do
not hate him.

Nor is Lord Palmerston popular with the political artisans. He has
done nothing for them, and intends to do nothing. A cynic once said
that 'a constitutional statesman ought to live from hand to mouth.'
Of course, in its literal form, this is a nonsensical exaggeration, but
there is a latent vestige of truth in it which Lord Palmerston illustrates.
He *does* live from hand to mouth, and has always done so. He has
through life troubled himself with the principal matters of the moment,
and troubled himself about nothing else. He does so now. Thinking
people see that the vast and intelligent working classes of this country
cannot always—cannot long continue to be excluded from all political
power. Every man who sees beyond the present moment perceives
this, and thinks how it may best be done,—how the most numerous
class in the nation can be admitted to some power without swamping
all other classes and absorbing all power. But Lord Palmerston does
not perceive it. In the old times, when the middle classes were in subjection, when Bradford had no member, when only a few far-seeing
men foresaw that there must be a reform, Lord Palmerston was not a
reformer. He was a Canningite, and Mr. Canning laughed at reform.
He was a member of Lord Liverpool's government, the most illiberal
and the least improving of all governments. Most people then were of
that way of thinking, and, therefore, he was of that way too. He
did not wish to enfranchise the middle class,—he let it go on till it
enfranchised itself. Just so now. He does nothing for the working
men; he laughs at them and plays with them. If they *would* have power,
he would let them have it. He would accept their dynasty and be
happy under it, as he accepted and enjoyed all others.

Perhaps we cannot sum up these qualities which mar Lord Palmerston's almost universal popularity better than by saying that he was born before *earnestness* was thought to be a virtue. That is a new word and a new merit. In the days of the Regency, when Lord Palmerston was young, there was no 'Social Science.' Men eat and drank, and married, and gave in marriage, and no intellectual care troubled them. It is not so with us. A haunting atmosphere of reflection is around and about us. Take up a speech of Mr. Gladstone's, you may agree with it or disagree with it, but you cannot help saying that there is a grave intensity which marks the man and marks his time. He is always revolving difficult problems, and so is the present age. But Lord Palmerston is of an older and lighter race. He follows the wise old maxim of a shrewd old banker, 'Live, sir, from day to day, and do not trouble yourself.' Therefore, there are many of us with whom he can never be very popular, the depth of whose natures he can never touch; but we all admire his many great and manly qualities, and are deeply interested in him, as the representative of an age which has passed away,—as an historical phenomenon which has become unique by lapse of time, and is likely never to occur again.

Richard Cobden

Introductory note

Richard Cobden (1804–1865) was born at Heyshott, Sussex, the son of William Cobden, a farmer. At the age of fifteen Cobden became a clerk, and then a commercial traveller for his uncle, who was a London calico merchant. In 1828 he became a partner in a calico firm and in 1831 established a calico factory in Lancashire. Cobden settled in Manchester in 1832. He now began to repair his neglected education, and although he learned French and attempted other formal studies, his chief reading was in newspapers, Hansard, and generally in current affairs. He began to write on economics in the Manchester *Examiner*, and in 1835–6 published the pamphlets which opened his career. In these he stated the theory which was to be his policy all his life, that the only sound policy for Great Britain lay in free trade and non-intervention. Between 1835–38 he travelled in America, Germany, and the East. In 1838 he joined the movement with which his name has ever since been connected; in October a group of Manchester merchants formed a new association which grew to be the Anti-Corn-Law League. Cobden gave the League his unsparing devotion; he had considerable talent for organisation and a gift for presenting difficult ideas to untrained minds. He became M.P. for Stockport in 1841, and early made his mark in parliamentary debate. His chief labours for the Anti-Corn-Law League, however, were on the platform, and with John Bright he travelled the country year after year. In 1845 Cobden altered the focus of his arguments against the Corn Laws to their agricultural aspect, since the revival of trade in 1844 had weakened his arguments against them on grounds of the duties on corn being an obstacle to foreign demand for British goods. After Peel's resignation in 1845, Cobden set about persuading *any* government of the necessity for total repeal of the Corn Laws, and when the bill for total repeal of them was passed in 1846 after Peel's return to office, Peel acknowledged Cobden's untiring and disinterested concern in the matter. Cobden had been privately financially ruined while he had expended all his

energies and attention on the Anti-Corn-Law League. A public sub-
scription was raised for him in commemoration of his services, and
£80,000 was collected. A further £40,000 was collected for him in
1860. In the general election of 1847 he became M.P. for the West
Riding of Yorkshire as well as Stockport. During the next decade
he advocated international arbitration and disarmament, and with
Bright stood out against the Crimean War, which earned him a great
public repulse. In 1857 he defeated the government on the question
of the Chinese war, but when Palmerston at once appealed to the
country, Cobden found that his action during the Crimean War had
lost him his chance of retaining his Yorkshire seat, and when he stood
for Huddersfield he was defeated. In 1859 he was returned as M.P. for
Rochdale. During the next year he negotiated the commercial treaty
with France. Palmerston offered him a baronetcy or a privy-councillor-
ship, both of which he refused. Cobden died in London in 1865.

Mr. Cobden[1]

WE have already said what seemed necessary on the controversy between Mr. Cobden and Mr. Delane. Since we wrote, some additional letters have been published, but they do not change the essence of the matter. Mr. Cobden, as well as Mr. Bright had some right to complain of the original articles,—but there was no ground for Mr. Cobden's violence. Still less was there a reason for his sudden intrusion upon the useful privacy of newspaper writing. As we lately showed, anonymous writing is almost essential to the existence of newspapers as distinct properties, and it is of great moment that newspapers should be steadied and guided by the instincts of property, rather than distracted and impelled by the momentary caprices of casual writers. We return to the subject of this lamentable correspondence, not in the least for its intrinsic interest, but because it affords a reasonable opportunity for a few remarks upon the late career of a very remarkable man.

Mr. Cobden for many years, we might say during his whole political career, has been an *outsider* in politics. At first this was necessary. He and others, to whom England is indefinitely indebted, took up, as the sole subject of political pursuit, a subject which was almost neglected by professional politicians, which formed no part of the special creed of Whig or Tory, but which at the time was more important than any disputed topic in either creed, or than any subject which politicians were discussing. Free Trade was unspeakably more important to England than the 'Appropriation Clause,' or such matters. It was then right to be an outsider, for the politicians inside the world of politics had neglected the one thing needful, and were cumbering themselves with comparative trifles. Mr. Cobden was wise in saying he would vote for any Ministry which would carry Free Trade, for the good to be effected by that measure far outweighed any other harm a ministry might do. He did right to be one-idead and solitary,—for in their solitude he and his friends could brood and did brood over the one idea of most importance in contemporary politics.

[1] This article was first published in *The Economist* for December 26 1863; Volume XXI, pp. 1443–4.

But this conjuncture was exceptional and temporary. Free Trade was carried,—at least the Corn Laws were repealed. The citadel was captured, and the true principle was admitted. There was no other great idea outside English politics which justified political segregation. Politicians may have defects: they make great omissions. In this case they had the defect of omitting the greatest topic of their age from party politics,—the only politics for which most politicians will ever care. Still such great errors are rare. Politicians do not in most generations commit such a blunder, and hardly in any generation do they commit more than one. Since the Corn Laws were repealed, and the Anti-Corn-Law League disbanded, our government, our parties, and our Parliament have upon the whole, and with rare exceptions, been fittingly occupied with the greatest contemporary topics. Mr. Cobden's separate faith had become the common and accepted creed; he had converted all politicians, and it would have seemed that he should no longer be alone among politicians. He had converted the ministerial hierarchy, and he should have become a minister.

There was much that he could have taught to common statesmen, and much, too, which he could have learned from them. It would be very untrue to quote of the English world the trite saying that the world is governed with little wisdom. There probably never was a nation governed, on the whole, with greater average sense, with greater continuity of practical discretion, than ours. Certainly, no contemporary nation is governed, taken as a whole, with nearly as much. Louis Napoleon has a sort of far-sightedness which our statesmen have not, and which would be useless to them if they had it, for the nation at large could not follow nor comprehend it. And even he has strange veins of weakness and theatricality, which make his statesmanship peculiar and remarkable, as we acknowledge it to be inferior, in the long run and on the whole, to the tame and even course of our parliamentary statesmen. Of French officials and of American we need not speak; every one will admit that they are inferior to our own. Nevertheless, our statesmen have great defects. England is governed with much sense, but with little originality. Our parliamentary statesmen are grave, cautious, and decorous. They have habits of business and the manners of gentlemen. They are all men of respectable ability : as a class, and as compared with ordinary men, they are men of considerable ability. But as a class, and with exceptions, they are not irritably suggestive. It is not from them that we expect new schemes, or novel hints, or strange ideas. Lord Macaulay, who lived among them, has said, that he should sooner expect a great original work on political science,—such a work, for example, as *The Wealth of Nations*— from an apothecary in a country town, or from a minister in the Hebrides, than from a parliamentary statesman of long standing. Every close and good observer must confirm the remark. A certain easy monotonous sense characterises our higher class. They have no favourite schemes or original ideas; they mean *well*, but they do not mean *much*. Some have ascribed this to the early age at which most of our statesmen enter subordinate offices, in which they are expected to follow blindly the doctrine of a cabinet, to whose deliberations they are not admitted. It has been said, 'Years of acquiescing in proposals as to which he has not been consulted, of voting for measures which he did not frame, and in the wisdom of which very often did not believe, of arguing for proposals from half of which he dissents,— usually *disintellectualise* a parliamentary statesmen before he comes to half his power.' There is truth in this, and even more generally it may be said that parliamentary statesmen, who, knowing that they cannot propose any scheme for which the nation is not prepared, discourage rather than cultivate a far-reaching originality, which can seldom be advantageous and which may often be troublesome. Other reasons too might be added, but we are not now concerned with them: our busi- ness is only with the fact. All observers will agree that our highest political class is not excitably suggestive, and that its members are remarkable for judgment rather than imagination—for a sedate selec- tion rather than for copious proposals.

Mr. Cobden was the man to be of use in a class like this, just because he is the exact opposite to it. He has not, we may be pardoned for saying, great administrative ability, but we heard a very competent judge, not now among us, once say, 'Cobden is most valuable in counsel: very shrewd and suggestive, and not at all extreme.' He could not help starting and thinking of many considerations on many sub- jects which most of our statesmen would hardly dream of, and which it would take them some trouble to comprehend. There is plenty of torpidity, if we may say it with respect, in our official life, and a little of animated suggestion would be most valuable there. As a rule, there is plenty of sense to reject what is unsound, but there is not enough of *vis insita*—of irritable energy to venture on proposals. There is

much in Mr. Cobden which he might beneficially impart to our governing class—much which they might learn from him.

There is much too which they might teach him. If they are over-
ballasted with discretion, he is not so. The speciality of his mind is to
seize on some one aspect of a subject, and work it out exclusively and
to the omission of all others. If we may be pardoned the saying, he is
like a clever boy from a small school, who has been very well taught
what he knows, but who is not conscious of the incompleteness of his
knowledge, and whose knowledge often stops very abruptly. At a
university these idiosyncracies are rubbed off, and these limitations are
removed; men gain a wider and more universal culture, and learn also
how limited that enlarged knowledge is and must be. The great
university of the world has the same effect. But Mr. Cobden has not
entered it. He has travelled widely, but among a special class. He has
been *consigned* from Free-trader to Free-trader. He has often enlarged
his latitude and longitude, but never his thoughts and ideas. In close
counsel with responsible statesmen he might have gained the reliability in which he is wanting. At present he is *par excellence* a man to
hear, but not a man to follow. He suggests invaluable elements for
judgment, but he does not shape that judgment himself.

His position as an *outsider* has caused the principal defeats of Mr.
Cobden's career. Such a position teaches a man nothing. Responsible
office, and even responsible opposition, teach much: the very errors
of to-day are to an improving statesman the lessons of to-morrow.
Mr. Cobden has learned little or nothing. We chanced a week or two
ago to look over an old and fragmentary collection of his anti-Corn
Law speeches. Even now they are pleasant reading; there is an effectual
simplicity about them as rare in oratory as in action. But Mr. Cobden
has not advanced beyond those speeches; we do not say he has never
spoken so well as then, though a harsh critic might say so, but certainly
he has never spoken better. Seventeen years have passed away since
the dissolution of the League, but his mind has not grown during that
long period. What he is, he was—what he was, he is. Contrast such
a career with that of other statesmen. What a world of thought Mr.
Gladstone has developed in those years. Who supposed in 1846 he
would be a great Chancellor of the Exchequer, that he would be the
most masterly explainer, and the most advancing and reforming
financier of the age? In 1846 he was one of the Peelites, and men now
immeasurably his inferiors were reckoned as his equals. Or take Lord

Palmerston, a far older man than Mr. Cobden, and one, therefore, who could be less asked to display new excellences. During the last ten years he has developed the highest faculty of parliamentary statesmanship,—the faculty of premiership. Ten years ago we used to discuss eagerly whether he was a good foreign minister or a bad, but no one guessed that he possessed the instinct and genius of a great Prime Minister. If Mr. Cobden were a small man, we should not have complained of his want of development and growth. But he has not a poor nature. As we believe, he might have improved into something far greater than he is if he had chosen the true means,—if he had chosen a position in which there was to be much learnt instead of one in which nothing.

Mr. Cobden's irritability arises in part from natural sensitiveness, but in part, also, from his unfavourable position. It is not pleasant to be out of power; and it is least pleasant to the most suggestive men. It is not in human nature that Mr. Cobden should not be vexed that the English would go forward with so little aid of guidance from him. He must wish, he *ought* to wish to impress his mind on events; yet he must feel that very rarely, that only on very isolated occasions, he does so effectually. This is the real source of his attacks on Lord Palmerston and his attacks on *The Times*. These are the powers that be; the exponents of our present governing opinions; the statesman and the newspaper which partly guide and partly follow, but always aim to coincide with the national will. Mr. Cobden must hate them because that national opinion is often erroneous, and the national action accordingly perverted.

We hear it said that Mr. Cobden has lost himself! Mr. Cobden will never lose himself. Much greater faults than he has would not ruin a man so great as he is. He will remain a man of genius; he will retain his 'unadorned eloquence;' he will be as before the apostle of Free Trade. We shall still owe to him the repeal of the Corn Laws and the French treaty. He will still have a fair chance of some posthumous fame. But he must not expect that which is yet dearer to human nature,—contemporary respect and consideration. The daily respect of an age is given to those who do its daily work—to those who bear the burden and the heat of common affairs. The best counsellors from without are in comparison but little regarded, and they should not repine or murmur at it.

Mr. Cobden[1]

Twenty-three years ago—and it is very strange that it should be so many years—when Mr. Cobden first began to hold Free-trade meetings in the agricultural districts, people there were much confused. They could not believe the Mr. Cobden they saw to be the 'Mr. Cobden that was in the papers.' They expected a burly demagogue from the North, ignorant of rural matters, absorbed in manufacturing ideas, appealing to class prejudices—hostile and exciting hostility. They saw 'a sensitive and almost slender man, of shrinking nerve, full of rural ideas, who proclaimed himself the son of a farmer, who understood and could state the facts of agricultural life far better than most agriculturalists, who was most anxious to convince every one of what he thought the truth, and who was almost more anxious not to offend any one.' The tradition is dying out, but Mr. Cobden acquired, even in those days of Free-trade agitation, a sort of agricultural popularity. He excited a personal interest—he left what may be called a *sense* of himself among his professed enemies. They were surprised at finding that he was not what they thought; they were charmed to find that he was not what they expected; they were fascinated to find what he was. The same feeling has been evident at his sudden death,—death at least what was to the mass of occupied men sudden. Over political Belgravia—the last part of English society Mr. Cobden ever cultivated —there was a sadness. Every one felt that England had lost an *individuality* which it could never have again, which was of the highest value, which was in its own kind altogether unequalled.

What used to strike the agricultural mind as different from what they fancied and most opposite to a Northern agitator was a sort of playfulness. They could hardly believe that the lurking smile, the perfectly magical humour which they were so much struck by, could really be that of a 'Manchester man.' Mr. Cobden used to say, 'I have as much right as any man to call myself the representative of the

[1] This article was first published in *The Economist* for April 8 1865, Volume XXIII, pp. 397–8.

tenant-farmer, for I am a farmer's son, and the son of a Sussex farmer.' But agriculturists keenly felt that was not the explanation of the man they saw. Perhaps they could not have thoroughly explained, but they perfectly knew that they were hearing a man of singular and most peculiar genius, fitted as if by 'natural selection' for the work he had to do, and not wasting a word on any other work or anything else, least of all upon himself.

Mr. Cobden was very anomalous in two respects. He was a *sensitive* agitator. Generally, an agitator is a rough man of the O'Connell type, who says anything himself, and lets others say anything. You 'peg into me and I will peg into you, and let us see which will win,' is his motto. But Mr. Cobden's habit and feeling was utterly different. He never spoke ill of any one. He arraigned principles, but not persons. We fearlessly say that after a career of agitation of thirty years, not one single individual has—we do not say a valid charge, but a producible charge—a charge which he would wish to bring forward against Mr. Cobden. You can't find the man who says 'Mr. Cobden said this of me, and it was not true.' This may seem trivial praise, and on paper it looks easy. But to those who know the great temptations of actual life it means very much. How would any other great agitator, O'Connell, or Hunt, or Cobbett, look if tried by such a test? Very rarely, if even ever in history, has a man achieved so much by his words—been victor in what was thought at the time to be a class struggle—and yet spoken so little evil as Mr. Cobden. There is hardly a word to be found, perhaps, even now, which the recording angel would wish to blot. We may on other grounds object to an agitator who lacerates no one, but no watchful man of the world will deny that such an agitator has vanquished one of life's most imperious and difficult temptations.

Perhaps some of our readers may remember as vividly as we do a curious instance of Mr. Cobden's sensitiveness. He said at Drury Lane Theatre, in tones of feeling, almost of passion, curiously contrasting with the ordinary coolness of his nature: 'I *could* not serve with Sir Robert Peel.' After more than twenty years, the curiously thrilling tones of that phrase still live in our ears. Mr. Cobden alluded to the charge which Sir Robert Peel had made, or half made, that the Anti-Corn-Law League and Mr. Cobden had, by their action and agitation, conduced to the actual assassination of Mr. Drummond, his secretary, and the intended assassination of himself, Sir Robert Peel. No excuse or palliation could be made for such an assertion except the most important one, that Peel's nerves were as susceptible and sensitive as Mr. Cobden's. But the profound feeling with which Mr. Cobden spoke of it is certain. He felt it as a man feels an unjust calumny, an unfounded stain on his honour.

Mr. Disraeli said on Monday night (and he has made many extraordinary assertions, but this is about the queerest) 'Mr. Cobden had a profound reverence for tradition.' If there is any single quality which Mr. Cobden had not, it is traditional reverence. But probably Mr. Disraeli meant what is most true, that Mr. Cobden had a delicate dislike of offending other men's opinions. He dealt with them tenderly. He did not like to have his own creed coarsely attacked, and he did— he could not help doing—as he would be done by; he never attacked any man's creed coarsely, or roughly, or in any way except by what he in his best conscience thought the fairest and justest argument.

This sensitive nature is one marked peculiarity in Mr. Cobden's career as an agitator, and another is that he was an agitator *for men of business*. Generally speaking, occupied men charged with the responsibilities and laden with the labour of grave affairs are jealous of agitation. They know how much may be said against any one who is responsible for anything. They know how unanswerable such charges nearly always are, and how false they easily may be. A capitalist can hardly help thinking 'Suppose a man was to make a speech against *my* mode of conducting my own business, how much he would have to say.' Now it is an exact description of Mr. Cobden that by the personal magic of a single-minded practicability, he made men of business abandon this objection. He made them rather like the new form of agitation. He made them say, 'How business like, how wise, just what it would have been right to do.'

Mr. Cobden of course was not the discoverer of the Free-trade principle. He did not first find out that the Corn Laws were bad laws. But he was the most effectual of those who discovered how the Corn Laws were to be repealed—how Free-trade was to change from a doctrine into a doctrine of *The Wealth of Nations*, into a principle of tariffs, and a fact of real life. If a thing was right, to Mr. Cobden's mind it ought to be done, and as Adam Smith's doctrines were admitted on theory, he could not believe that they ought to lie idle, that they ought to be 'bedridden in the dormitory of the understanding.'

Lord Houghton once said, 'In my time political economy books used to begin, Suppose a man upon an island.' Mr. Cobden's speeches never began so. He was altogether a man of business speaking to men of business. Some of us may remember the almost arch smile with which he said the House of Commons 'does not seem quite to understand the difference between a cotton mill and a print work.' It was almost amusing to him to think that the first assembly of the first mercantile nation could be, as they were, and are very dim in their notions of the most material divisions of their largest industry. It was this evident and first hand familiarly with real facts and actual life which enabled Mr. Cobden to inspire a curiously diffused confidence through all commercial—we may say through all matter-of-fact men. He diffused a kind of 'economical faith.' People in these days had only to say 'Mr. Cobden said so,' and other people went and believed it.

Mr. Cobden had nothing in the received sense classical about his oratory, but it is quite certain that Aristotle, the greatest teacher of the classical art of rhetoric, would very keenly have appreciated his oratory. This sort of economical faith is exactly what he would most have valued,—what he most prescribed. He said: 'A speaker should convince his audience that he was a likely person to know.' This was exactly what Mr. Cobden did. And the matter-of-fact philosopher would have much liked Mr. Cobden's habit of coming to the point.' It would have been thoroughly agreeable to his positive mind to see so much of clear, obvious argument. He would not indeed, have been able to conceive a 'League meeting.' There has never, perhaps, been another time in the history of the world when excited masses of men and women hung on the words of one talking political economy. The excitement of these meetings were keener than any political excitement of the last twenty years—keener infinitely than any which there is now. It may be said, and truly, that the interest of the subject was Mr. Cobden's felicity, not his mind; but it may be said with equal truth, that the excitement was much greater when he was speaking than when any one else was speaking. By a kind of keenness of nerve, he said the exact word to touch, not the bare abstract understanding, but the quick individual perception of his hearers.

We do not wish to make this article a mere panegyric. Mr. Cobden was far too manly to wish such folly. His mind was very peculiar, and, like all peculiar minds, had its sharp limits. He had what we may call a *supplementary* understanding—that is a bold, original intellect, acting on a special experience, and striking out views and principles not known to, or neglected by, ordinary men. He did not possess the traditional education of his country, and did not understand it. The solid heritage of transmitted knowledge had more value, we believe, than he would have accorded to it. There was a defect in business not identical, but perhaps not altogether without analogy. The late Mr. Wilson used to say 'Cobden's administrative powers I do not think much of, but he is most valuable in counsel, always original, always shrewd, and not at all extreme.' He was not altogether equal to meaner men in some beaten tracks and pathways of life, though he was far their superior in all matters requiring an original stress of speculation, an innate energy of thought.

It may be said, and truly said, that he has been cut off before his time. A youth and manhood so spent as his well deserved a green old age. But so it was not to be. He has left us, quite independently of his positive works, of the repeal of the Corn Laws of the French treaty, a rare gift—the gift of *unique* character. There has been nothing before Richard Cobden like him in English history, and perhaps there will not be anything like it. And his character is of the simple, emphatic, picturesque sort which must easily, when opportunities are given as they were to him, go down to posterity. May posterity learn from him. Only last week we hoped to have learned something more ourselves.

> But what is before us we know not,
> And we know not what shall succeed.

John Bright
Introductory note

John Bright (1811–1889) was born at Rochdale, Lancashire, the son of Jacob Bright, owner of a spinning-mill, and of Martha Wood. In his youth he worked in his father's mill. He made his first public speech in 1830 in defence of the temperance movement and gained his reputation as an orator by his steady opposition to the principle of church rates, between 1834–41. He also advocated the abolition of capital punishment. His lifelong friendship with Cobden began during this period, probably in 1835. In 1840 he became treasurer of the Rochdale branch of the Anti-Corn-Law League, and in 1842 began agitation in London against the Corn Laws, which was later carried on in the Midlands and in Scotland. In 1843 he became M.P. for Durham, and in 1847 and 1852 M.P. for Manchester. In 1848 he advocated disestablishment in Ireland and increased occupation for the peasantry by partition of landed property. In 1849 he joined Cobden in forming 'The Commons' League' for parliamentary reform. In 1851 he opposed Russell's excluding Sir David Salomons from the House as a Jew. In 1853–4 he opposed the Crimean War. He was defeated in the election for Manchester in 1857, but elected for Birmingham and subsequently re-elected in 1858, 1865, 1868, 1873, 1874, and 1880–85. In 1859 Bright opposed the government reform bill in a speech insisting on the need for redistribution of seats. He negotiated the preliminary treaty of commerce with France in 1860. He was President of the Board of Trade in Gladstone's first ministry, 1868–70. He became Chancellor of the Duchy of Lancaster in 1873, which position he resigned in 1882 on British intervention in Egyptian affairs. In 1885 he became M.P. for the central division of Birmingham, and in 1887 made his last parliamentary speech, an attack on Gladstone's Home Rule Bill of 1886. He and Cobden were the two leading representatives of the manufacturing class as a force in English politics after the Reform Act of 1832. Bright died in Rochdale in 1889.

Mr. Bright at Manchester[1]

MR. BRIGHT's speeches are for the moment as important as events, and they are always eloquent, but nevertheless they are just a little wearisome. He will persist in arguing so exclusively with those whom he calls Tories, those who object entirely to Reform. He has not a word to bestow upon those who agreeing with every word he said in his great speech at Manchester, nevertheless oppose Mr. Gladstone's Reform Bill. Mr. Bright was as effective on Monday as usual, indeed more so, for he was unusually moderate, but he really affirmed nothing new. He asserted that about five millions of grown Englishmen out of seven were without votes; that the little boroughs had a number of seats out of all proportion to their population, their wealth, and their contributions to the revenue; that the county representation was 'dead,' being in the hands of the landlords; that the little towns were very much bribed; that the Tories had fought the Reform Bill unfairly; that they had as a party endorsed Mr. Lowe's severe strictures on the workmen; that Mr. Gladstone's Bill was moderate, admitting only 200,000 workmen; that the degradation of many classes in England was a discredit to those who governed them; that workmen in power would insist on free education, and compel rulers to leave off worrying the 'dry bones' of theology; that the prosperity of the country was mainly due to Free Trade; that Free Trade was mainly due to him and his followers; that Lord Derby had opposed almost every sound measure brought forward of late years, and that if Lord Derby brought forward a Reform Bill it would be a trick. Most of these things are more or less truths, many of them truisms. We do not ourselves see why county representation is dead, when it avowedly represents the greatest county interest, the land, but we quite admit it is not quite so much alive as it might be. Nor can we recognise the implied assertion that seven millions of voters have a perfect right to govern the British Empire which contains 260 millions of people, while a million have

[1] This article was first published in *The Economist* for September 29 1866, Volume XXIV, p. 1134.

only an imperfect right. As the Empire must be governed by a section of its inhabitants, the limit of that section must be a matter of policy and consideration and not of abstract right. But accepting Mr. Bright's point of view, all he says is true, and how does it all prove that a blank reduction of the suffrage is the true remedy? He says workmen are not ignorant, venal, or degraded. Quite true, but neither are bishops, but we are not going to trust the government of Great Britain to bishops only. He says an addition of 200,000 workmen to the register is a very moderate demand. So it is, perhaps even too moderate, for it is not sufficient to enable the electoral body to resist further pressure from without, but then why insist on a Bill which gives us those 200,000 *and* a certainty of 2,000,000 more? An addition of 2,000,000 working votes to the register is not moderate, and that addition is at no distant date the inevitable consequence of the Reform Bill as proposed last session. He says the workmen would give us universal education, which is we believe and trust correct, but then if they will, why urge so strongly a Bill which besides securing that great good will ensure also so many evils. He believes the only correctives for bribery are large constituencies and the ballot; but surely that is no argument for a Bill which does not contain the ballot, and retains most of the petty boroughs with the addition of a few electors considerably worse, in those boroughs, than the existing constituency. His whole argument tends to prove that workmen have not their due share of power, as against or by the side of the landlords and the rich, and then he fights for a scheme which will in scores of boroughs intensify the power of the purse, which gives the workmen but few certain representatives in the House of Commons, and which clears the way to the almost certain disfranchisement of every class but one. As against Tories his argument is unanswerable, or answerable only on Mr. Lowe's base, that an oligarchy is a good working form of government; but as against moderate Liberals, who really wish for a large infusion of popular strength, but do not want to see the flavour of the wine quite destroyed by the quantity of alcohol introduced into it, it can have little weight.

Mr. Bright will probably reply that his object is not to argue, but to stir the people, to answer once for all the assertion that the masses do not care for the franchise. That is a perfectly legitimate object, and he has succeeded in it, aided no doubt by Mr. Lowe, whose speech has done more to make Reform certain than all Mr. Bright has ever said; but why impair the greatness of that effort by scarcely-veiled appeals to physical force, and by attributing to one party a monopoly of the right to do justice? In his speech at the banquet, he defended force as a moral agent, quite forgetting that the argument cuts two ways; that if the people have a right to coerce the aristocracy into carrying out their views, the aristocracy must also have a right to use their existing powers by refusing to obey. We do not go the length of asserting force to be always immoral, either on the popular or the official side; but on either side its exercise can only be legitimate on certain conditions, the first of which is that it is visibly impossible to attain the end in any legal way. Mr. Bright knows that in this instance there is no impossibility, knows that it is the first doctrine of English statesmen, of Lord Derby as well as Mr. Gladstone, never to refuse to the people that which they emphatically desire. If they desire Reform, and it is becoming clear they do desire it, they will have Reform, and apologies for force are useless and dangerous invitations to lawlessness. Above all, why refuse a good Reform Bill at Lord Derby's hands? We are not very likely, perhaps, to get one, but we may; and till we see it, who is to pass an opinion? Mr. Bright apparently believes that Reform is a medicine, the efficacy of which depends on the character of the nurse who holds the spoon—an electuary into which poison might be introduced without anybody perceiving it. He forgets that the prescription must be written in a hospital, in presence of other and more learned doctors, of scores of eyes at once keen and hostile. If Lord Derby can really do what Mr. Bright seems to suspect he will do, frame a Reform Bill which shall satisfy the workmen, soothe the Liberals, pass the Tories, deceive Mr. Bright, and be really Conservative after all, why, clearly, Lord Derby is at least in power of brain, the fittest person to rule Great Britain.

Mr. Bright's Retirement[1]

THE retirement of Mr. Bright from the Cabinet, owing to failing health, will give all the older readers of *The Economist* a peculiar feeling of sadness. A new generation is attaining life and vigour to whom the 'Anti-Corn-Law League' is a matter of history. If you chance to speak of it as '*the* League,' as we always used to speak of it, they ask '*what* League?' But the great majority of active men still remember the details of that great agitation, the triumphs of 'Drury Lane and Covent Garden' meetings, and how Mr. Bright's voice rung full and penetrating, second in power only to one, if second to any, over those great open stages. That Mr. Bright has to abandon active administration will come home to many as an unwelcome hint that it is time for them to give up themselves.

If, as has been said, 'it is a proud thing to have millions of opponents and *no* enemy,' Mr. Bright has a full right to be proud. Persons at a distance who disapprove of his principles, and who only think of him as an incarnation of them, undoubtedly hate him with a strong political hatred; but no one brought close to him does so. There is an evident sincerity and bluff *bona fides* about him, which goes straight to the hearts of Englishmen. We have been often amused to see how much, in the depths of Tory districts where 'John Bright' was bitterly execrated, the regular residents were puzzled because their own M.P.'s and the most conservative people who went to London always mentioned him with geniality and toleration, and if young, would say, in the modern dialect—'Well, after all, he is a great *institution*.'

Perhaps great orators, more than any other men, are liable to be utterly misconceived. Their power—more penetrative at the moment than any literature—brings home to thousands and thousands *some* notion, but it can never be a true notion. An orator works under severe conditions. He can only express the sort of thoughts an audience will hear, and the sort of feelings they will apprehend; and every

[1] This article was first published in *The Economist* for December 24 1870, Volume XXVIII, pp. 1545–6.

orator of finer nature has much sentiment which is too subtle for the multitude, and many conclusions which will not suit public meetings. There are many things, too, which can only be said in a still, small voice, and not in the stentorian tones which alone public meetings can take in. No audience, still less any distant hearer of a speech, gives an orator credit for that which he has to leave out in order to speak effectually. They fancy that there is nothing in him but the sort of things which he says, especially if he is continually saying them; but an orator of finer genius feels much which he never says, much which under the inevitable conditions of his art he could not say. It is the pursuing penalty of every great orator that he is, in a sense, *mis*known everywhere, for he is compelled to diffuse among mankind a picture of himself in a deceiving light, with some traits aggravated, with other traits diminished—like him of course in many respects, yet to those who have real knowledge, in nearly as many utterly unreal and unlike.

Mr. Bright has had his full share of such misconceptions. In the agricultural districts he is even yet looked upon as an excessively pacific person, who cared little for the honour of England, and who would sacrifice that or anything else for peace at any price; but as Lord Granville said—'There are not many persons who have more of the popular "John Bull" character' than Mr. Bright, and among the many ingredients of that character, a certain pugnacity is not the one for which he is the least remarkable.

Again, Mr. Bright is often imagined to be a wild incendiary, who would be glad to pull down every present institution, and who would not much care to inquire with what substitutes these institutions were to be replaced. But in the present Cabinet, unless consistent rumour speaks false, his voice has more usually been a Conservative voice than the contrary. And in fact, though Mr. Bright has wanted much to change many things, and still may want to change them, he is much too characteristic an Englishman to like change for change's sake, or not to have a full share of the Conservative instinct which if possible clings to the 'tried,' and will not without plain and clear reason consent to migrate to the unknown and inexperienced.

If Mr. Bright has been somewhat misconceived in his own time, he will probably have the compensation of being—we may risk a prophecy—of all our own contemporary politicians the best known to posterity. His speeches are very amusing reading, and, as a rule, those are best known to posterity who can amuse posterity. Nothing can in general be more fleeting than the fame of an orator. A great budget speech is heard with the most eager attention, and criticised at the time with vehement interest. But who cares for it a few years afterwards? Who but a very few economical inquirers has the slightest remembrance of the financial speeches of Pitt or Peel? But there is a certain mixture of racy fun and sentiment in Bright's speeches which make them capital reading even now—reading which you can read when you are tired, but which yet has something in it; and this is the sort of literature which travels farthest and lives longest.

We are not now reviewing Mr. Bright's career. It is not yet closed. Though we trust he will never again attempt administrative labours, we hope that his powerful tones may often be heard again in the great assemblages of his countrymen. If we had to sketch his life, there would be something to blame as well as much to praise. But we need not go into that now. We have only to express our regret at his retirement, and to wonder at the strange dispensations of Providence, which mixed a fine, and to some extent incapacitating, thread of nervous delicacy in a mind so healthy, so vigorous, and on most points so emphatically robust.

Mr. Bright's Return to Parliament[1]

EVERYBODY will feel the liveliest satisfaction that one of our greatest orators, most imaginative political thinkers, and at bottom, we firmly believe, most sensible public men, should be able to return to his place in Parliament. Mr. Bright is, with all his reputation for passion and vehemence of speech, a thoroughly sober, and, in a certain sense, even Conservative, politician; in fact, we should be disposed to say that he does not intellectually give half enough weight to considerations which seem to have no root in British history, that his mind, as a reformer, is somewhat limited by the political ways and methods of the country in which he has grown up. His presence therefore in Parliament, and his presence as an independent member, will do more than anything else to moderate that irritability of desire for change which has attacked some of the younger members of the party, and has gained a certain influence also amongst the people. If any single man can check the premature and eccentric attacks on the Constitution which have lately sprung into fashion, Mr. Bright is the man. Besides this, he has gained all his influence by his thorough-going radicalism. He is known as a rather extreme economist. His speeches prove him to be a not unwilling satirist of the House of Lords. He has the dissenter in his very blood. Hence neither republicans, nor economists, nor reformers of the peers, nor the friends of secular education can despise his authority; and we may be sure that, on the whole, that authority will be used on the side of moderation. The great 'tribune of the people,' as he used to be called, has mellowed in later life into a statesman who, though he has not deserted one of his old principles, has gained the reputation of standing on the ancient ways in his mode of supporting them.

But when it is said that Mr. Bright's return to Parliament will be of great service to the existing ministry, we confess that we feel the gravest doubts. That his influence will be, on the whole, a moderating

---

[1] This article was first published in *The Economist* for November 25 1871, Volume XXIX, pp. 1428–9.

influence, and that it will tend to diminish the power of the left wing of the Liberal party, we have admitted, and so far, it might be supposed, that it must serve the Government. That is exactly what we doubt. Mr. Bright can hardly be anything else than what we may call a Radical patron of the Government,—as Sir Roundell Palmer has so long been a Conservative patron of it. In that capacity he may very well contrive to diminish the severity of the attacks upon it, and to win it some victories which it might not otherwise achieve. But it is quite a mistake to suppose that governments necessarily gain by victories which are not due to their own intrinsic strength, or even that they lose much by defeats which it is admitted that they could not, unassisted, avoid. Governments may lose, and lose greatly, in moral influence by victories which they only obtain through the aid of a powerful ally. And they might easily lose even less by absolute defeat. Of all dangers to a government supposed to be at all shaky, perhaps the very greatest is the reputation of its living only by virtue of the ægis thrown over it by a private member. And Mr. Gladstone's Government will not only certainly incur this danger, it will probably incur it in a far more exaggerated form than the truth will actually warrant. We shall be told on almost every occasion of victory that the Cabinet owed its success to the intervention of Mr. Bright or Sir Roundell Palmer. The Government will not get even the credit it really deserves for strength and decision. All its failures will be enhanced by the remark that even Mr. Bright could not save them; all its successes diminished by the hint that it was Mr. Bright's imputed merit to which the Government owed its escape. A private protector is about the greatest danger any government can have. It would certainly be far better for it to dispense with the aid, than to have credit for a vast deal more than it really receives.

Nor will the case be much better if on some great questions Mr. Bright should disapprove, as he is very likely to disapprove, of the policy of the Cabinet. It is not very easy to suppose, for instance, that he would really have heartily supported the extra military estimates voted last year; and had he then been in the House, his vote thrown into the opposite scale would have had enormous weight against the Government, though his support of these measures would not have had the moral effect of adding any prestige to their policy. It is far from impossible that he may on some points go pretty strongly with the Nonconformists against Mr. Forster's education policy; and if he should do so, the adhesion of the Cabinet's 'own familiar friend' to the ranks of the malcontents will be held as proof positive, with a large section of the country, that the Government has really played into the hands of the Conservatives. In short, nothing is more difficult, we might almost say more impossible, than for a popular leader of the first rank so to act, *outside* a government, as to give it any real assistance. If he opposes it, however moderately, he carries all the greater weight with the people, because he is known to be friendly in sentiment. If he supports it he diminishes its prestige by the very act of extending his protection. Mr. Bright in the Government, involved in all its responsibilities, was a very powerful auxiliary. Mr. Bright, independent of it, but favourable to it so far as he honestly can be, will be likely to do quite as much to relax its cohesion as to diminish the external pressure upon it. In fact, the diminution of external pressure on a government is not always a service to it. It is by external pressure, and the resistance it elicits, that a government gains its authority, and by the absence of it that it is apt to lose it.

But Sir Roundell's Palmer's assistance, it will be said, has not had this effect in any great degree on the Government. His interventions have usually diminished the pressure of the Conservatives without really carrying the demoralising effect of patronage. No doubt. But that is because Sir Roundell Palmer, eminent as he is, is really little more than an individual, and not the representative of a popular party. His assistance has helped the Government almost purely by its intellectual force, and the moral respect his character commands. It is always an advantage for a government to have distinguished adherents whose help tells only by the intrinsic weight of its argument, and not by virtue of any following which it commands. But Mr. Bright's help is a very different matter. He is not merely an Achilles whose aid is courted for its individual value,—he is the chief of a great party in the country, and a small party in the House, whose complaints are more or less silenced by his word. Hence no one can really estimate what votes he brings or keeps away, and it is quite certain that a government which is beginning to lose popularity will be credited with having got a great deal more help from such an alliance than it has, and will be deserted a great deal more freely if the leader of this alliance abandons it, than it would have been without such an example to quote.

On the whole, then, while we are quite sure that parliamentary debate will gain immensely by Mr. Bright's presence, and are disposed to think that direct Radical pressure on the Government will be reduced by it, we are strongly disposed to think that it will not prove a beneficial influence in the long run. Governments cannot afford to be protected by private influence; nor can a government that is losing popularity afford to be overruled or defeated by it. There is every reason to think that either the one risk or the other must be incurred by the Government, when Mr. Bright returns to his seat in the House, and either of them is of a very dangerous and solvent kind.

Mr. Bright on Landowning[1]

MR. BRIGHT has a controversy with Lord Derby as to the number
of landowners in the country, and especially in Scotland, as to the
figures of which we shall not say anything. But there are some underlying points of principle in the matter to which sufficient attention is
not, we think, given.

First, certainly in England, and probably in Scotland too, the number of nominal proprietors is very greatly less than that of the real
owners. The habit of England as to land is *family* ownership. The
estate is settled in such a way as to secure the wife, to secure the
children, to regulate the enjoyment of the property in a settled way as
the family convenience provides; to prevent its being wasted and the
whole family made penniless by the fault of any single person. How
much of the land of England is held in 'family tenure,' if we may
coin a word for it, we cannot tell; but it is very large indeed, and you
could not get at it by any return of nominal proprietors. In most cases,
such a return would only give the names of trustees who have no
real interest in the property at all; to get at the real truth, the deeds of
every family must be examined, the equitable as well as legal interests
counted, and the results tabulated, which would be impossible. A
'Doomsday book' for the nineteenth century, for which Lord
Derby once wished, is an unattainable ideal, to which in England there
can be hardly any approximation. The present species of conjoint
ownership is too complex to be described in any return. But nothing
can be more strange than that Mr. Bright should wholly ignore its
existence; he never mentions the word family settlement; he does not
seem to know that any such arrangements exist.

The singularity is greater because this is the cardinal difficulty
which impedes every attempt to simplify English land tenure. The
great obstruction to the free transfer of the soil is that so many people
are more or less interested in it. A conveyancer, when he examines a

[1] This article was first published in *The Economist* for January 29 1876, Volume XXXIV,
pp. 121–3.

title, has to see that all the existing owners convey, and that all those whom he sets down as extinct owners are really such, and have passed away. How far this system is good—whether the security of families is a better or worse thing than the free transfer of land—whether some of the advantages of that security may not be gained without sacrificing so much as we sacrifice now—are questions; but it is not a question, for it is certain, that what now impedes land-dealing is this system of many owners, and not, as Mr. Bright says, a system of single ones. Mr. Bright thinks too that the English laws of land tenure are constructed on feudal principles. But the greatest characteristic of these laws, as compared with all others which have descended from the middle ages, is the quickness and the facility with which they emancipated themselves from feudalism. Though perpetual, or very long entails, prevailed almost everywhere else in Europe, they have long been abolished here; and the tying up of property has been restricted to limits which may be too long or too short, but have nothing to do with feudality.

And the proof that they have nothing to do with it is that they extend to money which never was 'feudal,' as well as to land which was. The funds can be tied up just as long as land, and in fact are so. A very large sum in them is so set apart for the security of families just as land is, and by deeds whose operation lasts just the same time. No good can, but much harm must come from discussing the transfer of land, ignoring the main obstruction, and inventing an imaginary one.

But there is a second and worse mistake in Mr. Bright's reasoning. He assumes—he does not try to prove, he simply takes for granted—that cheap and easy transfer of land will tend in England to produce a class of peasant proprietors. But there cannot be a greater error. A little examination will, we think, establish that an increased cheapness of land transfer would consolidate the main part of the land of England in the hands of the monied classes even more effectually than now, and that the working men who cultivate the fields would own just as little of them.

The principle is that a dear thing will, as a rule, and in the long run, be bought by those who can give most for it. And in England, as in all old countries, land is a very dear thing. If land is at £80 an acre, five acres would take £400, and to suppose that an English agricultural labourer is likely to possess £400 is to go out of the present world. His imagination could not rise to the magnitude of such a sum; if he had only the tenth part of it he would be off to the beer-house, and be drunk for some weeks. And even the small farmer who has such a capital can employ it much better in cultivating a farm say of 100 acres than in buying five of his own. Land in England will scarcely pay 3 per cent. on the purchase money, whereas a small farmer, looking after things himself, and watching each item of outlay, probably makes 15 per cent., or more. Nothing, therefore, is more ruinous to such a farmer than to change him to a proprietor. In so doing you would at once make a poor man of him.

In the long run, when countries have attained a certain measure of intelligence, money goes with quickness and certainty where there is most to be made of it—at any rate, it is bad political economy, and most unsafe besides, to expect to create a whole new class of men on the assumption that money will not so go. But every attempt to create peasant proprietors in England by making land cheap really assumes this, and will, therefore, fail. Persons of small capital who know how to cultivate land will find they can live far better by cultivating a fair quantity of other people's land than by keeping to a petty patch of their own.

In the present state of agriculture this becomes palpable, because there are so many things to illustrate its principle. Nothing could be more wasteful or more absurd than for a small farmer to own his own steam plough. Such a man would at once say he could not afford to lock up so much capital. But his buying land is in its financial effect just the same, for land is but one instrument of cultivation just as this plough is another.

We shall be asked, if peasant proprietorship is thus economically unprofitable, why does it exist in so many countries? The continent of Europe is pretty well exclusively so cultivated. The answer is that the continent inherited this system from the middle ages, and that now, though it might be economically advantageous to extricate itself from it, the fixed habits of society forbid, and the system cannot be changed. In early times this method of cultivation is substantially the only one possible. There is, then, no scientific agriculture, no large moving capital, no steam ploughs, or other machines. The only way, then, to till the soil is to get some peasant with his own hands to do so. All through mediæval Europe some serf—some villain—some *adscriptus glebæ*—is to be found fixed to the land, and cultivating it. Gradually, being fixed to the soil, he obtains fixed rights in it; he comes to pay some settled rent or payment, or sort of service to his lord, and all above is more or less his. Thus a hundred years ago there was in most European states a double ownership, a *seigneur* under some name claiming services or dues, and a peasant under some name paying them. In many places this exists still; but in the best parts, either by revolution or purchase, the lord has ceased to exist. He has been either bought out or thrust out; and so peasants have become the sole proprietors. But it is a system which would not now create itself. It remains, because man is not a purely economical animal; because these peasants love their lands with an intense passion. But it remains in the richest parts with difficulty. Even in France wealth begins to make inroads upon it.

The growth of this system was interrupted in England by the demand for labour, which made the 'villain' glad to leave the land and seek town wages; and by the growth of sheep-farming natural when this country was an exporter of wool, as well as a great manufacturer of it. We never had peasant proprietors, because the labourers could go elsewhere (which on the continent they could not), and the landowners were glad they should (which on the continent they were not). That the English agricultural labourer is now ill paid is true, but this is mainly the result of improvident multiplication, stimulated by a disastrous poor-law; originally it was prosperity—comparative prosperity, as compared with the continent—which unfixed him from the soil, and prevented his acquiring an interest in it. But it will be urged there are peasant proprietors not only on the continent, where they have thus inherited them, but in the United States, and almost everywhere in English colonies. But the reply is, that there the economical conditions are different. Land is very cheap, and a person of a little capital can acquire quite as much of it as he is able to cultivate. No one there will work on other people's land, because virgin land worth only a trifle is lying idle. In such a place and period peasant proprietorship arises like a weed in the soil. Nothing else is possible then and there. But you cannot infer from its naturalness in new countries the possibility of transplanting it to an old country like England, where economical circumstances are not such as to favour, but such as to oppose it.

Mr. Bright seems to approve of the French law of compulsory equal division at a father's death between children. But this does not seem to be the best French opinion. Putting aside the effect on land, which is not so formidable in France, where population is so nearly stationary, as it would be in England, where it augments fast, the result on business is pernicious. A capitalist in various undertakings cannot leave one to one son and another to another, and portion off the daughters as he can here, but the law gives all equal shares in each. At each generation the most complex affairs are thrown into a compulsory and often ill-assorted partnership, which often causes evil, and the apprehension of which discourages enterprise. Instead of a rich and active capitalist being able, as with us, to feel that he can provide comfortably for his children by a proper adjustment of bequests to circumstances, he feels in France that after his death his family must squabble in a vain attempt at an unattainable equal division. No law could be devised more likely to make men shun business or to make them uncomfortable in it.

Some years ago peasant proprietorship was much pressed, because it gave the mass of the people the sanction of property, and so settled society on a stable basis. But now France, the great educator of Europe by her misfortunes, has taught us a new lesson in this matter. We now know that peasant proprietorship spreads not only the sense of property but a panic of property. The one idea of a French *paysan* is that he may lose his *terre*. All politics to him begin and end in finding some one to keep it safe for him. A main difficulty in the way of— perhaps an insuperable obstruction to—free government in France, is the fright of small holders about their plots of land, which makes them hate agitation, fear discussion, and be always ready to run to a despot.

We can imagine nothing, therefore, less in the spirit of the present time, or less likely to happen, than the creation of a peasant proprietorship in England, and we are glad to feel sure that the Liberal party will not, as Mr. Bright advises, agitate for it, for they would only be binding themselves to attempt an undesirable impossibility.

The Conservative Vein in Mr. Bright[1]

IT seems a paradox to say that there are few more typical Conservatives in the House of Commons than Mr. Bright; and yet the assertion is in one sense certainly true. Vehemently as he has fought for the cause of popular right, and eloquently as he has, at times, attacked the privileged classes who resisted these reforms, Mr. Bright's political notions are,—and this is the characteristic of a Conservative,—probably more strictly prepossessions and traditions, less the result of inner deliberation and intellectual judgment, than those of any Conservative in the House of Commons, immeasurably more so than those of the Conservative Leader. We doubt very much whether even Mr. Gathorne Hardy has as much right to represent the Conservative whose political mind is the product of deep traditional, and, we may say, hereditary preoccupations, as Mr. Bright. Of course it is not merely the accident that a man's traditional feelings on politics represent the tendencies of the future rather than the tendencies of the past, which makes him in this sense a Liberal rather than a Conservative. We are now using the word rather in relation to character than in relation to the progress of events. And in this sense we should say that while the Liberal turn of mind denotes the willingness to admit new ideas, and the perfect impartiality with which those ideas, when admitted, are canvassed and considered, the Conservative turn of mind denotes adhesiveness to the early and probably inherited ideas of childhood, and a very strong and practically effective distrust of the novel intellectual suggestions which come unaccredited by any such influential associations. Now in this sense, it hardly needed Mr. Bright's very able speech on Wednesday, against Women's Suffrage, to show that constitutionally, though not in the sense which the accident of chronology attaches to the word, Mr. Bright is a Conservative. Mr. Bright has been throughout his life a very warm friend of what is called progress on all subjects on which he inherited from

[1] This article was first published in *The Economist* for April 29 1876, Volume XXXIV pp. 506–7.

his early traditions the ideas of progress. But it is not possible to mention a single subject on which he has abandoned the traditions of his youth in favour of the newer ideas of his maturity, and of the age in which that maturity has been cast. Let us cast a glance all round the political world. In relation to the question of throne or republic, it cannot be doubted that he inherited from his forefathers a sort of abstract preference for a republic, together with a very decided disposition to let well alone, and acquiesce in a throne so long as that throne is dignified by high character and personal virtues. And this is precisely the shade of policy which he has always represented whenever such matters have come into discussion at all. That Mr. Bright has always been the first to claim a kindly and cordial consideration for the republic ultimately founded by the descendants of the Pilgrim Fathers in the United States of America, we all know. But we also all know how, whenever anything like a taunt has been cast at the institution of royalty in England, Mr. Bright has been foremost to lend the shield of his personal enthusiasm to the present wearer of the British crown. When the Queen is in question it would be impossible to name a more cordial Conservative than Mr. Bright. His feelings are kindled, like the feelings of a cavalier of old, at the mere mention of her name, as Mr. Ayrton has had occasion to know.[2] No doubt it is in great measure the simplicity and worth of the present monarch which endears her so much to Mr. Bright. But that, again, shows that old associations and emotions, not mere intellectual convictions, are at the root of his feelings. He does not desire to discriminate between the institution and the form which the institution takes at the present moment. The mixed feelings which he has always felt grow stronger with his years. He is as earnest as ever in his abstract admiration for republics. He is more earnest than ever in his concrete loyalty to the throne.

Or take questions of constitutional reform, and consider his attitude on them. He has always been eager for the enlargement of the franchise up to the point of a household franchise. He holds that family life is a sort of guarantee for English sobriety—a notion very dear to the British middle class, but not perhaps very adequately sustained by the

---

[2] Ayrton was Liberal M.P. for Tower Hamlets (1857–74), and held office as Parliamentary Secretary to the Treasury, First Commissioner of Works and Judge Advocate General. In 1866, addressing a meeting of working men in his constituency, he reflected severely on the Queen's retirement from public life owing to the death of the Prince Consort. He was rebuked with dignity by John Bright who happened to be present at the meeting.—Ed.

testing of experience. For that inherited idea he has fought gallantly till he has succeeded in making it part of the British constitution, at least as regards the boroughs, and he is pledged of course to extend it to the counties. But while he is eloquent on behalf of the guarantee given by a householder's responsibility and ties, and would be the last, we suspect, to ask us to dispense with it, as a condition of the suffrage, any attempt to take guarantees of another sort, which were not familiar to his childhood—like that known as cumulative voting, or representation of minorities—he has always hated with an intensity and inexorability almost amusing. But some one will say that this only shows that Mr. Bright is really Liberal, and not Conservative,—that he sees these suggestions advanced by those who grudge the democracy its triumphs, and not by those who trust the people. Well then take this question of the women's franchise. Our readers are aware that we have advocated that change partly on the ground that in the working class, at least,—the most numerous class,—the women are often more careful, and intelligent, and scrupulous, and competent to vote, than the men,—partly because we have regarded them as likely to be themselves the better for an extension of their practical interests. But Mr. Bright, after voting once reluctantly for it, has at last been unable to suppress the disgust with which this proposal to turn family life and traditions (as they have been transmitted to him) upside down, affects him, and has broken through the trammels of personal ties to speak with all the force and vigour of his character on behalf of traditions so deeply ingrained into it. This metamorphosis, as it seems to him, of the true functions of women, revolts him far more than it revolts the bulk of the Conservative party, some of whom, indeed, may, perhaps have adopted the cry for women's suffrage out of party motives, but most of whom, no doubt, sympathised far more deeply with Mr. Bright than with any of their own leaders. Indeed, Mr. Bright dwelt on the idea that a revolution rather than a reform was involved in the proposal, with the genuine Conservative horror of revolution. There was not much evidence in his speech that he had carefully weighed the probable results of the change, and found them dangerous. On the contrary, the speech went to prove that the change, if adopted, must be adopted on the ground of considerations fundamentally different from those which had recommended the various reforms of the franchise already adopted. And this seemed to be almost enough for him. Prove that it was a proposal not only new in detail, but new in principle, and it lost all charm for him. Revolution is as much a term of reproach to Mr. Bright as it is to Mr. Gathorne Hardy, though it means somewhat different things in the two men's mouths. In each of them alike it represents the antithesis of all the cherished traditions of early years.

In short, Mr. Bright's political constitution vehemently repels the new ideas of modern statesmanship. He cannot bear the agitation for the election of labourers or artisans as members of Parliament—a new idea which seems to him subversive of political traditions. He wisely snubs Home Rule. He will not listen with patience to any argument for the fair representation of minorities. He declines all invitations to join the Alliance League for the diminution of public-houses. His Liberal sympathies are confined to the causes which he found popular among his people long before he was a great personage on the political stage—to Free-trade, economy, peace, a popular franchise of the old kind, the ballot; and enthusiasm for these causes is really in him political Conservatism. And the manner of his advocacy is as Conservative as the matter. He always addresses the political affections rather than the political reason, and this is no doubt the great secret of his true popularity. The creed of the Mr. Bright of 1876 is probably far less altered from the creed of the Mr. Bright of 1840 than is the creed of the Duke of Richmond of 1876 from the creed of the same peer in 1840. The Duke of Richmond has reluctantly abandoned many articles of his old creed—Mr. Bright has abandoned none.

James Wilson

Introductory note

James Wilson (1805–1860) was born in Hawick, Roxburghshire, the fourth son of William Wilson, a woollen manufacturer, and of Elizabeth Richardson. At the age of sixteen he was apprenticed to a hat manufacturer in Hawick, and three years later moved to London where he eventually set up his own business with his brother William. In 1839 he published *Influences of the Corn Laws*, and in 1841 *The Revenue*. He founded *The Economist* in 1843 'to discuss financial questions in their wider social and commercial aspect', and was its editor until 1860. He was M.P. for Westbury, Wiltshire in 1847 and 1852, and for Devonshire from 1857–9. He became Joint-Secretary to the Board of Control in 1848; Financial Secretary to the Treasury in 1853, a post he held until 1858; Vice-President of the Board of Trade and Paymaster-General in 1859, and was made a Privy Councillor in that year. He went to India as Financial Member of the Council of India, established a paper currency and reformed the system of public accounts. James Wilson died in Calcutta in 1860. His eldest daughter Eliza married Walter Bagehot in 1857.

Memoir of the Right Honourable
James Wilson [1]

PERHAPS some of the subscribers to *The Economist* would not be unwilling to read a brief memoir of Mr. Wilson, even if the events narrated were in no respect peculiar. They might possibly be interested in the biography of an author of whose writings they have read so many, even if the narrative related no marked transitions and no characteristic events. But there were in Mr. Wilson's life several striking changes. The scene shifts from the manufactory of a small Scotch hatter, in a small Scotch town, to London—to the Imperial Parliament,—to the English Treasury,—to the Council Board of India. Such a biography may be fairly expected to have some interest. The life perhaps of no *Political Economist* has been more eventful.

James Wilson was born at Hawick, in Roxburghshire, on the 3rd of June 1805. His father, of whose memory he always spoke with marked respect, was a thriving man of business, extensively engaged in the woollen manufacture of that place. He was the fourth son in a family of fifteen children, of whom, however, only ten reached maturity. Of his mother, who died when he was very young, he scarcely retained any remembrance in after life. As to his early years little is now recollected, except that he was a very mild and serious boy, usually successful during school hours, but not usually successful in the playground.

As Mr. Wilson's father was an influential Quaker, he was sent when ten years old to a Quaker school at Ackworth, where he con-

[1] This essay was first published as a special supplement to *The Economist* of November 17 1860, Volume XVIII, pp. 1287–1300. James Wilson had actually died in India on August 11 1860 but the news did not reach his family in England until September 12, when one of his daughters, Julia, read it in *The Times*. *The Economist* for September 15, bordered in black, contained an announcement of his death, together with a lengthy quotation from *The Times* obituary. Bagehot and Hutton wisely decided to publish a fuller memoir later and this appeared on November 17. Emily Russell Barrington, James Wilson's youngest daughter, later wrote her father's biography *The Servant of All* published by Longmans in 1927. She also includes a chapter on Wilson in her *Life of Walter Bagehot*, Longmans, London 1915.

tinued for four years. At that time—it may surprise some of those who knew him in later life to be told—he was so extremely fond of books as to wish to be a teacher; and as his father allowed his sons to choose their line in life, he was sent to a seminary at Earlscome in Essex, to qualify himself for that occupation. But the taste did not last long. As we might expect, the natural activity of his disposition soon induced him to regret his choice of a sedentary life. He wrote to Hawick, 'I would rather be the most menial servant in my father's mill than be a teacher'; and he was permitted to return home at once.

Many years later he often narrated that, after leaving Earlscome, he had much wished to study for the Scottish bar, but the rules of the Society of Friends, as then understood, would not allow his father to consent to the plan. He was sometimes inclined half to regret that he had not been able to indulge this taste, and he was much pleased at being told by a great living advocate that 'if he had gone to the bar he would have been very successful.' But at the time there was no alternative, and at sixteen he accordingly commenced a life of business. He did not, however, lose at once his studious predilections. For some years at least he was in the habit of reading a good deal, very often till late in the night. It was indeed then that he acquired most of the knowledge of books which he ever possessed. In later life he was much too busy to be a regular reader, and he never acquired the habit of catching easily the contents of books or even of articles in the interstices of other occupations. Whatever he did, he did thoroughly. He would not read even an article in a newspaper if he could well help doing so; but if he read it at all, it was with as much slow, deliberate attention as if he were perusing a treasury minute.

At the early age we have mentioned he commenced his business life by being apprenticed to a small hat manufacturer at Hawick; and it is still remembered that he showed remarkable care and diligence in mastering all the minutiæ of the trade. There was, indeed, nothing of the *amateur* man of business about him at any time. After a brief interval, his father purchased his master's business for him and for an elder brother, named William, and the two brothers in conjunction continued to carry it on at Hawick during two or three years with much energy. So small a town, however, as Hawick then was, afforded no scope for enterprise in this branch of manufacture, and they resolved to transfer themselves to London.

Accordingly, in 1824, Mr. Wilson commenced a mercantile life in

London (the name of the firm being Wilson, Irwin, and Wilson), and was very prosperous and successful for many years. His pecuniary gains were considerable, and to the practical instruction which he then obtained he always ascribed his success as an economist and a financier. 'Before I was 20 years of age,' he said at Devonport in 1859, 'I was a partner in a firm in London, and I can only say if there is in my life one event which I regard with satisfaction more than another, it is that I had then an opportunity of obtaining experience by observation which has contributed in the main to what little public utility I have since been to my country. During these few years I became acquainted—well acquainted—with the middle classes of this country. I also became acquainted in some degree with the working classes; and also, to a great extent, with the foreign commerce of this country in pretty nearly all parts of the world; and I can only say the information and the experience I thus derived have been to me in my political career of greater benefit than I can now describe.'

In 1831, the firm of Wilson, Irwin, and Wilson was dissolved by mutual consent. But Mr. Wilson (under the firm of James Wilson and Co.) continued to carry on the same kind of business, and continued to obtain the same success. He began in 1824 with £2,000, the gift of his father, and in 1837 was worth nearly £25,000,—a fair result for so short a period, and evincing a steady business-like capacity and judgment; for it was the fruit not of sudden success in casual speculation, but of regular attention during several years to one business. From circumstances which we shall presently state, he was very anxious that this part of his career should be very clearly understood.

During these years Mr. Wilson led the usual life of a prosperous and intellectual man of business. He married,* and formed an establishment suitable to his means, first near his manufactory in London, and afterwards at Dulwich. He took great pleasure in such intellectual society as he could obtain; was especially fond of conversing on political economy, politics, statistics, and the other subjects with which he was subsequently so busily occupied.† Through life it was

* He was married on 5th January, 1832, to Miss Elizabeth Preston, of Newcastle, and this has given rise to a statement that he was once in business at Newcastle. This is, however, an entire mistake. He was never in business anywhere except at Hawick and London. It may be added, that on the occasion of his marriage he voluntarily ceased to be a member of the Society of Friends, for whom he always, however, retained a high respect. During the rest of his life he was a member of the Church of England.

† Among his friends of this period should be especially mentioned Mr. G. R. Porter, of the Board of Trade, the author of *The Progress of the Nation*, whose mind he described twenty years later as the most accurate he had ever known.

one of his remarkable peculiarities to be a *very animated* man, talking by preference and by habit on *inanimate* subjects. All the *verve*, vigour, and life which lively people put into exciting pursuits, he put into topics which are usually thought very dry. He discussed the currency or the Corn Laws with a relish and energy which made them interesting to almost every one. 'How pleasant it is,' he used to say, 'to talk a subject out,' and he frequently suggested theories in the excitement of conversation upon his favourite topics which he had never thought of before, but to which he ever afterwards attached, as was natural, much importance. The instructiveness of his conversation was greatly increased as his mind progressed and his experience accumulated. But his genial liveliness and animated vigour were the same during his early years of business life, as they were afterwards when he filled important offices of state in England and in Calcutta. Few men can have led a more continuously prosperous and happy life than he did during those years. Unfortunately it was not to continue.

In 1836, or thereabouts, Mr. Wilson was unfortunately induced to commence a speculation in indigo, in conjunction with a gentleman in Scotland. It was expected that indigo would be scarce, and that the price would rise rapidly in consequence. Such would indeed appear to have been the case for a short period, since the first purchases in which Mr. Wilson took part yielded a profit. In consequence of this success, he was induced to try a larger venture,—indeed to embark most of his disposable capital. Unfortunately, the severe crisis of 1837 disturbed the usual course of all trades, and whether from that cause or from some other, indigo, instead of rising rapidly, fell rapidly. The effect on Mr. Wilson's position may be easily guessed. A very great capitalist would have been able to hold till better times, but he was not. 'On the first of January,' he said at Devonport, 'in a given year, my capital was nearer £25,000 than £24,000, and it was all lost.' Numerous stories were long circulated—most of them exaggerated, and the remainder wholly untrue, as to this period of misfortune in Mr. Wilson's life; but the truth is very simple. As is usual in such cases, various arrangements were proposed and agreed to, were afterwards abandoned, and others substituted for them. A large bundle of papers carefully preserved by him records with the utmost accuracy the whole of the history. The final result will be best described in his own words at Devonport, which precisely correspond with the balance sheets and other documents still in existence. They are part of a speech in answer to a calumnious rumour that had been circulated in the town:—

'Now, how did I act on this occasion? and this is what this placard has reference to. By my own means alone I was enabled at once to satisfy in full all claims against me individually, and to provide for the early payment of one-half of the whole of the demands against the firm, consisting of myself and three partners. I was further enabled, or the firm was enabled, at once to assign property of sufficient value, as was supposed, to the full satisfaction of the whole of the remainder of the liabilities. An absolute agreement was made, an absolute release was given to all the partners; there was neither a bankruptcy nor an insolvency, neither was the business stopped for one day. The business was continued under the new firm, with which I remained a partner, and from which I ultimately retired in good circumstances. Some years afterwards it turned out that the foreign property which was assigned for the remaining half of the debts of the old firm, of which I was formerly a partner, proved insufficient to discharge them. The legal liability was, as you know, all gone; the arrangement had been accepted—an arrangement calculated and believed by all parties to be sufficient to satisfy all claims in full; but when the affairs of the whole concern were fully wound up, finding that the foreign property had not realised what was anticipated, I had it, I am glad to say, in my power to place at my banker's, having ascertained the amount, a sum of money to discharge all the remainder of that debt, which I considered morally, though not legally due. This I did without any kind of solicitation— the thing was not named to me, and I am quite sure never were the gentlemen more taken by surprise than when a friend of mine waited on them privately in London, and presented each of them with a cheque for the balance due to them. Now, perhaps, I have myself to blame for this anonymous attack. I probably brought it on myself, for I always felt that if this matter were made public, it might look like an act of ostentatious obtrusion on my part, and therefore, when I put aside the sum of money necessary for the purpose, I made a request, in the letter I wrote to my bankers, desiring them as an especial favour that they would instruct their clerks to mention the matter to no one; and in order that it should be perfectly private, I employed a personal friend of my own in the city of London, in whose care I placed the whole of the cheques, to wait on those gentlemen and present each of them with a cheque, and I obtained from him a promise, and he from them, not to name the circumstance to any one.' The secrecy thus enjoined was well preserved. Many of the most intimate friends of Mr. Wilson, and his family also, were entirely unacquainted with what he had done, and learnt it only through the accidental medium of an electioneering speech. It may be added, too, that some of those who knew the circumstances, and who have watched Mr. Wilson's subsequent career, believe that at no part of his life did he show greater business ability, self-command, and energy, than at the crisis of his mercantile misfortunes.

It is remarkable that the preface to Mr. Wilson's first pamphlet, on the 'Influences of the Corn Laws,' is dated 1st March, 1839, the precise time at which he was negotiating with his creditors for a proper arrangement of his affairs; and to those who have had an opportunity of observing how completely pecuniary misfortune unnerves and unmans men—mercantile men, perhaps, more than any others—it will not seem unworthy of remark that a careful pamphlet, with elaborate figures, instinct in every line with vigour and energy, should emanate from a man struggling with extreme pecuniary calamity, and daily harassed with the painful details of it.

After 1839 Mr. Wilson continued in business for several years, and with very fair success, considering that his capital was much diminished and that the hat manufacture was from temporary circumstances in a state of transition. He finally retired in 1844, and invested most of his capital in the foundation and extension of *The Economist*.

These facts prove, as we believe, the conclusion which he was very desirous to make clear—that, though unfortunate on a particular occasion, Mr. Wilson was by no means, as a rule, unsuccessful in business. He did not at all like to have it said that he was fit to lay down the rules and the theory of business, but not fit to transact business itself. And the whole of his life, on the contrary, proves that he possessed an unusual capacity for affairs—an extraordinary *transacting* ability.

It may, however, be admitted that Mr. Wilson was in several respects by no means an unlikely man to meet with, especially in early life, occasional misfortune. To the last hour of his life he was always sanguine. He naturally looked at everything in a bright and cheerful aspect; his tendency was always to form a somewhat too favourable judgment both of things and men. One proof of this may be sufficient;

—he was five years Secretary of the Treasury, and he did not leave it a suspicious man.

Moreover, Mr. Wilson's temperament was very active and his mind was very fertile. And though in many parts of business these gifts are very advantageous, in many also they are very dangerous, if not absolutely disadvantageous. Frequently they are temptations. Capital is always limited; often it is *very* limited; and therefore a man of business, who is managing his own capital, has only defined resources, and can engage only in a certain number of undertakings. But a person of active temperament and fertile mind will soon chafe at that restriction. His inventiveness will show him many ways in which money might easily be made, and he cannot but feel that with his energies he would like to make it. If he have besides a sanguine temperament, he will believe that he can make it. The records of unfortunate commerce abound in instances of men who have been unsuccessful because they had great mind, great energy, and great hope, but had not money in proportion. Some part of this description was, perhaps, applicable to Mr. Wilson in 1839, but exactly how much cannot, after the lapse of so many years, be now known with any accuracy.

Mr. Wilson's position in middle life was by no means unsuitable to a writer on the subjects in which he afterwards attained eminence. He had acquired a great knowledge of business through a long course of industrious years; he had proved by habitual success in business that his habitual judgment on it was sound and good. If he had been a man of only ordinary energy and only ordinary ability, he would probably have continued to grow regularly richer and richer. But, by a single error natural to a very sanguine temperament and a very active mind, he had destroyed a great part of the results of his industry. He had a new career to seek. He was willing to expend on it the whole of his great energies. He was ready to take all the pains which were necessary to fit himself for success. When he wrote his first pamphlet, he used to say that he thought 'the sentences never would come right.' In later life he considered three leading articles in *The Economist*, full of facts and figures, an easy morning's work, which was quite compatible with the transaction of much other business. Mr. Wilson was a finished man of business obliged by necessity to become a writer on business. Perhaps no previous education and no temporary circumstances could be conceived more likely to train a great financial writer and to stimulate his powers.

In 1839, Mr. Wilson published his 'Influences of the Corn Laws'; in 1840, the 'Fluctuations of Currency, Commerce, and Manufactures'; in 1841, 'The Revenue; or, What should the Chancellor do?' in September, 1843, he established *The Economist*. The origin of the latter may be interesting to our readers. Mr. Wilson proposed to the editor of the *Examiner* that he should furnish gratuitously a certain amount of writing to that journal on economical and financial subjects; but the offer was declined, though with some regret, on account of the expense of type and paper. A special paper was therefore established, which proved in the end as important as the *Examiner* itself. From the first, Mr. Wilson was the sole proprietor of *The Economist*, and though he obtained pecuniary assistance—especially from the kindness of Lord Radnor—he embarked some capital of his own in it from the first, and afterwards repaid all loans made to him for the purpose of establishing it.

It would not be suitable to the design of this memoir to give any criticism of Mr. Wilson's pamphlets, still less would it become *The Economist* to pronounce in any manner a judgment on itself. Nevertheless, it is a part of the melancholy duty we have undertaken to give some account of Mr. Wilson's characteristic position as a writer on political economy, and of the somewhat peculiar mode in which he dealt with that subject.

Mr. Wilson dealt with political economy like a practical man. Persons more familiar with the literature of the science might very easily be found. Mr. Wilson's faculty of reading was small, nor had he any taste for the more refined abstractions in which the more specially scientific political economists had involved themselves. 'Political economy,' said Sydney Smith, 'is become in the hands of Malthus and Ricardo, a school of metaphysics. All seem to agree what is to be done; the contention is how the subject is to be divided and defined. *Meddle with no such matters.*' We are far from alleging that this saying is just; nor would Mr. Wilson have by any means assented to it. But though he would have disavowed it in theory, it nevertheless embodies his instinctive feeling and characteristic practice. He 'meddled with no such matters'; though he did not deny the utility of theoretical refinements, he habitually and steadily avoided them.

Mr. Wilson's predominating power was what may be called a business-imagination. He had a great power of conceiving transactions. Political economy was to him the science of buying and selling, and of the ordinary bargains of men he had a very steady and distinct conception. In explaining such subjects he did not begin, as political economists have been wittily said to do, with 'Suppose a man upon an island,' but 'What they *do* in the city is this.' 'The real course of business is so and so.' Most men of business will think this characteristic a great merit, and even a theoretical economist should not consider it a defect. The *practical* value of the science of political economy (the observation is an old one as to *all* sciences) lies in its 'middle principles.' The extreme abstractions from which such intermediate maxims are scientifically deduced lie at some distance from ordinary experience, and are not easily made intelligible to most persons, and when they *are* made intelligible, most persons do not know how to use them. But the intermediate maxims themselves are not so difficult; they are easily comprehended and easily used. They have in them a practical life, and come home at once to the 'business' and the 'bosoms' of men. It was in these that Mr. Wilson excelled. His 'business-imagination' enabled him to see 'what men did,' and 'why they did it'; 'why they ought to do it,' and 'why they ought not to do it.' His very clear insight into the real nature of mercantile transactions made him a great and almost an instinctive master of *statistical selection*. He could not help picking out of a mass of figures those which would tell most. He saw which were really material; he put them prominently and plainly forward, and he left the rest alone. Even now if a student of parliamentary papers should alight on a return 'moved for by Mr. Wilson,' he will do well to give to it a more than ordinary attention, for it will be sure to contain something attainable, intelligible, and distinct.

Mr. Wilson's habit of always beginning with the facts, always arguing from the facts, and always ending with a result applicable to the facts obtained for his writings an influence and a currency more extensive than would have been anticipated for any writings on political economy. It is not for *The Economist* to speak of *The Economist*; but we may observe that through the pages of this journal certain doctrines, whether true or false, have been diffused, far more widely than they ever were in England before,—far more widely than from their somewhat abstract nature we could expect them to be diffused,—far more widely than they are diffused in any other country but this. The business-like method and vigorous simplicity of Mr. Wilson's arguments converted very many ordinary men of business, who would have distrusted any theoretical and abstruse disquisition, and would not have appreciated any elaborate refinements. Nor was this special influence confined to mercantile men. It penetrated where it could not be expected to penetrate. The Duke of Wellington was, perhaps, more likely to be prejudiced against a theoretical political economist than any eminent man of his day; he belonged to the 'pre-scientific period'; he had much of the impatient practicality incident to military insight; he was not likely to be very partial to the 'doctrines of Mr. Huskisson'; —nevertheless, the Duke early pointed out Mr. Wilson's writings to Lord Brougham as possessing especial practical value; and when the Duke at a much later period was disposed to object to the repeal of the Navigation Laws, Mr. Wilson had a special interview to convince him of its expediency.

Nor is this faculty of exposition by any means a trifling power. On many subjects it is a common saying 'that he only discovers who proves'; but on practical politics we may almost say that he only discovers who convinces. It is of no use to have practical truths received by extraordinary men, unless they are also accepted by ordinary men. Whether Mr. Wilson was exactly a great writer we will not discuss: but he was a great *belief producer*; he had upon his own subjects a singular gift of *efficient* argument;—a peculiar power of bringing home his opinions by convincing reasonings to convincible persons.

The time at which Mr. Wilson commenced his career as an economical writer was a singularly happy one. An economical century has elapsed since 1839. The Corn Laws were then in full force, and seemed likely to continue so; the agriculturists believed in them, and other classes acquiesced in them; the tentative reforms of Mr. Huskisson were half-forgotten; our tariff perhaps contained some specimen of every defect—it certainly contained many specimens of most defects; duties abounded which cramped trade, which contributed nothing to the exchequer, which were maintained that a minority might believe they profited at the expense of the majority; all the now settled principles of commercial policy were unsettled; the 'currency' was under discussion; the Bank of England had been reduced to accept a loan from the Bank of France; capitalists were disheartened and operatives disaffected; the industrial energies, which have since multiplied our foreign commerce, were then effectually impeded by legislative fetters and financial restraints. On almost all of these restraints Mr. Wilson had much to say.

Upon the Corn Laws Mr. Wilson developed a theory which was rare when he first stated it, but which was generally adopted afterwards, and which subsequent experience has confirmed. He was fond of narrating an anecdote which shows his exact position in 1839. There had just been a meeting of the Anti-Corn Law League at Manchester, and some speakers had maintained, with more or less vehemence, that the coming struggle was to be one of class against class, inasmuch as the Corn Laws were beneficial to the agriculturists, though they were injurious to manufacturers. The tendency of the argument was to set one part of the nation against another part. Mr Wilson was travelling in the North and was writing in a railway carriage part of the 'Influences of the Corn Laws.' By chance a distinguished member of the League, whom Mr. Wilson did not know, happened to travel with him, and asked him what he was about. 'I am writing on the Corn Laws,' said Mr. Wilson, 'something in answer to the rubbish they have been talking at Manchester.' 'You are a bold man,' was the reply; 'Protection is a difficult doctrine to support by argument.' But it soon appeared that Mr. Wilson was the better Free-trader of the two. He held that the Corn Laws were injurious to all classes; that the agriculturists suffered from them as much as the manufacturers; that, in consequence, it was 'rubbish' to raise a class-enmity on the subject, for the interest of all classes was the same. 'We cannot too much lament,' he says in his 'Influences of the Corn Laws,' 'and deprecate the spirit of violence and exaggeration with which this subject has always been approached by each party, which no doubt has been the chief cause why so little of real truth or benefit has resulted from the efforts of either; the arguments on either side have been supported by such absurd and magnified statements of the influences of those prohibitory laws on their separate interests, as only to furnish each other with a good handle to turn the whole argument into ridicule. It therefore appears to be necessary to a just settlement of this great question, that these two parties should be first reconciled to a correct view of the real influences thus exerted over their interests, and the interests of the country at large; to a conviction that the imaginary fears of change on the one hand, and the exaggerated advantages expected on the other hand, are equally without foundation; that there are in reality no differences in the solid interests of either party; and that *individuals*, *communities*, or *countries* can only be prosperous in proportion to the prosperity of the whole.' And he proposed to prove 'that the agricultural interest has derived no benefit but great injury, from the existing laws; and that the fears and apprehensions entertained of the ruinous consequences which would result to this interest by the adoption of a free and liberal policy with respect to the trade in corn are without any foundation; that the value of this property, instead of being depreciated, in the aggregate, would be rather enhanced, and the general interests of the owners most decidedly benefited thereby;' and, 'that, while incalculable benefit would arise to the manufacturing interest and the working population generally, in common with all classes of the community, from the adoption of such policy, nothing can be more erroneous than the belief that the price of provisions or labour would on the average be thereby cheapened, but that, on the contrary, the tendency would rather be to produce, by a state of general increased prosperity, a higher average rate of each.'

Whatever might be thought in 1839, in 1860 we can on one point have no doubt whatever. The repeal of the Corn Laws has been followed by the exact effect which Mr. Wilson anticipated. Whether his argument was right or wrong, the result has corresponded with his anticipation. The agriculturists have prospered more,—the manufacturers, the merchants, the operatives, all classes in a word have prospered more, since the Corn Laws were repealed than they ever did before. As to abstract questions of politics there will always be many controversies; but upon a patent contemporaneous fact of this magnitude there cannot be a controversy.

It is indisputable also that, for the purposes of the Anti-Corn Law agitation, Mr. Wilson's view was exceedingly opportune. Mr. Cobden said not long ago (we quote the substance correctly even if the words are wrong), 'I never made any progress with the Corn Law question while it was stated as a question of class against class.' And a careful inquirer will find that such is the real moral of the whole struggle. If it had continued to be considered solely or mainly as a manufacturer's question, it might not have been settled to this hour. In support of this opinion Mr. Wilson made many speeches at the meetings of the Anti-Corn League, though he had little taste for the task of agitation.

We cannot give even an analysis of Mr. Wilson's arguments—our space is too brief—but we will enumerate one or two of the principal points.

He maintained that, under our protective laws, the agriculturists never had the benefit of a high price, and always suffered the evil of a low price. When our crop was scanty, it was necessary to sell the small quantity at a high price, or the farmer could not be remunerated. But exactly at that moment foreign corn was permitted by law to be imported. In consequence, during bad years the farmer was exposed to difficulty and disaster, which were greater because, in expectation of an English demand, large stocks were often hoarded on the Continent, and at once poured in to prevent the home-grower compensating himself for a bad harvest by an equivalent rise of price.

Nor was the farmer better off in very plentiful years. There was a surplus in this country, and that surplus could not be exported, for the price of wheat was always lower abroad than here. The effect is evident. As corn is an article of the first necessity, a certain quantity of it will always be consumed, but more than that quantity will not be readily consumed. A slight surplus is, therefore, invariably found to lower the price of such articles excessively. In very good years the farmer had to sell his crop at an unremuneratingly low price, while in very bad years he was prevented from obtaining the high price which alone could compensate him for his outlay. Between the effects of the two sorts of years his condition was deplorable, and parliamentary committees were constantly appointed to investigate it.

Mr. Wilson also explained how much these fluctuations in price contracted the home demand for agricultural produce. The manufacturing districts were, he showed, subjected by the Corn Laws to alternate periods of great excitement and great depression. When corn was very cheap, the mass of the community had much to spend on other things; when corn was very dear, they had very little to spend on those things. In consequence, the producers of 'other things' were sometimes stimulated by a great demand, and at other times deadened by utter slackness. The labouring classes in the manufacturing districts acquired in periods of plenty a certain taste for what to them were luxuries, and in periods of scarcity were naturally soured at being deprived of them. The manufacturers were frequently induced to invest additional capital by sudden augmentations of demand, and were often ruined by its sudden cessation. It was therefore impossible that the manufacturing classes could be steady customers of the agriculturists, for their own condition was fluctuating and unsteady.

Mr. Wilson also showed that if the landed interest was injured by the effects of the Corn Laws, this was of itself enough to injure the manufacturing interests. 'The connection,' he wrote, 'between the manufacturer and the landed interest in this country is much closer than is generally admitted or believed; not only is the manufacturer dependent on the landed interest for the large portion of his goods which they immediately consume, but also for a very large portion of what he exports to the most distant countries. All commerce is, either directly or indirectly, a simple exchange of the surplus products of one country for those of another. It is therefore a first essential that we should be able to take the cotton of America, the sugar and coffee of India, the silk and teas of China, before they can take our manufactures; and if this be necessary, then must it follow that in proportion to the extent to which we can take their produce, will they be enabled to take our manufactures. Therefore, whatever portion of these products is consumed in this country by the landed interest, must to that extent enable the manufacturer to export his goods in return; and thus any causes which increase this ability on the part of the landed interest to consume, must give a corresponding additional ability to the manufacturers to export. Every pound of coffee or sugar, every ounce of tea, every article of luxury, the produce of foreign climes, whether consumed within the castles and halls of our wealthiest landowners, or in the humble cottages of our lowliest peasantry, alike represent some portion of the exports of this country. On the other hand, the dependence of the landowner is no less twofold on the manufacturer and merchant. He is not only dependent upon them for their own immediate consumption, but also for the consumption of whatever food enters into the cost price of their goods. Although the English farmer does not export his *corn* or his other produce in the exact shape and form in which he produces them, they constitute not the less on that account a distinct portion of the exports of this country, and that in the best of all possible forms. Just as much as the manufacturer exports the wool or the silk which enters into the fabrics of those materials, does he export the corn which paid for the labour of spinning and weaving them. It would be an utter impossibility that this country could consume its agricultural produce but for our extensive manufacturing population; or that the value of what would be consumed could be near its present rate. If without this aid our agricultural produce were as great as it now is, a large portion would have to seek a market in distant countries: it would then have to be exported in the exact form in which it is produced; the expenses of which being so large would reduce very greatly from its value and net price, and the landed interest would be immediately affected thereby. But, as it is, the produce of the land is exported in the condensed form of manufactured goods, at a comparatively trifling expense, which secures a high value to it here. Thus, for example, a few bales of silk or woollen goods may contain as much wheat in their value as would freight a whole ship. To this advantage the landed interest is indebted, exclusively, for the very superior value of property and produce in this country to any other; because, by our great manufacturing superiority, a market is found for our produce over the whole world, conveyed in the cheapest and most condensed form. While the Chinese, or Indians, buy our cottons, our silks, or our woollens, they buy a portion of the grain and other produce of the land of this country; and therefore the producer here, while indulging in the delicacies or luxuries of oriental climes, may only be consuming a portion of the golden heads of wheat which had gracefully waved in his own fields at a former day. Is it not, therefore, sufficiently clear that no circumstance whatever can. either improve or injure one of these interests without immediately in the same way affecting the other? The connection is so close that it is impossible to separate or distinguish them. Any circumstance which limits our commerce must limit our market for agricultural produce; and any possible circumstance which deteriorates the condition of our agriculturists must deteriorate our commerce, by limiting our imports, and consequently our exports. These are general principles, and are capable of extension to the whole world, in all places, and at all times; and the same principle as is thus shown to connect and combine the different interests of any one country, just as certainly operates in producing a similar effect between different countries; and we ardently hope, ere long, to find not only the petty jealousies between different portions of the same community entirely removed, but that all countries will learn that a free and unrestricted co-operation with each other in matters of commerce can only tend to the general benefit and welfare of all.'

We do not say that these propositions were exactly discoveries of Mr. Wilson. During the exciting discussion of a great public question, the most important truths which relate to it are 'in the air' of the age; many persons see them, or half-see them; and it is impossible to trace the precise parentage of any of them. But we do say that these opinions were exactly suited to the broad and practical understanding of Mr.

MEMOIR OF THE RIGHT HONOURABLE JAMES WILSON

Wilson; that they were very effectively illustrated by him—more effectively probably than by any other writer; that he thought them out for himself with but little knowledge of previous theories; that they, principally, raised Free Trade from a class question to a national question; that to them, whether advocated by Mr. Wilson or by others, the success of the Anti-Corn Law agitation was in a great measure owing; that whatever doubt may formerly have been felt, an ample trial has now proved them to be true.

Mr. Wilson's pamphlet entitled 'The Revenue; or, What should the Chancellor do?' which attracted considerable attention when it was published in 1841, is worth reading now, though dated so many years ago, for it contains an outline of the financial policy which Sir Robert Peel commenced, and which Mr. Gladstone has now almost completed. This pamphlet, which is rather long (27 moderate pages), was begun as an article for the *Morning Chronicle*, but proved too long for that purpose. It was written with almost inconceivable rapidity—nearly all we believe in a single night,—though its principles and its many figures will bear a critical scrutiny even now.

In the briefest memoir of Mr. Wilson it is necessary to say something of the currency; but it will not be advisable to say very much. If however we could rely on the patience of our readers, we should say a good deal. On no subject perhaps did Mr. Wilson take up a more characteristic position. He saw certain broad principles distinctly and steadily, and to these he firmly adhered, no matter what refined theories were suggested, or what the opinion of others might be.

Mr. Wilson was a stern bullionist. He held that a five-pound note was a promise to pay five pounds. He answered Sir Robert Peel's question, 'What is a pound?' with Sir Robert's own answer. He said it was a certain specified quantity of gold metal. He held that all devices for aiding industry by issuing inconvertible notes were certainly foolish, and might perhaps be mischievous. He held that industry could only be really aided by additional *capital*—by new machines, new instruments, new raw material; that an addition to a paper *currency* was as useless to aid deficient capital, as it was to feed a hungry population.

Mr. Wilson held, secondly, that the *sine qua non*, the great pre-requisite to a good paper currency, was the maintenance of an adequate reserve by the issuer. He believed that a banker should look at his liabilities as a whole—the notes which he has in circulation and the deposits he has in his ledger taken together; and should retain a sufficient portion of them (say one-third) in cash, or in something equivalent to cash, in daily readiness to pay them at once. Mr. Wilson considered that bankers might be trusted to keep such a reserve, as they would be ruined, sooner or later, if they did not; and if the notes issued by them were always convertible at the pleasure of the holder, he believed that the currency would never be depreciated.

He thought however that, as bank-notes must pass from hand to hand in the market, and as in practice most persons—most traders especially—must take them in payment whether they wish to do so or not, some special security might properly be required for their payment. He would have allowed any one who liked to issue bank-notes on depositing Consols to a sufficient amount—the amount, that is, of the notes issued, and an adequate per centage in addition.

Lastly, Mr. Wilson believed that the bank-note circulation exercised quite a secondary and unimportant influence upon prices and upon transactions, in comparison with the auxiliary currency of cheques and credits which has indefinitely augmented during the last thirty years. So far from regarding the public as constantly ready for an unlimited supply of bank-notes, he thought that it was only in times of extreme panic, when this auxiliary currency is diminished and disturbed, that the bank-notes in the hands of the public either could or would be augmented. He believed that the public only kept in their hands as many notes as they wanted for their own convenience, and that all others were in the present day paid back to the banker immediately and necessarily.

Unfortunately, however, the currency is not discussed in England with very exact reference to abstract principles. The popular question of every thinker is, 'Are you in favour of Peel's Bill, or are you against it?' And this mode of discussing the subject always placed Mr. Wilson in a position of some difficulty. He concurred in the aim of Sir Robert Peel, but objected to his procedure. He wished to secure the convertibility of the bank-note. He believed that the Act of 1844 indirectly induced the Bank directors to keep more bullion than they would keep otherwise, and in so far he thought it beneficial; but he also thought that the advantages obtained by it were purchased at a needless price; that they might have been obtained much more cheaply; that the machinery of the Act aggravated every panic; that it tended to fix the attention of the public on bank-notes, and so fostered the mischievous delusion that the augmented issue of paper currency would strengthen industry; that it neglected to take account of other forms of credit which are equally important with bank-notes; that '*for one week in ten years*'—the week of panic—it created needless and intense apprehension, and so tended to cause the ruin of some solvent commercial men. In brief, though he fully believed the professed object of Sir Robert Peel—the convertibility of the bank-note—to be beneficial and inestimable, he as fully believed the special means selected by him to be inconvenient and pernicious.

Opinions akin to Mr. Wilson's, if not identical with them, are very commonly now entertained, both by practical men of business and by professed economists. The younger school of thinkers who have had before them the working of the Act of 1844 and the events of 1847 and 1857, and are not committed by any of the older controversies, are especially inclined to them. Yet from peculiar causes they have not been so popular as Mr. Wilson's other opinions. His views of finance and of the effect of Free Trade, which were half heresies when he announced them, have now become almost axioms. But the truth of his currency theory is still warmly controverted. The reason is this:— Sir Robert Peel's Act is a sort of compromise which is suited to the English people. It was probably intended by its author as a preliminary step; it undoubtedly suits no strict theory; it certainly has great marks of incompleteness; but 'it works tolerably well'; if it produces evils at a crisis, 'crises come but seldom'; in ordinary times commerce 'goes on very fairly.' The pressure of practical evil upon the English people has never yet been so great as to induce them to face the unpleasant difficulties of the abstract currency question. Mr. Wilson's opinions have, therefore, never been considered by practical men for a practical object, and it is only when so considered that any opinions of his can be duly estimated. Their essentially moderate character, too, is unfavourable to them—not, indeed, among careful inquirers, but in the hubbub of public controversy. The only great party which has as yet attacked Sir Robert Peel's Bill is that which desires an extensive issue of inconvertible currency; but to them Mr. Wilson was as much opposed as Sir Robert Peel himself. The two watchwords of the controversy are 'caution' and 'expansion': the advocates of the Act of 1844 have seized on the former, the Birmingham school on the latter; the intermediate, and, as we think, juster opinions of Mr. Wilson have had no party cry to aid them, and they have not as yet therefore obtained the practical influence which he never ceased to anticipate and to hope for them. No more need be said upon the currency question,— perhaps we have already said too much; but to those who knew Mr. Wilson well, no subject is more connected with his memory: he was so fond of expounding it, that its very technicalities are, in the minds of some, associated with his voice and image.

But it was not by mere correctness of economical speculation that Mr. Wilson was to rise to eminence. A very accurate knowledge of even the more practical aspects of economical science is not of itself a productive source of income. By the foundation of *The Economist* Mr. Wilson secured for himself during the rest of his life competence and comfort, but it was not solely or simply by writing good political economy in it. The organisation of a first-rate commercial paper in 1843 required a great inventiveness and also a great discretion. Nothing of the kind then existed; it was not known what the public most wished to know on business interests; the best shape of communicating information had to be invented in detail. The labour of creating such a paper and of administering it during its early stages is very great; and might well deter most men even of superior ability from attempting it. At this period of his life Mr. Wilson used to superintend the whole of *The Economist*; to write all the important leaders, nearly all of the unimportant ones; to make himself master of every commercial question as it arose; to give practical details as to the practical aspects of it; to be on the watch for every kind of new commercial information; to spend hours in adapting it to the daily wants of commercial men. He often worked till far into the morning, and impressed all about him with wonder at the anxiety, labour, and exhaustion he was able to undergo. As has been stated, for some months after the commencement of this paper he was still engaged in his former business; and after he relinquished that, he used to write the City article and also leaders for the *Morning Chronicle*, at the very time that he was doing on this paper far more than most men would have had endurance of mind or strength of body for. Long afterwards he used to speak of this period as far more exhausting than the most exhausting part of a laborious public life. 'Our public men,' he once said, 'do not know what anxiety means; they have never known what it is to have their own position dependent on their own exertions.' In 1843, and for some time afterwards, he had himself to bear extreme labour and great anxiety together; and even his iron frame was worn and tried by the conjunction.

Within seven years from the foundation of *The Economist*, Mr. Wilson dealt effectively and thoroughly with three first-rate subjects, —the railway mania, the famine in Ireland, and the panic of 1847, in addition to the entire question of Free Trade, which was naturally the main topic of economical teaching in those years. On all these three topics he explained somewhat original opinions, which were novelties, if not paradoxes then, though they are very generally believed now. To his writings on the railway mania he was especially fond of recurring, since he believed that by his warnings—warnings very effectively brought out and very constantly reiterated—he had 'saved several men their fortunes' at that time.

The success of this paper, and the advantage which the proprietor of it would derive from a first-hand acquaintance with political life, naturally led him to think of gaining a seat in Parliament, and an accidental conversation at Lord Radnor's table fixed his attention on the borough of Westbury. After receiving a requisition, he visited the place, explained his political sentiments at much length 'from an old cart,' and believed that he saw sufficient chances of success to induce him to take a house there. He showed considerable abilities in electioneering, and a close observer once said of him, 'Mr. Wilson may or may not be the best political economist in England, but depend upon it he is the *only* political economist who would ever come in for the borough of Westbury.' Though nominally a borough, the constituency is half a rural one, much under the influence of certain Conservative squires. The Liberal party were in 1847 only endeavouring to emancipate themselves from a yoke to which they have now again succumbed. Except for Mr. Wilson's constant watchfulness, his animated geniality, his residence on the spot, his knowledge of every voter by sight, the Liberal party might never have been successful there. A certain expansive frankness of manner and a wonderful lucidity in explaining his opinions almost to any one, gave Mr. Wilson great advantages as a popular candidate, and it was very remarkable to find these qualities connected with a strong taste for treating very dry subjects upon professedly abstract principles. So peculiar a combination had the success which it merited. In the summer of 1847 he was elected to serve in Parliament for Westbury.

Mr. Wilson made his first speech in the House of Commons on the motion for a Committee to inquire into the commercial distress at that time prevalent.[2] And it was considered an act of intellectual boldness for a new member to explain his opinions on so difficult a subject as the currency, especially as they were definitely opposed to a measure supported by such overwhelming parliamentary authority as the Act of 1844 then was. Judging from the report of the speech in 'Hansard,' and from the recollections of some who heard it, the speech was a successful one. It is very clear and distinct, and its tone is very emphatic, without ever ceasing to be considerate and candid. It contains a sufficient account of Mr. Wilson's tenets on the currency—so good an account, indeed, that when he read it ten years later, in the panic of 1857, he acknowledged that he did not think he could add a word to it. At the time, however, the test of its Parliamentary success was not the absolute correctness of its abstract principles, but, to use appropriate and technical language, 'its getting a rise out of Peel.' Sir Robert had used some certainly inconclusive arguments in favour of his favourite measure, and Mr. Wilson made that inconclusiveness so very clear that he thought it necessary to rise 'and explain,' which, on such a subject, was deemed at the moment a great triumph for a first speech.

As might be expected from so favourable a commencement, Mr. Wilson soon established a parliamentary reputation. He was not a formal orator, and did not profess to be so. But he had great powers of exposition, singular command of telling details upon his own subjects, a very pleasing voice, a grave but by no means inanimate manner—qualities which are amply sufficient to gain the respectful attention of the House of Commons. And Mr. Wilson did gain it. But speaking is but half, and in the great majority of cases by far the smaller half, of the duties of a member of Parliament. Mr. Wilson was fond of quoting a saying of Sir Robert Peel's, 'That the way to get on in the House of Commons was to take a place and sit there.' He adopted this rule himself, was constant in his attendance at the House, a good listener to other men, and always ready to take trouble with troublesome matters. These plain and business-like qualities, added to his acknowledged ability and admitted acquaintance with a large class of subjects upon which knowledge is rare, gave Mr. Wilson a substantial influence in the House of Commons in an unusually short time. The Corn Laws had been repealed, the pitched battle of Free Trade had been fought and won, but much yet remained to be done in carrying out its

[2] On November 30 1847.—Ed.

principles with effective precision, in applying them to articles other than corn, in exposing the fallacies still abundantly current, and in answering the exceptional case which every trade in succession set up for an exceptional protection. These were painful and complex matters of detail, wearisome to very many persons, and rewarding with no *éclat* those who took the trouble to master and explain them. But Mr. Wilson shrank from no detail. For several years before he had a seat in the House, he had been used to explain such topics in countless conversations with the most prominent Free-traders and in *The Economist*. He now did so in the House of Commons, and his influence correspondingly increased. He was able to do an important work better than any one else could do it, and, in English public life, real work rightly done at the right season scarcely ever fails to meet with a real reward.

That Mr. Wilson early acquired considerable parliamentary reputation is evinced by the best of all proofs. He was offered office before he had been six months in the House of Commons, though he had, as the preceding sketch will have made evident, no aristocratic connections—though he was believed to be a poorer man than he really was—though writing political articles for newspapers has never been in England the sure introduction to political power which it formerly was in France—though, on the contrary, it has in general been found a hindrance. In a case like Mr. Wilson's, the prize of office was a sure proof of evident prowess in the parliamentary arena.

The office which was offered to Mr. Wilson was one of the Secretaryships of the Board of Control. Mr. Wilson related at Hawick his reluctance to accept it, and his reason. Never having given any special attention to Indian topics, he thought it would be absurd and ridiculous in him to accept an office which seemed to require much special knowledge. But Lord John Russell, with 'that knowledge of public affairs which long experience ensures,' at once explained to him that a statesman, under our parliamentary system, must be prepared to serve the Queen 'whenever he may be called on'; and accordingly that he must be ready to take *any* office which he can fill, without at all considering whether it is that which he can *best* fill. After some deliberation, Mr. Wilson acknowledged the wisdom of this advice, and accepted the office offered him. Long afterwards, in the speech at Hawick to which we have alluded, he said that without the preliminary knowledge of India which he acquired at the Board of Control, he would never have been able to undertake the regulation of her finances.

When once installed in his office, he devoted himself to it with his usual unwearied industry. And at least on one occasion he had to deal with a congenial topic. The introduction of railways into India was opposed on many grounds, most of which are now forgotten,—such as 'the effect upon the native mind,' 'the impossibility of inducing the Hindoos to travel in that manner,' and the like; and more serious difficulties occurred in considering the exact position which the Government should assume with regard to such great undertakings in such singular circumstances,—the necessity on the one hand, in an Asiatic country where the state is the sole motive power, of the Government's doing something,—and the danger on the other hand of interfering with private enterprise, by its doing, or attempting to do, too much. Mr. Wilson applied himself vigorously to all these difficulties; he exercised the whole of his personal influence, and the whole of that which was given to him by his situation, in dissipating the fanciful obstacles which were alleged to be latent in the unknown tendencies of the oriental mind; while he certainly elaborated,—and he *believed* that he originally suggested,—the peculiar form of state guarantee upon the faith of which so many millions of English capital have been sent to develop the industry of India.

Besides discharging the duties of his office, Mr. Wilson represented the Government of the day on several committees connected with his peculiar topics, and especially on one which fully investigated the Sugar question. Of the latter, indeed, he became so fully master that some people fancied he must have been in the trade; so complete was the familiarity which he displayed with 'brown muscovado,' 'white clayed,' and all other technical terms which are generally inscrutably puzzling to parliamentary statesmen. On a parliamentary committee Mr. Wilson appeared to great advantage. Though sufficiently confident of the truth of his own opinions, he had essentially a fair mind; he always had the greatest confidence that if the facts were probed the correctness of what he believed would be established, and, *therefore*, he was always ready to probe the facts to the bottom. He was likewise a great master of the Socratic art of inquiry; he was able to frame a series of consecutive questions which gradually brought an unwilling or a hostile witness to conclusions at which he by no means wished to arrive. His examination-in-chief, too, was as good as his cross-examination, and the animated interest which he evinced in the subject relieved the dreariness which a rehearsed extraction of premeditated answers commonly involves. The examination of Lord Overstone before the Committee of 1848 on Commercial Distress, that of Mr. Weguelin before the Committee on the Bank Acts in 1857, and several of the examinations before the Committee on Life Insurance, of which he was the chairman, may be consulted as models in their respective kinds. And it should be stated that no man could be less overbearing in examination or cross-examination; much was often extracted from a witness which he did not wish to state, but it was always extracted fairly, quietly, and by seemingly inevitable sequence.

Mr. Wilson continued at the Board of Control till the resignation of Lord John Russell's Cabinet in the spring of 1852. He took part in the opposition of the Liberal party to Lord Derby's Government, and was very deeply interested in the final settlement of the Free Trade question which was effected by the accession of the protectionist party to office. After a very severe contest he was re-elected for Westbury in July, 1852, and on the formation of the Aberdeen Government he accepted the office of Financial Secretary to the Treasury, which he continued to hold for five years, until the dissolution of Lord Palmerston's administration in the spring of 1857, and upon his efficiency in which his remarkable reputation as an official administrator was mainly based.

The Financial Secretaryship of the Treasury is by no means one of the most conspicuous offices in the Government, and but few persons who have not observed political life closely are at all aware either of its difficulty or of its importance. The office is, indeed, a curious example of the half grotesque way in which the abstract theory of our historical constitution contrasts with its practical working. In the theory of the constitution—a theory which may still be found in popular compendiums—there is an officer called the Lord High Treasurer, who is to advise the Crown and be responsible to the country for all public monies. In practice, there is no such functionary: by law his office is 'in commission.' Certain Lords Commissioners are supposed to form a Board at which financial subjects are discussed, and which is responsible for their due administration. In practice, there is no such discussion and no such responsibility. The functions of the Junior Lords of the Treasury, though not entirely nominal, are but slight. The practical administration of our expenditure is vested in the First Lord of the Treasury, the Chancellor of the Exchequer, and the Financial Secretary of the Treasury. And of these three the constitutional rule is, that the First Lord of the Treasury is only officially responsible for decisions in detail when he chooses to interfere in those decisions. Accordingly, when a First Lord, as was the case with Sir Robert Peel, takes a great interest in financial questions, the Chancellor of the Exchequer does the usual work of the Secretary of the Treasury, and the Secretary of the Treasury has in comparison nothing to do. But when, as was the case in the governments of Lord Aberdeen and Lord Palmerston, the Prime Minister takes no special interest in Finance, the Chancellor of the Exchequer is very fully employed in the transaction of his own proper business, and an enormous mass of work, some of it of extreme importance, falls to the Secretary of the Treasury. Of late years, the growth of the miscellaneous civil expenditure of the country has greatly augmented that work—great as it was before. In general, it may be said that the whole of the financial detail of our national expenditure is more or less controlled by the Secretary of the Treasury; that much of it is very closely controlled by him; and that he has vast powers of practical discretion if only he be a man of ability, industry, and courage.

For such an office as this Mr. Wilson had very peculiar qualifications. He was perfectly sure to be right in a plain case; and by far the larger part of the ordinary business of the Government, as of individuals, consists of plain cases. A man who is thoroughly sure to decide effectually and correctly the entire mass of easy obvious cases, is a safer master of practical life than one eminently skilled in difficult cases, but deficient in the more rudimentary qualification. Nor is the power of certainly deciding plain cases rightly, by any means very common, especially among very intellectual men. A certain taint of subtlety, a certain tendency to be wise above the case in hand, mars the practical efficiency of many men whose conversation and whose powers would induce us to expect that they would be very efficient. Mr. Wilson had not a particle of these defects. He struck off each case with a certain sledge-hammer efficiency, and every plain case at least with infallible accuracy.

It might seem overstrained eulogy—a eulogy which he would not have wished—to claim for Mr. Wilson an equally infallible power of deciding complicated cases. As to such cases there will always be a doubt. Plain matters speak for themselves: they do not require a dissertation to elucidate them: every man of business, as soon as he hears the right decision of them, knows that it is the right decision.

But with more refined matters it is not so; as to points involving an abstract theory, like that of the currency, there will and must be differences of judgment to the end of time. We would not, therefore, whatever may be our own opinion, claim for Mr. Wilson as infallible a power of deciding difficult questions as he certainly possessed of deciding plain questions. But we do claim for him even in such matters the greatest secondary excellence, if, indeed, a secondary excellence it be. Mr. Wilson was perfectly certain to be *intelligible in the most difficult case.* Whether he did right or did wrong, must, as we have said, be from the nature of the subject-matter very arguable. But *what* he did and *why* he did it, was never in doubt for a moment. The archives of the Treasury contain countless minutes from his pen, most of them written with what most men would call rapidity, just while the matter was waiting for decision, and on all sorts of subjects, many of them very complicated ones,—yet it may be doubted whether any one of those minutes contains a single sentence not thoroughly and con- spicuously clear. The same excellence which has been shown in countless articles in *The Economist* appears in his business-like docu- ments. Wherever his leading articles were written and under whatever circumstances,—and some of the most elaborate of them were written under rather strange circumstances (for he could catch up a pen and begin to write on the most involved topic, at any time, in any place, and, as a casual observer would think, without any premeditation),— but wherever and however these articles might be written, it may be safely asserted that they do not contain a sentence which a man of business need read twice over, or which he would not find easily and certainly intelligible. At the Treasury it was the same. However complicated or involved the matter to be decided might be,—however much it might be loaded with detail or perplexed by previous con- troversy,—Mr. Wilson never failed to make immediately clear the exact opinion he formed upon it, the exact grounds upon which he formed it, and the exact course of action which he thought should be adopted upon it. Many persons well acquainted with practical life will be disposed to doubt whether extreme accuracy of decision is not almost a secondary merit as compared with a perfect intelligibility. In many cases it may be better to have a decision which every one can understand, though with some percentage of error, than an elaborately accurate decision of which the grounds and reasons are not easily grasped, and a plan of action which, from its refined complexity, is an inevitable mystery to the greater number of practical persons. But, putting aside this abstract discussion, we say without fear of contradiction or of doubt, that Mr. Wilson added to his almost infallible power of deciding plain cases, an infallible certainty of being entirely intelligible in complicated cases. Men of business will be able to imagine the administrative capacity certain to be produced by the union of extreme excellence in both qualities.

One subsidiary faculty that Mr. Wilson possessed, which was very useful to him in the multifarious business of the Treasury, was an extraordinary memory. On his own subjects and upon transactions in which he had taken a decisive part, he seemed to recollect anything and everything. He was able to answer questions as to business transacted at the Treasury after the lapse of months and even of years without referring to the papers, and with a perfect certainty of substantial accuracy. He would say, without the slightest effort and without the slightest idea that he was doing anything extraordinary: 'Such and such a person came to me at the Treasury, and said so and so, and this is what I said to him.' And it is quite possible that he might remember the precise sums of money which were the subject of conversation. A more useful memory for the purposes of life was perhaps never possessed by any one. In the case of great literary memories, such as that of Lord Macaulay and of others, the fortunate possessor has a continued source of pleasurable and constantly recurring recollections; he has a full mind constantly occupied with its own contents, recurring to its long loved passages from its favourite authors constantly and habitually. But Mr. Wilson never recurred to the transactions in which he had been engaged except when he was asked about them; he lived as little in the past perhaps as is possible for an intellectual person; but the moment the spring was touched by a question or by some external necessity, all the details of the past transaction started into his memory completely, vividly, and perfectly. He had thus the advantage of always remembering his business, and also the advantage of never being burdened by it. Very few persons can ever have had in equal measure the two merits of a fresh judgment and a full mind.

Mr. Wilson's memory was likewise assisted by a very even judgment. It was easier to him to remember what he had done, because, if he had to do the same thing again, he would be sure to do it in precisely the same way. He was not an intolerant person, but the qualities he tolerated least easily were flightiness and inconsistency of purpose.

He had furnished his mind, so to say, with fixed principles, and he hated the notion of a mind which was unfurnished.

All these mental qualities taken together go far to make up the complete idea of a perfect administrator of miscellaneous financial business, such as that of the English Treasury now is. And Mr. Wilson had the physical qualities also. An iron constitution which feared no labour, and was very rarely incapacitated even for an hour by any illness, enabled him to accomplish with ease and unconsciously an amount of work which few men would not have shrunk from. In the country, where his habits were necessarily more obvious, he habitually spent the whole day from eleven till eight, with some slight interval for a short ride in the middle of the day, over his treasury bag; and as such was his notion of a holiday, it may be easily conceived that in London, when he had still more to do in a morning, and had to spend almost every evening in the House of Commons, his work was greater than an ordinary constitution could have borne. And it was work of a rather peculiar kind. Some men of routine habits spend many hours over their work, but do not labour very intensely at one time; other men of more excitable natures work impulsively, and clear off every thing they do by eager efforts in a short time. But Mr. Wilson in some sense did both. Although his hours of labour were so very protracted, yet if a casual observer happened to enter his library at any moment, he would find him with his blind down to exclude all objects of external interest, his brow working eagerly, his eye fixed intently on the figures before him, and, very likely, his rapid pen passing fluently over the paper. He had all the labour of the chronic worker, and all the labour of the impulsive worker too. And those admitted to his intimacy used to wonder that he was never tired. He came out of his library in an evening more ready for vigorous conversation—more alive to all subjects of daily interest—more quick to gain new information—more ready to expound complicated topics, than others who had only passed an easy day of idleness or ordinary exertion.

By the aid of this varied combination of powers, Mr. Wilson was able to grapple with the miscellaneous financial business of the country with very unusual efficiency. Most men would have found the office work of the Secretary of the Treasury quite enough, but he was always ready rather to take away labour and responsibilities from other departments than to throw off any upon them. Nor was his efficiency confined to the labours of his office. The Financial Secretary of the Treasury has a large part of the financial business of the House of Commons under his control, and is responsible for its accurate arrangement. The passing a measure through the House of Commons is a matter of detail; and in the case of the financial measures of the Government, a large part of this—the dullest part, and the most unenvied—falls to the Secretary of the Treasury. He is expected to be the right hand of the Chancellor of the Exchequer in all the most wearisome part of the financial business of the House of Commons; and we have the best authority for stating that, under two Chancellors of the Exchequer very different from one another in many respects, Mr. Wilson performed this part of his duties with singular efficiency, zeal, and judgment.

The Financial Secretary of the Treasury is likewise expected to answer all questions asked in the House as to the civil estimates—a most miscellaneous collection of figures, as any one may satisfy himself by glancing at them. Mr. Wilson's astonishing memory and great power of lucid exposition enabled him to fulfil this part of his duty with very remarkable efficiency. He gave the dates and the figures without any note, and his exposition was uniformly simple, emphatic, and intelligible even on the most complicated subjects. The great rule, he used to say, was to answer exactly the exact question: if you attempted an elaborate exposition, collateral issues were necessarily raised, a debate ensued, and the time of the House was lost.

Mr. Wilson's mercantile knowledge and mercantile sympathies were found to be of much use in the consolidation of the customs in 1853, and he took great interest in settling a scheme for the payment of the duties in cheques instead of bank-notes, by which the circulation has been largely economised and traders greatly benefited. During the autumn of 1857, his long study of the currency question, and his first-hand conversancy with the business of the City, were valuable aids to the Administration of the day in the anxious responsibilities and rapidly shifting scenes of an extreme commercial crisis. It would be impossible to notice the number of measures in which he took part as Secretary of the Treasury, and equally impossible to trace his precise share in them. That office ensures to its holder substantial power, but can rarely give him legislative fame.

On two occasions during his tenure of office at the Treasury, Mr. Wilson was offered a different post. In the autumn of 1856 he was offered the Chairmanship of Inland Revenue, a permanent office of considerable value then vacant, which he declined because he did not consider the income necessary, and because (what some people would think odd) it did not afford sufficient occupation. It was a 'good pillow,' he said, 'but he did not wish to lie down.' The second office offered him was the Vice-Presidency of the Board of Trade in 1855, which would have been a step to him in official rank, but which would have entailed a new election, and he did not feel quite secure that the electors of Westbury would again return him. He did not, however, by any means wish for the change, as the Vice-Presidency of the Board of Trade, though nominally superior, is in real power far inferior to the Secretaryship of the Treasury.

In the general election of 1857, Mr. Wilson was returned for Devonport, for which place he continued to sit till his departure for India. He went out of office on the dissolution of Lord Palmerston's Administration in the spring of 1858, and took an active part in the Liberal opposition to Lord Derby's Government, though it may be remarked that he carefully abstained from using the opportunities afforded him by his long experience at the Treasury, of harassing his less experienced successors in financial office by needless and petty difficulties.

On the return of the Liberal party to power, Mr. Wilson was asked to resume his post at the Treasury, but he declined, as, after five years of laborious service, he wished to have an office of which the details were less absorbing. He accepted, however, the Vice-Presidency of the Board of Trade—an office which is not in itself attractive, but which gives its possessor a sort of claim to be President of the Board at the next vacancy. The office of President is frequently accompanied by a seat in the Cabinet, and Mr. Wilson's reputation on all subjects connected with trade was so firmly established that in his case it would have been practically impossible to pass him over, even if it had been wished. He had, however, secured so firm a position in official circles by his real efficiency, that the dispensers of patronage were, as he believed, likely to give him whatever he desired as soon as the exigencies of party enabled them to do so.

He had not been long in office before he had good reason for thinking that he would be offered by the Government the office of Financial Member of the Council of India under very peculiar circumstances. There had never before been such an officer. One member of Council had since 1833 been always sent out from England, but he had always been a lawyer, and his functions were those of a jurist and a regulative administrator, not those of a financier. The mutiny of the Sepoys in 1857 had, however, left behind it a deficit with which the financiers of India did not *seem* to be able to cope, and which a cumbrous financial system did not give them the best means of vanquishing. There was a general impression that some one with an English training and English habits of business would have a better chance of overcoming the most pressing difficulty of India than any one on the spot. And there was an equally general impression that if any one were to be sent from England to India with such an object, Mr. Wilson was the right person. He united high financial reputation, considerable knowledge of India acquired at the Board of Control, tried habits of business, long experience at the English Treasury, to the sagacious readiness in dealing with new situations which self-made men commonly have, but which is commonly wanting in others.

On personal grounds Mr. Wilson was disinclined to accept the office. He was on the threshold of the Cabinet here; he was entitled by his long tenure of office at the Treasury to a pension which would merge in the salary of Indian Councillor; the emoluments of the latter office were not necessary to him; his life was very heavily insured for the benefit of his family; though he had never during his tenure of office at the Treasury been connected directly or indirectly with any kind of commercial undertaking (*The Economist* alone excepted), some investments which he made in land and securities had been very fortunate; since the year 1844 everything of a pecuniary kind in which he had been concerned had not only prospered, but remarkably prospered; he felt himself sufficiently rich to pursue the career of prosperous usefulness and satisfied ambition that seemed to be before him here. There was no consideration of private interest which could induce him to undertake anxious and dangerous duties in India; he even ran some pecuniary risk in leaving this country, as it was possible that in the vicissitudes of newspaper property this journal might again need the attention of its proprietor and founder. On public grounds, however, he believed that it was his duty to accept the office; he took a keen interest in Indian finance; believed that the difficulties of it might be conquered, and thought that in even *attempting* to conquer them he would be doing the greatest and most lasting public service that it was in *his* power to accomplish.

He accordingly accepted the office of Financial Member of the Council of India, and proceeded to make somewhat melancholy arrangements for leaving this country. He broke up his establishment here; bade farewell to his constituents at Devonport and to the inhabitants of his native place; attended some influential public meetings in towns deeply interested in the commerce of India; and on 20th of October, 1859, left England, as it proved for ever.

Of Mr. Wilson's policy in India it would not be proper to give more than a very brief sketch here. That policy is still fresh in the memory of the public; it has been very frequently explained and discussed in *The Economist*; it is still being tried, and, though he was fully persuaded of the expediency of his measures, he would not have wished for too warm a eulogy of them while they are as yet untested by the event. In almost the last letter which the present writer received from him, there was a sort of reprimand for permitting this journal to draw too great an attention to his plans, and to ascribe the merit of them too exclusively to him, and too little to the Government of which he was a member.

On his arrival in India he found that the Governor-General was on a tour in the Upper Provinces of India, and before doing any business of importance at Calcutta he travelled thither. This journey he thought very advantageous, because it gave him a great insight into the nature of the country, and enabled him to consult the most experienced revenue officers of many large districts on their respective resources, and on the safest mode of making those resources available to the public. He was much struck with the capabilities of the country, and wrote to England almost in so many words 'that it was a fine country to *tax*.' On the other hand, however, he was well aware of the difficulty of his task. The only two possible modes of taxation are direct and indirect, and in the case of India there is a difficulty in adopting either. If we select indirect taxation and impose duties on consumable commodities, the natives of India meet us by declining to consume. Their wants are few, and they will forego most of them if a tax can be evaded thereby. On the other hand, if we adopt in India a direct tax on property or income, there is great difficulty in finding out what each man's property or income is. In England we trust each person to tell us the amount of his income, but even here the results are not wholly satisfactory; and it would be absurd to fancy that we can place as much reliance upon the veracity of orientals as upon that of Englishmen.

These difficulties, however, Mr. Wilson was prepared to meet. On the 18th February, 1860, he proposed his budget to the Legislative Council at Calcutta, and the reception given to it by all classes was remarkably favourable. He announced, indeed, a scheme of heavy taxation, but the Indian public had been living for a considerable time under a sentence of indefinite taxation, and they were glad to know the worst. Anything distinct was better than vague suspense, and, as usual, Mr. Wilson contrived to make his meaning *very* distinct. His bearing also exercised a great influence over the Anglo-Indian public. In England he had been remarkable among official men for his constant animation and thorough naturalness of manner: in his office he was as much himself as at a dinner table or in the House of Commons: he had no tinge of supercilious politeness or artificial blandness. In any new scene of action—especially in such a scene as British India—these qualities were sure to tell beneficially. Plain directness and emphatic simplicity were the external qualities most likely to be useful at Calcutta, and these were Mr. Wilson's most remarkable qualities.

The principal feature of Mr. Wilson's budget was the income tax, which he avowedly framed after the English fashion. It is true that but little reliance can, perhaps, be placed on the statements of orientals as to their wealth. It is very possible that the complicated machinery of forms and notices which is in use here may not be applicable in India. All this Mr. Wilson well knew. But he thought that our Indian subjects should have an opportunity of stating their income before they were taxed upon it. If they should state it untruly, or should decline to state it, it might be necessary to tax them arbitrarily. But he did not think it would be decent—that it would be civilised—to begin with an arbitrary assessment. By the Income Tax Act which he framed, it is enacted that other modes may be substituted if in any instance the English mode of assessment should prove inapplicable. In other words, if our oriental fellow-subjects will not tell us the truth when they are asked, we must tax them as best we can, and they cannot justly complain of unfairness and inequality. *We* would have been mathematically just, if *they* had given us the means.

The reception of Mr. Wilson's budget was universally favourable until the publication of the minute of Sir Charles Trevelyan, which, as was inevitable, produced a serious reaction. Heavy taxation can never be very pleasant, and in the Presidency of Madras Sir Charles gave the sanction of the Government—of the highest authority the people saw —to the hope that they would not be taxed. The prompt recall of Sir Charles, however, did much to convince the natives of the firm determination of the English Government, and Mr. Wilson hoped that the ordeal of criticism through which his measures had to pass would ultimately be favourable to them. It certainly secured them from the accusation of being prepared in haste, but it purchased this benefit at the loss to the public of much precious time, and to Mr. Wilson of precious health. Of the substance of this minute it is sufficient to say that its fundamental theory that additional taxation of any sort was unnecessary in India, has scarcely been believed by any one except its author. Almost every one has deemed it too satisfactory to be true.

On another point Mr. Wilson's budget has been criticised in England, though not in India. It has been considered to be a protective budget. The mistake has arisen from not attending to what that budget is. The changes made by Mr. Wilson in the import duties were two. 'The first was a reduction from twenty to ten per cent. upon a long list of articles, including haberdashery, millinery, and hosiery, all part of the cotton trade; the second was an increase in the duty upon cotton yarn from five to ten per cent., thus creating a uniform tariff of ten per cent.'* Of these two, it is plain the reduction from twenty per cent. to ten was not a change that would operate as a protection to Indian industry; and the increase of the duty on yarn has a contrary tendency. Yarn is an earlier, cloth a later, stage of manufacture, and in Mr. Wilson's own words, 'it is a low duty on yarn and a high duty on cloth that encourages native weaving.' For the effect of the general system of high customs duties in India Mr. Wilson is not responsible, but his predecessors. What *he* did has no protective tendency.

If the income tax should, as may be fairly hoped, become a permanent part of the financial system of India, it will serve for a considerable period to keep Mr. Wilson's name alive there. So efficient an expedient must always attract the notice of the public, and must in some degree preserve the remembrance of the minister by whom it was proposed.

Mr. Wilson, however, undertook two other measures of very great importance. One of these has been frequently described as the introduction into India of the English system of public accounts. But it

* *The Economist* of Sept. 8th, 1860, p. 977.

would be more truly described as the introduction of a rational system of public accounts. There are three natural steps in national finance, which are certainly clearly marked in our English system, but which have a necessary existence independent of that recognition. These three are—first, the estimate of future expenditure; secondly, what we call the Budget, that is the official calculation of the income by which the coming expenditure is to be defrayed; thirdly, the audit which shows what the expenditure has been and how it has been met. The system of finance which Mr. Wilson found in India neglected these fundamental distinctions. There were no satisfactory estimates of future expenditure, and no satisfactory calculation of future income. In consequence, the calculations of the official departments have been wrong by millions sterling, and English statesmen have felt great difficulty not only in saying how the deficit was to be removed, but likewise in ascertaining what the amount of the deficit was. At the time of his death Mr. Wilson was eagerly occupied in endeavouring to introduce a better system.

Mr. Wilson will likewise be remembered as the first minister who endeavoured to introduce into India a government paper currency. On the 3rd March, 1860, he introduced into the Legislative Council an elaborate plan for this purpose, which, with a slight modification by Sir Charles Wood—curious in the theory of the currency, but practically not very important—will speedily, it is probable, be the fundamental currency law—the 'Peel's Act' of British India.

The exact mode in which Mr. Wilson regarded these great objects, will perhaps be better explained by two extracts from his latest letters than by any other means. On 4th of July he wrote to a friend:—

'Firmness and justice are the only policy for India;—no vacillation, or you are gone. They like to be governed; and respect an iron hand, if it be but equal and just. I have I think more confidence than ever that the taxes will be established and collected, and without disturbance. But the task is still an enormous one. I must retrench yet at least 3½ millions, and get the same sum from my *new* taxes to make both ends meet. I am putting the screw on very strongly, but rather by an improved policy in army and police than in reductions of salaries and establishments, which cannot be made. I have set myself *five* great points of policy to introduce and carry out.

'1. To extend a system of sound taxation to the great trading classes who hitherto have been exempted, though chiefly benefited by our enormously increased civil expenditure.

'2. To establish a paper currency.

'3. To reform and remodel our financial system, by a plan of annual budgets and estimates, with a Pay Department to check issues, and keep them within the authorised limits,—and an effective audit.

'4. A great police system of semi-military organisation, but usually of purely civil application, which, dear though it be, will be cheaper by half a million than our present wretched and expensive system,— and by which we shall be able to reduce our native army to at least one-third—and by which alone we can utilise the natives as an arm of defence without the danger of congregating idle organised masses.

'5. Public works and roads, with a view to increased production of cotton, flax, wool, and European raw materials.

'The four first I have made a great progress in: the latter must follow. But you will call it 'a large order.' However, you have no idea of the increased capacity of the mind for undertaking a special service of this kind when removed to a new scene of action, and when one throws off all the cares of engagements less or more trivial by which one is surrounded in ordinary life, and throws one's whole soul into such a special service, and particularly when one feels assured of having the power to carry it out. I cannot tell you with what ease one determines the largest and gravest question here compared with in England; and I am certain that the more one can exercise real power, there is by far the greater tendency to moderation, care, and prudence.'

In a second letter, dated July 19, he wrote to the same friend from Barrackpore:—

'The Indian Exchequer is a huge machine. The English Treasury is nothing to it for complexity, diversity, and remoteness of the points of action. Our great enemies are time and distance; and with all our frontier territories there is scarcely a day passes that we have not an account of some row or inroad. It is a most unwieldy Empire to be governed on the principle of forcing civilisation at every point of it. One day it is the frontier of Scinde and a quarrel with our native chiefs which our Resident must check: another, it is an intrigue between Heraut and Cabul, with a report of Russian forces in the background: the next, there is a raid upon our Punjab frontiers to be chastised: then come some accounts of coolness, or misunderstanding, or unreasonable demands from our ally in Nepaul: then follow some

inroads from the savage tribes which inhabit the mountains to the rear
of Assam and up the Burrampootra: then we have reported brawls in
Burmah and Pegu, and disputes among the hill tribes whose relations
to the British and the Burmah Governments are ill defined: then we
have Central India, with our loyal chiefs Scindiah and Holkar, independent princes with most turbulent populations, which could not
be kept in order a day without the presence of British troops and of
the Governor-General's Agent. Besides all these, we have among
ourselves a thousand questions of internal administration, rendered
more difficult by the ill-defined relations between the Supreme and
the Subordinate Governments—the latter always striving to encroach,
the former to hold its own. Hence, questions do not come before us
simply on their merits, but often as involving these doubtful rights.
Then we have Courts of Justice to reform, as well as all other institutions of a domestic kind not to reform alone, but to extend to new
territories. Then we have a deficit of £7,000,000, and had a government teaching the people that all could be done without new taxes.
But unfortunately all, except the taxes, are a present certainty—*they* are
a future contingency. What will they yield? I have no precise knowledge. I think from three to four millions a year when in full bloom:—
this financial year not more than a million.

'I have now got a Military Finance Commission in full swing: a
Civil Finance Commission also going: I am reorganising the Finance,
Pay, and Accountant-General's Department, in order to get all the
advantage of the English system of estimates, Pay Office and Audit:—
and this with as little disturbance of existing plans as possible. The
latter is a point I have especially aimed at. On the whole, and almost
without an exception, I have willing allies in all the existing offices.
No attempt that I see is anywhere made to thwart or impede.'

'You can well understand, then, how full my hands are, if to all
these you add the new currency arrangements, you will not then wonder that my health has rendered it necessary to come down here for a
day or two to get some fresh air.'

It will be observed that in the last extract Mr. Wilson alludes to his
impaired health. For some time after his arrival in India he seemed
scarcely to feel the climate. He certainly did not feel it as much as
might have been anticipated. He worked extremely hard; scarcely
wrote a private letter, but devoted the whole of his great energies to
the business around him. His letters for a considerable time abound

with such expressions as 'Notwithstanding all my hard work my health is excellent.' From the commencement of the rainy season at Calcutta, however, he ceased to be equally well, his state began to arouse the apprehensions of experienced observers, and he was warned that he should retire for a short time to a better climate. He would not, however, do so until his financial measures had advanced sufficiently far for him to leave them. His position was a very peculiar one. In general, if one administrator leaves his post, another is found to fill it up. But Mr. Wilson was a unique man at Calcutta. He was sent there because he had certain special qualifications which no one there possessed; and, accordingly, he had no one to rely on in his peculiar functions save himself. His presence on the spot was likewise very important. The administration of a department can be frequently transacted by letter, but the organisation of new departments and new schemes requires the unremitting attention of the organiser— the impulse of his energy. The interest, too, which Mr. Wilson took in public business was exceptionally great, and no one who knew him well would suppose that *he* would leave Calcutta while necessary work, or what he deemed so, was to be done there.

Nor was labour the sole trial to which his constitution was exposed. The success of measures so extensive as his, must ever be a matter of anxious doubt until the event decides; and in his case there were some momentary considerations to aggravate that anxiety. There was no experience of such taxation as he had proposed, and the effect of it must therefore be difficult to foresee. Moreover, for a brief period a famine seemed to be imminent in Upper India, which must have disturbed the whole operation of his financial schemes. In his debilitated state of health this last source of anxiety seemed much to weigh upon him.

About the middle of July he went for a week to Barrackpore, near Calcutta. The change was, however, too slight, and, as might be expected, he returned to Calcutta without any material benefit. From that time the disease gradually augmented, and on the evening of the 2nd August he went to bed never to rise from it again. For many days he continued to be very ill, and his family experienced the usual alternations of hope and fear. He was quite aware of his critical state, and made all necessary arrangements with his habitual deliberation and calmness.

Lord Canning saw him on the 9th for the last time, and was much struck with the change which illness had made in him. He believed that he saw death in his face, and was deeply impressed with the vivid interest, which, even in the last stage of weakness, he took in public affairs, with his keen desire for the success of his plans, and with the little merit which he was disposed to claim for his own share in them.

It was hoped that he would be strong enough to bear removal, and it was intended to delay the mail steamer for a few hours to take him to sea—the usual remedy at Calcutta for diseases of the climate. But when the time came there was no chance that his strength would be adequate to the effort. During the whole of the 11th he sank rapidly, and at half-past six in the evening he breathed his last.

The mourning in Calcutta was more universal than had ever been remembered. He had not been long in India, but while he had been there he filled a conspicuous and great part: he had done so much, that there were necessarily doubts in the minds of some as to the expediency of part of it. No such doubts, however, were thought of now. 'That he should have come out to die here!'—'That he should have left a great English career *for this!*'—were the phrases in every one's mouth. The funeral was the largest ever known at Calcutta. It was attended by almost the entire population, from the Governor-General downwards, and not a single voice, on any ground whatever, dissented from the general grief.

Very little now remains to be said. A few scattered details, some of them perhaps trivial, must complete this sketch.

Mr. Wilson's face was striking, though not handsome. His features were irregular, but had a peculiar look of mind and energy, while a strongly marked brow and very large eyebrows gave to all who saw him an unfailing impression of massive power and firm determination.

Mr. Wilson's moral character in its general features resembled his intellectual. He was not a man of elaborate scruples and difficult doubts, and he did not much like those who were. His conscientiousness was of a plain but very practical kind; he had a single-minded rectitude which went straight to the pith of a moral difficulty—which showed him what he ought to do. On such subjects he was somewhat intolerant of speculative reasoning. 'The common sense is so and so,' he used to say, and he did not wish to be plagued with anything else.

In one respect his manner did not uniformly give a true impression of him. He always succeeded in conveying his meaning, in stating what he wished to have done and why he wished it: he never failed to convince any one of his inexhaustible vigour and his substantial ability; but he sometimes did fail in giving a true expression to his latent generosity and real kindliness. He shrank almost nervously from the display of feeling, and sometimes was thought by casual observers to feel nothing, when in reality he was much more sensitive than they were. Another peculiarity which few persons would have attributed to him aided this mistake. It may seem strange in a practised Secretary of the Treasury, but he used to say that through life he had suffered far more from shyness than from anything else. Only very close observers could have discovered this, for his manner was habitually impressive and unfaltering. But common acquaintances, sometimes even persons who saw him on business, erroneously imputed to unthinking curtness that which was due in truth to nervous hesitation.[3]

In the foregoing sketch Mr. Wilson has of necessity been regarded almost exclusively as a public man, but his private life has many remarkable features, if it were proper to enlarge on them. His enjoyment of simple pleasures, of society, of scenery, of his home, was very vivid. No one who saw him in his unemployed moments would have believed that he was one of the busiest public men of his time. He never looked worn or jaded, and always contributed more than his share of geniality and vivacity to the scene around him. Like Sir Walter Scott, he loved a bright light; and the pleasantest society to him was that of the cheerful and the young.

The universal regret which has been expressed at Mr. Wilson's death is the best tribute to his memory. It has been universally felt that on his special subjects and for his peculiar usefulness he was 'a finished man,' and in these respects he has left few such behind him. The qualities which he had the opportunity of displaying were those

---

[3] Morgan and Hutton have the following paragraph which does not appear in the original article in *The Economist*.

With his subordinates in office he was, however, very cordial. He discussed matters of business with them, listened carefully to their suggestions or objections, and very frequently was guided by their recommendations. He had no paltry desire to monopolize the whole credit of what might be done. He probably worked harder than any Secretary of the Treasury before or since, but so far from depressing those below him, he encouraged their exertions, co-operated with them, and was ever ready to bear hearty testimony to the tried merit of efficient public servants. He was also quite willing to forget the temporary misunderstandings which are so apt to occur among earnest men who take different views of public affairs: he was eminently tolerant,—though he had almost always a strong conviction of his own, he never felt the least wish to silence discussion. Believing that his own opinions were true, he was only the more confident that the more the subject was discussed, the more true they would be found to be. Few men ever transacted so much important business with so little of the pettiness of personal feeling.

of an administrator and a financier. But some of those who knew him best believed that he only wanted an adequate opportunity to show that he had also many of the higher qualities of a statesman; and it was the feeling that he would perhaps have such an opportunity which reconciled them to his departure for India. As will have been evident from this narrative, he was placed in many changing circumstances, and in the gradual ascent of life was tried by many increasing difficulties. But at every step his mind grew with the occasion. *We* at least believe that he had a great sagacity and a great equanimity, which might have been fitly exercised on the very greatest affairs. But it was not so to be.

———————

The intelligence of Mr. Wilson's death was formally communicated by the Indian to the Home Government in the following despatch:—

To the Right Honourable Sir Charles Wood, Bart., G.C.B.,
Secretary of State for India.

SIR,—The painful task is imposed upon us of announcing to Her Majesty's Government the death of our colleague, the Right Honourable James Wilson.

2. This lamentable event took place on the evening of Saturday, the 11th, after an illness of a few days.

3. We enclose a copy of the notification by which we yesterday communicated the mournful intelligence to the public. The funeral took place at the time mentioned in the notification; and the great respect in which our lamented colleague was held was evinced by a very large attendance of the general community, in addition to that of the public officers, civil and military.

4. We are unable adequately to express our sense of the great loss which the public interests have sustained in Mr. Wilson's death. We do not doubt, however, that this will be as fully appreciated by Her Majesty's Government as it is by ourselves, and as we have every reason to believe it will be by the community generally throughout India.

5. But we should not satisfy our feelings in communicating this sad occurrence to Her Majesty's Government, if we did not state our belief that the fatal disease which has removed Mr. Wilson from among us was in a great degree the consequence of his laborious application to the duties of his high position, and of his conscientious determination not to cease from the prosecution of the important measures of which he had charge until their success was ensured. Actuated by a self-denying devotion to the objects for which he came out to this country, Mr. Wilson continued to labour in-

defatigably long after the general state of his health had become such as to cause anxiety to the physician who attended him, and it was within a few days only after the Income Tax had become law, and when, at the earnest request of his medical adviser, he was preparing to remove from Calcutta for the remainder of the rainy season, that he was seized with the illness that has carried him off.

6. It is our sincere conviction that this eminent public servant sacrificed his life in the discharge of his duty.—We have, &c.,

CANNING.

H. B. E. FRERE.

C. BEADON.

Fort William, the 13th August.

Sir George Cornewall Lewis

Introductory note

George Cornewall Lewis (1806–1863) was born in London, the elder son of Sir Thomas Lewis and Harriet Cornewall. He was educated at Eton and Christ Church, Oxford. He entered Parliament as Liberal M.P. for Herefordshire in 1847, and was Secretary to the Board of Control in that year. In 1848 he was Under-Secretary for the Home Department and from 1850–2 Financial Secretary to the Treasury. Having become M.P. for the Radnor Boroughs in 1855, he became Chancellor of the Exchequer in the same year, a post he held until 1858. From 1859–61 he was Home Secretary and from 1861–3 Secretary for War. He edited the *Edinburgh Review* from 1852–5. In 1852 he published *A Treatise on the Methods of Observation and Reasoning in Politics* and in 1855 his *Enquiry into the Credibility of the Early Roman History*. He died at Harpton Court, Radnorshire, in 1863.

Sir George Cornewall Lewis [1]

FEW more curious sights were, not long since, to be seen in London than that of Sir George Lewis at the War Office. What is now a melancholy recollection was, when we used to see it, an odd mixture of amusing anomalies. The accidental and bit-by-bit way in which all minor business is managed in England has drifted our public offices into scattered, strange, and miscellaneous places. It has drifted the war minister into the large drawing-room of an old mansion, which is splendid enough to receive fashionable people, and large enough to receive a hundred people. In this great and gorgeous apartment sat, a few months since, a homely scholar in spectacles, whose face bore traces of sedentary labour, and whose figure was bent into the student-stoop. Such a plain man looked odd enough in such a splendid place. But it was much more odd to think that that man in that place supremely regulated the War Department of England. The place should have been a pacific drawing-room, and the man was a pacific student. He looked like a conveyancer over deeds, like a scholar among treatises, like a jurist making a code; he looked like the last man to preside over martial pomp and military expeditions.

So *unique* a man as Sir George Lewis has, in truth, rarely been lost to this country. Most men, most politicians even especially fall easily into some ready-made classification, belong to one of the recognised groups of ordinary character. Political life has gone on so long that we have ascertained the principal species of statesmen, and have a fixed name ready for each. But Sir George Lewis, as all who knew him in the least well will testify, did not belong exactly to any received type. People were puzzled how to classify a man who wrote on the Astronomy of the Ancients, the Fables of Babrius, and Roman History *before* there was history, and who was yet able to fill three difficult cabinet offices in quick succession. He wrote what most cabinet ministers would think it too much and too hard to read. No German

[1] *A Dialogue on the Best Form of Government*, by the Right Hon. Sir G. C. Lewis, Bart. M.P. London, 1863. This essay was first published in the *National Review* for October 1863, Volume XVII, pp. 492–524.

professor, from the smoke and study of many silent years, has ever put forth books more bristling with recondite references, more exact in every technicality of scholarship, more rich in matured reflection, than Sir George Lewis found time, mind, and scholarlike curiosity, to write in the very thick of eager English life. And yet he was never very busy, or never seemed so. In the extremity of the *Trent* difficulty, when, as he was inclined to think, a war with America was impending, when a war minister might be pardoned for having no time for general reflection, Sir George Lewis found time, at three o'clock on a busy parliamentary day, to discuss with the writer of these lines, for some twenty minutes, the comparative certainty, or rather *un*certainty, of the physical and moral sciences. It was difficult to know what to make of such a man.

The difficulty was the greater because he made no pretence to be a marvel of versatile ability. When Lord Brougham was Chancellor, he was always doing—his enemies said for display, his friends said from a certain overflow of miscellaneous activity—many out-of-the-way matters. According to one legend, he even wrote a treatise on hydro-statics for the Society of Useful Knowledge which was so full of blunders that it could not be published. Many statesmen have had the vanity of variety. But if ever there was a plain man, an unpretending man, a man who in matters of business affected to be *par negotiis neque supra*, that man was Sir George Lewis. The objection to him was that he was too prosaic, too anxiously safe, too suspicious of every thing showy. It was not possible for an enemy or for an opponent—for he had no enemies—to hint that Sir George Lewis's miscellaneous books were written from a love of display. They were written from a bent of nature—from the born love of dry truth.

To those, however, who had an opportunity of accurately observing Sir George Lewis there was no difficulty in making him out. He was so simple and natural that he explained himself. His principal qualities were all of a plain and homely species, and though it may not be possible to give a likeness of them, yet a brief description may easily give an idea and an approximation.

The specialty of his mind was a strong simplicity. He took a plain, obvious view of every subject which came before him. Ingenuities, refinements, and specious fallacies might be suggested around him in any number or in any variety, but his mind was complication-proof. He went steadily through each new ambiguity, each new distinction, as it presented itself. He said, in unadorned but apt English, 'The facts are these and these; the new theory concerning them is so and so: it accounts for facts Nos. 1, 2, and 3, but fails to account for facts Nos. 4, 5, and 6.' Of course he was not uniformly right. We shall show that there were some kinds of facts, and some sorts of events, which he was by mental constitution not able wholly to appreciate. But his view of every subject, though it might not be adequate, though it might be limited, was always lucid. His mind was like a registering machine with a patent index. It took in all the data, specified, enumerated them, and then indicated with unmistakable precision what their sum-total of effect precisely was. The index might be wrong, though it pretty generally was right; but nobody could ever mistake for a moment what it meant and where it was.

Few men ever kept apart, in civil matters, so well what, in medical matters, would be called the diagnosis and the prescription. Most men mix, even to themselves, their view of what is with their suggestion of what should be. You could not have made Sir George Lewis mix the two. His mind on such points was almost a tedious formality. He would say, 'The facts proved are so and so; from these there are the following probable inferences. If you wish to alter the present circumstances and to produce others, you must do so and so.' When a man came to him with a plan, he asked, 'What is your object?' Until he got a plain answer to that, and a proof that the object was good, he never looked at the plan. All this in theory may seem very obvious and very trite. Nothing is so easy as to be sensible on paper. The only true theory of transacting business is a simple matter which has been known for hundreds of years. Any part of that theory in print looks stupid, and not worth saying. Yet in real life, especially in political life, how few great actors are there! In politics the issues to be determined are for the most part plain and simple; but they are exciting, are embedded in rhetoric, and overlaid with irrelevant matter. A certain strong simplicity sweeps all these outside matters away. Talking to Sir George Lewis on a pending political matter was like reading a chapter of Aristotle's Politics; you might think the view incomplete, but there were the same pregnant strength and matter-of-fact simplicity.

One great advantage of this sort of mind Sir George Lewis noted in an article in the *Edinburgh Review*, which, though when published anonymous, may now be quoted as his: 'When Demosthenes was asked what was the first and second and third qualification of an orator, he answered, "Delivery;" in like manner, if we were asked what is the first and second and third qualification of an English statesman, we would answer, "Intelligibility." As in oratory the most eloquent words and the wisest counsels will avail but little if they are not impressed by voice and manner upon the minds of an audience; so integrity and public spirit will fail to command confidence, if the course adopted is intricate or inextricable.' Sir George Lewis could not have described his own sort of mind better if he had been trying to do so; he *could* not be intricate or perplexed. On those rare occasions in politics when it is useful to be ambiguous he failed. When he was Home Secretary he could not diffuse that useful mist over delicate difficulties which was now and then desirable, and in which Sir George Grey has succeeded. An unbroken fluency in indefinite half-truths was simply impossible to Sir George Lewis. He could not be said to fail in it, for he did not attempt it. His mind was unsuited to ambiguity, whether artful or natural. But on those all but universal occasions when only a plain intelligible statement of an important proposition was required his solid vigour was appropriate. He could never have appealed to the people by the felicitous attraction of his words, but he had an even surer source of popularity in the certain intelligibility of his plans.

The last words of his last book show the sort of grave moderation with which he regarded politics, as wise as any of which he ever made use. They are the judgment in which the reflective man of the world sums up the arguments of the advocates of different forms of government.

'Each one of you, in to-day's discussion, has been able to show specious, perhaps strong, grounds in favour of his opinion. Monarchicus can say with truth that the testimony of experience is in his favour; that the vast majority of nations, now and at all former periods of time, have been governed by monarchs; and that a plural or republican government is an intricate machine, difficult to work, and constantly tending to relapse into monarchy. Aristocraticus can argue that aristocracy is the government of intelligence and virtue; and that it is a just medium between the two extremes of monarchy and democracy; while Democraticus can dwell upon the splendid vision of a community bound together by the ties of fraternity, liberty, and equality, exempt from hereditary privilege, giving all things to merit, and presided over by a government in which all the national interests are faithfully represented. But even if I were to decide in favour of one of these forms, and against the two others, I should not find myself nearer the solution of the practical problem. A nation does not change the form of its government with the same facility that a man changes his coat. A nation in general only changes the form of its government by means of a violent revolution. This is not a moment when reason is in the ascendant, and when the claims of force can be safely disregarded. The party which is uppermost in the revolution dictates the form of government, and pays little attention to abstract theories, unless it be those which coincide with its own views. The past history of a nation, its present interests, its present passions and antipathies, the advice of favourite leaders, the intervention of foreign governments, all exercise a powerful influence at such a crisis in determining the national decision. Such is the rude process by which one form of government is actually converted into another; very unlike the gentle and rational method which is assumed by the constructors of Utopias. Besides, the political preferences of a people are in general determined by habit and mental association; and though the newly introduced constitution may be intrinsically better than its predecessor, yet the people may dislike it, and refuse it the benefit of a fair trial. It may therefore fail, not from its own defectiveness, but through the ill-will and reluctance of those by whom it is worked.

'There are some rare cases in which a nation has profited by a revolution. Such was the English revolution of 1688, in which the form of the government underwent no alteration, and the person of the king was alone changed. It was the very minimum of a revolution; it was remarkable for the absence of those accompaniments which make a revolution perilous, and which subsequently drew upon it a vindictive reactionary movement. The late Italian revolution has likewise been successful; by it the Italian people have gained a better government, and have improved their political condition. It was brought about by foreign intervention; but its success has been mainly owing to the moderation of the leaders in whom the people had the wisdom to confide, and who have steadily refrained from all revolutionary excesses.

'The history of forcible attempts to improve governments is not, however, cheering. Looking back upon the course of revolutionary movements, and upon the character of their consequences, the practical conclusion which I draw is, that it is the part of wisdom and prudence to acquiesce in any form of government which is tolerably well administered, and affords tolerable security to person and property. I would not, indeed, yield to apathetic despair, or acquiesce in the persuasion that a merely tolerable government is incapable of improvement. I would form an individual model, suited to the character, disposition, wants, and circumstances of the country, and I would make all exertions, whether by action or by writing, within the limits of the existing law, for ameliorating its existing condition, and bringing it nearer to the model selected for imitation; but I should consider the problem of the best form of government as purely ideal, and as unconnected with practice; and should abstain from taking a ticket in the lottery of revolution, unless there was a well-founded expectation that it would come out a prize.'

This sober simplicity is not to the taste of many people. Many wish to find in politics a sort of excitement. They wish that public affairs should be managed in a rather theatrical way, in order that they themselves may have the pleasure of reading a stimulating series of brilliant events. People who went to Sir George Lewis for excitement were very likely to be disappointed. He was sure to knock the gloss off things. 'People,' he would observe, 'who know how things are managed, know that the oftener cabinets meet the better. Ignorant persons fancy that when cabinets meet often there is something wrong; but that is a mistake. It is in the long vacation and in the country that some ministers do something brilliant and extraordinary that is much objected to. When ministers get together, they can agree on something plain and satisfactory.' He always talked of the Cabinet as if it were a homely sort of committee.

At bottom, perhaps, he did not much object to be thought a little commonplace. 'In *my* opinion,' he said (and perhaps there is no harm in adding that it was in reference to the Suez canal), 'in nine cases out of ten cure is better than prevention. If it be ever necessary to hold Egypt, then fight for Egypt. By looking forward to all possible evils, we waste the strength that had best be concentrated in curing the *one* evil which happens.' Those who wish that the foreign affairs of England should be managed according to a far-seeing and elaborate policy will not like such voluntary shortsightedness; but the English people themselves rather like to have the national course fixed by evident, palpable, and temporary circumstances.

Some people thought Sir George Lewis obstinate, and in one sense he was so. No one was a better colleague; no one, after full discussion, was readier to take a share in the responsibility for measures of which he did not entirely approve the whole. But though he gave up his proposals, he did not alter his opinion. It may be said of him that he could not alter it. Most men's conclusions are framed upon fluctuating considerations, some of which are very indistinctly present to their minds, and most of which it would puzzle them to state shortly. Sir George Lewis knew exactly what were the facts upon which he grounded his opinion, and what his inference from those facts. Unless you gave him new facts, he could not help drawing the same inference. This was one of the comforts of dealing with him. You always knew exactly where you would find his mind. Unless the data had altered, you might be sure his inference from the data would be unchanged.

It may be added that his inference was almost sure to be exactly sound. His *data* might be limited. As we shall show, there were some kinds of facts which, from a limitation of nature, he did not thoroughly appreciate. When such facts were in question, his conclusion was likely enough to be wrong; for he was arguing rightly on incomplete premisses. But no one could gainsay that correctness of his inference from what he did see. He was the soundest judge of probability we have ever known. The facts being admitted to be so and so, what will be the consequence of those facts? Upon this question few judgments, if any, in England were better than that of Sir George Lewis.

It is this judgment of probability which makes the man of business. The data of life are accessible; their inference uncertain: a sound judgment on these data is the secret of success to him who possesses it, and the reason why others trust him. It is this that men call a *sound* understanding; it is this that Napoleon had in mind when he said that a man should be *carré à la base*.

To this straightforward simplicity of understanding Sir George Lewis added the most complete education perhaps of any man of his time. He did not believe in what has been called *speciality*; at least he confined it to the lower grades of practical life and literary labour. He has observed: 'The permanent officers of a department are the depositories of the official traditions, they are generally referred to by the political head of the office for information upon questions of official practice; and knowledge of this sort acquired in one department would be useless in another. If, for example, the chief clerk of the criminal department of the Home Office were to be transferred to the Foreign Office or to the Admiralty, the special experience which he has acquired

373

in the Home Office, and which is in daily and hourly requisition for the assistance of the Home Secretary, would be utterly valueless to the Foreign Secretary or to the First Lord of the Admiralty. . . . The same person may be successively at the head of the Home Office, the Foreign Office, the Colonial Office, and the Admiralty; he may be successively President of the Board of Trade and Chancellor of the Exchequer; but to transfer an experienced clerk from one office to another would in general be like transferring a skilful naval officer to the army, or appointing a military engineer officer to command a ship of war. A similar distinction may be observed in other branches of practical life; thus, an architect may direct the execution of different classes of buildings; he may give plans for palaces, churches, courts of justice, bridges, private dwellings; but the subordinate workmen whom he employs retain their separate functions unchanged—a carpenter does not become a mason, a painter or glazier does not become an ironmonger or plasterer.'

He sincerely believed (and perhaps acted to excess on the belief) that a well-educated man was competent to undertake any office and to write on any subject. He would have acknowledged the truth of the saying, that the end of education was to make a good *learner*. He was at the day of his death perhaps the best learner in England; there was no sort of definite information, whether relating to public business or to books, which he did not know how to acquire and where to find. Some public men may know where to find as much political information; some scholars may know where to find as much learned information; but what other man knows so precisely the best sources of both kinds of knowledge?

He had a nearly perfect mastery over the keys of knowledge. He derived from Eton and Oxford a perfect knowledge of the classical languages, and he extended it to the day of his death. An article published in *Notes and Queries* within a week or two of that time showed that he had read Mr. Freeman's history,—a rather formidable work, which we elsewhere review, relating to the Ætolian and other Greek leagues, which was only then just published, and which is as much as many busy men read in ten years. Many English statesmen have been good classical scholars, and it is happily not difficult for those who have once well learned the languages of antiquity to retain a familiarity with its masterpieces. The very business of life, indeed, adds to these masterpieces an additional charm, for it reveals touches of discerning thought, and traits of eternal human knowledge, which the writers learned from experience, and which no one can appreciate without it. Mr. Pitt, Mr. Canning, Lord Grenville, the Marquis Wellesley, and many others of our conspicuous statesmen, have had this sort of scholarship. The knowledge of the classics was to them an intellectual luxury. But Sir George Lewis had a far more laborious scholarship than this. He had read and knew, not only the classical writers themselves, but also terrific German treatises, in many volumes and upon the worst paper, *about* the classics, which no intellectual voluptuary would touch or look at.

In addition to his Eton and Oxford scholarship, Sir George Lewis was excellently acquainted with modern languages, and had a fair knowledge of mathematics. But a mere enumeration of this sort does not in the least give a notion of the sort of knowledge he had—a phrase, not of the purest English, alone expresses it: it was a knowledge which 'turned up' every where. Hardly a subject could be started on which he could not throw an unexpected light, and to which he could not add some new fact. The sort of way in which this happened is aptly enough illustrated by Lord Stanhope's *Miscellanies*, published last year: 'Mr. Windham,' writes Lord Stanhope, 'in his speech of December 9, 1803, observes of the Martello towers that they were so called from a place of that name in Corsica; and I have quoted that sentence from him in my *Life of Pitt*.

'Since my own publication, however, there has been suggested to me, by a very high authority upon all such subjects, a derivation far more probable than Mr. Windham's, and certainly, as I conceive, the right one.

S.

'*Right Hon. Sir George C. Lewis to Earl Stanhope.*

[Extract.]   'April 2, 1862.

'The origin of Martello towers I believe to have been that when piracy was common in the Mediterranean, and pirates like the Danes made plundering descents upon the coasts, the Italians built towers near the sea in order to keep watch and give warning if a pirate ship was seen to approach the land. This warning was given by striking on a bell with a hammer; and hence these towers were called *Torri da Martello*.

'*The same to the same.*

'May 7, 1862.

'I think that I have discovered, with the assistance of a friend, the

375

origin of Windham's statement respecting Martello towers. An attack was made on the tower of Mortella, in Corsica, by the British forces both by sea and land, in February 1794. The tower was taken after an obstinate defence, but the two attacking ships were beaten off. This circumstance is likely to have given rise to the confusion between Martello towers generally and this tower of Mortella.'

And Lord Stanhope adds some additional facts showing that the derivation suggested by Sir George Cornewall Lewis was correct. Again, in p. 40, Lord Stanhope gives an extract from a letter of Sir George Lewis:

'Lord Grenville told my father that Pitt had formed a plan for abolishing all Customs Duties, and that he would have carried it into effect, if the war of the French Revolution had not broken out, which defeated all his financial and commercial schemes. Lord Grenville said that the amount of the public expenditure at that time rendered such a plan quite feasible.'

These are two instances casually occurring in one little volume. But any one who knew Sir George Lewis would know that these sort of miscellaneous odd facts were accumulated in his memory, to what seemed an infinite number, and were at once brought out when they could be useful in illustrating any thing.

As a writer this great knowledge, especially when connected with the strong love of bare truth which led him to acquire that knowledge, was not advantageous to him. He gave a mistaken credit to his readers; he fancied they loved fact and truth as much as he did. 'Woe to the writer,' goes a wise saying, 'that exhausts his subject; his readers are exhausted first.' Sir George Lewis always exhausted his subject if he could, and you could not have persuaded him not to do so. In proposing the dowry of the Princess Royal he amused the House of Commons by an elaborate reference, not only to the dowry of George III's daughters, who seemed quite far enough back for an impatient audience that wanted its dinner, but also to a perfectly forgotten Princess Royal who was George III's aunt. Most of his books are too full of citations and explanations; and to the last he would have been more read and more influential if he had thought often of Sidney Smith's precept, 'Now, remember Noah, and be *quick*.'

But though a tendency to overlay a subject with superfluous erudition was one of Sir George Lewis's defects, the possession of that available erudition was one of his greatest powers. In the present day the usefulness of a public man is largely measured by the number of subjects which he can get up—Sir George Lewis could get up any subject. There was no probable topic on which he could not form, from the very best sources, with ease and pleasure, a clear, determinate, and exact opinion. His memory helped him. It has been compared to Macaulay's—not that it was equal to such marvellous displays, but that it contained as much, or nearly as much, miscellaneous knowledge. And there was this peculiarity in it. Macaulay's memory, like Niebuhr's, undoubtedly confounded not unfrequently inference and fact: it exaggerated; it gave, not what was in the book, but what a vivid imagination inferred from the book. Sir George Lewis had none of this defect: his memory was a dry memory, just as his mind was a dry light; if he said a thing was at page 10, you might be sure it was at page 10. Somebody called him a 'sagacious dictionary,' and there was felicity in the expression.

Apart from this massive simplicity of understanding, and this immense accumulation of exact knowledge, there was nothing *very* remarkable in Sir George Lewis. It would be the greatest injustice to his memory, and be the very last thing which he would have desired, to mar the picturesque outlines of his character by concealing its limitations. He had, as we explained, some great qualities in an extraordinary measure, but in other respects he was no more than an ordinary man, and in some he was even less than one.

There was a want of brisk enthusiasm about him both in appearance and in reality. He looked like a scholar, a thinker, and a man of business; he did not look like—he was not—a buoyant ruler or a popular orator. He was quite conscious of this himself, and would sometimes allude to it. The late Mr. Wilson—a very vivacious and active man—who was Secretary of the Treasury when Sir George Lewis was Chancellor of the Exchequer, used to relate, that when he once was urging something rather strongly, Sir George answered: 'No; I can't do it. The fact is, Wilson, you are an animal, and I am a vegetable.' Taken literally, this would have been a satire on himself, but it indicated his main defect. He had always, or nearly always, sufficient judgment for a great statesman, but he had not always sufficient impulse.

He was *puzzled* about the passions of mankind; he had so little passion himself that it seemed to him an unknown force which might take men to a distance which it was impossible to foresee, and in a direction that could not be calculated. 'When,' we have heard him say, 'you know a man will act for his own interest, you know how to deal with him; but if he is likely to be guided by feeling, it is impossible to predict his course.' Such extreme calmness of mind is not favourable to a statesman; it is good to be without vices, but it is not good to be without temptations. It would always have been a difficulty to Sir George Lewis that he did not share the impetuous part of human nature whether for good or evil. He was ever liable to impute to a settled design and intellectual self-interest what was in fact owing to an impulse of philanthropy or a gust of mere passion. He was apt to be thought cynical in opinion, though goodnatured in manner and action,—and in some sense he was so. He took too external a view of human nature, and ascribed to consistent selfishness what was really produced by mixed motives and a close combination of good and evil.

He was so defective in the more conspicuous sorts of imagination, that he was often thought to have no imagination. But this was an error. He could conceive well the working of a polity, the operation of a scheme, the details of a plan. His criticism on the working, say of the American Constitution, would show great power of conceiving distant causes, and of predicting and analysing strange effects. He had the business imagination. But he had no other. He could not imagine great passions, or overwhelming desires, or involved character; he knew that there were such things, but he had no image of them in his mind and no picture. He was like a man on the edge of a volcano, who dreaded an eruption, but had no vision of the flames. He was thus apt to be out of sympathy with, and even to be impatient of, some elements in ordinary men's judgment. He was a little too critical of public opinion, too critical, that is, for a parliamentary statesman, for one who should try to sympathise with the master whom he must obey. Sir George Lewis hated exaggeration as much as he could hate any thing,—and popular opinion is always exaggerated. 'There is,' said Sir Stafford Northcote, 'no quality for which Sir George Lewis is more remarkable than for a quiet courage, which emboldens him to give utterance from time to time, and sometimes without any apparent necessity for his doing so, to propositions of the most alarmingly unpopular nature.' And such courage is admirable. In this day it is much to have a statesman who, on any occasion and for any object, will withstand public opinion. But such opposition should be reserved for great occasions, and too much must not be expected from the mass of men. A vague tendency and loose approximation to what is right is all we can hope of miscellaneous popular opinion; and it is not wise in a statesman to criticise too nicely, or to attempt to give to the rough practical judgment of men a fine accuracy which it can never in fact possess. Sir George Lewis was the antithesis of a demagogue; he could not take a test without a qualification; he was sure to distrust, and apt to despise, a popular dogma.

A slight survey—and we have only space or powers for a very slight one—will show that these qualities were as conspicuous in Sir George Lewis's writings as in his political career. Indeed, if there ever was a man whose mind was always and every where one and the same, Sir George was that man. He had not really a versatile mind, though his pursuits were varied. He was far too modest and wise to aim at what was impossible to him, and nature had given him sharp limitations. It was said by *The Times* of Lord Brougham, 'that he might have been any *one* of ten first-rate kinds of men, but that he had tried to be *all* ten, and had failed.' Sir George Lewis had none of this flexibility, and none of this vanity. He never tried to be a great poet or a great orator, or to be any thing else but what nature made him— a shrewd and solid thinker. He had a great faculty of research, but his matter is every where of the same sort. It is the same imperturbable homely sense upon finance in his budgets, upon the Egyptology of Baron Bunsen in his Ancient Astronomy.

Sir George Lewis's principal writings may be divided into two classes, the historical and the speculative; and it is hardly too much to say that the whole of the historical are developments in many forms of one central idea. He always devotes himself to the refutation of an hypothesis: some previous writer has elaborated a theory which, Sir George Lewis maintains, rests on no basis of evidence, and which he wishes to dispel. Some one has seen a *mirage*, and related it as a fact; Sir George Lewis wishes to dispel the mirage.

His earliest work of this sort was the *Origin and Formation of the Romance Language*. M. Raynouard, a distinguished French scholar, had expounded a very curious and remarkable theory as to the breaking-up of the Latin language. It is certain that good Latin was once spoken at Rome; it is certain that the Romans conquered the rest of Italy, France, and Spain; it is certain that in each of these countries a modern language, analogous to the Latin, and derived from the Latin, is now spoken. How, then, did the Latin break up? how, then, were the new languages formed? M. Raynouard maintained that they were formed by means of an intermediate language. He held that the Romance language, which was purely spoken in the times of the Troubadours, and which is still corruptly spoken in Provence, was a language once used in the same form all over Europe; that it was the same tongue in France, in Portugal, in Italy, and in Spain; and that as a person who spoke Latin would have been universally intelligible at one time, so a person who spoke Romance would have been universally understood at a subsequent time. This idea of a single diffused Middle-Age language Sir George Lewis undertakes to dispel; he thinks it a dream and a theory. He says that the Latin broke up under different circumstances, with different velocities, and in different modifications, in the different states of Europe. There was a certain general resemblance, he holds, in the changes which were in progress, whether in Italy or Spain, France or Portugal, because those changes in all these countries were produced by the same causes. The invasion of the barbarians, the fall of the Roman empire, and the somewhat mysterious movement which tends to break up the old rhetorical and synthetic languages, and replace them by analytic and conversational languages, were common causes, operating alike in all countries where Latin had been spoken. But though the change in all the languages was in the same general direction, it was not at the same rate, nor was it identical in details. There has, according to Sir George Lewis, never been a single vernacular language spoken through Europe since Latin was so spoken. The theory of Raynouard is, according to Sir George Lewis's characteristic language, an 'unsupported and imaginary hypothesis.'

This essay on the Romance language was republished by Sir George within a few months of his death, and is worth reading as an illustration of his mode of thought and argument. The burden of proof is upon Raynouard. He says there was a common language at a certain date; where, then, is that language? what were its parts of speech, its verbs, its pronouns, and its substantives? Let us look at them in the different countries of Europe at the time in question, and prove that the language was uniform by the identity of its forms. Accordingly Sir George Lewis goes through the earliest known forms of the Italian, Spanish, Provençal, and French languages, and he shows that at the earliest stage they were *not* identical. He characteristically says, 'The importance and interest of the philological problem which is treated in the following pages are much increased by the fact that it lies entirely within the historical period; and that not only the original and the derivative languages, but also the circumstances attending the transition, are known by authentic evidence and by an unbroken tradition. It is therefore a problem which admits of solution by demonstrative arguments, and without recourse to a series of hypotheses and conjectures, weakening as the chain lengthens.' Sir George Lewis revels, we may almost say, in the plentifulness of the evidence. He has lists of the 'tenses and inflexions of Romance nouns,' 'new Romance nouns formed by affixes,' of the degrees of comparison, pronouns, and numerals, in the Romance language, with endless similar information. He elaborately compares the earliest stages of the Italian, Spanish, and French languages with the earliest form of the Provençal; and he shows clearly and fully, what was probable enough in itself, that the earliest forms of these languages differ; that they have pursued a different history; that the Provençal is only one of the derived languages, with a history of its own; that there never was any one derived language generally diffused through Europe; that as soon as the use of Latin ended, distinctions of speech began. A very close political observer, who did not himself easily relinquish any thing, once described Sir George Lewis as the most pertinacious man he had ever known: 'He returns,' it was added, 'to the charge again and again, and he hardly ever fails.' This was said by one who seldom read any thing, who had read very little of Sir George Lewis's writing, who assuredly had never opened the treatise on the Romance languages. But if he had studied the treatise, he could not have described it better. Sir George returns again and again, with verbs and pronouns, to the charge, and he hardly ever fails. A student who continued to believe Raynouard's theory must be impervious to argument and detail-proof.

The largest of all Sir George Lewis's writings, and his acutest, strikes with the same tactics at a nobler game upon a larger field. The reception of Niebuhr's *History of Rome* is one of the most curious of recent literary phenomena. Though he really is a bold theorist on Roman history, though his narrative is by admission constructed by the imagination, he has obtained something like the credit due to an almost contemporary authority—to a person who had some special information. He believed he had acquired, by long study and brooding, a special faculty, a peculiar divination. He tells us, 'All my faculties

were directed to a single object for sixteen months, without any inter-
mission except now and then for a few days. My sight grew dim in its
passionate efforts to pierce into the obscurity of the subject, and unless
I was to send forth an incomplete work, which sooner or later would
have had to be wholly remodelled, I was compelled to wait for what
Time might gradually bring forth. Nor has he been niggardly, but,
though slowly, has granted me one discovery after another.' 'The true
account, it must be owned, is not always the most probable. But when
an inquirer, after gazing for years with ever renewed undeviating
steadfastness, sees the history of mistaken, misrepresented, and forgotten events rise out of mists and darkness, and assume substance and
shape, as the scarcely visible aerial form of the nymph in the Sclavonic
tale takes the body of an earthly maiden beneath the yearning gaze of
love,—when by unwearied and conscientious examination he is
continually gaining a clearer insight into the connexion of all its parts,—
and discerns that immediate expression of reality which emanates
from life,—he has a right to demand that others, who merely throw
their looks by the way on the region where he lives and has taken up
his home, should not deny the correctness of his views, because they
perceive nothing of the kind. The learned naturalist, who has never
left his native town, will not recognise the animal's track, by which
the hunter is guided: and if any one, on going into Benvenuto's prison,
when his eyes had for months been accustomed to see the objects
around him, had asserted that Benvenuto like himself could not
distinguish any thing in the darkness, he would surely have been
somewhat presumptuous.' It is beautiful to see the heavy care and
sluggish diligence with which Sir George Lewis reckons all this poetry
back into mere prose.

'The history of Niebuhr,' he tells us, 'has thus opened more questions than it has closed, and it has set in motion a large body of com-
batants, whose mutual variances are not at present likely to be settled
by deference to a common authority, or by the recognition of any
common principle.

'The main cause of the great multiplicity and wide divergence of
opinions, which characterise the recent researches into early Roman
history, is the defective method, which not only Niebuhr and his
followers, but most of his opponents, have adopted. Instead of employing those tests of credibility which are consistently applied to
modern history, they attempt to guide their judgment by the indica-

tions of internal evidence, and assume that the truth can be discovered by an occult faculty of historical divination. Hence, the task which they have undertaken resembles an inquiry into the internal structure of the earth, or into the question, whether the stars are inhabited. It is an attempt to solve a problem, for the solution of which no sufficient data exist.

'The consequence is, that ingenuity and labour can produce nothing but hypotheses and conjectures, which may be supported by analogies, and may sometimes appear specious and attractive, but can never rest on the solid foundation of proof. There will, therefore, be a series of such conjectural histories; each successive writer will reject all or some of the guesses of his predecessors, and will propose some new hypothese of his own. But the treatment of early Roman history, though it will be constantly moving, will not advance; it will not be stationary, but neither will it be progressive; it will be unfixed and changeable, but without receiving any improvement; and it will perpetually revolve in the same hopeless circle. Like the search after the philosopher's stone, or the elixir of life, it will be constantly varying its aspect, under the treatment of different professors of the futile science; but truth and certainty, the aim of all rational employment of the intellect, will always be equally distant. Each new system of the early Roman constitution will be only (to use Paley's words) one guess among many; whereas he alone discovers who proves. There is indeed no doubt that long habit, combined with a happy talent, may enable a person to discern the truth where it is invisible to ordinary minds, possessing no peculiar advantages. This may be observed, not only in historical researches, but in every other department of knowledge. In order, however, that the truth so perceived should recommend itself to the convictions of others, it is a necessary condition that it should admit of proof which they can understand. Newton might have perceived, by a rapid and intuitive sagacity, the connexion between the fall of an apple and the attraction of the earth to the sun; but unless he could have demonstrated that connexion by arguments which were intelligible and satisfactory to the scientific world, his discovery would have been useless, except as a mere suggestion. In like manner, we may rejoice that the ingenuity and learning of Niebuhr should have enabled him to advance many novel hypotheses and conjectures respecting events in the early history, and respecting the form of the early constitution, of Rome. But unless he can support those hypotheses by sufficient evidence, they are not entitled to our belief. It is not enough for a historian to claim the possession of a retrospective second-sight, which is denied to the rest of the world; of a mysterious doctrine, revealed only to the initiated. Unless he can prove as well as guess; unless he can produce evidence of the fact, after he has intuitively perceived its existence, his historical system cannot be received. The oases of truth which he discerns amidst the trackless expanses of fiction and legend, may be real; but until their existence can be verified by positive testimony, we have no certainty that these "green spots in memory's waste" may not be mere mirage and optical delusion. It is an excellence in a historian of antiquity, who has sufficient data to proceed upon, that he should form a vivid conception of the events described; that he should live, as it were, among the persons whose acts he recounts; and that he should carry his reader back into the bygone times in which his drama is placed. On the other hand, it is a fault in the modern writers who first narrated Roman history that they should have related the events as if they had never happened. But when there is a want of solid evidence, we do not render the history true by treating the events as if they were real.'

Almost the whole of Sir George Lewis's two volumes are an expansion and development of this passage. He turns Niebuhr's revelations into fancies, and his divinations into mere guesses. Since Sir George Lewis's work on Roman history, no English scholar at least has ventured to defend Niebuhr's essentially arbitrary treatment of legendary history. An historian, it is now agreed, cannot accept one legend because it suits a preconceived hypothesis, and reject another because it is inconsistent with that hypothesis. He must take both or must reject both. We may not, and perhaps have not, attained to a complete and accepted theory of the value of traditional evidence; there are many points on that subject which require much more delicate handling than they have received. But no one will ever revive Niebuhr's notion of an occult tact. A long acquaintance and a familiar meditation upon any sort of *truth* does indeed give an instinctive sense with respect to that truth. A constant habit of comparing accurate truth with legendary versions of the same truth would really give a student a verified knowledge, and even a quick instinctive idea what sort of inventions popular tradition is prone to. But Niebuhr had studied legends as to times of which there are only legends; he had not compared truth with fiction, but fiction with fiction. He had not acquired a test of truth by a contact with truth; but his hot brain had brooded so long on a favourite subject that he mistook its own fancies for realities. Sir George Lewis did not mistake them.

It is sometimes said that Sir George Lewis would accept no fact of which there was not contemporary evidence, and that he set no value whatever upon any tradition in any case. But this is a mischievous exaggeration. Sir George Lewis was not the most exacting of historical critics. He considered Polybius as too strict and sceptical. Polybius thought that an historian without books, and with only oral information, could not be sure of events more than twenty years before his own birth. Sir George Lewis held that a sort of memory of leading events, accurate in substance though probably inaccurate in detail, might be preserved by tradition for about a hundred years, and that special events from special circumstances might be remembered longer; but that in such cases it was only the general outline which could be faintly traced, and only events of interest that would be preserved. After about a hundred years—after the period about which a man could hear from his grandfather—he thought, for the most part, there was no reliable knowledge.

Sir George Lewis's Ancient Astronomy might seem a deviation from his general studies. Astronomy is a physical science, and Sir George, though well enough acquainted with such sciences, did not profess to have made them a special study. He was often enough heard to say, half in jest but still with a certain meaning, 'That on matters of practical interest the physical sciences were less certain than the moral: as long as you are dealing with abstractions, with perfectly elastic beams and a world without friction, physical science is quite certain; but as soon as you introduce the actual conditions of life, and talk of the real world in which we live, most physical sciences become as uncertain as any moral science. Take, for example, physic. If you will question your medical man, you will find that, if he cures you, it will not be by the goodness of his *arguments*. A great deal of what is set down upon that subject in grave treatises appears to me to be inconsistent rubbish. And my experience at the War Office shows me that scientific evidence may be accumulated in almost any quantity for any given invention and against any given invention.' A man who talked in this spirit was scarcely likely to devote many hours out of the scanty leisure of English public life to the history of physical science. Nor was Sir George Lewis attracted to the subject by its abstract scientific interest. He is at great pains to explain that he makes no pretension to such abstract mathematical knowledge as was possessed by Delambre and others, his predecessors, and that astronomy is conversant with obvious realities which have always excited human curiosity. In truth, he encountered ancient astronomy in his investigations of ancient history. He found many pretensions to ancient scientific knowledge which it was much in his way to scrutinise and disbelieve; he was in all his inquiries compelled to deal with ancient chronology, which is not to be understood except with reference to the astronomical notions of those who framed it. Such questions as, Was there a Roman year of ten months?, met him at every step. He was thus led to write a clear, compendious, and popular account of the rise of astronomical science in ancient Greece. It is not exhaustive, as most of his treatises are exhaustive; it is not, like his other treatises, supported by an available accumulation of all appropriate knowledge, for he was in some places cramped by the deficiency of his mathematics. It is not, therefore, one of the works on which his fame as a great scholar will hereafter rest. But it is a very clear, sensible, and interesting account of the interesting subject to which it relates.

But bound up with the history of Ancient Astronomy, and having but a very slender relation to it, are three essays: one on the Early History and Chronology of the Egyptians; another on the Early History and Chronology of the Assyrians; and a third on the Navigation of the Phœnicians. Here Sir George Lewis is all himself, dealing with the subjects which he liked best and dealing with them as he liked best. Any body who wishes to know the sort of mind he had may read —and it is not unamusing reading—his criticism on the Egyptian history of Baron Bunsen. At the risk of tediousness we will condense a little of it:

'The principal manipulator,' says Sir George Lewis, 'of the ancient Egyptian chronology is Baron Bunsen, who, in his recent work on Egypt, has avowedly applied the method of Niebuhr to Egyptian antiquity. Now the method with which Niebuhr treated the early history of Rome was to reject the historical narrative handed down by ancient, and generally received by modern writers; and to substitute for it a new narrative reconstructed on an arbitrary hypothetical basis of his own. Every thing that is original and peculiar in Niebuhr's historical method, and in its results, is indeed unsound. But it possessed advantages, when employed in the transmutation of Roman antiquity, which are wanting to it when applied to Egyptian antiquity. The early Roman history, whatever may be its authenticity, presents at least a full and continuous narrative, most parts of which are related in discordant versions by different classical writers. As none of these versions rests on an ascertained foundation, or can be traced to coeval attestation, great facility is afforded for ingenious conjecture, for bold and startling combinations, for hypothetical reconstruction by means of specious analogies, and for the display of imposing paradox and dazzling erudition. But the so-called history of ancient Egypt consists of little more than chronology. It is, for the most part, merely a string of royal names. Now this is a most unattractive field for the hypothetical historian: he is condemned to make bricks without straw. Instead of demolishing and rebuilding constitutions, instead of creating new states of society out of obscure fragments of lost writers, he is reduced to a mere arithmetical process. Accordingly, the operations of Bunsen and other modern critics upon the ancient history of Egypt rather resemble the manipulation of the balance-sheet of an insolvent company by a dexterous accountant (who, by transfers of capital to income, by the suppression or transposition of items, and by the alteration of bad into good debts, can convert a deficiency into a surplus), than the conjectures of a speculative historian, who undertakes to transmute legend into history.

'Egyptology has a historical method of its own. It recognises none of the ordinary rules of evidence; the extent of its demands upon our credulity is almost unbounded. Even the writers on ancient Italian ethnology are modest and tame in their hypotheses, compared with the Egyptologists. Under their potent logic all identity disappears; every thing is subject to become any thing but itself. Successive dynasties become contemporary dynasties; one king becomes another king, or several other kings, or a fraction of another king; one name becomes another name; one number becomes another number; one place becomes another place.

'In order to support and illustrate these remarks, it would be necessary to analyse Bunsen's reconstruction of the scheme of Egyptian chronology. Such an analysis would be inconsistent with the main object of the present work; but a few examples will serve to characterise his method.

'Sesostris is the great name of Egyptian antiquity. Even the builders of the pyramids and of the labyrinth sink into insignificance by the side of this mighty conqueror. Nevertheless, his historical identity is not proof against the dissolving and recompounding processes of the Egyptological method. Bunsen distributes him into portions, and identifies each portion with a different king. Sesostris, as we have already stated, stands in Manetho's list as third king of the twelfth dynasty, at 3320 B.C., and a notice is appended to his name clearly identifying him with the Sesostris of Herodotus. Bunsen first takes a portion of him, and identifies it with Tosorthrus (written Sesorthus by Eusebius), the second king of the third dynasty, whose date is 5119 B.C., being a difference in the dates of 1799 years—about the same interval as between Augustus Cæsar and Napoleon; he then takes another portion, and identifies it with Sesonchosis, a king of the twelfth dynasty; a third portion of Sesostris is finally assigned to himself. It seems that these three fragments make up the entire Sesostris; who, in this plural unity, belongs to the Ancient Empire; but it is added that the Greeks confounded him with Ramesses, or Ramses, of the New Empire, a king of the nineteenth dynasty, whose date is 1255 B.C.; who, again, was confounded with his father, Sethos; which name again was transmuted into Sethosis and Sesosis.

'Lepsius agrees with Bunsen that Sesostris in the Manethonian list, who stands in the twelfth dynasty, at 3320 B.C., is not Sesostris; but, instead of elevating him to the third dynasty, brings him down to the nineteenth dynasty, and identifies him with Sethos, 1326 B.C.; chiefly on account of a statement of Manetho, preserved by Josephus, that Sethos first subjugated Cyprus and Phœnicia, and afterwards Assyria and Media, with other countries further to the east. Lepsius, moreover, holds that Ramses, the son of Sethos, was, like his father, a great conqueror, but that the Greeks confounded both father and son under the name of Sesostris.

'We therefore see that the two leading Egyptologists, Bunsen and Lepsius, differing in other respects, agree in thinking that Sesostris is not Sesostris. The notice appended to his name in Manetho, which identifies him with the Sesostris of Herodotus, Diodorus, and other Greek writers, is regarded by Lepsius as spurious. But here their agreement stops. One assigns Sesostris to what is called the Old, the other to what is called the New Empire, separating his respective dates by an interval of 3793 years. What should we think, if a new school of writers on the history of France, entitling themselves Francologists, were to arise, in which one of the leading critics were to deny that Louis XIV lived in the seventeenth century, and were to identify him with Hercules, or Romulus, or Cyrus, or Alexander the Great, or Cæsar, or Charlemagne; while another leading critics of the same school, agreeing in the rejection of the received hypothesis as to his being the successor of Louis XIII, were to identify him with Napoleon I and Louis Napoleon?'

It is well known that all these conjectures on early Egyptian history are supported by the recent discovery of the true meaning of the long-unintelligible hieroglyphic inscriptions. But Sir George Lewis does not believe they have discovered their meaning. He states the problem certainly with formidable force. It is something like this: 'Here you have inscriptions composed in a lost *language*, and written down in a *character* which is also lost. Is it to be believed that the imagination of man can first guess rightly the system of written symbols, and then guess the meaning too? It is the old story; you have to interpret the dream without knowing what it is. Even supposing that you have found out, as you think, one set of written symbols, and made a language in these symbols which you can read, who will assure us that some other person will not find another set of symbols with another set of meanings in a new imaginary language?' 'The question,' says Sir George Lewis, 'as to the possibility of interpreting a language whose tradition has been lost, is further confused by a deceptive analogy derived from the process of deciphering. A cipher is a contrivance for disguising the alphabetical writing of a known language by a conventional change of characters. The explanation of this conventional change is called the *Key*. If a document written in cipher falls into the possession of a stranger ignorant of the *Key*, and if he can conjecture with tolerable certainty the language in which it is written, he can proceed to apply to it the rules for deciphering, which are founded upon the comparative frequency of certain letters and certain words in the given language. This process, if the document be tolerably long, is almost infallible. It is difficult to devise a cipher, sufficiently simple for frequent use, which cannot be deciphered by a skilful and experienced decipherer. But this operation supposes the language to be understood; it is a merely alphabetical process; it does not determine the meaning of a single word; it merely strips the disguise off a word, and reproduces it in its ordinary orthography. No process similar to deciphering can afford the smallest assistance towards discovering the signification of an unknown word, written in known alphabetical characters. The united ingenuity of the most skilful decipherers in Europe could not throw any light upon an Etruscan or Lycian inscription, or interpret a single sentence of the Eugubine Tables. In like manner, assuming an Egyptian hieroglyphical text to be correctly read into alphabetical characters, no process of deciphering could detect the meaning of the several words.'

It is possible, for example, that Champollion may have discovered by comparison of some proper names some phonetic characters, and it is also possible that the ancient Egyptian may have had some analogy with the modern Coptic,—the same sort of analogy, perhaps, which Italian bears to Latin. But it is very difficult to be satisfied that any great knowledge could be derived from the spelling of a few letters, and the guessing of a few words as expressed in these letters. 'Where,' says Sir George Lewis, 'the tradition of a language is lost, but its affinity with a known language is ascertained or presumed, the attempts to restore the significations of words proceed upon the hypothesis that the etymology of the word can be determined by its resemblance, more or less close, to a word in the known language, and that the etymology of the word is a certain guide to its meaning. But although there is a close affinity between etymology and meaning, yet etymology alone cannot be taken as a sure index to meaning. When the signification of a word is ascertained, it is often difficult to determine the etymology. The Lexilogus of Buttmann, the Romance Dictionary of Diez—in fact, any good etymological vocabulary—will furnish ample evidence of this truth. But when the process is inverted, and it is proposed to determine the signification of the words of an entire language from etymological guesses, unassisted by any other knowledge, the process is necessarily uncertain and inconclusive, and can be satisfactory only to a person who has already made up his mind to accept *some* system of interpretation.

'Thus in Italian the word *troja* signifies a sow. Diez refers the origin of this word to the old Latin expression *porcus Trojanus*, which meant a pig stuffed with other animals and served for the table; the name being an allusion to the Trojan horse. He conceives that this phrase first became *porco di troja*, and afterwards *troja* simply, with the signification of a pregnant sow. Assuming this etymology to be true, what possible ingenuity could have enabled any body to invert the process, and to discover the meaning by the etymology, if the meaning were unknown?'

The alphabet of Baron Bunsen is very complicated. He has four classes and an extra, or later class. He has 1000 characters altogether:

Ideographics	620
Determinatives	164
Phonetics	130
Mixed	55
Later alphabet	100
	1069

And he can read a very large number of words; but we are not surprised to hear that 'the system of reading the hieroglyphic characters, as expounded by the Egyptologists, is flexible and arbitrary. It involves the hypothesis of homophones; that is to say, of a plurality of signs for the same sound. It likewise involves a mixture of ideographic and phonetic symbols.'

Altogether, though Sir George Lewis may not be right in his bold assertion that *no* early Egyptian history is possible, he is clearly successful in proving that Baron Bunsen's history is untrue. As he expelled the conjectures of Niebuhr from Roman history, so he has expelled the conjectures of Niebuhr's great pupil from Egyptian history. Nobody who reads Sir George Lewis can doubt that Bunsen, for the most part, indulges in conjecture as to the language, as to the written character, and as to the history of ancient Egypt. *His* theories in future will not be accepted as facts. A better feat of iconoclasm has seldom been performed.

These historical works might well have exhausted the leisure of a man almost always occupied in civil business. But Sir George Lewis wrote another long series of books on philosophical politics also. We have not left ourselves much space to speak of them at great length, and we do not think that they need be spoken of at such great length as his historical works. We think that they represent less perfectly the best parts of his mind, and that they bear more marks of his deficiencies.

The earliest and among the most curious is an essay on the *Use and Abuse of certain Political Terms*, published in 1832. It is curiously characteristic of Sir George Lewis that, at a time when England was convulsed by the almost revolutionary struggle of the Reform Bill, when all Europe still gazed with wonder at the prosperous effect of the most happy of French revolutions, Sir George Lewis should have sat down, to write not on the facts of political revolution, but on the *words* of political science. After he became a practical statesman he became more alive to political passions and less occupied with political terms; but to the last he was too apt to wonder at great conflicts, and to be pleased with verbal inquiries. In 1833 he was under the mastery of a remarkable teacher. The late Mr. Austin had little fame in his lifetime, and was so discouraged by neglect that he could not nerve himself to complete great works, of which he had finished what most men would consider the difficult part, and had only to add that which most people would think the easy part. He in this point resembled Coleridge. That great thinker has left no work which embodies his philosophy, and yet his philosophy has permeated his generation. Mr. Austin seized hold, some thirty years ago, of several strong minds, and by the help of these great minds he greatly influenced his time. You will find thoughts distinctly traceable to him far away among people who never heard of him. His few lectures and his years of conversation were a peculiar source of nice expression and accurate thought for more than half a century; a little bit of just though almost pedantic thought cropped suddenly up in our crude and hasty English life. Thirty years ago Mr. Austin, at the London University, explained what may be called the necessary part of political science, and illustrated it by the best of all illustrations—Roman law. He analysed not a particular government, but what is common to all governments; not one law, but what is common to all laws; not political communities in their features of diversity, but political communities in their features of necessary resemblance. He gave politics not an interesting aspect, but a new aspect; for, by giving men a steady view of what political communities *must* be, he stopped in the bud many questions as to what they ought to be, or ought not to be. As a gymnastic of the intellect, and as a purifier, Mr. Austin's philosophy is to this day admirable,—even in its imperfect remains; a young man who will study it will find that he has gained something which he wanted, but something which he did not *know* that he wanted; he has clarified a part of his mind which he did not know needed clarifying. Sir George Lewis was deeply penetrated by this abstract teaching; to the last day of his life, in the unphilosophical atmosphere of the War Office, he would use the phrases of, and would like allusions to, this philosophy. One source of his power as a political thinker was, that he had, under Mr. Austin's guidance, studied political questions as it were in their skeleton. Once a jurist, always a jurist. The vast and easy command of the whole sources of juridical literature which Sir George Lewis showed in his essay *On Foreign Jurisdiction, and the Extradition of Criminals,* and elsewhere, is largely due to his early studies. Yet it may be doubted whether Mr. Austin's influence was entirely favourable to him. A certain school of thinkers magnify the effects of human language. Calm and simple-minded students, when they see the hasty world of human beings using inaccurate and vague words, are apt to ascribe all their errors to those words, and to believe that, if you could put human language right, you would set the world in order. There is no greater mistake. Men are mainly deceived by their passions and their interests; they care but little for abstract truth, and rush forward to small, petty, but concrete, objects. They catch hastily at any sort of word that justifies what they wish to do, and if it sounds well care little for fallacies and ambiguities. The language is inaccurate no doubt, but it is a symptom only of a mental disease. You cannot calm the passions of men by defining their words. Mr. Austin's school was apt to forget this. The early treatise of Sir George Lewis on the *Use and Abuse of Political Terms,* and some of his later too, are not exempt from this defect, though his strong sense and really practical turn of mind always kept it in check. A person wishing to watch his intellectual history, should look carefully at this book; it is a series of exercises in Mr. Austin's class-room.

A more serious defect mars the popularity of Sir George Lewis's writings, and we think Mr. Austin is partly to blame for that too. Mr. Austin was always talking of the 'formidable community of fools;' he had no popularity; little wish for popularity; little respect for popular judgment. This is a great error. The world is often wiser than any philosopher. 'There is some one,' said a great man of the world, 'wiser than Voltaire, and wiser than Napoleon, *c'est tout le monde.*' Popular judgment on popular matters is crude and vague, but it is right. And it is even more certain that a great writer on morals and politics ought not to adopt a mode of writing which excludes him from popularity. Mr. Austin's mere style did this for him. He wrote on the principle that people would be sure to comprehend what was completely expressed, but could never be trusted to supply an *hiatus* in what was incompletely expressed. His writings accordingly read like a legal document; every possible case is provided for, every ambiguity is guarded against, and—hardly any one can read them.

The ordinary human mind cannot bear that method of expressing every thing; it is more puzzled by such elaborate precision than by any thing else. Sir George Lewis did not err in mere language, but he erred in treatment. Mr. Austin expands all thoughts, new and old, at just the same length; and he taught Sir George Lewis to do so also. In the present state of the moral sciences, this is absurd. Much of them is very well, though a little vaguely, understood by the world at large. It is often of great consequence to reduce them to a principle; it is often of great importance to add new truths, and to give a new edge to old truth. But it is not advisable to begin with a principle and to work steadily through all its possible applications at the *same* length. If you do, the reader will say, 'How this man *does* prose! why, I knew that;' and he did know it. Some of the applications of a principle are new, and should be treated at length; some are of pressing importance, and should be treated at length too; but all the consequences should not be worked out like a sum. An atmosphere of commonplace hangs over long moral didactics, and an equal expansion of what the world knows and what it does not know will not be read by the world.

Sir George Lewis did his fame serious harm by neglecting this maxim. He wrote, for example, *An Essay on the Influence of Authority in Matters of Opinions*, which was described by a hasty thinker as a book to prove that when 'you wanted to know any thing, you asked some one who knew something about it.' The essay certainly abounds in acute remarks and interesting illustrations, and if these remarks and these illustrations had been printed separately, it would have been a good book. But the systematic treatment has been fatal to it. The different kinds and cases of authority are so systematically enumerated, that the reader yawns and forgets.

The case is even worse with his great treatise *On the Methods of Observation and Reasoning in Politics*, in two large volumes. Scarcely any one has read these volumes, and those who have are sure that their bulk was a mistake. They are written upon the principle that 'two and two make four' is as much unknown to the mass of men as the integral calculus. Easy things are explained exactly with the same care as difficult things, and in consequence very few people read the explanations. There are many admirable parts and essays in the book. It contains an account and criticism of 'political induction' as described by Mr. Mill, and an account and criticism of jurisprudence as described and understood by Mr. Austin. Both these discussions are very good, and the speculations of the two thinkers are well spliced together; but they are overlaid with long explanations of what requires no explanation, and discussions of what need never have been discussed. Charles Fox used to say of a very dull but able speaker, 'I always listen to that man, and then speak his speech over again.' A dishonest writer might well do so with Sir George Lewis's writings. There are many thoughts, and a million facts in them, which the world would be glad to hear, though it cannot extract them from the rest. A writer of this sort naturally did not look for profit from his laborious writings; few men have done more gratuitous work. He was disposed to agree with Mr. Mill, that the notion of 'thinkers giving out doctrines for bread was a mistake,' and even to hold that speculators should *pay* for the opportunity of placing their opinions before the world.

We own that we much regret this misconception of the conditions of modern writing, now that Sir George Lewis's career has been cut short in the midst. When he had life before him, it seemed less important that he should throw away fame; but now that all is over we wish he had desired popularity more, for he would have been remembered better. He really had considerable powers of pointed writing. The little treatise at the head of this article shows that when he did not aim at completeness he could write easily that which would be easily read. He had not, indeed, the powers of a great literary artist; it was not in his way to look at style as an alluring art; he wanted to express his opinion, and cared for nothing else. He had no literary vanity; and without the vanity that loves applause few indeed cultivate the tact that gains applause. 'If you can do without the world,' says the cynic, 'the world can do without you;' and it is as true to say that few, if any, gain literary fame who do not long and hunger after it.

As a sort of compensation, Sir George Lewis rose more rapidly as a parliamentary statesman than any of his contemporaries. He was in the first rank of the Liberal party, yet he entered Parliament five years after Mr. Cardwell, fifteen years after Mr. Gladstone, nineteen years after Sir Charles Wood, and forty years after Lord Palmerston. It is curious at first sight that he should have done so. He was not an attractive speaker, he wanted animal spirits, and detested an approach to any thing theatrical. He had very considerable command of exact language, but he had no impulse to use it. If it was his duty to speak, he spoke; but he did not want to speak when it was not his duty.

Silence was no pain, and oratory no pleasure to him. If mere speaking were the main qualification for an influence in Parliament,—if, as is often said, parliamentary government be a synonym for the government of talkers and *avocats*,—Sir George Lewis would have had no influence, would never have been a parliamentary ruler. Yet we once heard a close and good observer say: 'George Lewis's influence in the House is something wonderful; whatever he proposes has an excellent chance of being carried. He excites no opposition, and he commands great respect, and generally he carries his plan.' The House of Commons, according to the saying, is wiser than any one in it. There is an elective affinity for solid sense in a practical assembly of educated Englishmen which always operates, and which rarely errs. Sir George Lewis's influence was great not only on his own side of the House, but on the other. He had, indeed, probably more real weight with moderate Conservatives than with extreme Liberals. Enterprise neither seemed to be nor was his *forte*, and bold men thought him rather tame. His influence was like that of Lord Palmerston: he was liked by the moderate members, whether Whigs or Tories, who think just alike, whatever they call themselves; and who are likely nowadays to rule the country, whatever name the party in power may chance to bear. He was a safe man, a fair man, and an unselfish man. He had a faculty of 'patient labour,' which, as he himself remarked, *'was as sure* to be appreciated when Englishmen meet together to transact business, as wit or eloquence;' and therefore it was that he had great influence in the House of Commons; therefore it was that he rose rapidly.

He filled three cabinet offices; the first was that of Chancellor of the Exchequer, and this was the one which he liked best, and for which he conceived himself best qualified. He had no easy time, however, during his actual tenure of the office. He had to find money for the Crimean war, the heaviest draft on the resources of the exchequer since Waterloo; he had to break the 'fundamental law of the currency,' as he called it, Peel's Act, in the unexpected panic of 1857. He gave universal satisfaction as finance minister, and especial satisfaction in the City. He was clear, considerate, and it was at once felt that argument would move him if good argument could be found. He had to borrow much money, and he so managed as to be able to borrow it without undue charge to the state, and with that immediate success which sustains the credit of the state, and secures a *prestige* in the money-market. It is scarcely possible to speak of him as finance minister without alluding to his differences with Mr. Gladstone in the Cabinet and out of it. Yet it is not possible to discuss the subject accurately. Mr. Gladstone's views of the budget of 1860, we all know; but Sir George Lewis's views have never been set forth at length, and it is not wise to base an argument on scraps of oral conversations. It may be as well, however, to point out that, in addition to their intrinsic and considerable differences of temperament and character, they approached finance from two different and even opposite points of view. Mr. Gladstone is the successor, the legitimate inheritor of the policy of Sir Robert Peel. He made his reputation as a financier and as a statesman by the budget of 1853, in which the prominent object is to remove old taxes, that cramp and harass industry. He regards the public purse as donative, out of which trade may be augmented and industry developed. Sir Robert Peel used the public purse in that manner, and Mr. Gladstone has done so also. Sir George Lewis was led, perhaps from temperament, and certainly from circumstances, to take a stricter and simpler view of finance. He came into office on a sudden, during a great war, and he had to find the resources for that war. He had to consider, not how taxation could be adjusted so as to help trade, but how the exchequer could be filled to pay soldiers. On all financial matters he looked solely at the balance of the account, Will there be a deficit, or will there not be? Forms of account, and all minor matters, were in his mind of very small importance; he looked to the simple question, How much will there be in the till at the end of the year? With two such different prepossessions as these, it is no wonder that men so intrinsically different as Sir George Lewis and Mr. Gladstone did not very well agree upon finance; it is rather a wonder that they could act together at all. There is no use, over Sir George Lewis's grave, in reviving financial controversies; every body will now admit that while he was in office and responsible he was a sound and sure Chancellor of the Exchequer.

In the panic of 1857, we have heard, he was even amusing. His perfect impassivity and collectedness contrasted much with the excitement of eager men; and in a panic most men are eager. A deputation of Scotch bankers attended at the Treasury to ask Sir George to induce the Bank of England to make advances to them in certain possible cases. Sir George said, 'Ah, gentlemen, if I were to interfere with the discretion of the Bank, there would be a run upon me much greater than any which there has ever been upon you.' He was a man who probably *could* not lose his head.

At the Home Office he had the opportunity of displaying great judicial faculties. The Home Office is the high court of appeal in cases of criminal justice. When any one is to be hung, it is almost always argued before the Home Secretary that he should not be hung. If Sir George Lewis had practised at the bar, for which he studied, he would have been a bad advocate; his mind was not fertile[2] in ambiguous fallacies, and was incapable of artificial belief; and a great pleader should excel in these. One of the greatest judges of our generation, when at the bar, could only state the point once, and when the court did not understand him, could only mutter, 'What fools they are! awful fools, infernal fools!' Sir George Lewis would not have indulged in these epithets, but he would have been nearly as little able to invent ingenious suggestions and out-of-the-way arguments. He probably would have said, 'I have explained the matter. If the court *will* not comprehend it, *I* cannot make them.' But no man was fitter for a judge than himself. He would never have shirked labour,—which is not unknown even among judges,—and his lucid exposition of substantial reasons would have been consulted by students for years. At the Home Office he could not display all these qualities, but he was able to display some of them.

At the War Office he shone far less. It did not suit his previous pursuits; and no other man with such pursuits would have taken it, or, indeed, would have been asked to take it. He pushed in this case too far the notion that an able and educated man can master any subject, and is fit for any office. The constitutional habit in England of making a civilian supreme over military matters, though we believe a most wise habit, has its objections, and may easily look absurd. It *did* look rather absurd when the most pacific of the pacific, the most erudite of the erudite, Sir George Lewis, was placed at the head of the War Department. In great matters, it cannot be denied, he did well. When the capture of the *Trent* made a war with the Federal States a pressing probability, the arrangements were admitted to be admirable. Much of the credit must belong in such a case to military and other subordinates,—all the details must be managed by them; but the superior minister must have his credit too. He brought to a *focus* all

---

[2] The *National Review* (p. 521) has 'futile' for 'fertile' but this seems an obvious misprint and I have substituted 'fertile'.

which was done; he summed-up the whole; he could say distinctly why every thing which was done was done, and why every thing left undone was left undone. He would have been ready with a plain intelligible reason on all these matters in Parliament and elsewhere. And this was not an easy matter for a civilian after a few months of office. But on minor matters Sir George Lewis was not so good at the War Department as at the Exchequer or the Home Office. He had been apprenticed to the Home Office as Under-Secretary, and to the Exchequer as Financial Secretary to the Treasury; but he had never been apprenticed to the War Office. On matters of detail he was obliged to rely on others. He held, and justly, that a parliamentary chief of temporary, perhaps *very* temporary, tenure of office should be very cautious not to interfere too much with the minor business of his department. He should govern, but he should govern through others. But the due application of this maxim requires that the chief minister should know, as it were by intuition and instinct, which points are important and which are not important. And no civilian introduced at once to a new department like that of War can at once tell this. He *must* be in the hands of others. In the House of Commons, too, Sir George Lewis could never answer questions of detail on war matters in an offhand manner. He had to say, 'I will inquire, and inform the honourable member.' At the Home Office he could have answered at once and of himself. It was an act of self-denial in him to go to the War Office. He felt himself out of place there, and was sure that his administration of military matters could not add to his reputation. But he was told it was for the interest of the Government that he should accept the office, and he accepted it. Perhaps he was wrong. The reputation of a first-rate public man is a great public power, and he should be careful not to diminish it. The weight of the greatest men is diminished by their being seen to do daily that which they do not do particularly well. A cold and cynical wisdom particularly disapproves of most men's *best* actions. Few men were less exposed to the censure of such wisdom than Sir George Lewis; but his acceptance of the War Office was a sacrifice of himself to the public, which injured him more than it advantaged the public,—which it would be better not to have made.

The usefulness of men like Sir George Lewis is not to be measured by their usefulness in mere office. It is in the Cabinet that they are of *most* use. Sir George Lewis was made to discuss business with other men. 'If,' we have heard one who did much business with him say,—

'if there is any fault in what you say, he will find it out.' In council, in the practical discussions of pending questions, a simple masculine intellect like that of Sir George Lewis finds its greatest pleasure and its best use. He was *made* to be a cabinet minister.

The briefest notice of Sir George Lewis should not omit to mention one of the most agreeable, and not one of his least rare, peculiarities— his good-natured use of great knowledge. It would have been easy for a man with such a memory as his, and such studious habits as his, to become most unpopular by cutting-up the casual blunders of others. On the contrary, he was a most popular man; for he used his knowledge with a view to amend the ignorance of others, and not with a view to expose it. His conversation was superior either to his speeches or his writings. It had—what is perhaps rarer among parliamentary statesmen than among most people—the flavour of exact thought. It is hardly possible for men to pass their lives in oratorical efforts without losing some part of the taste for close-fitting words. Well-sounding words which are not specially apt, which are not very precise, are as good or better for a popular assembly. Sir George Lewis's words in political conversation were as good as words could be; they might have gone to the press at once. We have compared it to hearing a chapter in Aristotle's Politics, and perhaps that may give an idea that it was dull. But pointed thought on great matters is a very pleasant thing to hear, though, after many ages and changes, it is sometimes a hard thing to read. The conversation of the Dialogue at the end of his treatise on 'The Best Form of Government' has been admired, but it is very inferior to the conversation of the writer. There was a delicate flavour of satire lurking in the precise thought which could not be written down, and which is now gone and irrecoverable.

'When,' says Lord Brougham, commenting on the death of a states-man once celebrated and now forgotten,—'when a subject presented itself so large and shapeless, and dry and thorny, that few men's fortitude could face, and no one's patience could grapple with it; or an emergency occurred demanding on the sudden access to stores of learning, the collection of many long years, but arranged so as to be made available at the shortest notice,—*then* it was men asked where Lawrence was.' And now, not only when information is wanted, but when counsel is needed,—when parties are confused,—when few public men are trusted,—when wisdom, always rare, is rarer even than usual,—many may ask, in no long time, 'Where is Lewis now?'

The Tribute at Hereford to Sir George Cornewall Lewis[1]

NOTHING could be in more perfect taste than the proceedings at Hereford on the uncovering of the statue of Sir George Lewis. These local events are local casualties. It is impossible to foretell whether the principal local person is not a loquacious fool of good intentions who will say just what he should not, or whether he is a man of feeling and judgment who will say what he should say with taste and propriety. There is nothing which Sir George Lewis would so much have disliked as an exaggerated *éloge* over his grave: those who knew him would have had his quiet smile of utter contempt present to them while they read it. Happily, nothing of this sort was attempted. The sober and modest nature of the man was duly honoured in the quiet and unobtrusive nature of the remembrance. Both Mr. Clive and Lord Palmerston spoke of Sir George Lewis with guarded care, as English gentlemen wish to be spoken of, as one English gentleman, therefore, should speak of another. Sir George Lewis had no enemies, but if he had, no enemy could have taken a just exception to the praises of his friends. He would have exactly desired this. He cared very little, perhaps nothing, for passing popularity: he would have been prepared with various classical quotations upon the mutability of the vulgar judgment, but he would deeply value a restrained expression of deep respect by neighbours and friends who knew him well; he would believe that they were the legitimate 'authority'—the persons who ought to speak on that matter.

It is very curious that Lord Palmerston, who spoke, so to say, Sir George Lewis's epitaph, should have had the slowest, and that Sir George Lewis should have had the most rapid, political rise of our time. Unquestionably, Lord Palmerston is in some sense a buoyant man, and Sir George Lewis was in some sense a heavy man, yet the latter came to the surface far quicker. Lord Palmerston was a quarter

[1] This article was first published in *The Economist* for September 10 1864, Volume XXII, pp. 1136–7.

of a century in Parliament before he was anything at all, before he was any more than a subaltern official; Sir George Lewis was only thirteen years in Parliament altogether, and in that time he was Secretary of the Treasury, Chancellor of the Exchequer, Home Secretary, Secretary for War, and had acquired the perfect respect and confidence of the House of Commons. He finished his whole career as a statesman in about half the number of years that it took Lord Palmerston to become a statesman at all.

The causes which so much delayed Lord Palmerston's rise are not to the present purpose, but the cause which so much accelerated that of Sir George Lewis is very simple. He had, above every other statesman of the age, the gift of inspiring confidence. Coleridge said of Southey that he inspired every one with a confidence in his *reliability*, and this is an almost exact description of Sir George Lewis. Political opponents and political friends both felt that he had fairly applied a strong and unfettered mind to vast accumulated information, and that his measures were the result of that application. People thought twice before they opposed a grave and business-like measure, proposed by Sir George Lewis in that grave and business-like manner.

In one most important respect he was like Lord Palmerston, though in every other most unlike. His opinions were always plain and simple opinions. People who went to him with the notion that he was a great philosopher and scholar were often puzzled at this plainness. They expected something farfetched and recondite, and certainly they did not get it. He held as a principle that difficult schemes, fine calculations, *unintelligible* polities were as such beyond the range of popular government. Perhaps too he hated them as if they were a kind of mysticism. At all events, a person who could not understand Sir George Lewis's conversation on political business must have been unfit for every kind of business. It had exactly the homely exactitude that English people like. We have heard it remarked of Sir Robert Peel's speeches, that he generally made a remark which seemed to have been left by every one on purpose for him: it was so sensible, when made, that every one believed he could have made it. It was much the same with Sir George Lewis. What he said seemed so credible and sensible that, in an hour or two, you were apt to believe that you had always thought so.

Possibly this distinctness of aim has been rather deficient in our policy for a year past. We certainly believe that Sir George Lewis could have cross-examined Lord Russell on the Danish policy rather acutely. 'What,' he would have said, 'is the object you desire? When we are agreed on that, we will discuss the *modus operandi*; but it is a mistake to deliberate on expedients, when there is a fundamental discrepancy respecting ends.' At any rate we should *like* to hear Lord Russell answer Sir George Lewis on this subject. This need of a definite aim ran through all his speculations. To take an example from the foreign politics now most interesting to us—American politics: 'I have never,' said Sir George Lewis in a letter of March, 1861, now lying before us, 'been able, either in conversation or by reading, to obtain an answer to the question, What will the North do if they beat the South? To restore the old Union would be an absurdity. What other state of things does that village lawyer Lincoln contemplate as the fruit of victory? It seems to me that the men now in power at Washington are much such persons as in this country get possession of a disreputable joint stock company. There is almost the same amount of ability and honesty.' After nearly three years of experience, it would be difficult to describe Washington more justly. But we do not cite the instance to prove Sir George Lewis's power of prediction, so much as to prove his unfailing desire for a distinct aim.

The political precision of Sir George Lewis is peculiarly English, but it is not at all more English than his scholarship. Persons who do not read such books may fancy that 'scholars' books' are much the same in all countries. But such is not the case. Mr. Grote's *History*, to take an instance, could no more have been written in Germany than Bacon's *Novum Organum* could have been written by Socrates. That history belongs to the intellectual atmosphere of England, as plainly as our parliamentary debates. There is in it the constant sense of evidence,—the habitual perception of tested probability which the atmosphere of a free country produces, and must produce. Sir George Lewis's books have this instinctive sense of the real value of evidence even more than Mr. Grote's. He could not help feeling it; he did not wish to forget it, and he could not have forgotten it if he had wished.

Sir George Lewis is gone, but he has left a remembrance in many minds which will not grow cold while they are still warm. For many years it will to many be much to have known one who was learned and yet wise; just but yet kind; considerate and observing, and yet never in the least severe.

Albert Prince Consort
Introductory note

Albert Francis Charles Augustus Emmanuel, later Prince Consort of Britain, was born at Rosenau near Coburg in 1819, the second son of Ernest, duke of Saxe-Coburg-Gotha, and of Louise, daughter of Augustus, duke of Saxe-Gotha-Altenburg. Prince Albert visited England in 1836, when the Princess Victoria expressed her willingness to accept him as consort. After some travelling and the continuing of his education, Prince Albert became betrothed to Queen Victoria in 1839, and they were married in 1840. In this year, Prince Albert was appointed Regent in case of the Queen's death. Throughout their married life Prince Albert gave the Queen great assistance in the performance of her political duties. The Prince Consort took an active part in the life of the nation: he projected the idea of the Great Exhibition of 1851; he gave valuable advice throughout the Crimean War, and he showed great sympathy with the condition of the working classes. Prince Albert died in London in 1861.

The Late Prince Consort[1]

S o much has ere this been said upon the life and character of Prince Albert, that scarcely anything now remains except to join very simply and plainly in the regret and sympathy which have been everywhere expressed by all classes of the nation, the low as well as the high. A long narrative of a simple career would now be wholly needless, for our contemporaries have supplied many such, and any protracted eulogy would be unsuitable both to our business-like pages and to the simple character of him whom we have lost.

If our loss is not, as has been extravagantly said, the greatest which the English nation could have sustained, it is among the most irreparable. Our parliamentary Constitution in some sense renews itself, or tends to do so. As one old statesman leaves the scene, a younger one comes forward in the vigour of hope and power to fill his place. When one great orator dies, another commonly succeeds him. The opportunity of the new aspirant is the departure of his predecessor; on every vacancy some new claimant—many claimants probably—strive with eager emulation to win it and to retain it. Every loss is in a brief period easily and fully repaired. Even, too, in the hereditary part of our Constitution most calamities are soon forgotten. One monarch dies, and another succeeds him. A new court, a new family, new hopes and new interests spring up and supersede those which have passed away. What was is forgotten; what is is seen. But now we have the old court without one of its mainstays and principal supports. The royal family of last week is still (and without change) the royal family of to-day; but the *father* of that family is removed. For such a loss there is not in this world any adequate resource or any complete compensation. In no rank of life can any one else be to a widow and children what the deceased husband and father would have been. In the court as in the cottage, such loss must not only be grief now, but perplexity, trouble, and perhaps mistake hereafter.

[1] This article was first published in *The Economist* for December 21 1861, Volume XIX, page 1401.

The present generation, at least the younger part of it, have lost the idea that the court is a serious matter. Everything for twenty years has seemed to go so easily and so well, that it has seemed to go of itself. There is no such thing in this world. Everything requires anxiety, and reflection, and patience. And the function of the court, though we easily forget it when it is well performed, keeps itself much in our remembrance when it is ill performed. Old observers say that some of the half-revolutionary discontent in the times preceding the Reform Bill was attributable to the selfish apathy and decrepit profligacy of George the Fourth. The Crown is of singular importance in a divided and contentious free state, because it is the *sole* object of attachment which is elevated above every contention and division. But to maintain that importance, it must create attachment. We know that the Crown now does so fully; but we do not adequately bear in mind how much rectitude of intention, how much judgment in conduct, how much power of doing right, how much power of doing nothing, are requisite to excite the loyalty and to retain the confidence of a free people.

Some cynical observers have contrasted the unlimited encomiums of the last week with the 'cold observance' and very measured popularity of Prince Albert during his life. They remember the public hisses of 1855, and perhaps recall many hints and whispers of politics that have passed away. But the most graphic of our contemporaries have found nothing to record of Prince Albert so truly characteristic as this change. His circumstances, and perhaps his character, forbade him to attempt the visible achievements and the showy displays which attract momentary popularity. Discretion is a quality seldom appreciated till it is lost, and it was discretion which Prince Albert eminently possessed.

The Prince Consort and Lord Palmerston[1]

Mr. Martin's *Life of the Prince Consort* has been published so soon after Mr. Evelyn Ashley's 'Life of Lord Palmerston,' and the two books so often refer to the same political transactions, that no one can read them both without being tempted into a comparison of the two men, both as speculative and as practical statesmen. Indeed, the comparison is in many respects very instructive. Lord Palmerston was one of those statesmen of very mature years whom the process of 'natural selection,' as it is applied in the conflicts of parliamentary life, had brought to the head of affairs,—a man of singular tenacity and vigour of will, and of very considerable self-will, who understood well the world and its ways, who had much careless humour, a most active ambition, and plenty of *savoir faire*, but who was never a very considerate politician, one rather who scrambled his way into a policy and scrambled his way out of it again without either looking forward very much, to avoid making a mistake, or back very much after he had made one, but who fought his way through his difficulties with a good deal of valour, and a very hand-to-mouth species of reflectiveness. The Prince Consort on the other hand was a young man who, though carefully educated for his position, had had no sifting in the battle of life, and perhaps hardly had at any time the physique requisite to bear a very hard sifting of that kind; he was not wanting in such knowledge of the world as a life spent among courts, and a naturally observant nature give, but he wanted that ease and carelessness of manner which are so much more effective in inoculating men of the world with new ideas and aims, than are the most carefully prepared arrays of reasons. But he was a very considerate politician, who always took pains to master the general principles which governed the political conditions of any problem before him, and very seldom made any mistake as to the character of those principles. There was not a trace in the Prince of either the animal buoyancy of Lord Palmerston, or the political self-

[1] This article was first published in *The Economist*, Volume XXXIV, p. 1282, November 4 1876.

will which so often accompanies that kind of buoyancy. He was always ready to renounce his own wishes, eager to look at every question in as purely impartial a light as it would admit of, and desirous so to shape the course taken, that it would not hamper the highest policy of the future. He would have done more, we think, practically to mould the policy of England than he did, if he had seemed to be a little less painstaking, and had imperceptibly infected, rather than directly indoctrinated, the statesmen around him, with the results of his sagacious and careful reflections. It is evident from Mr. Martin's *Life* that he had not the knack of dropping seed without appearing to sow it—which is an important art for a prince who has to deal with tough old statesmen of wills as headstrong and habits as fixed as Lord Palmerston's. But though he may not have had the best knack of carrying his own way, his way was apt to be not unfrequently very much better worth carrying than that of the statesmen whom he chiefly tried to influence. Especially was this the case in relation to foreign policy. The Prince Consort had some of the cosmopolitan culture which fitted him to view these questions from a point of view above that of our insular interests. Lord Palmerston, on the contrary, was very apt to have no notion of a Foreign Office question, except that which he had got from looking at it like an Englishman, and discussing it, and hearing it discussed in Parliament. He did not ask himself, as the Prince Consort always did, what a policy would lead to—whether it could be consistently developed and carried out—what, in fact, it really implied, and whether what it implied was something which it was worth our while to battle for steadily and of set purpose. When Lord Palmerston as an Englishman received a shock, he immediately felt the importance of making the person who caused it receive a shock in return, and if possible, a worse shock than had been given; and so his diplomacy sometimes amounted to very little more than the part of a valiant diplomatic boxer, who was likely enough to get the best of the game at which he was playing, but had no sort of security that when he had got the best of it he should not be found to have secured for himself and for his country a very doubtful advantage, if not an inheritance of positive mischief.

Of course, the best illustration we can give of this power of the Prince to understand a great question far better than the minister whose mind he would have impressed, if he could, with his own larger view, is the memorandum which he wrote when Turkey had declared war on Russia in 1853, and the Prince, presuming that we should be drawn into taking part with Turkey, was doing his best to impress on the Queen's ministers the grave responsibility of such a step; and especially the great danger that it might commit us to a general support of Turkish policy instead of that very limited and conditional support of Turkey against external aggression, to which he was so anxious to limit it. His words are words which can hardly be now read by any English statesman of that day to whom they were submitted, without producing a certain sense of shame, if not self-reproach, that they did not effect more in the way of warning us from a dangerous policy, and guiding us into a wise one. 'In acting,' he said, 'as auxiliaries to the Turks, we ought to be quite sure that *they* have no object in view *foreign* to our duty and interests; that they do not drive at war while we aim at peace; that they do not, instead of merely resisting the attempt of Russia to obtain a Protectorate over the Greek population, incompatible with their own independence, seek to obtain themselves the power of imposing a more oppressive rule of two millions of fanatic Mussulmen, over twelve millions of Christians; that they do not try to turn the tables upon the weaker power, now that backed by England and France, they have themselves become the stronger. There can be little doubt, and it is very natural, that the fanatic party at Constantinople should have such views; but to engage our fleet as an auxiliary force for such purposes, would be fighting against our own interests, policy, and feelings. From this it would result, that if our forces are to be employed for any purpose, however defensive, as an auxiliary to Turkey, we *must insist* upon keeping not only the conduct of the negotiation, but also the power of peace and war in our own hands, and that Turkey refusing this, we can no longer take part *for her*. It will be said that England and Europe have a strong interest, setting all Turkish considerations aside, that Constantinople and the Turkish territory should not fall into the hands of Russia and that they should, in the last extremity, even go to war to prevent such an overthrow of the balance of power. This must be admitted, and such a war may be right and wise. But this would be a war, not for the maintenance of the *integrity of the Ottoman Empire*, but merely for the interests of the European powers and of civilisation. It ought to be carried on unshackled by obligations to the Porte, and will probably lead, in the peace which must be the object of that war, to the obtaining of arrangements more consonant with the well-understood interests of

Europe, of Christianity, liberty, and civilisation, than the reimposition of the ignorant, barbarian, and despotic yoke of the Mussulman over the most fertile and favoured provinces of Europe.'

It is sufficiently evident from Lord Palmerston's reply to this memorandum, how far in advance of Lord Palmerston was the Prince Consort in his conception of the true character of the Ottoman rule, and the danger to be apprehended from giving it artificial support. Lord Palmerston's mind at the time was riveted on one point, and one point alone,—the excessive pretensions and ambition of Russia. He had no room in his mind for any second idea. He had not, like the Prince Consort, the power of looking to other almost inevitable consequences of the war he was contemplating, besides the one which he wished to bring about,—consequences which would be, in all probability, as mischievous as those on which his attention was centred might have been beneficial. In his communication, addressed to Lord Aberdeen, on the Prince Consort's memorandum, he writes thus:—

'It is said also that the Turks are re-awakening the dormant fanaticism of the Mussulman race, and that we ought not to be helping instruments to gratify such bad passions. I believe these stories about awakened fanaticism to be fables invented at Vienna and Petersburg; we have had no facts stated in support of them. I take the fanaticism which has been thus aroused to be the fanaticism which consists in burning indignation at a national insult, and a daring impatience to endeavour to expel an invading enemy. This spirit may be reviled by the Russians, whose schemes it disconcerts, and may be cried down by the Austrians, who had hoped to settle matters by persuading the Turks to yield, but it will not diminish the goodwill of the people of England, and it is a good foundation on which to build our hopes of success.' No more shortsighted passage was ever written by an able statesman; but much of Lord Palmerston's action at the time was even more onesided and cavalier still. For example, before even Turkey had declared war at all,—and of course, long before England and France had declared war, which was not till several months later,—Lord Palmerston wrote to Lord Aberdeen (on 7th October, 1853) saying, that he wished to propose to the Cabinet, 'first, that instructions should be sent to Constantinople that in the event of war having been declared' [by Turkey] 'the two squadrons should enter the Black Sea, and should send word to the Russian Admiral at Sebastopol that, in the existing state of things, any Russian ship of war found cruising in the Black

Sea would be detained, and given over to the Turkish Government.'
A rasher and more violent proposal could hardly be imagined. Of
course we now know that war between the Allies and Russia was not
avoided, and we are apt to think that even then it was inevitable. But
at the time the statesmen of the day were clearly bound to consider
all the best means by which it could be avoided and the Russian
aggression nevertheless repelled—and of such means it is perfectly
clear that Lord Palmerston's violent and self-willed proposal was not
one. A better recipe for ensuring war between the Western Powers and
Russia than the proposal which Lord Palmerston desired to press upon
the Cabinet could hardly have been imagined. Indeed, if Lord Aberdeen contributed to bring on the war by too great hesitancy, we can
all admit now that his excuse was great in having for his foreign
minister a colleague whose impulses were so obviously violent and
self-willed, and not marked by the reticence and self-control of a true
statesman. On the whole, no thoughtful man will compare the statesmanship of the Prince Consort during the years 1853–4 with the
statesmanship of Lord Palmerston, without some sense of regret that
the more farsighted, the more sober, and the more effectually self-
controlled statesman did not gain the ascendancy which he deserved
over the far more impetuous and imperious, though much older
adviser, who at that time guided the policy of England.

William Gladstone

Introductory note

William Ewart Gladstone (1809–1898) was born in Liverpool, the third son of John Gladstone, merchant and Tory M.P., and of his second wife, Anne Robertson. He was educated at Eton and Christ Church, Oxford. Largely through the patronage of the Duke of Newcastle, Gladstone was elected to Parliament as a Tory in 1832.* He became Junior Lord of the Treasury in 1834, and Under-Secretary for War and the Colonies in 1835. At this period he denounced liberal innovation and parliamentary reform. In 1841 Gladstone became Vice-President of the Board of Trade under Sir Robert Peel, and in 1843 he became President of the Board and a member of the Cabinet. He resigned in 1845 over the government's proposal to assist Catholic education in Ireland. In 1845 he became Colonial Secretary, but because of his free-trade views lost his seat in the Commons. In 1847 he was elected M.P. for the University of Oxford. Gladstone had seceded from the Tory party when Sir Robert Peel did so, and in the next few years he was moving towards Liberalism. In 1852 he contributed very largely to the fall of the Derby-Disraeli ministry by his attack on Disraeli's budget. In the succeeding ministry of Lord Aberdeen, Gladstone was Chancellor of the Exchequer, and his great budget of 1853 enhanced his already considerable reputation as financier and orator. He resigned office in 1855, and from then until 1859 devoted most of his attention to attacking Palmerston's policies; nevertheless he joined Palmerston as Chancellor of the Exchequer and so became one of the leaders of the new Liberal party. He introduced a series of budgets leading towards more complete free trade. His moderate parliamentary Reform Bill of 1866 was defeated, but his speeches at that time did much to mould Disraeli's Reform Bill the following year. At the retirement of Lord John Russell in 1868, Gladstone became leader of the Liberal party and Prime Minister. His first administration from 1868–74 was marked by a series of reform measures. The Anglican Church in

---

* He did not actually take his seat until January 1833.

I reland was disestablished, freeing the people from supporting a church to which most of them did not belong; the Irish Land Act of 1870 gave a degree of security to Irish tenant farmers. Religious tests for entry to Oxford and Cambridge were abolished; the secret ballot was introduced in elections; trade unions were legalised; and the judiciary was entirely reorganised. These changes provoked much opposition, and the Liberals were defeated in the election of 1874. In 1875 Gladstone relinquished leadership of the Liberal party, but did not retire from politics. The Near Eastern question and his alarm at Disraeli's adventurous foreign and colonial policy roused him to action, and by 1877 he was embarked on an active political campaign against the government. Gladstone was again Prime Minister from 1880–5, in 1886, and from 1892–4. The landmarks of his various ministries after Bagehot's time were the Land Act of 1881, the third Parliamentary Reform Act of 1884, the Boer War, which ended disastrously for England in 1881, the revolt in Egypt of Arabi Pasha, and the Irish Home Rule Bills, which were both rejected and the last of which brought Gladstone's last ministry to defeat. Gladstone died at Hawarden in 1898.

Mr. Gladstone[1]

W E believe that Quarterly essayists have a peculiar mission in relation to the characters of public men. We believe it is their duty to be personal. This idea may seem ridiculous to some of our readers; but let us consider the circumstances carefully. We allow that personality abounds already, that the names of public men are for ever on our lips, that we never take up a newspaper without seeing them. But this incessant personality is wholly fragmentary; it is composed of chance criticism on special traits, of fugitive remarks on temporary measures, of casual praise and casual blame. We can expect little else from what is written in haste, or is spoken without limitation. Public men must bear this criticism as they can. Those whose names are perpetually in men's mouths must not be pained if singular things are sometimes said of them. Still *some* deliberate truth should be spoken of our statesmen; and if Quarterly essayists do not speak it, who will? We fear it will remain unspoken.

Mr. Gladstone is a problem, and it is very remarkable that he should be a problem. We have had more than ordinary means for judging of him. He has been in public life for seven-and-twenty years; he has filled some of the most conspicuous offices in the state; he has been a distinguished member of the Tory party; he *is* a distinguished member of the Liberal party; he has brought forward many measures; he has passed many years in independent opposition, which is unquestionably the place most favourable to the display of personal peculiarities in Parliament; he is the greatest orator in the House of Commons; he never allows a single important topic to pass by without telling us what he thinks of it;—and yet, with all these data, we are all of us in doubt about him. What he will do, and what he will think, still more, why he will do it, and why he will think it, are *quæstiones vexatæ* at every political conjuncture. At the very last ministerial crisis, when the government of Lord Derby was on the verge of extinction, when

[1] *Speech of the Chancellor of the Exchequer on the Finance of the Year and the Treaty of Commerce with France.* Delivered in the House of Commons, on Friday, February 10 1860. Corrected by the Author. This essay was first published in the *National Review* for July 1860, Volume XI, pp. 219–43.

every voice on Lord John's resolution[2] was of critical importance, no one knew till nearly the last hour how Mr. Gladstone would vote; and in the end he voted against his present colleagues. The House of Commons gossips are generally wrong about him. Nor is the uncertainty confined to parliamentary divisions; it extends to his whole career. Who can calculate his future course? Who can tell whether he will be the greatest orator of a great administration; whether he will rule the House of Commons; whether he will be, as his gifts at first sight mark him out to be, our greatest statesman? or whether, below the gangway, he will utter unintelligible discourses; will aid in destroying many ministries and share in none; will pour forth during many hopeless years a bitter, a splendid, and a vituperative eloquence?

We do not profess that we can solve all the difficulties that are suggested even by the superficial consideration of a character so exceptional. We do not aspire to be prophets. Mr. Gladstone's destiny perplexes us—perhaps as much as it perplexes our readers. But we think that we can explain much of his past career; that many of his peculiarities are not so unaccountable as they seem; that a careful study will show us the origin of most of them; that we may hope to indicate some of the material circumstances and conditions on which his future course depends, though we should not be so bold as to venture to foretell it.

During the discussion on the budget, an old Whig who did not approve of it, but who had to vote for it, muttered of its author, 'Ah, Oxford on the surface, *but* Liverpool below.' And there is truth in the observation, though not in the splenetic sense in which it was intended. Mr. Gladstone does combine in a very curious way many of the characteristics which we generally associate with the place of his education with many of those which we usually connect with the place of his birth. No one can question the first part of the observation. No man has through life been more markedly an Oxford man than Mr. Gladstone. His *Church and State*, published after he had been several years in public life, was instinct with the very spirit of the Oxford of that time. His *Homer*, published the other day, bears nearly equal traces of the school in which he was educated. Even in his ordinary style there is a tinge half theological, half classical, which recalls the

[2] Lord John Russell moved a resolution on March 21 1859 to reject Lord Derby's parliamentary reform bill as not going far enough. The resolution was carried and Lord Derby asked for a dissolution and appealed unsuccessfully to the country.—Ed.

studies of his youth. Many Oxford men much object to the opinions of their distinguished representative, but none of them would deny that he remarkably embodies the peculiar results of the peculiar teaching of the place.

And yet he has something which his collegiate training never would have given him, which it is rather remarkable it has not taken away from him. There is much to be said in favour of the University of Oxford. No one can deny to it very great and very peculiar merits. But certainly it is not an exciting place, and its education operates as a narcotic rather than as a stimulant. Most of its students devote their lives to a single profession, and we may observe among them a kind of sacred torpidity. In many rural parsonages there are men of very great cultivation, who are sedulous in their routine duties, who attend minutely to the ecclesiastical state of the souls in their village, but who are perfectly devoid of general intellectual interests. They have no anxiety to solve great problems; to busy themselves with the speculations of their age; to impress their peculiar theology—for peculiar it is both in its expression and its substance—on the educated mind of their time. Oxford, it has been said, 'disheartens a man early.' At any rate, since Newmanism lost Father Newman, few indeed of her acknowledged sons attain decided eminence in our deeper controversies. Jowett she would repudiate, and Mansel is but applying the weapons of scepticism to the service of credulity. The most characteristic of Oxford men labour quietly, delicately, and let us hope usefully, in a confined sphere; they hope for nothing more, and wish for nothing more. Even in secular literature we may observe an analogous tone. The *Saturday Review* is remarkable as an attempt on the part of 'University men' to speak on the political topics and social difficulties of the time. And what do they teach us? It is something like this: 'So-and-so has written a tolerable book, and we would call attention to the industry which produces tolerable books. So-and-so has devoted himself to a great subject, and we would observe that the interest now taken in great subjects is very commendable. Such-and-such a lady has delicate feelings, which are desirable in a lady, though we know that they are contrary to the facts of the world. All common persons are doing as well as they can, but it does not come to much after all. All statesmen are doing as ill as they can, and let us be thankful that *that* does not come to much either.' We may search and search in vain through this repository of the results of

'University teaching' for a single truth which it has established, for a single high cause which it has advanced, for a single deep thought which is to sink into the minds of its readers. We have, indeed, a nearly perfect embodiment of the corrective scepticism of a sleepy intellect. 'A B says he has done something, but he has not done it; C D has made a parade of demonstrating this or that proposition, but he does not prove his case; there is one mistake in page 5, and another in page 113: a great history has been written of this or that century, but the best authorities as to that period have not been consulted, which, however, is not very remarkable, as there is nothing in them.' We could easily find, if it were needful, many traces of the same indifferent habit, the same apathetic culture, in the more avowed productions of Oxford men. The shrewd eye of Mr. Emerson, stimulated doubtless by the contrast to America, quickly caught the trait. 'After all,' says the languid Oxford gentleman of his story, 'there is nothing true and nothing new, and no matter!'

To this, as to every other species of indifferentism, Mr. Gladstone is the antithesis. Oxford has not disheartened *him*. Some of his colleagues would say they wished it had. He is interested in every thing he has to do with, and often interested too much. He proposes to put a stamp on contract notes with an eager earnestness as if the destiny of Europe, here and hereafter, depended upon its enactment. He cannot let any thing alone. 'Sir,' said an old distributor of stamps in Westmoreland, 'my head, sir, is worn out. I must resign. The Chancellor, sir, is imposing of things that I can't understand.' The world is not well able to understand them either. The public departments break down under the pressure of the industry of their superior. Mr. Gladstone is ready to work as long as his brain will hold together—to make speeches as long as he has utterance (words he is sure to have); but the subordinate officials will not work equally hard. They have none of the excitement of origination; they will not share the credit of success. They do, however, share the discredit of failure. In the high-pressure season of this year's budget, Acts of Parliament have been passed in which essential provisions were not to be found, in which what was intended to be enacted was omitted or exceeded, in which the marginal notes were widely astray of the text. In his literary works Mr. Gladstone is the same. His book on Homer is perhaps the most zealous work which this generation has produced. He has the enthusiasm of a German professor for the scholastic detail, for the exact meaning of word No. 1, for the precise number of times which word No. 2 is used by the poet; he has the enthusiasm of a lover for Helen, the enthusiasm of an orator for the speeches. Of his theological books we need not speak; every reader will recall the curious succession of needless *quæstiunculæ* by which their interest is marred.

Some of this energy Mr. Gladstone probably owes to the place of his birth. Lancashire is sometimes called 'America-and-water;' we suspect it is America and very little water. The excessive energy natural to half-educated men who have but a single pursuit cannot, indeed, in any part of England, produce the monstrous results which it occasionally produces in the United States; it is kept in check by public opinion, by the close vicinity of an educated world. But in its own pursuit, in commerce, we question whether New York itself is more intensely eager than Liverpool,—at any rate, it is difficult to conceive how it can be. Like several other remarkable men whose families belong to the place, Mr. Gladstone has carried into other pursuits the eagerness, the industry,—we are loth to say the rashness, but the boldness—which Liverpool men apply to the business of Liverpool. Underneath the scholastic polish of his Oxford education, he has the speculative hardihood, the eager industry of a Lancashire merchant.

Such is one of the principal peculiarities which Mr. Gladstone's character presents even to a superficial observer. But something more than superficial observation is necessary really to understand a character so complicated and so odd. We will touch upon some of the traits which are among the most important; and if our minute analysis has, or seems to have, some of the painfulness of a vivisection, we would observe that a defect of this kind is in some degree inseparable from the task we have undertaken. We cannot explain the special peculiarities of a singular man of genius without a somewhat elaborate and a half-metaphysical discussion.

It is needless to say that Mr. Gladstone is a great orator. Oratory is one of the pursuits as to which there is no error. The criterion is ready. Did the audience feel? were they excited? did they cheer? These questions, and others such as these, can be answered without a mistake. A man who can move the House of Commons— still, after many changes, the most severe audience in the world— must be a great orator. The most sincere admirers and the most eager depreciators of Mr. Gladstone are agreed on this point, and it is almost the only point on which they are agreed.

It will be well, however, to pause upon this characteristic of Mr. Gladstone's genius, and to examine the nature of it rather anxiously, because it seems to afford the true key to some of his most perplexing peculiarities. Mr. Gladstone has, beyond any other man in this generation, what we may call the oratorical *impulse*. We are in the habit of speaking of rhetoric as an art, and also of oratory as a faculty, and in both cases we speak quite truly. No man can speak without a special intellectual gift, and no man can speak well without a special intellectual training. But neither this gift of the intellect nor this education will suffice of themselves. A man must not only know what to say, he must have a vehement longing to get up and say it. Many persons, rather sceptical persons especially, do not feel this in the least. They see before them an audience,—a miscellaneous collection of odd-looking men,—but they feel no wish to convince them of any thing. 'Are not they very well as they are? They believe what they have been brought up to believe.' 'Confirm every man in *his own* manner of conceiving,' said one great sage; 'A savage among savages is very well,' remarked another. You may easily take away one creed and then not be able to implant another. 'You may succeed in unfitting men for their own purposes without fitting them for your purposes:'—thus thinks the *cui bono* sceptic. Another kind of sceptic is distrustful, and speaks thus: 'I know *I can't* convince these people; if I could, perhaps I would, but I can't. Only look at them! they have all kinds of crotchets in their heads. There is a wooden-faced man in spectacles. How can you convince a wooden-faced man in spectacles? And see that other man with a narrow forehead and compressed lips—is it any use talking to him? It is of no use; do not hope that mere arguments will impair the prepossessions of nature and the steady convictions of years.' Mr. Gladstone would not feel these sceptical arguments. He would get up to speak. He has the *didactic* impulse. He has the 'courage of his ideas.' He will convince the audience. He knows an argument which will be effective, he has one for one and another for another; he has an enthusiasm which he feels will rouse the apathetic, a demonstration which he thinks must convert the incredulous, an illustration which he hopes will drive his meaning even into the heads of the stolid. At any rate, he will try. He has *a nature*, as Coleridge might have said, towards his audience. He is sure, if they only knew what he knows, they would feel as he feels, and believe as he believes. And by this he conquers. This living faith, this enthusiasm, this confidence, call it as we will, is an extreme power in human affairs. One *croyant*, said the Frenchman, is a greater power than fifty *incrédules*. In the composition of an orator the hope, the credulous hope, that he will convince his audience is the *primum mobile*, it is the primitive incentive which is the spring of his influence and the source of his power. Mr. Gladstone has this incentive in perhaps an excessive and dangerous measure. Whatever may be right or wrong in pure finance, in abstract political economy, it is certain that no one save Mr. Gladstone would have come down with the budget of 1860 to the Commons of 1860. No other man would have believed that such a proposal would have a chance. Yet after the warning,—the disheartening warning of a reluctant cabinet,—Mr. Gladstone came down from a depressing sick-bed, with semi-bronchitis hovering about him, entirely prevailed for the moment, and three-parts conquered after all. We will not say that *the world* is given to men of this temperament and this energy; on the contrary, there is often a turn in the tide, the ovation of the spring may be the prelude to unpopularity in the autumn; but we see that *audiences* are given them; we see that unimpressible men are deeply moved by them,—that the driest topics of legislation and finance are for the instant affected by them,—that the prolonged effects of that momentary influence may be felt for many years, sometimes for centuries. The orator has a dominion over the critical instant, and the consequences of the decisions taken during that instant may last long after the orator and the audience have both passed away.

Nor is the didactic impulse the only one which is essential to a great political orator, nor is it the only one which Mr. Gladstone has. We say it with respect, but he has the *contentious* impulse. He illustrates the distinction between the pacific and the peaceful. On all great questions, on the controversies of states and empires, Mr. Gladstone is the most pacific of mankind. He hates the very rumour of war; he trusts in moral influences; he detests the bare idea of military preparations. He will not believe that preparations are necessary till the enemy is palpable. In the early part of 1853 he did not believe that the Russian war was impending; after the conversations of the Emperor Nicholas with Sir Hamilton Seymour, he proposed to Parliament a scheme for converting some portions of the national debt, which could only be successful if peace continued, and which, after the outbreak of the war, failed ignominiously. In 1860, *mutatis mutandis*, he has done the same. He staked his financial reputation upon a fine calculation; he gave us a budget in which the two ends scarcely met. The Chinese war came, and they no longer meet. We believe Mr. Gladstone so much hates the bare idea of the possibility of war, that after many warnings, after at least one failure, which must have been painful, and which should have been instructive, he has refused to take even the contingency of hostilities into his calculations. Some one said he was not only a Christian, but a morbid Christian. He cannot imagine that any thing so coarse as war will occur; when it does occur, he has a tendency to disapprove of it as soon as he can. During the Russian war he soon joined, in fact if not in name, the peace-at-all-price party; he exerted his finest reasonings and his most persuasive eloquence against a war which was commenced with his consent. At the present moment no Englishman, not Mr. Bright himself, *feels* so little the impulse to arm. He will not believe in a war till he sees men fighting. He is the most pacific of our statesmen in theory and in policy.—When you hear[3] Mr. Gladstone he is about the most combative. He can bear a good deal about the politics of Europe, but let a man question the fees on vatting, or the change in the game-certificate, or the stamp on bills of lading—what melodious thunders of loquacious wrath! The world, he hints, is likely to end at such observations, and that they should be made by the honourable member who made them,—'by the honourable member who four years ago said so-and-so, and five years before that moved, &c. &c.' The number of well-intentioned and tedious persons that Mr. Gladstone annually scolds into a latent dislike of him must be considerable.

But though we may smile at the minutiæ in which this contentious impulse sometimes shows itself, we must remember that the impulse itself is essential to a great political orator, every where in some degree, but in England especially. To be an influential speaker in the House of Commons, a man must be a great debater. He must excel not only in elaborate set speeches, but likewise in quick occasional repartee. No one but a rather contentious person will ever so excel. Mr. Fox, the most genial of men, was asked why he disputed so vehemently about some trifle or other. He said, 'I *must* do so; I can't live without discussion.' And this is the temperament of a great debater. It must be a positive pain to him to be silent under questionable assertions, to hear others saying that which he cannot agree with. An indifferent sceptic, such as we formerly spoke of, endures this very easily. 'He

---

[3] The *National Review* has 'see' for 'hear'.—p. 226.

thinks, no doubt, what the speaker is saying is quite wrong; but people do not understand what he is saying; very likely they won't understand the answer: besides, we've a majority; what is the use of arguing when you have a majority? Let us outvote him on the spot, and go to bed.' And so report says have whips argued to Mr. Gladstone, but he is ever ready. He takes up the parable of disputation at a quarter-past twelve, and goes on till he has exhausted argument, illustration, ingenuity, and research. To hardly any man have both the impulses of the political orator been given in so great a measure: the didactic orator is usually felicitous in exposition only; the great debater is, like Fox, only great when stung to reply by the *æstus* of contention. But Mr. Gladstone is by nature, by vehement overruling nature, great in both arts; he longs to pour forth his own belief; he cannot rest till he has contradicted every one else.

In addition to this oratorical temperament, Mr. Gladstone has in a high degree the most important intellectual talent of an orator; he has what we may call an adaptive mind. He has described this himself better than most people would describe it. 'Poets of modern times have composed great works, in ages that stopped their ears against them. 'Paradise Lost' does not represent the time of Charles the Second, nor the 'Excursion' the first decades of the present century. The case of the orator is entirely different. His work, from its very inception, is inextricably mixed up with practice. It is cast in the mould offered to him by the mind of his hearers. It is an influence principally received from his audience (so to speak) in vapour, which he pours back upon them in a flood. The sympathy and concurrence of his time is, with his own mind, joint parent of his work. He cannot follow nor frame ideals; his choice is, to be what his age will have him, what it requires in order to be moved by him, or else not to be at all. And as when we find the speeches in Homer, we know that there must have been men who could speak them, so, from the existence of units who could speak them, we know that there must have been crowds who could feel them.' We may judge of the House of Commons in the same way from the great 'budget' speech. No one, indeed, half guides, half follows the moods of his audience more quickly, more easily, than Mr. Gladstone does. There is a little playfulness in his manner, which contrasts with the dryness of his favourite topics, and the intense gravity of his earnest character. He has the same sort of control over the minds of those he is addressing that a good driver has over the animals he guides; he feels the minds of his hearers as the driver the mouths of his horses.

The species of intellect that is required for this task is pre-eminently the advocate's intellect. The instrument of oratory, at least of this kind of oratory, is the *argumentum ad hominem*. It is 'inextricably mixed up with practice.' It argues from the data furnished to him 'by the mind of his hearers.' He receives his premises from them 'like a vapour,' and pours out his 'conclusions upon them like a flood.' Such an orator may believe his conclusions, but he can rarely believe them for the reasons which he assigns for them. He may be an enthusiast in his creed, he may be a zealot in his faith, but not the less will he be an advocate in his practice; not the less will he catch at disputable premises because his audience accepts them; not the less will he draw inferences from them which suit his momentary purpose; not the less will he accept the most startling varieties of assertion, for he will imbibe from one audience a different 'vapour' of premises from that which he will receive from another; not the less will he have the chameleon-like character which we associate with a consummate advocate; not the less will he be one thing to-day, with the colour of one audience upon him; not the less will he be another to-morrow, when he has to address, persuade, and influence some different set of persons.

We scarcely think with Mr. Gladstone that this style of oratory is the very highest, though it is very natural that he should think so, for it exactly expresses the oratory in which he is the greatest living master. Mr. Gladstone's conception of oratory, in theory and in practice, is the oratory of Pitt, not the oratory of Chatham or of Burke: it is the oratory of adaptation. We do not deny that this is the kind of oratory which is most generally useful, the only kind which is commonly permissible, the only one which in general would not be a *bore*; but we must remember that there is an eloquence of great principles which the hearers scarcely heed, and do not accept—such as, in its highest parts, is the eloquence of Burke,—we must remember that there is an eloquence of great passions, of high-wrought intense feeling, which is nearly independent of the peculiarities of its audience, because it appeals to our elemental human nature,—which is the same, or much the same, in almost every audience, which is every where and always susceptible to the union of vivid genius and eager passion. Such as this last was, if we may trust tradition, the eloquence of Chatham, the source of his rare, magical, and occasional power. Mr. Gladstone has neither of these. Few speakers equally great have left so few passages which can be quoted,—so few which embody great principles in such a manner as to be referred to by coming generations. He has scarcely given us a sentence that lives in the memory; nor is his declamation, facile and effective as it always is, the very highest declamation: it is a nearly perfect expression of intellectualised sentiment, but it wants the volcanic power of primitive passion.

The prominence of advocacy in Mr. Gladstone's mind is in appearance, though not in reality, diminished by the purity and intensity of his zeal. There is an elastic heroism about him. When he begins to speak, we may know that we are going to hear what we shall not agree with. We may believe that the measures he proposes are mischievous; we may smile at the emphasis with which some of their minutiæ are insisted upon; but we inevitably feel that we have left the ordinary earth. We know that high sentiments will be appealed to by one who feels high sentiments; that strong arguments will be strongly stated by one who believes that argument should decide controversy. We know that we are beyond the realm of Sir William Hayter,[4] we have left behind us the doctrine that corruption is the ruling power in popular assemblies, that patronage is the purchase-money of power. We are not alleging that in the real world in which we live there is not some truth—more or less of truth—in these lower maxims; but they do not rule in Mr. Gladstone's world. He was not born to be a Secretary of the Treasury. If he tried his hand at it, he would perplex the borough attorneys out of their lives. And he *could* not keep the office a month; he would evince a real disgust at detestable requests, and guide with odd impulsiveness the delicate and latent machinery. His natural element is a higher one. He has—and it is one of the springs of great power—a real faith in the higher parts of human nature; he believes, with all his heart and soul and strength, that there *is* such a thing as truth; he has the soul of a martyr with the intellect of an advocate.

Another of Mr. Gladstone's characteristics is an extraordinary love of labour. We have alluded several times to his taste, we might almost say whimsical taste, for *minutiæ*. He is ready with whatever detail may be necessary on any subject, no matter of what kind. He covers his greatest schemes with a crowd of irrelevant appendages, till it is

[4] Sir William Hayter was the patronage secretary.—Ed.

425

difficult to see their outline. The budget of 1860 was large enough and complicated enough, one would have thought, in its essential irremovable features; but its author did not think so. He had supplementary provisions respecting game-certificates, respecting the transmission of newspapers by the post, respecting 'several other minuter changes with which he was almost ashamed to trouble the committee.' The labour necessary to all these accessories must have been enormous. Many of the alterations may have—must have—been lying ready in his memory, or in some old note-book, for many years. But the industry to furbish them up, to get them into a practicable, or even into a proposable, shape, would frighten not only most persons, but most laborious persons. And Mr. Gladstone's energy seems to be strictly intellectual. Nothing in his outward appearance indicates the iron physique that often carries inferior men through heavy tasks. Whatever he does that is peculiar, he does by the peculiarity of his mind. He is carried through his work, or seems to be so, by pure will, zeal, and effort.

The last characteristic of Mr. Gladstone which is very remarkable, or which we shall mention, is his scholastic intellect. We have not much of this in conspicuous men in the present day; but in former times there was a good deal of it. Lord Bacon had something like it in his eye when he spoke of minds which were not 'discursive' or skilful in discovering analogies, but were '*discriminative*' or skilful in detecting differences. The best scene for training this sort of intellect is the law-court. Lord Bacon must have seen much of it in the work of Gray's Inn when he was young, and traces of the discipline which he then underwent may perhaps be found even in books which were written by him many years afterwards. When, as in positive law, the first principles are fixed, there is no room for the highest originality; the only admissible controversy is whether a particular case comes or does not come within a particular principle. On this point there is room for endless distinctions and eternal hair-splitting. When the principles settled by authority are not entirely consistent, the function of this kind of distinguishing reason is even greater; it has to suggest nice refinements, which may reconcile the apparent differences between the principles themselves, as well as to settle the exact relation of the case on the facts to the doctrine of the authorities. Accordingly, the scholastic theologians of mediæval times were the most expert masters of the discriminative ratiocination which the world has ever seen.

They had to reconcile the recognised authorities of the Catholic Church—authorities vast in size, and scattered over centuries in time—with one another, with good sense, with the facts of special cases, with the general exigencies of the age. By their labour was formed that acute logic, that subtle, if unreal, philosophy which fell at the Reformation, when the authorities of the Catholic Church were no longer conclusive, and the art of arranging them was no longer important. We have learned to smile at the scholastic distinctions of former times; the inductive philosophy, which is now our most conspicuous pursuit, does not need them; the popular character of our ordinary discussion does not admit of them. In a free country we must use the sort of argument which plain men understand,—and plain men certainly do not appreciate or apprehend scholastic refinements. So at least we should say beforehand. Yet Mr. Gladstone is the states-man whose expositions have, for good or for evil, more power than those of any other; his voice is a greater power in the country of plain men than any other man's; nevertheless his intellect is of a thoroughly scholastic kind. He can distinguish between any two propositions; he never allowed, he could not allow, that any two were identical: if any one on either side of the House is bold enough to infer any thing from any thing, Mr. Gladstone is ready to deny that the inference is correct,—to suggest a distinction which he says is singularly im-portant,—to illustrate an apt subtlety which, in appearance at least, impairs the validity of the deduction. No schoolman could be readier at such work. We may find the same tendency of mind even more strikingly illustrated in his writings. At the time of the Gorham case, for example, he wrote a pamphlet on the Royal Supremacy. For the purposes of that case, it was of the last importance to determine the exact position of the Crown with respect to ecclesiastical affairs, and especially to the offence of heresy. The law at first seems distinct enough on the matter. The 1st of Elizabeth provides 'that such juris-dictions, privileges, superiorities, and preëminences, spiritual and ecclesiastical, as by any spiritual or ecclesiastical power or authority hath heretofore been or may lawfully be exercised or used for the visitation of the ecclesiastical state and persons, and for reformation, order, and correction of the same, and of all manner of errors, heresies, schisms, abuses, offences, contempts, and enormities, shall for ever, by authority of this present parliament, be united and annexed to the imperial crown of this realm.' These words would have seemed distinct and clear to most persons. They would have seemed to give to the Crown all the power it could wish to exercise—all that any spiritual authority had ever 'theretofore exercised'—all that any temporal authority could ever use. We should think it was clear that Queen Elizabeth would have applied a rather summary method of instruction to any one who attempted to limit the jurisdiction conferred by this enactment. If Mr. Gladstone had lived in the times about which he was writing, he might have had to make a choice between being silent and being punished; but in the times of Queen Victoria he is not subjected to an alternative so painful. He writes securely:

'We have now before us the terms of the great statute which, from the time it was passed, has been the actual basis of the royal authority in matters ecclesiastical: and I do not load these pages by reference to declarations of the Crown, and other public documents less in authority than this, in order that we may fix our view the more closely upon the expressions of what may fairly be termed a fundamental law in relation to the subject-matter before us.

'The first observation I make is this: there is no evidence in the words which have been quoted that the Sovereign is, according to the intention of the statute, the source or fountain-head of ecclesiastical jurisdiction. They have no trace of such a meaning, in so far as it exceeds (and it does exceed) the proposition, that this jurisdiction has been by law united or annexed to the Crown.

'I do not now ask what have been the glosses of lawyers—what are the reproaches of polemical writers—or even what attributes may be ascribed to prerogative, independent of statute, and therefore applicable to the Church before as well as after the Reformation. I must for the purposes of this argument assume what I shall never cease to believe until the contrary conclusion is demonstrated by fact, namely, that in the case of the Church justice is to be administered from the English bench upon the same principles as in all other cases— that our judges, or our judicial committees, are not to be our legislators—and that the statutes of the realm, as they are above the sacred majesty of the Queen, so are likewise above their ministerial interpreters. It was by statute that the changes in the position of the Church at that great epoch were measured—by statute that the position itself is defined; and the statute, I say, contains no trace of such a meaning as that the Crown either originally was the source and spring of ecclesiastical jurisdiction, or was to become such in virtue of the annexion to it of the powers recited; but simply bears the meanings, that it was to be master over its administration.'

So that which seems a despotism is gradually pruned down into a vicegerency. 'All the superiorities and preëminences spiritual and ecclesiastical,' which had ever been lawfully exercised are restricted to the single function of regulation; and by a judicious elaboration the Crown becomes scarcely the head of the Church, but only the *visitor* and corrector of it, as of several other corporations. We are not now concerned with the royal supremacy—we have no wish to hint or intimate an opinion on a vast legal discussion; but we *are* concerned with Mr. Gladstone. And we venture to say that a subtler gloss, more scholastically expressed, never fell from lawyer in the present age, or from schoolmen in times of old.

The great faculties we have mentioned give Mr. Gladstone, it is needless to say, an extraordinary influence in English politics. England is a country governed mainly by labour and by speech. Mr. Gladstone will work and can speak, and the result is what we see. With a flowing eloquence and a lofty heroism; with an acute intellect and endless knowledge; with courage to conceive large schemes, and a voice which will persuade men to adopt those schemes,—it is not singular that Mr. Gladstone is of himself a power in parliamentary life. He can do there what no one else living can do.

But the effect of these peculiar faculties is by no means unmixedly favourable. In almost every one of them some faulty tendency is latent, which may produce bad effects—in Mr. Gladstone's case has often done so, perhaps does so still. His greatest characteristic, as we have indicated, is the singular vivacity of his oratorical impulse. But great as is the immediate power which a vehement oratorical propensity, when accompanied by the requisite faculties, secures to the possessor, the advantage of possessing it, or rather of being subject to it, is by no means without an alloy. We have all heard that Paley said he knew nothing against some one *but* that he was a popular preacher. And Paley knew what he was saying. The oratorical impulse is a *disorganising* impulse. The higher faculties of the mind require a certain calm, and the excitement of oratory is unfavourable to that calm. We know that this is so with the hearers of oratory; we know that they are carried away from their fixed principles, from their habitual tendencies, by a casual and unexpected stimulus. We speak commonly of the power of the orator. But the orator is subject himself to much the same calamity. The force which carries away his hearers must first carry away himself. He will not persuade any of his hearers unless he has first succeeded, for the moment at least, in persuading his own mind. Every exciting speech is conceived, planned, and spoken with excitement. The orator feels in his own nerves, even in a greater degree, that electric thrill which he is to communicate to his hearers. The telling ideas take hold of him with a sort of *seizure*. They fasten close upon his brain. He has a sort of passionate impulse to tell them. He hungers, as a Greek would have said, till they are uttered. His mind is full of them. He has the vision of the audience in his mind. Until he has persuaded these men of these things, life is tame, and its other stimulants are uninteresting. So much excitement is evidently unfavourable to calm reflection and deliberation. Mr. Pitt is said to have thought more of the manner in which his measures would strike the House than of the manner in which, when carried, they would work. Of course he did—every great orator will do so, unless he has a supernatural self-control. An ordinary man sits down—say to make a budget: he arranges the accounts; adds up the figures; contrasts the effects of different taxes; works out steadily hour after hour their probable incidence, first of one, then of another. Nothing disturbs him. With the orator it is different. During that whole process he is disturbed by the vision of his hearers. How they will feel, how they will think, how they will like his proposals,—cannot but occur to him. He hears his ideas rebounding in the cheers of his hearers, he is disheartened at fancying that they will fall tamely on an inanimate and listless multitude. He is subject to two temptations; he is turned aside from the conceptions natural to the subject by an imagination of his audience; his own eager temperament naturally inclines him to the views which will excite that audience most effectually. The tranquil deposit of ordinary ideas is interrupted by the sudden eruption of volcanic forces. We know that the popular instinct suspects the judgment of great orators; we know that it does not give them credit for patient equanimity; and the popular instinct is right.

Nor is cool reflection the only higher state of mind which the oratorical impulse interferes with; we believe that it is singularly unfavourable also to the exercise of the higher kind of imagination. Several great poets have written good dramatic harangues; but no great practical orator has ever written a great poem. The creative imagination requires a singular calm: it is 'the still unravished bride of quietness,' as the poets say —'the foster-child of silence and slow time.' No great work has ever been produced except after a long interval of still and musing meditation. The oratorical impulse interferes with this. It breaks the exclusive brooding of the mind upon the topic; it brings in a new set of ideas, the faces of the audience and the passions of listening men; it *jerks* the mind, if the expression may be allowed, just when the delicate poetry of the mind is crystallising into symmetry. The process is stayed, and the result is marred.

Mr. Gladstone has suffered from both these bad effects of the oratorical temperament. His writings, even on imaginative subjects, even on the poetry of Homer, are singularly devoid of the highest imagination. They abound in acute remarks; they excel in industry of detail; they contain many animated and some eloquent passages. But there is no central conception running through them; there is no binding idea in them; there is nothing to fuse them together; they are elaborate aggregates of varied elements; they are not shaped and consolidated wholes. Nor, it is remarkable, has his style the delicate graces which mark the productions of the gentle and meditative mind; there is something hard in its texture, something dislocated in its connections. In his writings, where he is removed from the guiding check of the listening audience, he starts off, just where you least expect it. He hurries from the main subject to make a passing and petty remark. As he has not the central idea of his work vividly before him, he overlays it with tedious, accessory, and sometimes irrelevant detail.

His intellect has suffered also. He is undeniably defective in tenacity of first principle. Probably there is nothing which he would less like to have said of him, and yet it is certainly true. We speak of course of intellectual consistency, not of moral probity. And he has not an *adhesive* mind; such adhesiveness as he has is rather to projects than principles. We will give—it is all we have space to give—a single remarkable instance of his peculiar mutability. He has adhered to his project of reducing the amount levied in England by indirect taxation in the year 1860. He announced in 1853 that he would do so, and, what was singular enough, he was able to do it when the time came. But this superficial consistency must not disguise from us the entire inconsistency in abstract principle between the budget of 1853 and the budget of 1860. The most important element in English finance at present is the income-tax. In 1853 that tax was, Mr. Gladstone explained to us, an occasional, an exceptional, a sacred reserve. It had done much that was wonderful for our fathers in the French War; Sir Robert Peel had used it with magical efficiency in our own time; but it was to be kept for first-rate objects. In 1860 the income-tax has become the tax *of all work*. Whatever is to be done, whatever other tax is to be relinguished, it is but a penny more or a penny less of this ever-ready and omnipotent impost. We do not blame Mr. Gladstone for changing his opinion. We believe that an income-tax of moderate amount should be a permanent element in our financial system. We think that additions to it from time to time are the best ways of meeting any sudden demand for exceptional expenditure. But we cannot be unaware of the transition which he has made. His opinion as to our most remarkable tax has varied, not only in detail, but in essence. It was to be a rare and residuary agency; it is now a permanent and principal force. The inconsistency goes further. He used to think that he would be guilty of a 'high political offence' if he altered the present mode of assessing the income-tax, if he equalised the pressure on industrial and permanent incomes. But he is now ready to *consider* any plan with that object,—in other words, he is ready to do it if he can. A great change in his fundamental estimate of our greatest tax has made an evident and indisputable change in his mode of viewing proposed reforms and alterations in it.

Mr. Gladstone's inclination—his unconscious inclination for the art of advocacy—increases his tendency to suffer from the characteristic temptations of his oratorical temperament. It is scarcely necessary to say that professional advocacy is unfavourable to the philosophical investigation of truth; a more battered commonplace cannot be found any where. To catch at whatever turns up in favour of your own case; to be obviously blind to every thing which tells in favour of the case of your adversary; to imply doubts as to principles which it is not expedient to deny; to suggest with delicate indirectness the conclusive arguments in favour of principles which it is not wise directly to affirm,—these, and such as these, are the arts of the advocate. A political orator has them almost of necessity, and Mr. Gladstone is not exempt from them. Indeed, without any fault of his own, he has them, if not to an unusual extent, at least with a very unusual conspicuousness. His vehement temperament, his 'intense and glowing mind,' drive him into strong statements, into absolute and unlimited assertions. He lays down a principle of tremendous breadth to establish a detail of exceeding minuteness. He is not a 'hedging' advocate. He does not understand the art which Hume and Peel,—different as were their respective spheres,—practised with almost equal effect in those spheres. Mr. Gladstone dashes forth to meet his opponents. He will believe easily,—he will state strongly whatever may confute them. An incessant use of ingenious and unqualified principles is one of Mr. Gladstone's most prominent qualities; it is unfavourable to exact consistency of explicit assertion, and to latent consistency of personal belief. His scholastic intellect makes matters worse. He will show that any two principles are or may be consistent; that if there is an apparent discrepancy, they may still, after the manner of Oxford, 'be held together.' One of the most remarkable of Father Newman's Oxford sermons explains how science teaches that the earth goes round the sun, and how scripture teaches that the sun goes round the earth; and it ends by advising the discreet believer to accept *both*. Both, it is suggested, may be accommodations to our limited intellect—aspects of some higher and less discordant unity. We have often smiled at the recollection of the old Oxford training in watching Mr. Gladstone's ingenious 'reconcilements.' It must be pleasant to have an argumentative acuteness which is quite sure to extricate you, at least in appearance, from any intellectual scrape. But it is a dangerous weapon to use, and particularly dangerous to a very conscientious man. He will not use it unless he believes in its results; but he will try and believe in its results in order that he may use it. We need not spend further words in proving that a kind of advocacy at once acute, refined, and vehement, is unfavourable both to consistency of statement and to tenacious sluggishness of belief.

In this manner the disorganising effects of his greatest peculiarities have played a principal part in shaping Mr. Gladstone's character and course. They have helped to make him annoy the old Whigs, confound the country gentlemen, and puzzle the nation generally. They have contributed to bring on him the long array of depreciating adjectives, 'extravagant,' 'inconsistent,' 'incoherent,' and 'incalculable.'

Mr. Gladstone's intellectual history has aggravated the unfavourable influence of his characteristic tendencies. Such a mind as his required, beyond any man's, the early inculcation of a steadying creed. It required that the youth, if not the child, should be father to the man; it required that a set of fixed and firm principles should be implanted in his mind in its first intellectual years,—that those principles should be precise enough for its guidance, tangible enough to be commonly intelligible, true enough to stand the wear and tear of ordinary life. The tranquil task of developing coherent principle might have calmed the vehemence of Mr. Gladstone's intellectual impulses,—might have steadied the impulsive discursiveness of his nature. A settled and plain creed which was in union with the belief of ordinary men might have kept Mr. Gladstone in the common path of plain men—might have made him intelligible and safe. But he has had no such good fortune. He began the world with a vast religious theory; he embodied it in a book on Church and State; he defended it, as was said, mistily,—at any rate, he defended it in a manner which requires much careful pains to appreciate, and much preliminary information to understand; he puzzled the ordinary mass of English Churchmen; he has been half out of sympathy with them ever since. The creed which he had chosen, or which his Oxford training stamped upon him, was one not likely to be popular with common Englishmen: it has a scholastic appearance and a mystical essence which they dislike almost equally; but this was not its worst defect. It was a theory which broke down when it was tried. It was a theory with definite practical consequences, which no one in these days will accept—which no one in these days will propose. It was a theory to be shattered by the slightest touch of real life, for it had a definite teaching which was inconsistent with the facts of that life—which all persons who were engaged in it were, on some ground or other, unanimous in rejecting. In Mr. Gladstone's case it has been shattered. He maintained that a visible Church existed upon earth; that every state was bound to be directed by that Church; that all members of that state should, if possible, be members of that Church; that at any rate none of the members should be utterly out of sympathy with her; that the state ought to aid her in her characteristic work, and refrain from aiding all her antagonists in that work; that within her own sphere the Church, though thus aided, is substantially independent; that she has an absolute right to elect her own bishops, to determine her own creed, to make her own definitions of orthodoxy and heresy. This is the high Oxford creed; and, in all essential points, it was Mr. Gladstone's first creed. But a curious series of instructive events proved that England at least would not adopt it,—that the actual Church of England is not the Church of which it speaks,—that the actual English state is by no means the state of which it speaks. The additional endowment of the Maynooth College which Sir Robert Peel proposed was an express relinquishment of the principle that the Church of England had an exclusive right to assistance from the state; it proved that the Conservative party—the special repository of constitutional traditions—was ready to aid a different and antagonistic communion. The removal of the Jewish disabilities struck a still deeper blow: it proved that persons who could not be said to participate in even the rudiments of Anglican doctrine might be prime ministers and rulers in England. The theory of the exclusive union of a visible Church with a visible State vanished into the air. The real world would not endure it. We fear it must be said that the theory of the substantial independence of the English Church has vanished too. The case of Dr. Hampden proved conclusively that the intervention of the English Church in the election of her bishops was an ineffectual ceremony; that it could not be galvanised into effective life; that it was one of those lingering relics of the past which the steady English people are so loth to disturb.[5] Undisputed practice shows that the Prime Minister, who is clearly [a] secular prince, is the dispenser of ecclesiastical dignities. And the judgment of her Majesty's Council in the Gorham case went further yet. It touched on the finest and tenderest point of all. It decided that, on the critical question, heresy or no heresy, the final appeal was not to an ecclesiastical court, but to a lay court—to a court, not of saintly theologians, but of tough old lawyers, to men of the world most worldly. The Oxford dream of an independent Church, the Oxford dream of an exclusive Church, are both in practice forgotten; their very terms are strange in our ears; they have no reference to real life. Mr. Gladstone has had to admit this. He has voted for the endowment of Maynooth; he has voted for the admission of Jews to the House of Commons; he has acquiesced in the Hampden case; he sees daily the highest patronage of the Church distributed by Lord Palmerston, the very man who, on any high-church theory, ought not to dispense it, to the very men who, on any high-church theory, ought not to receive it. He wrote a pamphlet on the Gorham case, but he does not practically propose to alter the constitution of the judicial committee of the Privy Council; he has never proposed to bring in a bill for that purpose; he acquiesces in the supreme decision of the most secular court which can exist over the most peculiarly ecclesiastical questions that can be thought of. These successive changes do credit to Mr. Gladstone's good sense; they

[5] Dr. Hampden was made Bishop of Hereford by Lord John Russell in 1847 despite strong opposition from many of the clergy who accused him of 'rationalism'.—Ed.

show that he has a susceptible nature, that he will not live out of sympathy with his age. But what must be the effect of such changes upon any mind, especially on a delicate and high-toned mind. They tend, and must tend, to confuse the first principles of belief; to disturb the best landmarks of consistency; to leave the mind open to attacks of oratorical impulse; to foster the catching habit of advocacy; to weaken the guiding element in a disposition which was already defective in that element. The 'movement of 1833,' as Father Newman calls it, has wrecked many fine intellects, has broken many promising careers: it could not do either for Mr. Gladstone, for his circumstances were favourable, and his mental energy was far too strong; but it has done him harm, nevertheless; it has left upon his intellect a weakening strain and a distorting mark.

Mr. Gladstone was a likely man to be enraptured with the first creed with which he was thrown, and to push it too far. He wants the warning instincts. Some one said of him formerly, 'He may be a good Christian, but he is an atrocious pagan;' and the saying is true. He has not a trace of the protective morality of the old world, of the *modus in rebus*, the μέσον, the shrinking from an extreme which are the prominent characteristics of the ethics of the old world, which are still the guiding creed of the large part of the world that is scarcely altered after two thousand years. And this much we may concede to the secular moralists,—unless a man have from nature a selective tact which shuns the unlimited, unless he have a detective instinct which unconsciously but sensitively shrinks from the extravagant, he will never enjoy a placid life, he will not pass through a simple and consistent career. The placid moderation which is necessary to coherent success cannot be acquired, it must be born.

Perhaps we may seem already to have more than accounted for the prominence of Mr. Gladstone's characteristic defects. We may seem to have alleged sufficient reasons for his being changeable and impulsive, a vehement advocate, and an audacious financier. But we had other causes to assign which have aggravated these faults. We shall not, indeed, after what we have said, venture to dwell on them at length. We will bear in mind the precept, 'If you wish to exhaust your readers, exhaust your subject.' But we will very slightly allude to them.

A writer like Mr. Gladstone, fond of deriving illustration from the old theology, might speak of public life in England as an *economy*.

It is a world of its own, far more than most Englishmen are aware of. It presents the characters of public men in a disguised form; and by requiring the seeming adoption of much which is not real, it tends to modify and to distort much which is real. An English statesman in the present day lives by following public opinion; he may profess to guide it a little; he may hope to modify it in detail; he may help to exaggerate and to develop it; but he hardly hopes for more. Many seem not willing to venture on so much. And what does this mean except that such a statesman has to follow the varying currents of a varying world; to adapt his public expressions, if not his private belief, to the tendencies of the hour; to be in no slight measure the slave—the petted and applauded slave, but still the slave—of the world which he seems to rule. Nor is this all. A minister is not simply the servant of the public, he is likewise the advocate of his colleagues. No one supposes that a Cabinet can ever agree; when did fifteen able men—fifteen able men, more or less rivals—ever agree on any thing? We are aware that differences of opinion, more or less radical, exist in every Cabinet; that the decisions of every Cabinet are in nearly every case modified by concession; that a minority of the Cabinet frequently dissents from them. Yet all this latent discrepancy of opinion is never hinted at, much less is it ever avowed. A Cabinet minister comes down to the House habitually to vote and occasionally to speak in favour of measures which he much dislikes, from which he has in vain attempted to dissuade his colleagues. The life of a great minister is the life of a great advocate. No life can be imagined which is worse for a mind like Mr. Gladstone's. He was naturally changeable, susceptible, prone to unlimited statements—to vehement arguments. He has followed a career in which it is necessary to follow a changing guide, and to obey more or less, but always to some extent, a fluctuating opinion; to argue vehemently for tenets which you dislike; to defend boldly a given law to-day, to propose boldly that the same law should be repealed to-morrow. Accumulated experience shows that the public life of our parliamentary statesmen is singularly unsteadying, is painfully destructive of coherent principle; and we may easily conceive how dangerous it must be to a mind like Mr. Gladstone's— to a mind, by its intrinsic nature, impressible, impetuous, and unfixed.

What, then, is to be the future course of the remarkable statesman whose excellences and whose faults we have ventured to analyse at such length? No wise man would venture to predict. A wise man does not predict much in this complicated world, least of all will predict the exact course of a perplexing man in perplexing circumstances. But we will hazard three general remarks.

First, Mr. Gladstone is essentially a man who cannot impose his creed *on* his time, but must learn his creed *of* his time. Every parliamentary statesman must, as we have said, do so in some measure; but Mr. Gladstone must do so above all men. The vehement orator, the impulsive advocate, the ingenious but somewhat unsettled thinker, is the last man from whom we should expect an original policy, a steady succession of mature and consistent designs. Mr. Gladstone may well be the expositor of his time, the advocate of its conclusions, the admired orator in whom it will take pride; but he cannot be more. Parliamentary life rarely admits the autocratic supremacy of an original intellect; the present moment is singularly unfavourable to it; Mr. Gladstone is the last man to obtain it.

Secondly, Mr. Gladstone will fail if he follow the seductive example of Sir Robert Peel. It is customary to talk of the unfavourable circumstances in which the latter was placed, but in one respect those circumstances were favourable. He had very unusual means of learning the ideas of his time. They were forced upon him by a loud and organised agitation. The repeal of the Corn-Laws, the repeal[6] of the Catholic disabilities,—the two acts by which he will be remembered,—were not chosen by him, but exacted from him. The world around him clamoured for them. But no future statesman can hope to have such an advantage. The age in which Peel lived was an age of destruction; the measures by which he will be remembered were abolitions. We have now reached the term of the destructive period. We cannot abolish all our laws; we have few remaining with which educated men find fault. The questions which remain are questions of construction,—how the lower classes are to be admitted to a share of political power, without absorbing the whole power; how the natural union of Church and State is to be adapted to an age of divided religious opinion, and to the necessary conditions of a parliamentary government. These, and such as these, are the future topics of our home policy. And on these the voice of the nation will never be very distinct. Destruction is easy, construction is very difficult. A statesman who will hereafter learn what our real public opinion is, will not have to regard loud

[6] The *National Review* has 'the revival of the Catholic disabilities' but 'repeal' is clearly meant—p. 241.

agitators, but to disregard them; will not have to yield to a loud voice, but to listen for a still small voice; will have to seek for the opinion which is treasured in secret rather than for that which is noised abroad. If Mr. Gladstone will accept the conditions of his age; if he will guide himself by the mature, settled, and cultured reflection of his time, and not by its loud and noisy organs; if he will look for that which is thought rather than for that which is said,—he may leave a great name, be useful to his country, may steady and balance his own mind. But if not, not. The coherent efficiency of his career will depend on the guide which he takes, the index which he obeys, the δαίμων which he consults.

There are two topics which are especially critical. Mr. Gladstone must not object to war because it is war, or to expenditure because it is expenditure. Upon these two points Mr. Gladstone has shown a tendency,—not, we hope, an uncontrollable tendency, but still a tendency—to differ from the best opinion of the age. He has been unfortunately placed. His humane and Christian feelings are opposed to war; he has a financial ideal which has been distorted, if not destroyed, by a growing expenditure. But war is often necessary; finance is but an end; money is but a means. A statesman who would lead his age must learn its duties. It may be that the defence of England, the military defence, is one of our duties; if so, we must not sit down to count the cost. If so, it is not the age for arithmetic. If so, it is for our statesmen—it is especially for Mr. Gladstone, who is the most splendidly gifted amongst them—to sacrifice cherished hopes; to forego treasured schemes; to put out of their thoughts the pleasant duties of a pacific time; to face the barbarism of war; to vanquish the instinctive shrinkings of a delicate mind.

Lastly, Mr. Gladstone must beware how he again commits himself to a long period of bewildering opposition. Office is a steadying situation. A minister has means of learning from his colleagues, from his subordinates, from unnumbered persons who are only too ready to give him information what the truth is, and what public opinion is. Opposition, on the other hand, is an exciting and a misleading situation. The bias of every one who is so placed is to oppose the ministry. Yet on a hundred questions the ministry are likely to be right. They have special information, long consultations, skilled public servants to guide them. On most points there is no misleading motive. Every minister decides, to the best of his ability, upon most of the questions which come before him. A bias to oppose him, therefore, is always dangerous. It is peculiarly dangerous to those in whom the contentious impulse is strong, whose life is in debate. If Mr. Gladstone's mind is to be kept in a useful track, it must be by the guiding influence of office; by an exemption from the misguiding influence of opposition.

No one desires more than we do that Mr. Gladstone's future course should be enriched, not only with oratorical fame, but with useful power. Such gifts as his are amongst the rarest that are given to men; they are amongst the most valuable; they are singularly suited to our parliamentary life. England cannot afford to lose such a man. If in the foregoing pages we have seemed often to find fault, it has not been for the sake of finding fault. It is *necessary* that England should comprehend Mr. Gladstone. If the country have not a true conception of a great statesman, his popularity will be capricious, his power irregular, and his usefulness insecure.

Oxford and Mr. Gladstone [1]

FORTY years ago Mr. Canning said, in a speech on Catholic Emancipation, 'I was warned when the question first crossed my path that I must relinquish the most cherished object of my life—the representation of the University of Oxford. I made my choice. The occasion is past, I will speak of it no more.' Oxford has been curiously consistent. When Mr. Canning so spoke, her voice in Parliament was a peculiar voice. It was a conspicuous advantage,—a 'blue ribbon' in the speech of those aristocratic days, when visible symbols had a meaning, that the mere largeness of the cultivated world prevent their having now. To sit then for Oxford gave then of itself an unequalled prestige both in the House and out of it. The political world of that day, mostly educated at two universities, recognised in the most fascinating and aristocratic of these universities an inherent charm. All this is now gone. Parliament has been reformed, and a race of men educated 'nowhere,' as would have been said once, but quite able intellectually to hold their own, throng the lower House. And Oxford has herself to blame. It is she that has dissolved the charm which she inherited. The new race of members were deeply susceptible of cultivated influence, or why did Mr. Gladstone's words so fascinate Liverpool and Manchester? But Oxford will choose her worst men and will not choose her best. The cause lies deep in her teaching and that of the public schools. She gives, as Eton gives, a splendid teaching to the few, and a contemptible teaching to the many. Consequently, the products of her teaching in no way represent her teachers. The mass of men who, for the sake of orders, or for any other reason, take a common degree, no more represent Oxford than a common Eton fag represented the knowledge of Dr. Hawtrey. You cannot make a good university constituency where the necessary attainments of a graduate represent a feeble and irregular culture. To create great men is not enough; Oxford has quite done her share of that in this generation.

[1] This article was first published in *The Economist* for July 22 1865, Volume XXIII, pp. 877–8. On July 18 1865 Gladstone had been defeated at Oxford a seat he was defending in the general election of that year. Gladstone had represented Oxford in parliament for 18 years.

To cite but one case, she has trained both Newman and Jowett, the greatest leader of Anglican anti-liberalism and the greatest leader of Anglican liberalism which the age has produced. But Oxford has produced (as we have heard a tutor regret) a 'stupid average,' and it is this average which rules the poll. It is this average which excluded Mr. Canning, which rejected Sir Robert Peel, which rejected Mr. Gladstone,—which, in a word, refused to elect the three statesmen who were in their generations the best products of her teaching, and who were alike in this—that they each at least tried to combine the true Conservatism and the true Liberalism—the inheritance of the past and the necessities of the present. Everybody understands the errors of their fathers, but it is not every Oxford man who sees that in rejecting Mr. Gladstone he has repeated the error of those who rejected Sir Robert Peel and excluded Mr. Canning.

It is better, however, for England that Oxford has decided as she has. It is of great importance that the statesmen of England should sit for constituencies of a proper class. There are two sorts of seats, one of which we may call special and peculiar, and the other of which we may call neutral and judicial. The first have particular opinions and interests; they have singular wants and notions, and their representatives are sent to express them. Accordingly, these representatives assume almost inevitably the character of advocates. They have a case which they wish to bring before the House; they have a lesson to teach it foreign to the experience and different from the notions of ordinary educated men. There ought to be some special constituencies in Parliament for every such special type of thought—some for the shipowner, some for the manufacturer, some for the landlord, some for the clergy; but there ought to be a vastly greater number of constituencies of no aberrant type, no eccentric idiosyncracy, which simply represent the common voice of educated men, which must hear what the commissioned advocates of classes allege, weigh their arguments, estimate their often conflicting assertions, and in the last resort decide. Oxford is, as will be admitted both by her admirers and by her critics, a special constituency, and therefore she ought not to be represented by a ruling statesman. She must enforce upon him special notions, singular ideas, unusual thoughts; she must, if she does her duty, press upon him the advocacy of her characteristic creed. But a great statesman cannot be a class advocate. He should sit for a constituency which is the judge of other constituencies—which can hear and listen—which represents the general voice of all England, not the special dialect of any bit of England.

South Lancashire is, upon the whole, and subject to some exceptions, such a constituency. There was an idea in some not very instructed quarters, that if Mr. Gladstone were returned for South Lancashire, he would be pressed into Radicalism by his constituents. We will not discuss the personal compliment to Mr. Gladstone, but look at the constituency. South Lancashire returns two Conservatives, Liverpool two more, and Manchester excludes Mr. Bright's brother because he is Mr. Bright's brother. South Lancashire is a constituency which will wish its representative to coincide in judgment with the entire people of England.

Oxford could have done Mr. Gladstone no greater service than by compelling him to make these speeches at this critical moment. They are statesmanlike speeches. The words in the Manchester speech on reform will remove many misconceptions:—'I have ever been, and I still am, opposed to every sudden and violent change. Never have I spoken a word which, fairly interpreted, gave the smallest countenance to the schemes—if such schemes there be—of any who might view with indifference the passing of precipitate and extensive measures that might endanger by their very suddenness the true and just balance of the powers of the constitution; but this I say, that the true and just balance of those powers would not be destroyed, but improved, by a fair and liberal and sensible—not a sweeping nor overwhelming—admission of our brethren of the labouring community to the privileges of the suffrage.' And the whole of these speeches advertise his genius. No other man could make one such oration at three o'clock in the afternoon, and another great oration at eight o'clock in the evening. The impression of his facility in Manchester is wonderful. They say, 'He goes down to make a great speech at the Free Trade Hall just as another man goes to eat his lunch.' So much effectual, telling, producible power has not been exhibited in England for many a long day. One fact is very significant. The practical question now is, Shall Mr. Disraeli or Mr. Gladstone lead the next House of Commons? In Mr. Gladstone's case, there has been vehement criticism and eager admiration. He has, to quote again a phrase of Schiller which he himself once quoted, 'been much hated and also much beloved.' But of Mr. Disraeli there has been no affectionate word. No one has ventured to say that he wishes to have any confidence in him, or that he wishes to be led by him.

Mr. Gladstone's Resolutions[1]

MR. GLADSTONE'S resolutions on the Irish Church—wise and
necessary as they seem to us—are, no doubt, likely to be accepted
with considerable reluctance by a good many honest Liberals. No
institution, which has lived for 300 years, and which has doubtless
improved rather than deteriorated of late years, can be swept away
by a *coup de main* without giving rise to many compunctions and many
groans. The resolutions of which Mr. Gladstone has given notice
point, without any opening for doubt, to the absolute termination,
within the limits of the generation now living, of all state-payment of
the officials of the Anglican Church in Ireland. What the state will do
with the property over which it will thus resume its right of disposal,
as the individual claimants for the revenue die, is a question, of course,
for any government which may carry the proposed disendowment into
execution. In all probability, Mr. Bright's advice would be followed,
and something at least given in absolute property to each of the three
great churches in Ireland, to break their fall to voluntaryism—something to the Protestant Church, in order not to strip it at once of all
revenue independent of voluntary contributions; something to the
Presbyterians, to break the blow of the withdrawal of the *regium
donum*; something, also, to the Catholics, to compensate for the disendowment of Maynooth, and to put them in a position of perfect
equality with the rival sects. But this proposal is not embodied in Mr.
Gladstone's resolutions, though it has received his emphatic approval,
and seems to be the natural course. It would be cruel not to recognise
that a Church, which has been hitherto aided by the State, can hardly
attain the position of a flourishing voluntary Church in a single generation. Nearly all the flourishing voluntary churches have attained their
position by the labour and sacrifice of many generations. A Church

---

[1] This article was first published in *The Economist* for March 28 1868, volume XXVI,
pp. 347–8. On March 16 1868 in Parliament Gladstone had first declared his support for
disestablishment of the Irish Church. He followed this up on March 23 by giving notice
of three resolutions to the effect that establishment in Ireland should be brought to an
end.

taught to depend on external aid could not be expected to take even a fair relative position in the race, if it were stripped naked and driven out into the wilderness without any property of its own. The state must and will recognise its responsibility for having encouraged the habit of dependence upon itself, and will be morally bound to give it a fair start in its new career when the old career is finally terminated. But though there can be no doubt that any government which undertakes the duty of carrying Mr. Gladstone's resolutions into effect will be susceptible, perhaps even too susceptible to considerations of this kind, they are very properly not embodied in Mr. Gladstone's resolutions; which affirm (1) the necessity of disestablishment, subject to the vested interests now in being; (2) the duty of preventing the creation of new vested interests by the further exercise of public patronage; and (3) the expediency of an immediate address to the Crown, requesting the Queen 'to place at the disposal of Parliament her interest in the temporalities of the archbishoprics, bishoprics, and other ecclesiastical dignities and benefices.' The two latter resolutions are the mere logical consequents of the first,—proving that the first is not to be a mere abstract resolution, but to take effect at once. Taken together, they will mean, if carried, that the House of Commons has finally condemned the Irish Church, though without expressing any opinion as to the proper mode of dealing with the public property to be gradually acquired as a result of this resumption by the state of its ecclesiastical property and endowments. And that there will be many politicians, and not a few Liberals, who will stand aghast at the audacity of this resolve, is only human nature. They will say, of course, that this Church property has never been really coveted by the Catholics; that it supports a very popular, genial, if not always a very hard-worked, body of men; that, in Ireland, as Mr. Disraeli said the other day, the wise policy is rather 'to create than to destroy;' that the resolutions, if carried, will destroy much and create nothing; that the Protestants will be outraged, and be more disposed than ever to wreak their outraged feelings on the Catholics; that the Catholics, though they may feel their pride somewhat gratified, will gain nothing to make them thoroughly grateful, and to make them compensate by their gratitude for the new irritation inspired in the Protestants; in short, that while you make one section (the minority) fiercely vindictive, you will lend very little warmth to the loyalty of the other and major section. Finally, it will be constantly reiterated, as Mr.

Disraeli's letter to the Earl of Dartmouth warns us that the Prime Minister himself intends to insist, that it is not so much an Irish as an English question which is now at issue; that the union between Church and State is threatened in Great Britain as much as in Ireland; and that if that union is severed in the latter island, it cannot long stand in the former. All this will be said, and will probably be believed to be true, by some Liberals, as well as many Tories.

Still, every genuine Liberal should find it easy to see his way through these objections, and to give a cordial and unflinching support to Mr. Gladstone's resolutions. For we may remark that if these objections are good at all, they are good for an indefinite time, and really mean that you should never begin at all to undo the injustice, theoretically admitted, of applying national property to sectional uses. There is no more abruptness in what is now proposed than in any action long delayed, which follows only too tardily in the path of conviction. For years politicians have been saying strongly, and saying continually, that the only clear grievance of Ireland is the established Protestantism,—that neither England nor Scotland would tolerate for a moment an established Catholicism,—that the Protestant establishment in Ireland is quite indefensible, and that it is only waiting the growth of an equitable opinion to be removed. This is what we have all been saying,—the tremblers no less than the resolute,—for it has always been an intellectual satisfaction to the tremblers to admit a theoretical case, on condition that they are not asked practically to act upon it. But now, when there seems a fair chance that opinion is ripe to remove this last grievance under which Ireland is smarting, and to give some practical evidence of our wish to govern Ireland as we would wish to be governed ourselves, the very persons who professed to be waiting for an equitable opinion to ripen, are the first to take offence at the notion that it is already ripe enough. They are quite willing, it seems, to hope for a fitting season in future, on condition that that future shall never turn into a present. It is part of their faith in the grievance, that it shall never be redressed till every one shall be equally willing to redress it. They now point out, with irresistible truth, that if you are to right the Catholics, you must irritate the Protestants, who think the present system perfectly just;—and, on that account, they would have us sit still until Protestant churchmen, whose communion profits by the establishment, are as willing as the Catholics to see their endowments withdrawn. We call this mere political trifling. To admit an injustice which you decline to remedy until those who do not admit it, and find their interests in not admitting it, agree with you, is simply to declare that you hold a conviction to which you never intend to accommodate your conduct. Yet this is precisely what these Liberals will do, who vote against Mr. Gladstone's resolutions on the ground that they are premature, when the only evidence that they *are* premature is their own voting, and the voting of those who think with them. Men who declare that Mr. Gladstone is precipitate, and manufacture for themselves the only proof that he is so by voting against him, really demonstrate not that he is precipitate, but that they are reluctant,—and averse to believe that the hour for justice has arrived. If the followers hang back, the leader may be said to be precipitate,—but, then, you cannot fairly say that they hang back *because* he is precipitate, since he would not be precipitate unless they chose to hang back. If this went on for another twenty years, and the tremblers still hung back, the leader would be just as precipitate then as now. All that Mr. Gladstone can fairly be asked to consider is, whether or not there is a wide-spread and deep conviction in the Liberal party that the Irish minority Church is a grievance which England, for herself, would never tolerate; and, next, whether there is not at the present moment a very eager and timely desire among the Liberals to prove at once to Ireland that we intend to wash our hands of the policy of inflicting on her, because we are strong, what we would never tolerate for ourselves, and what we well know that Ireland would never tolerate if allowed to govern herself after her own fashion. If both these propositions are true, Mr. Gladstone has no right to deem his resolutions premature. They are not premature in relation to Liberal *conviction*, and the leader of a party is scarcely the man to accuse it openly of choosing to approve a principle of action on which it has no intention of acting.

This premised, we are in a position to traverse directly all the excuses put forward for delay. It is quite true, as Mr. Disraeli said, that in Ireland, as a general rule, it is better to create than to destroy. But *which* creates the most and destroys the least?—the policy which creates faith in the justice of government amongst four-fifths of the population, and destroys a monopoly enjoyed by one-fifth,—or the policy which maintains, that is, declines to destroy, the latter, and thereby continues to prevent or arrest the growth of all hearty Irish faith in our British justice. The repeal of the Corn Law was in this sense a destructive policy; it destroyed a monopoly; it destroyed the confidence of the monopolists in government; but it created a new confidence in the millions, a new cordiality between the Government and the governed, and in this alone, apart from the stimulus it gave to trade, it created infinitely more than it destroyed.

Then, it is said that you will create a far more bitter animosity in the Protestant Irish than you can compensate by the increased loyalty of the Catholic Irish. Possibly you may: the privileged classes never like to be reduced to equality with the unprivileged classes; they are sullen for a time; they growl and sulk; but they are not dangerous, for they well know it is useless to agitate for a restoration of privileges. The intrinsic justice of the case tells against them after all, whether they admit it or not. Put a real slur on the Irish Protestants,—subject them to a disability of any kind to which you refuse to subject the Catholics, and you would never hear the end of it; you would have agitation, resistance, rebellion, if you did not yield. But it cannot be so with relation to any policy which simply cancels the unjust favour shown to them, and they well know it. They will growl for a time, but they well know their own impotence. They will accommodate themselves to equality as fast as they can, and in the meantime, they will not be insane enough to swell the political disaffection. They will never cry out for a republic of Catholic Irishmen in which they themselves would have no influence, and perhaps no liberty. We confess that the temporary anger of the Irish Protestants—and it can be only temporary—seems to us perfectly insignificant, if it be incurred in pursuance of a strictly just policy towards the whole nation. At all events, it is a plea which is either good for ever against all reform, or not good at all,—and least of all now, when we wish to mark specially our desire to do justice towards those who accuse us of having for centuries been partial to the few Protestants of Ireland, and unjust to the millions.

Finally, to Mr. Disraeli's argument, that the fall of the establishment in Ireland will be the death-blow of the establishments in England and Scotland, we can only say that we believe exactly the reverse to be true. You might just as well say that to suspend the *habeas corpus* in Ireland, where Fenianism is wide-spread, involves its suspension in England and Scotland, where it scarcely exists at all. To abolish an institution which is utterly unsuited to the wishes and wants of the country, furnishes no argument at all for abolishing one that is perfectly well suited to the wishes and wants of the country. On the contrary, the former discredits the latter far more than the latter can palliate the former. If we are to extend all we do in Ireland to England, without having the motives here which we have there, we may just as well do the same for India and Australia, and Canada and Jamaica. There cannot be a sillier argument than that which proceeds upon identity of system for totally different circumstances. You might as well wear thin things in winter because you wear them in summer, as abolish an establishment which is popular and dear to the nation, because you have abolished another establishment which is unpopular and unwelcome to another nation. When men are driven to such arguments as these, they are driven to their last defences, and may as well give up the contest at once.

Mr. Gladstone's Chapter
of Autobiography[1]

MR. GLADSTONE'S account of his change of opinion on the subject
of the Irish Church is full of character, both intellectual and moral.
The intellectual interest lies in the curious process by which the very
substance of his present creed on the relation of Church to State is
developed from that minute germ of *exception* to his former creed
which he stated incidentally in his letter to Mr. (afterwards Lord)
Macaulay in 1839. The moral interest lies partly in the delicate and
scrupulous honour by which Mr. Gladstone guarded himself from the
danger of succumbing to mere self-interested motives, and partly
in the evidence that his intellect was completely moulded into his
present opposite views by causes infinitely more powerful than any
self-interested motives could possibly have exerted over his mind—
namely, that sympathy with the growing political freedom of the day
which compelled him year by year to assign an ever-increasing importance to influences wholly unprovided for in his early creed and
yet clamorously demanding recognition in any practical view of the
future relations between Church and State.

Mr. Gladstone started with a theory of the relation of Church to
State, which characteristically enough admitted two exceptions—both
of them exceptions which we should have thought of a very alarming
kind for the prospects of the theory itself, yet both evincing how
utterly *unable* Mr. Gladstone was even in his youth, and even in the
ardour of youthful theorising, to ignore the results already attained
by the movement of public thought in England. His theory of the
State in relation to the Church was that the state is not only able to

---

[1] This article was first published in *The Economist* for November 28 1868, Volume
XXVI, pp. 1357–8. 'A Chapter of Autobiography' was published in November 1868.
Gladstone was troubled by the inconsistency between his current attitude to the relation
of Church and State (which included a determination to disestablish the Irish Church)
and that expressed in his book *The State in its Relations with the Church* (1838) published thirty years earlier. 'A Chapter of Autobiography' was intended to justify his change
of views to himself and to the public.

discern moral truth and to act upon it, but that it is able to discern religious truth and to act upon it; from which his general inference was that the state should not be indifferent to the religious faith of its own servants, but should regard that faith as at least a matter of the first moment in selecting them; and secondly, that it is bound in general to spread the truth in which it believes, and consequently to refuse assistance to all error in which it does not believe. The first inference led Lord Macaulay to suppose that Mr. Gladstone lamented the repeal of the Test Act, and would wish to re-enact it. The second inference would have led any one to suppose that Mr. Gladstone was opposed to the Maynooth grant, and would repeal that. In both cases the conclusion was or would have been rash. Mr. Gladstone, though a theorist and a warm theorist, was then as now acutely sensitive to the limits of practicability in the political condition of the nation within which he lived. He had an exception covering each case. He explained to Lord Macaulay that he did not regret the repeal of the Test Act, and did not wish it re-enacted. Although he thought that the orthodoxy of any man, proposed as a servant of the Crown, was not only not an irrelevant but a really important matter, he would give range and verge enough for taking into account other considerations which might be, in the special case, of even greater moment. He would admit men of other than the prescribed faith into office if there was sufficient reason for overruling this very important objection to them; but he would not admit that it was not an objection. On the other hand, though his theory would not in any way admit of *future* assistance to error, he admitted the plea of a special *covenant* as binding on any government, and such a covenant having been given in the case of Maynooth, the moral obligation to fulfil it necessarily over-ruled the moral objection to giving it. By these subtle and yet most characteristic and sincere exceptions, Mr. Gladstone just brought his theory abreast of the moment in which he launched it—1838; that is, he did not compel himself or any one else who might adopt it, to agitate for a retrogressive step in the direction of repealing the Test Act, or withdrawing the grant from Maynooth. But the theory, clogged with its double exception, was like the astronomical hypothesis of cycles and epicycles to account for the movements of the planets before the adoption of the Copernican theory. It would have been clear to most men of Mr. Gladstone's intellectual force that either the main theory must encroach on and subvert the exceptions, or that the exceptions must, like parasitic plants, destroy the theory to which they clung, but it was not clear to him. His mind reflected most powerfully every actual movement of the day, and he evidently never anticipated for a moment that the theory would subvert the exceptions. But neither did he anticipate *then* that the exceptions would encroach upon and destroy the main structure of his theory. His own religious hopes and wishes were at the bottom of his theory; his clear apprehensions of the condition of public thought were at the bottom of the exceptions he admitted to it; and yet there was at that time so complete an equilibrium between the inner religious current of his own mind and the flowing tide of political thought outside him which met and just balanced the force of that current, that he does not seem to have anticipated that this momentary rationale of the relation of State to Church need be disturbed.

The first shock came in 1844, when Mr. Gladstone had just become a member of Sir Robert Peel's Cabinet, in Sir Robert Peel's proposal to extend and remodel the Maynooth grant, as a sort of concession to the Catholic claims in Ireland. Mr. Gladstone saw at once that the ground was giving way under him, but he could not trust himself— and most honourable to him was it that he would not trust himself—to form an impartial opinion on the subject with so violent a personal inducement as beset him in his desire to remain with his colleagues in the high post which he had just achieved, and which then seemed very naturally almost the goal of his political ambition. He resigned, not to oppose Sir Robert Peel, but to enable himself to reconsider freely convictions which he had so deliberately formed out of office. In the end he assented as an independent member to the proposal, but he felt very justly that only as an independent member could he even have trusted his own sincerity in retracting his theory. Those who laugh scornfully at his scrupulousness should remember, what they are apt to forget, that very few politicians could ever have conceived and believed so subtle and complex a theory as Mr. Gladstone's, and that those who could, are just the very men who would most emphatically need very clear moral guarantees of their own sincerity in afterwards rejecting it. It is the subtle-minded who most need to guard themselves against self-deception. Mr. Gladstone—except so far as he is checked by his strong sympathy with popular tendencies—is eminently subtle-minded. No statesman has ever felt more keenly the need of guaranteeing himself by external tests against the fear that he might be deceiving himself as to his political motives. No statesman has ever given stronger and more complete guarantees for the perfect purity and disinterestedness of his public conduct. And he has found a double recompense, in a manly self-confidence, which is the secret of much of his influence, and the ample and enthusiastic trust of the people who confer power upon him.

But though Mr. Gladstone assented to the extension of the Maynooth grant, which was in fact giving up his principle that the Government should lend its aid only to the propagation of religious truth, he had already perceived that the *other* exception he had admitted to his theory,—the exception permitting persons out of the communion of the national Church to be admitted, on sufficient grounds, to office and influence in the state,—was already demanding much larger and speedier concessions, making in fact much more rapid encroachments on his ecclesiastical theory than the first. He saw that the admission of absolute political equality between English subjects of different religions—the necessity of ignoring altogether objections founded on dissent or other religious differences—was becoming more and more imminent every day. And he evidently felt that the drift of opinion was rather in the direction of removing all real grievances by abating privilege than in that of removing grievances by multiplying privileges—by 'levelling down' rather than 'levelling up.' He wisely and courageously protested against the silly Ecclesiastical Titles Bill, which proposed to make it penal for Roman Catholic prelates to assume territorial titles in the United Kingdom. But since then the whole current of his opinion has obviously set in the direction of removing Irish grievances, not by granting new privileges to the Catholics, but by taking away those which had long ago been unjustly granted to the Protestants.

It will be noticed as one of the most curious features of this autobiographical chapter that Mr. Gladstone has never seemed to feel the need of what we may call an overruling principle—that he began by being satisfied with a principle engrafted with glaring exceptions, and that when the exceptions grew into a theory, as they have at last done, he still feels no annoyance at being entangled with his original principle, in the form (now) of an exception. It is perhaps one of his great merits as a practical statesman that he rather enjoys superimposing a subtle exception on the general theory, if practical conditions require it. But it is curious to note that the principle with which he started, that a government *can* ascertain religious truth and if so ought to propagate it, is, though abandoned as a principle, still retained as an exception to his new principle, that the political equality of all religions must be assumed as the basis of a national life like ours. He admits emphatically that a self-governing nation with a great variety of religious creeds cannot possibly agree upon any single form of religious truth to propagate. But then he makes, wisely enough for practical purposes, this exception in favour of the English Establishment, that as it has come down from times when the members of the Government were not mere spokesmen of the nation, but were in some sense guardians of the nation,—as in those times they were quite warranted in propagating their own faith in the nation,—and as that faith still remains the basis of a great institution, which is on the whole very popular with all classes and which does much good,—it ought still to be sanctioned by Parliament, even though it may have to be admitted that Parliament itself is wholly incapacitated by its own heterogeneous religious composition from again choosing any special form of Christian faith as 'the truth,' or even from adhering to the present form, and sanctioning it as true. Mr. Gladstone still seems to cling to the idea that the established religion should be supported, not merely as highly *useful* to the nation, but as in some sense spreading 'the truth.' But whose truth? Not Parliament's, for it is admitted that Parliament contains the most opposite forms of belief; not any existing political power's view of truth—only the view of truth adopted by an English government three hundred years ago. What possible duty can Parliament have to propagate such a body of 'truth' as neither it holds itself nor any other assignable organ of the people hold? Surely while the great *usefulness* of the English Church may readily be conceded, Mr. Gladstone can scarcely mean that it *now* rests on any higher political foundation than that of a high moral expediency. It does great good. But can any statesman say that it spreads, or is capable of spreading, the view of truth adopted by any existing English government as its own?

Mr. Gladstone on Home Rule for Ireland[1]

THE Prime Minister's speech at Aberdeen cannot at any rate be
charged with that tendency to intellectual hesitation and finesse which
is the favourite taunt of his opponents. In speaking of the Irish cry
for Home Rule, Mr. Gladstone drew no fine distinctions, and came to
no ambiguous conclusion. He asked if the United Parliament was to
be broken up because it could not or would not do justice to Ireland,
or only to please the Irish fancy. If the former were alleged, the
answer was that for the last three years the United Parliament has been
eagerly engaged in doing for Ireland what it would hardly have done
for either England or Scotland—no doubt because neither England
nor Scotland stood in need of the measures granted as Ireland did,—
but none the less did this sufficiently demonstrate the perfect willingness and capacity of the United Parliament to redress all real Irish
grievances. If the latter were alleged, that the Irish do not *choose* to
take even good government from the hands of a United Parliament,
then the answer is that on that head the Irish have only the right to
vote with the other members of the Union; the whole Union has a
right to decide what is in this respect for the common benefit, and
unless any party can allege that their individual interests are trampled
on by the Union, the whole Union has a right to say whether union
or separation will best promote the interests of all. And this in point of
fact, as everybody knows, Great Britain has long ago decided. In
Mr. Gladstone's own vigorous words—'Can any sensible man, can
any rational man, suppose that at this time of day, in this condition
of the world, we are going to disintegrate the great capital institutions
of this country for the purpose of making ourselves ridiculous in the
sight of all mankind, and crippling any power we possess for bestowing
benefits through legislation on the country to which we belong?'
    That is clear, forcible language, which may, we hope, have the
effect of showing the Home Rule party in Ireland that while Ireland

[1] This article was first published in *The Economist*, for September 30 1871, Volume
XXIX, p. 1175.

MR. GLADSTONE ON HOME RULE FOR IRELAND

may gain almost anything that is reasonable and just from the Imperial Parliament, she will not gain the repeal of the Union for which that party is now crying out, and which would be indeed in many respects far more mischievous to British interests, and perhaps even to Irish interests, than absolute independence.

Indeed it is hard to conceive anything more mischievous than the opening of an indefinite, and indefinitely increasable, number of debatable issues between Great Britain and Ireland, such as would be not merely suggested but forced on the public by the division of duties between an Irish and British parliament. It is difficult enough to divide the sphere of properly municipal or country from properly central and parliamentary powers, and almost impossible to do so beneficially without giving Parliament an absolute overriding power in case of conflict. But this difficulty would not only be enhanced a thousand times by the great importance, unity, and national coherence of an Irish parliament, but it would be quite impossible to give the Imperial (or as it would then be, federal) Parliament a power to over-ride the decisions of an Irish parliament without provoking something like a rebellion on every separate occasion. It may be said perhaps that this difficulty has never been felt in the United States, where the state powers and the federal powers are divided by a hard and fast line, which neither state nor federation have the power to overleap. But in point of fact the difficulty has been felt and felt very keenly, and though not for precisely the same reasons as it would be felt in this case, yet for a similar class of reasons—namely, because the genius and policy of a certain group of the states diverged very widely from the genius and policy of the remainder. The Secession War was in fact a state revolt against the central power, and though that secession was due not to race, but to a 'domestic institution' of a most potent and mischievous kind, yet difference of race and religion conjointly are certainly quite capable of producing as great a chasm of feeling between the different members of a federation as is any difference in 'domestic institutions.' Only consider for a moment what an Irish parliament would be disposed to feel if it found itself compelled to impose taxes for a war in which the sympathies of Ireland were directly opposed to the sympathies of Great Britain, or were even hindered from imposing taxes for some purely Irish object by the weight of the taxation for Imperial purposes which it disapproved. Is it even conceivable that such a parliament could long exist without becoming a centre of the fiercest disloyalty and even treason? Or put aside questions of finance, and look only at ecclesiastical policy. Would not it be very probable that one of the first efforts of Ireland's separate Parliament would be to re-establish a Church in Ireland, but not this time a Protestant but a Catholic Church—an effort which would probably give rise to civil war unless England interfered to thwart the wish of the Catholic party, in which case the danger of a violent disruption would arise again from another cause? It is in fact as plain as common sense can make it to all who look at the condition of Ireland with impartial eyes, that 'Home Rule' would be but the first step in a series of virulent disputes as to the political relations of the two islands, which could hardly end except in separation, or re-conquest with all the evils that that would bring in its train. The Home Rule party would certainly be imprudent, but they would be far more logical, if they were to raise a cry at once for an independent Irish Republic.

Mr. Gladstone and the People[1]

MR. GLADSTONE'S speech at Greenwich marks a new era in English politics,—not that it is for him a very great speech, and still less that it is the speech of a statesman as such,—if it *had* been, in that place and delivered to such an audience it would probably have been a great mistake and a sad failure,—but that it marks the coming of the time when it will be one of the most important qualifications of a prime minister to exert a direct control over the masses—when the ability to reach them, not as his views may be filtered through an intermediate class of political teachers and writers, but *directly* by the vitality of his own mind, will give a vast advantage in the political race to any statesman. We are not saying that the power of addressing twenty-five thousand people for two hours, and holding their attention and interest in spite of plenty of hostile elements in the great crowd, is one which above all others we delight to see in a leading statesman. As far as our own tastes go, we might prefer the sort of statesman who could only reach the nation through comparatively select audiences like Parliament, whose power is reserved for the higher regions of statesmanship, and who possesses none of the notes of the great popular orator. All we are saying is that the time is evidently approaching when such statesmen will be at a considerable disadvantage, even as heads of an administration, when a power like that evinced by Mr. Gladstone will be of the very first importance even for his position as Leader of the House of Commons and first minister of the Queen. Criticise Mr. Gladstone's speech as you will—virulently, contemptuously, patronisingly, compassionately, or from any other point of view, however depreciating,—no politician in his senses will deny that it has added greatly to the strength of the Government's position; that it has to some extent neutralised much of the political result of the process of many months' slow decay and demolition of his power. If Parliament were to meet again to-morrow, Mr. Gladstone's position would be

[1] This article was first published in *The Economist* for November 4 1871, Volume XXIX, pp. 1330–1.

quite changed. It would be at once felt by all his discontented allies as well by his party foes that Mr. Gladstone's direct command over the people is still immense,—that the result of an appeal to the people by him against a divided and hostile Parliament would very probably end in his full reinstatement in power, with as large a majority as ever. Mr. Gladstone has illustrated most remarkably his reserve power outside Parliament. No English minister probably ever had less of a personal parliamentary following than Mr. Gladstone. There he has no phalanx like Lord Russell's Whig phalanx, and Lord Palmerston's personal admirers. In Parliament he has no body-guard. But he has shown once more how easily he can get the ear of the electors themselves, and that under circumstances of no little difficulty,—circumstances in which both his policy and his shortcomings as a local representative combined to make him unpopular with his audience. Parliament fully appreciates this reserve power in a prime minister, which secures him, as it were, a separate and private appeal to the people,— an appeal not simply through the people's representatives, and what the people may or may not understand of his reported parliamentary speeches, but by direct personal influence. Parliament may not like it, —may think it even a dangerous power,—may echo the grumblings of three years ago over Mr. Gladstone's stumping tour in Lancashire; but Parliament will recognise and respect it as a new store of political force, as a guarantee that the Premier has more direct relations to the people than any other premier of our times, and that if he becomes unpopular with the representatives of the people, he may still be more popular with the people themselves than even those representatives. Undoubtedly Mr. Gladstone's Greenwich speech will serve as a conspicuous mark for the date when it first became advisable for a minister to cultivate the gifts of a great popular orator,—an orator who can deal with political topics in the broad, easy, and animated style which touches the people, and without any of that subtle flavour of parliamentary skill which only suits the statesman.

Mr. Gladstone not only displayed this sort of power in a very remarkable degree at Greenwich, but what is quite as remarkable as anything else, it is a late-acquired power. He was from the first no doubt a good parliamentary speaker. Lord Macaulay, in his review of Mr. Gladstone's early book on Church and State, speaks of his parliamentary promise in high terms. But the constitution of his mind was so complex, and his style of argument so little popular, that no one certainly then thought of him as a popular orator. Sir Robert Peel, if we remember his words rightly, says in his political memoranda, that Mr. Gladstone brought 'his high character and great attainments' to the aid of the Conservative ministry, but evidently thought little of his oratorical powers. Indeed, it was not till he busied himself with finance,—*i.e.*, with very definitely marked-out subject-matter, in which there was no room for subtleties, though much for explanatory and expository dissertation,—that his remarkable faculty as an orator, his artistic power of planning out his subjects, his ease and vivacity in making them interesting to others, his skill in illustrating principles, his animation in recounting facts, began to be generally understood. And it was far later again that he acquired any of that power of fascinating and influencing a genuine multitude, by which Mr. Bright first became noticeable. Mr. Gladstone's rhetorical powers, at first as little popular as great fluency and earnestness could well be, have gradually worked themselves out into a real command of popular sympathies and the popular intelligence, and the fact is one that at so critical a moment as this will hardly fail to be of the greatest significance to his but recently tottering Government.

We are quite willing to admit that the speech itself, though a very powerful and lively speech from a prime minister to his constituents, was in no sense the speech of the head of a great administration declaring and expounding his policy. Such a speech could hardly have been made to 25,000 people in the open air under the conditions of time and space under which he spoke. A man who has to exert his voice to its utmost, and to interest a great crowd for a considerable time, cannot by any possibility trace out the fine lines of a national policy, even if he had spare energy enough to concentrate his mind upon them in the face of such physical difficulties. But as the speech of a prime minister who is also a representative to his constituents, it is not easy to overestimate its ability and its interest. The historical illustration of the difficulty of keeping together large parliamentary majorities, as introductory to his own expression of confidence in his colleagues and himself, and his complete refusal to admit that this address was his 'last dying speech and confession,'—his bold expression of continued confidence in his Irish policy,—his reply to the charge of niggardly economies, which was as far from any yielding of principle as it was from any unfair attack on those Conservative predecessors who had yet, as he showed, economised (and quite rightly economised) more labour in the national dockyards than ever he and his colleagues,—his defence of his military policy,—the moderate and just stand he took upon his education policy,—and finally, his extremely lively and true remarks on the fundamental popularity of the House of Lords, even with the working classes, and the undesirability therefore of doing away with the hereditary principle,—were all treated with a lightness and yet energy of touch, and connected together in so natural and taking a manner, that Mr. Gladstone taught the audience, which he was also amusing, without letting them know that he was teaching them. And the last part of his speech on the mistake made by the representatives of skilled labour in their negotiations with certain peers and baronets, through Mr. Scott Russell, and in venturing to hope that legislation could do for them what really nothing but individual energy and self-denial could ever achieve, was more than instructive and lively; it went thoroughly home to his audience, and made them feel how thoroughly Mr. Gladstone understood their position, and how steadily he could resist unwise demands, even while heartily entering into their most urgent wants.

Thus when Mr. Gladstone left the Greenwich hustings, his Government certainly stood in a far stronger position than it has done for many months back. The nation has again learnt to realise that its Prime Minister understands both its unwise wishes and its genuine wants better than almost any other man in it, and that even if misunderstandings must arise between the Cabinet and Parliament, there will be a very strong disposition on the part of the masses to believe what the Prime Minister says of Parliament, more easily than what Parliament says of the Prime Minister.

Mr. Gladstone's Ministry[1]

Mr Gladstone's ministry still exists, but in a very short time it must cease to do so. It has become a provisional government; its successor is already designated. There is nothing premature in endeavouring to estimate it, for its history is, in substance, ended.

On such a matter it is not possible to be impartial; the coolest bystanders are part of their age, and their judgment is perturbed by the atmosphere of sentiment in which they live. But being as impartial as we can, our judgment is that the ministry of Mr. Gladstone has had a better combination of great ministers than any ministry since the first Reform Act. Some administrations have surpassed it in this or that particular, but, upon the whole, it has done the most and been the best.

Most governments since 1832 have been deficient in the essence of a government—power. They have not been backed by a sufficient majority to enable them to do what they liked; sometimes they have not had a majority at all; generally they have had only a 'working majority,' as it is called—a majority, that is, enough to enable them to transact the common work of Parliament, but not enough to enable them to enact their own ideas or to propose large reforms adverse to great interests. There have, indeed, been only two governments of immense power since 1832. The first is the Whig Government which followed the Reform Act of that time; and that was no doubt a Government which achieved much, and which has a great name in history. But Mr. Disraeli long ago pointed out its defect: it was not 'presided over by a guiding and original mind.' Lord Grey belonged to a past period; he represented a great tradition, but he was not a great reality. When he passed the Reform Act his special work was almost done. Lord Althorp was a country gentleman of strong charac-

---

[1] This article was first published in *The Economist* for February 14 1874, Volume XXXII, pp. 189–90. In the general election of January–February 1874 the Conservatives were victorious. Mr. Gladstone did not wait to meet parliament as was then still the normal custom (Disraeli's resignation in 1868 was considered exceptional), and offered the Queen his resignation at Windsor on February 16.

ter, but he had no great abilities, and had no taste for office, and wished, as he said, that he was 'back among his pheasants and his fowling-piece.' The influence of Lord Russell, defective as it was, did not begin to predominate till the omnipotence of the Whigs was passed; before he ruled, the Conservative reaction of those years had begun. In consequence the efforts of the Whig Cabinet of 1832 wanted effect and unity; they were often most excellent, but they were never so impressive as they ought to have been, and they are now most insufficiently borne in mind because they did not emanate from, and were not associated with, a single mind of vast vigour and ability. The commanding element in life and history is a great person. One Napoleon is worth fifty common generals; he can do far more, and what he does will be infinitely better remembered. No cabinet can effectually rule this country if it is a cabinet only—if it is not itself ruled by a great prime minister. The element of greatness nobody will deny to Mr. Gladstone's Government. Any time this five years it has been easy to hear almost every kind of criticism on Mr. Gladstone; it is particularly easy now when everybody is finding out that they have always been Conservatives. But no one ever hinted that on a great subject, and when his mind was made up, he did not carry his Cabinet before him, and penetrate their whole policy with his peculiar personality.

The only other government of similar power since 1832 is that of Sir Robert Peel, which succeeded the election of 1841. This government was followed by a great majority, and ruled by a great prime minister; but it was utterly weak in another way—it had no characteristic measures, and is now known by uncharacteristic measures. It was elected to maintain Protection, and it abolished Protection; to maintain the Corn Laws, and it abolished the Corn Laws. Except the Bank Act of 1844, which is an outlying matter, the Government of Sir Robert Peel is known only by its recantations. A first-rate government embodies in acts and laws the principle of a preconceived policy, but Sir Robert Peel's government abandoned its own previous policy and adopted that of its adversaries.

In this respect the Government of Mr. Gladstone is indisputably superior. It has, as everybody admits, been faithful to the principles which it announced. A single mistake in the Education Act is the sole exception which can even be fancied. The Government entered office with a list of congenial measures, and it passed these and others.

The result of our comparison therefore is that the administration of Mr. Gladstone is much superior to all others since 1832, save two, in force and power; and that to one of these two it is superior in possessing a suitable great man, and to the other in having passed suitable great measures. When posterity compares the two, it will probably say that Mr. Gladstone is not by several degrees so great an administrator as Sir Robert Peel, but that he is by at least as many degrees a greater orator. To equal or rival Mr. Gladstone's budget speeches we must go farther back; to those of Pitt, and the remains of Pitt's speeches are too fragmentary to enable us to say what was their merit in comparison. Neither Sir Robert Peel nor Mr. Gladstone can of course be put in the first order of statesmen; both their careers have one fatal fault: they were converted assailants—they ended by enacting what they began by opposing. But Mr. Gladstone has been far more fortunate. Sir Robert Peel, by changes of opinion, twice destroyed his party and Government; but Mr. Gladstone has never destroyed either, and lived to enact his truest and best ideas with the approbation of our strongest recent party and the aid of our strongest recent Government. But in another respect Sir Robert Peel was far happier. He left a school of able and attached political pupils; but, whether from difference of time or character, Mr. Gladstone will leave none. When he retires there will be no Gladstonite[s?], though there were Peelites for so many years.

Of the other members of the Government we have so often said so much that we need now say very little. The world, we believe, has been unjust to Mr. Lowe. He was not a great Chancellor of the Exchequer, neither his previous studies nor his former life had prepared him for a finance minister, and he suffered from physical defects great enough to be a serious obstacle to a highly trained mind. But he showed, as he always shows, strong character and great abilities, and the so-called scandals, amid which he left the Exchequer, were at the worst slight errors, of which all Ministers commit many. But no minister equals Mr. Lowe in the art of advertising his blunders, and of irritating those who can take advantage of them. Mr. Goschen and Mr. Cardwell, though at first sight no one would think them much fit to administer the army and navy, have in fact administered them so well that it will puzzle the Conservatives excessively to find for them suitable successors. We own that of late Mr. Forster has disappointed us; he has shown an obstinacy in adhering to the *ipsissima verba* of the

Education Act which the principles of religious education did not require, and which now gives Mr. Disraeli a great advantage that he has begun to use. But notwithstanding all this, Mr. Forster has passed by far the most efficacious Education Act we have ever seen in England, and his massive common sense has made a deep impression through the country. As to the enterprising foreign policy with which we are threatened, we should be much frightened if we thought that we should ever see it. But we do not think so. If Lord Derby is the next Foreign Secretary, he will act much as Lord Granville has acted. He will not probably have so fine a tact, but he will decide from the same anxiety to be sound and the same dislike to be showy, which have made Lord Granville successful. Our foreign policy will go on in its recent path, and we do not believe that it is possible at present to find a better one.

But, it will be asked, if Mr. Gladstone's is so good a government, why does not the country wish to keep it? We answer that, though a good government, it has not the particular species of goodness which the public for the moment want. It is in its nature an active and innovating government, and the country just now wishes a passive and non-innovating government. There is no great change for which the country is now prepared, and therefore it fears a government which will propose changes, and desires a Government which will oppose them. Mr. Gladstone's Government fails, notwithstanding its merits, because those merits are unsuited to its place and time.

In this respect, and in this respect almost alone, Mr. Gladstone has been much less fortunate than Sir Robert Peel. He has left on the country the impression that he was the minister of a party. There are many persons who imagine that he has a settled desire to keep the Liberals in office at any price and any hazard. They believe that he will accept any measure which the extreme Liberals require as the price of their support, and will impose it on the rest of the Liberals and on the country. How false this idea is can be best learned by talking to the extreme Liberals. They, on the other hand, say that Mr. Gladstone 'has lost their confidence; that he believes all manner of superstition; that he is the worst of Conservatives—a Conservative in disguise.' But the world has incurably received the contrary impression; it thinks that Mr. Gladstone is ready for any changes, however violent— nay, that he prefers them even when they are most violent. This is probably the price which an eager orator must pay for his fire and vivacity. He sweeps away a hundred obstacles by his intensity and his eloquence, but he imparts inevitably the notion that he is incapable of calm and moderation. This first impression is clearly wrong; many vehement orators have been very deficient in decision and determination. But it has been Mr. Gladstone's misfortune to spread it through England, and it is one of the most powerful causes that have contributed to his fall. Time passes on and brings a thousand changes; but unless past experience is a bad guide, it will be many years before we see a ministry of so much power and so much mind again.

Mr. Gladstone on Ritualism [1]

W E hear it said 'that Mr. Gladstone ought not to write on ritualism; that he ought to keep his pen quiet; that the head of a great party is a kind of trustee for that party, and that he should primarily consider its interest in all which he says and in all which he writes. Particularly he ought not as a political leader to take up an unpopular cause out of the sphere of politics.' Whether ritualism is out of the sphere of politics may, we think, be denied, but further than that, if the Liberal party think that Mr. Gladstone will think of their immediate interest in that way, a great experience goes to show that they have mistaken their man. Mr. Gladstone has never considered *his own* interest in that way. He has always been doing something contrary to his immediate interest. Every one who is conversant with the political talk of the last twenty or twenty-five years must have heard a hundred times—'Gladstone is done for; Gladstone never can recover from this again; he is his own worst enemy; no one but himself could have done himself fatal harm, and now he has himself done it.' But, in fact, within a month after each of the hundred fatal failures Mr. Gladstone has arisen again and is just where he was before. He has made some great speech or proposed some great measure which has caused everything which was objected to to be forgotten. Every public man wins or loses by the balance which there is in his favour, but there are two ways of gaining that balance. Some statesmen have almost nothing put to their debit, so that all which they do, be it ever so little, goes with only slight deduction to their credit; others have a good deal put to their debit, but then, on the other hand, an immense sum is every now and then paid to their credit. Mr. Gladstone is of the latter class; he 'turns over,' as we should say in the City, 'a very large amount,' and at the end of the year the balance to his advantage is most considerable, after charging him with all that he ought to be charged with.

[1] This article was first published in *The Economist* for October 3 1874, Volume XXXII, pp. 1185–6. The Public Worship Regulation Act of 1874 had made ritualism a topic of lively discussion. Gladstone set out his views on the matter in an article in the *Contemporary Review* entitled 'Ritualism and Ritual.' Gladstone opposed the Act and put forward six resolutions to form a basis for alternative legislation.

We may seem to imply that we do not think that the publishing of Mr. Gladstone's essay on 'Ritualism' was the wisest of his public acts, and we own we do not think so. Of course you would never have induced by any offer steady and regular English statesmen, such men as Lord Cardwell or Lord Derby, to put their names at such a time to, or to write, such a paper, but we should not have thought that conclusive. As we have explained, Mr. Gladstone is not a man who ever can or ever will run in the common groove. Our objection is to the substance of the paper, because we think it improperly changes the issue and diverts attention from the point to which it is most expedient that it should be directed.

Mr. Gladstone says, and very truly, that there has been in all religious communities a great reaction in favour of suitable cere-monial of late years; that in all the odd and bleak style of former years is getting more out of fashion; that in all the 'outward and visible' tends to assume a place which previous generations would certainly have refused to it, and which probably they would have been shocked at its even claiming. Mr. Gladstone's instances do not go beyond the body of orthodox persons—dissenters or church people. But the reaction in favour of the 'outward and visible' went much wider. We could name a Unitarian chapel so finely built and with so much of ecclesiastical expression that a high churchman who saw it uttered 'Confound their impudence.' Mr. Gladstone could have insisted on nothing more justly than on the augmented respect now paid in almost all sects to the exterior symbol.

But this does not come to the main point. If the outcry were really against an increased respect for the outward and visible, it ought to extend to all sects, for in all of them that respect for the outward and visible is to be seen more or less. But, as we are aware, this is not so. It is only one kind of 'symbol' which is execrated; only one sect in which the dislike is held; only one kind of 'Ritualism' which people ever think of or Parliament ever discusses. Nor is it to the purpose to insist, as Mr. Gladstone does with much truth and much ingenuity, on the want of artistic sense in Englishmen, and their unfitness to find good outward symbols for inward things; for this unfitness is common to all sects and classes, and if it were the source of the present cry, that cry would pervade all sects, and attack all additional symbols and all new forms of ceremonies. But, as we know, that cry does nothing of the sort; its object is limited to one set of persons and to one kind of ceremonial. There must be something special in this.

There *is* something special. It is true that all kinds of religion tend to form to themselves a ritual; but it is not true that all have that tendency equally—some have it much more than others. Those which have it most are those which are based most on the sacramental principle. We cannot go fully into the reasons for this. Theological disquisition is not suitable to these pages; but roughly we may put the matter in this way. The essence of a 'sacrament' is that the officiating person performs an invisible supernatural act; he changes the elements of bread and wine into something which is no longer bread and wine; he gives the mere water of baptism a supernatural efficiency which does not belong to it in reality. The essence, the leading and cardinal point of religions based on this principle, is the public working of an imperceptible but efficacious miracle. The special characteristic of other kinds of worship is that something is said or felt or believed, but here that characteristic is something done. Inevitably this great act tends to surround itself with other minor acts. A worship of prayer and preaching may be content with prayer and preaching, but a worship of supernatural acts tends naturally to surround itself with preparatory natural acts; it jars human nature to begin with so great a thing, it requires to be introduced by some minor thing. As a matter of experience sacramental churches have been churches of ceremonial; the churches which have completely rejected the sacraments principle have been those in which the worship has been the plainest and the ritual the least. And the theory of human nature would lead us to expect that it would be so.

In one of his most remarkable books the greatest Roman Catholic writer of this age describes the point forcibly. He introduces a recent convert as saying:—'I could attend masses for ever, and not be tired. It is not a mere form of words, it is a great action, the greatest action that can be on earth. It is not the invocation merely, but, if I dare use the word, the evocation of the Eternal. He becomes present on the altar in flesh and blood, before whom angels bow and devils tremble. This is that awful event which is the scope, and is the interpretation of every part of the solemnity. Words are necessary, but as means, not as ends; they are not mere addresses to the throne of grace, they are instruments of what is far higher, of consecration, of sacrifice.' Minds in this temper try to procure for themselves the most striking ceremonial which they can procure; they endeavour to accompany the invisible drama with a visible drama as lofty, as exciting, and as little inappropriate as they can.

The moment that we understand that ritualism is the natural accompaniment of this kind of religion we also understand why the English dislike ritualism, for they dislike this form of religion— dislike it more than they dislike any other; 'popery' is the best-known instance and the most striking development of it, and the English people hate 'popery.' The idea of such a kind of worship besides seems alien to them, and to run counter to their instincts. The idea of an invisible supernatural act performed close to them startles them, shocks them, and seems, as they say, 'carrying things to an extreme.' And they would not like it any the better, but much the worse, because the power of performing so great an act, if once believed and admitted, inevitably gives to those who perform it diffused prestige and influence; this doctrine establishes a priesthood in the world, and the English people hate a priesthood. The most striking ritualism is accordingly hated in England, because the species of religion which most tends to be strikingly ritualistic is equally hated.

We should not have thought it necessary to write on a subject far from those most usual to us if we had not thought that the matter was very serious to us. In so saying, we give of course no opinion on the truth or falsity of any theological doctrine. Ours are not columns in which such topics can be spoken of. We mean that the political consequences of 'ritualism,' in the sense in which we have explained it, and in the manner in which in truth it arises in the real world, are very serious. It endangers the establishment of the Church in England, both if it retains within its limits those who sympathise with ritualism and if it expels them. If it retains them it is in danger, because it identifies itself with a kind of religion which the English people dislike exceedingly and which they fear exceedingly. The connection between the Church and the State in England may easily be severed if that Church gives a home to those whom the common feeling of the nation particularly dislikes and at whom it is particularly irritated. On the other hand, if the Church expels those who sympathise in this movement and those who take part in it, it runs into danger because it narrows its boundaries; because it loses the support of an eager and earnest body; because no one can know how deeply notions akin to this permeate society, and how many may be affected by measures directed against them; and because, owing to many circumstances, the same class of men no longer enter the Church that used to do so, so that she has to be content with inferiors; and because, therefore, any new exclusion would be the diminution of a class already diminished, and the weakening of a power already impaired. Either way, the result to the Establishment is important.

We are grateful to Mr. Gladstone for what he has given us, but we own we think he ought to have done less or more. Either he ought not to have written on a subject on which he was sure to offend many, or he ought to have grappled with that subject in its practical aspect, and upon the side on which, far more than any other, it influences our politics.

Mr. Gladstone's Resignation[1]

In one respect Mr. Gladstone is unique. Many statesmen have written books in retirement, and some have ostentatiously commended it. But ordinarily those books are tame and those commendations forced. Now that they feel no longer the excitement of the senate or of office all else seems tasteless to them, and you can trace that languor in every phrase they utter. But no one can say this of Mr. Gladstone. His writings in retirement may or may not be too many; they may or may not be models of style; but no one can say that they do not show the keenest interest in their subjects. If he writes in the 'Quarterly,' you wonder at the usual vigour of the anonymous contributor; if he writes on the 'Vatican Decrees,' you admire the minute research and the zeal of disputation which no divine can surpass. In Homeric criticism his eagerness is almost greater: it has long been said of him that he 'cared as much about the sons of Priam as if they had votes on a division'; and, in fact, he can pursue, with elastic energy, inquiries which most bookworms would call tedious. And in all this exceptional earnestness there is not a vestige of affectation. It is the simple expression of an intense nature, which singular to say is both variable and concentrated, which pours itself in a hundred pursuits, but which for the time being is absorbed in each.

This is the real explanation of Mr. Gladstone's resignation. He can withdraw into comparative retirement, because he can be absorbingly occupied in retirement. If he hears from a distance the din of Parliamentary battle, he is not overpowered with melancholy musing; his compensations are at hand; his study is no place of calm to him, for it is alive with 'hot thought' and rings with controversies for which he cares.

That Mr. Gladstone has judged wisely for himself in resigning the leadership of the Liberal party we cannot doubt. There can be little

[1] This article was first published in *The Economist* for January 16 1875, Volume XXXIII, p. 58. Gladstone announced his resignation from the leadership of the Liberals on January 13 1875 just before the publication of this article. He resumed it on becoming Prime Minister in 1880.

pleasure in leading that party in its present state, and there must be much vexation. It will be impossible to please everybody, and easy not to please anybody. The toil of attending Parliament merely to 'watch the proceedings;' to sit opposite to a government in anxious hope that it may make some mistake, and with little to say if it does not; to detect errors in figures and poke amendments into clauses,— is an excellent training for young members, but a dismal employment for a finished statesman. In Mr. Gladstone's case it would be particularly melancholy, for it would be a striking contrast to his own Government. After just having achieved much of which even those who question the policy do not doubt the greatness, it would be pitiable to be occupied for session after session in framing minute criticism on measures of which those who approve the object cannot deny the mediocrity.

The task would be the less pleasing because it is a kind of parliamentary work, probably the only kind, for which Mr. Gladstone is not well fitted. In framing or explaining great measures, in great replies—in short, in all first-class combats—he is without a rival in our time; Lord Russell, no partial judge, seems to think, without a rival during his immense parliamentary experience. But exactly the qualities which fit Mr. Gladstone for these great combats unfit him for much small work. He is not a man to hold, as the lawyers say, a 'watching brief.' The best requisites for that task are—first, taciturnity, so as not to be hurried into premature objection; and next, a light way of handling small objections, so as not to make too much, and yet to make enough of them. But no one would praise Mr. Gladstone for these gifts; he has greater ones, but he has not these.

If anything could incline a statesman in Mr. Gladstone's place to resign the leadership of the Liberal party, we should say that it would be the speeches which have been made during the recess by liberal members. At first sight these speeches all look complimentary, for they are unanimous in professions of allegiance; but when carefully examined their purport is less pleasing, for most of the speakers expect their fealty to be recompensed, and to be recompensed by the achievement of an impossible task. The Liberal party is, by admission, divided: what some wish others reject; what some think an indispensable good others think an irreparable calamity. And many expect Mr. Gladstone to discover the word of the enigma—the measure which is to bring them together. But he cannot do so at this moment, nor can anyone else. Such measures must 'grow;' they cannot be made. A new race of ideas must be formed. Long controversies and many agitations will be necessary before the Liberal party will be united upon a single plan, and before the nation will be prepared to accept it of them.

For himself therefore, as we believe, Mr. Gladstone has judged wisely. What will be the effect of that decision on the Liberal party is another question. For the moment it will, we cannot doubt, be unfavourable. In the first place the party will lose the enormous advantage of being led by a man of genius. Indeed it seems as if genius would soon be banished from practical statesmanship. If anything should happen to the present Prime Minister, and if Mr. Gladstone perseveres in retiring, two great parties in the state will be left with what in the cotton market would be called 'best middling' statesmen and with no others. And we believe that the effect will be to make politics as a study less elevating and less instructive to the English people than they have been used to find it. The spectacle of the contentions of first-rate men on subjects which the many care for is the best and almost the only way of bringing home to the many what high mental ability really is, and how completely they are themselves destitute of it. What such men do by intentional benefit is less instructive than that which they confer by the unintentional spectacle of what they are. This, it appears likely, we may before long much want. As a contemporary of Pitt and Fox said when they had passed away, 'We are left with pigmies whom we know to be pigmies, because we have measured them with giants.'

The want of an intellectual bond in the Liberal party will also be much more felt now that Mr. Gladstone has retired than it was before. The allegiance paid to him might often be, perhaps often was, hollow; still it was an allegiance. The consequent tie might be a frail tie, still it was a tie which there is nothing to replace. There is no one whom all sides of the Liberal party can even profess to reverence in the same way. Between the two extremes of the party—between men like Mr. Chamberlain and men like Lord Cardwell—how weak is now the bond, and how wide is now the contrast.

The most pleasant aspect of the subject is that, though Mr. Gladstone retires from the leadership of the Liberals, he does not retire from Parliament or from public life. We shall still be instructed by his occasional efforts, though not, as we have for so many years been, by his daily and constant efforts. And this will be a considerable compensation, especially as compared with the times most recent. It is impossible not to imagine that a nature at once so eager and so peculiar as Mr. Gladstone's must have suffered much in fulfilling a representative function as a party leader. He must have had to suppress much he would have said if he had been left unshackled, and have said much that he did say in a different way. It must have been painful to think that common people had a kind of veto on his words; that they had a kind of right to say, 'Our leader ought not to say that; we ought not to be bound by this sort of thing.' And as so often happens in a struggle against nature, we think Mr. Gladstone not unfrequently overdid what was necessary. We should be inclined to say that throughout very many of his speeches while minister there was, notwithstanding their other great merits, a want of the idiosyncratic and individual charm to which we are used. The minister was great, but the man, such as we had known him for years, and as doubtless he still is, seemed somehow disguised and eclipsed. From all hindrance of this sort we shall now be freed. Parliament will again have the most chosen thoughts of the most peculiar statesman of the age uttered not only in most eloquent but in most characteristic words, and it will be a great refreshment.

Benjamin Disraeli
Introductory note

Benjamin Disraeli (1804–1881) was born in London, the son of Isaac D'Israeli, an Italian Jew who made a fortune as a London merchant, and of Miriam Basevi. He was privately educated and in 1821 was articled to a solicitor; he entered Lincoln's Inn in 1824 and kept nine terms, but left the law for unsuccessful ventures in stocks and in journalism. In 1826 he published his first novel, *Vivian Grey*, in 1831 *The Young Duke*, and in 1832 *Contarini Fleming*. Disraeli stood for Parliament as a Radical in 1832 and 1834, but then changed over to the Tory party. He expounded his contention that it was possible to be both a Conservative and a democrat in three pamphlets published during 1835 and 1836. After two more defeats Disraeli was elected for Maidstone in 1837. Although he was refused a position in Sir Robert Peel's government in 1841, he acquired a position of considerable influence in Tory circles. He differed from Peel in believing that the interests of wealthy manufacturers were not the interests of England, and Disraeli became the spokesman of a small group of younger Tories, nicknamed 'Young England,' who defended the landed interests against the proposed repeal of the Corn Laws, and the working classes against exploitation by the factory owners. His novels *Coningsby*, 1844, and *Sybil*, 1845, embodied these ideas. When Peel's ministry fell after the repeal of the Corn Laws in 1846, Disraeli became the leader of the Conservative party in the Commons. In 1847 he supported the Liberals in removing Jewish exclusion from Parliament and in the same year published *Tancred*, his last political novel. In 1852 Lord Derby took office, with Disraeli as Chancellor of the Exchequer, but the ministry soon fell as a result of Gladstone's attacks on Disraeli's budget. The second Derby-Disraeli cabinet was from 1858–9. Their third administration was from 1866–8, and was notable for the passage of the second parliamentary Reform Bill in 1867, for which Disraeli was largely responsible. He yielded to the more moderate demands of the Liberal opposition, knowing that they would pass the Bill if the Conservatives did not. The Bill added more than a million voters to the register. Lord Derby retired in 1868, and Disraeli became Prime Minister, but his ministry fell almost immediately over the issue of the disestablishment of the Anglican Church in Ireland, a measure supported by the Liberals. While Leader of the Opposition, Disraeli published *Lothair* (1870), a novel chiefly concerned with religious conflicts. After Gladstone's defeat in 1874, Disraeli again became Prime Minister. Although he carried through some necessary legislation for social reform, his real interest was in foreign policy, which was characterised by a vigorous imperialism. He purchased shares in the Suez Canal in 1875, from the bankrupt Khedive of Egypt, so securing English interests in the canal. He gained for Queen Victoria the title of Empress of India in 1876, after which he was raised to the peerage as the Earl of Beaconsfield. The Russo-Turkish war of 1877 was precipitated by the open support that Disraeli had given to Turkey; he played a large part at the Congress of Berlin in 1878, which resulted in a treaty depriving Russia of much of the reward of victory. Disraeli retired on the defeat of the Conservatives in the elections of 1880, and completed his retrospective novel, *Endymion*. He died at Hughenden Manor, Buckinghamshire, in 1881.

Mr. Disraeli[1]

'THE career of the late Chancellor of the Exchequer,' said one of Mr. Disraeli's political friends soon after his comparative failure as a minister in 1852, 'is not closed; we believe its brightest portion is in the future. We have invariably observed that whenever Mr. Disraeli has received a check, it has only been the herald of a great advance; and that when the world has believed him beaten, he has always been on the eve of his greatest victories.' Read by the light of recent events, this was undoubtedly a remarkable prophecy. Mr. Disraeli has never held a position so eminent as that which he now holds. He was the life and soul of the late administration. Without him it could not have lasted a single week. He has resigned without accepting any reward. Lord Derby has taken the blue ribbon. Lord Malmesbury and Sir John Pakington have had the Order of the Bath. Mr. Disraeli, who was far more essential to the Government than either of them,—whose management of the House of Commons won him on this occasion universal admiration, whose recent speeches have scarcely been rivalled for insight, point, and individual character, by any statesman of our day,—has retired with a dignity that will deservedly increase his influence in entering on the leadership of the powerful Conservative Opposition. It is not, therefore, an inappropriate time to make a few remarks on his general capacity and character as a statesman. He has proved, in the last year, that his great abilities are matured, and his character weighted, by experience. He has shown that he can do, what in 1852 at least he had not yet learned to do,—lead with dignity, and fail with dignity after personal exertions which, so far as their intellectual character is concerned, might well have earned ample success. What are the principal characteristics of his strange and brilliant career?

Mr. Disraeli is chiefly remarkable for the unusual combination which his mind presents of individual tenacity of purpose, with a flexibility

[1] This article was first published in *The Economist* for July 2 1859, Volume XVII, pp. 725-6.

and pliancy of intellect rarely found in men of so much audacity and strength. There never was a statesman of eminence who, when he entered on public life, was so strangely in need of the lessons of experience; there never was one who was so apt a learner; there never was one who was more resolute to turn that ready faculty to the best account. From the day of his maiden speech, now more than twenty-one years ago, when he appealed in vain to the House of Commons for a cheer, and sat down with the warning, 'I am not at all surprised at the reception I have experienced. I have begun several times several things, and I have often succeeded at last. I will sit down now, but the time will come when you will listen to me,' up to the day when, amid the breathless attention of the House, he delivered his gallant, eloquent, and adroit defence of the late Government, Mr. Disraeli has never quailed beneath the difficulties of his arduous career, and never failed in that self-possession, which knows how to turn every error, every false step into the materials of a future success. Beginning without rank, without connection, without wealth,—with every difficulty in his path which the prejudices of race could conjure up,—without entering into the convictions or understanding the political traditions either of the party he was to defend or of the party he was to assail,— wholly destitute of the kind of practical sagacity which most easily inspires Englishmen with confidence,—with an ill-regulated literary ambition and a false melodramatic taste that were well calculated to increase tenfold the existing prejudices against him, it is difficult to conceive a greater marvel than the brilliant success which Mr. Disraeli has achieved, singlehanded, in a sphere of life usually thought singularly exclusive and inaccessible to unassisted adventurers.

The success of this great party-leader is, we believe, traceable to two principal gifts—a very sensitive and impressible, but extremely unoriginal imagination, and a dexterity seldom equalled in working up all the impressions he receives into materials for personal attacks. Had Mr. Disraeli been a man of deeper and more original imagination than he is, he could not have surrendered as he has done, at every crisis in his career, to the ascendant influence of the hour. He has never had a political faith,—he probably does not know what it means. No man has invented so many political theories. No living politician's fancy has been half so prolific of suggestions for new bases of political creed. No statesman has ever been so 'viewy.' But notwithstanding all his strictures on Sir Robert Peel for want of originality and imagination, there probably never was a statesman so unoriginal as himself. His efforts at originality,—whether political or literary,—have ever been of that excessively theatrical kind which seem, as it were, to be always gasping for breath; and he is never successful except when he desists from such efforts, and simply adopts or delineates what he sees in the actual life around him. Whether as a novelist or as a statesman, his efforts at original construction have always been rhapsodical. Those who knew his early fictions and 'Coningsby' well, recognised last session, in India Bill No. 2, unmistakeable traces of the same mind. The same unsound imagination which filled Mr. Disraeli's novels with the most flimsy and eccentric theories of history, society, and political organisation,—which invented the 'Venetian-Doge' theory of the English Constitution,—the doctrine of the absolute ascendancy of the 'Caucasian' race,—the gospel of 'Young England,'—the historical hypothesis that Charles the First was a martyr to the principle of direct taxation,—the identity of Tory principles with those of Free Trade,—the theory that the 'tendency of civilisation is to pure monarchy,'—that 'an educated nation recoils from the imperfect vicariat of what it calls a 'representative government,' and a thousand others,— has been equally visible whenever Mr. Disraeli has attempted to win the admiration of the House of Commons by any proposition of a directly constructive nature. No politician has ever shown, in the bad sense of the word, so *romantic* a political imagination,—in other words a fancy so little imbued with the laws of real life, so ready to revolt against those laws, and put feeble idealities in their place. His ideal measures, like his ideal heroes, have always seemed the inventions of a mind on the rack to produce something grand or startling, instead of something true and life-like; there is no trace in them of the genius which breathes in his criticisms of actual measures, and his delineations of actual men. Nothing has really impeded his progress more than his efforts after originality. His mind was made to receive impressions and to interpret the tendencies of others. When he has limited himself to this he has been marvellously successful. When he has striven to engrave something new upon his age, he has fallen far below the standard of even average English sense.

On the other hand, if there have been no statesmen of eminence so devoid of constructive genius as Mr. Disraeli—if, even, he has fallen far below his great adversary Sir Robert Peel in his attempts to create, simply because he has been possessed with the desire to astonish, instead of with the desire to interpret, his age,—there has seldom been a statesman with so great a power for understanding and delineating all that comes within the actual range of his experience, and turning it into a weapon of the most formidable efficiency. Mr. Disraeli has made himself a *power* in the House of Commons exactly by this art. Whenever he has lost way, it has been by attempts at original statesmanship; but, when he has confined his efforts to showing how well he understands both the weak and strong points of those around him, he has been terrible and quite unsurpassed. Whether in fiction or in debate, there are few who have drawn so many true and subtle sketches of those whom they have actually seen and known. His power seems limited to direct experience. He has no insight into past history,—no power of giving or restoring life to characters with which he has not come into personal contact. But he is an absolute master of personalities of all kinds, whether purely critical, flattering, or caustic; and it it is by the unsparing use of this formidable literary weapon that, in spite of all blunders, he has won his way to the eminence on which he now stands. He has said, in one of his works, 'nothing is great but the personal,' and for him, at least, it has been so. He has adopted the opinions of parties as he would adopt a national costume. 'Tory,' 'Radical,' 'Tory-Radical,' 'Free-Trader,' 'Protectionist,' 'Conservative,' 'Reformer,' no creed has come amiss to him, and amidst them all he has maintained the same clear eye for the personal qualities of those around him, and the same determined will to use them for individual or party ends.

In short, Mr. Disraeli owes his great success to his very unusual capacity for *applying* a literary genius, in itself limited, to the practical purposes of public life. Had his genius been really deeper than it is, it would have absorbed him, and he would have devoted his life to the exercise of an imagination which, as it is, he has principally valued as a formidable political weapon. While his combative instinct has been strong, and so determined him to seek a fair field for its practical satisfaction, his literary insight has been only of that depth which irritates and fires the intellect without absorbing it. It has not been deep enough to engross his powers; it has been quite deep enough to give him the sense of power. He forms, in this respect, a remarkable contrast to Sir E. B. Lytton, who, with probably greater literary genius, has nothing like the same power of wielding it as a practical instrument,—the same art of turning his literary ploughshares and pruning hooks into swords and spears. Indeed, practical politics is not an attractive field for men who care to delineate life more than they care to influence it. Statesmen must usually be occupied more with measures, social tendencies, public wants, national convictions, than with the niceties of individual character. Mr. Disraeli is just enough of a literary man to indicate clearly in all his speeches that these things do not seriously occupy him,—that he compels himself to use them as instruments for ends which interest him far more deeply. When we read his speeches we feel, by a kind of instinct, that there is nothing very real or very deep,—nothing which seems to him of essential importance,—as long as he stays in the field of dry argument and exposition. But when we come to the personal phases of the question, all is changed and living. The telling epithets, the graphic hints, the signs of living insight, are all reserved for those passages in which he addresses himself not to measures but to men, in which he throws off a happy picture of a statesman's career, or delineates with life-like touches the demeanour of the House of Commons. He has nothing of the statesman's power of imaging forth the actual effect and operation of the measures he advocates,—nothing of the statesman's power of penetrating to the heart of a deep national conviction. When he attempts these things, he is apt to produce some romantic failure that brings scorn upon himself; but, though almost all his power is limited to the use of a keen and delicate weapon very susceptible of abuse, he has at least recently shown that the responsibility of a high position can make him generous and dignified,—with here and there even a certain touch of chivalry,—in the wielding of a talent so individual and so pungent as his own.

Why Mr. Disraeli has Succeeded[1]

MR DISRAELI once said that those 'who went down to posterity were about as rare as planets;' but he will succeed in going down there himself. The Reform Act of 1867 will be remembered as long as the Constitution of England is remembered. Why so great a change was made so silently and with so little national discussion will amaze our children,—just as we of this generation cannot comprehend the Reform discussions of 1832, and why so much was hoped from a measure upon its face so prosaic. But Mr. Disraeli is identified with it. His name was the first on the back of the Bill of the names of those who brought it in, and his will be the name which posterity will think of with it. And the reward is just. It *is* Mr. Disraeli's Bill. Without professing to know what happened in the Cabinet, so much as this is certain. Mr. Disraeli all along wished to go down very low, to beat the Whigs—if possible, the Radicals too—by basing the support of the Conservative party upon a lower class than those which they could influence. For this end he induced his party to surrender their creed and their policy; he altered what his followers had to say, even more than the Constitution under which they are going to live. How then did he attain such a singular success?

It is usual to say that he attained it by fraud and deceit. And we certainly are not about to defend his morality. On the contrary, we have attacked it often, and, if need were, would attack it now. But a little study of human affairs is enough to show that fraud alone— fraud by itself—does not succeed; it is too ugly and coarse for man to bear; it is only when disguised in great qualities, and helped on by fine talents, that it prospers. What, then, in this case, were the accompanying aids?

Mr. Disraeli is one of the most observant students of human life in England. He said many years since of Sir Robert Peel, 'He was a bad judge of character. The prosperous routine of his youth was not

[1] This article was first published in *The Economist* for September 7 1867, Volume XXV, pp. 1009–10.

favourable to this talent. He never had to *struggle*.' But Mr. Disraeli has had to struggle. His career is of his own making; it has no precedent; he is the one literary adventurer, who has led the House of Commons, or who is likely, perhaps, to lead it, if wealth is strengthened by the new Bill as much as seems probable. In the course of his aspiring youth he observed all classes of men,—not deeply and profoundly perhaps; it is only the very greatest men who do that; but distinctly, and in their plain traits. His early novels are studies of conspicuous life. In them all the obvious momentary part of English society is sketched very vividly and very well.

The whole of this observant faculty, which was trained in social life, has been concentrated on Parliament. For years he has sat almost silent,—never raising petty discussions and confusing old people who thought a Leader of [the] Opposition ought to be always opposing, but watching day by day the course of events till he has, perhaps, the best and nicest parliamentary memory of his generation. Probably he required all this culture. He has not—at least experience seems to show that he has not—instinctive tact. There is even at times an inaptitude to comprehend those around him. When he asked last Session 'Why, what opinions have we changed?' there was a roar as much from his own side of the House as from the opposite; and, perhaps, there was hardly a man there who did not understand better than Mr. Disraeli why it was *gauche* to say that. He failed egregiously in his first speech, though it would be absurd to press that by itself, as many great speakers have failed at first, and most learn by paining their hearers, but there was a sort of opaque, undiscerning vanity about the performance, which was singularly unpromising. Indeed, as for instinctive tact, Mr. Disraeli has made stupendous blunders:— a Budget which everybody was to like, but which no one would accept; an Indian Bill, at which everybody laughed; speeches in Opposition innumerable, which made men say, till Lord Palmerston died, 'That Dizzy was the Whigs' best friend.' But now, with the training of years, he has developed a sort of second-hand tact by memory, which serves him well, and is surer than any he has to fight against.

Mr. Disraeli is not profound in the least, and perhaps he would laugh at telling what he thinks his best creed. But he has a fatal facility in suggesting hazy theories which would puzzle an Aristotle. The driest and hardest thinker could never get right if he persisted in tying his words into the pretty puzzles which Mr. Disraeli delights in, and which so often take. His language upon abstract subjects, for upon those of this world he can talk plainly enough, is to that of a thinker by profession—to the language, say, of Mr. Mill—what discolouring artificial light is to daylight. You never know what he is talking about, or whether it means much or little. But, though not deep, Mr. Disraeli's mind is beyond measure quick, and, as far as it penetrates, original. There is nothing routine about him. He got the House of Commons to sit at unheard of hours—from 2 till 7—and seemed to think nothing of it, though some grave members thought it almost a Reform Bill in itself. It has been said, not very wisely, that the best general is he who best knows how to repair a defeat and if that were translated, it might be said that Mr. Disraeli was the best Leader of the House of Commons, for he knows how to glide out of a scrape better than anyone.

To this quickness of a keen man, he joins, by some freak of nature, the imperturbability of an apathetic man. Whether he is quite as impassive as he seems, may, indeed, be doubted. Very near observers are said to be able to detect shades of wincing. But very impassible he must be; and it is a sort of 'double first' in skirmishing talent to be so quick to hit, and so hard to *be* hit. No doubt the opportunities of his career have been favourable,—at least, they look so now that he has made a good use of them. He found the Tory party at the death of Lord George Bentinck almost barren of great ability in the House of Commons. The trained official Peelites who before led the party had followed Sir Robert Peel. The grade of gentry who fill the country seats, and mostly compose the Conservative party in the Commons, are perhaps the least able and valuable part of English society. They have neither the responsibilities nor the culture of great noblemen, and they have never felt the painful need of getting on, which sharpens the middle class. They have a moderate sort of wealth which teaches them little, and a steady sort of mind fit for common things, but they have no flexibility and they have no ideas. Almost the worst of the class, too, are often sent to Parliament, and the best left out, because a foolish prejudice requires that the member shall have land within the county. Mr. Disraeli found himself with the most ingenious and manipulating intellect of his generation at the head of the 'Army of Fogies,' and the result is what we see.

What have been the consequences of the slow honesty of the Tory party, and the quick dishonesty of the Tory leader, future years will unfold better than we can understand them now. But it is well for us to see exactly what the forces were; and that it was not fraud itself which won, but fraud in a convenient place, and with singular ability.

Mr. Disraeli's Administration[1]

Mr. Disraeli's Administration has lasted nominally only nine months; but, in fact, we may fairly assume that he has had the practical guidance of the Tory policy since the resignation of Lord Russell's Government in 1866. It is impossible now not to cast back a glance at his use of the power which he had gained for himself by his brilliant talents and pertinacity. Has that use of power been worthy or unworthy of the skill and tact and undaunted perseverance which Mr. Disraeli displayed in climbing to his high office from that obscure position in which it is said, on good authority, that he deliberately resolved on attaining the eminence he has at last reached?

This is not precisely an easy question to reply to. That Mr. Disraeli has shown as Prime Minister precisely the same qualities, without any trace at all of degeneration in their kind, by which he reached the top of the ladder, we entirely believe. There has been, as far as we see, no sign of failing power in his administration. He has acted as Prime Minister, and as virtual Tory leader before he was Prime Minister, very much as any shrewd observer would have been disposed to expect, though perhaps with even more moderation and judgment. But whether the class of abilities which were specially fitted for the great political climbing feat which Mr. Disraeli has performed were of the class likely to be particularly useful, or as well adapted to Mr. Disraeli's position at the summit as they were adapted to the labour of ascent, is certainly very much more doubtful. When the end is attained, we naturally look for the display of new qualities which would justify the laborious appliance of means. We want to see whether the climber climbed—like Lord Clive in his boyhood when he ascended the church steeple—simply for the sake of the gymnastic feat, simply because he was conscious of a great climbing power, or because he was conscious of powers which could not be adequately exerted except at the highest point of political influence. We may say at once that we see no trace of power of this kind in Mr. Disraeil;

[1] This article was first published in *The Economist* for December 12 1868, Volume XXVI, pp. 1414-5.

that his abilities seem to us to be much more extraordinary when we look at the position he has won, than when we attempt to estimate the use which he has made of it; that he seems to us to have displayed Herculean powers in reaching a position wherein he found not very much that he cared to do, except occupying it, and still less that it was of any great advantage either to his own party or to the country that he should do. He has been a shrewd, composed, intelligent, and generally dignified Prime Minister; but he has not gained fresh credit for his party; he has not developed any original policy; he has not inspired as first minister any fresh confidence in himself.

It has been Mr. Disraeli's misfortune throughout his main political career to lead a party of very strong prejudices and principles, without feeling himself any cordial sympathy with either the one or the other. No doubt that is precisely the fact which has enabled him on most great emergencies to be of use to his party. His completely external intelligence has been to them what the elephant driver's—the mahout's —is to the elephant, comparatively insignificant as a force, but so familiar with all the habits of the creature which his sagacity has to guide, and so entirely, if it only knew, at its mercy, that all his acuteness is displayed in contriving to turn the creature's habits and instincts to his own end, profit, and advantage,—which, however, cannot be done without also carefully preserving the creature itself from great dangers, and guarding it against the violence of its own passions. In this way Mr. Disraeli has necessarily been of great use to the Tory party. But something more than this is needed for a great and successful Tory statesman. There must be at least some sympathy as well as professional counsel. There must be some power to inspire enthusiasm as well as to create intellectual respect. There must be some sense of common conviction as well as of common interest. There must be some identity of sentiment as well as of mutual dependence. Mr. Disraeli when he had reached the summit of his ambition naturally needed more than ever this community of faith and purpose, in order to teach him how to use his power both for his party's benefit and his own. But he had it not. He could only calculate the chances of success without reference to their aims and wishes; and the effect of course was to diminish his influence over them, without even giving the appearance of individual conviction and personal self-denial to his.policy. It seemed a policy in the air, calculated to succeed, not calculated for any special object higher and better than success.

If we look at Mr. Disraeli's legislative policy, no one can avoid the criticism that while it was in one great instance at least *not* a policy favourable to his own party, it affected to be so, and was forced upon them on the plea that it would prove so. Mr. Disraeli proposed as a Conservative policy, because it would 'dish the Whigs,' that which was not really Conservative and which dished the Conservatives if anybody; and so he had neither the party success of a clever strategic move, nor the national success of sacrificing party to the people's welfare. With regard to Reform this was conspicuously the case. What he proposed in pointed opposition to Mr. Gladstone, and in order to deprive the Liberals of that 'prætorian guard' of select artisans, to secure whose aid Lord Russell's borough franchise was, Mr. Disraeli thought, specially adapted,—namely, household suffrage in boroughs, —proved specially fatal to his party. Instead of getting at the supposed Conservatism and Toryism of the most ignorant and most prejudiced class, it evoked a far stronger Liberalism in the boroughs than we had ever reached before. On the contrary, the county franchise, which was not due to any *finesse* of Mr. Disraeli's, which was taken with no practical alteration from the Liberal bill, did in fact evoke a certain additional Conservative force on which Mr. Disraeli had never counted. His strategy wholly failed. What he proposed to do for party objects failed of those objects. And, unfortunately, he never professed or proposed to sink party in the welfare of the nation. In the Reform Act as a strategist he unquestionably outflanked himself.

And on the Irish Church,—the only other great legislative conflict which falls within the period of his administration, and for this indeed he alone, and not in any degree Lord Derby, is responsible,—he again failed in doing the absolutely best thing for his party, without succeeding in even the appearance of sacrificing party to country. It was a great mistake to throw out feelers in the direction of endowing the Roman Catholic Church, not only without being prepared to follow them up by a frank declaration of policy, but even when he was prepared to disavow them and creep out of them as best he could. He weakened and disheartened the mere Conservatives, without winning the credit of a generous sacrifice of power for a policy which many would have thought farseeing and statesmanlike. In this case as in the last, Mr. Disraeli's difficulty was that he had no personal preferences, no political convictions either in common with his party or divergent from them. He acted as he felt, like a statesman living from hand to mouth, *using* his party rather than expressing its feelings or rallying its forces. Against a party that was convinced, led by a statesman whose convictions were deep, he naturally found himself almost powerless.

But if in strategy and in legislation Mr. Disraeli's administration has not been admirable, any fair politician will admit that on the whole his ministerial use of official power in selecting the men for the appointments he has had to fill up has been most shrewdly, even wisely used. In distributing the offices amongst his own colleagues his choice was always considerate and acute, though this may be originally due to Lord Derby. Mr. Gathorne Hardy showed himself a very able administrator both at the Poor Law Board and at the Home Office. Lord Cranborne was perhaps as good an Indian Secretary as was ever appointed, and Lord Carnarvon was excellent at the Colonial Office. Sir Stafford Northcote has unquestionably made an able Indian Secretary since Lord Cranborne's resignation, and if the other officials of Mr. Disraeli's Government have been less remarkable for administrative ability, it is less from any fault of their chief than from the radical poverty of his materials. But it is in the external appointments, especially since Mr. Disraeli became solely responsible for them, that he has, except in one notable instance, shown the greatest ability and insight, and the greatest freedom from partisan feeling. Lord Mayo's appointment to be Governor-General of India appears to most men a very remarkable exception to this rule. Mr. Disraeli, however, asserts positively that he believes him to be eminently fitted for the post, and though the public have absolutely no access to his data for that apparently eccentric view, it is still quite fair that, considering the spirit shown in his other appointments, he should have full credit for sincerity. In his ecclesiastical appointments undoubtedly Mr. Disraeli has shown disinterestedness and the acuteness of an impartial man of the world, judging by the qualities which he hears on all sides ascribed to the most eminent candidates for promotion. And it is remarkable that he has evidently regarded a high and impressive moral energy as a quality of the first importance for his episcopal appointments. The promotion of the Dean of Cork to the bishopric of Peterborough, and the translation of the Bishop of London to the see of Canterbury, are conspicuous instances of this. Mr. Disraeli might have been satisfied with learning and a spotless reputation. He has seen that something more was desirable in a leader of the Church—a certain originality of moral nature as well. On the whole, we must recognise in his use of patronage a very dispassionate and, in some sense, elevated judgment, which even Mr. Gladstone may scarcely succeed in rivalling. In statesmanship, Mr. Disraeli's administration has been a failure; in the choice of officials, it has been in some sense even a distinguished success.

Mr. Disraeli as a Member of the House of Commons[1]

Nothing could be more out of place or premature than to review as yet Mr. Disraeli's career. That career is not yet ended. But some remarks may be made of him as a member of the House of Commons, in which he has sat for forty years, and where he obtained his political eminence and power. That part of his career is certainly over, for he has chosen to leave its peculiar scene.

During this long period Mr. Disraeli has filled four parts. First,—that of a political free lance or outsider. And it was in this that he first obtained fame. The best opportunity for such a man is when parties are breaking up,—when secret feelings are in many minds; when cautious men do not know what to say. The latter part of Sir Robert Peel's ministry was such a period. From the time when he became conspicuously and obviously a Free-trader there was always a secret anger in the Conservative ranks which craved for an outlet, but which no 'regular man' could express. This Mr. Disraeli spoke out. From the time of Mr. Milne's sugar amendment, in 1844, till the completion of the disruption of the Tories, in 1846, Mr. Disraeli poured epigram upon epigram and innuendo on innuendo on the 'organised hypocrisy' of his professed leader; and there is no doubt that Sir Robert Peel suffered exceedingly under the smart. He was, in every way, a most sensitive man, and he was especially sensitive in all that related to the House of Commons, which was the scene of his life, and to his position there. But now he was, for the first time in his life, exposed to a style of attack to which he had not the sort of power to reply, but which was for the moment the most effective style of any; and he was pained accordingly. No 'free lance,' perhaps, has ever achieved so much and so suddenly as Mr. Disraeli then did. Upon this part of his career an historical examiner would give him first-rate marks—much greater than he would give to any competitor.

[1] This article was first published in *The Economist* for August 19 1876, Volume XXXIV, pp. 969–70.

The next, and far the longest, of Mr. Disraeli's parliamentary parts, is that of Leader of [the] Opposition. And in this he showed eminent mind—not equal to that of his free-lance period, but still very great. His powers of epigram and amusing nonsense gave an infinite aid, year after year, to a party that was to be beaten. And after his fashion he showed a high magnanimity and conscience in not opposing or hampering the ministry on great questions—say of foreign policy, when his so doing would hurt the country. But this praise must end here. On all minor parliamentary questions Mr. Disraeli has simply no conscience at all. He regards them as a game—as an old special pleader regarded litigation, to be played so as to show your skill, and so as to win, but without any regard to the consequences. Indeed, Mr. Disraeli at bottom believes that they have no consequences—that all is settled by questions of race, 'Caucasian or Semitic,' and that it is simple pedantry in such things to be scrupulous. And still worse than this, which is an amusing defect after all, and excusable—(for there *are* many deeper issues and causes than are dreamed of in parliamentary philosophy),—Mr. Disraeli often showed in opposition a turn for nonsense, which was *not* amusing. He has many gifts, but he has not the gift of thinking out a subject, and when he tries to produce grave thought he only makes platitudes. And some of his 'mares' nests,' like his difficulty in the Franco-German War, from our guarantee to the Saxon provinces of Prussia, are incredible, and could only have been reached by a mind which, with many elements of genius, has also an element of hare-brained recklessness. Drearier hearing, or drearier reading, than Mr. Disraeli's Opposition harangues, when they were philosophical, can hardly anywhere be found. But still, though with these and other defects, he *did* lead the Tory Opposition through long melancholy years, when one did not know who else *could* have or who *would* have.

The next of Mr. Disraeli's parliamentary parts was the leader of a ministry in a minority, where again he was first-rate. He showed sometimes—in 1852, in 1858, and in 1866—a nimbleness, a tact, and dexterity far surpassing, probably anything that Parliament has ever seen similar. He 'hit the House'—to use a phrase which Burke used of a like but very inferior person—he 'hit the House between the wind and the water,' and cut with a light witticism knots insoluble by solemn argument. If, by a series of 'selections,' nature had made a man so fit for this kind of work, it would have been a marvel. But Mr. Disraeli drifted in it, as if by chance, from quite another calling and another sphere.

Lastly, Mr. Disraeli has been lately, and was but yesterday, leader of a ministry in a majority. And here there was a wonderful contrast. So far from being first-rate, he was ninth-rate. He seemed to resemble those guerilla commanders who, having achieved great exploits with scanty and ill-trained troops, nevertheless are utterly at a loss and fail when they are placed at the head of a first-rate army. In 1867, he made a minority achieve wonderful things, but in 1876, when he had the best majority—the most numerous and obedient—since Mr. Pitt, he did nothing with it. So far from being able to pass great enactments, he could not even despatch ordinary business at decent hours. The gravest and sincerest of Tory members—men who hardly murmur at anything—have been heard to complain that it *was* hard, after voting so well and doing so little, they should be kept up so very late. The session just closed will be known in parliamentary annals as one of the least effective or memorable on record, and yet one of the most fatiguing. And this collapse is no accident in Mr. Disraeli's career, but a thing essentially characteristic of the man, and which might have been predicted by anyone who had analysed the traits which he had shown before. If we may be pardoned the metaphor—though his chaff is exquisite, his wheat is poor stuff. The solid part of his mind—the part fit for regulating bills and clauses—is as inferior to that of an ordinary man of decent ability as the light and imaginative part is superior. An incessant and almost avowed inaccuracy pervades him. And if you ask such a man to regulate the stupendous business of Parliament—to arrange, and if possible effect, the most complex *agenda* that ever was in the world,—failure is inevitable. It is like entering a light hack for a ploughing-match. In the last parliamentary situation, Mr. Disraeli has scarcely seemed to be what he used to be, and this because that situation was the one for which he was the least suited, and the last in which he should have been placed. As so often happens, having obtained the ambition of his life—to be a minister with power—he found he had only got where he ought not to be— he found that he could not wield the power.

And two things have been common to Mr. Disraeli all through these positions. In them all he has charmed the House, and has given debates in which he took part a kind of nice and literary flavour which other debates had not, and which there is no one left to give to them. He was the best representative which the 'Republic of Letters' has ever had in Parliament, for he made his way by talents—especially by a fascination of words—essentially literary. And on the other hand, though he charmed Parliament he never did anything more. He had no influence with the country. Such a vast power over Englishmen as has been possessed by Lord Palmerston and by Mr. Gladstone was out of his way altogether. Between Mr. Disraeli and common Englishmen there was too broad a gulf—too great a difference. He was simply unintelligible to them. 'Ten miles from London,' to use the old phrase, there is scarcely any real conception of him. His mode of regarding parliamentary proceedings as a play and a game is incomprehensible to the simple and earnest English nature. Perhaps he has gained more than he has lost by the English not understanding him. At any rate, the fact remains that the special influence of this great gladiator never passed the walls of the amphitheatre; he has ruled the country by ruling Parliament, but has never had any influence in Parliament reverberating from the nation itself.

Edward Stanley, fourteenth Earl of Derby

Introductory note

Edward George Geoffrey Smith Stanley (1799–1869), the son of Edward Smith Stanley, thirteenth Earl of Derby, was born at Knowsley Park, Lancashire. He was educated at Eton and at Christ Church, Oxford. Between 1822 and 1844 he was Whig M.P. for Stockbridge, Preston, Windsor and North Lancashire successively. From 1827–30 he was Under-Secretary of State for the Colonies, and from 1830–3 was Chief Secretary for Ireland. In 1832 he introduced the Reform Bill for Ireland, having already instituted the Irish Board of Works and introduced the Irish Education Act in 1831. In 1833 he carried the Peace Preservation Act and the Irish Church Temporalities Act. In 1833 he carried the Act for the abolition of slavery. He was opposed to the appropriation of Irish church revenues for secular purposes, and resigned over this in 1834. He joined the opposition and was Colonial Secretary under Peel from 1841–4. On Peel's declaration of immediate free trade, he resigned, and accepted leadership of the anti-free traders. In 1851 he succeeded to the earldom of Derby. In 1852 he formed a protectionist ministry but failed to secure a majority at the general election, and resigned after a defeat on the budget. During his second premiership from 1858–9 he settled disputes with France, Naples, and America concerning rights of search. When he introduced a bill for equalising the town and country franchise he was defeated and dissolved parliament. His last administration was from 1866–8, during which he and Disraeli framed the Reform Bill of 1867. Lord Derby resigned through ill health in 1868, and died at Knowsley Park in 1869.

The late Lord Derby and
the Conservative Party[1]

WE have not very much respect for the fine-spun theories by which
some of our contemporaries endeavour to explain the ascendancy of
the late Lord Derby in the Conservative party. It seems to us that he
ruled by virtue of a very intelligible qualification—that he was the
most Conservative politician among politicians competent to rule at
all. That he was a great peer is true, but there are peers who represent
the aristocratic sentiment quite as fully, and whose families are as
illustrious in our history, who never obtain any influence at all. It is
true also that he was rich, but there are richer peers who are nobodies;
and to do Englishmen justice, although they make competence a
condition of success, and cordially respect wealth, they do not regulate
their loyalty to a leader by calculations as to his income. A little too
much is made also of the popular regard attracted to Lord Derby by
his courage, and chivalry, and interest in the turf, and splendid classical
scholarship. His scholarship has been rather against Mr. Gladstone.
We doubt if Lord Derby ever was a very popular personage, in the
usual sense of those words,—in the sense, for example, in which they
are often applied to describe Lord Palmerston's hold upon the country.
The mob out of Liverpool knew very little about him. He ruled the
Lords, and he led his party, but he never acquired a personal following
as Sir Robert Peel did, and never gained—as really popular statesmen
do—a genuine appreciation from the other side, while the regret for his
death has, out of Lancashire, nothing of a national character about it.
His leadership was due, we conceive, mainly to this—that on all the
points for which Conservatives sincerely care he was genuinely
Conservative, while most persons of his parliamentary rank, eloquence,
and capacity of deciding in emergencies are not. Conservatives desire
mainly four things—that the social system should not be materially
changed, but remain based on a code favourable to aristocracy; that

[1] This article was first published in *The Economist* for October 30 1869, Volume XXVII,
pp. 1279–80.

the established Church should retain a definite and legal pre-eminence among the churches of the land; that land should be made of all kinds of property the safest and most dignified; and that Liberals should be defeated whenever possible and snubbed always; and Lord Derby desired all these things as strongly as they did. Much of his character is still obscure—for example, the *kind* of mental fear which influenced him in dealing with the Hyde Park riots—and will remain obscure till more of his recent history is known; but to doubt that he was sincerely and heartily an aristocrat, a friend of the Church, a champion of 'the land,' and an enemy of the Whigs, is to misread his whole career, and these were the things his party expected him to be, and reverenced him for being. In trying to secure their ends he might err, and very often did err, but he always wanted to secure them, and being confident of that, and unable to suggest wiser schemes than his own, they followed him with persistent devotion. Even in the single case in which he seemed to postpone his predilections to a desire for power, it is most probable that he was not postponing them—that he really imagined, like hundreds of abler men, that his reform bill would yield a majority highly friendly to Conservatism as he understood the word; and indeed he was not altogether wrong. The Bill did increase Conservative power in the counties, and in the towns which Lord Derby best understood, the towns of Lancashire; and he was only wrong because he judged too much by the evidence of his own eyes, and forgot the kingdom he did not see. He was a *fitting* Conservative leader, and on the whole, though a rash and unsuccessful one, he was not incompetent. He kept the upper House very firmly together; he fought hopeless battles like protection very resolutely; he preserved the Irish Church for twenty years after it ought to have perished; he organised a 'country party'; and he always avoided ruinous collisions with the majority of the people. He had, too, one statesmanlike quality, very often indeed wanting to men who are conscious that their attitude is one of resistance,—he could take a decision when it involved immense responsibility. He quitted a cabinet to save the Irish Church; he risked a quarrel with the Crown to prevent the creation of life Peers; he accepted household suffrage, and adhered to it when some of his ablest lieutenants shrank; and in the Trent affair he made up his mind to a great war so decisively that he is credibly declared to have conveyed an assurance of support to Lord Palmerston. In nine cases out of ten he was wrong in his political forecast, his political wishes, and his political action; but he was never—except perhaps once—more wrong than his followers, and as he was more eloquent, more decisive, and more influential with his order than they, we cannot affect to wonder at his ascendancy in their councils.

His decease will, we believe, be found to leave a greater blank than is at present expected. Whether he was a statesman or not, and we believe he was not, he was undoubtedly a man who could and did rule a party. There is no one now who in a grand emergency can walk down to the House of Lords and be quite sure that if he likes to run the risk he can veto a great Liberal measure; and the disappearance of that reserved power, a power which it should be remembered he used with almost timid caution, will greatly affect the position of the Tories. The fact that they could in the last resort always arrest movement was one which greatly increased, if not their influence with the country, at least their weight with the ministry of the day, which never wanted if it could help it to be driven to revolutionary or coercive measures. Nor is there any man quite sure of the support of the unbroken party in the Commons. Mr. Disraeli is not, and Mr. Gathorne Hardy is not, and the party must range itself behind one of those two men, and if they quarrel there is no one to settle the dispute. This is a great loss, and for the present an irreparable one, for the Earl leaves no successor. Lord Salisbury cannot, while Mr. Disraeli lives, have his influence in the Commons; and Lord Stanley, who might acquire as much, does not stand in the same relation to Conservatism in the country or to the general body of Peers. He is sure to defend landed property, and nearly sure to see upheld the aristocratic constitution of society; but he is not sure to hate the Whigs, and is very lukewarm indeed in his devotion to the Church. That he will become a Liberal we doubt, for the Liberalism of our day tends more and more to become sympathetic,—to depart from that cold, strict line of reasoning which attracts Lord Stanley towards what may be called the economic school. He could accompany Liberals in an attack upon land-laws which clearly diminished rent, or production of physical comfort; but the moment they began to legislate to make tenants more independent, to raise the standard of manhood, even at the sacrifice of wealth, he would draw back, or remain quiescent. On the other hand he can hardly become a genuine Tory, for belief in establishments is of the very essence of that creed, and even if he did, the party would hardly follow him. They would always suspect him of being too sensible, and of seeing the other side too clearly, and he has none of the eloquence which could overcome that latent doubt. He will have, we suspect, either to stand aside awaiting the formation of that party of Moderates which some politicians expect, or devote himself still more sedulously to the study of foreign affairs, the branch of state service which of all others he is said to like best. In either case he cannot fill his father's place, and Conservatives will, we imagine, find that that place was very useful to them; that to a party which is lost if it divides, an ultimate referee, sure to sympathise with their views, even if he carried them out badly, was almost invaluable. Lord Derby could, and except in the Irish Church debates did, make those Conservatives who trust Mr. Disraeli and those who distrust him pull together, and we question if there is anyone left in either House who can do that. The keystone has fallen out, and a reconstructed party, like a reconstructed house, is never quite the same.

Edward Henry Stanley, fifteenth Earl of Derby

Introductory note

Edward Henry Stanley (1826–1893) was born at Knowsley Park, Lancashire, the eldest son of Edward Stanley, fourteenth Earl of Derby, and of Emma, daughter of Lord Skelmersdale. He was educated at Rugby and at Trinity College, Cambridge. Member of Parliament for King's Lynn from 1848–69, he became Under-Secretary for Foreign Affairs in 1852. In the second Derby Ministry, 1858–9 he was Colonial Secretary and, after the passing of the India Bill, Indian Secretary. From 1866–8 he was Foreign Secretary under his father Lord Derby and Disraeli, and mediated between France and Prussia in 1867. He supported the Reform Bill of 1867 but led the opposition to the Irish disestablishment bill very half-heartedly. He succeeded to the earldom in 1869. From 1874–8 he was Foreign Secretary in Disraeli's second ministry. In 1880 he left the Conservatives and eventually joined the Liberal Unionists, and led them in the House of Lords. He died at Knowsley Park in 1893.

Lord Derby on the
Conservative Situation[1]

I⊤ is always satisfactory to politicians who care less for the immediate
party vicissitudes of the day than for the general result of all such
vicissitudes, to see the ranks of the Conservatives led by a statesman
who thoroughly represents the true genius of English Conservatives.
There is of course much in Lord Derby's able speech at Liverpool on
Tuesday with the tendency of which we wholly differ; but we cannot
help rejoicing to see any man taking the lead of English Conservatives
who succeeds to the place occupied by the late Sir Robert Peel—who
is, above all things, sober, who is not only sober but of the English
school of sobriety, who is Conservative more because he distrusts
novelties intellectually than because he has any romantic respect for
the past, who fights Liberalism rather by forcing it to show good cause
for every step it takes, than by springing on it brand-new sensational
theories as to the significance and grandeur of British institutions—in
a word, one who talks the political dialect of English country gentlemen, and does not suppose that he can unite his party by clever
rhodomontade, or annihilate the Radicals by the showy flashes of a
romancing imagination. If Lord Derby could but lead the Conservatives we should find the Conservatives at once moderated and united
by his strong common sense and his frigid lucidity. There could be
no greater benefit to the Liberal party. It would compel them to be
prudent, it would force them to be united, it would curb their vagaries,
it would temper their sanguineness, it would stimulate their administrative zeal and caution. An opposition led by such a leader as Lord
Derby would be the best of all resisting media in which the party of
reform could move. We should be more likely to exhaust existing
administrative power before attempting the always questionable
resource of new legislative powers; and we should be far less likely
to put forward legislative schemes of imposing outlines for which the

---

[1] This article was first published in *The Economist* for January 13 1872, Volume XXX,
pp. 33-4.

mind of the country is as yet unprepared. Moreover, with Lord Derby at the head of the Opposition, the practical difference of tendency between the two parties would be very much narrowed, and therefore much more distinct. No one clearly knows what Mr. Disraeli may approve or disapprove. He is a sort of unknown quantity in politics. Lord Derby always makes his drift distinct, and always lets us see its reason—a quality greatly tending to clear away the obscurities of a political contest. The more Mr. Disraeli cedes the guidance of his party to Lord Derby, the better it will be not only for Conservative prospects, but also for Liberal unity and consistency of purpose. It is quite worth while to follow Lord Derby briefly over the more important heads of his speech, just to show where and how his principles differ from those of the shrewdest part of the Liberal party, and how much we should gain by having the difference thoroughly canvassed and definitely measured.

On the sarcasms at the catastrophes which have injured, and the errors which have somewhat discredited, the present Government, it is not necessary to follow Lord Derby—as these are just the sort of hits which, whether deserved or undeserved, are independent of political principle. His discussion of principles he begins with the House of Lords, on which he takes exceedingly moderate ground, amounting precisely to this, that till a better and more popular alternative can be discovered, the House of Lords will certainly not be overthrown. That is true of course, and many Liberals have said the same; but Lord Derby exaggerates his case grossly when he says that the defence for an hereditary house of the legislature is much better than that for an hereditary throne, on the ground that there must be some sensible persons in a great number even of hereditary peers, while the chance in favour of a sensible hereditary monarch is to say the least much smaller. That may be true, but it does not prove Lord Derby's point. A sensible monarch in a country where the political prerogative of the monarch is so closely limited as it is in England is not of the first importance; still less does it matter that his sense, if he have sense, shall sway towards the popular side of politics. But in relation to a co-ordinate House of Parliament it is not only sense, but sense with a particular bias, that is desirable; and if you have sense with a strong and tenacious opposite bias, the more sense there is, the worse almost it may be for the country. We are quite inclined to agree practically with Lord Derby that a few good life-

peers and a sound tradition for the guidance of the House of Lords—
we would say in short, such a leader as himself—are about the only
feasible improvements we can hope to make at present. But we differ
from him greatly as to the extent of the anomaly, and hold that the
constitutional monarchy may well contrive to outlast long the much
more dangerous institution of a house of the legislature in which
there is and must be a steady and chronic inclination to differ widely
from the representatives of the people. Such an institution as this might
become profoundly unpopular, and go down before a sudden burst of
popular impatience almost at any moment. It will no doubt take a
great deal of imprudent guidance to excite such a burst of impatience
among a people so slow to embrace great changes as the English.
Still it may come at any time, and how long it may be deferred must
depend on the sagacity of the leaders and members of this curious
political anomaly.

Then there is the Church question and the education question on
which Lord Derby's tone is of course the very model of moderation.
His counsel comes to this, that the policy of disestablishing the Irish
Church of the minority would lead logically to a similar disestablishment of the English Church of the moiety of the nation, but that in
English politics we do not go by logic, and that while churchmen can
agree inside the Church there will be no difficulty in routing Mr.
Miall and his allies.[2] That is an unusually cautious way of insinuating
—if Lord Derby really meant to insinuate—that the establishment of
some religion in any state is right on principle, and that the Irish
disestablishment was therefore wrong on principle, but a precedent
not likely to be followed in a state where there is so little grievance
in the right policy as there is in England. The difference between
what Lord Derby's language suggested, and was possibly meant to
suggest, and the sound Liberal principle, was simply this—that while
he seems to indicate that the principle of an establishment is never to be
attacked, moderate Liberals think it entirely a matter of expediency,
and would discuss the question in every individual case solely on the
special circumstances of that case, and with regard to the consequences
to which a particular establishment might be shown to lead. We can
quite conceive a time coming,—though we do not say it will come,—

---

[2] Edward Miall, a Congregationalist minister and founder of *The Nonconformist*, was
an implacable enemy of the Establishment and a supporter of the complete separation
of Church and State—Ed.

when the English Establishment itself might be an evil to be removed. Lord Derby's language half implies that in a case where an establishment inflicted an extreme injustice—that of Ireland—it was politically *wrong* to remove it; but he also intimates his opinion that unless English churchmen pull well together, the English institution may in fact fall like the sister Establishment. So the issue between the Liberal and Conservative party is surely narrow enough,—the former maintaining that the question is always one of a large political expediency; the latter not conceding this, but still quite disposed to discuss the question of expediency, and to admit that if that was decided against them, there is not practically much chance of holding their ground.

Then Lord Derby comes to the licensing and sanitary and social questions, and on these there is even less difference between him and the Liberal party. He holds that on all these subjects new legislation can do comparatively little, that we must look chiefly to negative measures, the energy of private enterprise, and the enforcement of good administrative regulations. On the proposed Alliance measure, the so-called permissive bill,[3] Lord Derby puts forward genuine Liberal doctrine with the utmost force. 'Their theory is that if by any means you can persuade two-thirds of the ratepayers of a district that beer is objectionable, they shall have the right to impose that rule of diet on the remaining third. Now, that is sheer tyranny and intolerance of the worst sort. It would be just as reasonable to lay it down that where two-thirds of the population of any district were Protestants, no Catholic should be allowed to open a place of worship, or that where two-thirds were Liberals, no Conservative should be allowed to set up a newspaper.' We cannot conceive of an answer to that argument. Whether Lord Derby is right in preferring 'to have the trade open to all competitors,' and to try and prevent abuses by enforcing strict regulations, is, we think, very doubtful. Beerhouses and gin palaces, when multiplied beyond a certain number, become public nuisances and sources of very gross annoyance to all quiet people, and of active temptation to the poor. Now, if two-thirds of the inhabitants of any parish have no right to prescribe a diet to the other third, still less has the minority of ratepayers the right to impose a great nuisance on the majority. We suspect that without limiting the

[3] The United Kingdom Alliance was a temperance organisation which had been striving to have an Act passed for some years on the lines described by Lord Derby in his speech. Mr Wilfred Lawson M P introduced such a measure in 1864, it seems to have eventually secured a second reading but later lapsed and appears to have come to nothing.—Ed.

licences in some reasonable way, no real reform can be effected. But here clearly Lord Derby is a Liberal and not a Conservative at all. And nothing can be better than his attack on the foolish proposals of Mr. Scott Russell and his friends to remove pauperism by legislation, when the only good that it is proposed to do can be done far better, and with much less danger of abuse, by building societies and co-operative stores. As Lord Derby remarks, the greatness of the English nation is not of government manufacture. It is the result of private energy, and without the full development of that energy England will not grow greater.

On foreign policy of course Lord Derby has a sneer at the American Treaty and the Black Sea Treaty, and thinks that Lord Granville will not greatly pride himself on either. Perhaps not, but he will certainly have less cause to reproach himself for sinning deliberately against light, than has Lord Derby to reproach himself for the treaty concerning Luxembourg, to which we objected so earnestly at the time, and of which every subsequent year has tended to show the mischievousness and the folly.

On the whole, it is clear that Lord Derby's Conservatism differs from the wisest form of the Liberalism opposed to him only by a much more deeply ingrained distrust of change, but not by a radically different set of political axioms and principles. Lord Derby comes nearer to the type of the late Sir Robert Peel than any other Conservative statesman of his day; and it is in competition with such a type of Conservatism as this that the Liberal party will become welded most closely together, and will learn the firmness and the caution of wise audacity.

John Laird Mair Lawrence, first Baron Lawrence

Introductory note

John Laird Mair Lawrence (1811–1879) was born in Richmond, Yorkshire, the eighth of twelve children of Lieutenant-Colonel Alexander Lawrence. He was educated at Bristol, Londonderry, Bath and Haileybury. He went to Calcutta in 1830 to work for the East India Company. From 1830–4 he was assistant-magistrate and collector at Delhi. Between 1834 and 1844 he was in charge first of the northern and then of the southern divisions of the Delhi territory. From 1844–6 he was magistrate and collector in Delhi, and from 1846–8 administrator of the newly constituted district, the Jullundur Doab. Between 1848 and 1857 he was first a member of the board of administration and then chief commissioner for the Punjab. In 1858 Lawrence received a baronetcy, after the capture of Delhi from the mutineers in 1857, which had been achieved through his advice and action. He became a Privy Councillor in 1858, and was in England at the India Office from 1859–62. From 1863–9 he was Viceroy of India; the chief aims of his administration being irrigation, sanitation, railway extension, and peace. In 1869 he was created Baron Lawrence of the Punjab and of Grately. He died in London in 1879.

Lord Lawrence[1]

THE elevation of Sir John Lawrence to the peerage, gazetted on Tuesday, deserves we think more than a passing word. No man of our time belonging so clearly to the middle class has ever compelled such complete and universal recognition by the aid of those qualities alone which distinctively belong to the middle class—has ever shown so completely what those qualities are, wherein they succeed, and wherein they are found wanting. The son of an Irish officer with a large family and limited means, forced into the civil service almost against his own will, John Lawrence took to the work of governing Asiatics in the same spirit and using the same powers as a self-made engineer or contractor, a Brindley or Brassey, employs in some great material undertaking. Throughout his life till he became viceroy he was always engaged in reducing something or somebody to order, compelling men and things to work in the groove in which they could be of most use to the common weal as he judged the common weal to be. Now the obstacle was a mountain to be bored, and then a swamp to be filled up; here was a province choked with nobles to be tamed; there a great city to be rescued from anarchy; now there were mountaineers to be bridled, and again there were mutineers to be pulverised; but whatever it was the work was always done,—done promptly, done thoroughly, and done by the shortest road. The first work of a new government, particularly in Asia, is always of this kind, and for that first work there probably never was a foreman like John Lawrence. His men, to begin with, were always in hand, because if they were not they were smashed, flung aside, driven out of the way by the plainest and severest of rebukes. It was not of the slightest use talking about heavy work or inadequate pay or mental idiosyncrasies; there was the work to be done, and you had to do it or go, though if you did it efficiently you were left very much to your own discretion. Till he became Viceroy, and indeed afterwards, Sir John Lawrence governed his subordinates

[1] This article was first published in *The Economist* for April 3 1869, Volume XXVII, pp. 384–5.

very much as a foundry foreman governs his—by distinct orders, by emphatic rebukes, by a perpetual repetition of the command to get on, to get the work done, and leave off arguing. On the whole this method succeeded in the Punjab better than any finer one would have done. Men of great originality or deep insight or genius could not endure it, and gradually slipped away, or accepted positions in which the goad was more seldom applied; but the majority of officials like to be driven when the coachman is able as well as severe, and Sir John Lawrence gradually organised a troupe most efficient for doing any visible work. Invisible work they could not do, and of all 'the Punjabees,' as they were latterly called, perhaps not one per cent has ever added anything to the domain of thought or raised the mental character of the people he governed, or excited any feeling towards the government except a respectful fear. The work again was always attacked in the same direct fashion. There were many brigands among the states on the hither side of the Sutlej; but Mr. Lawrence had not ruled there a year before they all felt brigandage far too unprofitable a trade. The social evils which produce the crime were not removed, but the crime ceased, because men were not brave enough to go on with it. There were eternal bickerings among the princes; Sir John Lawrence did not reconcile them; but by determinately making himself master, he extinguished them for the time. When Lord Hardinge was fighting the Sikhs, Delhi was disaffected; but Sir John Lawrence was ruling there, and though he cured no disaffection, every ruffian in that Alsatia knew that if he acted on his inclinations he would be hanged out of hand. Subsequently in the Punjab, the Government wanted revenue. Sir John Lawrence said the great fiefholders should be taxed like other people. His far greater, yet far less capable brother, Sir Henry,—a man with ten times Lord Lawrence's genius, and not a tithe of his efficiency,—talked of native ideas and the use of aristocracies, and the development of native society in its own grooves; but to the strong middle-class man, the deficit in the exchequer was a Chat Moss to be filled, and in went the feudal system, and with it British chance of ever being loved in the Punjab. The mountain tribes kept making raids, just as our own Highlanders did and for the same motives—want of money and envy of the wealth stored up in the plains. Sir John did not make them devoted loyalists as Pitt did—did not try to do it, but opened a debtor and creditor account with them, and for every penny they stole took back five farthings, and they, though as predatory as ever, had to leave off stealing. In seven years the Punjab was transformed from a native state, in which anarchy was universal and careers numberless, into a British province in which order was as settled as in Kent, and nobody was allowed to do anything except make money. The hill had been bored, the Moss had been filled, and there was the engine on a level road. Then came the mutiny and, as it chanced, a bit of work with it which exactly suited the genius of the Chief Commissioner. It was not necessary that he should eradicate causes of disaffection, or reawaken loyalty, or change the current of native feeling, but it was necessary that he should take Delhi. So he took it. Columbus never battled with obstacles as Sir John did during those five months of 1857. Stephenson never gave such an example of perseverance and self-reliance. No matter what county was denuded of troops, no matter how dangerous the Sikh levies might seem, no matter how the ground might quake under his feet, till Delhi had been entered the engine could not move, and entered it should be. And at last, in September, when all was nearly over, when the Sikhs had fixed a day for revolt, and the besieging army was on the verge of retreat, the energy of the man broke out into flame, and the peremptory telegram 'take Delhi' risked, and saved the Empire. Everything had been flung into the Moss, but it was firm ground at last.

Sir John Lawrence was not as successful as viceroy, for the work to be done was too invisible,—it was not building a railway, but devising an organisation to manage railways well. His system of driving instead of stimulating his subordinates, so successful while he could guide his team himself, failed when applied to a dozen teams driven by other men. He had colleagues, and superiors far away, and work to do which he did not personally quite understand, and comparatively he failed to get it done. We say comparatively, because his administration was after all an exceedingly good one, only not so good as those who had observed his career in the Punjab thought they had a right to expect. Whatever he did himself was done well, as for example foreign negotiation, but he infused no extra or unusual strength into other men. It has been observed, and with some truth, that Sir John Lawrence never finds efficient agents in men to whom he cannot give direct and repeated orders,—that he never succeeds in making them do precisely what he wants, either leaving them too much to themselves, or failing to choose the right persons. The Bootan campaign was a series of muddles, and the Orissa famine a catastrophe. The viceroy too disposed of his patronage too much in the Punjab style—that is, he selected men whom he knew to be efficient, without reflecting that other men whom he did not know, but who had prior claims, might be efficient too. The men promoted were strong according to his conception of strength—that is, they could always do well what they were bidden to do, but the services were disheartened, and the prosperity of an empire depends more upon the general spirit of its services than on the capacity of a few individuals in prominent place. There was great foresight in the viceroy and great incisiveness of vision, but he wanted the aristocratic quality—a certain largeness of field, and the quality of the highest genius for government, that of evoking new power. British rule in India is neither better founded nor more enlightened in its ends for his rule; it is only a little stronger. There was a tendency in the viceroy towards hand-to-mouth politics, to do daily work and to do it well; but to evade very great questions and all questions which did not immediately press. Strict, stern, and clear as his finance for example had been in the Punjab, he sanctioned very bad imperial budgets,—one for example was instantly cancelled at home,—and his mode of dealing with Oude showed that the value of a great social experiment was beyond his grasp. No man looked forward till to-morrow more clearly, but he could not think of half a century hence. It was the same kind of limitation to his mind which made him as viceroy keep up so little state and show. Calcutta declared that it was parsimony,—Sir John being in gifts one of the most liberal of mankind,—but it was really an inability to recognise the uses of 'representation.' Ceremonial was unreal, consequently he would have no ceremonial, forgetting that scenic effect, though made up of paint and canvas and lime light, has its place in the world as well as in the theatre. His views on education and on the relation of government to the creeds of the peninsula were all of the missionary kind— very good in their way, very clear, and very easily carried out, but narrower than beseemed the ruler of so many races in so many stages of civilisation. Sir John Lawrence was in fact a middle-class ruler, a workman in politics rather than a thinker, an administrator rather than a politician, a man who had every faculty except those which are essential to the founder. There probably never was a better soldier, or a man who more thoroughly understood how to raise mercenary armies; but he quits India without having rendered it less necessary to use white troops to watch dark troops, or more possible to allow the native army breech-loading rifles. No man perhaps ever used his strength more efficiently or better deserved a peerage, but in none have the limits of that strength been so clearly revealed. He is a Nasmyth hammer which can chip an egg or flatten an iron bar, but only within its groove.

George William Frederick Villiers, fourth Earl of Clarendon, and fourth Baron Hyde

Introductory note

George William Frederick Villiers (1800–1870) was born in London, the eldest son of George Villiers and Theresa Parker. He entered the diplomatic service at an early age, and became attaché at St. Petersburg in 1820. In 1823 he became a commissioner of customs, and from 1833–9 was ambassador at Madrid. He succeeded to the peerage in 1838 on the death of his uncle. Lord Clarendon was Lord Privy Seal from 1839–41, and in 1846 became President of the Board of Trade. From 1847–52 he was Lord-Lieutenant of Ireland. From 1853–8 Lord Clarendon was Foreign Secretary and so was responsible for the conduct of the Crimean War and the terms of the Treaty of Paris in 1856. He was Chancellor of the Duchy of Lancaster in 1864, and Foreign Secretary from 1865–6 and again from 1868–70. Lord Clarendon died in London in 1870.

The late Lord Clarendon[1]

THE late Lord Clarendon belonged to a very small and very remarkable class of peers. There are many peers, as the lawyers, who have no birth, but who worked hard in their youth; and there are also many who have the highest birth, and have never worked the least. There are many who have earned rank, and many who have inherited rank. But it is rare to find a peer who inherits his rank and yet who has known what it is to earn his bread. Of the eminent peers there is perhaps hardly more than one now living of whom this is true. Lord Salisbury has indeed a right to feel that circumstances cannot ruin him, that a revolution may come, that the House of Lords may perish, that estates may be confiscated, but that his abilities as a popular writer will earn him money as they did before. Though in a different way Lord Clarendon was of this class also. When he was in the Excise office in Dublin, and all through his younger life, there was but a distant probability of his coming to the title, and he had to work really for his bread. And the training of his youth was probably of use to him always. To the last week of his life[2] he was a curiously unremitting worker. With somewhat peculiar hours and times he got through more work probably in the twenty-four hours than most administrators of his time, and finished it all with care and accuracy. There were none of the gratuitous blunders and hurried errors which mostly characterise the work of one who is much praised for great activity; everything was carefully considered and carefully executed.

Perhaps it is not unconnected with this praise that there was an indescribable repose about Lord Clarendon's manner and appearance. No one who saw him, in his later years at least, would have ever thought him a specially active man. He seemed a very calm, sensible, and singularly courteous old gentleman; and it would scarcely have occurred to a casual observer that he was an exceedingly indefatigable worker. But those who have watched the habits of men of business in

[1] This article was first published in *The Economist* for July 2 1870, Volume XXVIII, pp. 813–14.
[2] *The Economist* has 'death' for 'life'—p. 814.

politics and out of it will have seen many cases in which a still and quiet man who does not seem to be doing much, and probably is talking of something quite different, has in matter of fact and at the week's end accomplished much more than the 'rushing mighty wind;' —the very energetic man who is never idle or at rest and who has no thought but his office business. A still man like Lord Clarendon has time to think what he will do, and most incessant men are apt to act before they have thought, and therefore land where they should not, or else lose half their time in sailing back again.

It was, perhaps, the result of Lord Clarendon's early training that he always took great interest in commerce, and whenever he had the power steadily used the agency of the Foreign Office for its advantage. He was much too thoroughly on a level with his time to do this by an aggressive foreign policy. The old notion of fighting for foreign markets, or of intriguing for their exclusive use, had so completely died out that he cannot be praised for being exempt from it. Lord Clarendon used only the legitimate functions for trade purposes. He was especially eager for the collection of actual statistical information by our foreign consuls and embassies. The commencement of their reports on these subjects, and the establishment of the statistical department of the Board of Trade, were largely owing to his great interest in these objects.

That Lord Clarendon showed great originality as a Foreign Minister will hardly be contended, and some, among whom we are ourselves to be found, will have grave doubts whether extreme originality in such office is either possible or desirable. The cases of great invention are rare in all business, but they are particularly rare in those kinds of business which require the constant consent of many persons—and of these the English foreign policy is one. Not, indeed, that at the moment of taking his decision, the Foreign Minister is particularly trammelled. In great cases he must consult the Prime Minister and perhaps the Cabinet. But if these stood by themselves, having the power of peculiar information, he could probably mostly carry with him the minds of men occupied with near and pressing questions, and not in general ready to acquire disagreeable and uncertain detail as to remote topics and strange events. But the great obstacle to originality is the English nation. In a free country a minister can only do that which the nation is prepared for, and if he tries to do more the nation will disown him. Within special limits, and on minor questions, he can give an effectual guidance and control decision, but beyond those limits, and on vital matters, he has no power at all. The subtle power which we call 'opinion,' which is the product of so long a history and the offspring of so many causes, hems him in, and he cannot do as he would but if he stays must act as he would not. An irritable farseeing originality is commonly a vice in business, and in a Foreign Minister it would be an intolerable nuisance. It was exactly because Lord Clarendon had a delicate instinct of the limits of his power that he was so truly useful and so really influential.

In one respect we are not inclined to join in the universal praise which within the last few days Lord Clarendon has received. He has been greatly praised as a writer, and no doubt he wrote not only with great facility but with much elegance. But there is one great difficulty about almost all his despatches. Each sentence is clear, and no word brings you to a stop; but yet after a few paragraphs a careful reader suddenly pauses to think where he is and what he has assented to. And even when he reads the paragraphs over again he will not always find it easy to be sure that he sees the limits of what was meant and the limits of what was not meant. The limpid flow of delicate words takes him steadily on, but where at any precise instant he is he cannot be very confident. For the old intercourse of foreign courts this sort of style has immense advantages: it gives no present offence, and, having no marked sentences, leaves no barbed words for after irritation. And in Lord Russell we had a warning of the evils of the opposite style. He wrote as he used to speak in the House of Commons. With a certain cold acumen he 'pitched' (there is no less familiar word adequate) 'into' the foreign courts, as he used to pitch into Sir Robert Peel; and not being used to parliamentary plainness the foreign courts did not like it. Lord Russell hardly conducted a foreign controversy in which the extreme intelligibility of his words did not leave a sting behind them. Of Lord Clarendon the very contrary may be said,—he scarcely left a sting, never an unnecessary one. But, on the other hand, Lord Russell's despatches, hard and unpleasant as they often are, never left anyone in doubt as to their precise meaning. If they did mislead some foreign courts it is because they could not understand that a minister would blurt out all his meaning in that *gauche* manner; but to a common reader they are as plain as words can make them. And, as in the present day, great despatches, being published, are really addressed to whole nations of common readers as well as to small courts of special training, they ought to be so written as to combine the gentle sauvity that suits the one with the unmistakeable plainness which is essential to the other. It was exactly the gliding urbanity of Lord Clarendon's style which pleased the courts while it perplexed the common people.

But we do not need now to dwell at length on a point so subordinate. It is much for a man of Lord Clarendon's standing to have written nearly perfectly in the old style; it is no ground for serious blame to him that he did not invent a new style. He will be remembered by posterity as a minister singularly suited to the transition age in which he lived, and as possessing both the courtly manners which are going out, and also the commercial tastes and the business knowledge which are coming in. Some critics will, as we have said, find fault with his want of special designs and of a far reaching policy. But to this generation of Englishmen this was no fault at all. We wish that foreign nations should, as far as may be, solve their own problems; we wish them to gain all the good they can by their own exertions, and to remove all the evil. But we do not wish to take part in their struggles. We fear that we might mistake what was best; we fear that in so shifting a scene we might find years hence, when the truth is known, that we had in fact done exactly the reverse of what we meant, and had really injured what we meant to aid. We fear that amid the confusion our good must turn to evil, and that our help would be a calamity and not a blessing. And for an age like this Lord Clarendon was a fitting minister, for he had a wise sagacity to interfere as little, and to refrain from acting as much as prudence rendered possible.

Samuel Robert Graves

Introductory note

Samuel Robert Graves, a Liverpool merchant and shipowner, was senior Conservative M.P. for Liverpool from 1865–73. He died in London in 1873.

The late Mr. Graves[1]

THE generality of the sorrow at the sudden death of Mr. Graves, and the depth of the respect shown for his memory, almost prove that both must be deserved. That a man of Irish birth, who started in Liverpool with but little fortune and with no particular connections, should, at so early an age as fifty-five, be member for that great city, have an almost universal popularity there, receive at his election more votes than any borough member ever obtained before, attain an excellent position in parliament, and receive at his unlooked-for death marks of attachment and grief from all ranks of persons, and even from royalty itself, is very remarkable, but it would be quite incomprehensible without real and great merit. Only fine qualities of some kind could enable a man who began with so few advantages to obtain so much influence over so many and so various persons, and to win so much regard from them.

Those best acquainted with the sphere of action will admit that business ability alone would never have given Mr. Graves the position he held, or have attracted such multitudes to his funeral. Business ability is not an uncommon quality in Liverpool; a very considerable number of persons could be named there who can transact commercial affairs almost as well as it is possible to transact them. No skill in money matters could elevate anyone much above many of them, for their skill in such matters is almost perfect. And though commercial ability gains money it does not win hearts, and it is plain that Mr. Graves gained at Liverpool and elsewhere a sympathy and an affection which can never be obtained by mere transacting power. Nor was Mr. Graves's success in his constituency and in Parliament due to any singular gift of oratory. On the contrary, there are plenty of men who speak quite as well as Mr. Graves whom no one cares for, either in parliament or out of it, and on whose death, however sudden, no one would grieve except a small circle just around them. Nor would mere

[1] This article was first published in *The Economist* for January 25 1873, Volume XXXI, pp. 91–2.

'hard work,' to which we have seen Mr. Graves's success, both in life and parliament, ascribed, at all account for the peculiar nature of that success. The genuine faculty of hard work is not a common quality, and we quite agree that Mr. Graves possessed it; but we could name men even in parliament who work quite as hard for whom no one cares—who have won no sympathy, and attained no respect.

The real secret of Mr. Graves's peculiar success was his singularly unique character. He possessed in combination two important qualities, which are not very common singly, which are very rarely joined together, but the combination of which has singular power. A *very* high degree of fairness and honesty is not so very common in mercantile or in any other line of life. A certain decent amount of honesty is very fairly diffused; the higher kind of nicety and honour, which everyone feels though no one can precisely describe it, is unhappily not common. And everyone who met Mr. Graves, even casually, became at once convinced that he possessed this delicate and indefinable quality, and those who knew him long and well were unanimous that this casual conviction was justified. He was a man whom no one need watch, and who might be trusted implicitly, and with anything.

And besides this he was a consummate manager and manipulator of men. For the most part there is about people so honest as he was a certain rigidity of manner and stiffness of mind. They do not easily enter into the thoughts and minds of others; they are blunt and decided, and go to their object in a plain straightforward way. They do not perceive instinctively what others are thinking of; in consequence they are bad negotiators. They do not see what is in the minds of the other side, and so they say the wrong thing, and negotiation fails. But Mr. Graves was a warm negotiator. He could not help seeing what was in the minds of those with whom he was concerned. He adapted himself to it instinctively; was astonished that anyone could help seeing it. He was as pliable as a diplomatist could be, and he was as honest as it was possible to be. Indeed, an honest negotiator is the honestest of men, for it is in the making of delicate arrangements, and in the nice manipulation of men, that the highest honesty is tested most nicely.

We do not at all mean that Mr. Graves's powers were of a moral kind only. The intellectual qualities required for a good diplomatist are of an extremely high kind. To have in a large measure the comprehension to understand and the tact to manage other men, is very rare, and Mr. Graves had these gifts in singular abundance. We need not say that besides these, he had all the qualities of a man of business, and that he had commercial knowledge and a fine practical understanding. All this has been said for the last few days so often that it is needless to repeat it. We have only tried to analyse a little his character, so as to give to those who did not know him some vague idea of his peculiar gifts and power.

That we have done so with a painful feeling we need not say. There is a charm about men like him which no analysis can reach, and no pen can set down. And those who have that charm are perhaps most apt to be taken from us. A coarse and hard man of business might have done Mr. Graves's work and more, and been with us still; but the crush of parliamentary and the struggle of commercial life are most trying to the finer fibres of human nature. In such scenes we should always watch with the most anxiety the lives of those whom we can least spare, and whom we should most wish to keep.

Henry Fawcett

Introductory note

Henry Fawcett (1833–1884) was born in Salisbury, the son of William Fawcett, a draper, and of Mary Cooper. He was educated at King's College School, London, and Peterhouse, Cambridge. He became a student at Lincoln's Inn in 1854. In 1858 he lost his eyesight in a shooting accident. From 1863 until his death he was professor of political economy in Cambridge. Fawcett became Liberal M.P. for Brighton in 1865, and played an important part in the passing of the Reform Bill in 1867. From 1871–3 and again in 1874 he sat on committees on Indian Finance. He was elected for Hackney in 1874 and in 1880. During Gladstone's second administration in 1880, Fawcett was Postmaster General. He died in Cambridge in 1884.

Mr. Fawcett[1]

I T is not the lot of *The Economist* often to agree completely with Mr. Fawcett, but we do not know that there is a more useful member in the House of Commons, in which he occupies a somewhat exceptional position. Debarred by a physical infirmity from office, and not possessed of popular arts, Mr. Fawcett can hardly be regarded as the leader of any section of the Commons, and yet he is received on rising as no mere borough member ever is received. A scholar, a doctrinaire, and at the same time member for the radical majority of one of the most radical constituencies in the kingdom, Mr. Fawcett is listened to by Tories of the 'highest' type, and his speeches frequently tell distinctly on divisions. He is not popular, he is not eloquent in the sense in which Mr. Gladstone or Mr. Bright is eloquent, and he is not a man of business; but nevertheless his weight in the conduct of national affairs is seldom on any question inappreciable, and on one or two questions, such as India, is so marked as to excite considerable jealousy in official quarters. Part of his influence is no doubt due to his courage, to the coolness with which he defends doctrines known to be unpopular; but the major portion of it is due, we believe, to the hard common sense, and adherence to scientific principles, by which his radicalism is modified. The most prominent defect of the radicalism of the present day is a new one,—one quite unknown to the great radicals of our history,—a certain pulpiness or sentimentality which we are accustomed to attribute only to the liberal politicians of the continent, and from this Mr. Fawcett is entirely free. Believing that force is an element, and a great element, in human affairs, he never allows himself to talk nonsense about the inutility of armies and navies, but in a hard, cool way argues that we must not have too much or too little navy or army. Believing that finance is a necessary element in politics, he never allows himself to be drawn into absurdities about reductions or about expenditures, but maintains that this or that tax

---

[1] This article was first published in *The Economist* for February 8 1873, Volume XXXI, pp. 154–5.

or reduction is good or bad, for such and such reasons; that the treasury must be kept full, and that if taxation hurts people, well, it is the essential quality of taxation to hurt very much. Believing that we ought to keep India, he never makes wild speeches against Indian administration, but accepts the duty, and labours with all his might to have the duty done in the way he approves. We do not agree on the whole with his way, thinking him deceived by an agrarian crotchet, but we do most heartily honour the immense labour and energy with which he has fought for his thesis—that taxation is the crux of the Indian administration, and that Indian administrators have, on the whole, mismanaged it. The point however on which his speciality comes out most strongly is the law of property. Radicals believe in property like other men, but they are always apt to leave an impression that they at heart hold all property to belong to the state, and to be leased in trust for the public convenience, or rather for the convenience of any section of the public which happens to want some of it. Mr. Fawcett never will give in to that tone at all. Whatever the subject he always defends the well understood economic laws, whether they are popular or unpopular, with the most hearty belief in their accuracy, venturing, for instance, to say that the poor ought not to be exempt from taxation in proportion because that is robbery of the rich. Why are they to be robbed? The 'hard,' or, to use a common expression, the cruel, consequences that flow from economic laws do not strike him any more than the hard consequences which flow from any other laws regulating the economy of the world. If a good person does not save, a good person will want, and that seems to modern philanthropy very hard, hard enough to justify taking something from a bad person to give to the good one. 'No,' says Mr. Fawcett, 'property is independent of goodness and badness. If a good person puts his finger in the candle, his finger will be burnt, and you have no right, because of that, to burn the bad man's finger.' We are not of course quoting under any form, however condensed, but that is the drift of one or two of his recent speeches, and hard, sound sense of that sort, when coming from a member whose radicalism is not doubtful, is in its way almost invaluable. It would have little effect coming from Mr. Henley,[2] because he would be supposed to be wishing to keep up the

[2] Joseph Henley was Tory M.P. for Oxfordshire 1841–78, at one time President of the Board of Trade, from which office he resigned in 1859 because of his opposition to parliamentary reform and especially the changes proposed in the county franchise.—Ed.

old order of things; but coming from a member known not to wish that, it has a decided effect. It puts an end to a great many fears, and it prevents a great many silly proposals which but for the certainty of Mr. Fawcett's dangerous opposition might exercise a certain influence over the public mind. The member for Brighton in fact compels his whole party to think before they speak, to try their ideas by facts, to ascertain—to speak plain English—before they produce their proposals how they will appear to men who are not moved by phrases, who will in their commonplace, clearheaded way see what effect any given law or project of law is to have on the ultimate prosperity of the nation. He makes radicalism intelligible and tolerable to men who have something to lose. A member of this kind, whether his hearer agrees with him or not—and we, for example, very often disagree—is most valuable to the House of Commons, where Mr. Fawcett often makes a speech which, to men heated with oratory and sentimentalities and exaggerated ideas of their constituents' wishes, has the bracing and tonic effect of a cold douche very heartily thrown.

Mr. Fawcett's speech on Monday at Brighton was not one of the best illustrations of his especial utility, but still it was full of it. His main idea was a statesmanlike one, the necessity of considering the Treasury before considering everybody's complaint. All manner of half-considerate people have been asking during the recess all manner of contradictory things,—want, for instance, the malt tax abolished, the income tax abolished, the rates thrown on the general treasury, and expenditure for a host of philanthropic schemes. Well, asks Mr. Fawcett, at some length, who is going to pay the bill? How do these people propose to empty the state till and make it pay everything, to add new charges and abolish old revenue, to, in fact, 'surpass the dreams of the old alchemists, and extract wealth out of nothing?' If you abolish the malt tax you must, at all events, keep the rates. If you abolish the income tax, you must give up great expensive schemes like state-aided emigration. Mr. Fawcett does not speak as many radicals would have spoken against the landed interest, which is making, or supposed to be making, these demands, or declare rates a blessing, or assert that the income tax is unimproveable, but he brings the orators to book summarily with hard common sense. Their proposals, good or bad, cost money. Where is it to come from? Some people advocate the abolition of schedule D, and the substitution of a tax on property. Why, asks Mr. Fawcett, should we tax a man who has bought something with his savings to exempt the man who might save £20,000 a year? Others ask the total abolition of the tax, but many of them want also a free breakfast table. There is a very general and a very useless moan over the frequency of strikes. They are very injurious, says Mr. Fawcett, but until capital and labour have identical pecuniary interests they cannot be prevented, they are our mode of fighting the battle, and a mild one, leading us on through inconveniences into a happier future. Others again are indignant with the expenditure on the army and navy; but after all, says Mr. Fawcett, the prodigal expenditure of other nations upon means of attack must exercise some influence upon our expenditure on means of defence. These seem to many men almost platitudes, but they are only platitudes because they are truths, and they are uttered before a popular constituency by a man who accepts what is called the radical creed quite heartily, and, as far as appears, carries his radical followers heartily with him. Mr. Fawcett, in fact, does find means to bring the extreme Liberals into full connection with the quiet mass of hard-headed opinion existing in the country, and that is a very creditable and beneficial feat to perform. We do not want parties to be divided in this country as they are in France, till one set of men scarcely understand another set, and till the rule of the majority is regarded by minorities almost as the rule of an invading enemy. Mr. Fawcett talks a radicalism Whigs can understand, and therefore a radicalism which inclines them to examine all radicalism a little more closely, and to dread it a little less.

John Stuart Mill
Introductory note

John Stuart Mill (1806–1873) was born at Pentonville, London, the son of James Mill, the utilitarian philosopher, and of Harriet Burrow. He was educated entirely by his father, and received a most rigorous academic training from a very early age. He became a junior clerk in the India House in 1823. At about this time he formed the Utilitarian Society which met to read and discuss essays, and in 1826 was one of the founders of the Speculative Society. His *System of Logic* was published in 1843, and *Principles of Political Economy* in 1848. On the dissolution of the East India Company in 1858, Mill retired with a pension. From 1865–8 he was M.P. for Westminster and a follower of Gladstone. After leaving parliament he returned to literary pursuits. He published *The Subjection of Women* in 1869, *Chapters and Speeches on the Irish Land Question* in 1870, his *Autobiography* in 1873. *Three Essays on Religion* was posthumously published in 1874. Mill died and was buried at Avignon in 1873.

Mr. Mill's Address to the Electors of Westminster[1]

WHETHER it be wise for Mr. Mill to enter Parliament; whether the position he will take there will be adequate either to his great abilities or to his paramount reputation; whether the time and strength which he will have to spend within its walls, listening to dreary speakers and grappling with wearisome details, would not be better employed in following out those philosophical principles which he, far beyond any other writer of this age, is fitted to handle; whether in a word the man of speculation and of thought will not be somewhat lost and wasted among the men of action and routine:—these are questions which may well admit of doubt. But that his presence in the House of Commons will be an ornament and a strength, an addition to its wisdom and its fame; that it ought to contain such men as he, though not to consist of such; that the electors of Westminster will do themselves singular credit by choosing him; and that the representative system, under which so fearless a thinker and so independent and uncompromising a candidate is returned to parliament by one of the most numerous and most popular constituencies in the kingdom, will stand in far less need of reform than we are accustomed to believe;—these are points which admit of no doubt whatever. For ourselves, differing as we do in the strongest manner from many of Mr. Mill's political opinions, we should vote for him in preference to any other candidate, partly because we know no man whose voice is better entitled to be heard in the senate of a great country, and partly because *our* senate is conspicuously distinguished by the absence of that original, philosophic, and thorough-going honesty of thought which Mr. Mill would bring into it;—and if the radical electors of Westminster have the manhood and good sense to select a wise and good man as their representative merely because he is wise and good, though he will neither spend money nor canvas votes, though he will repeat none of their favourite

[1] This article was first published in *The Economist* for April 29 1865, Volume XXIII, pp. 497–8.

watchwords, though he has stripped bare many of their commonest fallacies, and though he caricatures, by transcending, some of their most cherished doctrines,—why we shall think more highly of them than we ever did before.

Mr. Mill's confession of political faith, as contained in his letter (through Mr. Beal to the electors of Westminster), is one of the most remarkable addresses ever delivered by any candidate to any constituency,—especially in respect to the qualities of honesty, simplicity, and courage. It shows the lofty vantage ground which on such occasions is occupied by a man who cares little whether he enters parliament or not, but who cares much that if he does enter it, he shall enter it without having paid down a single concession as the price of his success, without having stooped to ask election as a favour, without having condescended to modify or to conceal a single opinion, or to fetter himself by a single pledge. It is almost the first time within our remembrance when the relation between a candidate and a constituency has been placed on its true footing; and the electors of Westminster will do themselves signal honour if they answer to the implied appeal in a corresponding spirit.

It is astonishing how a thorough logical capacity, unflinching integrity of purpose, and a profound knowledge of the facts and principles involved, even in the hands of a radical, shatter all the ordinary radical fallacies into dust. Mr. Mill assuredly is an advanced Liberal, if ever there was one; yet there is scarcely one of his doctrines which does not fly in the face and strike at the root of the official creed of the advanced Liberal party. His differences with *them* are differences of principle not of detail:—*we* on the contrary can agree with him in everything, except in the degree to which he would push some of the applications of his principle;—and even there we differ with him chiefly because we think his practice would negative his principle and defeat his aim. We need scarcely say a word as to his claim for the extension of the suffrage to all adult women:—no party, and scarcely any individual politician save himself, holds this theory, and it will be long before it becomes a practical question. When it does, we entertain little doubt that Mr. Mill will have altered his views on the matter, as he has done on the ballot; for he will probably have discovered that out of the two or three million of women whom he would thus endow—including half-a-million of maid-servants—not above ten thousand would have any political opinions at all, or any *political* preferences for one candidate over another; and that in consequence to give them votes would merely be giving extra votes vicariously to their fathers, their husbands, their masters, their lovers, or their priests. Mr. Mill, of course, would hope and wish that all women should be enlightened and rational enough to hold his enlightened and rational opinions:—but conceive the position of an unhappy woman, embracing his views, to whom an 'advanced Liberal,' a radical of Mr. Bright's school, stood in any of the relations we have specified! how she would be snubbed by her father, *boudé* by her husband, deserted by her lover, bullied by her master, and excommunicated by her priest! But to proceed to the other and more practical items of Mr. Mill's creed.

The radicals pin their faith upon the Ballot:—Mr. Mill, as we know, repudiates it altogether:—deeming that it is unnecessary, that the evil of it would outweigh the good, and considering also, as we gather from his language, that a constituency, meriting the suffrage he would bestow upon it, ought not to require or wish for the secrecy solicited for it. *Again*: the radicals are vehement in their clamour for the substitution of exclusively direct taxation instead of our present mixed system,—wishing, in the first place, to exonerate the working classes from taxation altogether, and, in the second place, to diminish the revenue insidiously by making a large revenue difficult if not impossible of collection. Mr. Mill, on the contrary, like all thinkers, prefers the combination of direct with indirect taxes, on the double ground of justice and morality. *Thirdly*, the radicals are striving hard to erect into an article of the national creed that England must never interfere in foreign affairs except where her own national interests are concerned:—Mr. Mill, more nobly and more justly, declares that such interposition on the side of liberty, to countervail interposition on the side of oppression, is a right and may become a duty. *Fourthly*, the radicals go in for retrenchment and the reduction of our armaments wholesale and without reference to possible danger or ultimate consequence:—Mr. Mill will have nothing to say to such short-sighted and unpatriotic parsimony; he would economise, not by cutting down either army or navy, but by spending our money more efficiently upon both. The radicals would at once abolish purchase in the army as utterly bad:—Mr. Mill reminds them that there is one system which is worse, and which, as matters at present stand, would probably be substituted for it; and hints that it can scarcely be considered a reform to get rid of one evil merely to replace it by another. The radicals, true to their shallow system of going, *tête baissée* and with their eyes shut, at a practice which is abused, instead of at the abuse of the practice, insist upon the total abolition of flogging. Mr. Mill quietly corrects their blindfold zeal, and, like most sensible men, would abolish it only where indefensible, and retain it where it is specially appropriate. And, lastly, Mr. Mill with all his leanings towards the claims of labour and of the poor, is too sound an economist and too just a man not to see the fallacy and the hopelessness of the schemes, now so popular among many philanthropists and radicals, for legislating between masters and men, and preventing strikes and lock-outs by arbitrary arbitration, and hits the nail on the head in one single sentence. 'I see nothing which law can do in the matter, *except to protect from violation the equal liberty of all to combine or to refrain from combining.*' This one phrase contains the gist of the whole matter. When once workmen shall be effectually liberated from the tyranny of their fellow-workmen and left free to belong to trades' unions or not as they please, and to work or leave work as they individually wish, secure against intimidation from any quarter, no lockouts and few strikes will be needed to adjust the disputes between capital and labour. Labour, if thoroughly free, will always command its own fair terms; and capital, if unterrified by its dangers, be always too selfish to combine to defraud labour or oppress it.

It is, however, Mr. Mill's views in regard to the extension of the suffrage which most gratify us (with one exception), and which we apprehend will most disgust the ordinary and *doctrinaire* radical. While, with the courageous simplicity of a man who has laid firm grasp upon a principle, he goes much further towards universal suffrage than any leaders of the advanced party have yet ventured, he declares that class ascendancy in any shape or in any hands is such an abomination in his eyes, that in any system of franchise extension ample precautions must be taken to 'prevent any class, even though it be the most numerous, from being able to swamp all other classes taken together.' He is resolute for the representation of minorities. 'I think (he says) that all considerable minorities in the country, or in a locality, should be represented in proportion to their numbers.' This, as our readers know, is the great principle for which we have always contended. If it can be secured and practically carried out, the most liberal extension of the franchise may be comparatively innocuous and even to a certain extent just and beneficial. If it be neglected, then such extension will assuredly become an injustice, a mischief, and a danger. But it is precisely this provision for the fair representation of minorities that Mr. Bright and the radicals as a party most utterly detest. With the instinct of hatred—far more unerring in its sagacity than the instinct of love—they perceive that it would be virtually fatal to that class ascendancy, that preponderance of mere numbers, that transfer of political power into the hands of that section of the community they hope and believe would be their votaries, which it is the object of all *their* reform schemes to secure. They are well aware that an extension of the franchise to something even far short of universal would place the (potential) command of the representation in the hands of the working class and the lower portion of the middle class, whenever they could induce these to pull together; they believe that these classes, as a rule, would adopt their dogmas and return their nominees; and their aim, therefore, is to obtain the virtual disfranchisement of the educated and propertied portion of the nation which it is the object of Mr. Mill to preserve from such virtual disfranchisement. Thus the objects and purposes of Mr. Bright and Mr. Mill are altogether discrepant and at variance;—and the candour with which the one leader avows his ultimate design, and the disingenuousness with which the other evades that avowal, are more at variance still.

We have left ourselves little room to comment on almost the only point of Mr. Mill's creed from which we seriously dissent; and indeed there is little need. We said a few words on the subject last week. But few more are wanted. Mr. Mill would so arrange the suffrage and the securities against the exclusion of minorities as practically to 'give to the labouring classes a clear half of the national representation.' Now to this proportion there seem to us to be at least two conclusive objections (not to mention minor and secondary ones)—objections so conclusive that we are satisfied that Mr. Mill himself will be among the first to admit their cogency. *First*, such an arrangement would give the absolute command of a parliamentary majority,—that is virtually the decision of the nation's policy,—into the hands of the members returned by the working men, whenever they chose to pull together, and whenever, as a matter of bad political economy, of vicious temper, of jobbing, of ultra-montanism, of anti-Saxonism,—or from any motive of intrigue whatever—they could induce any considerable section of the Irish members to coalesce with them,—a danger neither the probability nor the gravity of which should be underestimated or overlooked.—And *secondly*, such an arrangement, Mr. Mill we apprehend would agree with us in thinking, would often entirely sacrifice what is the second, if not the first, purpose of the representative system, —*viz.*, to secure the selection of the wisest and ablest and fittest men in the nation to be its legislators and rulers, and not merely those who most accurately mirror the *average* mind of the nation,—to make the House of Commons the faithful representative of the people in the sense of being the representative of all classes in their best moods, in their best influences, in their best specimens.

Mr. Mill on Ireland[1]

THERE are many quiet, excellent people about the world, who are much puzzled by Mr. Mill's recent career. They cannot be induced to believe that he is really honest; they say—'Here is a philosopher who publishes pamphlets on Reform, full of checks of democracy,—half-inspired, as one would think, by the dread of democracy,—who writes an elaborate treatise on parliamentary government, conceived in the same spirit, and inculcating the same doctrine; and yet this philosopher, when he comes into parliament, becomes almost a mere radical, loving democracy, desiring democracy, ready to sacrifice nearly everything for democracy. First read the recent political works of Mr. Mill, and then read his late speeches, and you will involuntarily imagine that the two do not come from the same mind. Who is simple enough to believe that both are genuine? Who does not see that the love of popular applause, that the necessities of the member for Westminster have corrupted the sage, have changed him into a demagogue?' Such language is, no doubt, natural, but it is also wholly wrong. An honester or a more simple-minded man than Mr. Mill—a man more ready, in season or out of season, to maintain an unpopular doctrine—does not live. But the fact is, he is easily excitable and susceptible; the evil that is in his mind at the moment seems to him the greatest evil,—for the time nearly the only evil,—the evil which must be cured at all hazards. Thus, before he entered public life, when he was a recluse student, living in a radical atmosphere, and talking mainly to a few radical admirers, he was impressed principally by the evils of radicalism; his large and catholic intellect was vexed at its shortcomings and its defects. But when he entered the House of Commons, when he saw face to face the Tory party on the opposite side,—when he saw beside him the half-Tory party on the Liberal side,—they had on him the same effect that a red rag has on a bull; he could see nothing but their enormities, and roared (as far as a philosopher

[1] This article was first published in *The Economist* for February 22 1868, Volume XXVI, pp. 201–3.

can roar) to subdue and end them. Then, as ever, the evil before him was the greatest evil; he did not change a single opinion, but he changed wholly his expressed sentiment; and naturally so, for his mind was hurried away by a current of feeling very different from the quiet tendencies of former times.

It is this singular union of very susceptible and animated feeling with philosophical tastes and a patient widely-searching intellect, that gives Mr. Mill both his peculiarity and his power. If he had been a mere dry economist,—a McCulloch or a *James* Mill,—a crowd of ardent admirers, a small body even of earnest disciples, would not have gone out into the streets of Westminster and compelled the voters to elect him. If he had been a mere excitable philanthropist, nobody would have cared—as every one does care—to have his careful opinion on complex matters. It is the curious composition that confers his strength: as a metropolitan wit said:—'Mr. Mill is Tom Hughes bound up with Ricardo.'

He now shows exactly the same susceptibility of mind on Ireland. Not three years ago, he told us in the last edition of his *Political Economy*,—in so saying, erasing and unsaying the most striking part of his first edition—that Ireland no longer needed 'heroic remedies,' and that the quiet course of ordinary improvements would be enough to raise her, if not to real prosperity, at least to sufficient well-being. But since then Fenianism has broken out, and Fenianism has upset Mr. Mill's conclusions wholly. He now thinks a *most* heroic remedy— a remedy many people would call revolutionary—imperiously requisite. Fenianism, he admits, is only a form of the same discontent which Ireland has so long nurtured; it is of the same species as Whiteboyism, Ribandism, and the rest. But this sober consideration has not steadied Mr. Mill's thoughts; the sudden flaring evil has excited his mind, as such evils so often do.

Mr. Mill's diagnosis is that the present land tenure is the fundamental disease of Ireland, and his cure is as follows:—He would have a compulsory enfranchisement of all the land in Ireland, just such as we have had in England of the copyhold land; he would have the fair rent of each acre assessed, and have it enacted that the present tenant should pay, in time to come, neither more nor less than this. This provision is, of course, for the benefit of the tenant. For the benefit of the landowner, he proposes that the present rent, whether more than the 'fair rent' or not, should be guaranteed by the English government.

If he likes (and, if wise, of course he would like), he may take consols for the amount and be quit of the land for ever. Of course, where the fair rent is as much as the present rent, the English Government will lose no money; it will receive with one hand what it guarantees or has to pay on the other. But when the present rent is more than the fair rent, the sum which the landlord will have to receive is greater than that which the tenant will have to pay, and the state must find the difference. In a word, if Mr. Mill's plan becomes law, the present tenants of Ireland will be the future owners of the Irish soil,—subject always to the fixed rent-charge.

Mr. Mill's reasoning in favour of his plan is twofold—economical and political. As to the first, he says that the cottier tenancy of Ireland is of a kind perfectly different from any which prevails in England. The farmer of England is a capitalist, who need not pay more rent than he likes: but the farmer of Ireland is a peasant, who must have land to live, who will pay the maximum possible in order to get that land, and would pay far more than a capitalist would even consider; who would, in fact, make over all the produce of the soil to his landlord, *minus* just enough to keep him and his alive in misery. And no doubt this cottier tenancy is a most wretched system. But is it a system which demands an 'heroic'—a revolutionary—remedy? Mr. Mill has himself told us not. He accounts for the change in the modes of treating Ireland, prescribed in the first and the last edition of his great work, by an alteration of circumstances in the seventeen years between. He says— 'The principal change consists in the great diminution, holding out a hope of the entire extinction, of cottier tenure. The enormous decrease in the number of holdings attested by the statistical returns sufficiently proves the general fact, and all testimonies show that the tendency still continues.' Surely it is not necessary to adopt a plan which is thought to be, and will have the moral effect of, confiscation, in order to get a tenure which already of itself is dying out, which natural common causes are killing. But Mr. Mill's main argument is political. He says his plan would cure Irish disaffection. But would it? Some shrewd observers say, no. They say—'Whatever you do, do not make England the landlord of Ireland,—it is too much so already. If you give the Irish their own soil subject to a Saxon quit-rent, they will never be satisfied till they get rid of the quit-rent too. You are offering to the peasantry of Ireland a premium on independence; you are enforcing on them a heavy payment while they adhere to England,

and palpably showing them that they need not pay it when her yoke is broken, and she ceases to own their soil.' And even beyond this there is a further difficulty. No land legislation—such is the axiom of the subject—will cure Irish discontent which does not cure Irish misery. Now, would Mr. Mill's plan effect that cure? We cannot but doubt it.

Our answer is that land, like so many other things, is a blessing only to those who can use it, and a poison to those who cannot. A race disciplined to labour, trained in the elements of forethought, if it should obtain the possession of land, would improve both in industry and prudence. But a race, from whatever cause, and by whatever history, improvident, reckless, and thoughtless, if given land without supervision, will only use it to become more idle, more reckless, more improvident. Upon the well-disposed, the possession of land acts as a stimulant, because it is a means of gaining future comfort; upon the idly-inclined, it acts as a narcotic, because it is an opportunity of present idleness. To which of the two classes the Irish population belong no one doubts. They have been trained and disciplined in the bad use of land—they have acquired worse habits of labour, probably, than any other race of equal mind. Who can be sure (and of a revolutionary measure we ought to *know* the efficiency, since we risk so many evils on its account), who can be sure that the absolute concession of all the land to such a people will bring happiness, and that it will not increase misery?

Suppose this case: The cottier tenant now pays more than a fair rent—more, that is, than a capitalist would pay—a rent unduly raised by the eager bidding of wretched competitors: the state would have to pay the landlord the difference; but what would become of the land? Surely the tenant, according to Irish habits, would turn landlord himself; *he* would not work; *he* would not improve the land; he would simply let some or all his land at a higher rent, and enjoy the difference. This was put on record by the most impartial of Irish observers many years since. 'It may be observed,' says Sir George Lewis, 'that if an Irish landlord resist the temptation of a high offer, and lets his land at what he considers a fair rent, he often creates a set of intermediate tenants who make a profit-rent by subletting the ground to persons who live in the extreme of misery.' There are already a great number of long leases and 'perpetuities' in Ireland which are universally underlet in this way, and are the worst abodes of misery.

Mr. Mill says that these old perpetuities failed because the rent

charged upon them was too low, and that so they encouraged subletting. But this is the unavoidable difficulty. If you take only a fair
rent from the cottier you must encourage subletting; you enable your
tenant to start at an advantage above those around him, and depend
on it he will make something out of them. The miserable are quite as
hard as the rich, or harder, to those more miserable. Or if you give up
the doctrine of a fair rent, and say the tenant shall pay the existing
rent, only to the state instead of to the landlord, you are landed in still
worse difficulties. The state will have to collect a rack-rent from a
squalid population; and the old scenes of the tithes collection would
be revived and aggravated. And after all, the state would get little.
It *could* not collect these petty rents; only an individual, and a stern,
not tender-hearted, individual, could collect them. The state must
have an army of collectors, for we are dealing with a whole island; it
would spend much, and it would receive very little.

Mr. Mill says subletting, if necessary, might be prevented; but how
prevented? and at what cost of money? and with what inevitable
unpopularity by the *English* Government through *all* Ireland? The
following quotation will illustrate the sort of cases of which many
might happen yearly in any part of the country; the passage is long,
but we do not apologise for it, since it is only by seeing the actual
detail and real life of the Irish difficulty that we can understand the
problem. Mr. Fennell, a landowner and magistrate, is asked before the
Devon Commission:—

'Can you give us any instances of that subdivision?—Yes, I can.
A tenant of my own held a few years ago thirty-six Irish acres of
land himself, under a lease directed to himself, not under the restriction
of the Subletting Act. He had a lease for lives prior to that. After a
bit he got one of his sons married, and gave him one-third of the farm,
and planted him on it. A little after he got a second son married,
and planted him on it, and gave him one-third. One of those men not
being industrious, and matters going wrong, could not pay his rent
for his third, and to relieve himself out of the difficulty he gives half
of his third to a fourth party, getting some money for it.

'Were you before this division took place aware of it, and did you
try to remonstrate with this person?—I did, and his reply was what else
could he do with his sons? And now the stranger is not paying anything, or paying badly, and he looks to me to get the man out for him.

'Is the lease still in existence?—Yes, there are three lives in existence still. I wish to state another instance about the division of land, and the way they deal with the land. About sixteen years ago, a tenant died in this place. He left me executor to his will, and guardian to his two infant daughters. He had but ten acres of land. ... An allowance of 5s an acre had been made for some time, and up to this time. Still I think he was paying the value. His will was that on the eldest girl attaining the age of nineteen, she was to get married; and upon her getting married, either to give half the ground to her other sister, or secure her in £50. On her attaining the age of nineteen, in one month afterwards she did get married, and her husband passed notes for the £50 to the other girl, instead of dividing the land, which £50 must still go out of my land, or I must have another tenant on it. I could instance hundreds of cases of that kind. ... I may notice one more particularly—a case of that kind. Another man died, leaving two sons. He had only nine acres of land. He divided this ground between them by will. One was married. The unmarried man he bound in his will to give £30 to his sister on marriage, having only four acres and a half of land. He did secure her in it, and has been three years in paying it. He has discharged it, but I believe he is beggared by it. He is pauperised. He had to sell his only cow and mule he had for the use of his farm, to provide the £30 for his sister.'

Who can believe that a half foreign government could ever regulate all these minute family transactions through a large island? And yet, unless you do that, you do nothing. You have still the same misery —the same Ireland which you now have.

But if Mr. Mill's plan does not cure the misery of Ireland, it will intensify, not alleviate, its political discontent. It will give that discontent exactly all it wants—an available weapon. Suppose that at a moment of political excitement—at such a crisis, say, as this of Fenianism,—the whole Irish people do not pay their rent to the English Government. What is to be done? You cannot serve a writ of eviction upon a whole nation? You will have enabled them to perplex you by a kind of treason which you can hardly permit, and yet you can hardly punish.

Mr. Mill appeals both to foreign precedent and to Indian precedent, but neither help him at the stress of the argument. There is no case where complete fixed ownership was conceded to a people before quite destitute of it, in which the result was good. Still less, where that people were demoralised by long habits of bidding more than they ought for land, because it was a necessity, and of neglecting and dividing the land when they got it, because it suited their idleness and inclination. All the continental peasant-proprietors grew out of the feudal system; fixity of tenure grew up vaguely and gradually, though, in the end, it was defined by law. In India, Mr. Mill himself tells us, that under all the native governments there was some old idea of a fixed standard, which might, indeed, be in practice infringed, but which was yet the right and just standard,—the rule which ought to be observed, even if it was not. The successful cases of land legislation have been the gift of a property completely fixed, in lieu of one partially, but incompletely, fixed; it has been a gift to persons prepared by a fitting experience, not to persons spoiled by a degrading past.

Mr. Mill appeals, too, to some continental philosophers who have recommended something like his plan. But it was very natural that they should think Ireland more like France or Prussia than it really is. They looked at the little properties, and they saw an analogy. But the secret of the Irish character—not, of course, of that character originally and in itself, but only of that character as we really find it after a long history and after many temptations—was not seen by them. Passing strangers do not see so deep.

Mr. Mill relies, too, more than he should upon a sort of intellectual terror; he tries to frighten us into his plan by hinting, or even saying, that we shall be thought fools if we do not agree with him. In substance, he says—'Posterity will agree with me; great thinkers agree with me; all persons on a level with their age agree with me; do not you—a mere student—incur the contempt of all competent minds both present and to come, by disagreeing with me.' But this language always reminds us of that which was so common in the city some two years since in the speculative times. How often have we heard—'Do not you be so slow; do not keep to your stupid old trade; go into these companies; look at the names of the directors, men of the first standing in the city, and you will get 20 per cent.; all people "up to the day" go into companies and get 20 per cent.; in ten years no one will do anything else. Do not be an old-fashioned fool, but do as others do.' And yet the events of the last two years have shown that there is some use in being old-fashioned; some truth in old maxims; some danger in new schemes. What the sober maxims teach may be done for Ireland we may soon discuss; but we cannot be tempted. We are rather frightened by the glowing 'Prospectus' of Mr. Mill.

The late Mr. Mill[1]

THE sudden death of Mr. Mill has caused a deep feeling in all the intellectual part of England. Few living philosophers have had so much influence; fewer still have inspired so much personal respect —we might say so much personal affection—among many who had never seen and who were never likely to see him. The personal attachment of the inner circle of his followers was far greater. To that inner circle we can make no claim to belong; we can only trace slightly, and in a manner which may not satisfy them, a rough outline of what seem to us the peculiarities of his mind and the sources of his influence.

To treatises such as Mr. Mill's *Logic* and his *Political Economy*, it is not usually easy to give important praise which no one will deny. The subjects with which they deal, the *Logic* particularly, are too full of doubts and too fertile in animosities. But no one, we think, will deny that hardly ever, perhaps never, in the history of philosophy, have two books so finished and so ample been written by a man who had only his leisure moments to give to them, and who had a day's work to do besides. The quantity of writing in these four thick volumes is not small; but many men, in detached essays and on varied points, equal or surpass that quantity. Even a daily occupation in laborious business is easily compatible with much desultory labour. But Mr. Mill's *Logic* and his *Political Economy* are not collections of desultory remarks; they are orderly, systematic works, in which the beginning has reference to the end, and almost every part has some relation, often a very close relation, to most other parts. To compose such books requires an incessant reminiscence of the past, and an equally incessant foresight of the future; and both these, more almost than anything else, strain and fatigue the brain. Only men with their whole time and whole strength can usually accomplish such tasks. But Mr. Mill wrote both these books when a laborious man of business,

[1] This article was first published in *The Economist* for May 17 1873, Volume XXXI, pp. 588–9.

who had daily difficult and exhausting duties to perform as well. Instead of wondering at occasional faults in such books, we should rather wonder that they exist at all.

The great merit of Mr. Mill, we think, was the merit of intellectual combination. Many philosophers—several contemporaries even— were much more eminent for absolute originality. But no one comes near Mr. Mill in the art—the invaluable art when, as now, philosophy is at once rich and fragmentary—of piecing together. In Mr. Mill's great works theories are placed in just juxtaposition which were wide apart before, and thirteen are named in the same sentence, where one would have hardly comprehended how they could be coupled together. Mr. Grote thus described the *Logic* in the *Westminster Review*—the other day as we may say—in 1865:—

'The *System of Logic* appears to us to present the most important advance in speculative theory which the present century has witnessed. Either half of it, the Ratiocinative or the Inductive, would have surpassed any previous work on the same subject. The Inductive half discriminates and brings into clear view, for the first time, those virtues of method which have insensibly grown into habits among consummate scientific inquirers of the post-Baconian age, as well as the fallacies by which some of these authors have been misled. The Ratiocinative half, dealing with matters which had already been well handled by Dutrieu and other scholastic logicians, invests their dead though precise formalism with a real life and application to the actual process of finding and proving truth. But besides thus working each half up to perfection, Mr. Mill has performed the still more difficult task of overcoming the repugnance, apparently an inveterate repugnance, between them, so as chemically to combine the two into one homogeneous compound; thus presenting the problem of Reasoned Truth, Inference, Proof, and Disproof, as one connected whole. For ourselves, we still recollect the mist which was cleared from our minds when we first read the *System of Logic*, very soon after it was published. We were familiar with the Syllogistic Logic in Burgersdicius and Dutrieu; we were also familiar with examples of the best procedure in modern inductive science; but the two streams flowed altogether apart in our minds, like two parallel lines never joining nor approaching. The irreconcilability of the two was at once removed, when we had read and mastered the second and third chapters of the Second Book of the *System of Logic*; in which Mr. Mill explains the functions and value of the Syllogism, and the real import of its major premiss.'

We do not altogether agree with Mr. Grote in his estimate of this particular doctrine, and on this particular instance we should have much to say if this were the place to say it. But the general description of the *Logic* which Mr. Grote gives is true and admirable. For the first time, an attempt was made to consider together the modern methods of scientific inference and, as Sir John Herschel[2] describes, the ancient methods of scholastic inference as mediæval writers set them forth. The two were never set so completely side by side before, or so fully made to illustrate one another.

Such a book, it will at once be seen, requires a most delicate art of exposition. For these comparisons, the style of a writer must describe not only 'meanings' but shades of meaning—not large ideas in the rough, but nice ideas with nice finish. And for this Mr. Mill was well fitted both by genius and by culture. He inherited a philosophical acumen from his father (and, we suspect, from a long line of Scotch and argumentative ancestors), and an education in France had given him the French gift of precise and graceful explanation. That he also caught a little, though only a little, of the tendency to diffuseness of modern French philosophers must, we admit, be acknowledged; but he also gained the literary talents most useful to a comprehensive philosopher—there extreme clearness and their wonderful readability.

In political economy there was an eminent field for Mr. Mill's peculiar powers of comparison. There is little which is absolutely original in his great work; and much of that little is not, we think, of the highest value. The subject had been discussed in detail by several minds of great acuteness and originality, but no writer before Mr. Mill had ever surveyed it as a whole with anything like equal ability; no one had shown with the same fulness the relation which the different parts of the science bore to each other; still less had any one so well explained the relation of this science to other sciences, and to knowledge in general. Since Mr. Mill wrote, there is no excuse for a political economist if his teaching is narrow-minded or pedantic; though, perhaps, from the isolated state of the science, there may have been

[2] Sir John Herschel was a noted astronomer and mathematician who restored mathematical science in England by introducing differential notation and the continental method of analysis. He played an important part in the founding of the Royal Astronomical Society.—Ed.

some before. Mr. Mill had another power, which was almost of as much use to him for his special occupations as his power of writing, he was a most acute and discerning reader. The world hardly gave him credit for this gift before the publication of his book on Sir William Hamilton. But those who have read that book will understand what Mr. Grote means when, in the essay we quoted before he speaks of Mr. Mill's 'unrivalled microscope which detects the minutest breach or incoherence in the tissue of his philosophical reasoning.' And he used this great faculty both good naturedly and conscientiously—he never gave heedless pain to any writer, and never distorted any one's meaning.

In fact, and partly for the reasons we have stated, Mr. Mill's two great treatises have had a unique and immense influence. In political economy the writer of these lines has long been in the habit of calling himself the last man of the ante-Mill period. He was just old enough to have acquired a certain knowledge of Ricardo and the other principal writers on political economy before Mr. Mill's work was published; and the effect of it has certainly been most remarkable. All students since begin with Mill and go back to all previous writers fresh from the study of him. They see the whole subject with Mr. Mill's eyes. They see in Ricardo and Adam Smith what he told them to see, and it is not easy to induce them to see anything else. Whether it has been altogether good for political economy that a single writer should have so monarchical an influence may be argued, but no testimony can be greater to the ability of that writer and his pre-eminence over his contemporaries. In a wider field the effect of the *Logic* has also been enormous. Half the minds of the younger generation of Englishmen have been greatly coloured by it, and would have been sensibly different if they had not been influenced by it. And there is no other book of English philosophy of which the same can be said, even with a pretext of truth.

A complete estimate of Mr. Mill would include an account of his career in parliament, and also an account of some peculiarities of his mind, which gave him, considering the dry nature of most of his pursuits and studies, a most singular influence. To very many younger minds he was not so much a political economist as a prophet, not so much a logician as a seer. He had, besides his rare power of arguing and analysing, an equally rare kind of contagious enthusiasm, which influenced a multitude of minds, and made them believe as he did. But an estimate of these peculiarities would be little suited to these pages; nor should we at this moment like to say much which, in our judgment, it would be necessary to say in order to make this estimate just. We have preferred to say that which is plainly true, and which could give no pain to anyone.

Thomas Carlyle and Edward John Eyre

Introductory note

Thomas Carlyle (1795–1881), the eldest son of James Carlyle, a mason, and of Janet Aitken, was born at Ecclefechan, Scotland. He was educated at Annan grammar school and at Edinburgh University. He became a schoolmaster at Kirkcaldy, read law at Edinburgh, was a tutor for a short time and contributed to various journals including the *Edinburgh Review.* He moved to London in 1834, and in 1837 published his *French Revolution,* which established his reputation. His other chief works were *Frederick the Great,* published between 1858–65, *Oliver Cromwell,* 1845, *Past and Present,* 1843, and *Chartism,* 1839. Carlyle was widely read, discussed and reverenced by the Victorian public. After the death of his wife in 1866 he became something of a recluse, and Eyre's case was one of the few public causes to which he gave his support. Another was the Franco-Prussian war, in which he favoured Prussia and wrote a pamphlet in support of the Prussian cause in 1870. Carlyle died in London in 1881.

Edward John Eyre (1815–1901) was born at Hornsea, Yorkshire, the third son of Anthony Eyre, the incumbent of Hornsea, and of Sarah Mapleton. He emigrated to Australia in 1833 and became a sheep-farmer. In 1836 he began to undertake journeys into the unknown interior as magistrate and protector of the Aborigines. From 1846–53 he was Lieutenant-Governor of New Zealand, and Governor of St. Vincent from 1854–60. He was appointed Governor of Jamaica in 1864, and in the following year proclaimed martial law after forcibly suppressing a native rebellion in Morant Bay. He confirmed the sentence of death for high treason which had been passed on a coloured member of the legislature, George William Gordon, and more than 600 other persons by Lieutenant Brand. Eyre was denounced in England for cruelty, temporarily suspended, and 'tried' by a royal commission of inquiry at Kingston, between January and March 1866. He was censured for unnecessary rigour, and recalled. He found supporters in Carlyle, Ruskin and Tennyson, but was condemned by

J. S. Mill, Huxley, Herbert Spencer and Goldwin Smith. Eyre was defendant in legal proceedings which aimed at bringing him to trial for murder, in 1867 and 1869, but the action was never brought, and Eyre's legal expenses were paid from public funds. He received a pension as a retired colonial governor in 1874, and died in Devonshire in 1901.

Mr. Carlyle on Mr. Eyre[1]

MR. THOMAS CARLYLE has come out of his retirement and scornful remoteness from public affairs to 'run into' one of the 'public noises' of the day. In the tranquillity of 'Ripple Court, Ringwould, Dover,' having received a 'call' from one 'Hamilton Hume, Esq., Hon. Sec. Eyre Defence Fund,' to join the committee of that enlightened body, Mr. Carlyle answered by declaring 'the clamour raised against Governor Eyre' to be 'disgraceful to the good sense of England;' Mr. Eyre being 'a just, humane, and valiant man,' who, by slaying some hundreds of coloured folk of an 'inhuman and half-brutish type,' causing a political opponent to be hanged on suspicion, and burning some thousand houses, thereby rendered services of 'incalculable value' to this empire. Mr. Gordon, and the man who was stuck up at four hundred yards like a Wimbledon target, to be shot at, and those who were beaten with wire whips, only got, it seems, in the estimation of Mr. Carlyle, 'their wages for their sad industry.' Mr. Carlyle, after a deliberate survey of the conduct of Mr. Eyre, is of opinion that 'this Governor merits,' not 'penalty and clamour,' but 'honour, and thanks, and *wise imitation*.' Consequently the whole weight of Mr. Carlyle's conviction and good wishes go with Mr. Hume and the other *con amore* defenders of Mr. Eyre and his cruelties to his political opponents and the coloured folk generally. Should there be a riot in London or Birmingham, Glasgow or Dublin, the 'governors' there for the time being have in Mr. Eyre a model. They are to imitate his conduct and hold a six weeks' carnival, proclaiming martial law, hanging, slaying, flogging, using God's own image for target practice at 400 yards, and then, when the festival of Justice, Humanity, and Valour is over, they are to have honour and thanks from the survivors. Is it possible to carry further the worship of brute force and of the sort of order in which brute force delights? If this is the authentic outcome of hero worship, it justifies, apart from other grounds, the distrust with which

[1] This article was first published in *The Economist* for September 15 1866, Volume XXIV, p. 1080.

that new religion is regarded,—a religion which dethrones law in favour of caprice, and thrusts an usurping personal wilfulness into the seat of justice. The English nation undoubtedly 'loves order and the prompt suppression of seditions,' but we are not aware that the nation holds in reverence the names of Jeffreys and Kirke, or worships the authors of the massacre of Glencoe, or thinks those persons the perfection of their species who charged with the yeomanry at Peterloo. The English nation applauds the prompt suppression of seditions, but up to this time it has not applauded the perpetration of unnecessary cruelties in the process, and it has guarded, or sought to guard, in a thousand ways, against slaying on suspicion, and especially the slaying of a political opponent. Mr. Carlyle's defence of Mr. Eyre means, if it means anything, that we are to reverse our system of government by law, based as nearly as may be on principles of justice, sweep away all the safeguards of personal liberty, and set up instead the will of one man, who may be an Aristides, but who may also be an Eyre. We say this would be a step backward towards barbarism—nay, it would *be* barbarism, for it would carry us back to the strife of the strong with the strong, and whether strength and justice were allied would be mere accident. On Mr. Carlyle's principles of judging human actions, as exemplified in this Eyre case, Philip II and Alva have a right to the honour and thanks of posterity. Hoorn, Egmont, and William the Silent only got their 'wages for their sad industry,' when they were slain. In a small way the exploits of Mr. Eyre in Jamaica were not unlike those of the Council of Blood. Yet he had far less on him the stress of necessity. After the fifteenth he might have brought every criminal to justice without the aid of martial law, and, great as was his offence in causing Mr. Gordon to be hanged, his greatest offence is that he put an affront on the majesty of the law, and, for the time, cancelled the ripest fruits of ages of civilisation by abolishing the distinction between the savage and the cultivated man. That is the greatest offence of Mr. Eyre, who could only 'govern' on the very rudest principles of club law, and we should certainly 'consider it of evil omen to the country and to its highest interests in these times,' to use Mr. Carlyle's own words, had there been no 'clamour raised against Governor Eyre.' That would have been indeed 'disgraceful,' not only to the 'good sense,' but to the sense of justice of England. And it is because the English nation has *not* changed, and has some regard for its honour, that there is this clamour which is naturally so distasteful to the great prophet of physical force. Up to a certain point Mr. Eyre showed promptitude and energy in suppressing a riot; and for that let him have honour and thanks, but after that point promptitude and energy settled down into deliberate cruelty and malignity; and self-respect and the 'highest interests' of the country bid us condemn these.

We cannot help thinking that this strange championship of a purely muscular morality by men of high intellectual reputation will have a very detrimental effect. If this is seen to be the legitimate outcome of literary culture, depend upon it literary culture will be more distrusted in the world of politics than ever it has been before. Even the squires, unless they are bitten by Mr. Bright, looking on these Jamaica transactions by the light of Quarter Sessions, feel that game itself would not tempt them to commit such acts of naked injustice. It is of little importance that men of the stamp of Lord Cardigan should patronize wholesale illegality. Nothing better is expected of them. But Mr. Carlyle, and even Mr. Ruskin, occupy a far other place in the public estimation, and exercise a far other influence than the hero of the black bottle, to whose level for the moment they have descended; and we say that when they go out of their way to become the advocates of Jamaica—we shall no longer talk of Jedburgh—justice, they do a very grievous injury to the common cause which they as well as we have really at heart. If the active intervention of very highly cultivated men would bring about a feeling of ready acquiescence in the conduct of affairs based on an imitation of Mr. Eyre, then the less these very highly cultivated persons intervene the better for us and them, for they would stand quite as good a chance of sharing the fate of Gordon as we or any other of Her Majesty's subjects. It is absolutely necessary in the interests of the highest as well as the meanest of Englishmen that the contemptuous disregard of the safeguards of personal liberty shown by Mr. Carlyle and his colleagues should receive public repro- bation; and it is far more painful to witness their serious errors— because they ought to know better—than to read of the crimes and blunders of the poor coloured folk of Jamaica, whose very inferiority should have secured them the justest treatment.

George Joachim Goschen
Introductory note

George Joachim Goschen (1831–1907) was born in Stoke Newington, London, the eldest son of William Goschen, a City of London banker, and of Harriet Ohmann. Educated at Rugby and at Oriel College, Oxford, he then entered his father's banking firm. He became Director of the Bank of England in 1858. His *Theory of the Foreign Exchanges*, published in 1861, attracted wide attention. From 1863–80 he was Liberal M.P. for the City of London. In 1865 he joined Lord Russell's ministry as Vice-President of the Board of Trade, and in 1866 entered the cabinet as Chancellor of the Duchy of Lancaster. Goschen was president of the Poor Law Board in Gladstone's first administration, from 1868–71. He helped to reform the system of local government. From 1871–4 he was First Lord of the Admiralty, and it was his refusal to reduce estimates which was largely responsible for the dissolution of the Government in 1874. Goschen was M.P. for Ripon, 1880–5, for East Edinburgh 1885–6, and for St. George's, Hanover Square, 1887–1900. He strenuously opposed Gladstone's Home Rule Bill in 1886 and in 1893. From 1886–92 he was Chancellor of the Exchequer in Lord Salisbury's government, and was First Lord of the Admiralty from 1895–1900 in Salisbury's third administration. Goschen was created a Viscount in 1900, and died at Seacox Heath, Kent, in 1907.

Mr. Goschen's Acceptance of Office[1]

As we not long since expressed a hope that office would be offered to Mr. Goschen, and that he would accept it, it might seem that we had now merely to express our satisfaction when it has been offered to him and he has accepted it. And, as far as he is personally concerned, there is nothing more to say. Mr. Goschen's presage for the future is his history during the last four years; in that time he has written an excellent book on one of the most complicated topics of political economy, in which he had very peculiar means of information; he has made several good speeches, and, what is much more difficult, gained a wide and deep influence in parliament; he has put himself at the head of the poll in the City of London against a very formidable opposition, and in preference to three colleagues, all much respected and all much older than he is. Such a career as this, though so brief, shows a variety of mind and a stability of character which must gain him future eminence, and which makes present eulogy unnecessary.

We refer to Mr. Goschen's change from the City to Whitehall, because it indicates a growing modification in the constitution and structure of our political class which is not always sufficiently observed, and which will produce very grave effects when it has attained its full development. The common sense of Englishmen looked especially for two things in a political class. First, *ease* in money matters. They wished and wish that the emoluments of office, though a good makeweight, and a desirable accessory, should not be the main object of a politician's life. If a man now serve the Queen for money, he had better serve the City. There is far more hard cash to be made by the same mind and the same effort east than west of Temple Bar. Probably, though this is not the time to pursue the subject, we have gone too far in this direction; the usages of our politics and the expensiveness of our society have too much restricted politics to very rich men. But though we may have exaggerated the idea, it was, when limited,

[1] This article was first published in *The Economist* for November 25 1865, Volume XXIII, pp. 1421–2.

an invaluable idea. The first thought in a minister's mind, at a crisis, ought not to be 'Shall or shan't I lose my salary?' It was said that if Mr. Pitt had been obliged—as seemed likely—to leave office in 1787, he must have gone back to the western circuit. Mr. Pitt's contempt of money was so well known, that no one suspected him of clinging to office to keep it, or of wishing office to gain it. But all men are not like Mr. Pitt, and looking to the upshot of his money matters, it is as well they are not. The sound judgment of Englishmen wisely exacts that conspicuous statesmen shall give security for their political independence by the known possession of a large and sure income. Secondly, we require of our statesmen what a Catholic theologian would call *detachment* in their money matters. They must not be mixed up in the changing money market of the world, nor even much in its shifting industry. At the outbreak of the American war, we remember recalling this to our readers' memories. Here was a case in which one of the most considerable industries in England—what was then thought to be a vital industry—was popularly imagined to be ruined, and was in fact deeply impaired, by a political cause; yet all the political questions relating to it were considered by officials, not one of whom could be suspected of a sinister interest in cotton. Whether Sea Islands were 8d a pound or two shillings did not matter, and was not fancied to matter, to a single member of Lord Palmerston's Cabinet. The curious gulf that separates our Treasury from the City is still more useful. Certain French ministers are said to see a stock-jobber or two every morning; and the large fortunes they gain are attributed to the skilful use of official knowledge and state influence. But the very accusation could not be made in England; the wildest satirists would not so slander any now conspicuous politician. We exact not only ease in money matters, but fixity in money matters, from our statesmen, and we get it.

Till lately, people of large landed property were the only persons who could fulfil these strict conditions. There was little other fixed settled wealth, except the funds; and large fundholders have always been very few: if people want a small interest for a large capital, they generally choose to get it from land, where they get social consequence into the bargain. Most other wealth was, in the French phrase, 'mobile,' depending on passing events, imperceptible circumstances, here to-day but gone to-morrow; it was, to use the vague, but yet useful word, *unrealised.* Now, a vast mass of industrial property exists which is quite as certain as anything in this world can be certain. A man may have property in railway debentures, canal shares, in nine-tenths of the many thousand securities enumerated in the *Investors' Manual*, and yet be as independent of political events, as careless whether he goes out or stays in, as if he owned half a county. The new sort of realised property is as politically serviceable as the old sort.

Mr. Goschen is an instance to prove that it is even better, and this is his exceptional peculiarity. He comes out of the City to take office, and he brings to office what nothing but the City could have taught him. There is a tinge of the amateur about every man of business who has not lived by business. There is a want which is hard to describe and impossible to define about him. A coarse attorney once said of a delicate advocate fresh from university honour, 'Ah, dear me! he is a good young man, but he has never tasted blood.' And a certain indistinctness, a certain tendency to fall short on a sudden and when you least expect it, a diffidence at heart often contrasting with an outward audacity, characterise as a rule and as a class those who have not known real business—the getting a livelihood by business. Those whose fortunes, great or small, have depended on the correctness of their decisions, acquire a correct decisiveness which does not waste time in irrelevant details, which is often even careless of accessory order, but which smites to the root whatever is most critical and needful in the topic on hand. It is because Mr. Goschen has had in high perfection this consummate training, that we expect far more from him than if he had been reared in the external technicalities of a public office, or belonged to the rank of the county aborigines.

Robert Lowe, Viscount Sherbrooke

Introductory note

Robert Lowe (1811–1892) was born at Bingham, Nottinghamshire, the second son of Robert Lowe, rector of Bingham, and of Ellen Pyndar. He was educated at Winchester and at University College, Oxford. After studying at Lincoln's Inn he was called to the bar in 1842, and went to Sydney where he practised law until 1850, when he returned to England and became a leader-writer on *The Times*. From 1852–9 he was M.P. for Kidderminster and from 1859–67 represented Calne. He was Joint-Secretary of the Board of Control from 1852–5; from 1855–8 Vice-President of the Board of Trade and Paymaster-General; and Vice-President of the committee of the council on education from 1859–64. In 1868 he became the first M.P. for London University and held the seat until 1880. From 1868 until 1873 he was Chancellor of the Exchequer and Home Secretary from 1873–4. Robert Lowe was created Viscount Sherbrooke in 1880. He died at Warlingham, Surrey, in 1892.

Mr. Lowe as Chancellor of the Exchequer[1]

'An oak,' said a great Irish orator, who did not succeed so well as
he expected in England, 'an oak should not be transplanted at fifty.'
And we believe that to be the reason why Mr. Lowe—though in
many respects he has shown great ability as finance minister—upon
the whole has not as yet succeeded better than many much stupider
men, or as well as his genius deserved. Mr. Lowe, before he began his
finance studies, had already 'invested' so much mind that most men
would have had no more left. His career at Oxford was unusually long;
he was not a mere student who took high honours. After that he
stayed several years as a working tutor, and has described to a royal
commission how steadily he worked for ten hours a day as a 'coach,'
and how little in consequence he accepts the 'romance' of tuition.
And the inevitable result has been that Mr. Lowe has become a scholar,
not only as young students become such, but as men of maturer years,
who mean to earn money by it, become so. A certain part of the
substance of his mind is embarked in that pursuit, and cannot now be
transferred to any other. After leaving Oxford Mr. Lowe made himself
not only an excellent English lawyer, but an admirable general jurist.
He is acquainted not only with the technicalities of English law, but
with the structure of other systems of law, and with the principles of
scientific jurisprudence. He has studied what Bentham said law 'ought'
to be, and what Austin said law 'must' be. And this too is a very
exhausting study, requiring, if the knowledge is really to be acquired
as Mr. Lowe has acquired it, and retained as he retains it, a great
'capital' of mind. No one can wonder that, when on the verge of
threescore, he was suddenly made finance minister, he should not
possess or display so much free and applicable mind as some younger
man. Great mind he must always display. But he has not displayed
proportionate mind—proportioned, we mean, to the immense abilities
which everyone knows he has. After all, there is only room in even

[1] This article was first published in *The Economist* for May 20 1871, Volume XXIX,
pp. 594–5.

the largest head for a certain number of thoughts, and Mr. Lowe had crowded his, long before he had tried finance, with many dissimilar and occupying ideas.

It is true that under our parliamentary system ministers of as mature an age as Mr. Lowe are not unfrequently transferred from post to post, and are placed in charge of offices with whose subjects they have no knowledge. No one supposes that Mr. Cardwell knew much of military business before he was made Secretary for War, and yet unquestionably he has pulled the Army Regulation Bill better through Parliament than the planners who contrived it, or the soldiers who will act on it. But these transferable statesmen commonly belong to a different class from Mr. Lowe. Like Mr. Cardwell, they are trained parliamentary advocates. They have learned to know the House of Commons, and the way of putting an argument so as to suit the House of Commons, as a long-practised advocate knows the sort of arguments which suit a jury, and the most telling way in which to state them to a jury. Sir Robert Peel was once said to know how to 'dress up a case for parliament' better than anyone else. And in this art there are two secrets, of which Mr. Cardwell is an eminent master. The first is always to content yourself with the minimum of general maxims, which will suit your purpose and prove what you want. By so doing you offend as few people as possible, you startle as few people as possible, and you expose yourself to as few retorts as possible. And the second secret is to make the whole discussion very uninteresting—to leave an impression that the subject is very dry, that it is very difficult, that the department had attended to the dreary detail of it, and that on the whole it is safer to leave it to the department, and a dangerous responsibility to interfere with the department. The faculty of disheartening adversaries by diffusing on occasion an oppressive atmosphere of businesslike dulness is invaluable to a parliamentary statesman.

But these arts Mr. Lowe does not possess. He cannot help being brilliant. The quality of his mind is to put everything in the most lively, most exciting, and most startling form. He cannot talk that monotonous humdrum which men scarcely listen to, which lulls them to sleep, but which seems to them the 'sort of thing you would expect,' which they suppose is 'all right.' And Mr. Lowe's mode of using general principles not only is not that which a parliamentary tactician would recommend, but is the very reverse of what he would advise. Mr. Lowe always ascends to the widest generalities: the *axiomata media*, as logicians have called them,—the middle principles, in which most minds feel most reality and on which they find it most easy to rest—have no charms for him. He likes to go back to the bone, to the abstract, to the attenuated, and if he left these remote principles in their remote unintelligibility, he would not suffer so much. But he makes the dry bones live. He wraps them in illustrations which Macaulay might envy. And he is all the more effective, because he uses our vernacular tongue. The phrases that 'the money market must take care of itself,' and that 'it was not the business of the Treasury to cocker up the Bank of England,' will long be remembered, and will longer impair his influence with grave, quiet, and influential persons. Mr. Lowe startles those who do not like to be startled, and does not compose those who wish to be composed—those who need a little commonplace to assure them that they are acting on safe principles, that they are not, according to the saying, 'lighting the streets with fireworks.'

These defects would be felt in any new office; but besides these, Mr. Lowe has one—a physical one—to which he has often himself alluded, and which hampers him beyond expression. In our younger days he would have been cited in books of 'entertaining knowledge' as a conspicuous instance of the 'pursuit of knowledge under difficulties.' Being unable to read books with his own eyes, he knows more about books than almost anyone who has eyes. A wonderful memory, and an intense wish to know the truth, have filled his head with knowledge; but though great powers may compensate for inherent defects, none, not even the greatest, can annihilate those defects. They are ineradicable, and the consequences of them will come back again to lessen every victory, and to enhance every disaster. It is so with Mr. Lowe in this case. A man who cannot easily read figures for himself, who cannot manipulate them for himself, who cannot throw them into various shapes, as it were, on trial for himself, cannot be a great financier. Our greatest financiers, Pitt, Peel, and Gladstone, have all of them been men who did not take their figures from others, but who spent a great—almost an excessive—labour on the *minutiæ* of them for themselves. It is from no lack of labour, and no lack of mind, that Mr. Lowe does not do this. By physical constitution he is incapable of it.

Something of this is at the bottom of Mr. Lowe's occasionally defective dealing with small financial forms, which was the only point that Mr. Disraeli made against him on Thursday night. It is hardly possible that a man with such immense disadvantages for business can have his tackle quite as ready and quite as perfect as those who are more fortunate. And Mr. Disraeli is scarcely the man who ought to have made the taunt. No one regards these legal forms with more sublime indifference than he does when it suits his office. 'Gentlemen of the long robe,' he used to say when in office, 'will attend to these details;' and he would have deemed it absurd that a minister, charged with the fate of cabinets and the policy of measures, should ever consider them. And perhaps he was right; perhaps it would have been absurd. But what is unnecessary for one minister cannot be incumbent on another similar minister. It was not for Mr. Disraeli, who has scarcely seemed to be able to see details and technicalities (so exclusively did he look on them from the most elevated points of policy), to reproach Mr. Lowe with a few trivial, innocuous, and excusable deficiencies in them.

The result of all this is very plain. It is that Mr. Lowe is under peculiar difficulties in finance—that it is not a region in which his great powers can ever show to the best advantage—that on the contrary, it is a region in which they will frequently be seen at the greatest disadvantage. But there is a profound truth in the saying that 'men of pre-eminent ability are always safe;' not of course that so wide a phrase is to be taken exactly to the letter, but that there is a 'reserve fund' in the highest ability which will enable it to pull through scrapes, to remedy errors, to surmount disasters, which would ruin and bury common men. Mr. Lowe will certainly not have an unchequered reign at the Exchequer; but he may reign long, he may do much good, and notwithstanding many failures and defects, may leave the special stamp and impress of his mind on many great budgets and important measures.

End of Volume III